YOUR BABY'S FIRST YEAR

This invaluable volume was prepared under the editorial direction of distinguished pediatrician Steven P. Shelov, M.D., M.S., F.A.A.P., and draws on the contributions and practical wisdom of more than seventy-five pediatric specialists and a six-member AAP editorial review board. Written in a warm, accessible style and richly illustrated with helpful drawings and diagrams, this book gives you the information you need to know to safeguard your child's most precious asset: his or her health.

In *Your Baby's First Year* you'll find:

- Detailed guidance on basic infant care, including milestones for physical, social, and cognitive growth
- "Health Watch" features that alert you to potential problems at each stage
- A list of age-appropriate toys and activities that stimulate infant brain growth and development
- Advice on how to handle common ailments, such as colds, ear infections, and rashes—and when you should call your pediatrician

Plus reliable information on:

- Nutrition, with advice on breastfeeding and bottle-feeding, and when to introduce solid foods
- Sleep habits and problems
- Baby-proofing your home
- Bathing and diapering your baby, plus skin and nail care
- Up-to-date immunization schedules

Child Care Books from the American Academy of Pediatrics

Caring for Your Baby and Young Child
Birth to Age 5

Caring for Your School-Age Child
Ages 5 to 12

Caring for Your Adolescent
Ages 12 to 21

Guide to Your Child's Symptoms
Birth Through Adolescence

YOUR BABY'S FIRST YEAR

Steven P. Shelov, M.D., M.S., F.A.A.P.,
Editor-in-Chief
Professor and Chairman of Pediatrics
Maimonides Medical Center, State
University of New York—Brooklyn

BANTAM BOOKS
NEW YORK • TORONTO • LONDON • SYDNEY • AUCKLAND

Your Baby's First Year

A Bantam Book published by arrangement with
the American Academy of Pediatrics

Bantam edition/June 1998

A note about revisions:
Every effort is made to keep YOUR BABY'S FIRST YEAR consistent with the most recent advice and information available from the American Academy of Pediatrics. In addition to major revisions identified as "Revised Editions," the text has been updated as necessary for each additional reprinting listed above.

ISBN 0-553-57904-5

Published simultaneously in the United States and Canada

Bantam Books are published by Bantam Books, a division of Random House, Inc. Its trademark, consisting of the words "Bantam Books" and the portrayal of a rooster, is Registered in U.S. Patent and Trademark Office and in other countries. Marca Registrada. Bantam Books, 1540 Broadway, New York, New York 10036.

PRINTED IN THE UNITED STATES OF AMERICA

OPM 20 19 18 17 16 15

Reviewers and Contributors

Editor-in-Chief
Steven P. Shelov, M.D., M.S.

Associate Editor
Robert E. Hannemann, M.D.

Editorial Board
Catherine DeAngelis, M.D.
Paul H. Dworkin, M.D.
Morris Green, M.D.
Robert J. Haggerty, M.D.
Andrew P. Mezey, M.D.
Jack P. Shonkoff, M.D.

AAP Board of Directors Reviewer
Donald E. Cook, M.D.

American Academy of Pediatrics
Executive Director: Joe M. Sanders, Jr., M.D.
Associate Executive Director: Roger F. Suchyta, M.D.
Director, Department of Communications: Linda L. Martin
Director, Division of Public Education: Lisa R. Reisberg
Project Manager, Division of Public Education: Mark T. Grimes
Project Coordinator, Division of Public Education: Kate Larson

Contributors
Henry Adam, M.D.
Watson Arnold, M.D.
Susan S. Aronson, M.D.
Elizabeth Ascher, M.D.
Sami Labib Bahna, M.D., Dr. P.H.
James Bale, M.D.
William F. Balistreri, M.D.
Joel L. Bass, M.D.
Judith Ann Bays, M.D.
Cheston Berlin, M.D.
Bram Bernstein, M.D.
Phillip Berry, M.D.
Scott J. Boley, M.D.
Margaret Bowden, M.A.
John T. Boyle, M.D.
William E. Boyle, Jr., M.D.
Patrick E. Brookhouser, M.D.
Philip Alfred Brunell, M.D.
Marilyn Bull, M.D.
Michael Robert Bye, M.D.
Linda Cahill, M.D.
Ralph Cash, M.D.

William J. Cochran, M.D.
Herbert J. Cohen, M.D.
J. Carl Craft, M.D.
Murray Davidson, M.D.
William Dietz, M.D., Ph.D.
Harold Diner, D.D.S.
Chester M. Edelmann, Jr., M.D.
Howard Eigen, M.D.
Ralph D. Feigin, M.D.
Vincent A. Fulginiti, M.D.
Lawrence W. Gartner, M.D.
Carol Roberts Gerson, M.D.
Fredda Ginsberg-Fellner, M.D.
Peter Gorski, M.D.
John Green, M.D.
Joseph Greensher, M.D.
Donald Gromisch, M.D.
Robert Gross, M.D.
Ken Grundfast, M.D.
Dennis Gurwitz, M.D.
Howard Gutgesell, M.D.
Roy Haberkern, M.D.
Katerina Haka-Ikse, M.D.
Ronald C. Hansen, M.D.
Terry Hatch, M.D.
Alfred Healy, M.D.
Frederick M. Henretig, M.D.
Robert N. Hensinger, M.D.
Alan R. Hinman, M.D.
Marjorie Hogan, M.D.
Judy Hopkinson, Ph.D.
Nancy Hutton, M.D.
Barbara J. Ivens, M.S.R.D.
Michael Steven Jellinek, M.D.
Murray Katcher, M.D.
John Kattwinkel, M.D.
Robert Kay, M.D.
Connie Keefer, M.D.
Avanelle Kirksey, Ph.D.
Ronald Ellis Kleinman, M.D.
Barry Allan Kogan, M.D.
Harold P. Koller, M.D.
John Kraft, M.D.
Richard Krugman, M.D.
Ruth A. Lawrence, M.D.
Moise Levy, M.D.
Nathan Litman, M.D.
Martin I. Lorin, M.D.
Stephen Ludwig, M.D.
Ronald B. Mack, M.D.
M. Jeffrey Maisels, M.D.
S. Michael Marcy, M.D.
Robert W. Marion, M.D.
Morri Ezekiel Markowitz, M.D.
Karin McCloskey, M.D.
Anna McCullough, M.S.R.D.
Lotti Mendelson, R.N., P. N.P.
Robert A. Mendelson, M.D.
Peter Miller, M.D.
Claes Moeller, M.D., Ph.D.
Howard C. Mofenson, M.D., F.A.A.C.T.
James H. Moller, M.D.
Corinne Montandon, Dr. P. H.
Douglas Moodie, M.D.
Dennis Murray, M.D.
Edwin Myer, M.D.
George Nankervis, M.D.
Kathleen G. Nelson, M.D.
Buford L. Nichols, Jr., M.D.
Lucy Osborn, M.D.
Mark Papania, M.D.
Jack L. Paradise, M.D.
James Perrin, M.D.
Peter Pizzutillo, M.D.
Stanley Alan Plotkin, M.D.
Shirley Press, M.D.
Gary S. Rachelefsky, M.D.
Isabelle Rapin, M.D.
Peter Rappo, M.D.
Leonard Rome, M.D.

Arnold Rothner, M.D.
Lawrence Schachner, M.D.
Edward L. Schor, M.D.
Gwendolyn Scott, M.D.
Jay Selcow, M.D.
Janet Silverstein, M.D.
James E. Simmons, M.D.
Frank R. Sinatra, M.D.
Lynn T. Staheli, M.D.
Russell Steele, M.D.
Martin Stein, M.D.
Ruth E. K. Stein, M.D.
George Sterne, M.D.
James Anthony Stockman III, M.D.
Robert R. Strome, M.D., F.A.C.S.
Janice Stuff, R.D.
Ciro Valent Sumaya, M.D.
Lawrence T. Taft, M.D.
Edward Tank, M.D.
Daniel M. Thomas, M.D.
George R. Thompson, M.D.
Deborah Tinsworth
Vernon Tolo, M.D.
David Tunkel, M.D.
Renee Wachtel, M.D.
Ellen R. Wald, M.D.
Esther H. Wender, M.D.
Claire Wenner, R.D.
Mark Widome, M.D.
Eugene S. Wiener, M.D.
Catherine Wilfert, M.D.
Modena Hoover Wilson, M.D.
Peter F. Wright, M.D.
Michael W. Yogman, M.D.

Acknowledgments

Illustrations:
Wendy Wray (Part I)
Alex Grey (Part II)

Writer:
Richard Trubo

Editor:
Robin Michaelson

Designer:
Richard Oriolo

Secretarial Support:
Debbie Carney
Patti Coffin
Debbie Cruz
Christine Esposito-Torres
Helen Fischman
Donita Kennedy
Delores Menting
Giselle Reynolds
Gale Ringeisen
Nancy Wagner
Mary Ellen Watson

Additional Assistance:
Susan A. Casey
Michelle Esquivel
Sarah Hale
Eleanor Hannemann
Hope Hurley
Christine Kang
Marlene Lawson, R.N.
Aimée Liu
Nancy Macagno
Leslie Nadell
Marsha L. Shelov, Ph.D.
Mary Claire Walsh
Kathy Whitaker, R.N.

This book is dedicated to
all the people who recognize that children
are our greatest inspiration in the present
and our greatest hope for the future.

PLEASE NOTE

The information contained in this book is intended to complement, not substitute for, the advice of your child's pediatrician. Before starting any medical treatment or medical program, you should consult with your own pediatrician, who can discuss your individual needs and counsel you about symptoms and treatment. If you have any questions regarding how the information in this book applies to your child, speak with your child's pediatrician.

The information and advice in this book apply equally to children of both sexes (except where noted). To indicate this, we have chosen to alternate between masculine and feminine pronouns throughout the book.

The American Academy of Pediatrics constantly monitors new scientific evidence and makes appropriate adjustments in its recommendations. For example, future research and the development of new childhood vaccines may alter the regimen for the administration of existing vaccines. Therefore, the schedule for immunizations outlined in this book is subject to change. These and other potential situations serve to emphasize the importance of always checking with your pediatrician for the latest information concerning the health of your child.

Contents

Resources from the American Academy of Pediatrics

The American Academy of Pediatrics develops and produces a wide variety of public education materials that teach parents and children the importance of preventive and therapeutic medical care. These materials include books, magazines, television programming, videos, brochures, and other educational resources. Examples of these materials include:

- Brochures and fact sheets on allergies, child-care issues, divorce and single parenting, growth and development, immunizations, learning disabilities, nutrition and fitness, sleep problems, substance abuse, and television
- Videos on immunizations, newborn care, nutrition education, allergies, bicycle safety, child abuse prevention, hospital and surgery preparation, and injury prevention and first aid
- First-aid and growth charts, child health records, children's activity booklets, educational computer software programs and video games, and books for parents and children

All of the above materials and more are listed in the AAP *Parent Resource Guide*, a comprehensive listing of patient education materials for adults and children.

For a copy of the Academy's *Parent Resource Guide*, send a self-addressed, stamped #10 envelope to:

American Academy of Pediatrics
Department PRG
141 Northwest Point Blvd.
P.O. Box 927
Elk Grove Village, IL 60009-0927

For help in finding a qualified pediatrician or pediatric subspecialist, contact the "Pediatrician Referral Source" of the American Academy of Pediatrics by sending the name of your town (or those nearby) and a self-addressed, stamped envelope to:

American Academy of Pediatrics
Department C—Pediatrician Referral
141 Northwest Point Blvd.
P.O. Box 927
Elk Grove Village, IL 60009-0927

Foreword

Your Baby's First Year is one of several child-care books developed by the American Academy of Pediatrics. The other books include *Caring for Your Baby and Young Child: Birth to Age 5, Caring for Your School-Age Child: Ages 5 to 12, Caring for Your Adolescent: Ages 12 to 21,* and *Guide to Your Child's Symptoms: Birth Through Adolescence.*

The American Academy of Pediatrics is an organization of 53,000 primary care pediatricians, pediatric medical subspecialists, and pediatric surgical specialists committed to the attainment of optimal physical, mental, and social health for all infants, children, adolescents, and young adults. This book is part of the Academy's ongoing education efforts to provide parents with quality information on a broad spectrum of children's health issues.

What distinguishes this child-care book from the many others in bookstores and on library shelves is that it has been developed and extensively reviewed by members of the American Academy of Pediatrics. A six-member editorial board developed the initial material with the assistance of more than seventy-five contributors and reviewers. The final draft was then reviewed by countless numbers of pediatricians. Because medical information on children's health is constantly changing, every effort has been made to ensure that this book contains the most up-to-date information available.

It is the Academy's hope that this book will become an invaluable resource and reference guide for parents. We believe it is the best source of information on matters of children's health and well-being. We are confident readers will find the book extremely valuable, and we encourage them to use this book in concert with the advice and counsel of their own pediatrician who will provide individual guidance and help on issues related to the health of their children.

Joe M. Sanders, Jr., M.D.
Executive Director
American Academy of Pediatrics

Introduction: The Gifts of Parenthood

Your baby is the greatest gift you will ever receive. From the moment you first hold this miracle of life in your arms, your world will be broader and richer. You will experience a flood of feelings, some of wonder and joy and others of confusion and of being overwhelmed and wondering whether you can ever measure up to the needs of your new baby. These are feelings you could barely imagine before—feelings that no one can truly experience without having a child.

Even describing them is difficult because the bond between parent and baby is so intensely personal. Why do tears come to your eyes the first time your baby smiles or reaches for you? Why are you so proud of her first words? Why does your heart suddenly start to pound the first time you watch her stumble and fall?

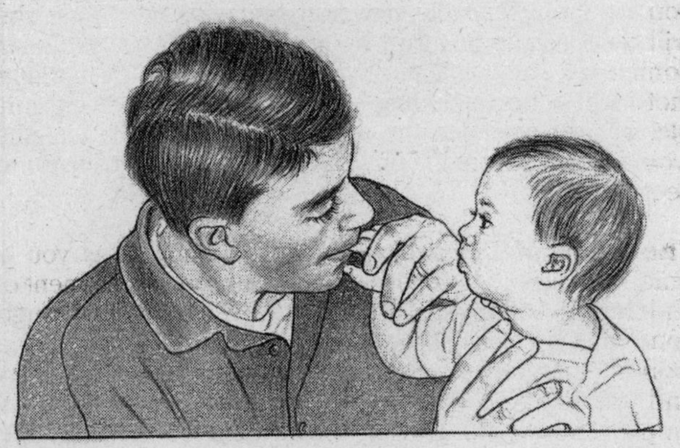

The answer lies in the unique two-way giving relationship between you and your baby.

Your Baby's Gifts to You

Although simple, your baby's gifts to you are powerful enough to change your life positively.

Unqualified Love. From birth, you are the center of your child's universe. He gives you his love without question and without demand. As he gets older, he will show this love in countless ways, from showering you with his first smiles to giving you his handmade valentines. His love is filled with admiration, affection, loyalty, and an intense desire to please you.

Your Baby's Gifts to You

- Unqualified love
- Absolute trust
- The thrill of discovery
- The heights of emotion

Absolute Trust. Your child believes in you. In her eyes, you are strong, capable, powerful, and wise. Over time, she will demonstrate this trust by relaxing when you are near. Sometimes, she will lean on you for protection from things that frighten her, including her own sensitivities. For example, in your presence she may try out new skills that she would never dare alone or with a stranger. She trusts you to keep her safe.

The Thrill of Discovery. Having a baby gives you a unique chance to rediscover the pleasure and excitement of childhood. Although you cannot relive your life through your child, you can share in his delight as he explores the world. In the process, you probably will discover abilities and talents you never dreamed you possessed. Feelings of empathy mixed with growing self-awareness will help shape your ability to play and interact with your growing child. Discovering things together, whether they be new skills or words or ways to overcome obstacles, will add to your experience and confidence as a parent and will better prepare you for new challenges that you never even envisioned.

The Heights of Emotion. Through your child, you will experience new heights of joy, love, pride, and excitement. You probably also will experience anxiety, anger, and frustration. For all those delicious moments when you hold your baby close and feel her loving arms around your neck, there are bound to be times when you feel you cannot communicate. For you as a parent, the challenge will be to accept and appreciate all the feelings your baby expresses herself and arouses in you, and to use them in giving her steady guidance.

The Gifts You Give Your Baby

As his parent, you have many vital gifts to offer your child in return. Some are subtle, but all are very powerful. Giving them will make you a good parent. Receiving them will help your baby become a healthy, happy, capable individual.

The Gifts You Give Your Baby

- Unconditional love
- Self-esteem
- Values and traditions
- Joy in life
- Good health
- Secure surroundings
- Skills and abilities

Unconditional Love. Love lies at the core of your relationship with your child. It needs to flow freely in both directions. Just as she loves you without question, you must give her your love and acceptance absolutely. Your love shouldn't depend on the way she looks or behaves. It shouldn't be used as a reward, or withheld as a threat. Your love for your baby is constant and indisputable, and it's up to you to convey that. Love must be held separate and above any fleeting feelings of anger or frustration over her conduct. Never confuse the actions with the child. The more secure she feels in your love, the more self-assurance she will have as she grows up.

Self-Esteem. One of your most important gifts as a parent is to help your child develop self-esteem. It's not an easy or quick process. Self-respect, confidence, and belief in oneself, which are the building blocks of self-esteem, take years to become firmly established. Beginning in infancy, your child needs your steady support and encouragement to discover his strengths. Loving him, spending time with him, listening to him, and praising his accomplishments are all part of this process. If he is confident of your love, admiration, and respect, it will be easier for him to develop the solid self-esteem he needs to grow up happy and emotionally healthy.

Values and Traditions. Regardless of whether you actively try to pass on your values and beliefs to your child, she is bound to absorb some of them just by living with you. She'll participate in family rituals and traditions and think about their significance. Give her guidance and encouragement, not only commands. Encourage questions and discussions, when age and language permit, instead of trying to force your values on your child. If your beliefs are well reasoned and if you are true to them, she will probably adopt many of them. If there are inconsistencies in your actions, something we all live with, often your children are the ones who will make that clear to you, either subtly by their behavior or, when they are older, more directly by disagreeing with you. The road to developing values is not straight and unerring. It demands flexibility built on firm foundations. While the choice of values and principles will ultimately be hers to make, she depends on you to give her the foundation through your thoughts, shared ideas, and most of all, your actions and deeds.

Joy in Life. Your child doesn't need to be taught to be joyful, but he does need your permission and occasional encouragement to let his natural enthusiasm fly free. The more joyful you are, particularly when you are with him, the more delightful life will seem to him and the more eagerly he will embrace it. When he hears music, he'll dance. When the sun shines, he'll turn his face skyward. When he feels happy, he'll laugh. This exuberance is often expressed through his being attentive and curious, willing to explore new places and things, and eager to take in the world around him and incorporate the new images, objects, and people into his own growing experience. Remember, different babies have different temperaments, some more apparently exuberant than others, some more noisily rambunctious, some more playful, some more reserved. But all babies demonstrate their joy in life in their own ways, and you as the parent will discover what those ways are and nurture your baby's joy. This is a gift every child deserves.

Good Health. Your baby's health depends significantly on the care and guidance you offer her. You begin during pregnancy, by taking good care of yourself and by arranging for obstetric and pediatric care. By taking your baby to the doctor regularly for consultations, keeping her safe from accidents, providing a nutritious diet, and encouraging exercise throughout childhood, you help protect and strengthen her body. You'll also need to maintain good health habits yourself, while avoiding unhealthy ones, such as smoking, excessive drinking, drug use, and lack of adequate physical activity. In this way, you'll give your child a healthy example to follow as she grows up.

Secure Surroundings. You naturally want to give your baby a safe, comfortable home. This means more than a warm place to sleep and a collection of toys. As important as it is to provide shelter that is physically safe and secure, it is even more important to create a home that is emotionally secure with a minimum of stress and a maximum of consistency and love. Your child can sense problems between other family members and may be very troubled by them, so it's important that *all* family problems, even minor conflicts, be dealt with directly and resolved as quickly as possible through cooperation. This may entail seeking advice, but remember, your family's well-being maintains an environment that promotes your baby's development and will allow him to achieve his potential. The family's dealing effectively with conflicts or differences will ultimately help him feel secure in his ability to manage conflicts and disagreements and will provide him a positive example for resolving his own challenges.

Skills and Abilities. As your child grows up, she'll spend most of her time developing and polishing a variety of skills and abilities in all areas of her life. You should help her as much as possible by encouraging her and providing the equipment and instruction she needs. It's also important not to forget some of the most important learning tools: Your baby will learn best when she feels secure, confident, and loved; she will learn best when information is presented in a way that she will respond to positively. Some information is best presented through play—the language of children. Young children learn a tremendous amount through play, especially when with parents or playmates. Other information is best learned or incorporated through actual experience. This may mean learning through exposure to diverse places, people, activities, and experiences. Other things are learned through stories, picture books, and activity books. Still other things are learned by watching—sometimes just watching you, sometimes watching other children or adults.

If you enjoy learning and making discovery fun for your baby, she will soon recognize that achievement can be a source of personal satisfaction as well as a way to please you. The secret is to give her the opportunities and let her learn as best fits her style and at her own rate.

How to Make Giving a Part of Your Daily Family Life

Giving your baby the guidance and support he needs to grow up healthy involves all the skills of parenthood: nurturing, guiding, protecting, sharing, and serving as an example or model. Like other skills, these must be learned and perfected through practice. Some will be easier for you than others. Some will seem easier on certain days than on others. These variations are a normal part of raising a child, but they do make the job challenging. The following suggestions will help you make the most of your natural parenting skills so you can give your child the best possible start.

Enjoy Your Baby as an Individual. Recognize that your baby is unique—different from everyone else—and appreciate her special qualities. Discover her special needs and strengths, her moods and vulnerabilities, and especially her sense of humor, which starts to show itself early in infancy. Let her show you the joy of play. The more you enjoy your baby and appreciate her individuality, the more successful you'll be in helping her develop a sense of trust, security, and self-esteem. You'll also have a lot more fun being a parent!

Educate Yourself. You probably know much more than you think you do about being a parent. You spent years observing your own parents and other families. Perhaps you've taken care of other people's children. And you have many instinctive responses that will help make you a giving parent. In other times, this probably would have been all the preparation you needed to raise a baby. However, our society is extremely complex and is constantly changing. In order to guide their children in this new world, parents often benefit from some extra education. Talk to your pediatrician and other parents, and ask questions. Read about issues and problems that affect your family. Contact local religious organizations, child-care centers, parent education classes, and other groups that specialize in child-related concerns. Often these groups serve as networks for concerned and interested parents. These networks will help you feel more comfortable and secure when issues seem puzzling or frustrating, a not uncommon state today.

As you gather advice, sift through it for information that is right for you and your baby. Much of what you receive will be very valuable, but not all of it. Because child rearing is such a personal process, there is bound to be disagreement. You are not obligated to believe everything you hear or read. In fact, one of the purposes of educating yourself is to protect your baby from advice that does not fit your family. The more you know, the better equipped you'll be to decide what works best for your family.

Be a Good Example. One of the ways your baby shows her love for you is by imitating you. This is also one of the ways she learns how to behave, develop new skills, and take care of herself. From her earliest moments she watches you closely and patterns her own behavior and beliefs after yours. Your examples become permanent images, which will shape her attitudes and actions for the rest of her life.

Setting a good example for your child means being responsible, loving, and consistent not only with her but with all members of the family. The way you conduct your marriage, for example, teaches your child about male and female roles and how she's "supposed" to behave as she gets older. Show your affection and take time for yourselves as a couple. If your child sees her parents communicating openly, cooperating, and sharing household responsibilities, she'll bring these skills to her own relationship.

Setting good examples also means taking care of yourself. As an eager, well-meaning parent, it's easy to concentrate so hard on your family that you lose sight of your own needs. That's a big mistake. Your baby depends on you to be physically and emotionally healthy, and she looks to you to show her how to keep herself healthy. By taking care of yourself, you express your self-esteem, which is important for both you and your baby. Getting a sitter and resting when you're overtired or ill will teach your child that you respect yourself and your needs. Setting aside time and energy for your own work or hobbies teaches your child that you value certain skills and interests and are willing to pursue them. Ultimately, she will pattern some of her own habits after yours, so the healthier and happier you keep yourself, the better it will be for both of you.

Show Your Love. Giving love means more than just saying "I love you." Your baby can't understand what the words mean unless you also treat him with love. Be spontaneous, relaxed, and affectionate with him. Give him plenty of physical contact through hugging, kissing, rocking, and playing. Take the time to talk, sing, and read with him every day. Listen and watch as he responds to you. By paying attention and freely showing your affection, you make him feel special and secure, and lay a firm foundation for his self-esteem.

Communicate Honestly and Openly. One of the most important skills you teach your child is communication. The lessons begin when she is a tiny baby gazing into your eyes and listening to your soothing voice. They continue as she watches and listens to you talking with other members of the family and, later, as you help her sort out her concerns, problems, and confusions. She needs you to be understanding, patient, honest, and clear with her.

Good communication within a family is not always easy. It can be especially difficult when both parents are working, overextended, or under a great deal of stress, or when one person is depressed or angry. Preventing a communications breakdown requires commitment, cooperation among family members, and a willingness to recognize problems as they arise. Express your own feelings, and as your child grows, encourage her to be equally open with you. Look for changes in her behavior that may signal sadness, fear, frustration, or worry, and show that you understand these emotions.

Listen to yourself as well, and consider what you say to your child *before* the words leave your mouth. In anger or frustration it's sometimes easy to make harsh, even cruel, statements, which you don't really mean but which a child may never forget. Phrases like "You stupid idiot" or "Don't bother me" make your growing baby feel worthless and unwanted and may seriously damage her self-esteem. If you constantly criticize or put her off, she may also back away from you.

Spend Time Together. You cannot give your child all that he needs if you only spend a few minutes a day with him. In order to know you and feel confident of your love, he has to spend a great deal of time with you, both physically and emotionally. Spending this time together is possible even if you have outside commitments. You can work full-time and still spend some intimate time with your baby every day. The important thing is that it be time devoted *just* to him, meeting his needs and your needs together. Is there any fixed amount? No one can really say. One hour of quality time is worth more than a day of being in the same house but in different rooms. You can be at home full-time and never give him the undivided attention he requires. It's up to you to shape your schedule and direct your attention so that you meet his needs.

It may help to set aside a specific block of time for your baby each day and devote it to activities he enjoys. Also make an effort to include him in all family activities.

Nurture Growth and Change. When your child is a newborn, it may be difficult for you to imagine her ever growing up, and yet your main purpose as a parent is to encourage, guide, and support her growth. She depends on you to provide the food, protection, and health care her body needs to grow properly, as well as the guidance her mind and spirit need to make her a healthy, mature individual. Instead of resisting change in your baby, your job is to welcome and nurture it.

Guiding your child's growth involves a significant amount of discipline, both for you and for your child. As she becomes increasingly independent, she needs rules and guidelines to help her find what she can do and enlarge that. You need to provide this framework for her, establishing rules that are appropriate for each stage of development and adjusting them as your child changes so they encourage growth instead of stifling it.

Minimize Frustrations and Maximize Success. One of the ways your child develops self-esteem is by succeeding. The process starts in the crib with his very first attempts to communicate and use his body. If he achieves his goals and receives approval, he soon begins to feel good about himself and eager to take on greater challenges. If, instead, he's prevented from succeeding and his efforts are ignored, he may eventually become so discouraged that he quits trying and either withdraws or becomes angry and even more frustrated.

As a parent, you must try to expose your child to challenges that will help him discover his abilities and achieve successes while simultaneously preventing him from encountering obstacles or tasks likely to lead to too great a series of frustrations and defeats. This does not mean doing his work for him or keeping him from tasks you know will challenge him. Success is meaningless unless it involves a certain amount of struggle. However, too much frustration in the face of challenges that really are beyond your child's current abilities can be self-defeating and perpetuate a negative self-image. The key is to moderate the challenges so they're within your baby's reach while asking him to stretch a bit. For example, try to have toys that are appropriate for his age level. See if you can find a variety of playmates, some older and some younger.

Recognize Problems and Get Help When Necessary. An enormous challenge, parenthood can be more rewarding and fun than any other part of your life. Sometimes, though, problems are bound to arise, and occasionally you may not be able to handle them alone. There is no reason to feel guilty or embarrassed about this. Healthy families accept the fact and confront difficulties directly. They also respect the danger signals and get help promptly when it's needed.

Sometimes, all you need is a friend. If you're fortunate enough to have parents and relatives living nearby, your family may provide a source of support. If not, you could feel isolated unless you create your own network of neighbors, friends, and other parents. One way to build such a network is by joining organized groups, such as "Mommy and Me" and baby gym classes at your local YMCA or community center. The other parents in these groups can be a valuable source of advice and support. Allow yourself to use this support when you need it.

Occasionally, you may need expert help in dealing with a

specific crisis or ongoing problem. Your personal physician and pediatrician are sources of support and referral to other health professionals, including family and marriage counselors. Don't hesitate to discuss family problems with your pediatrician. Many of these problems can eventually adversely affect the family's health if not resolved. Your pediatrician should know about them and is interested in helping you resolve them.

Your journey with your baby is about to begin. It will be a wondrous time filled with many ups and downs, times of unbridled joy and times of sadness or frustration. The chapters that follow provide a measure of knowledge intended to make fulfilling the responsibilities of parenthood a little easier and, hopefully, a lot more fun.

PART I

1

Preparing for a New Baby

Pregnancy is a time of anticipation, excitement, preparation, and, for many new parents, uncertainty. You dream of a baby who will be strong, healthy, and bright—and you make plans to provide her with everything she needs to grow and thrive. You probably also have fears and questions, especially if this is your first child, or if there have been problems with this or a previous pregnancy. What if something goes wrong during the course of your pregnancy, or what if labor and delivery are difficult? What if being a parent isn't everything you've always dreamed it would be? Fortunately, most of these worries are needless. The nine months of pregnancy will give you time to have your questions answered, calm your fears, and prepare yourself for the realities of parenthood.

Some of these preparations should begin when you first learn you're pregnant. The best way to help your baby develop is to take good care of yourself, since medical attention and good nutrition will directly benefit your baby's health. Getting plenty of rest and exercising moderately will help you feel better and ease the physical stresses of pregnancy. Talk to your physician about prenatal vitamins and avoiding smoking and alcohol.

As pregnancy progresses, you're confronted with a long list of related decisions, from planning for the delivery to decorating the nursery. You probably have made many of these decisions already. Perhaps you've postponed some others because your baby doesn't yet seem "real" to you. However, the more actively you prepare for your baby's arrival, the more real that child will seem, and the faster your pregnancy will appear to pass.

Eventually it may seem as though your entire life revolves around this baby-to-be. This increasing preoccupation is perfectly normal and healthy and may actually help prepare you emotionally for the challenge of parenthood. After all, you'll be making decisions about your child for the next two decades—at least! Now is a perfect time to start.

Here are some guidelines to help you with the most important of these preparations:

Giving Your Baby a Healthy Start

Virtually everything you consume or inhale while pregnant will be passed through to the fetus. This process begins as soon as you conceive. In fact, the embryo is most vulnerable during the first two months, when the major body parts (arms, legs, hands, feet, liver, heart, genitalia, eyes, and brain) are just starting to form. Chemical substances such as those in cigarettes, alcohol, illegal drugs, and certain medications can interfere with the developmental process, as well as with later development, and some can even cause congenital abnormalities.

Take smoking, for instance. If you smoke cigarettes during pregnancy, your baby's birthweight may be significantly decreased. Even inhaling smoke from the cigarettes of others (passive smoking) can affect your baby. Stay away from smoking areas and ask smokers not to light up around you. If you smoked before you got pregnant, and still do, this is the time to stop—not just until you give birth, but forever. Children who grow up in a home where a parent smokes have more ear infections and more respiratory problems during infancy and early childhood, and also have been shown to be more likely to smoke themselves when they grow up.

There's just as much concern about alcohol consumption. Excessive alcohol intake during pregnancy increases the risk of miscarriage. It also can cause a condition called fetal alcohol syndrome, which causes birth defects and below-average intelligence. To date, no one has determined exactly how much alcohol is too much for a pregnant woman, but there is evidence that the more you drink, the greater the risk to the fetus. Until there is more data, it is safest not to drink alcoholic beverages during pregnancy.

You should also avoid all medications and supplements except those your physician has specifically recommended for use during pregnancy. This includes not only prescription drugs that you may have already been taking, but also non-prescription or over-the-counter products such as aspirin, cold medications, and antihistamines. Even vitamins can be dangerous if taken in quantities larger than the recommended doses. (For example, excessive amounts of vitamin A have been known to cause congenital abnormalities.) Consult with your physician before taking drugs or supplements of any kind during pregnancy.

Your caffeine intake also should be limited while you are pregnant. While no adverse effects from normal caffeine intake have yet been proven, caffeine does tend to keep adults awake and make them irritable, which can only make things less comfortable and restful for you.

Another cause of congenital abnormalities is illness during pregnancy. Some of the most dangerous diseases you should take precautions against include:

German measles (rubella), which can cause mental retardation, heart abnormalities, cataracts, and deafness. Fortunately, this illness can now be prevented by immunization, though *you must not be immunized against rubella while pregnant.*

The majority of adult women are immune to German measles because they had the disease during childhood or have already been immunized against it. If you're not sure whether you're immune, ask your obstetrician to order a blood test for you. In the unlikely event that the test shows you're not immune, you must do your best to avoid young sick children, especially during the first three months of your pregnancy. It is then recommended that you receive immunization after giving birth to prevent this same concern in the future.

Chickenpox is particularly dangerous if contracted shortly before delivery. If you have not already had chickenpox, you should avoid anyone who might have or might be coming down with this disease, particularly young children who have been around others with chickenpox. If you have not had chickenpox, you should receive the preventive vaccine when you are not pregnant.

Toxoplasmosis is primarily a danger for cat owners. This illness is caused by a parasitic infection common in cats. The infected animal excretes a form of the parasite in its stools, and anyone who comes in contact with infected stools could themselves become infected.

If you own a cat, have it checked for toxoplasmosis before you become pregnant or as early as possible in your pregnancy. You can reduce the chances that your cat will con-

Where We Stand

The Academy message is clear—don't smoke when pregnant. Many studies now show that if a woman smokes during pregnancy, the baby's birthweight and growth during the first year of life may be reduced. The range of indisputable effects runs from depressed breathing movements during fetal life to cancer, respiratory disorders, and heart disease in later years.

If you smoke, quit. If you can't quit, don't smoke around children (especially indoors or in the car). Children of parents who smoke have more respiratory infections, bronchitis, pneumonia, and reduced pulmonary function than children of nonsmokers. The Academy supports legislation that would prohibit smoking in public places frequented by children. The Academy also supports a ban on tobacco advertising, harsher warning labels on cigarette packages, and an increase in the cigarette excise tax.

tract toxoplasmosis by feeding it only commercially prepared cat food, which is processed in a way that destroys the organisms. Also, to decrease your own chances of being infected, have someone who is not pregnant clean the litter box daily. (The toxoplasmosis organisms cannot infect humans until forty-eight hours after the cat excretes them.) If you do clean the litter box or handle cat litter, make sure to wash your hands thoroughly.

Also, avoid eating uncooked or partially cooked meat or fish (such as sushi), and practice good hand-washing techniques after handling uncooked meat products.

Choosing a Pediatrician

Every pediatrician is committed to helping parents raise healthy children with the greatest possible ease, comfort, pleasure, and success. However, different pediatricians have different approaches, so you may want to interview several pediatricians before selecting the one who best suits your family's particular preferences and needs. Conduct these visits *before* the baby arrives, so the pediatrician you choose can give your newborn her very first exam.

Here are some considerations to help you make your choice:

The Training of Pediatricians

Pediatricians are graduates of four-year medical schools with three additional years of residency training solely in pediatrics. Under supervised conditions, the pediatrician-in-training acquires the knowledge and skills necessary to treat a broad range of conditions, from the mildest childhood illnesses to the most serious diseases.

With the completion of residency training, the pediatrician is eligible to take a written examination given by the American Board of Pediatrics. If he or she passes this examination, a certificate is issued, which you will probably see on the pediatrician's office wall. If you see the initials FAAP after a pediatrician's name, it means he or she is a Fellow (member) of the American Academy of Pediatrics. Only Board-certified pediatricians can become members of this professional organization.

Following their residency, some pediatricians elect an additional one to three years of training in a subspecialty, such as neonatology (the care of sick and premature newborns) or pediatric cardiology (the diagnosis and treatment of heart problems in children). These pediatric subspecialists are generally called upon to consult with general pediatricians when a patient develops uncommon or special problems. If a subspecialist is ever needed to treat your baby, your regular pediatrician will help you find the right one for your baby's problem.

How to Find a Pediatrician for Your Baby

A good place to start looking for a pediatrician is by asking your obstetrician for referrals. He or she will know local pediatricians who are competent and respected within the medical community. Other parents also can recommend pediatricians who have successfully treated their children.

Once you have the names of several pediatricians you wish to consider, arrange a personal interview with each of them during the final months of your pregnancy. Most pediatricians routinely grant such preliminary interviews. Both parents should attend these meetings if possible, to be sure you both agree with the pediatrician's policies and philosophy about child rearing. Don't be afraid or embarrassed to ask any questions. Here are a few suggestions to get you started:

- ***How soon after birth will the pediatrician see your baby?***

Most hospitals ask for the name of your pediatrician when you're admitted to deliver your baby. The delivery nurse will then call that pediatrician or his associate on call as soon as your baby is born. If you had any complications during either pregnancy or delivery, your baby should be examined at birth. Otherwise, the examination can take place anytime during the first twenty-four hours of life. Ask the pediatrician if you can be present during that initial examination. This will give you an opportunity to learn more about your baby and get answers to any questions you may have.

- ***When will your baby's next exams take place?***

Pediatricians routinely examine newborns and talk with parents before the babies are discharged from the hospital. This lets the doctor identify any problems that may have arisen and also gives you a chance to ask questions that have occurred to you during your hospital stay, before you take the baby home. Your pediatrician will also let you know when to schedule the first office visit for your baby (as early as one day after discharge), and how he or she may be reached if a medical problem develops before then.

■ ***When is the doctor available by phone?***
Many pediatricians have a specific call-in period each day when you can phone with questions. If members of the office staff routinely answer these calls, you should find out what their training is. Also ask your pediatrician for guidelines to help you determine which questions can be resolved with a phone call and which require an office visit.

■ ***What hospital does the doctor prefer to use?***
Ask the pediatrician where to go if your baby becomes seriously ill or is injured. If the hospital is a teaching hospital with interns and residents, find out who would actually care for your infant if he was admitted.

■ ***What happens if there is an emergency?***
Find out if the pediatrician takes her own emergency calls at night. If not, how are such calls handled? Also, ask if the pediatrician sees patients in the office after regular hours or if you must instead take your baby to an emergency room. When possible, it's often easier and more efficient to see the doctor in her office, because hospitals frequently require lengthy paperwork and extended waits before your child receives attention. On the other hand, serious medical problems are usually better handled at the hospital, where staff and medical equipment are always available.

■ ***Who "covers" the practice when your pediatrician is unavailable?***
If your physician is in a group practice, it's wise to meet the other doctors, since they may treat your child in your pediatrician's absence. If your pediatrician practices alone, he probably will have an arrangement for coverage with other doctors in the community. Usually your pediatrician's answering service will automatically refer you to the doctor on call, but it's still a good idea to ask for the names and phone numbers of all the doctors who take these calls—just in case you have trouble getting through to your own physician.

If your baby is seen by another doctor at night or on the

weekend, you should check in by phone with your own pediatrician the next morning (or on Monday). Your doctor will probably already know what has taken place, but this phone call will give you a chance to bring him up to date and reassure yourself that everything is being handled as he would recommend.

■ ***How often will the pediatrician see your baby for checkups and immunizations?***
The American Academy of Pediatrics recommends checkups by one month, and at two, four, six, nine, twelve, fifteen, eighteen, and twenty-four months, and annually after that. If the doctor routinely schedules examinations more or less frequently than this, discuss the difference with her. The American Academy of Pediatrics immunization schedule is on page 82.

■ ***What are the costs of care?***
Your pediatrician should have a standard fee structure for hospital and office visits as well as after-hours visits and home visits (if he makes them). Find out if the charges for routine visits include immunizations. If not, ask how much they will cost. Also, if you are covered by a managed-care system (HMO, etc.), check whether the pediatrician is on the panel of physicians.

After these interviews, you need to ask yourself if you are comfortable with the pediatrician's philosophy, policies, and practice. You must feel that you can trust him and that your questions will be answered and your concerns handled compassionately. You should also feel comfortable with the staff and the general atmosphere of the office.

Once your baby arrives, the most important "test" of the pediatrician you have selected is how he cares for your infant and responds to your concerns. If you are unhappy with any aspect of the treatment you and your baby are receiving, you should talk to the pediatrician directly about the problem. If the response does not address your concerns properly, or the problem simply cannot be resolved, don't hesitate to change physicians.

Issues to Discuss with Your Pediatrician

Once you have found a pediatrician with whom you feel comfortable, let her help you plan for your infant's basic care and feeding. Certain decisions and preparations should be made before the baby arrives. Your pediatrician can advise you on such issues as:

When Should the Baby Leave the Hospital?

The fact that a short hospital stay (less than forty-eight hours) for term healthy infants can be accomplished does not mean that it is appropriate for every mother and baby. Each mother and baby should be evaluated individually to determine the best time of discharge. The timing of the discharge should be the decision of the physician caring for the infant, not the insurance company.

Should the Baby Be Circumcised?

If you have a boy, you'll need to decide whether or not to have him circumcised. Unless you are sure you're having a girl, it's a good idea to make a decision about circumcision ahead of time, so you don't have to struggle with it amid the fatigue and excitement following delivery.

Circumcision has been practiced as a religious rite for thousands of years. In the United States most boys are

Circumcision

At birth, most boys have skin that completely covers, or almost covers, the end of the penis. Circumcision removes some of this foreskin so that the tip of the penis (glans) and the opening of the urethra, through which the baby urinates, are exposed to air. Routine circumcisions are performed in the hospital within a few days of birth. When done by an experienced physician, circumcision takes only a few minutes and is rarely complicated. A few doctors provide local anesthesia in an effort to reduce the stress for the baby, but most circumcisions are done without medication. The option of using local anesthesia to minimize discomfort is one that should be carefully considered, since there are potential complications associated with its use.

circumcised, but usually for social rather than religious reasons. It is done because "all the other men in the family were circumcised," or because parents don't want their sons to feel "different."

At present, there is controversy over whether or not circumcision is advisable from a medical standpoint. New information suggests there are potential medical benefits to circumcision. Recent studies have concluded that male infants who are not circumcised may be more likely to develop urinary tract infections than those who are. Further studies are needed to confirm this observation.

Cancer of the penis, a very rare condition, has long been known to occur almost exclusively in uncircumcised men. New reports find that cervical cancer may be more common among females whose partners are uncircumcised. Thus far, these reports are inconclusive. Also inconclusive is new evidence regarding the relationship of circumcision to sexually transmitted diseases.

Circumcision does, however, pose certain risks such as infection and bleeding. If the baby is born prematurely, has an illness at birth, or has congenital abnormalities or blood problems, he should not be immediately circumcised. The procedure should be performed only on stable, healthy infants.

Where We Stand

The American Academy of Pediatrics believes that circumcision has potential medical benefits and advantages, as well as inherent disadvantages and risks. Therefore, we recommend that the decision to circumcise is one best made by parents in consultation with their pediatrician. Factors affecting the decision include medical conditions, aesthetics, religion, cultural attitudes, social pressures, and tradition. Your pediatrician should explain and discuss the benefits and risks of circumcision with you, and informed consent should be obtained before the procedure is performed.

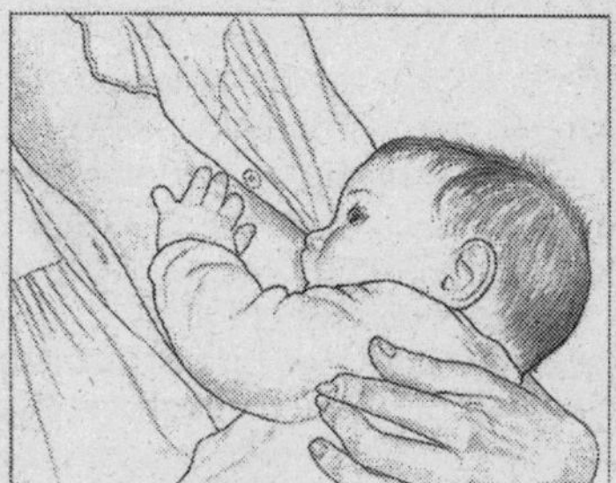

The American Academy of Pediatrics advocates breastfeeding as the optimal form of infant feeding.

Should I Breastfeed or Bottle-Feed?

Before your baby arrives, you'll want to decide whether you're going to breastfeed or feed formula. While not identical to breastmilk, most formulas are approximately as nutritious and digestible as human milk. Both approaches are safe and healthy for your baby and each has its advantages. *The American Academy of Pediatrics advocates breastfeeding as the optimal form of infant feeding.*

The most obvious benefits of breastfeeding are convenience and cost, but there are some real medical benefits, too. Breastmilk provides your baby with natural antibodies that help her resist certain kinds of infection. Breastfed babies also are less likely to suffer from allergies that occasionally occur in babies fed cow's milk formulas.

Mothers who nurse their babies also say that there are many emotional rewards. Once the milk supply is established and the baby is nursing well, both mother and child experience a tremendous sense of closeness and comfort, a bond that continues throughout infancy.

If you cannot breastfeed or you choose not to do so, you can still achieve similar feelings of closeness during bottle-feedings. Rocking, cuddling, stroking, and gazing into your baby's eyes will enhance the experience for both of you, regardless of the milk source.

Before making your decision on this issue, read Chapter 4, so that you thoroughly understand the advantages and disadvantages of breastfeeding and bottle-feeding, and you are aware of all the options available to you.

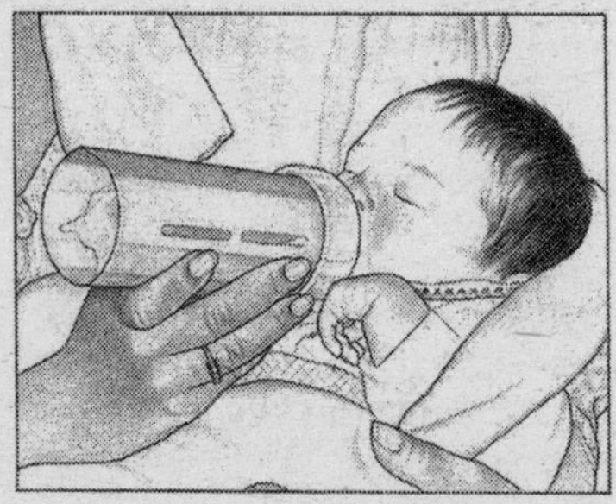

If you cannot breast-feed or you choose not to do so, you can still achieve similar feelings of closeness during bottle-feedings.

Preparing Your Home and Family for the Baby's Arrival

Choosing a Layette

As your due date nears, you'll need to acquire a layette, the basic collection of baby clothes and accessories that will get your newborn through his first few weeks. A suggested starting list includes:

3 or 4 pajama sets (with feet)
6 to 8 T-shirts
3 newborn sacques
2 sweaters
1 sleeping bag or bunting
2 bonnets
4 pairs of socks or booties
4 to 6 receiving blankets
1 set of baby washcloths and towels (look for towels with hoods)
3 to 4 dozen newborn-size diapers (plus diaper pins and 4 plastic pants if you use cloth diapers)

If you have other children, most of this layette probably will consist of hand-me-downs. If this is your first child, you may receive many of the items from friends and relatives. Here are some guidelines to help you make your selections for the rest of the items you need.

- Buy big. Unless your baby is born prematurely or is very small, he will probably outgrow "newborn" sizes in a matter of days—if he ever fits into them at all! Even three-month sizes may be outgrown within the first month. You'll want a couple of garments that your child can wear in the very beginning, but concentrate on larger sizes for the rest of the wardrobe. Your baby won't mind if his clothes are slightly large for a while.
- To avoid injury from burning garments, all children should wear flame-retardant sleepwear and clothing. Make sure the label indicates this. These garments should be washed in laundry detergents, not soap, because soap will wash out the flame retardant. Check the garment labels and product information to determine which detergents to use.
- Make sure the crotch opens easily for diaper changes.
- Avoid any clothing that pulls tightly around the neck, arms, or legs. These clothes are not only safety hazards but are also uncomfortable.
- Check washing instructions. Clothing for children of all ages should be washable and require little or no ironing.
- Do *not* put shoes on a newborn's feet. Shoes are not necessary until after he starts to walk. Worn earlier, they can interfere with the growth of his feet. The same is true of socks and footed pajamas if they're too small and worn for a prolonged period of time.

Buying Furniture and Baby Equipment

Walk into any baby store and you probably will be overwhelmed by the selection of equipment available. A few items are essential, but most things, while enticing, are not necessary. In fact, some are not even useful. To help you sort through the options, here is a list of the basic necessities you should have on hand when your baby arrives.

- A crib that meets all safety specifications (see *Cribs*, page 30). New cribs sold today must meet these standards, but if you're looking at used cribs, check them carefully to make sure they meet the same standards. Unless you have money to spare, don't bother with a bassinet. Your baby will outgrow it in just a few weeks.
- A crib mattress that is firm and covered with material that can be easily cleaned. If this covering is made of plastic or other nonabsorbent material, place a thick fabric pad on top of it so your baby won't lie in moisture caused by perspiration, drooling, or spit-up.
- Crib bumpers to keep your baby from hitting her head on the crib bars. Make sure these bumpers are tied to the crib railings, using all the strings. The bumpers should be removed when your child starts to stand; otherwise she may climb up on them and out of her crib. It is unnecessary and potentially dangerous to use pillows in a newborn's crib.
- Bedding for the crib, including a flannel-backed, waterproof mattress cover (which is cooler and more comfortable for your baby than plain plastic or rubber covers), and two fitted sheets. Never use infant cushions that have soft fabric coverings and are loosely filled with plastic foam beads or pellets. These cushions have been banned by the U.S. Consumer Product Safety Commission because they have been involved in thirty-six infant suffocations.
- A changing table that meets all safety specifications (see *Changing Tables*, page 314). It should be placed on a carpet or padded mat and against a wall, not a window, so there is no danger of your child falling. Put shelves or tables to hold diapers, pins, and other changing equipment within immediate reach (but away from the baby's reach), so you will not have to step away from the table—even for a second—to get anything.
- A 3-gallon diaper pail with deodorizer. If you are going to wash your own diapers, you'll need a second pail so you can separate wet diapers from "soiled" ones. If you use a diaper service, they usually will provide the pail.

- A large plastic washtub for bathing the baby. As an alternative to the washtub, you can use the kitchen sink to bathe your newborn, provided the faucet swings out of the way. After the first month, however, it's safer to switch to a separate tub, because the baby will be able to reach and turn on the faucet from the sink. Always make sure the bathing area is very clean prior to bathing your baby.

Safety Alert: Bassinets and Cradles

Many parents prefer to use a bassinet or cradle for the first few weeks, because it's portable and allows the newborn to sleep in the parents' room. But remember that infants grow very fast, so the cradle that is sturdy enough one month may be outgrown the next. To get the longest and safest possible use from your baby's first bed, check the following before buying:

1. The bottom of the cradle or bassinet should be well supported so it cannot possibly collapse.

2. The bassinet or cradle should have a wide base so it can't tip over even if someone bumps against it.

If the bassinet or cradle has folding legs, they should be locked straight whenever the bed is in use. Your baby should graduate to a crib around the end of the first month or by the time he weighs ten pounds.

Everything in the nursery should be kept clean and dust-free. (See Chapter 10 for safety specifications.) All surfaces, including window and floor coverings, should be washable. So should all toys that are left out. Although stuffed animals look cute around newborns (they seem to be a favorite shower gift), they tend to collect dust and may contribute to stuffy noses. Since your baby won't actively play with them for many months, you might consider storing them until she's ready for them.

If the air in the nursery is extremely dry, your pediatrician may recommend using a cool mist humidifier. This also may help clear your baby's stuffy nose when she has a cold. If you do use a humidifier, clean it frequently as directed in the package instructions and empty it when not in use. Otherwise, bacteria and molds may grow in the still water. Steam vaporizers are not recommended because of the danger of scalding.

One object that your baby is sure to enjoy is a mobile. Look for one with bright colors and varied shapes. Some also play pleasant music. When shopping for a mobile, look at it from below so that you'll know how it appears from your baby's point of view. Avoid the models that look good only from the side or above—they were designed more for your enjoyment than for the infant's. Make sure you remove the mobile at five months of age, or as soon as your baby can sit up, because that's when she'll be able to pull it down and risk injury.

A rocking chair, music box, and record or tape player are also wise additions to the nursery. The rocking motion of the chair will increase the soothing effect your baby feels when you hold her. Playing soft music for your baby will comfort her when you're not nearby and will help her fall asleep.

You will want to keep the lights in the nursery soft once your newborn has arrived, and leave a night-light on after dark. The night-light will allow you to check on the baby more easily, and as she gets older, it will reassure her when she awakens at night. Make sure all lights and cords are kept safely out of the baby's reach.

Safety Alert: Cribs

Your baby usually will be unattended when in his crib, so this should be a totally safe environment. Falls are the most common injury associated with cribs, even though they are the easiest to prevent. Infants are most likely to fall out of the crib when the mattress is raised too high for their height, or when the side rail is left down.

If you use a new crib or one manufactured since 1985, it will meet current safety standards. If you plan to use an older crib, inspect it carefully for the following features:

- Slats should be no more than 2⅜ inches apart so a baby's head cannot become trapped between them.
- There should be no cutouts in the headboard or footboard, as your baby's head could become trapped in them.
- If the crib has corner posts (sometimes called finials), unscrew them or cut them off. Loose clothing can become snagged on these and choke your baby.

Many older cribs were painted with lead-based paint, which can poison children if they gnaw on the crib rails (it does happen) and this lead accumulates in the body. Symptoms of slight lead poisoning may include mild learning disabilities; severe lead poisoning can produce permanent mental and physical retardation. As a precaution, strip the old paint and then repaint the crib using high-quality, new enamel. Let it dry thoroughly in a well-ventilated room. Then place plastic strips (available at most children's furniture stores) over the top of the side rails.

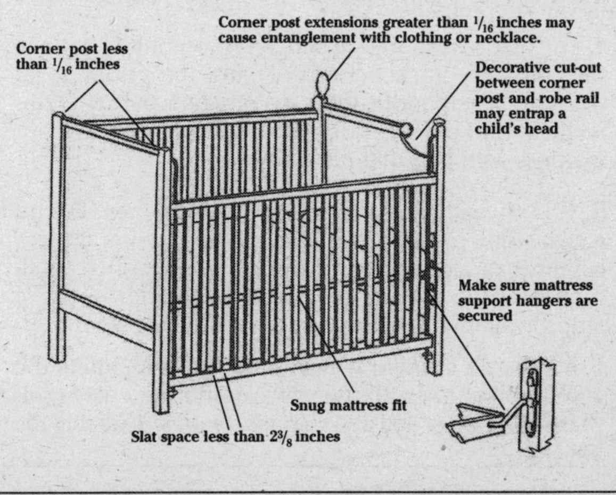

You can prevent other crib hazards by observing the following guidelines:

1. If you purchase a new mattress, remove and destroy all plastic wrapping material that comes with it, because it can suffocate a child. If you cover the mattress with heavy plastic, be sure the cover fits tightly; zippered covers are best.

2. As soon as your baby can sit, lower the mattress of the crib to the level where he cannot fall out either by leaning against the side or by pulling himself over it. Set the mattress at its lowest position by the time your child learns to stand. The most common falls occur when a baby tries to climb out, so move him to another bed when he is 35 inches tall, or the height of the side rail is less than three-quarters of his height.

3. When fully lowered, the top of the side rail of the crib should be at least 4 inches above the mattress, even when the mattress is set at its highest position. Be sure the locking latch that holds the side up is sturdy and can't accidentally be released by your infant. Always leave the side up when your baby is in the crib.

4. The mattress should fit snugly so your infant cannot slip into the crack between it and the crib side. If you can insert more than two fingers between the mattress and the sides or ends of the crib, replace the mattress with one that fits snugly.

5. Periodically check the crib to be sure there are no rough edges or sharp points on the metal parts, and no splinters or cracks in the wood. If you notice tooth marks on the railing, cover the wood with a plastic strip (available at most children's furniture stores).

6. Use a crib bumper when your child is an infant. Be sure the pad goes all the way around the crib and is secured with at least six straps or ties, to keep the bumper from falling away from the sides. To prevent strangulation, the ties should be no more than 6 inches long.

7. As soon as your baby can pull to a standing position, remove crib bumpers as well as any toys, pillows, or stuffed animals that are large enough to be used as a step for climbing out.

8. If you hang a mobile over your baby's crib, be sure it is securely attached to the side rails. Hang it high enough so your baby cannot reach it to pull it down, and remove it when he starts to sit, or when he reaches five months, whichever comes first.

9. Crib gyms should be removed as soon as your infant can get up on all fours. Even though these gyms are designed to withstand a child's grabbing and tugging, he could fall forward onto the gym and become entangled.

10. To prevent the most serious of falls, don't place a crib—or any other child's bed—beside a window.

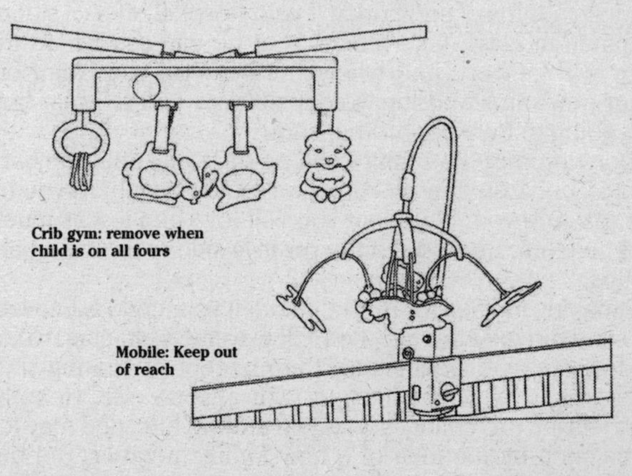

Crib gym: remove when child is on all fours

Mobile: Keep out of reach

Preparing Your Other Children for the Baby's Arrival

If you have other children, you'll need to plan carefully how and when to tell them about the new baby. A child who is four or older should be told as soon as you start telling friends and relatives. He should also be apprised of the basic facts about conception and pregnancy so he understands how he is related to his new brother or sister. Fables about storks and such may seem cute, but they won't help your youngster understand and accept the situation. Using one of the picture books published on the subject may help you to explain "where babies come from."

If your child is younger than four when you become pregnant, you can wait awhile before telling him. When he's this young, he's still very self-centered and may have difficulty understanding an abstract concept like an unborn baby. But once you start furnishing the nursery, bringing his old crib back into the house, and making or buying baby clothes, he should be told what's going on. Also take advantage of any questions he may ask about Mom's growing "stomach" to explain what's happening. Picture books can be helpful with very young children, too. Even if he doesn't ask any questions, start talking to your older child about the baby by the last few months of pregnancy. If your hospital offers a sibling preparation class, take him so that he can see where the baby will be born and where he may visit you. Point out other newborns and their older siblings, and tell him how he's going to be a big brother soon.

Don't promise that things will be the same after the baby comes, because they won't be, no matter how hard you try. But reassure your child that you will love him just as much, and help him understand the positive side of having a baby sibling.

Breaking the news is most difficult if your child is between two and three. At this age, he's still extremely attached to you and doesn't yet understand the concept of sharing time, possessions, or your affection with anyone else. He's also very sensitive to changes going on around him, and may feel threatened by the idea of a new family member. The best way to minimize his jealousy is to include him as much as possible in the preparations for the new baby. Let him shop with you for the layette and the nursery equipment. Show him pictures of himself as a newborn, and if you're recycling some of his old baby equipment, let him play with it a bit before you get it in order for the newcomer.

Any major changes in your preschooler's routine, such as toilet training, switching from a crib to a bed, changing bedrooms, or starting nursery school, should be completed before the baby arrives. If that's not possible, put them off until after the baby is settled in at home. Otherwise, your youngster may feel overwhelmed when the upheaval caused by the baby's arrival is added to the stress of his own adjustments.

Don't be alarmed if news that a baby is coming—or, later, the baby's arrival—prompts your older child's behavior to regress a little. He may demand a bottle, ask to wear diapers again, or refuse to leave your side. This is his way of demanding your love and attention and reassuring himself that he still has them. Instead of protesting or telling him to act his age, simply grant his requests, and don't get upset about it. A three-year-old toilet-trained child who demands a diaper for a few days, or the five-year-old who wants his outgrown (you thought long-forgotten) security blanket for a week, will soon return to his normal routine when he realizes that he now has just as important a place in the family as his new sibling.

Once the baby is home, encourage your toddler to help and play with the newborn, but don't force him. If he shows an interest, give him some tasks that will make him feel like a big brother, such as disposing of dirty diapers and picking out the baby's clothes or bath toys. And when you're playing with the baby, invite him to join you and show him how to hold and move the baby. Make sure he understands, however, that he's not to do these things unless you or another adult is present.

However busy or preoccupied you may be with your new arrival, make sure you reserve some special time each day just for you and your older child. Read, play games, listen to music, or simply talk together. Show him that you're interested in what he's doing, thinking, and feeling—not only in relation to the baby but about everything else in his life.

Preparing Yourself for Delivery

Toward the end of pregnancy, you may start feeling a little frantic. You'll be eager for the baby to arrive, but at the same time worried that your baby will be born before you have everything in perfect order. As your due date approaches (and in some cases, passes), you'll have to fend off countless callers who are almost as excited as you are, and also concerned about your welfare. This social pressure, added to the physical discomfort of late pregnancy, can make the ninth month seem endless. But the story does have a nice ending, so try to enjoy your leisure time as much as you can.

If you use this time wisely, you can get some chores out of the way that would otherwise have to be done after delivery. For example:

- Make a list of people who will receive birth announcements, select the announcement style, and address the envelopes in advance.
- Cook a number of meals and freeze them. You may not feel up to cooking for a while after the baby arrives.
- Look for child-care and/or housekeeping help if you can afford it, and interview candidates in advance. (See *Finding Temporary Child-Care Help,* page 194.) Even if you don't think you'll need extra help, you should have a list of names to call in case the situation changes.

Before entering your ninth month, make your last-minute preparations for delivery. Your checklist should include the following:

- Name, address, and phone number of the hospital
- Name, address, and phone number of the doctor or nurse-midwife who will deliver your baby, and of the person who covers the practice when your doctor is not available
- The quickest and easiest route to the hospital or birthing center
- The location of the hospital entrance you should use when labor begins
- The phone number of an ambulance service, in case you need such assistance in an emergency
- The phone number of the person who will take you to the hospital (if that individual does not live with you)

- A bag packed with essentials for labor and for the rest of your hospital stay, including toiletries, clothing, addresses and phone numbers of friends and relatives, reading material, and a receiving blanket and suit of clothes for the baby to wear home
- A safety seat for the car so you can bring the baby home safely. Make sure the seat meets all federal safety standards. Install it in the backseat facing the rear. Never place a rear facing car seat in front of an air bag. It should stay in this position until your baby reaches one year of age *and* weighs at least 20 pounds. Then position it facing forward. (See *Car Seats*, page 330 for complete details.)
- If you have other children, make arrangements for their care during the time you will be at the hospital

Once your baby finally arrives, all the waiting and discomforts of pregnancy will seem like minor inconveniences. Suddenly you'll get to meet this new person who's been so close and yet so mysterious all these months. The rest of this book is about the child she will become and the job that awaits you as a parent.

2

BIRTH AND THE FIRST MOMENTS AFTER

Giving birth is one of the most extraordinary experiences of a woman's life. Yet after all the months of careful preparation and anticipation, the moment of birth is almost never what you had expected. Labor may be easier or more physically demanding than you had imagined. You may end up in a delivery room instead of the birthing room you'd wanted, or you could have a Caesarean section instead of a vaginal delivery. Your health, the condition of the fetus, and the policies of the hospital will all help determine what actually happens. But fortunately, despite what you may have thought when you were pregnant, these are not the issues that will make your child's birth a "success." What counts is the baby, here at last and healthy.

ROUTINE VAGINAL DELIVERY

In a routine vaginal delivery, your first view of your baby may be the top—or crown—of his head, seen with the help of a mirror. After the head is delivered, the obstetrician will suction the nose and mouth, and your baby will take his first breath. He doesn't need to be slapped or spanked to begin breathing, nor will he necessarily cry; many newborns take their first breath quietly.

With the most difficult part of the birth now over, there is usually one last pause before the push that sends the rest of your infant's body, which is smaller than his head, gliding smoothly into the doctor's waiting arms. After another, more thorough suctioning of his nose and mouth, your baby may be handed to you to hold—and behold.

Even if you've seen pictures of newborns, you're bound to be amazed by the first sight of your own infant. When he opens his eyes, they will meet yours with curiosity. All the activity of birth may make him very alert and responsive to your touch, voice, and warmth. Take advantage of this attentiveness, which may last for the first few hours. Stroke him, talk to him, and look closely at this child you've created.

Fresh from birth, your newborn may be covered with a white cheesy substance called vernix. This protective coating is produced toward the end of pregnancy by the sebaceous (fat-producing) glands in his skin. He'll also be wet with amniotic fluid from the uterus. If there was an episiotomy (surgical cutting) or tearing of tissue in the vaginal area, he may have some of your own blood on him. His skin, especially on the face, may be quite wrinkled from the wetness and pressure of birth.

Your baby's shape and size also may surprise you, especially if this is your first child. On the one hand, it's hard to believe that a human being can be so tiny; on the other, it's incredible that this "enormous" creature could possibly have fit inside your body. The size of his head in particular may alarm you. How could it possibly have made it through the birth canal? The answer lies in its slightly elongated shape. The head was able to adapt to the contour of the passageway as it was pushed through, squeezing to fit. Now free, it may take up to several days to revert to its normal oval shape.

Your baby's skin color may be a little blue at first, but will gradually turn more pink as his breathing becomes regular.

His hands and feet will be cold, and may remain so, on and off, for several weeks until his body is better able to adjust to the temperature around him.

You also may notice that your newborn's breathing is irregular and very rapid. While you normally take twelve to fourteen breaths per minute, your newborn may take as many as sixty. An occasional deep breath may alternate with bursts of short, shallow breaths followed by pauses. Don't let this make you anxious. It's normal for the initial days after birth.

Delivery by Caesarean Section

More than twenty out of every hundred babies born in the United States are delivered by Caesarean section (also called C-section or, simply, section). In a C-section, surgery is performed so the baby can be taken directly from the uterus instead of traveling through the birth canal. Caesarean sections are most often done when the mother has had a previous baby by Caesarean delivery, or when the obstetrician feels that the baby's health might suffer if born vaginally. Usually, if the fetus's heartbeat slows abnormally or becomes irregular, the obstetrician will perform an emergency C-section instead of taking the chance of allowing labor to progress.

The birth experience with a C-section is very different from that of a vaginal delivery. For one thing, the whole operation ordinarily takes no more than an hour, and—depending on the circumstances—you may not experience any labor at all. An important difference is the need to use medication that affects both mother and baby. If given a choice of anesthetic, most women prefer to have a regional anesthesia, an injection in the back that blocks pain by numbing the spinal nerves, such as an epidural or a spinal. Administration of a regional anesthesia numbs the body from the waist down, has relatively few side effects, and allows you to witness the delivery. But sometimes, especially for an emergency C-section, a general anesthetic must be used, in which case you are not conscious at all. Your obstetrician and the anesthesiologist in attendance will advise you which approach they think is best, based on the medical circumstances at the time.

Because of the effects of the anesthesia, babies born by C-section sometimes have difficulty breathing in the beginning and need extra help. A pediatrician or other person skilled in newborn problems is usually present during a Caesarean section so that she can examine and assist the baby, if necessary, immediately after birth.

If you were awake during the operation, you may be able to see your baby as soon as she's been examined and proclaimed healthy. She then will be taken to the nursery to spend several hours in a temperature-controlled crib. This allows the hospital staff to observe her while the anesthesia wears off and she adjusts to her new surroundings.

If a general anesthesia was used during the delivery, you may not wake up for a few hours. When you do, you may feel groggy and confused. You'll probably also experience some pain where the incision was made. But you'll soon be able to hold your baby, and you'll quickly make up for the lost time.

Your C-section baby may look "prettier" than newborns delivered vaginally, because she didn't have to squeeze through the birth canal. As a result, instead of being elongated, her head retains its roundish shape.

Don't be surprised if your baby is still being affected by the anesthesia for six to twelve hours after delivery and appears a little sleepy. If you're going to breastfeed, try to nurse her as soon as you feel well enough. Even if she's drowsy, her first feeding will provide a reason for her to wake up and meet her new world—and you!

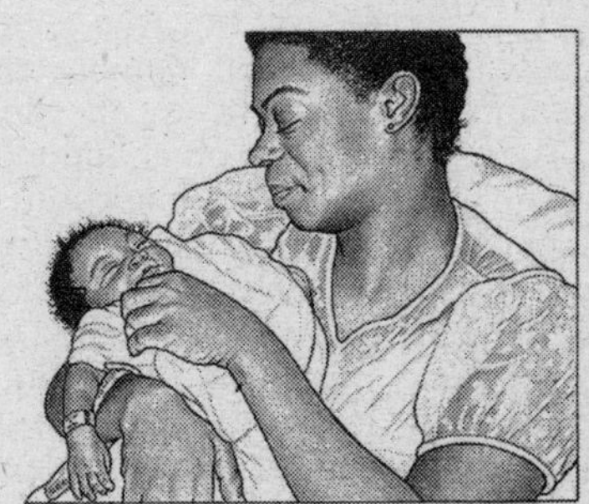

Even if you've seen pictures of newborns, you're bound to be amazed by the first sight of your own infant.

Delivery Room Procedures Following a Normal Vaginal Birth

As your baby lies with you following a routine delivery, his umbilical cord will still be attached to the placenta. For several minutes the cord may continue to pulsate, supplying the baby with oxygen while he establishes his own breathing. Once the pulsing stops, the cord will be clamped and cut. (Because there are no nerves in the cord, the baby feels no pain during this procedure.) The clamp will remain in place for twenty-four to forty-eight hours, or until the cord is dry and no longer bleeds. The stump that remains after the clamp is removed will fall off sometime between ten days and three weeks after birth.

Once you've had a few moments to get acquainted with your baby, he will be dried to keep him from getting too cold, and a doctor or nurse will examine him briefly to make sure there are no obvious problems or abnormalities. One minute after birth, and again at five minutes, he will be given Apgar scores (see page 46), which measure his overall responsiveness. Then he will be wrapped in a blanket and given back to you.

Depending on the hospital's routine, your baby may also be weighed, measured, and receive medication before leaving the delivery room. All newborns are slightly low in vitamin K, which is necessary for normal blood-clotting, so they are given an injection of this vitamin to prevent excessive bleeding.

Because bacteria in the birth canal can infect a baby's eyes, your baby will be given antibiotic eye drops or silver nitrate ointment, either immediately after delivery or later, in the nursery, to prevent any infection.

There's at least one other important procedure to be done before either you or your newborn leaves the delivery room: Both of you will receive matching labels bearing your name and other identifying details. After you verify the accuracy of these labels, one will be attached to your wrist and the other to your baby's. Each time the infant is taken from or returned to you while in the hospital, the nurse will check the bracelets to make sure they match. Many hospitals also footprint newborns as an added precaution.

Bonding

If you have a delivery without complications, you'll be able to spend the first hour or so after birth holding, stroking, and looking at your baby. Because babies are usually alert and very responsive during this time, researchers have labeled this the "sensitive period."

The first exchanges of eye contact, sounds, and touches between the two of you are all part of a process called bonding, which helps lay the foundation for your relationship as parent and child. While it will take months to learn your baby's basic temperament and personality, many of the core emotions you feel for him may begin to develop during this brief period immediately after birth. As you gaze at him and he looks back, following your movements and perhaps even mirroring some of your expressions, you may feel a surge of protectiveness and awe. This is part of the attachment process. It's also quite normal if you do *not* immediately have tremendously warm feelings for your baby. Labor is a demanding experience, and your first reaction to the birth may well be a sense of relief that at last it's over. If you're exhausted and emotionally drained, you may simply want to rest. That's perfectly normal. Give yourself a half hour or so until the strain of labor fades, and then request your baby. Bonding has no time limit.

Also, if your baby must be taken to the nursery right away for medical attention, or if you are sedated during the delivery, don't despair. You needn't worry that your relationship will be harmed because you didn't "bond" during this first hour. You can and will love your baby just as much, even if you weren't able to watch his birth or hold him immediately afterward. Your baby also will be fine, just as loving of you, and connected to you.

Procedures Following Premature Birth

About five or six out of every one hundred births in this country are premature. Because these babies are born before they are physically ready to leave the womb, they often have problems. For this reason, premature babies are given extra medical attention and assistance immediately after delivery. Depending upon how early the baby is, your pediatrician may call in another pediatrician (called a neonatologist), who specializes in premature intensive care, to help determine what, if any, special treatment the infant needs.

If your baby is born prematurely, she may neither look nor behave like a full-term infant. While the average full-term baby weighs about 7 pounds at birth, a premature newborn might weigh 5 pounds or even less. The earlier she arrives, the smaller she will be, the larger her head will seem in relation to the rest of her body, and the less fat she will have. With so little fat, her skin will seem thinner and more transparent, allowing you actually to see the blood vessels beneath it. Her features will appear sharper and less rounded than they would at term, and she probably won't have any of

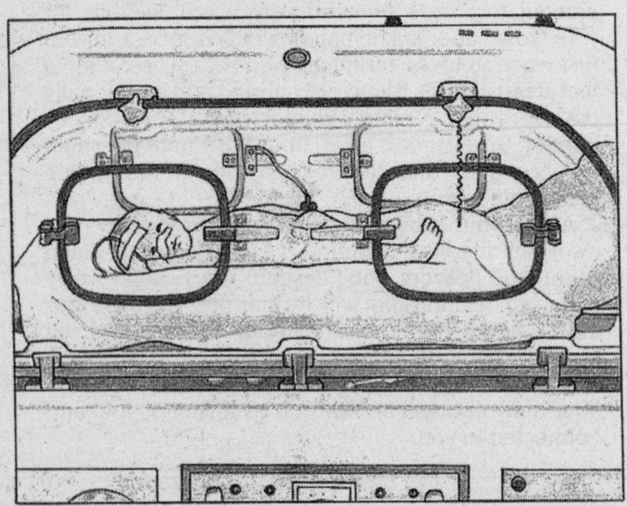

Your premature baby will be placed immediately after birth in an enclosed bed to keep her warm.

the white, cheesy vernix protecting her at birth, because it isn't produced until late in pregnancy.

Because she has no protective fat, your premature baby will get cold in normal room temperatures. For that reason she'll be placed immediately after birth in an enclosed bed in which the temperature can be adjusted to keep her warm. After a quick examination in the delivery room, she'll probably be moved to a special-care nursery.

You may also notice that your premature baby will cry only softly, if at all, and may have trouble breathing. This is because her respiratory system is still immature. If she's more than two months early, her breathing difficulties can cause serious health problems, because the other organs in her body may not get enough oxygen. To make sure this doesn't happen, your doctors will keep her under close observation. If she needs help breathing, she may be given extra oxygen, or special equipment may be used temporarily to do some of her breathing for her.

As important as this special care is for your baby's survival, her move to the nursery will probably be wrenching for you. On top of all the worry about her health, you may miss the experience of holding, breastfeeding, and bonding with her right after delivery. You won't be able to hold or touch her whenever you want, and you can't have her with you in your room.

What's your best defense against the stress of an experience like this? Ask to see your baby as soon as possible after delivery, and become as active as you can in caring for her. Spend as much time with her in the nursery as your condition—and hers—permit. Even if you can't hold her, touch her through the portholes of the enclosed bed. Breastfeed her if possible, or ask the nurses to help you express milk to feed her; this will stimulate your own milk production so you can nurse her when she's able.

The more you participate in her process of recovery and the more contact you have with her during this time, the better you'll feel about the situation and the easier it will be for you to care for her when she leaves the nursery. If you have questions, be sure to ask them of the doctors and nurses. Also, don't forget that your own pediatrician will be participating in, or at least will be informed about, your infant's immediate care. Because of this, he will be able to answer most of your questions.

Apgar Scores

As soon as your baby is born, a delivery nurse will set one timer for one minute and another for five minutes. When each of these time periods is up, a nurse or physician will give your baby her first "tests," called Apgars.

This scoring system (named after its creator, Virginia Apgar) helps the physician estimate your baby's general condition at birth. The test measures your baby's heart rate, breathing, muscle tone, reflex response, and color. It cannot predict how healthy she will be as she grows up or how she will develop; nor does it indicate how bright she is or what her personality is like. But it does alert the hospital staff if she is sleepier or slower to respond than normal and may be in need of assistance as she adapts to her new world outside the womb.

Each characteristic is given an individual score; then all scores are totaled. For example, let's say your baby has a heart rate of more than 100, cries lustily, moves actively, grimaces and coughs in response to the syringe, but is blue; her one-minute Apgar score would be 8. About nine out of ten newborns in this country score in the 8 to 10 range. Because their hands and feet remain blue until they are quite warm, few score a perfect 10.

If your baby's Apgar scores are between 5 and 7 at one minute, she may have experienced some problems during birth which lowered the oxygen in her blood. In this case, the staff will probably dry her vigorously with a towel while oxygen is held under her nose. This should start her breathing deeply and improve her oxygen supply so that her five-minute Apgar scores total between 8 and 10.

A small percentage of newborns have Apgar scores of less than 5. For example, babies born prematurely or delivered by emergency C-section are more likely to have low scores than infants with normal births. These scores may reflect difficulties the baby experienced during labor, or problems with her heart or respiratory system.

If your baby's Apgar scores are very low, a mask may be placed over her face to pump oxygen directly into her lungs. If she's not breathing on her own within a few minutes, a tube can be placed into her windpipe, and fluids and medications may be administered through one of the blood vessels in her umbilical cord to strengthen her heartbeat. If her Apgar scores are still low after these treatments, she will be taken to the special-care nursery for more intensive medical attention.

Apgar Scoring System

Score	**0**	**1**	**2**
Heart Rate	Absent	Less than 100 beats per minute	More than 100 beats per minute
Respiration	Absent	Slow, irregular; weak cry	Good; strong cry
Muscle Tone	Limp	Some flexing of arms and legs	Active motion
Reflex*	Absent	Grimace	Grimace and cough or sneeze
Color	Blue or pale	Body pink; hands and feet blue	Completely pink

* Reflex judged by placing a catheter or bulb syringe in the infant's nose and watching her response.

LEAVING THE DELIVERY AREA

If you've given birth in a birthing room or alternative birth center, you probably won't be moved right away. But if you delivered in a conventional delivery room, you'll be taken to a recovery area where you can be watched for problems such as excessive bleeding. Your baby may be taken to the nursery at that time, or he may receive his first physical examination by your side.

This exam will measure his vital signs: temperature, respiration, and pulse rate. The pediatrician or nurse will check his color, activity level, and breathing pattern. If he didn't receive his vitamin K and eye drops earlier, they will be administered now. And once he's warm, he'll be given his first bath and the stump of his cord may be painted with a blue antibacterial dye or other medication to prevent infection. Then he'll be wrapped in a blanket and, if you wish, returned to you.

After all this activity during his first couple of hours, your baby will probably fall into a deep sleep, giving you time to rest and think back over the exciting things that have happened since labor began. If you have your baby with you, you may stare at him in wonder that you could possibly have produced such a miracle. Such emotions may wipe away your physical exhaustion temporarily, but don't fool yourself. You need to relax, sleep, and gather your strength. You have a very big job ahead of you—you're a parent now!

Nursing After Delivery

Do you plan to breastfeed your baby? If so, ask ahead of time about the hospital's policies on nursing in the delivery area. Most hospitals today encourage immediate breastfeeding following routine delivery unless the baby's Apgar scores are low or he's breathing very rapidly, in which case nursing would be delayed temporarily.

Breastfeeding right away benefits the mother by causing the uterus to contract, thus reducing the amount of uterine bleeding. (The same hormone that stimulates milk production triggers the uterine contractions.)

The first hour or so after birth is a good time to begin breastfeeding, because your baby is very alert and eager. When put to the breast he will first lick it. Then, with a little help, he'll grasp the nipple and suck vigorously for several minutes. If you wait until later, he may be sleepier and have more difficulty holding the nipple effectively.

Breastmilk does not begin flowing for three to five days after delivery, but your baby does receive colostrum, a thin, yellowish fluid that contains protein and antibodies to protect him from infection. Colostrum doesn't provide as many calories or as much fluid as breastmilk, but it is still an important source of nutrition and immunity. (See page 96.) (For a complete discussion of breastfeeding, see Chapter 4.)

3

Basic Infant Care

When your baby first arrives, you may feel a bit overwhelmed by the job of caring for her. Even such routine tasks as diapering and dressing her can fill you with anxiety—especially if you've never spent much time around babies before. But it doesn't take long to develop the confidence and calm of an experienced parent, and you'll have help. While you are in the hospital, the nursery staff and your pediatrician will give you instructions and support your needs. Later, family and friends can be helpful; don't be bashful about asking for their assistance. But your baby will give you the most important information—how she likes to be treated, talked to, held, and comforted. She'll bring out parental instincts that will guide you quite automatically to many of the right responses, almost as soon as she's born.

The following sections address the most common questions and concerns that arise during the first months of life.

DAY TO DAY

Responding to Your Baby's Cries

Crying serves several useful purposes for your baby. It gives him a way to call for help when he's hungry or uncomfortable. It helps him shut out sights, sounds, and other sensations that are too intense to suit him. And it helps him release tension.

You may notice that your baby has fussy periods throughout the day, even though he's not hungry, uncomfortable, or tired. Nothing you do at these times will console him, but right after these spells, he may seem more alert than before, and shortly thereafter may sleep more deeply than usual. This kind of fussy crying seems to help babies get rid of excess energy so they can return to a more contented state.

Pay close attention to your baby's different cries and you'll soon be able to tell when he needs to be picked up, consoled, or tended to, and when he is better off left alone. You may even be able to identify his specific needs by the way he cries. For instance, a hungry cry is usually short and low-pitched, and it rises and falls. An angry cry tends to be more turbulent. A cry of pain or distress generally comes on suddenly and loudly with a long, high-pitched shriek followed by a long pause and then a flat wail. The "leave-me-alone" cry is usually similar to a hunger cry. It won't take long before you have a pretty good idea of what your baby's cries are trying to tell you.

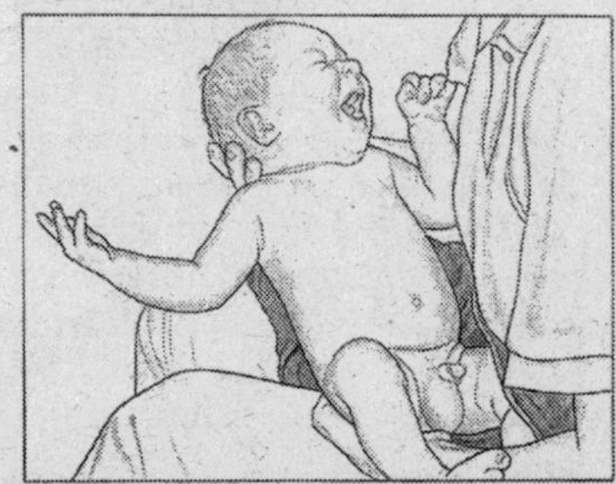

It won't take long before you have a pretty good idea of what your baby's cries are trying to tell you.

Sometimes different types of cries overlap. For example, newborns generally wake up hungry and crying for food. If you're not quick to respond, your baby's hunger cry may give way to a wail of rage. You'll hear the difference. As your baby matures his cries will become stronger, louder, more insistent. They'll also begin to vary more, as if to convey different needs and desires.

The best way to handle crying is to respond promptly to your infant whenever he cries during his first few months. You cannot spoil a young baby by giving him attention; and if you answer his calls for help, he'll cry less overall.

When responding to your infant's cries, try to meet his most pressing need first. If he's cold and hungry and his diaper is wet, warm him up, change his diaper, and then feed him. If there's a shrieking or panicked quality to the cry, you should consider the possibility that a diaper pin is open or a strand of hair is caught around a finger or toe. If he's warm, dry, and well fed but nothing is working to stop the crying, try the following consoling techniques to find the ones that work best for your baby:

- Rocking, either in a rocking chair or in your arms as you sway from side to side
- Gently stroking his head or patting his back or chest
- Swaddling (wrapping the baby snugly in a receiving blanket)
- Singing or talking
- Playing soft music

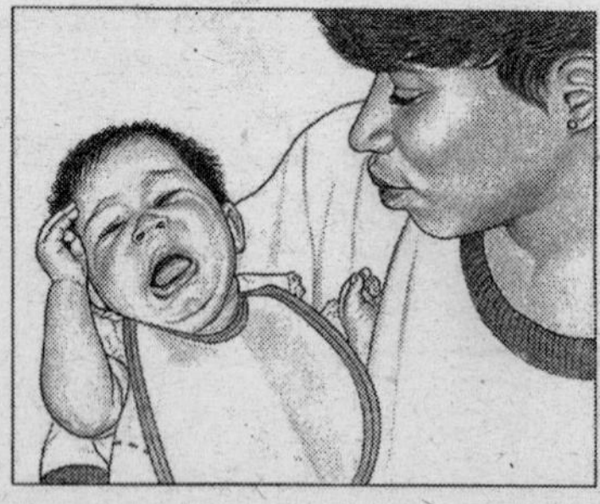

Respond promptly to your infant whenever he cries during his first few months. You cannot spoil a young baby by giving him attention.

- Walking him in your arms, a stroller, or a carriage
- Riding in the car
- Rhythmic noise and vibration
- Burping him to relieve any trapped gas bubbles
- Warm baths (*Most* babies like this, but not all.)

Sometimes, if all else fails, the best approach is simply to leave the baby alone. Many babies cannot fall asleep without crying, and will go to sleep more quickly if left to cry for a while. The crying shouldn't last long if the child is truly tired.

If your baby is inconsolable no matter what you do, he may be sick. Check his temperature (see *Taking a Rectal Temperature*, page 78). If it is over 100 degrees Fahrenheit (rectally), he could have an infection. Contact your pediatrician.

The more relaxed you remain, the easier it will be to console your child. Even very young babies are sensitive to tension around them and react to it by crying. Listening to a wailing newborn can be agonizing, but letting your frustration turn to anger or panic will only intensify your infant's screams. If you start to feel that you can't handle the situation, get help from another family member or a friend. Not only will this give you needed relief, but a new face can sometimes calm your baby when all your own tricks are spent. No matter how impatient or angry you feel, do not shake the baby. Shaking an infant hard can cause blindness, brain damage, or even death.

Above all, don't take your newborn's crying personally. He's not crying because you're a bad parent or because he doesn't like you. All babies cry, often without any apparent cause. Newborns routinely cry a total of one to four hours a day. It's part of adjusting to this strange new life outside the womb.

No mother can console her infant *every* time he cries, so don't expect to be a miracle worker with your baby. Instead, take a realistic approach to the situation, line up some help, get plenty of rest, and enjoy all those wondrous moments with your child.

Helping Your Baby Sleep

Initially, your infant doesn't know the difference between day and night. Her stomach holds only enough to satisfy her for three or four hours, regardless of the time, so there's no escaping round-the-clock waking and feeding for the first few weeks. But even at this age, you can begin to teach her that nighttime is for sleeping and daytime for play. Do this by keeping nighttime feedings as subdued as possible. Don't turn up the lights or prolong late-night diaper changes. Instead of playing, put her back down after feeding and changing her. If she's napping longer than three or four hours, particularly in the late afternoon, wake her up and play with her. This will train her to save her extra sleeping for nighttime.

Positioning for Sleep

For many years it has been recommended that infants, particularly in the age range from birth to four months, be placed on their stomachs for sleep. This was thought to be the best way to avoid aspiration (sucking food into the trachea or windpipe) in case of vomiting or spitting up. *Recent information, however, indicates that the back is a safer position, particularly as it relates to Sudden Infant Death Syndrome (SIDS). Therefore, the American Academy of Pediatrics recommends that healthy infants be placed on their backs for sleep.* The exact reason for this finding is not certain, but it may be related to the stomach-positioned infant getting less oxygen or eliminating less carbon dioxide because she is "rebreathing" air from a small pocket of bedding pulled up around the nose. Although sleep position is probably not the only reason for SIDS, it seemed to be so strongly related that the Academy felt obligated to make this recommendation. Please note that there are some exceptions to this new recommendation, which your pediatrician can discuss with you.

This recommendation applies to infants throughout the first year of life. However, the recommendation is particularly important for the first 6 months, when the incidence of SIDS is the highest.

It is also important to avoid placing your baby down for sleep on soft, porous surfaces such as pillows or quilts. Her airway may become blocked if her face becomes burrowed in such surfaces. A firm crib mattress covered by a sheet is the safest bedding.

As she gets older and her stomach grows, your baby will be able to go longer between feedings. In fact, you'll be encouraged to know that more than 90 percent of babies sleep through the night (six to eight hours without waking) by three months. Most infants are able to last this long between feedings when they reach 12 or 13 pounds, so if yours is a very large baby, she may begin sleeping through the night even earlier than three months. As encouraging as this sounds, don't expect the sleep struggle to end all at once. Most children swing back and forth, sleeping beautifully for a few weeks, or even months, then returning abruptly to a late-night wake-up schedule. This may have to do with growth spurts increasing the need for food, or, later, it may be related to teething or developmental changes.

From time to time you will need to help your baby fall asleep or go back to sleep. Especially as a newborn, she probably will doze off most easily if given gentle continuous stimulation. Some infants are helped by rocking, walking, patting on the back, or by a pacifier in the mouth. For others, music from a radio or a record or tape player can be very soothing if played at moderate volume. Even the sound of the television, played quietly, can provide comforting background noise. Certain stimulation, however, is irritating to any baby—for example, ringing telephones, barking dogs, and roaring vacuum cleaners.

There is no reason to restrict your baby's sleeping to her crib. If, for any reason, you want her closer to you while she sleeps, use her infant seat or bassinet as a temporary crib and move it around the house with you. (She'll be perfectly happy in a padded basket if you don't have an "official" bassinet.)

How Your Baby Sleeps

Even before birth your baby's days were divided between periods of sleep and wakefulness. By the eighth month of pregnancy or earlier, her sleep periods consisted of the same two distinct phases that we all experience:

1. Rapid eye movement (or REM) sleep, the times during which she does her active dreaming. During these periods her eyes will move beneath her closed lids, almost as if she were watching a dream take place. She may also seem to startle, twitch her face, and make jerking motions with her hands and feet. All are normal signs of REM sleep.

2. Non-REM sleep, which consists of four phases: drowsiness, light sleep, deep sleep, and very deep sleep. During the progression from drowsiness to deepest sleep, your baby becomes less and less active, and her breathing slows and becomes very quiet, so that in deepest sleep she is virtually motionless. Very little, if any, dreaming occurs during non-REM sleep.

At first your newborn will probably sleep about sixteen hours a day, divided into three- or four-hour naps evenly spaced between feedings.

Each of these sleep periods will include relatively equal amounts of REM and non-REM sleep, organized in the following order: 1. drowsiness; 2. REM sleep; 3. light sleep; 4. deep sleep; 5. very deep sleep.

After about two to three months the order will change, so that as she grows older she cycles through all the non-REM phases before entering REM sleep. This pattern will last into and through adulthood. As she grows older the amount of REM sleep decreases, and her sleep will become generally calmer. By the age of three, only one-third or less of total sleep time is spent in REM sleep.

Where We Stand

Based on an evaluation of current SIDS data, the American Academy of Pediatrics recommends that healthy infants, when being put down to sleep, be placed on their back. Despite common beliefs, there is no evidence that choking is more frequent among infants lying on their backs (the supine position) when compared to other positions. In some circumstances, there are still good reasons for placing certain infants on their stomachs for sleep. You are encouraged to discuss your individual circumstances with your pediatrician.

Diapers

Until disposable diapers were introduced about thirty-five years ago, the only choice was to use cloth diapers, and either launder them at home or use a commercial diaper service. Today, modern disposable diapers meet the needs and expectations of most parents, and make up 80% or more of all diaper changes in virtually all developed countries. However, diaper choice is a decision that every new parent faces. Ideally, you should choose between cloth and disposable diapers before the baby arrives, so you can stock up or make delivery arrangements ahead of time. In order to plan ahead, you should know that most newborns go through about ten diapers a day.

Disposable Diapers. Most disposable diapers today consist of an inner liner next to the baby to help keep wetness away from the skin, an absorbent core made of purified wood pulp and super absorbent polymers, and an outer waterproof covering. They may have elastics at the waist and legs to provide better fit and help prevent leaks, and have various kinds of fastening tapes to make application and removal easier. Over the years, disposable diapers have become thinner and lighter, while continuing to meet the needs for containment, comfort, ease of use, and skin care.

To fit a disposable diaper, place the baby on the open diaper so the fastening tapes are in back of the baby, and bring the front of the diaper between the baby's legs. Then bring the back edges of the diaper over the front and press the tapes into place to fasten. When changing a soiled diaper, dump loose stool into a toilet. Do not flush the diaper, because it can block your plumbing. Wrap the diaper in its outer cover, and discard in a waste receptacle.

Cloth Diapers. Like disposable diapers, reusable cloth diapers have improved over the years, and are available in a variety of absorbencies and textures. The original single-layer cotton diaper that is folded down to size has been largely replaced with the double-layered rectangular cotton diaper that has a multi-ply or fiber-filled center strip. Most parents fasten them with diaper pins. To prevent pricking the baby when using pins, you need to keep your hand between the pin and your baby's skin. You can also use diaper tape, which comes in a dispenser like household tape, and adheres to the cloth. The correct way to apply cloth diapers is shown in the diagrams. To prevent wet clothes and bedding, cloth diapers can be covered with a waterproof pant or overwrap. Cloth diapers are also available that combine the diaper and overwrap into a single unit.

If you want to use a diaper service, shop around before you make a choice. Ideally, a diaper service should pick up dirty diapers and drop off clean ones twice a week. Some services ask you to rinse the diapers yourself, while others prefer that you leave them intact, waste and all, in the diaper pail. If a diaper service is not available, or you choose to wash diapers yourself, keep them separate from other clothes. After dumping stool into a toilet, you should rinse diapers in cold water, then soak them in a mild detergent solution with bleach for 30 minutes. Wring them out, then wash in hot water with a mild detergent.

Diaper Choice. Diaper choice has been complicated in recent years by the debate on the environmental effects of diapers, mostly centered on the effects of disposable diapers on landfill space. Actually, both cloth and disposable diapers have environmental effects, including raw material and energy usage, air and water pollution, and waste disposal. A number of scientific studies have found that each diaper has some environmental effect. Disposable diapers add 1% to 2% to municipal solid waste, while cloth diapers use more energy and water in laundering and contribute to air and water pollution. It is difficult to judge whether solid waste issues are more important than energy, air, and water pollution issues. In the end, it is up to individuals to make their own decisions about diaper type based on their own concerns and needs.

When considering the cost of diapers, the use of disposable and cloth diapers from a diaper service is roughly equivalent. Laundering your diapers at home can save money, but you must decide whether this is a good way to spend your time and energy.

There are also some health aspects to consider. Excessively wet skin and contact with urine and stool can cause diaper rash. Because cloth diapers can't keep wetness away from your baby's skin as effectively as disposables, it's especially important to change cloth diapers quickly after they become wet or soiled. If you use cloth diapers, you might consider using disposables overnight and during trips and outings, when it is often less convenient to change them frequently.

Another health-related issue results from the ability of diapers to prevent leakage of urine and stool. This is particularly important in group child-care settings such as day care centers, where intestinal diseases can be easily transmitted among the children. Disposable diapers are generally able to prevent leaks better than cloth because their super absorbent polymers lock wetness inside. Because of the increased risk for leaks and diaper handling issues, many day care centers require the use of disposable diapers.

How to Diaper Your Baby

Before you start to change your baby, make sure you have all the necessary supplies within easy reach. *Never* leave your baby alone on the changing table—not even for a second. It won't be long before he will be able to turn over, and if he does it when your eyes or attention are diverted, a serious injury could result.

When changing a newborn, you will need:

- a clean diaper (plus fasteners if a cloth diaper is used)
- ointment or petroleum jelly (for use only if the baby has a rash)
- cotton balls and a small basin with lukewarm water and a washcloth (commercial diaper wipes can also be used, although some babies are sensitive to them; if any irritation occurs, discontinue use)
- baby powder (advisable at the direction of your pediatrician)

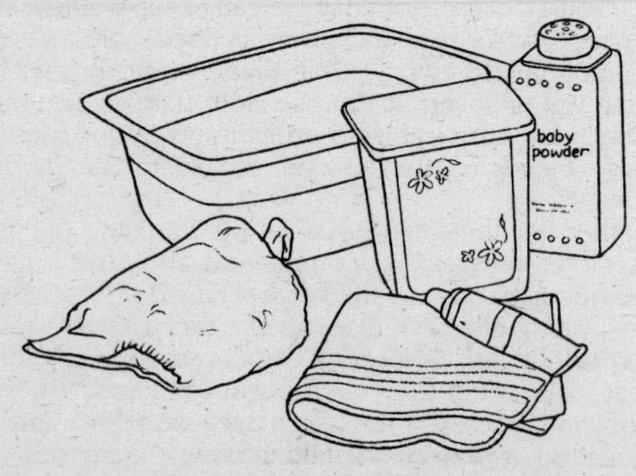

This is how you proceed:

1. Remove the dirty diaper and use the lukewarm water and cotton to gently wipe your baby clean (remember to wipe front to back on female infants).

2. Use the damp washcloth to wipe the diaper area.

3. Use the diaper rash preparation recommended by your pediatrician.

4. Put on the new diaper as shown on succeeding pages.

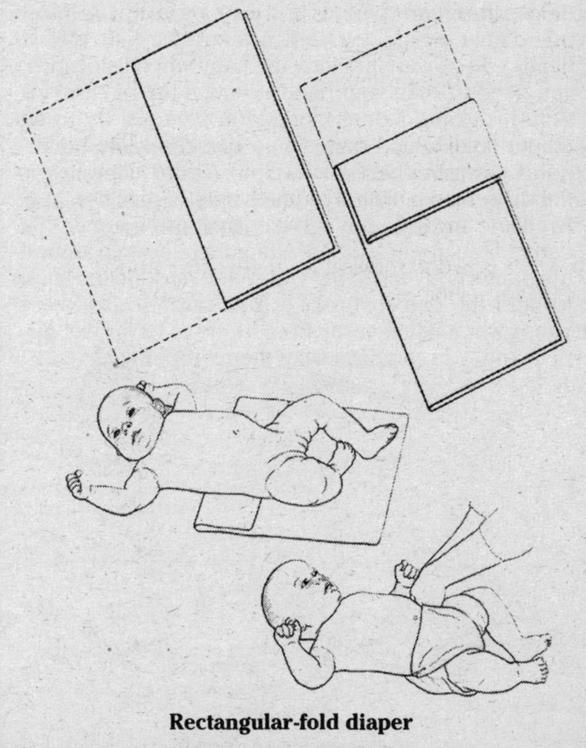

Rectangular-fold diaper

Cloth diapers are available either prefolded (14 by 20 inches) or in a 27-inch square which you can fold to fit your child precisely. Initially, you will need to fold about a third of the diaper down from the end so it's not too long. This also increases the absorbency. If the diapers have extra padding and your baby is a boy, place the padding in front. For girls, the padding goes in back.

The tape fasteners on disposables make the job of diapering very easy (except when petroleum jelly or lotion from your fingers gets onto the tape and prevents it from sticking), but there are also ways to fasten cloth diapers that many parents find just as convenient. Most use diaper pins (oversized safety pins with plastic heads). To prevent pricking the baby when using pins, you need to keep your hand between the pin and his skin. If this procedure makes you nervous, try using diaper tape, which comes in a dispenser like household tape and adheres to the cloth. A third alternative is the diaper wrap, which requires neither pins nor tape. Available from diaper services and most stores that carry baby supplies, diaper wraps literally wrap around the baby's body, fastening with Velcro around the waist to hold the diaper in place. You can also use these wraps when you're away from home to cover wet diapers until you can dispose of them properly.

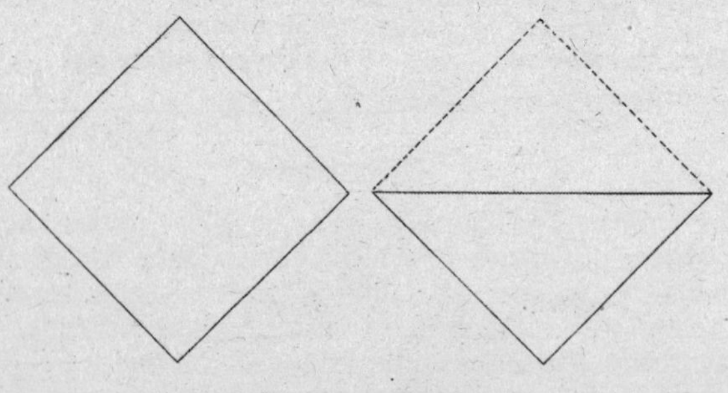

Triangular-fold diaper

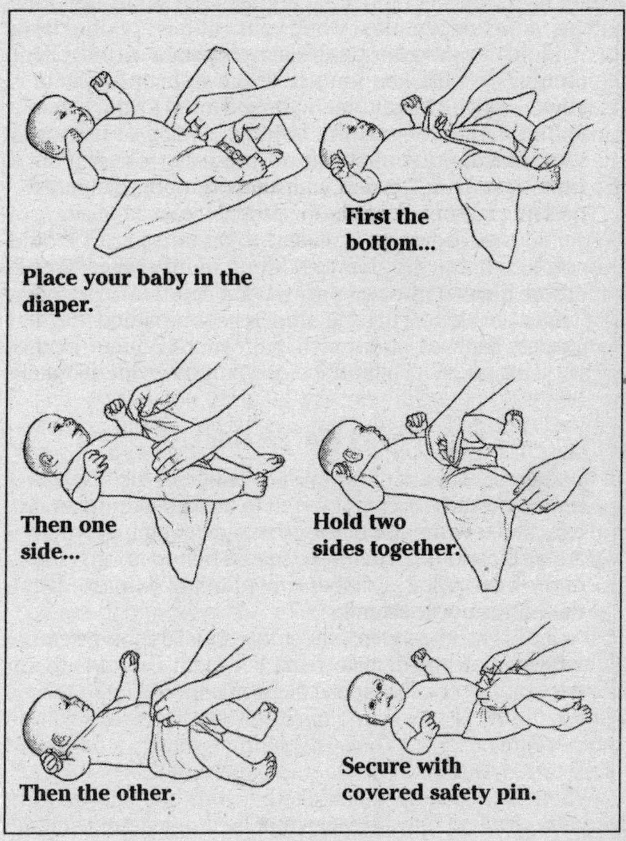

Urination

Your baby may urinate as often as every one to three hours, or as infrequently as four to six times a day. If she's ill or feverish, or when the weather is extremely hot, her usual output of urine may drop by half and still be normal.

Urination should never be painful. If you notice any signs of distress while your infant is urinating, notify your pediatrician, as this could be a sign of infection or some other problem in the urinary tract.

In a healthy baby, urine is light to dark yellow in color (the darker the color, the more concentrated the urine; the urine will be more concentrated when your child is not drinking a lot of liquid). Sometimes you'll see a pink stain on the diaper which may be mistaken for blood. But in fact, this stain is usually a sign of highly concentrated urine, which has a pinkish color. As long as the baby is wetting at least four diapers a day, there probably is no cause for concern, but if the pinkish staining persists, consult your pediatrician.

The presence of actual blood in the urine or a bloody spot on the diaper is never normal, and your pediatrician should be notified. It may be due to nothing more serious than a small sore caused by diaper rash, but it could also be a sign of a larger problem. If this bleeding is accompanied by other symptoms, such as abdominal pain or bleeding in other areas, seek medical attention for your baby immediately.

Bowel Movements

In the first few days of life your baby will have his first bowel movement, which is often referred to as passing meconium. This thick, dark green or black substance filled his intestines before birth, and it must be eliminated before normal digestion can take place. Once the meconium is passed, the stools will turn yellow-green.

If your baby is breastfed, his stools should soon resemble light mustard with seedlike particles. Until he starts to eat solid foods, the consistency of the stools should be soft, even slightly runny. If he's formula-fed, his stools usually will be tan or yellow in color. They will be firmer than in a baby who is breastfed, but no firmer than peanut butter.

Whether breastfed or bottle-fed, if your baby has hard or very dry stools, it may be a sign that he is not getting enough fluid, or that he is losing too much fluid due to illness, fever, or heat. Once he has started solids, hard stools might indicate that he's eating too many constipating foods, such as cereal or cow's milk, before his system can handle them. (Whole cow's milk is not recommended for babies under twelve months.)

Keep in mind that occasional variations in color and consistency of the stools are normal. For example, if the digestive process slows down because the baby has had a particularly large amount of cereal that day or foods requiring more effort to digest, the stools may become green; or if the baby is given supplemental iron, the stools may turn dark brown. If there is a minor irritation of the anus, streaks of blood may appear on the outside of the stools. However, if there are large amounts of blood, mucus, or water in the stool, call your pediatrician immediately. These symptoms may indicate severe diarrhea or an intestinal abnormality.

Because an infant's stools are normally soft and a little runny, it's not always easy to tell when a young baby has mild diarrhea. The telltale signs are a sudden increase in frequency (to more than one bowel movement per feeding), and unusually high liquid content in the stool. Diarrhea may be a sign of intestinal infection, or it may be caused by a change in the baby's diet. If the baby is breastfeeding, he can even develop diarrhea because of a change in the mother's diet.

The main concern with diarrhea is the possibility that dehydration can develop. If fever is also present and your infant is less than two months old, call your pediatrician immediately. If your baby is over two months and the fever lasts more than a day, check his urine output and rectal temperature; then report your findings to your doctor so she can determine what needs to be done.

The frequency of bowel movements varies widely from one baby to another. Many pass a stool soon after each feeding. This is a result of the gastrocolic reflex, which causes the digestive system to become active whenever the stomach is filled with food.

By three to six weeks of age, some breastfed babies have only one bowel movement a week and still are normal. This happens because breastmilk leaves very little solid waste to be eliminated from the child's digestive system. Thus, infrequent stools are not a sign of constipation and should not be considered a problem as long as the stools are soft (no firmer than peanut butter), and your infant is otherwise normal, gaining weight steadily, and nursing regularly.

If your baby is formula-fed, he should have at least one bowel movement a day. If he has fewer than this and appears to be straining because of hard stools, he may be constipated. Check with your pediatrician for advice on how to handle this problem. (See *Constipation*, page 420.)

Diaper Rash

Diaper rash is the term used to describe a rash or irritation in the area covered by the diaper. The first sign of diaper rash is usually redness or small bumps on the lower abdomen, buttocks, genitals, and thigh folds—surfaces that have been in direct contact with the wet or soiled diaper. This type of diaper rash is rarely serious, and usually clears in three or four days with appropriate care.

The most common causes of diaper rash include:

1. Leaving a wet diaper on too long. The moisture makes the skin more susceptible to chafing. Over time, the urine in the diaper decomposes, forming chemicals that can further irritate the skin.

2. Leaving a stool-soiled diaper on too long. Digestive agents in the stool then attack the skin, making it more susceptible to a rash.

Regardless of how the rash begins, once the surface of the skin is damaged, it becomes even more vulnerable to further irritation by contact with urine and stool.

Another cause of rash in this area is yeast infection. This rash is common on the thighs, genitals, and lower abdomen but almost never appears on the buttock.

While most babies develop diaper rash at some point during infancy, it happens less often in babies who are breastfed (for reasons we still do not know). Diaper rash occurs more often at particular ages and under certain conditions:

- among babies eight to ten months old
- if babies are not kept clean and dry
- when babies have frequent stools (especially when the stools are left in their diapers overnight)
- when a baby starts to eat solid food (probably due to the introduction of more acidic foods and

changes in the digestive process caused by the new variety of foods)

- when a baby is taking antibiotics (because these drugs encourage the growth of yeast organisms that can infect the skin)

To reduce your baby's risk of diaper rash, make these steps part of your diapering routine:

1. Change the diaper as soon as possible after a bowel movement. Cleanse the diaper area with a soft cloth and water after each bowel movement.

2. Change wet diapers frequently to reduce skin exposure to moisture.

3. Expose the baby's bottom to air whenever feasible. When using plastic pants or disposable diapers with tight gathers around the abdomen and legs, make sure air can circulate inside the diaper.

If a diaper rash develops in spite of your efforts and the skin is dried out, you may need to use a lotion or ointment; if it is a moist rash, use a drying lotion. The rash should improve noticeably within forty-eight to seventy-two hours. If it doesn't, consult your pediatrician.

Bathing

Your infant doesn't need much bathing if you wash the diaper area thoroughly during diaper changes. Two or three times a week during her first year is plenty. If she is bathed more frequently, it may dry out her skin.

During her first week or two, until the stump of the umbilical cord falls off, your newborn should have only sponge baths. In a warm room, lay the baby anywhere that's flat and comfortable for both of you—a changing table, bed, floor, or counter next to the sink will do. Pad hard surfaces with a blanket or fluffy towel. If the baby is on a surface above the

Baby towels with built-in hoods are the most effective way to keep your baby's head warm when she's wet.

floor, use a safety strap or keep one hand on her *at all times* to make sure she doesn't fall.

Have a basin of water, a damp, double-rinsed (so there is no soap residue in it) washcloth, and a supply of mild baby soap within reach before you begin. Keep your baby wrapped in a towel, and expose only the parts of her body you are actively washing. Use the dampened cloth first without soap to wash her face, so you don't get soap into her eyes or mouth. Then dip it in the basin of soapy water before washing the remainder of her body and, finally, the diaper area. Pay special attention to creases under the arms, behind the ears, around the neck, and, especially with a girl, in the genital area.

Once the umbilical area is healed, you can try placing your baby directly in the water. Her first baths should be as gentle and brief as possible. She will probably protest a little; if she seems miserable, you should go back to sponge baths for a week or two, then try the bath again. She will make it clear when she's ready.

Most parents find it easiest to bathe a newborn in a bathinette, sink, or plastic tub lined with a clean towel. Fill the basin with two inches of water that feels warm—not hot—to the inside of your wrist or elbow. If you're filling the basin from the tap, turn the cold water on first (and off last) to avoid scalding yourself or your child. In addition, make sure your hot water heater is set no higher than 120 degrees Fahrenheit.

Make sure that supplies are at hand and the room is warm before undressing the baby. You'll need the same supplies that you used for sponge bathing, but also a cup for rinsing with clear water. When your infant has hair, you'll need baby shampoo, too.

If you've forgotten something or need to answer the phone or door during the bath, *you must take the baby with you,* so keep a dry towel within reach. *Never leave a baby alone in the bath, even for an instant.*

If your baby enjoys her bath, give her some extra time to splash and explore the water. The more fun your child has in the bath, the less she'll be afraid of the water. As she gets older, the length of the bath will extend until most of it is taken up with play. Bathing should be a very relaxing and soothing experience, so don't rush unless she's unhappy.

When your infant comes out of the bath, baby towels with built-in hoods are the most effective way to keep her head warm when she's wet. Bathing a baby of any age is wet work, so you may want to wear a terry-cloth apron or hang a towel over your shoulder to keep you dry.

In the early months you may find it easiest to bathe your infant in the morning, when she's alert and the house is quiet and warm. By the time she graduates to the bathtub (usually when she's sitting up or outgrows the basin), you may want to shift to an evening schedule on the days she's bathed. The bath is a relaxing way to prepare her for sleep.

Bath toys are not really needed for very young babies, as the stimulation of the water and washing is exciting enough. Once a baby is old enough for the bathtub, however, toys become invaluable. Containers, floating toys, even waterproof books make wonderful distractions as you cleanse your baby.

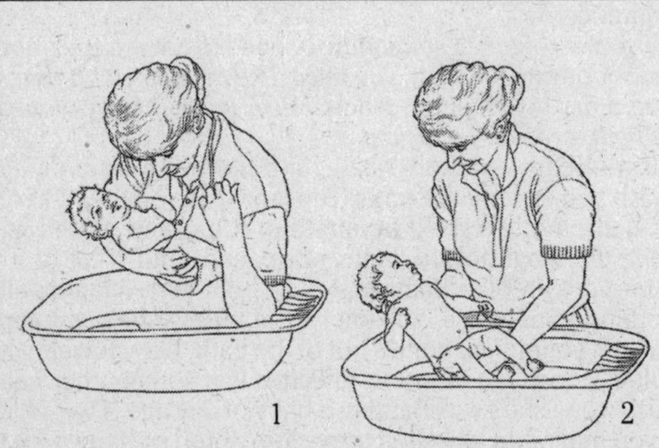
1 2

Fill the basin with 2 inches of water that feels warm—not hot—to the inside of your wrist or elbow. Once you've undressed your baby, place her in the water immediately so she doesn't get chilled. Use one of your hands to support her head and the other to guide her in, feet first. Speak to her encouragingly, and gently lower the rest of her body until she's in the tub. Most of her body and face should be well above the water level for safety, so you'll need to pour warm water over her body frequently to keep her warm.

3 4

Use a soft cloth to wash her face and hair, shampooing once or twice a week. Massage her entire scalp gently, including the area over her fontanels (soft spots). When you rinse the soap or shampoo from her head, cup your hand across her forehead so the suds run toward the sides, not into her eyes. Should you get some soap in her eyes, and she cries out in protest, simply take the wet washcloth and liberally wipe her eyes with plain, lukewarm water until any remains of the soap are gone, and she will open her eyes again. Wash the rest of her body from the top down.

Skin and Nail Care

Your newborn's skin may be susceptible to irritation from chemicals in new clothing, and from soap or detergent residue on clothes that have been washed. To avoid problems, double-rinse all baby clothes, bedding, blankets, and other washable items before exposing the baby to them. (Wash his new layette, too, before he uses it.) For the first few months, do your infant's wash separately from the family's.

Contrary to what you may read in ads for baby products, your infant does not ordinarily need any lotions, oils, or powders. If his skin is very dry, you can apply a small amount of nonperfumed baby lotion sparingly to the dry areas. Never use any skin-care products that are not specifically made for babies, because they generally contain perfumes and other chemicals that can irritate an infant's skin. Also avoid baby oil, which does not penetrate or lubricate as well as baby lotion. If the dryness persists, you may be bathing your child too often. Give him a bath just once a week for a while and see if the dryness stops. If not, consult your pediatrician.

The only care your infant's nails require is trimming. You can use a soft emery board, baby nail clippers, or blunt-nosed toenail scissors. A good time to trim nails is after a bath if your baby will lie quietly, but you may find it easiest to do when he's asleep. Keep his fingernails as short and smoothly trimmed as possible so he can't scratch himself (or you). In the early weeks his fingers are so small and his nails grow so quickly you may have to trim them twice a week.

By contrast, his toenails grow much more slowly and are usually very soft and pliable. They needn't be kept as short as

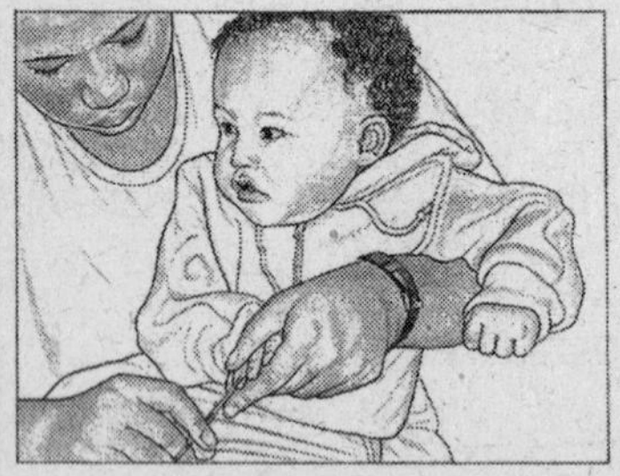

In the early weeks your baby's fingers are so small and his nails grow so quickly you may have to trim them twice a week.

the fingernails, so you may have to trim them only once or twice a month. Because they are so soft, they sometimes look as if they're ingrown, but there's no cause for concern unless the skin alongside the nail gets red, inflamed, or hard. As your baby gets older, his toenails will become harder and better defined.

Clothing

Unless the temperature is hot (over 75 degrees Fahrenheit), your newborn will need several layers of clothing to keep her warm. It's generally best to dress her in an undershirt and diapers, covered by pajamas or a dressing gown, and then wrapped in a receiving blanket. (If your baby is premature, she may need still another layer of clothing until her weight reaches that of a full-term baby and her body is better able to adjust to changes in temperature.) In hot weather you can reduce her clothing to a single layer, but be sure to cover her when in air-conditioned surroundings or near drafts. A good rule of thumb is to dress the baby in one more layer of clothing than you are wearing to be comfortable in the same environment.

If you've never taken care of a newborn baby before, the first few times you change her clothes can be quite frustrating. Not only is it a struggle to get that tiny little arm through the sleeve, but your infant may shriek in protest through the whole process. She doesn't like the rush of air against her skin, nor does she enjoy being pushed and pulled through garments. It may make things easier for both of you if you hold her on your lap while changing the upper half of her body, then lay her on a bed or changing table while doing the lower half. When you're dressing her in one-piece pajamas, pull them over her legs before putting on the sleeves. Pull T-shirts over her head first, then put one arm at a time through the sleeves. Use this opportunity to ask, "Where's the baby's hand?" As she gets older this will turn into a game, with her pushing her arm through just to hear you say, "*There's* the baby's hand!"

Dressing Your Baby

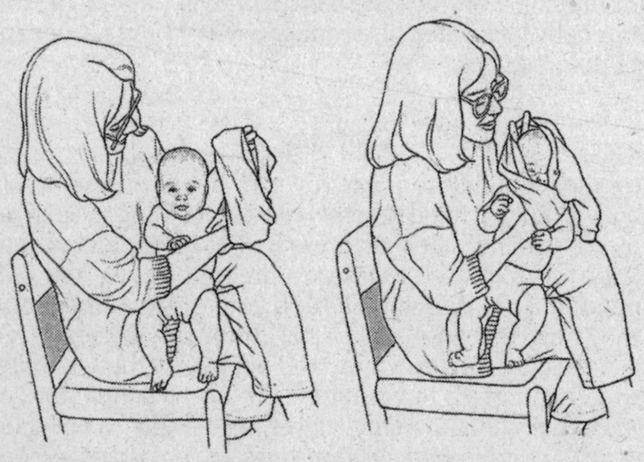

Supporting your baby on your lap, stretch the garment neckline and pull it over your baby's head, using your fingers to keep it from catching on her face or ears.

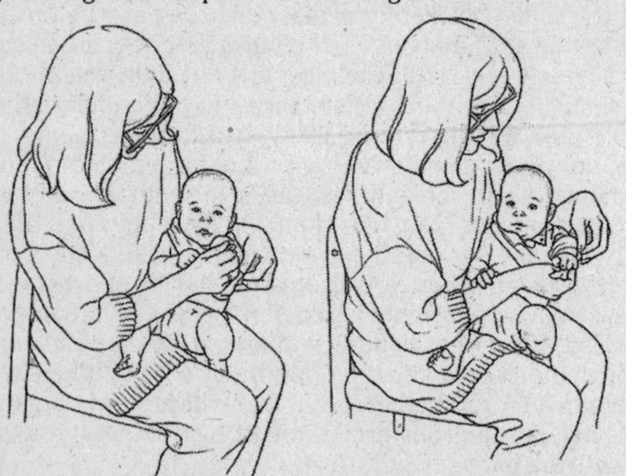

Don't try to push your baby's arm through the sleeve. Instead, put your hand into the sleeve from the outside, grasp your baby's hand, and pull it through.

Undressing Your Baby

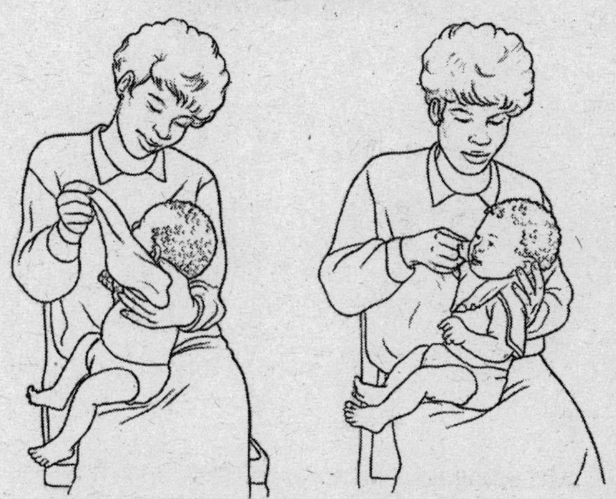

Take off the sleeves one at a time while you support your baby's back and head.

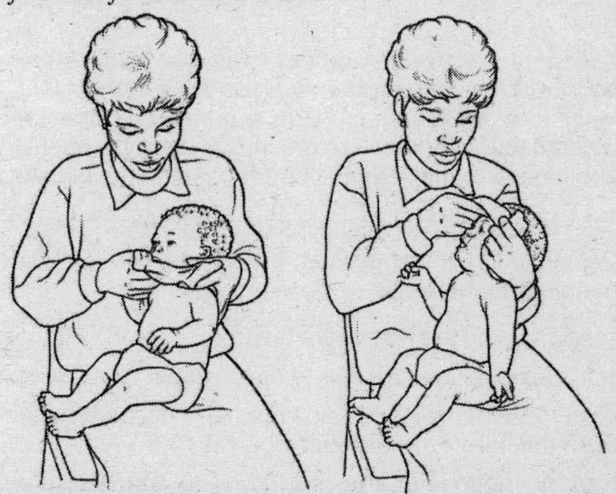

Then stretch the neckline, lifting it free of your baby's chin and face as you gently slip it off.

A Snug Bundle

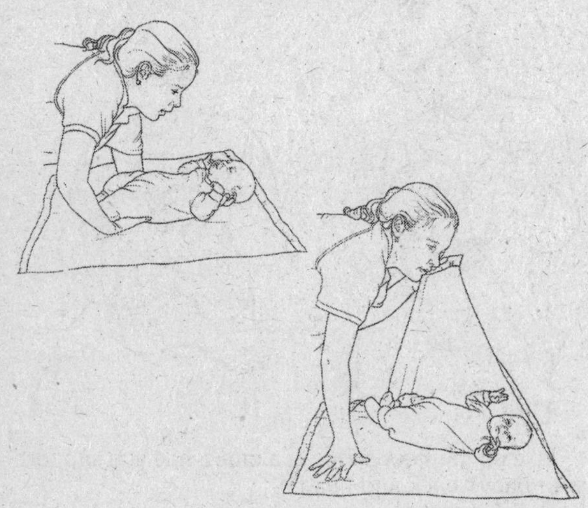

During the first few weeks, your baby will spend most of his time wrapped in a receiving blanket. Not only does this keep him warm, but the slight pressure around the body seems to give most newborns a sense of security. To make a snug bundle, spread the blanket

Certain clothing features can make dressing much easier. Look for garments that

- snap or zip all the way down the front, instead of the back
- snap or zip down both legs to make diaper changes easier
- have loose-fitting sleeves so your hand fits underneath to push the baby's arm through
- have no ribbons or strings to knot up, unravel, or wrap around the neck (which could cause choking)
- are made of stretchy fabric. (Avoid tight bindings around arms, legs, or neck.)

out flat, with one corner folded over. Lay the baby face-up on the blanket, with his head at the folded corner. Wrap the left corner over his body and tuck it beneath him. Bring the bottom corner up over his feet, and then wrap the right corner around him, leaving only his head and neck exposed.

Your baby will also need a blanket or quilt to cover her when sleeping. Place it over her loosely, without tucking it in. As she gets older and becomes more active, she's bound to kick off the covers occasionally. At that time you'll need either to dress her in warmer pajamas (with feet) or keep her room warm while she's sleeping. Try not to place your baby near air-conditioning or heating vents, open windows, or other sources of drafts.

YOUR BABY'S BASIC HEALTH CARE

Taking a Rectal Temperature

Very few babies get through infancy without having a fever, which is usually a sign of infection somewhere in the body. A fever indicates that the immune system is actively fighting viruses or bacteria, so—in this respect—it is a positive sign that the body is protecting itself. But if the body temperature gets too high too rapidly (over 104 degrees Fahrenheit, 40 degrees centigrade, rising more than several degrees an hour), there may be a possibility of a convulsion occurring.

An infant cannot hold a thermometer steady in his mouth for you to take an oral temperature, and "fever strips" that are placed on the baby's forehead are not accurate. The best way to measure fever in an infant is by taking a rectal temperature. Once you know how to take a rectal temperature, it is really quite simple; but it's best to learn the procedures in advance so you're not nervous about them the first time your child is actually sick.

Among your basic baby equipment, you should have at least one rectal thermometer with a short, round mercury bulb. Two are even better, since thermometers are breakable. Beware—it's very easy to smash the thermometer against the sink while shaking it down or to drop it while juggling your baby in your arms.

Rectal thermometer (with short, round bulb)

Reading a thermometer takes some practice, and you should learn how before a crisis arises. The trick is to hold the thermometer between your thumb and index finger (at the end opposite the bulb) and roll it slowly back and forth until you see the mercury column. The temperature reading corresponds to the end of the column. Digital thermometers are easier to read, but are also more expensive.

The procedure for taking a rectal temperature with a glass thermometer is as follows:

1. Shake the mercury column down until it reads below 96 degrees (35 degrees centigrade). To do this, hold the end opposite from the bulb tightly between your fingers and snap your wrist (*away* from any countertops or nearby objects).
2. Rub the bulb end with rubbing alcohol or soap and water, and rinse it with cool clear water.
3. Place a small amount of lubricant such as petroleum jelly on the bulb end.
4. Place your baby belly-down on a firm surface. If he's a tiny infant, you can lay him across your lap, but if he's larger or squirming, you'll find a changing table or even the floor much safer.
5. Firmly press the palm of one hand against the baby's lower back just above the buttocks. If he tries to roll over, increase the pressure to hold him still.
6. With your other hand, insert the lubricated thermometer ½ inch to 1 inch into the anal opening. Hold the ther-

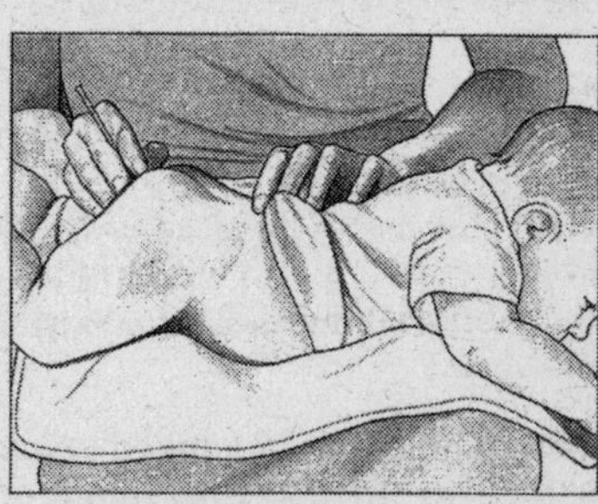

Taking a rectal temperature

mometer between your second and third fingers with the hand cupped over the baby's bottom. Hold in place for two minutes before removing and reading it.

7. A rectal reading over 100 degrees Fahrenheit (38 degrees centigrade) may indicate fever. If you think the temperature may be unusually high because your child has been physically active or too warmly clothed, retake the temperature in thirty minutes.

Visiting the Pediatrician

You probably will see more of your pediatrician in your baby's first year than at any other time. The baby's first examination will take place immediately after birth. The schedule below lists the minimum routine checkups for the rest of your baby's first two years. Your pediatrician may want to see your baby more often.

Ideally, both parents should attend these early visits to the doctor. These appointments give you and your pediatrician a chance to get to know each other and exchange questions and answers. Don't restrict yourself to medical questions; your pediatrician is also an expert on general child-care issues and a valuable resource if you're looking for child-care help, parent support groups, or other outside assistance. Many pediatricians hand out information sheets that cover the most common concerns, but it's a good idea to make a list of the questions you have before each visit so you don't forget any important ones.

If only one parent can attend, try to get a friend or a relative to join the parent who does. It's much easier to concentrate on your discussions with the doctor if you have a little help dressing and undressing the baby and gathering all of her things. While you're getting used to outings with your newborn, an extra adult can also help carry the diaper bag and hold doors.

The purpose of these early checkups is to make sure your baby is growing and developing properly and has no serious abnormalities. Specifically, the doctor will check the following:

Growth. You will be asked to undress your baby, and then he'll be weighed on an infant scale. His length may be measured lying on a flat table with his legs stretched straight. A special tape is used to measure the size of his head. All of these measurements should be plotted on a graph in order to determine his growth curve from one visit to the next. (You can plot your baby's growth curve in the same way using the charts on pages 150–53.) This is the most reliable way to judge whether he's growing normally, and will show you his position on the growth curve in relation to other children his age.

Head. The soft spots should be open and flat for the first few months. By two to three months of age, the spot at the back should be closed. The front soft spot should close before your child's second birthday (around eighteen months of age).

Ears. The doctor will look inside both ears with an otoscope, an instrument that provides a view of the ear canal and eardrum. This tells her whether there is any evidence of fluid or infection in the ear. You'll also be asked if the baby responds normally to sounds. Formal hearing tests are rarely given to an infant unless there is suspicion that a problem exists.

Eyes. The doctor will use a bright object or flashlight to catch your baby's attention and track his eye movements. She may also look inside the baby's eyes with a lighted instrument called an ophthalmoscope—repeating the internal eye examination that was first done in the hospital nursery. This is particularly helpful in detecting cataracts (clouding of the lens of the eye). (See *Cataracts*, page 500.)

Mouth. The mouth is checked for signs of infection and, later, for teething progress.

Heart and Lungs. The pediatrician will use a stethoscope on the front and back of the chest to listen to your baby's heart and lungs. This examination determines whether there are any abnormal heart rhythms, sounds, or breathing difficulties.

Recommended Childhood Immunization Schedule
United States, January – December 2001

Vaccines[1] are listed under routinely recommended ages. [Bars] indicate range of recommended ages for immunization. Any dose not given at the recommended age should be given as a "catch-up" immunization at any subsequent visit when indicated and feasible. (Ovals) indicate vaccines to be given if previously recommended doses were missed or given earlier than the recommended minimum age.

Age ▶ Vaccine ▼	Birth	1 mo	2 mos	4 mos	6 mos	12 mos	15 mos	18 mos	24 mos	4-6 yrs	11-12 yrs	14-18 yrs
Hepatitis B[2]		Hep B #1										
			Hep B #2			Hep B #3					(Hep B[2])	
Diphtheria, Tetanus, Pertussis[3]			DTaP	DTaP	DTaP		DTaP[3]			DTaP	Td	
H. influenzae type b[4]			Hib	Hib	Hib	Hib						
Inactivated Polio[5]			IPV	IPV		IPV[5]				IPV[5]		
Pneumococcal Conjugate[6]			PCV	PCV	PCV	PCV						
Measles, Mumps, Rubella[7]						MMR				MMR[7]	(MMR[7])	
Varicella[8]							Var				(Var[8])	
Hepatitis A[9]										Hep A-in selected areas[9]		

Approved by the Advisory Committee on Immunization Practices (ACIP), the American Academy of Pediatrics (AAP), and the American Academy of Family Physicians (AAFP).

1. This schedule indicates the recommended ages for routine administration of currently licensed childhood vaccines, as of 11/1/00, for children through 18 years of age. Additional vaccines may be licensed and recommended during the year. Licensed combination vaccines may be used whenever any components of the combination are indicated and its other components are not contraindicated. Providers should consult the manufacturers' package inserts for detailed recommendations.

2. Infants born to HBsAg-negative mothers should receive the 1st dose of hepatitis B (Hep B) vaccine by age 2 months. The 2nd dose should be at least one month after the 1st dose. The 3rd dose should be administered at least 4 months after the 1st dose and at least 2 months after the 2nd dose, but not before 6 months of age for infants.

Infants born to HBsAg-positive mothers should receive hepatitis B vaccine and 0.5 mL hepatitis B immune globulin (HBIG) within 12 hours of birth at separate sites. The 2nd dose is recommended at 1-2 months of age and the 3rd dose at 6 months of age.

Infants born to mothers whose HBsAg status is unknown should receive hepatitis B vaccine within 12 hours of birth. Maternal blood should be drawn at the time of delivery to determine the mother's HBsAg status; if the HBsAg test is positive, the infant should receive HBIG as soon as possible (no later than 1 week of age).

All children and adolescents who have not been immunized against hepatitis B should begin the series during any visit. Special efforts should be made to immunize children who were born in or whose parents were born in areas of the world with moderate or high endemicity of hepatitis B virus infection.

3. The 4th dose of DTaP (diphtheria and tetanus toxoids and acellular pertussis vaccine) may be administered as early as 12 months of age, provided 6 months have elapsed since the 3rd dose and the child is unlikely to return at age 15-18 months. Td (tetanus and diphtheria toxoids) is recommended at 11-12 years of age if at least 5 years have elapsed since the last dose of DTP, DTaP or DT. Subsequent routine Td boosters are recommended every 10 years.

4. Three *Haemophilus influenzae* type b (Hib) conjugate vaccines are licensed for infant use. If PRP-OMP (PedvaxHIB® or ComVax® [Merck]) is administered at 2 and 4 months of age, a dose at 6 months is not required. Because clinical studies in infants have demonstrated that using some combination products may induce a lower immune response to the Hib vaccine component, DTaP/Hib combination products should not be used for primary immunization in infants at 2, 4 or 6 months of age, unless FDA-approved for these ages.

5. An all-IPV schedule is recommended for routine childhood polio vaccination in the United States. All children should receive four doses of IPV at 2 months, 4 months, 6-18 months, and 4-6 years of age. Oral polio vaccine (OPV) should be used only in selected circumstances. (See MMWR *Morb Mortal Wkly Rep* May 19, 2000/49(RR-5);1-22).

6. The heptavalent conjugate pneumococcal vaccine (PCV) is recommended for all children 2-23 months of age. It also is recommended for certain children 24-59 months of age. (See MMWR *Morb Mortal Wkly Rep* Oct. 6, 2000/49(RR-9);1-35).

7. The 2nd dose of measles, mumps, and rubella (MMR) vaccine is recommended routinely at 4-6 years of age but may be administered during any visit, provided at least 4 weeks have elapsed since receipt of the 1st dose and that both doses are administered beginning at or after 12 months of age. Those who have not previously received the second dose should complete the schedule by the 11-12 year old visit.

8. Varicella (Var) vaccine is recommended at any visit on or after the first birthday for susceptible children, i.e. those who lack a reliable history of chickenpox (as judged by a health care provider) and who have not been immunized. Susceptible persons 13 years of age or older should receive 2 doses, given at least 4 weeks apart.

9. Hepatitis A (Hep A) is shaded to indicate its recommended use in selected states and/or regions, and for certain high risk groups; consult your local public health authority. (See MMWR *Morb Mortal Wkly Rep* Oct. 1, 1999/48(RR-12); 1-37).

For additional information about the vaccines listed above, please visit the National Immunization Program Home Page at www.cdc.gov/nip or call the National Immunization Hotline at 800-232-2522 (English) or 800-232-0233 (Spanish).

Abdomen. By placing her hand on the infant's abdomen and gently pressing, the doctor makes sure that none of the organs is enlarged and there are no unusual masses or tenderness.

Genitalia. The genitalia are examined at each visit for any unusual lumps, tenderness, or signs of infection. In the first exam or two, the doctor pays special attention to a circumcised boy's penis to make sure it's healing properly. She checks all baby boys to make certain both testes are down in the scrotum.

Hips and Legs. The pediatrician will move your baby's legs to check for dislocations or other problems with the hip joints. Later, after the baby starts to walk, the doctor will watch her take a few steps to make sure the legs and feet are properly aligned and move normally.

Developmental Milestones. The pediatrician will also ask about the baby's general development. Among other things, she'll observe and discuss when the baby starts to smile, roll over, sit up, and walk, and how he uses his hands and arms. During the exam she will test reflexes and general muscle tone. (See Chapters 5 through 9 for details of normal development.)

Immunizations

Your baby should receive most of his childhood immunizations before his second birthday. These will protect him against ten major diseases: polio, measles, mumps, chickenpox, rubella (German measles), pertussis (whooping cough), diphtheria, tetanus, *Haemophilus* (Hib) infections, and Hepatitis B. See page 82 for the schedule of immunizations recommended by the American Academy of Pediatrics.

DTaP or DTP Vaccines. At her two-month checkup your baby should receive her first DTaP or DTP vaccine immunizing her against diphtheria (D), tetanus (T), and either acellular pertussis (aP) or whole cell pertussis (P).

This vaccine is given in five injections, the first three at two, four, and six months. A fourth dose is given six to twelve months after the third dose, usually around eighteen months of age. Then your child will receive another shot before she enters school, between four and six years. This "booster" shot raises your child's immunity against these diseases to higher levels.

Within the first twenty-four hours after the shot, your baby may be irritable and less energetic than usual. The area where the vaccine was injected may be red and sensitive, and she may have a low-grade fever (less than 102 degrees Fahrenheit [38.9 degrees centigrade]). These normal reactions should last no more than forty-eight hours. They can be treated with acetaminophen given every four hours. (See the chart on page 520, for appropriate doses.) Do not use aspirin.

Notify your pediatrician if your baby displays any of the following less common reactions:

- Constant, inconsolable crying for more than three hours
- Unusual, high-pitched crying
- Excessive sleepiness or difficulty in waking up
- Limpness or paleness
- Temperature of 105 degrees Fahrenheit (40.6 degrees centigrade) or higher
- Convulsion (usually resulting from a high fever)

While these more serious side effects may sound alarming, there is less than a 1 percent chance that your baby will have *any* of them.

In 1992, a new type of pertussis vaccine that does not use the killed cell itself, but only part of it, was licensed for doses 4 and 5. This vaccine is called "acellular type" and is listed as DTaP. As of 1997, *DTaP is the preferred vaccine for all doses in the immunization schedule*. DTaP is less likely to cause the mild and moderate problems we see after regular DTP. Both are effective in preventing all three diseases. If your baby is not immunized, her risk of getting one of these diseases increases greatly. Diphtheria, tetanus, and pertussis are dangerous diseases. (See Chapter 24, *Immunizations*.)

The dangers include:

- Two out of ten people who get tetanus die from it.
- Before this vaccine was available, one out of fifteen people who got diphtheria died from it.
- One out of one hundred babies under two months who get pertussis die from it. (The overall death rate is one in one thousand, including older infants.)
- Nearly three out of every four infants who get pertussis require hospitalization, and one out of five develops pneumonia.

There has been controversy concerning the reactions to the DTP vaccine, but because the benefits so far outweigh the risks, *the American Academy of Pediatrics strongly recommends continuing the routine use of this vaccine or DTaP (preferred) beginning at age two months.*

There are, however, some babies who should have these vaccinations postponed, and a few who should not receive them at all. These include infants who have one or more of the following problems:

- A severe reaction to the initial immunization (allergic reaction or inflammation of the brain called encephalopathy)
- A previous convulsion, or the suspicion of having a progressive disease of the nervous system

If your baby has any of these difficulties, make sure that your pediatrician is aware of them *before* DTP immunization is given.

Polio Vaccine. Polio is a viral disease that can paralyze some muscles of the body. The illness may be mild to very serious, depending on the muscles involved and the severity of the involvement. Fortunately, wild polio virus has been eliminated from the United States because effective vaccines have been used to prevent the disease.

Vaccination is the best way to protect against polio. Children should receive four doses of polio vaccine before they enter school. There are two kinds of polio vaccines: IPV or inactivated polio vaccine, which is given as an injection in the leg or arm, and OPV or oral polio vaccine, which is given by mouth as drops. Polio vaccine is given at two, four, twelve to eighteen months, and again between four and six years. (For children who receive the all-OPV schedule, the third dose can be given any time between six and eighteen months of age.)

Both IPV and OPV provide excellent protection against polio. Parents can choose one of three recommended schedules—all-OPV, all-IPV, or combined IPV/OPV. Talk to your pediatrician about which schedule your baby should receive.

OPV provides excellent protection against polio and prevents the spread of wild polio virus from one person to another. No injections are required. Even though OPV contains a weakened polio vaccine virus, it can on very rare occasions cause vaccine-associated paralytic polio (VAPP) in an infant with a compromised immune system. It may also cause VAPP in a person who is in close contact with a baby who has received the oral vaccine, if that person has not been properly immunized (the virus will be present in the infant's stool shortly after vaccination). The chances of this occurring are very rare, however. The all-OPV schedule may be recommended if your baby is allergic to the antibiotics neomycin or streptomycin, which are used in the production of IPV.

IPV provides excellent protection against polio and has not been shown to cause any major problems except mild soreness at the site of the injection. IPV protects the infant who receives the injection, and, because it is made with an inactivated polio virus, does not cause VAPP. In the event of a polio outbreak, however, IPV is not as effective as OPV in preventing the spread of the wild polio virus. Your baby may need to get the all-IPV schedule if he, or anyone with whom he is in close contact, has a weakened immune system as the result of a disease such as cancer or AIDS. The IPV schedule may also be recommended for children who are receiving radiation or chemotherapy treatments or for those undergoing long-term steroid treatment for chronic illnesses.

By getting two doses of IPV followed by two doses of OPV (the combination schedule), your baby can get the benefits of both vaccines—excellent protection against polio with fewer injections; protection from epidemic polio; and less risk of contracting VAPP.

MMR Vaccine. At twelve to fifteen months, your child will receive a single shot immunizing her against mumps, measles, and rubella. Though these diseases are best known for the rashes (measles and rubella) and glandular swelling (mumps) they produce, each may also cause serious medical complications. Immunizations against these diseases rarely cause any serious side effects, but your child may experience the following reactions, beginning seven to ten days following the injection:

- A mild rash
- Slight swelling of the lymph nodes in the neck or diaper area
- Low-grade fever
- Sleepiness

If your child is allergic to eggs, a reaction to the vaccine may rarely occur (because eggs are used in the process of manufacturing it), so you should alert your pediatrician to the fact. Also, if your child is taking any medication that interferes with the immune system, or her immune system is weakened for any reason, she should not be given the MMR. Because not all children are immune to these diseases after one vaccination, and in order to give additional protection, a second MMR is recommended prior to the twelfth birthday. Many states recommend giving this second dose earlier (four to six years of age), so you must check with your pediatrician.

Chickenpox Vaccine. A vaccine to protect against chickenpox is recommended for all healthy children between twelve and eighteen months of age who have never had the disease. Children under thirteen who have not had chickenpox and were never vaccinated also should receive a single dose of the vaccine. Adolescents and young adults who have never had chickenpox or been vaccinated should receive two doses of vaccine separated by four to eight weeks. Although chickenpox will not cause complications in most healthy children, certain groups are at a higher risk of developing more severe problems. These include children who are under one year of age, have weak immune systems, have eczema and other skin conditions, have asthma, or are adolescents.

***Haemophilus Influenzae* Type B Vaccine (Hib).** A vaccine against bacterial infections caused by the bacteria *Haemophilus influenzae* type b is recommended for infants beginning at two months of age. (See also *Meningitis,* page 534.) Use of this vaccine has resulted in markedly reducing diseases caused by this bacteria.

Hepatitis B Vaccine. A vaccine to prevent hepatitis B has been added to the list of those recommended to be given to babies. Hepatitis B (sometimes called serum hepatitis) is a viral illness that affects the liver. It can occur at any age, including the newborn period. It can be passed from mother to infant at the time of birth or from one household member to another. It also can be spread through sexual intercourse or contact with infected blood from needles or contaminated surgical instruments.

Infants and young children can contract the disease and have mild to no symptoms until sometime later when they may develop chronic liver problems, including cancer.

Since the disease seems to be increasing and contact cannot always be predicted or avoided, health authorities, including the American Academy of Pediatrics, have recommended immunization in early infancy.

The vaccine is given in three doses beginning shortly after birth with a second dose one or two months later and a booster dose at six to eighteen months of age.

Older children, adolescents, and adults should also be immunized. Many child-care providers and public school systems require proof of vaccination for hepatitis B prior to school entry. Three doses of vaccine are also needed for these individuals with a time interval of one and six months between the first and second and third doses, respectively.

There have been no serious reactions to the vaccine. However, minor side effects such as fussiness and soreness, redness, or swelling at the site of the injection may be noted. The vaccine is contraindicated only in those persons severely allergic to yeast (rare in children).

This chapter has dealt in a general way with the topic of infant care. Your baby is a unique individual, however, so you will have some questions specific to him and him alone. These are best answered by your own pediatrician.

Where We Stand

The American Academy of Pediatrics believes that the benefits of immunization far outweigh the risks incurred by childhood diseases, as well as any risks of the vaccines themselves. Despite highly publicized cases of severe adverse effects associated with the vaccines—particularly the pertussis component of the DTP immunization—these unfortunate outcomes are very rare. The AAP believes that immunizations are the safest and most cost-effective way of preventing disease, disability, and death, and it urges parents to ensure that their children are immunized against dangerous childhood diseases.

With regard to chickenpox, the AAP recommends the varicella vaccine for universal use in early childhood and for susceptible older children and adolescents. A single dose should be given between 12 and 18 months of age, and can be given at the same time as the child's first MMR (measles, mumps, rubella) vaccination. Older children should be immunized with a single dose at the earliest convenient opportunity.

4

Feeding Your Baby: Breast and Bottle

Your baby's nutritional needs during the rapid-growth period of infancy are greater than at any other time in his life. He will approximately triple his birthweight during his first year.

Feeding your infant provides more than just good nutrition. It gives you a chance to hold your newborn close, cuddle him, and make eye contact. These are relaxing and enjoyable moments for you both, and they bring you closer together emotionally.

Before your baby arrives you should consider whether to breastfeed or give him infant formula. This is an important decision that requires serious consideration, so you should carefully evaluate both options before making your final decision. This chapter will provide the basic information you need to select the best option for you and your baby.

Because of its nutritional composition, human milk is the ideal food for human infants. Babies who are breastfed are at reduced risk of acquiring ear infections and severe diarrhea and of developing allergic reactions. In addition, there is some evidence that for mothers, breastfeeding reduces certain types of cancer and may prevent hip fractures later in life. As a result, most pediatricians urge expectant mothers to breastfeed.

But it's important not to feel guilty if you decide to bottle-feed your baby. Infant formula is an acceptable and nutritious alternative to human milk. Whatever your reason for not breastfeeding (and it could simply be that you don't want to), this is your choice. However, it's important that you give it serious consideration before your baby arrives, because starting with formula and then switching to breastmilk can be difficult, or even impossible if you wait too long. The production of milk by the breast (the process is called lactation) is most successful if breastfeeding begins immediately after delivery. If you begin breastfeeding and then, for any reason, decide that it's not right for you, you can always switch to formula.

Approximately 44 percent of newborns in the United States are breastfed at birth. By six months, only about 20 percent are being breastfed. The World Health Organization (WHO) and many experts encourage women to breastfeed as long as possible, one year or even longer, because breastmilk provides optimal nutrition and protection against infections. You may well use both methods with your infant before his first year is over—all the more reason to familiarize yourself in advance with the basic information about each one.

Advantages and Disadvantages of Breastfeeding

As we've already mentioned, human milk is the best possible food for any baby. Its major ingredients are sugar (lactose), easily digestible protein (whey and casein), and fat (digestible fatty acids)—all properly balanced to suit your baby and protect against such conditions as ear infections (otitis media), allergies, vomiting, diarrhea, pneumonia, wheezing, bronchiolitis, and meningitis. In addition, there are numerous minerals and vitamins, as well as enzymes that aid the digestive and absorptive process. Formulas only approximate this combination of nutrients and don't provide the enzymes, antibodies, and many other valuable ingredients of breastmilk.

There are many practical reasons to breastfeed, or nurse, your baby. Human milk is relatively low in cost. While maintaining a balanced diet yourself, you should increase your own caloric intake, but that costs only about half of what you'd have to spend for formula. Also, human milk needs no preparation and is instantly available at any time, wherever you may be. As an added advantage to the nursing mother, breastfeeding makes it much easier to get back into shape physically after giving birth, by using up about 500 calories a day and by helping the uterus tighten up and return more quickly to its normal size.

The psychological and emotional advantages of breastfeeding are just as compelling, for both mother and baby, as the physical benefits. Nursing provides direct skin-to-skin contact, which is soothing for your baby and pleasant for you. The same hormones that stimulate milk production may also promote feelings that enhance mothering. Almost all nursing mothers find that the experience makes them feel more attached and protective toward their babies and more confident about their own abilities to nurture and care for their infants. This advantage of breastfeeding can't be emphasized enough.

When breastfeeding is going well, it has no known disadvantages for the baby. The breastfeeding mother will find that there is some increased demand on her time because of the longer and more frequent feedings that occur as compared to the use of formula, but this increase in time with the infant is an important component of infant nurturing and development. It usually means that sleep time is shorter but more frequent than is usually the case, and that other family members may have to assume responsibility for other family tasks. After a few weeks these changes in routine are accepted as normal.

Other family members can actively share in all aspects of caring for the baby even though they do not directly feed milk to the baby. They can enjoy the fun of holding the baby during burping. An important role for the father of the breastfed infant is nonnutritive cuddling. A father is invaluable when comforting is necessary for baby and mother. He can hold, diaper, bathe, and carry the baby, and he can handle the feeding whenever an occasional bottle is required. The best protection against miscommunication is openly discussing the issue of feeding and making sure both parents understand and support the choice before the baby arrives. Most fathers want their children to receive the best possible nutrition from the start, and without question, that is mother's milk. Mothers who need to be away from the baby for a period of time (due to employment, for example, or to go shopping or pursue social activities) can continue to provide their milk to the baby by pumping and collecting breastmilk for frozen storage and bottle-feeding by father, other family members, or child-care workers.

Are there medical circumstances that may make breastfeeding inadvisable? Yes, but they are rare. If a mother is extremely ill, she may not have the energy or stamina to breastfeed without interfering with her own recovery. She may also be taking certain medications that would pass into her milk and be dangerous to her infant, although the great majority of medications are safe for breastfeeding.

If you are taking medications for any reason (prescription drugs or over-the-counter medications), let your pediatrician know before you start breastfeeding. Your pediatrician can advise you whether any of these drugs can pass through breastmilk and cause problems for your baby. Sometimes medicines can be switched to safer ones.

Occasionally, some mothers find continuing breastfeeding too great a strain. While breastfeeding may be uncomfortable at first, most of these early discomforts can be overcome with time, coaching, and experience. However, if breastfeeding does not begin to go smoothly by the end of the second month, and you really feel that the negatives of breastfeeding are far outweighing the positives, then it may be best to switch to formula feeding. Try not to feel a sense of letdown if this happens; you and your baby need to find the right combination for both of you to make the feeding experience positive in every way.

Advantages and Disadvantages of Bottle-Feeding

While recognizing the benefits of breastfeeding, mothers, and fathers too, may feel that bottle-feeding gives the mother more freedom and time for duties other than those involving baby care. Dad, grandparents, sitters, and even older siblings can feed an infant formula or breastmilk that has been expressed into a bottle. Not only does this give the mother more flexibility, but it helps everyone else in the family to bond with the baby.

There are other reasons why some parents feel more comfortable with bottle-feeding: They know exactly how much food the baby is getting, and there's no need to worry about the mother's diet or medications that might affect the milk.

Formula manufacturers have not yet found a way to reproduce the components that make human milk so unique. Although formula does provide the nutrients an infant needs, it lacks the antibodies and components that only mother's milk contains.

Formula-feeding is also costly and may be inconvenient for some families. The formula must be bought and prepared (unless you use the more expensive, ready-to-use types). This means trips to the kitchen in the middle of the night, as well as extra bottles, nipples, and other equipment. Unintended contamination of formula must also be considered a potential risk.

Breastfeeding Your Baby

Developing the Right Attitude

You can do it! This should be your attitude about breastfeeding from the beginning. There's plenty of help available and you should take advantage of the expert advice, counseling, classes, and group meetings that are available. For example, you can:

- Talk to your prenatal instructors or attend a breastfeeding class.
- Talk to your obstetrician and pediatrician. They can provide not only medical information but also encouragement and support when you need it most.
- Talk to women who are breastfeeding successfully and ask their advice.

- Talk to members of La Leche League in your community. This is a worldwide organization dedicated to helping families learn about and enjoy the experience of breastfeeding. Ask your pediatrician for information about how to contact La Leche League.
- Read about breastfeeding. Recommended books include *Bestfeeding,* by M. Renfrew and C. Fisher (Celestial Arts Publishing Co.); *The Complete Book of Breastfeeding,* by M. Eiger and S. Olds (Bantam); *Nursing Your Baby,* by K. Pryor (Harper & Row); and *The Nursing Mother's Companion,* by K. Huggins (Harvard Common Press).

Getting Started: Preparing the Breasts for Lactation

Whether or not you intend to nurse your infant, your body starts preparing to breastfeed as soon as you become pregnant. The area surrounding the nipples—the areola—becomes darker. The breasts themselves enlarge as the cells that will manufacture the milk multiply, and the ducts that will carry the milk to the nipple develop. Meanwhile, your body starts storing excess fat in other areas to provide the extra energy needed for lactation.

As early as the sixteenth week of pregnancy, the breasts are ready to produce milk as soon as the infant is born. The first milk fluid—a rich, though somewhat thick-appearing, orange-yellow solution that is produced for several days after delivery until replaced by mature milk—is called colostrum. Colostrum contains more protein, salt, antibodies, and other protective properties than later breastmilk, but less fat and fewer calories. Your body will produce colostrum for several days after delivery until your mature milk "comes in." The milk then thins out, becomes milklike in color, and begins to adjust to the baby's needs for the rest of the time that you breastfeed. Breastmilk changes its nutritional qualities to match the changing needs of your growing infant.

As your body naturally prepares for breastfeeding, there is very little that you need to do. Unless your nipples are flat or inverted, you *don't* have to stretch, pull, roll, or buff the nipples toward the end of pregnancy. The nipples do not need to be "toughened up" to withstand your baby's sucking.

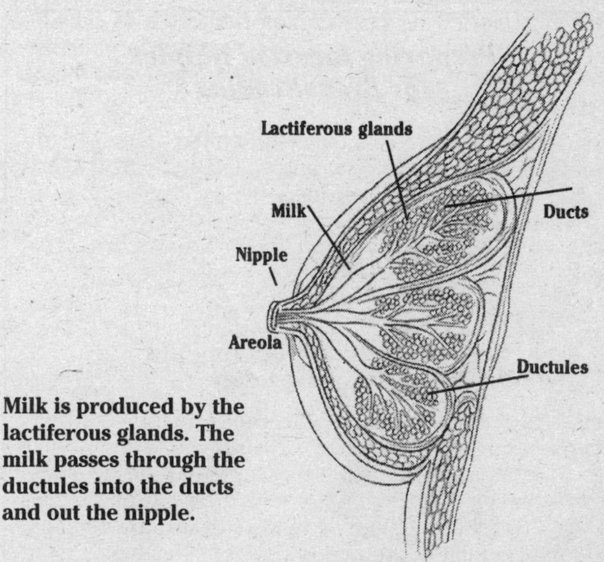

Milk is produced by the lactiferous glands. The milk passes through the ductules into the ducts and out the nipple.

In fact, some of these tactics may actually interfere with normal lactation by harming the tiny glands in the areola that secrete a milky fluid that lubricates the nipples in preparation for breastfeeding.

There's another reason: As you approach the end of your pregnancy, excessive nipple stimulation may also cause the release of hormones that make the uterus contract, and could possibly trigger early labor. So although occasional gentle stimulation—for example, during lovemaking—is harmless, you should avoid rigorous manipulation of the nipples. Normal bathing and gentle drying is the best way to care for your breasts during pregnancy.

Although many women rub lotions and ointments on their breasts to soften them, these are not necessary and may clog the skin pores. Salves, particularly those containing vitamins or hormones, are unnecessary and could cause problems for your baby if used while breastfeeding, as the substances in them can be absorbed into your system through the skin and transmitted to the baby through breastmilk.

Preparing Inverted Nipples for Breastfeeding

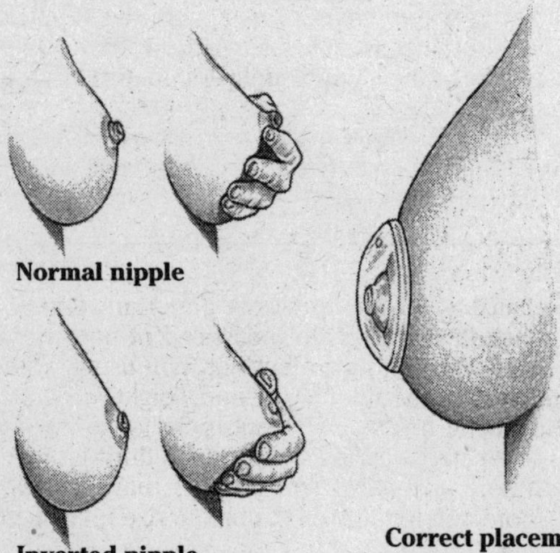

Normally, when you press the areola between two fingers, the nipple should protrude and become erect. If the nipple seems to pull inward and disappear instead, it is said to be "inverted" or "tied." This can interfere with successful breastfeeding because the baby may have difficulty grasping the areola and getting milk from the ducts. Fortunately, if the problem is diagnosed during pregnancy, it can easily be treated before the baby arrives.

The simplest treatment for an inverted nipple is a special breast shield worn inside the bra during waking hours for several weeks or months prior to delivery. This plastic device, available at most baby and drug stores, is shaped like a hollow dome. The underside, worn against the skin, has a hole for the nipple. The circular area around this hole creates a gentle, uniform pressure on the areola, causing the nipple to protrude through the hole. Eventually, the nipple takes on this shape even without the shield.

Rarely, in severe cases of inversion, the shield devices are not effective. Occasionally, inverted nipples may not be noticed until delivery. In this case the postpartum staff will assist you with drawing out the nipple with a breast pump before putting the baby to the breast. The baby's sucking at the breast will also help draw out the inverted nipple.

Proper support of the breasts is important during pregnancy (whether one plans to breastfeed or not) and lactation, because the breasts are heavier than usual. Without a good brassiere, the additional size and weight will stretch the ligaments of the breasts and contribute to future sagging. Some women start wearing nursing bras during pregnancy. They are more adjustable and roomier than normal bras, and are more comfortable as the breast size increases.

Letting Down and Latching On

After your baby is born and lactation begins, the breasts are ready to produce milk. As he nurses, your baby's actions will let your body know when to start and stop production. The process begins with the baby getting a good grip on the areola, not the nipple, and starting to suck. This is called

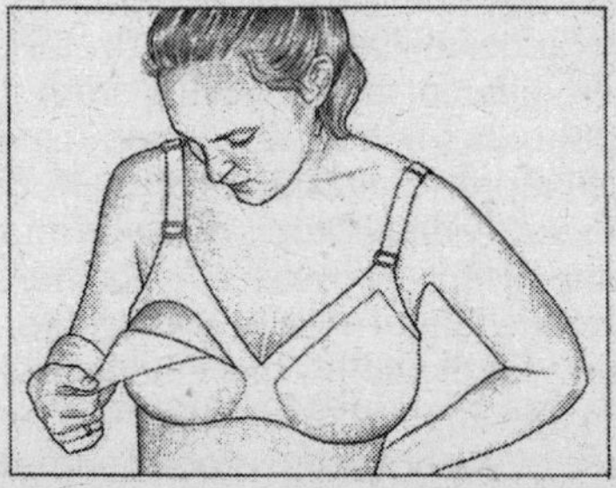

Proper support of the breasts is important during pregnancy and lactation.

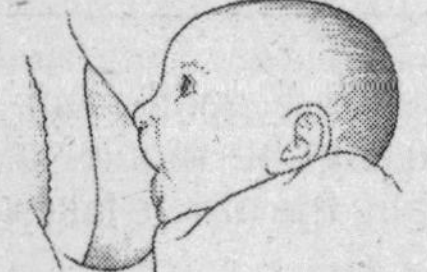

This baby has latched on to the breast correctly.

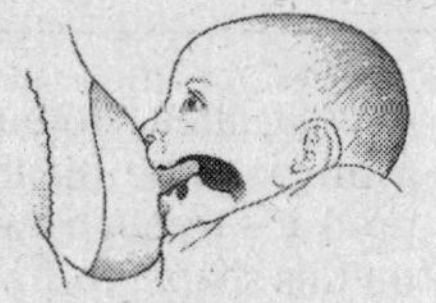

The entire areola and nipple are in his mouth.

"latching on." He should do this instinctively as soon as he feels the breast against his mouth. You can help him get started by holding him so that he squarely faces the breast, and then stroking his lower lip or cheek with the nipple. This stimulates the reflex that causes him to search for the nipple with his mouth (the rooting reflex). This will result in the infant opening the mouth widely, and at that moment the baby should be moved toward the breast.

As the baby takes the breast into his mouth, his jaws should close around the areola, not the nipple. His lips will separate and the gums will encircle the areola. His tongue will stroke upward, pressing the nipple against his palate and emptying the milk ducts with an undulating motion. Putting the baby to the breast in the first hour after delivery will establish good breastfeeding patterns at a time when infants are usually alert and vigorous. Later in the first day, they may get sleepy, but if they began nursing in the first hour, they are more likely to be successful breastfeeders.

In some cases an infant will have trouble latching on. This occurs most often in newborns who have been given bottles or pacifiers. They may simply lick, nibble, or chew with their jaws instead of using the tongue. These motions, however, won't stimulate the breast to make more milk, so it will be necessary to "teach" your baby how to latch on properly. Your delivery nurse or pediatrician can help you do this. Sucking from the breast is different from sucking from a nipple on a bottle. Some authorities believe that introducing a bottle early on may cause nipple confusion and interfere with the establishment of breastfeeding. Others disagree and feel that nonnutritive sucking (using the breast as a pacifier) does not interfere with breastfeeding—talk to your doctor.

Once your baby is sucking efficiently, his movements will stimulate the nerve fibers in the nipple. In turn, the emptying of the breast and the release of the hormone prolactin from the pituitary gland (see box on page 102) will release hormones that prompt the breasts to make more milk and increase its flow. Breast stimulation also starts milk flowing through the milk ducts, the "let-down reflex," due to the release of another hormone, oxytocin, by the pituitary gland.

This also causes the muscles of the uterus to contract. So, in the first days or weeks after delivery, you may feel "after pains," or cramping of the uterus, each time you nurse. While this may be annoying and occasionally painful, it helps the uterus return quickly to its normal size and condition and reduces postpartum blood loss. It also indicates that the breastfeeding is going well.

Once lactation has begun, it usually takes just a few minutes of sucking before the milk lets down (begins to flow). Just hearing your baby cry may actually be enough to trigger milk flow.

The signs that let-down is occurring vary from woman to woman, and change with the volume of milk the baby demands. Some women feel a subtle tingling sensation, while others experience a buildup of pressure that feels as if their breasts are swelling and overfull—sensations that are quickly relieved as the milk starts to flow. Some women never feel these sensations, even though they are nursing successfully and the infant is getting plenty of milk.

The way the milk flows also varies widely. It may spray, gush, trickle, or flow. It may also be quite different in each breast—perhaps gushing on one side and trickling on the

The Let-Down Process

As your baby sucks, several different hormones work together to produce milk and release it for feeding. From the moment she starts to nurse, here is what happens within her mother's body:

1. Her sucking movements stimulate nerve fibers in the nipple.

2. These nerve fibers carry the request for milk up the spinal column to the pituitary gland in your brain.

3. The pituitary gland responds to this message by releasing the hormones prolactin and oxytocin.

4. Prolactin stimulates the breasts to produce more milk.

5. Oxytocin stimulates contractions of the tiny muscles surrounding the ducts in the breasts. These contractions squeeze the ducts and eject the milk into the reservoir under the areola.

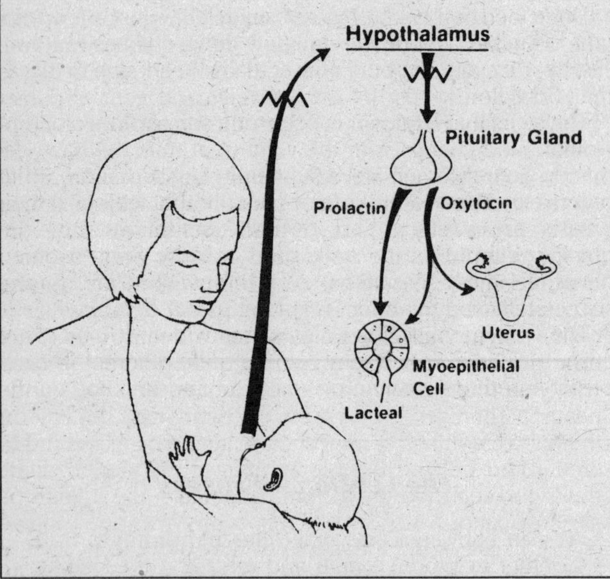

other. This is due to slight differences in the ducts on either side, and is no cause for concern.

The First Feeding

If you had a normal delivery, and you and your baby are alert and awake, you should nurse him as soon as he's born. If there were complications with the delivery, or your newborn needs immediate medical attention, you may have to wait a few hours. If the first feeding takes place within the first day or two, you should have no physical difficulty nursing. If nursing has to be delayed beyond that time, the nursing staff will assist you with pumping and hand expression.

If you do nurse immediately after delivery, you may find it most comfortable to lie on your side, with the baby lying facing you, opposite the breast. If you'd rather sit up, use pillows to help support your arms and cradle the baby at breast level, making sure his entire body, not just his head, is facing your body. Following a Caesarean section, the most comfortable position may be a side hold, or what's also called a "football hold," in which you sit up and the baby lies at your side facing you. Curl your arm underneath him, and support and hold his head at your breast. This position keeps the baby's weight off your abdomen, but the infant must squarely face the breast for the proper grasp.

If you stroke your newborn's lower lip or cheek with the nipple, he'll instinctively open his mouth wide, latch on, and begin to suck. He's been practicing this for some time by sucking his hand, fingers, and possibly even his feet in utero. (Some babies actually are born with blisters on their fingers caused by this prenatal sucking.) It takes little encouragement to get him to nurse, but you may need to help him properly grasp the areola. You may hold the breast with your thumb above the areola, fingers and palm underneath it. Then gently compress the breast and direct it into the baby's mouth. It is important to keep fingers behind the areola and be sure the nipple is level or pointed slightly down to keep the nipple from rubbing on the infant's palate. No matter which technique you try, you need to keep your fingers clear of the areola so the baby can grasp it. Be sure your fingers are no closer than two inches from the base of the nipple.

Let the baby nurse at the first side as long as he wishes, then put him on the other side, also until he stops by himself.

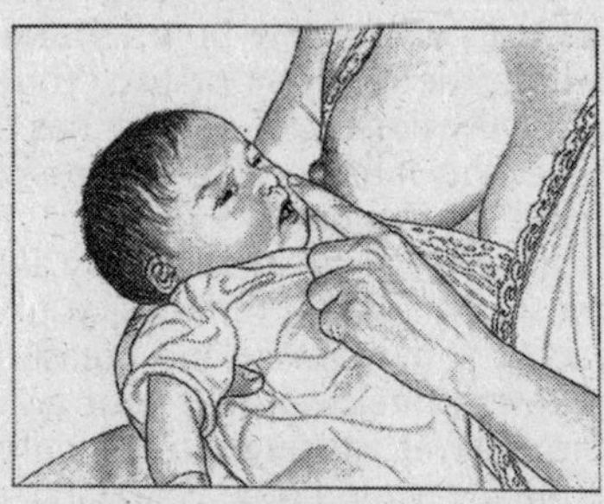

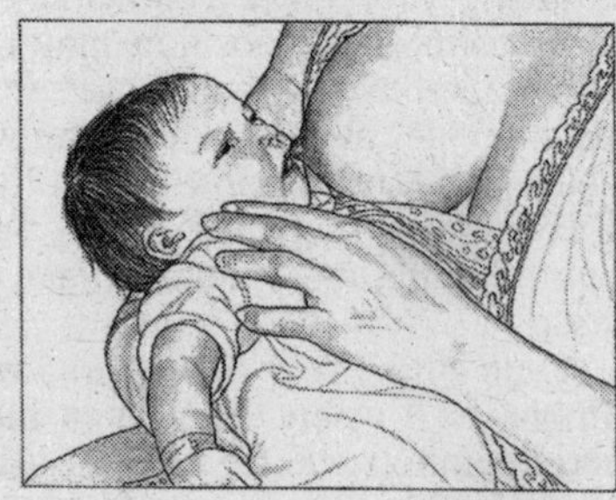

If you stroke your newborn's lower lip or cheek with your finger or with the nipple, he'll instinctively turn, latch on, and begin to suck.

Let-down, uterine cramping, swallowing sounds, and return to sound sleep by the baby are all signs of successful breastfeeding. It probably will take two or three minutes for let-down to occur in the first few feedings, after which he should receive all the available colostrum. Within a week or so, let-down will take place much more rapidly and your milk supply will increase dramatically.

If you are not sure you are letting down, just watch your baby. He should be swallowing after every few sucks at the start of the feeding. After five or ten minutes, he may switch to what's called nonnutritive sucking—a more relaxed sucking that provides emotional comfort rather than food. Another way to check your let-down is to expose the opposite breast while nursing and see if colostrum or, later, milk flows from it as the baby sucks. You can also slide your finger into the corner of your baby's mouth, breaking his suction to see if there is a flow from that breast.

The more relaxed and confident you feel, the quicker your milk will let down. The first feedings in the hospital may be

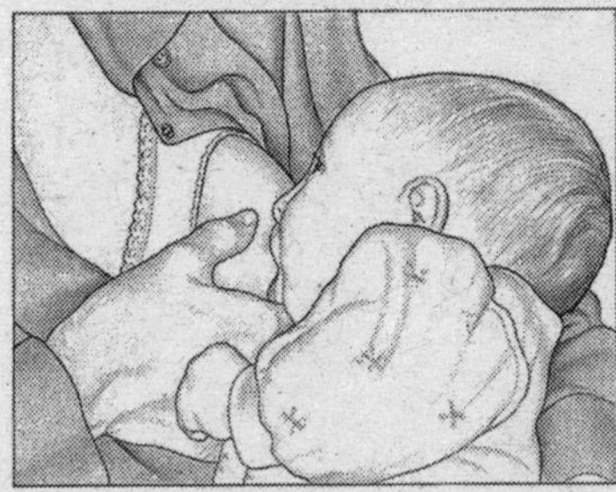

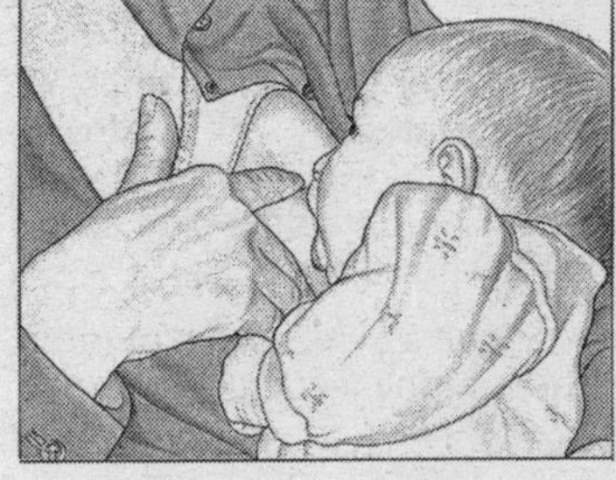

You may need to help him properly grasp the areola.

difficult because of excitement or, perhaps, your uncertainty about what to do. Breastfeeding should not cause sustained pain in the nipple, areola, or breast. If there is pain for more than a few moments at the beginning, ask the nurse, lactation consultant, or your doctor to evaluate the breastfeeding and suggest changes. Ask the hospital staff for help; they are very experienced at assisting nursing mothers and babies.

Once you are back home, try the following suggestions to help the let-down reflex:

- Sit in a comfortable chair, with good support for your back and arms. (Many nursing mothers recommend rocking chairs.)
- Make sure the baby is positioned so he squarely faces the breast and is sucking properly, not biting.
- Listen to soothing music and sip a nutritious drink during feedings.

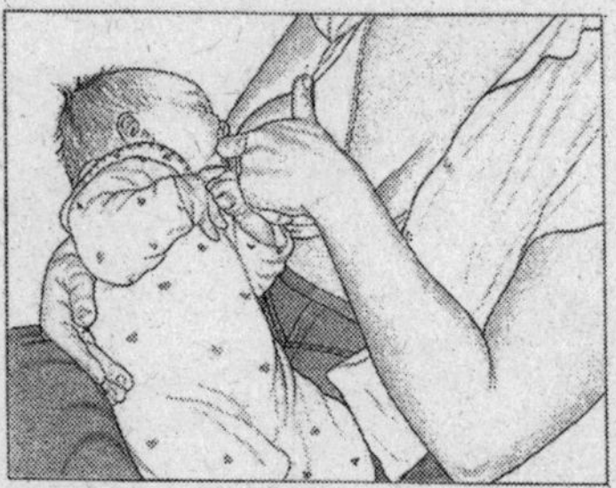

You can slide your finger into the corner of your baby's mouth, breaking his suction to see if there is a flow from the breast.

- Do not smoke, consume alcohol, or use illegal drugs, as all contain substances that can interfere with let-down, affect the content of breastmilk, and be harmful to the baby. Check with your obstetrician or pediatrician about any prescription drugs you may be taking.
- If your household is very busy, find a quiet corner or room where you won't be disturbed during feedings.

If you still are not letting down after trying these suggestions, contact your pediatrician for additional help. If you continue to have difficulties, ask to be referred to a lactation expert.

When Your Milk Comes In

For the first day or so after delivery, your breasts will be soft to the touch; but as the blood supply increases and milk-producing cells start to function efficiently, the breasts will become more firm. By the third or fourth day after delivery, your breasts will be producing transitional milk and may feel very full. At the end of the baby's first week, you will see only the white breastmilk (it may look like skimmed milk at first, but as the feeding continues, the amount of fat in the milk increases and it looks creamy), and you may feel engorged. Nursing the baby frequently and massaging the breasts during feeding may help minimize the fullness.

Engorgement occurs when the breasts become overfilled with milk. This can be very uncomfortable and at times

painful. The best solution to this problem is to nurse your baby whenever she is hungry, emptying both breasts about every two hours. Sometimes the breasts are so engorged that the baby has trouble latching on. If that happens, you can manually express some milk or use a mechanical breast pump before you start to nurse. This may help the baby get a better grasp and nurse more efficiently. Manual expression is done by placing your thumb on the breast, above the areola, and your fingers underneath. Gently but firmly roll and slide the thumb and fingers toward each other and onto the areola while compressing the breast tissue. Dripping a few drops into the baby's mouth will stimulate a lazy eater to start nursing. You can also try several techniques to ease the pain of engorgement, such as the following:

- Soak a warm cloth in warm water and put it on your breasts. Or take a warm shower.

- For severe engorgement, warmth may not help. In this case, you may want to use cold compresses as you express milk.
- Try feeding your baby in more than one way. Try sitting up, then lying down.
- Gently massage your breasts from under the arm and

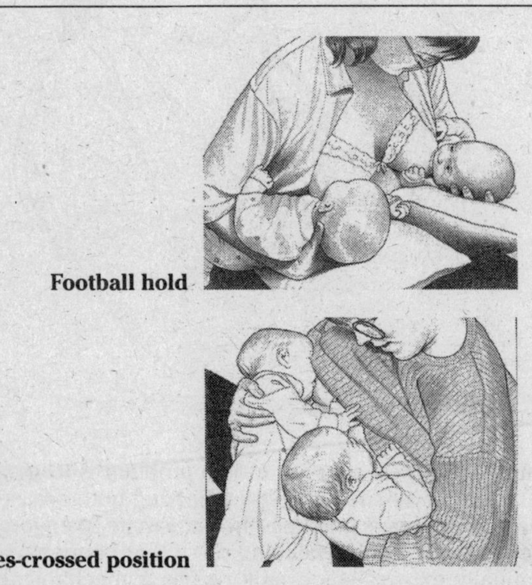

Football hold

Bodies-crossed position

Breastfeeding Twins

Twins present a unique challenge to the nursing mother. At first it's best to feed them one at a time, but after lactation is established, it's often more convenient to feed them simultaneously in order to save time. You can do this using the "football hold" to position one at each side, or cradle them both in front of you with their bodies crossing each other.

down the nipple. This will help reduce soreness and ease milk flow.

- Do not take any medications without approval from your doctor. Acetaminophen (nonaspirin pain reliever) may relieve pain and is safe to take occasionally during breastfeeding.

Fortunately, engorgement lasts only a few days while lactation is getting established. However, it can occur any time that feedings are skipped and the breasts are not emptied frequently in the first few weeks.

The volume of milk produced by the breasts increases dramatically over this first week. You may produce as little as ½ ounce (15 cc) at each feeding in the first couple of days. But by the fourth or fifth day, the volume may be up to 1 ounce (30 cc), and by the end of the week—depending on the size and appetite of the baby and the length of feedings—you may be producing 2 to 6 ounces (60 to 180 cc) at each feeding. At the end of your baby's first month, she should be receiving an average of 24 ounces (750 cc) of milk a day. See page 151 for information on how to tell if your baby is getting enough.

How Often and How Long?

Breastfed babies generally eat more frequently than formula-fed infants. Some newborns need to nurse every two hours; others, every three. As they get older, they are able to go longer between feedings, because their stomach capacity enlarges and their mothers' milk production increases. Breastfed babies get a smaller volume of milk early on when compared to bottle-fed infants.

What's the best feeding schedule for a breastfed baby? It's the one she designs herself. Your baby lets you know when she's hungry by waking and looking alert, putting hands toward mouth, making sucking motions, whimpering and flexing arms and hands, moving fists to mouth, becoming more active, and nuzzling against your breast (she can smell its location even through your clothing). It is best to start nursing the baby before crying starts. Crying is a late sign of hunger. Whenever possible, use these signals rather than the clock to decide when to nurse her. This way, you'll assure that

Getting to Know Your Baby's Feeding Patterns

Each baby has a particular style of eating. Years ago researchers at Yale University playfully attached names to five common eating patterns. See if you recognize your baby's dining behavior among them:

Barracudas get right down to business. As soon as they're put to the breast, they grasp the areola and suck energetically for ten to twenty minutes. They usually become less eager as time goes on.

Excited Ineffectives become frantic at the sight of the breast. In a frenzied cycle they grasp it, lose it, and start screaming in frustration. They must be calmed down several times during each feeding. The key to nourishing this type of baby is to feed him as soon as he wakes up, before he gets desperately hungry. Also, if the milk tends to spray from the breast as the baby struggles, it may help to manually express a few drops first to slow the stream.

Procrastinators can't be bothered with nursing until the milk comes in. As long as the reward is mere colostrum, they're not interested. These babies shouldn't be given bottles of water or formula. Continue to put them to the breast regularly, whenever they appear alert or make mouthing movements. Reluctant nursers sometimes benefit from being placed naked on the reclining mother's bare abdomen and chest for a period of time. They may spontaneously move toward the breast or they can be placed on the breast after a time. Advice on improved positioning and at-

she's hungry when she eats. In the process, she'll stimulate the breast more efficiently to produce milk.

Breastfeeding is generally most successful when you start nursing immediately after delivery (in the first hour), keep the baby with you as much as possible ("rooming in" with her in the hospital), and respond promptly to cues of hunger (a practice called demand-feeding). If you remain in the tachment also is helpful. For a baby who resists nursing for the first few days, you can use an electric or manual pump between feedings to stimulate milk production (see page 117). Just don't give up! Try to get some personal advice from mothers who have had similar problems, or seek professional evaluation and guidance.

Gourmets or *Mouthers* insist on playing with the nipple, tasting the milk first and smacking their lips before digging in. If hurried or prodded, they become furious and scream in protest. The best solution is tolerance. After a few minutes of playing, they do settle down and nurse well. Just be sure the lips and gums are on the areola and not on the nipple.

Resters prefer to nurse for a few minutes, rest a few minutes, and resume nursing. Some fall asleep on the breast, nap for half an hour or so, and then awake ready for dessert. This pattern can be confusing, but these babies cannot be hurried. The solution? It's best just to schedule extra time for feedings and remain as flexible as possible.

Learning your own baby's eating patterns is one of your biggest challenges in the first few weeks after delivery. Once this is established, it will be much easier to determine when he's hungry, when he's had enough, how often he needs to eat, and how much time is required for feedings. It is generally best to initiate a feeding at the earliest signs of hunger and before the baby cries. Babies also have unique positions that they prefer and will even show preference for one breast over the other.

hospital for several days and she sleeps in the nursery, her feeding schedule may be determined more by the needs of the staff than her own hunger pangs. In some cases this may be necessary. Once you're finally home, it may take several days for her to reset her internal clock, so in the meantime try feeding her every two to three hours even if she doesn't cry for nourishment. Sleepy babies should be awakened to

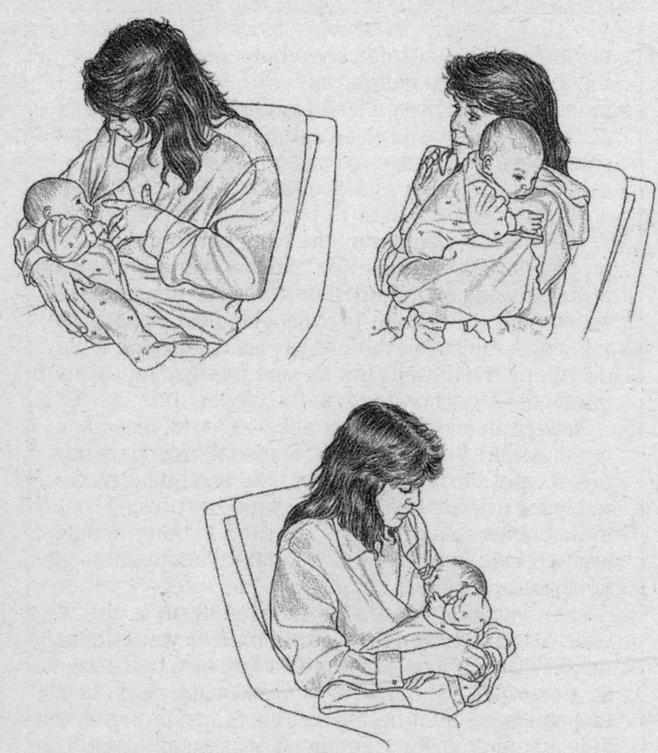

Each feeding should start with about ten minutes on one breast, followed by burping and a shift to the other breast.

feed after every three to four hours during the first few weeks of life.

Allow the baby to continue nursing on the first breast as long as desired. When she spontaneously stops for a prolonged period or falls off the breast, burp her. If your baby seems sleepy after the first breast, you may want to wake her up a bit by changing her diaper or playing with her a little before switching her to the second side. Since your infant sucks more efficiently on the first breast she uses, you should alternate from feeding to feeding the one she uses first. Some women place a safety pin or an extra nursing pad on the side where the baby last nursed as a reminder to start first on the other side at the next feeding.

Initially your newborn probably will nurse every couple of hours, regardless of whether it's day or night. By the end of her first month, she may start sleeping longer at night, perhaps going from 10:00 P.M. to 2:00 A.M. without a feeding, and then sleeping until 6:00 A.M. You can encourage this pattern by keeping her awake during the early part of the evening, giving her a long feeding at 10:00 P.M., and keeping her room dark, warm, and quiet at night. Don't turn on the light for the 2:00 A.M. feeding. Change her diaper quickly and without fanfare before this feeding and put her right back to sleep afterward. By four months she should be sleeping six hours or more at a stretch without awakening during the night. (See *Helping Your Baby Sleep,* page 54.)

You'll also find that your infant may require long feedings at certain times of the day and be quickly satisfied at others. She'll let you know when she's finished by letting go or drifting off to sleep between spurts of nonnutritive sucking. A few babies, if allowed to do so, would nurse around the clock to satisfy their sucking needs. If your baby falls into this category, you may have to set some limits. About ten minutes on each breast provides 90 percent of the available milk; beyond this time frame, she'll receive less and less milk per suck. On rare occasions, if she seems desperate to keep sucking for a prolonged period, you might try using a pacifier as a compromise—but don't count on its working and don't offer a pacifier until the infant is at least four to six weeks old. A baby who wants to keep nursing on and on (say, for twenty to thirty minutes per side) at every feeding may be having difficulty obtaining enough milk. If you are not sure why your baby wants to nurse so long, check with your pediatrician.

How Do You Know If Your Baby Is Getting Enough?

Your baby's diapers will provide clues about whether he is getting enough to eat. During the first month, if his diet is adequate, he should wet six to eight times a day and have at least two bowel movements daily (usually one little one after each feeding). Later, he may have less frequent bowel movements, and there may even be a day or more between them.

If your baby is otherwise thriving, this is quite normal. You can also hear your baby swallow, usually after several sucks in a row. Sleeping for a couple of hours right after a feeding is also a sign that he is getting enough. On the other hand, a baby who is not getting enough to eat over several days may become very sleepy and seem "easy" to care for. In the early weeks, a baby who sleeps for long periods (four hours or more) should be seen by the pediatrician.

Another way to judge your baby's intake over time is by weighing him once every week or two. During the first week of life, he may lose up to 7 to 10 percent of his birthweight (that's 6 to 12 ounces in an approximately 7½-pound full-term baby), but after that he should gain fairly steadily. By the end of his second week he ought to be back to his birthweight. If you've breastfed other children, lactation probably will get established more quickly this time around, so the new baby may lose very little weight and return to his birthweight in just a day or two. With each successive child, your milk will come in sooner and the volume will increase more rapidly.

Once your milk supply is established, your baby should gain about ⅔ ounce a day during his first three months. Between three and six months, his weight gain will taper off to about ½ ounce a day, and after six months, it will drop even further. If your baby is gaining less than this, you should discuss the situation with your pediatrician. Depend upon the scale at your pediatrician's office for the most accurate measurements.

The Supplemental Bottle

It is usually best to try to breastfeed your newborn around the clock. Having your baby with you in your hospital room as much as possible (called rooming-in at most hospitals) makes this much easier. Of course, you might be tempted to have your baby sleep in the nursery for one night so you can get an uninterrupted night's sleep. But research has shown that those mothers who keep their babies with them in their hospital room twenty-four hours per day sleep just as long in total as mothers whose babies are returned to the nursery. Also, if your baby is always with you, you can avoid any water or formula supplementation in those first few days, which may interfere with your ability to have a successful breastfeeding experience.

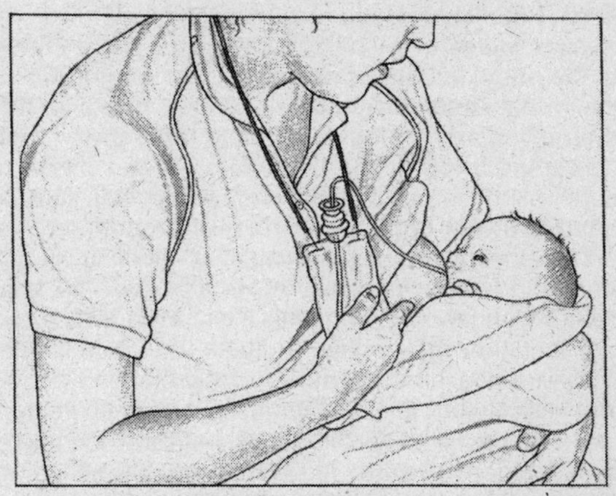

Nursing Trainers

The amount of milk your breasts produce depends on the amount of milk that is removed from them. So if you miss too many feedings, your body will automatically decrease production. This can occur even if you express milk during missed feedings, because pumps do not stimulate or empty the breasts nearly as efficiently as your baby's sucking.

If you miss a number of feedings because of illness or because your baby is unable to nurse for some reason, you may be able to keep your baby well fed while reestablishing your milk supply with the help of a device called a nursing trainer or supplemental nurser. Unlike a bottle, which trains the baby away from the breast, this device provides supplemental formula while the infant is at the breast.

It consists of a small plastic container that holds formula or expressed breastmilk and hangs from a ribbon around your neck. The container has a thin flexible tube that is held or taped along the breast with its tip adjacent to the nipple and placed in the corner of the baby's mouth as she sucks. Her suction draws the formula from the container into her mouth, so that even if you aren't producing much milk, she will still be getting a full meal. This reinforces her desire to nurse at the breast. At the same time, her sucking stimulates your body to step up milk production.

The nursing trainer, available at medical supply stores and some pharmacies, is also used to train babies with feeding problems. It can even help stimulate lactation in adoptive mothers, or mothers who have stopped breastfeeding for a prolonged period and wish to start again. Of course, there is no guarantee of success with these trainers, but for women who would otherwise have to give up on breastfeeding, supplemental nursers are worth a try.

Nursing trainers may also be used in some cases of breastmilk jaundice. Breastmilk jaundice is a condition that occurs in breastfed babies from ages 4 days to 2 weeks or so. This prolonged jaundice, which sometimes can be quite high, is due to elements in the breast milk interfering with the normal removal of bilirubin from the body. (Bilirubin is a chemical formed during the normal breakdown of old red blood cells. Everyone's blood contains small amounts of bilirubin, but newborns tend to have high levels because they have extra red blood cells at birth and their immature livers may have trouble processing the additional bilirubin that exists.) Rarely has this caused any difficulty, but if the jaundice is prolonged, your pediatrician will want to see your baby. Your pediatrician may recommend that you halt breastfeeding briefly.

But if you must miss several feedings in a row, the baby will need to be given either expressed breastmilk or formula. In that case, you will need to express milk, manually or mechanically, in order to stimulate continued milk production. Formula should be substituted for breastfeedings only when absolutely necessary during the first three to four weeks, and certainly no more than once every twenty-four hours. Bottle-feedings may get in the way of successful breastfeeding. In general, formula should be given to a breastfeeding newborn only if the mother is sick or must take medications that could temporarily pass into her milk and harm the baby. Most medications are safe for breastfeeding babies, but they should always be checked out by a knowledgeable physician or pharmacist.

Once breastfeeding is going well and the milk supply is established (usually three or four weeks after delivery), you may decide to use an occasional bottle of formula or expressed breastmilk so you can be away during some feedings. This probably won't interfere with your baby's nursing habits, but it may cause another problem: Your breasts may become engorged, and they can leak milk. You can relieve the engorgement by expressing milk to empty the breasts. Wearing nursing pads will help you manage the problem of leakage. (Some women need to wear nursing pads constantly during the first month or two of lactation.) Also, if you express milk in advance and store it, it can be used instead of formula for the bottle-feeding. In babies from families with a history of allergy, avoiding formula may be particularly important.

Milk can be expressed either by hand or by pump. If you choose to express manually, make sure your hands and the nipple area are clean, and use a sterile container to collect the milk. Hold the breast in one hand with fingers along the top and bottom of the areola, then press toward the chest wall with a rhythmic motion until the milk flows or squirts out. The manual technique described earlier also works as well. Transfer the milk into a sterile bottle, rigid plastic container, or specially made plastic bag for storage in the refrigerator. (See page 120.)

Most nursing mothers find using a pump easier than expressing milk manually. Hand pumps are available at most drug and baby stores. Avoid pumps that resemble a bicycle horn—this is an inefficient design that allows pumped milk

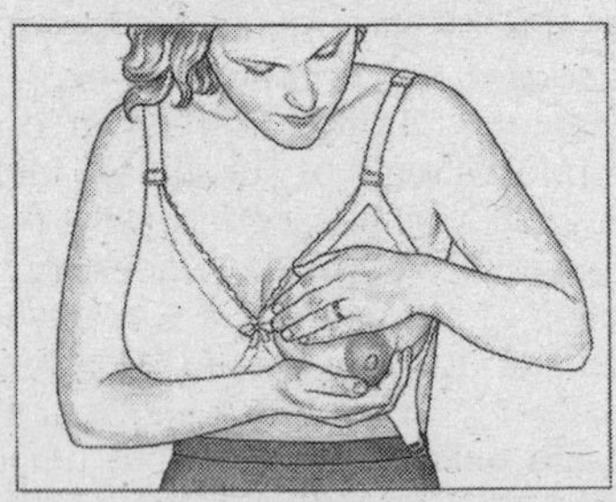

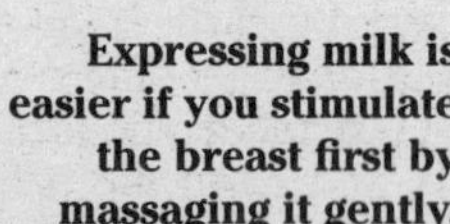

Expressing milk is easier if you stimulate the breast first by massaging it gently.

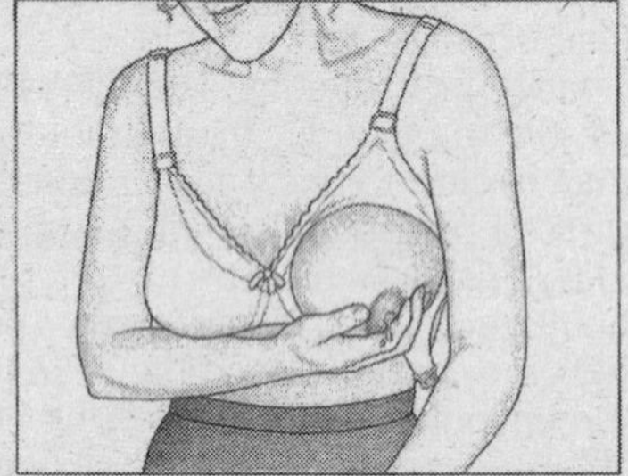

To express manually, hold the breast in one hand with fingers along the top and bottom of the areola, then press toward the chest wall with a rhythmic motion.

to flow back into the rubber bulb, which is virtually impossible to clean properly. As a result the milk can become contaminated.

What's a better choice? The most popular pumps consist of two cylinders, one inside the other, attached to a rigid device that looks like a funnel that fits over the breast. As you slide the outer cylinder up and down, negative pressure is created over the nipple area and milk collects in the bottom of the cylinder. This collecting cylinder can be used with a special nipple to feed your baby without transferring the milk, and the entire pump can be cleaned in the dishwasher. Several different companies manufacture variations on this basic design.

Some pumps use a squeeze bulb to create negative pressure and draw the milk into a bottle, and they work well for some women. They have a soft, pliable flange that fits around the nipple and produces a milking action on the areola while pumping.

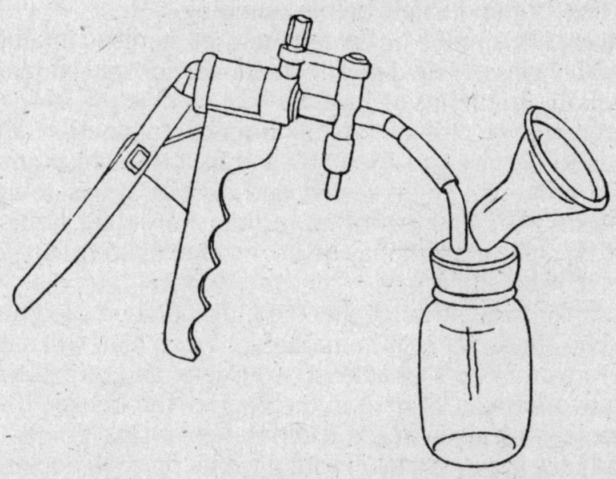

Hand pumps are available at most drug and baby stores.

Electric pumps stimulate the breast more effectively than manual expression or hand pumps. They are used primarily to induce or maintain lactation when a mother is unable to feed her infant directly for several days or more. These pumps are easier and more efficient than hand pumps—but they're vastly more expensive. The more elaborate ones cost over $1,000 apiece, so if you will need the pump for only a limited period, it's much more economical to rent one from a medical supply store, hospital, or a lactation rental agency. A small portable electric pump is also available, selling for around $75. If you return to work shortly after your baby is born and want to continue breastfeeding, obtaining a breast pump is essential.

When shopping for an electric pump to buy or rent, make sure it creates a steady milking action with variable pressure and is not simply a suction device. You may also want to consider a pump that expresses both breasts at the same time; such a pump will increase your milk volume as well as save time. No matter which type of pump you choose, make sure all parts that come in contact with skin or milk can be removed and sterilized (see page 128). Otherwise, the pump will become a breeding ground for bacteria and the milk will not be safe for your baby. Whenever using a pump, wash your hands immediately before pumping.

Breastmilk should be stored only in sterile containers, preferably glass or rigid plastic containers or special plastic bags. Baby bottle insert bags are not sufficiently strong or thick enough to protect the milk from contamination. If the milk is to be given to the baby within forty-eight hours, it should immediately be sealed and cooled. If this refrigerated milk goes unused for *more* than forty-eight hours, it should be discarded. It may be frozen after up to twenty-four hours of refrigeration.

If you know in advance that the milk won't be used for at least two days, freeze it immediately. Breastmilk will safely keep in your freezer for at least two weeks, and probably for up to two months. Store it in the back of the freezer. If you have a separate deep freeze, it can be kept for six months. It's a good idea to place a label with the date on each container so you can use the oldest milk first. It's useful to freeze milk in quantities of about 3 to 4 ounces—the amount of a single feeding. You can also freeze some 1-to-2-ounce portions; these will come in handy if the baby wants a little extra at any feeding.

When it's time to use this stored milk, keep in mind that your baby is accustomed to breastmilk at body temperature, so the milk should be heated to at least room temperature (68 to 72 degrees Fahrenheit) for feeding. The easiest way to warm refrigerated or frozen milk is to place the container in warm water and rotate it frequently. To speed up this process, place the container in a pan of water at low heat on the stove. You can also thaw milk by leaving it at room temperature, but this takes much longer and can lead to bacterial growth if left for many hours.

Microwave ovens should not be used for heating bottles. Microwaving overheats the milk in the center of the container. Even if the bottle feels comfortably warm to your touch, the superheated milk in the center can scald your baby's mouth. Also, the bottle itself can explode if left in the microwave too long.

Incidentally, once milk is thawed, its fat may separate, but it is still safe to drink. Just shake the container gently until the milk returns to a uniform consistency. Thawed milk should be used within four hours. Never refreeze it.

Not all breastfed babies react to the bottle the same way.

Some accept it easily, regardless of when it is first introduced. Others are willing to take an occasional bottle but not from the mother or when the mother is in the house.

You can increase the likelihood that your baby will accept a bottle the first few times if someone other than Mom offers it, and she is out of sight at the time. Once familiar with the bottle, he may be willing to take it in his mother's presence, possibly even from mother herself, but don't count on it. If you want to decrease resistance to the ultimate switch from breast to bottle, offer your baby a bottle at least once a week beginning in the baby's second month. On the other hand, an infant may never need a bottle and can be weaned directly to a cup.

Possible Problems

For some babies and mothers, nursing goes well from the start and there are never any problems. But breastfeeding can have its ups and downs, especially in the beginning. Fortunately, many of the most common difficulties can be resolved quickly if you know what to expect and how to respond. Here are some suggestions for dealing with them:

Food Sensitivities. At one time or another, almost everyone has eaten something that doesn't agree with him. In much the same way, food you eat may cause a reaction in your baby as part of it is transferred to her through breastmilk. She may respond by crying, fussing, nursing more frequently, and generally being inconsolable. It's easy to confuse this problem with colic, but there's a difference: While true colic occurs on a daily basis during the first three months (see *Colic*, page 179), colicky behavior caused by food sensitivity takes place only after the nursing mother eats the offending food, and it clears up in less than twenty-four hours.

Your baby may have a colicky reaction whenever you eat a certain food, or she may react only after you eat a large quantity of a particular food that causes no trouble in smaller amounts. "Gassy" foods, such as cabbage, onions, garlic, broccoli, and turnips, cause problems for some breastfed infants. Usually with food reactions, these types of symptoms last less than twenty-four hours and then disappear until the next time you eat the offending food.

In rare cases, babies may have a true allergy to cow's milk or other foods in the mother's diet and will have a colicky period several hours after their mothers eat any dairy product. In addition to the general fussiness typical of this short-lived colic, a food allergy may produce strong gastrointestinal discomfort, causing the baby to draw up her legs in pain. This should be discussed with your pediatrician before you eliminate the suspect foods from your diet for at least two weeks. (For dairy products this includes milk, cheese, yogurt, ice cream, and cottage cheese.) If the pattern of colic continues through these two weeks, then the baby's problem is more likely to be true colic rather than an allergy to a food that her mother is eating. If the baby's trouble disappears during this period, milk intolerance must be seriously considered. For infants of families with a history of allergy, nursing mothers may be advised to minimize or eliminate dairy products from their diets even if there are no signs of discomfort.

You can test to see if a particular food or group of foods is causing the reaction by returning these foods to your diet one at a time, with several days between each one to see if your baby has a reaction to any of them.

Caffeine is another food substance that sometimes creates problems for breastfeeding babies. Some of the caffeine that Mom ingests shows up in the breastmilk and can cause the baby to be irritable and feed more frequently than usual. Because infants don't eliminate caffeine from their bodies very efficiently, it tends to build up in their systems. Consequently, you may not notice any reaction in your baby until two or three weeks after she's born.

It is not necessary to eliminate caffeine entirely. However, even if you don't drink coffee, you may be getting more caffeine than you realize from soft drinks, chocolate, cocoa, and even some herb teas. These herb teas can be particularly troublesome because their manufacturers are not required to list the ingredients on the packaging. Don't forget, too, that many over-the-counter medications contain caffeine; you shouldn't use any drug without discussing its safety with your doctor.

Cracked Nipples. If your baby is not positioned properly or does not latch on well when you start breastfeeding, you may end up with cracked or sore nipples. Cracked nipples almost always result from incorrect positioning of the baby at the breast and incorrect latching on that allows the baby to bite or traumatize the nipple. Breastfeeding should not cause sustained pain or discomfort. If your nipple or other areas of the breast are painful, you should seek advice from an expert in lactation. Wash the breasts only with water, not soap. Creams, lotions, and more vigorous rubbing will not help, and may actually aggravate the problem. Also, try varying the baby's position at each feeding, and limiting the length of feedings to five or ten minutes (while adding more feedings to the schedule).

In humid climates the best treatments for cracked nipples are dryness, sunlight, and heat. Don't wear plastic breast shields or plastic-lined nursing pads, which hold in moisture; instead, expose your breasts to the air as much as possible, even using a hair dryer on low heat (and not too close) if it seems to help. Some women prefer to use a lamp with a 60-watt bulb positioned about 18 inches from the breasts for about twenty to thirty minutes several times a day. Also, after nursing, rinse the nipples to remove your baby's saliva, and then express a little milk from your breasts, letting it dry on the nipples. This dried milk will leave a protective coating that may help the healing process. In a dry climate, you might want to apply ointments or purified hypoallergenic lanolin. If these measures do not solve the problem, consult your doctor for further advice.

Engorgement. As we've already mentioned, your breasts can become severely engorged if your baby doesn't nurse often or efficiently during the first few days after your milk comes in. While some engorgement is to be expected when you start lactation, extreme engorgement causes swelling of the milk ducts in the breasts and of blood vessels across the entire chest area. The best treatment is to express milk between feedings, either manually or with a pump, and make sure the baby nurses at both breasts at every feeding. Since warmth encourages milk flow, it may also help to stand in a warm shower as you manually express the milk, or use warm compresses. You may also get some relief with the use of warm compresses during nursing and cool compresses between nursing.

If you have very severe engorgement, however, warmth

may aggravate the situation (it increases blood flow to the area). If this is the case, try using cold compresses or cool water instead as you express the milk. Some women even alternate cold and warm water between feedings. Whatever approach you use, the engorgement should subside on its own in a few days.

Mastitis. Mastitis is an infection of the breast caused by bacteria. Mastitis causes swelling, heat, and pain, usually in just one breast or part of the breast, and may cause a nursing mother to feel feverish and ill. If you experience any of these symptoms, notify your doctor at once so that he can begin treating the infection with antibiotics. Make sure he knows that you will be continuing to breastfeed so he will prescribe a medication that's safe for your baby. Be sure to take all the antibiotics even if you feel better. Do not stop nursing; this will worsen the mastitis and cause increased pain. The baby will not be harmed by nursing during the mastitis, and the milk will not change its composition because of the mastitis and the antibiotics.

Mastitis may be a sign that your body's immune defenses are down. Bed rest, sleep, and decreased activity will help you recover your stamina. Also, keeping the breasts drained will help prevent the infection from spreading. Take comfort in the fact that mastitis does not cause the milk itself to be infected, so there's no reason to stop nursing your baby. Rarely, a woman may find that it's too painful to have the baby nurse on the infected breast; in that case, open up both sides of your bra and let the milk flow from that breast onto a towel or absorbent cloth such as a clean diaper, relieving the pressure as you feed the baby on the opposite side. Then she can finish the feeding on the infected side with less discomfort.

The Cancer Question. Studies indicate that breastfeeding offers some protection against premenopausal breast cancer. If a woman has been diagnosed with cancer and has had a malignant tumor removed, the doctor may advise against breastfeeding. However, many doctors feel that breastfeeding is safe even if a woman has had a benign (noncancerous) lump or cyst removed.

Breastfeeding After Plastic Surgery on the Breasts. Plastic surgery to enlarge the breasts should not interfere with breastfeeding—provided the nipples have not been moved and no ducts have been cut. Questions have been raised recently about possible risks to the mother and nursing baby from leakage of silicone implants. This remains unresolved at this time, but most authorities recommend breastfeeding even after implant surgery. However, plastic surgery to reduce the size of the breasts is another matter; it often makes breastfeeding impossible, especially if the nipples are transplanted because the ducts or nerves have been cut. But many women who have been told by their surgeons that they will not be able to breastfeed find, to their surprise, that they are successful. It is worth trying.

Bottle-Feeding Your Baby

If you have decided to bottle-feed your baby, you'll have to start by selecting a formula. Your pediatrician will help you pick one based on your baby's needs. Twenty or thirty years ago, the majority of mothers made their own formula—a mixture of evaporated cow's milk, water, and sugar. Today, there are several prepackaged varieties and brands from which to choose.

Why Formula Instead of Cow's Milk?

Many parents ask why they can't just feed their baby regular cow's milk. The answer is simple: Young infants cannot fully digest this product as completely or easily as they digest formula. Also, cow's milk contains high concentrations of protein and minerals, which can stress a newborn's immature kidneys and can cause severe illness at times of heat stress, fever, or diarrhea. In addition, this feeding lacks the proper amounts of iron and vitamin C that infants need. It may even cause iron-deficiency anemia in some babies, since protein can irritate the lining of the stomach and intestine, leading to loss of blood into the stools. For these reasons your baby should not receive any regular cow's milk for the first twelve months of life.

A few families still prepare their own infant formula, but most pediatricians discourage this. When it is done, evaporated milk, which is cow's milk concentrate that is mixed with a special sugar product in precise amounts, should be prescribed and adjusted by your pediatrician. It is unwise to give your baby homemade formula without your pediatrician's advice.

Once your baby is past one year old, you may give him whole cow's milk—provided he has a balanced diet of solid foods (cereals, vegetables, fruits, and meats). But limit his intake of milk to one quart per day. More than one quart can provide too many calories, and may decrease his appetite for the other foods he needs. If he is not yet eating a broad range of solid foods, give him iron-fortified formula instead of cow's milk.

Do not give your baby any reduced-fat milk (2 percent or skimmed) before his second birthday. He needs the higher fat content of whole milk to maintain normal weight gain, and his body absorbs vitamins A and D better from whole milk. Also, nonfat, or skimmed, milk provides too high a concentration of protein and minerals and should not be given to infants or toddlers under age two. After two years of age, you should discuss your child's nutritional needs (including choice of milk products) with your pediatrician.

Choosing a Formula

When shopping for manufactured infant formula, you'll find three basic types:

Cow's milk-based formulas account for about 80 percent of the formula sold today. Though cow's milk is at its foundation, the milk has been changed dramatically to make it safe for infants. It is treated by heating and other methods to make the protein more digestible. More milk sugar (lactose) is added to make the concentration equal to that of breastmilk, and the fat (butterfat) is removed and replaced with vegetable oils and, in some formulas, animal fats that are more easily digested by infants.

Cow's milk formulas are available with added iron. Some infants do not have enough natural reserves of iron to meet their needs. So, the current recommendation is that iron-fortified formula be used for all bottle-fed infants from birth to one year of age. Additional iron is available in many baby foods, especially iron-fortified cereals.

Soy formulas contain a different protein (soy) and different carbohydrate (glucose polymers or sucrose) from milk-based formulas. They are recommended most commonly for babies unable to digest lactose, the main carbohydrate in cow's milk formula, although lactose-free cow's-milk-based formula is now also available. Many infants have brief periods when they cannot digest lactose, particularly following bouts of diarrhea, which can damage the digestive enzymes in the lining of the intestines. When these babies are placed on a lactose-free formula, the enzymes have a chance to return to normal. Depending on the severity and type of diarrhea, your infant may need to stay on the lactose-free formula for as little as a week or, rarely, as long as several months. Your pediatrician will tell you when it's safe to return to milk-based formula.

Another (and far less common) reason for placing an infant on soy formula is milk allergy, which can cause colic, failure to thrive, and even bloody diarrhea. This reaction can be so dangerous to a newborn that some doctors prescribe soy formula from birth as a preventive measure when there is a strong family history of allergies to cow's milk. Unfortunately, as many as half the infants who have milk allergy are also sensitive to soy protein, and they must be given a specialized formula or breastmilk.

Soy formula is also recommended for infants with a rare disorder called galactosemia. These babies have an intolerance to galactose, one of the two sugars that make up lactose. The carbohydrates used to replace lactose in most soy formulas are sucrose and corn syrup (or a combination of the two). Both are easily digested and absorbed by infants. Most of these formulas cost about the same as milk-based formulas and are supplemented with iron. Some states include the galactosemia test in the newborn screening. Infants with this very rare disorder must also be taken off breastmilk.

Soy formulas today contain a good source of protein, but not quite as good as cow's milk (which, in turn, is inferior to human milk). Also, your baby will absorb calcium and some other minerals less efficiently from soy formulas than from milk-based formulas. Because premature infants have higher requirements for these minerals, they usually are not given soy formula at all.

Healthy full-term infants should be given soy formula only when medically necessary. Some strict vegetarian parents choose to use soy formula because it contains no animal products.

Specialized formulas are manufactured for infants with particular disorders or diseases. There are also formulas made specifically for premature babies. If your newborn has special needs, ask your pediatrician which formula is best. Also be sure to check the package for details about feeding requirements (amounts, scheduling, special preparations), since these may be quite different from regular formulas.

Preparing, Sterilizing, and Storing Formula

Most infant formulas are available in ready-to-feed liquid forms, concentrates, and powders. Though ready-to-feed formulas are very convenient, they are also the most expensive. Formula made from concentrate is prepared by mixing equal amounts of concentrate and sterile water (i.e., one can of concentrate and one can of drinking water or one bottle at a time, leaving the can of concentrate covered in the refrigerator for no more than forty-eight hours). Powder, the least expensive form, comes either in premeasured packets or in a can with a measuring scoop. To prepare it, you'll add one level scoop of powder for every 2 ounces of water, and then mix thoroughly to make sure there are no clumps of undissolved powder in the bottle. The solution will mix more easily and the lumps will dissolve faster if you use slightly warmed water.

Aside from the price, one advantage of the powder is its light weight and portability. You can place a couple of scoops of powder in a bottle when you are going out with your baby, and then add water just before feeding. The powder will not spoil, even if it stays in the bottle several days before you add water. If you choose a formula that requires preparation, be sure to follow the manufacturer's directions exactly. If you add too much water, your baby won't get the calories and nutrients she needs for proper growth; and if you add too little water, the high concentration of formula could cause diarrhea or dehydration and will give your infant more calories than she needs.

Water to be used in formula (concentrate or powder) should be brought to a rolling boil for less than one minute before it is added to the formula. Also make sure all bottles, nipples, and other utensils you use to prepare formula—or to feed your baby—are clean. If the water in your home is chlorinated, you can simply use your dishwasher or wash the utensils in hot tap water with dishwashing detergent and then rinse them in hot tap water. If you have well water or nonchlorinated water, either place the utensils in boiling

Preparing Formula from Concentrate (one bottle at a time)

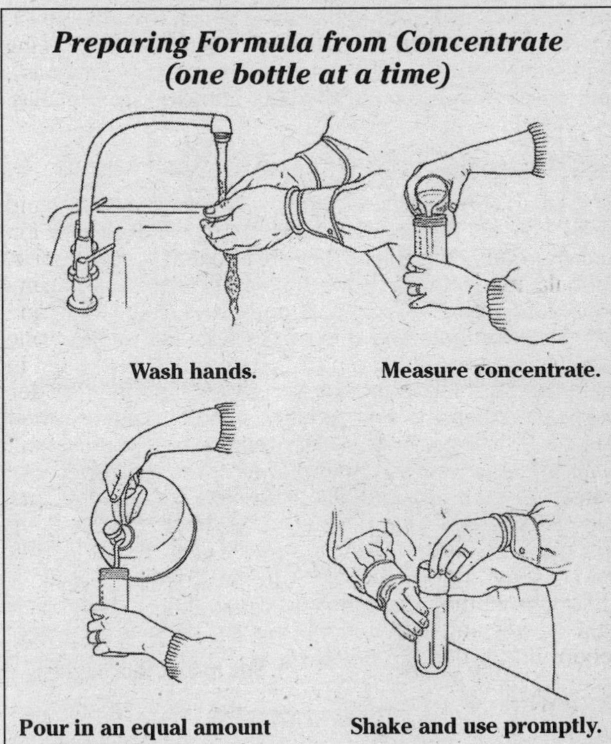

Wash hands. **Measure concentrate.**

Pour in an equal amount of sterile water. **Shake and use promptly.**

water for five to ten minutes or use a process called terminal heating.

In terminal heating, you clean, but do not sterilize, the bottles in advance. You then fill them with the prepared formula and cap them loosely. Next, the filled bottles are placed in a pan with water reaching about halfway up the bottles, and the water is brought to a gentle boil for about twenty-five minutes.

Any formula you prepare in advance should be stored in the refrigerator to discourage bacterial growth. If you don't use refrigerated formula within twenty-four hours, discard it. Refrigerated formula doesn't necessarily have to be warmed up for your baby, but most infants prefer it at least at room

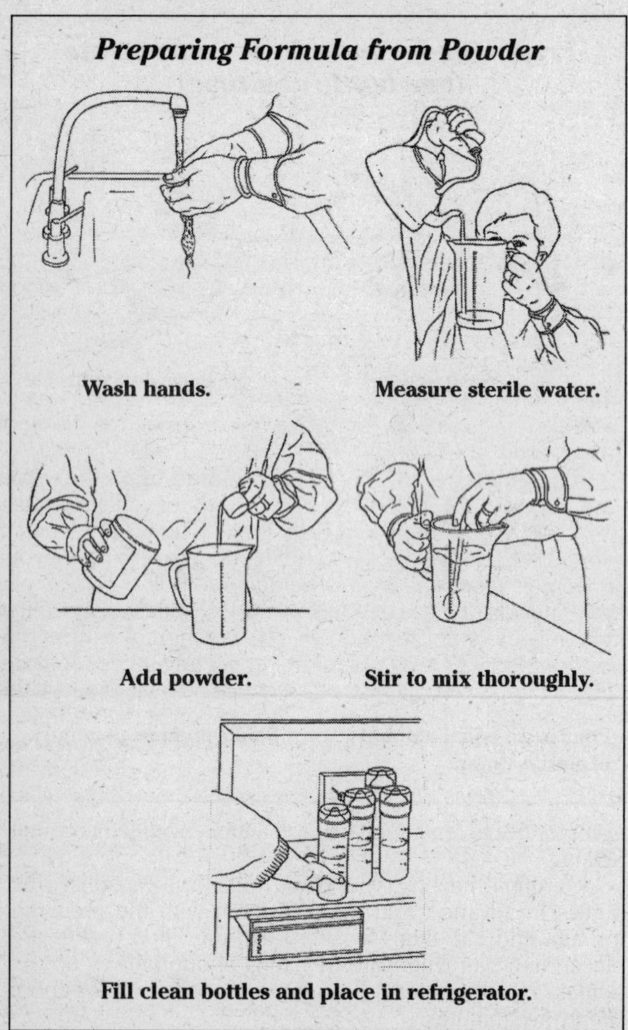

Preparing Formula from Powder

Wash hands.

Measure sterile water.

Add powder.

Stir to mix thoroughly.

Fill clean bottles and place in refrigerator.

temperature. You can either leave the bottle out for an hour so it can reach room temperature, or warm it up in a pan of hot water. (Again, do not use a microwave.) If you warm it or use it immediately after terminal heating, test it in advance to

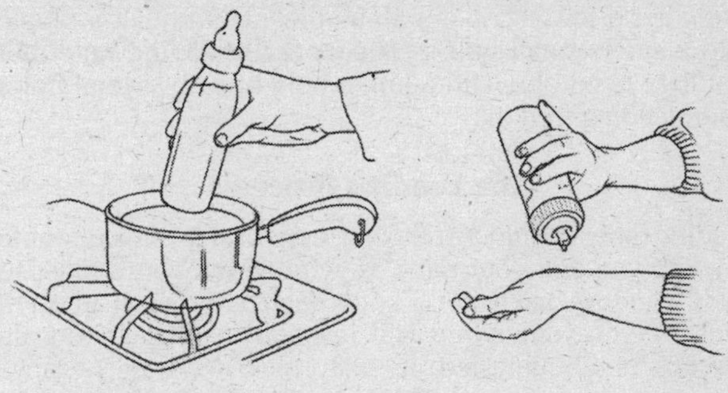

make sure it's not too hot for your child. The easiest way to test the temperature is to shake a few drops on the inside of your wrist.

The bottles you use may be glass, plastic, or plastic with a soft plastic liner. These inner liners are convenient to use, and may help prevent your baby from swallowing too much air as she sucks, but they are also the most expensive. As your baby gets older and begins holding the bottle herself, you should avoid the use of breakable glass bottles. Also, bottles that are designed to promote self-feeding are not recommended, as they may contribute to nursing-bottle tooth decay, by promoting constant feeding and exposure of the teeth to sugars throughout the day and night. When milk is permitted to collect behind the teeth, bacterial growth occurs. Self-feeding in a supine position (lying down on the back) has been shown to occasionally contribute to ear infections (see *Ear Infection,* page 485). Infants should not receive a bottle to suck on during the night. If a bottle is given at bedtime, it should be emptied in a relatively short period and taken away.

Ask your pediatrician which type of nipple she recommends. She'll choose from among the standard rubber nipples, orthodontic ones, and special designs for premature infants and babies with cleft palates. Whichever type you use, always check the size of the hole. If it's too small, your baby may suck so hard that she swallows too much air; if it's too big, the formula may flow so fast that she chokes. Ideally, formula should flow at a rate of one drop per second when you first turn the bottle upside down. (It should stop dripping after a few seconds.) Many parents find that a nipple with a single small hole is adequate for feeding water but that they need one with a larger hole or with several holes when feeding formula.

The Feeding Process

Feeding times should be relaxing, comforting, and enjoyable for both you and your baby. They provide opportunities to show your love and to get to know each other. If you are calm and content, your infant will respond in kind. If you are nervous or uninterested, he may pick up these negative feelings and a feeding problem can result.

You probably will be most comfortable in a chair with arms, or in one with pillows that let you prop up your own arms as you feed your infant. Cradle him in a semi-upright position and support his head. Don't feed him when he's lying down totally flat, because this will increase the risk of choking; it may also cause formula to flow into the middle ear, where it can lead to an infection.

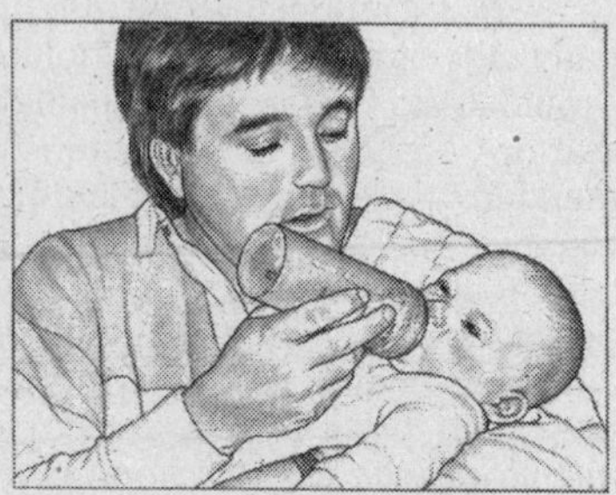

Hold the bottle so that formula fills the neck of the bottle and covers the nipple. This will prevent your baby from swallowing air as she sucks.

Hold the bottle so that formula fills the neck of the bottle and covers the nipple. This will prevent your baby from swallowing air as he sucks. To get him to open his mouth and grasp the nipple, stimulate his "rooting reflex" by stroking the nipple against the lower lip or cheek. Once the nipple is in his mouth, he will naturally begin to suck and swallow.

Amount and Schedule of Feedings

Your newborn will take from 2 to 3 ounces of formula per feeding, and will eat every three to four hours during her first

To get her to open her mouth and grasp the nipple, stimulate her "rooting reflex" by stroking the nipple against the cheek or lower lip.

few weeks. During the first month, if your baby sleeps longer than four to five hours and starts missing feedings, wake her up and offer a bottle. By the end of her first month, she'll be up to at least 4 ounces per feeding, with a fairly predictable schedule of feedings about every four hours. By six months, the amount consumed at each feeding should increase to 6 to 8 ounces and the feedings will number four or five in twenty-four hours.

On average, your baby should take in about 2½ ounces of formula a day for every pound of body weight. But she probably will regulate her intake from day to day to meet her own specific needs. So instead of going by fixed amounts, let her tell you when she's had enough. If she becomes fidgety or easily distracted during a feeding, she's probably finished. If she drains the bottle and still continues smacking her lips, she's probably still hungry. There are high and low limits, however. Most babies are satisfied with 3 to 4 ounces per feeding during the first month, and increase that amount by 1 ounce per month until they reach 8 ounces. If your baby consistently seems to want more or less than this, discuss it with your pediatrician. Your baby should drink no more than 32 ounces of formula in 24 hours.

As we mentioned in the section on breastfeeding, it's initially best to feed your newborn on demand, or whenever she cries because she's hungry. As time passes she'll begin to develop a fairly regular timetable of her own. As you become familiar with her signals and needs, you'll be able to schedule her feedings around her routine.

By two months (or 12 pounds) most babies no longer

need a middle-of-the-night feeding, because they're consuming more during the day and their sleeping patterns have become more regular, but this varies considerably from baby to baby. Their stomach capacity has increased, too, which means they can also go longer between daytime feedings—up to four or five hours at a time. If your baby still seems to want more frequent feedings at this age, try distracting her with play and an occasional bottle of water between scheduled feedings. This should make her hungrier for the next feeding, so she'll eat more at that time and be satisfied for a longer period.

The most important thing to remember, whether you breastfeed or bottle-feed, is that your baby's feeding needs are unique. No book can tell you precisely how much or how often she needs to be fed, or exactly how you should handle her during feedings. You will discover these things for yourself as you and your baby get to know each other.

Supplementation for Breastfed and Bottle-Fed Infants

Vitamin Supplements

Human milk contains a natural balance of vitamins, especially C, E, and the B vitamins, so if you and your baby are both healthy, and you are well nourished, your child may not require any supplements of these vitamins.

Some infants in urban settings who are not exposed to enough sunlight may need supplemental vitamin D. This vitamin is naturally manufactured by the skin when it is exposed to sunlight. If you live in a warm climate and take your baby out in the sunshine several times a week, even for brief periods, you and your baby will produce adequate vitamin D. A total of just fifteen minutes of sunlight a week is sufficient for fair-skinned infants. If he is dark-skinned and you live in a relatively cold climate—or if you cannot take him out in the sun on a regular basis—you will need to give him supplemental vitamin D drops beginning at birth and continuing as long as he is nursing. (Prepared formula has vitamin D added to it.) Your baby also will need vitamin D supplements if he was born prematurely or has certain medical problems. Discuss this issue with your doctor after your baby is born.

Some pediatricians recommend that nursing mothers continue taking a daily prenatal vitamin supplement just to ensure the proper balance, but there is no definitive evidence that this is necessary. A regular well-balanced diet should provide all the vitamins necessary for both you and the baby. If you are on a strict vegetarian diet, however, you may need to take an extra B-complex supplement, since certain B vitamins are available only from meat, poultry, or fish products. If your baby is on infant formula, he generally will receive adequate vitamins because formula has added vitamins.

Where We Stand

The American Academy of Pediatrics believes that healthy babies receiving a normal, well-balanced diet do not need vitamin supplementation over and above the recommended dietary allowances. Megadoses of vitamins—for example, large amounts of vitamins A, C, or D—can produce toxic symptoms, ranging from nausea to rashes to headaches and sometimes to even more severe adverse effects. Talk with your pediatrician before giving vitamin supplements to your baby.

Iron Supplements

Most babies are born with sufficient reserves of iron that will protect them from anemia. If your baby is breastfed, there is sufficient, well-absorbed iron to give her an adequate supply so that no additional supplement is necessary. When she is between four and six months old, you should be starting your breastfed infant on baby foods that contain supplemental iron (cereals, meats, green vegetables), which should further guarantee sufficient iron for proper growth.

If you are bottle-feeding your baby, it is now recommended that you use iron-fortified formula from birth through the entire first year of life. Supplemental vitamins or drops containing iron can be used as a last resort, but only with your pediatrician's advice and supervision. These medications are not as well tolerated, and have been known to stain the teeth.

Water

Until your baby starts eating solid foods, he'll get all the water he needs from breastmilk or formula. During very hot weather, offer a bottle-fed infant water between feedings but don't force it on him or worry if he rejects it. He may prefer to get the extra liquid from more frequent feedings. Breastfed infants generally do not need extra water.

Once your baby is eating solid foods, his need for liquid will increase. About 90 percent of all infants consume fruit juice by the time they are one year of age. The most common fruit juices are apple juice, grape juice, and, more recently, pear juice. Fruit juice has been recommended by pediatricians to provide extra free water for normal infants. However, if a baby drinks too much juice, sometimes it can't be digested properly, and can result in gas or diarrhea. Some fruit juices, such as white grape juice, may be digested more easily than others because they contain a balance of carbohydrates and no sorbitol, a natural sugar. To help regulate the amount of juice your infant drinks, make sure his daily juice intake does not exceed 4 to 6 ounces, offer your baby fruit juice with food to slow down the rate at which it's absorbed, and serve a combination of one-half juice and one-half water (see the table outlining fruit juices). If you offer him extra milk, formula, or juice at mealtimes, you may curb his appetite for solid foods, so instead try giving him water with his meals.

Your baby may also need extra water when he's ill, especially when he has a fever. Ask your pediatrician to help you determine how much water your baby needs at these times. The best fluid for a breastfed infant who is ill is breastmilk.

Mean Carbohydrate Content (G/100G) of Fruits and Fruit Juices

Fruit/Fruit Juice	*Fructose*	*Glucose*	*Sucrose*	*Sorbitol*
Prune	14.0	23.0	0.6	12.7
Pear	6.6	1.7	1.7	2.1
Sweet Cherry	7.0	7.8	0.2	1.4
Peach	1.1	1.0	6.0	0.9
Apple	6.0	2.3	2.5	0.5
Grape	6.5	6.7	0.6	trace
Strawberry	2.2	2.3	0.9	0.0
Raspberry	2.0	1.9	1.9	0.0
Blackberry	3.4	3.2	0.2	0.0
Pineapple	1.4	2.3	7.9	0.0
Orange	2.4	2.4	4.7	0.0

The table shows how many grams of different kinds of sugars are in the different juices. Juices high in sorbitol should probably be avoided when the child is recovering from diarrhea, as this sugar may increase loose stools. All other juices are fairly equivalent.

Fluoride Supplements

Babies do not require fluoride supplementation during the first six months of life. After that time, if they continue to receive breastmilk as their major source of milk and water, fluoride supplementation is advised if local drinking water contains less than .3 ppm of fluoride. Your pediatrician or pediatric dentist can advise you on the need for fluoride drops for your baby.

Formula-fed infants receive some fluoride from their formula and some from their drinking water (if it is fluoridated in their community). The Academy recommends that you check with your pediatrician to find out if any additional fluoride supplements are necessary.

Burping, Hiccups, and Spitting Up

Burping

Young babies naturally fuss and get cranky when they swallow air during feedings. Although this occurs in both breastfed and bottle-fed infants, it's seen more often with the bottle. When it happens, you're better off stopping the feeding than letting your infant fuss and nurse at the same time. This continued fussing will cause her to swallow even more air, which will only increase her discomfort and may make her spit up.

A much better strategy is to burp her frequently, even if she shows no discomfort. The pause and the change of position alone will slow her gulping and reduce the amount of air she takes in. If she's bottle-feeding, burp her after every 2 to 3 ounces. If she's nursing, burp her when she switches breasts.

How Do You Burp a Baby?

Here are a few tried-and-true techniques. After a little experimentation you'll find which ones work best for your infant.

1. Hold the baby upright with his head on your shoulder, supporting his head and back while you gently pat his back with your other hand.

If he still hasn't burped after several minutes, continue feeding him and don't worry; no baby burps every time. When he's finished, burp him again and keep him in an upright position for ten to fifteen minutes so he doesn't spit up.

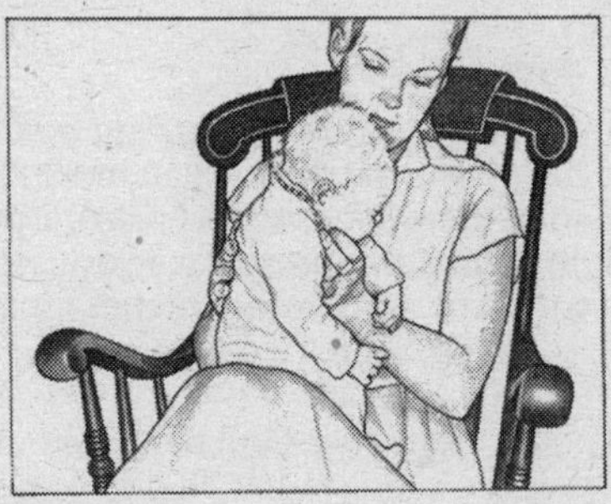

2. Sit the baby on your lap, supporting his chest and head with one hand while patting his back with your other hand.

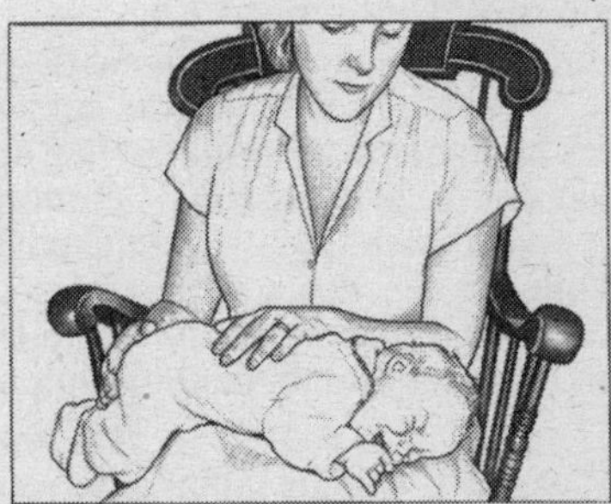

3. Lay the baby on your lap with his back up. Support his head so it is higher than his chest, and gently pat or rotate your hand on his back.

Hiccups

Most babies hiccup from time to time. This usually will bother you more than your infant, but if hiccups occur during a feeding, they may distress him. So change his position and try to get him to burp or relax. Wait until the hiccups are gone to resume feeding. If they don't disappear on their own in five to ten minutes, a few sucks of some water should stop them. If your baby gets hiccups often, try to feed him when he's calm and before he's extremely hungry. This will reduce the likelihood of hiccups during the feeding.

Spitting Up

Spitting up is another common occurrence during infancy. Sometimes spitting up means the baby has eaten more than her stomach can hold; sometimes she spits up while burping or drooling. Though it may be a bit messy, it's no cause for concern. It almost never involves choking, coughing, discomfort, or danger to your child, even if it occurs while she's sleeping.

Some babies spit up more than others, but most are out of this phase by the time they are sitting. A few "heavy spitters" will continue until they start to walk or are weaned to a cup. Some may continue throughout their first year.

You should be able to tell the difference easily between normal spitting up and true vomiting. Unlike spitting up, which most babies don't even seem to notice, vomiting is forceful and usually causes great distress and discomfort for your child. It generally occurs soon after a meal and produces a much greater volume than spitting up. If your baby vomits on a regular basis (one or more times a day), consult your pediatrician. (See *Vomiting*, page 439.)

While it is practically impossible to prevent all spitting up, the following steps will help you decrease the frequency of these episodes and the amount spit up:

1. Make each feeding calm, quiet, and leisurely.
2. Avoid interruptions, sudden noises, bright lights, and other distractions during feedings.
3. Burp your bottle-fed baby at least every three to five minutes during feedings.

4. Avoid feeding while your infant is lying down.
5. Place the baby in an upright position in an infant seat or stroller immediately after feeding.
6. Do not jostle or play vigorously with the baby immediately after feeding.
7. Try to feed her before she gets frantically hungry.
8. If bottle-feeding, make sure the hole in the nipple is neither too big (which lets the formula flow too fast) nor too small (which frustrates your baby and causes her to gulp air). If the hole is the proper size, a few drops should come out when you invert the bottle, and then stop.
9. Elevate the head of the entire crib with blocks (don't use a pillow) and put her to sleep on her back. This keeps her head higher than her stomach and prevents her from choking in case she spits up while sleeping.

As you can tell from the length and detail of this chapter, feeding your baby is one of the most important and, at times, confusing challenges you'll face as a parent. The recommendations in this section apply to infants in general. Please remember that your baby is unique and may have special needs. If you have questions that are not answered in these pages to your satisfaction, ask your pediatrician to help you find the answers that apply specifically to you and your infant.

5

YOUR BABY'S FIRST DAYS

After all the months of pregnancy, you may believe that you already know your baby. You've felt her kicks, monitored her quiet and active periods during the day, and run your hands over your abdomen as she nestled in the womb. Though all of this does bring you closer to her, nothing can prepare you for the sight of her face and the grip of her fingers around yours.

For the first few days after her birth, you probably won't be able to take your eyes off her. Watching her, you may see hints of yourself or other members of the family reflected in her features. But for the most part, she is unlike anyone else. And she'll have a definite temperament of her own that will start making itself known immediately. As she turns and stretches, only she knows what she wants and feels. She may, for example, protest wet or messy diapers from the first day after birth, complaining loudly until she is changed and fed and rocked back to sleep. Infants who behave like this not only tend to spend more time awake than other babies, but they may also cry and eat more. On the other hand, some newborns may not seem to notice when their diapers are dirty, and may object to having their bottoms exposed to the cold air during changes. These babies probably sleep a lot and eat less frequently than the more sensitive infants. Such individual differences are early hints of your child's future personality.

Some mothers say that after so many months of literally "possessing" her in the womb, it becomes difficult to view the baby as a separate human being, with thoughts, emotions, and desires of her own. Making this adjustment and respecting her individuality, however, are important parts of being a parent. If you can welcome her uniqueness now at birth, you'll have a much easier time accepting the person she becomes in the years ahead.

Your Newborn's First Days

How Your Newborn Looks

As you relax with your baby in your own room, unwrap his blankets and examine him from head to toe. You'll notice many details that escaped you in the first moments after birth. For instance, when he opens his eyes you'll see their color. Many Caucasian newborns have blue eyes, but they may change over the next year. Generally, infants with dark-skinned heritage have brown eyes at birth and they remain that color throughout life. If his eyes are going to turn brown, they'll probably become "muddy" during the first six months; if they're still blue at that time, they'll probably remain so.

You may notice a blood spot in the white area of one or both eyes. This, and the general puffiness of his face, are caused by pressures exerted during labor, but both will fade in a few days. If he was born by C-section, he won't have this puffiness and his eyes should be clear.

Bathed and dry, your baby's skin will seem very delicate. If he was born after his due date, he probably would have already lost his protective covering of vernix, and his skin

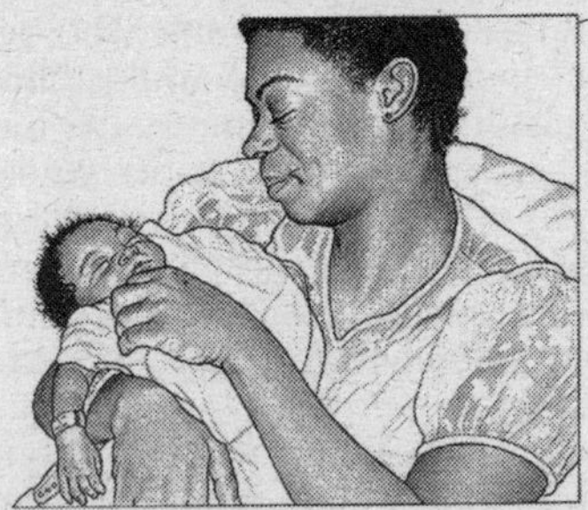

would have been wrinkled and peeling at birth. If he was born on time or early, he may peel a little now because of the sudden exposure to air after the vernix is washed away. This is a normal process and requires no treatment.

As you examine your baby's shoulders and back, you may notice some fine hair, called lanugo. Like the vernix, this hair is produced toward the end of pregnancy; however, it's usually shed before birth or soon thereafter. If your baby was born before his due date, he is more likely to have this hair still, and it may take a couple of weeks to disappear.

You may also notice a lot of pink spots and marks on your baby's skin. Some, like those that appear around the edges of his diaper, are simply due to pressure. Mottled or blotchy-looking patches are caused by exposure to cool air and will quickly disappear if you cover him again. If you find scratches, particularly on his face, trim his fingernails. (Keep his hands covered until you have a chance to do so.) Otherwise, he'll continue to scratch himself as he randomly moves his hands and arms.

Your baby may also have rashes and birthmarks. Most will fade quickly without treatment, but some may be permanent. These are the most common newborn rashes and birthmarks:

Salmon Patches or "Stork Bites." Patches of deep pink, usually located on the bridge of the nose, lower forehead, upper eyelids, back of the head, or neck. The most common birthmark, especially in light-skinned babies, they disappear over the first few months.

Mongolian Spots. Large, flat areas containing extra pigment, which appear green or blue (like a bruise) on the back or buttocks. Very common, especially in dark-skinned babies. They usually disappear by school age and are of no significance.

Pustular Melanosis. Small blisters that quickly dry and peel away, leaving dark spots like freckles. Some babies have only the spots, indicating that they had the rash before birth. The spots disappear in several weeks.

Milia. Tiny white bumps or yellow spots across the tip of the nose or chin, caused by skin gland secretion. They appear raised but are nearly flat and smooth to the touch. They disappear in the first two to three weeks of life.

Miliaria. A raised rash consisting of small fluid-filled blisters. The fluid is normal skin secretion and may be clear or milky-white. Miliaria usually disappears with normal skin cleansing.

Erythema Toxicum. A rash of red splotches with yellowish-white bumps in the centers. They generally appear only during the first day after birth, and disappear without treatment within the first week or so.

Capillary or Strawberry Hemangiomas. Raised red spots with a rough texture. For the first week or so, they may appear white or pale, then turn red later. Caused by dilated blood vessels in the top layers of the skin, they enlarge during the first few months, then gradually shrink and disappear without treatment.

Port Wine Stain. Large, flat, irregularly shaped red or purple areas, they're caused by a surplus of blood vessels under the skin. They won't disappear without treatment, which can be performed by either a plastic surgeon or a pediatric dermatologist when the child is older. (See also *Birthmarks*, page 559.)

If your baby was born vaginally, in addition to the elongated shape of her head, there also may be some scalp swelling in the area that was pushed out first during birth. If you press on this area, your finger may even leave a small indentation. This swelling is not serious and should disappear in a few days.

Swelling under the scalp also sometimes is visible several hours after birth, probably due to bleeding. (The bleeding occurs outside the skull bones, not inside the brain.) This swelling is often present on only one side of the head, and will seem to spring right back after you press on it. This, too, is caused by the intense pressure on the head during labor. It is not serious, though it usually takes six to ten weeks to disappear.

All babies have two soft spots, or fontanelles, on the top of the head. These are the areas where the immature bones of the skull are still growing together. The larger opening is on the top of the head toward the front; a smaller one is at the back. You needn't be afraid to touch these areas gently. They are covered by a thick, durable membrane that protects the skull's important contents.

Babies are affected by the large amount of hormones that were manufactured by their mothers during pregnancy. As a result, your baby's breasts may be enlarged temporarily and might even secrete a few drops of milk. This is equally likely in boy and girl babies, and normally lasts less than a week, although it can last several weeks. Don't try to compress or manipulate the breasts, since this won't reduce the swelling and could cause infection.

As you examine your baby's abdomen, it will seem prominent, and you may notice spaces between the abdominal muscles where the skin protrudes during crying spells. The spaces may be in a line down the center of the abdomen or in a circle at the base of the umbilical cord. This is normal and disappears within about one year.

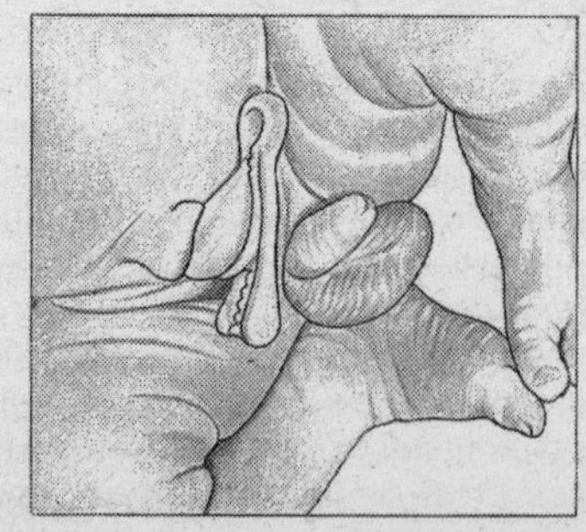

The stub of the umbilical cord is white, translucent, and shiny right after birth. The genitals of newborn babies often seem quite large for bodies so small.

The stub of the umbilical cord is white, translucent, and shiny right after birth. If it was painted with antibacterial dye, it may look blue, and quickly will begin to dry up and shrink. It should fall off within three weeks.

The genitals of newborn babies are often reddish and seem quite large for bodies so small. Girls may have clear, white, or slightly bloody vaginal discharge, caused by exposure to their mother's hormones during pregnancy. The scrotum of a baby boy may be smooth and barely big enough to hold the testicles; or it might be large and wrinkled. The testicles can move in and out of the scrotum. Sometimes they will retract as far as the base of the penis or even to the crease at the top of the thigh. As long as they are located in the scrotum most of the time, this is normal.

Some boys have a buildup of fluid in a sac called a hydrocele (see page 431) inside the scrotum. This will shrink gradually without treatment over several months as the fluid is reabsorbed by the body. If the scrotum swells up suddenly or gets larger when the baby cries, notify your pediatrician; this could be a sign of an inguinal hernia, which requires treatment.

At birth the foreskin is attached to the head, or glans, of the penis, and cannot be pushed back as it can in older boys and men. There is a small opening at the tip through which urine flows. If you have your son circumcised, the connections between the foreskin and the glans are artificially separated and the foreskin is removed, leaving the glans visible. Without a circumcision, the foreskin will naturally separate from the glans during the first few years.

While you're still in the hospital, the staff will watch carefully for your baby's first urination and bowel movement to make sure she has no problem with elimination. These may occur right after birth or up to a day later. The first bowel movement or two will be dark black-green and very slimy. They contain meconium, a substance that fills the infant's intestines during pregnancy, and which must be eliminated before normal digestion and passage of new stool can take place. If meconium is not passed within the baby's first forty-eight hours, it could mean that a problem exists in the lower bowel.

If you notice a little blood in the bowel movements during these first few days, it probably means that the infant swallowed some of her mother's blood during birth, or while nursing if she is breastfed. Although the baby won't be harmed by this in any way, it's best to let your pediatrician know about it so he can make sure this is really the reason behind it; if internal bleeding is the actual cause, immediate treatment will be necessary.

Care of the Penis

Caring for the Circumcised Penis. If you choose to have your son circumcised, the procedure probably will be performed on the second or third day after birth, unless it is delayed for religious reasons. Afterward, a light dressing such as gauze with petroleum jelly will be placed over the head of the penis. The next time the baby urinates, this dressing will usually come off. Some pediatricians recommend keeping a clean dressing on until the penis is fully healed, while others advise leaving it off. The important thing is to keep the area as clean as possible. If particles of stool get on the penis, wipe it gently with soap and water during diaper changes.

The tip of the penis may look quite red for the first few days, and you may notice a yellow secretion. Both indicate that the area is healing normally. Within a week the redness and secretion should gradually disappear. If the redness persists or there is swelling or crusted yellow sores that contain cloudy fluid, there may be an infection. This does not happen very often, but if you suspect that it is present, consult your pediatrician.

Usually, after the circumcision has healed, the penis requires no additional care. Occasionally a small piece of the foreskin remains. This should be pulled back gently each time the baby is bathed. Examine the groove around the head of the penis and make sure it's clean. Occasionally circumcision must be postponed because of prematurity or other medical problems. If it is not performed within the baby's first week, it is usually put off for several weeks or months. Your pediatrician will determine the best time for the circumcision. The follow-up care is the same, whenever it is performed.

Caring for the Uncircumcised Penis. In the first few months, your baby's uncircumcised penis should simply be cleaned and bathed with soap and water, like the rest of the diaper area. Initially, the foreskin is connected by tissue to the glans, or head, of the penis, so you shouldn't try to retract it. No cleansing of the penis with Q-Tips or antiseptics is necessary, but you should watch your baby urinate occasionally to make sure that the hole in the foreskin is large enough to permit a normal stream. If the stream consistently is no more than a trickle, or if your baby seems to have some discomfort while urinating, consult your pediatrician.

The doctor will tell you when the foreskin has separated and can be retracted safely. This will not be for several months to years. After this separation occurs, you should retract the foreskin occasionally to cleanse the end of the penis underneath. Once your son is out of diapers, you'll need to teach him how to do this himself so he can urinate and wash his penis.

Your Baby's Birthweight and Measurements

Did your baby weigh more or less than you had anticipated? His birthweight may actually be affected by a number of factors, including:

- Length of pregnancy before delivery: The later in the nine-month cycle he was born, the larger he may be.
- Parents' size: If both Mom and Dad are unusually large or small, the baby may follow suit.
- Complications during pregnancy: If the mother's blood pressure was high or she had certain other illnesses during pregnancy, the baby might be small. If she had diabetes during pregnancy, however, the baby might be larger than expected.

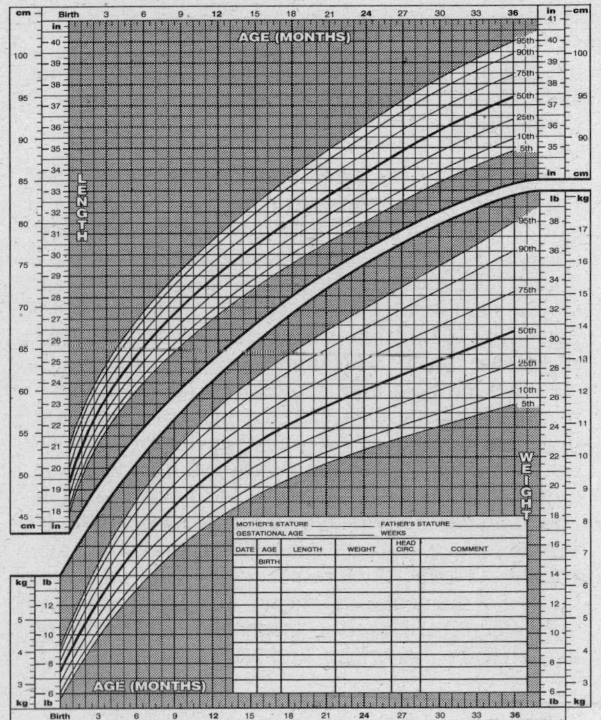

National Center for Health Statistics/Girls' Length for Age and Weight for Age Percentiles/Ages Birth-36 Months

- Nutrition during pregnancy: If the baby was not getting enough nourishment while inside the uterus, either because the mother's diet was very poor or because of a medical problem with pregnancy, the baby might be smaller than expected.
- Mother's smoking or alcohol or drug abuse during pregnancy.

If your baby is either much larger or much smaller than average, he's more likely to have problems adjusting to life

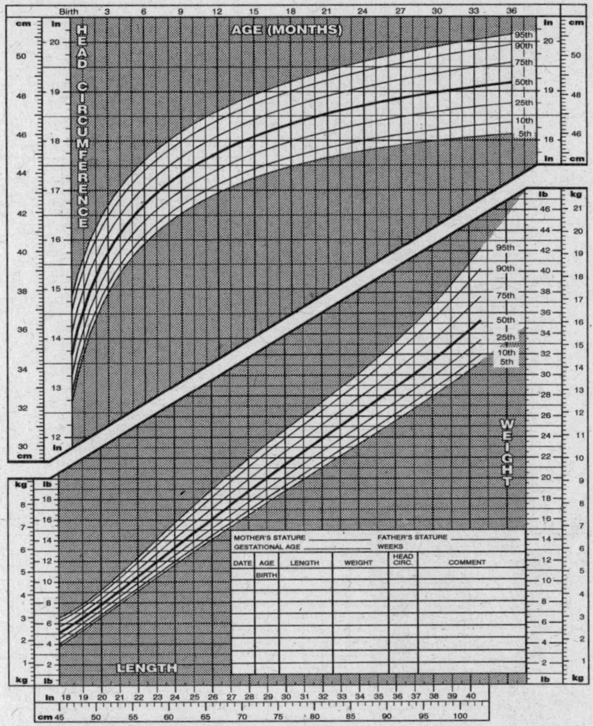

National Center for Health Statistics/Girls' Head Circumference for Age and Weight for Length Percentiles/Ages Birth-36 Months

outside the womb. To determine how his measurements compare with those of other babies born after the same length of pregnancy, your pediatrician will use this growth chart.

As you can see in this chart, eighty out of every one hundred babies born at forty weeks of pregnancy, or full term, weigh between 5 pounds 11 1/2 ounces and 8 pounds 5 3/4 ounces. This is a healthy average. Those above the ninetieth percentile on the chart are considered large, and those below the tenth percentile are regarded as small. Some large babies may initially have difficulty regulating their blood-sugar levels and require extra feedings to prevent hypoglycemia (low blood sugar). Small babies may have prob-

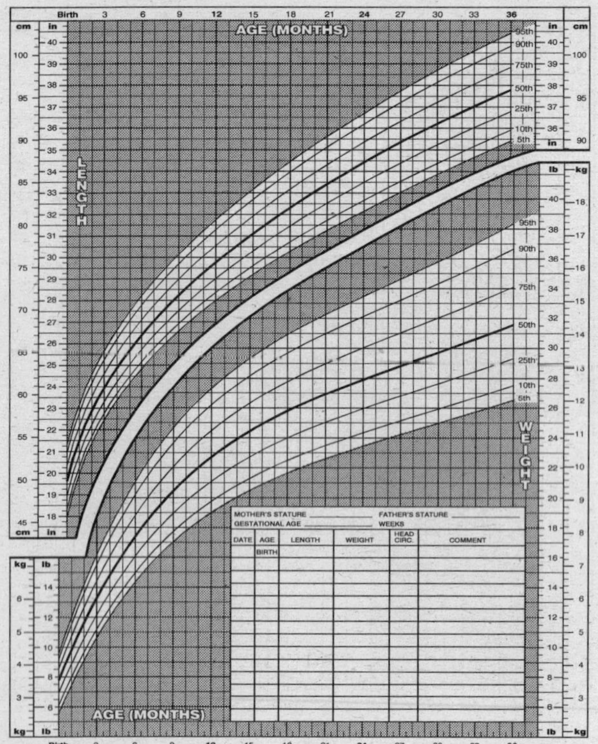

National Center for Health Statistics/Boys' Length for Age and Weight for Age Percentiles/Ages Birth-36 Months

lems feeding or regulating their body temperature. Incidentally, these early weight designations (large or small) do not predict whether you child will be above or below average when he grows up; but they do help the hospital staff determine whether he needs extra attention during the first few days after birth.

At every physical exam, beginning with the first one after birth, your pediatrician will take certain measurements. She'll routinely measure your baby's length, weight, and head circumference (the distance around his head) and will plot them on growth charts similar to the ones on pp. 150-53. In a healthy, well-nourished infant, these three measure-

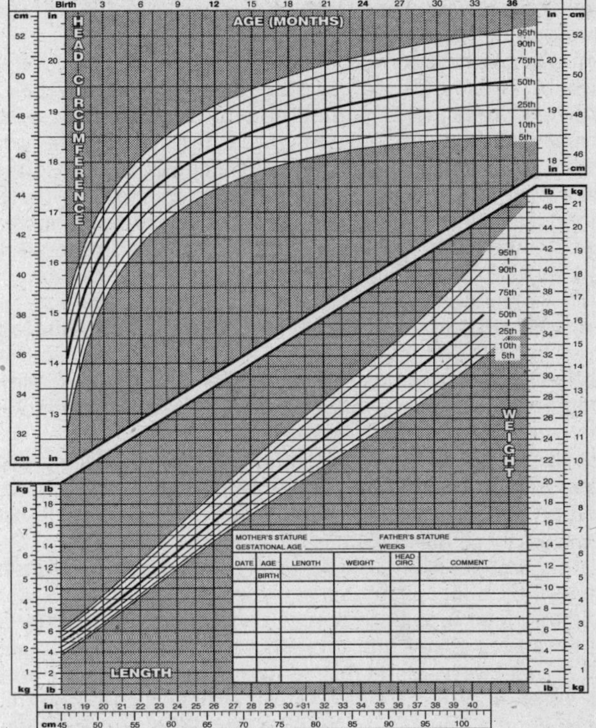

National Center for Health Statistics/Boys' Head Circumference for Age and Weight for Length Percentiles/Ages Birth-36 Months

ments should increase at a predictable rate. Any interruption in this rate cna help the doctor detect feeding, developmental, or medical problems.

How Your Newborn Behaves

Lying in your arms or in the crib beside you, your newborn makes a tight little bundle. Just as he did in the womb, he'll keep his arms and legs bent up close to his body and his fingers tightly clenched, though you should be able to straighten them gently with your hands. His feet will naturally curve inward. It may take several weeks for his body to unfold from this preferred fetal position.

You'll have to wait even longer for him to make the cooing or babbling sounds we generally think of as "baby talk." However, from the beginning he'll be very noisy. Besides crying when something is wrong, he'll have a wide variety of grunts, squeaks, sighs, sneezes, and hiccups. (You may even remember the hiccups from pregnancy!) Most of these sounds, just like his sudden movements, are reactions to disturbances around him; a shrill sound or a strong odor may be all it takes for him to jump or cry.

These reactions, as well as more subtle ones, are signs of how well your baby's senses are functioning at birth. After all those months in the womb, he'll quickly recognize his mother's voice (and possibly his father's as well). If you play soothing music, he may become quiet as he listens, or move gently in time with it.

By using his senses of smell and taste, he can distinguish breastmilk from any other liquid. Born with a sweet tooth, he'll prefer sugar water to plain water, and will wrinkle his nose at sour or bitter scents and tastes.

Your baby's vision will be best within an 8- to 12-inch range, which means he can see your face perfectly as you hold and feed him. But when you are farther away, his eyes may wander, giving him a cross-eyed or walleyed appearance. Don't worry about this. As his eye muscles mature and his vision improves, both eyes will remain focused on the same thing at the same time. This usually occurs between two and three months of age.

While your infant will be able to distinguish light from dark at birth, he will not yet see the full range of colors. So if you show him a pattern of black and white, or sharply

contrasting dark red and pale yellow, he will probably study it with interest; but if you show him a picture with lots of closely related colors, he may not respond at all.

Perhaps the newborn's most important sense is touch. After months of being bathed in warm fluid, his skin will now be exposed to all sorts of new sensations—some harsh, some wonderfully comforting. While he may cringe at a sudden gust of cold air, he'll love the feel of a soft blanket and the warmth of your arms around him. Holding your baby will give him as much pleasure as it does you. It will give him a sense of security and comfort, and it will tell him he is loved. Research shows it will actually promote his growth and development.

Going Home

If your baby was born in an alternative birthing center, you probably will go home within twenty-four hours. By contrast, you might spend up to three days in a hospital if yours was a routine delivery, and up to a week if you had a C-section or an especially difficult delivery. Recently however, even full-term babies who are well are going home within forty-eight hours after delivery.

From an emotional and physical standpoint, there are arguments for both the short and the long stay. Many women simply dislike being in the hospital; these women tend to feel more comfortable and relaxed at home. As soon as mother and baby are proclaimed healthy and able to travel, they're eager to leave. By keeping the hospital stay short, they'll certainly save themselves—or their insurance company—money. However, new mothers often cannot get

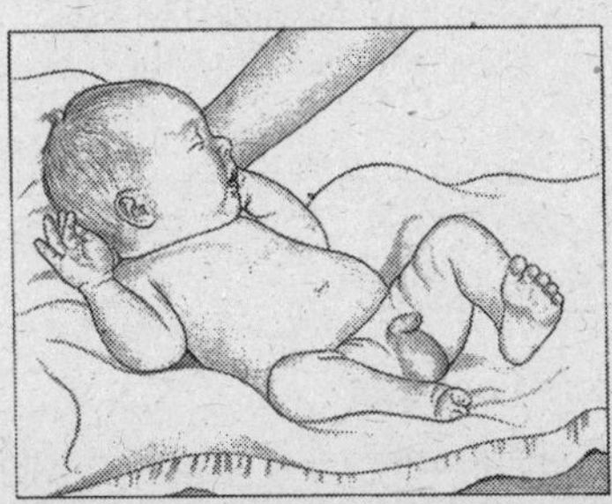

You have just given birth to a wonderful new being, but also to a new and awesome responsibility.

as much rest at home as in the hospital—especially if there are older children clamoring for attention. Nor is there the support of the hospital nurses during the first days of breast-feeding and baby care. You should weigh these advantages and disadvantages carefully prior to making your decision about when to go home.

Before you do leave the hospital, your home and car should be equipped with at least the bare essentials. At home you'll need a safe place for the baby to sleep, some diapers, and enough clothing and blankets to keep her warm and protected. If you're bottle-feeding, you'll also need a supply of formula. Finally, make sure you have a federally approved car seat in which your baby can ride on her trip home. The car seat should be in the back seat, securely attached by the car seat belt. Follow installation instructions carefully.

Where We Stand

The timing of discharge of a newborn from the hospital should be a mutual decision between the physician caring for the infant and the parents. The American Academy of Pediatrics believes that the health and well-being of the mother and her baby should take precedence over financial considerations. AAP policy establishes minimum criteria for early discharge of a mother and her baby and states it is unlikely these criteria can be accomplished in less than forty-eight hours. The Academy supports state and federal legislation based on AAP guidelines as long as physicians, in consultation with parents, have the final authority in determining when to discharge the patient.

Parenting Issues

Mother's Feelings

If you're like most new mothers, your first few days with your baby will be a mixture of delight, pain, utter exhaustion, and—especially if this is your first child—some apprehension about your capabilities as a parent. When the anxiety levels peak, it will be difficult to believe that you'll ever be an expert on baby care. But rest assured. As soon as you're home, things will start to fall into place. So instead of worrying while in the hospital, take advantage of the time to rest and let your body recover.

Quite often, women are so excited about their new arrival that they don't even notice how tired and sore they are. In spite of the fatigue, it may still be difficult to relax enough to fall asleep. If you're not careful, your rooming-in arrangements can add to the problem. However, having your baby sleep in the nursery may not give you the peace you thought if you then imagine that every crying baby you hear is your own. You can solve these problems by letting him sleep in his hospital-supplied bassinet next to you, so you can sleep when he does and hold him when he awakens.

On the other hand, particularly if you had a long, hard labor or a Caesarean section, you simply may not have the strength to keep the baby with you full-time. After having a C-section, you may find it uncomfortable to lift your baby for a few weeks; you may have to try different positions for holding and nursing him that put less strain on your stitches. These obstacles may make you feel that you're not bonding with your baby as you imagined you would; and you may feel especially disappointed if you had planned for a problem-free, natural delivery. Fortunately, your infant's major preoccupation during these first few days also will be sleeping and recuperating, and he won't much care where he does it as long as he's warm, dry, and fed when he's hungry. So for the moment, the hospital nursery will suit

Do not be afraid to ask for help if your concerns seem too great for you to handle.

him fine. You both will have plenty of time to form a secure bond with each other after your physical recoveries are complete.

If this is not your first child, there may be some questions on your mind, such as:

- ***Will this new baby come between you and an older child?***
  This needn't happen if you make a point of spending time separately with each child. When developing a routine during your first weeks home with the new baby, make sure to include special times with your older child.
- ***Will you be able to give the same intensity of love to the new baby?***
  In fact, each child is special and will draw out different responses and feelings from you. The way you relate to your newest child will have little to do with whether she's first, second, or third.
- ***How can you avoid comparing one to another?***
  You may find yourself thinking that the new baby is not as beautiful or alert as another child was right after birth, or you may worry because he's *more* attractive and attentive. In the beginning, these comparisons are inevitable, but as the new baby's own unique qualities begin to emerge, you'll become as proud of your children's differences as you are of their similarities.

On a more practical note, the prospect of taking care of two or more young children may worry you—and with good reason. Now, greater time demands and sibling rivalry loom before you, presenting a new, awesome challenge. Don't let yourself get overwhelmed by it. Given time and patience, all of you will adjust and learn to be a family.

If the newness, fatigue, and seemingly unanswerable questions push you to tears, don't feel bad. You won't be the first new mother to cry—or the last. If it makes you feel any better, your hormones are at least partly responsible for your fragile state.

The hormonal changes you went through as an adolescent, or experience during your menstrual cycle, are minor compared to the hormonal overhaul you're undergoing after giving birth. Blame it on the hormones, and rest assured that this, too, shall pass.

In addition to the hormonal effects, significant emotional changes are taking place. You have just given birth to a wonderful new being, but also to a new and awesome responsibility. There are significant changes taking place in your family life and your relationship with your husband. It is normal to think about these things, and easy to attach too much importance to them.

It is not wise to dwell on them, or take them *too* seriously, however. If you think you are doing that, you should discuss your concerns with your husband, obstetrician, pediatrician, and other people whose judgment you respect and value. Do not be afraid to ask for help if your concerns seem too great for you to handle, or if you feel increasingly depressed. Although a certain amount of postdelivery depression may be normal, it should not be overwhelming or last more than a few days.

Father's Feelings

As a new dad, your role is no less complicated than your wife's. No, you didn't have to carry the baby for nine months, but you did have to make adjustments physically and emotionally as the due date approached and preparations for the baby became all important. On the one hand, you may have felt as if you had nothing to do with this birth; but on the other, this is very much your baby, too.

When the baby finally arrived, you may have been tremendously relieved as well as excited and somewhat awed. In witnessing your baby's birth, feelings of commitment and love may have surfaced that you had worried you might never feel for this infant. You may also experience a greater admiration and love for your wife than you ever felt before. At the same time, contemplating the responsibility of caring for this baby for the next twenty years can be more than a little unnerving.

So how should you deal with all these conflicting emotions? The best approach is to become as actively involved in fathering as possible. For example, depending on the hospital and your own schedule, you may be able to "room in" with mother and/or infant until it's time to bring the baby home. This will help you feel less like a bystander and more like a key participant. You'll get to know your baby right from the start. It also will allow you to share an intense emotional experience with your wife.

Once the entire family is home, you can—and should—help diaper, bathe, and comfort your baby. Contrary to old-fashioned stereotypes, these jobs are not exclusively "woman's work." They are wonderful opportunities for all of you—mother, father, and even older siblings—to get to know and love this new family member.

Sibling's Feelings

Older children may greet a new baby with either open arms or closed minds. Their reaction will depend largely on their age and developmental level. Consider a toddler, for instance. There's little you can do to prepare her in advance for the changes that will come with a new sibling. To begin with, she'll be confused by the sudden disappearance of her parents when the baby is born. Upon visiting the hospital, she may be frightened by the sight of her mother in bed, perhaps attached to intravenous tubing.

She also may be jealous that her parents are holding someone else instead of her, and she may misbehave or begin acting younger—for example, by insisting on wearing diapers or suddenly having accidents several months after being toilet-trained. These are normal responses to stress and change, and don't deserve discipline. Instead of punishing her or insisting that she share your love for the new baby, give her extra love and reassurance. Her attachment to the baby will build gradually and naturally over time.

If your older child is a preschooler, she'll be better able to understand what's happening. By preparing her during the pregnancy, you can help ease her confusion, if not her jealousy. She can understand the basic facts of the situation ("The baby is in Mommy's tummy"; "The baby will sleep in my old crib") and she probably will be very curious about this mysterious person.

Once the baby is born, the older sibling still will miss her parents and resent the infant for being the new center of

Let the older sibling know frequently that there's enough room and love in your heart for both children.

attention. But praising her for helping out and acting "grown-up" will let her know that she, too, has an important new role to play. Make sure she still gets some time to be the "important one" and is allowed to "be the baby" when she needs to. And let her know frequently that there's enough room and love in your heart for both children.

If your older child is of school age, she shouldn't feel threatened by the newcomer in the family. She'll probably be fascinated by the process of pregnancy and childbirth, and be eager to meet the new baby. Once the infant arrives, you can expect the older child to be very proud and protective. Let her help take care of the little one, but don't forget that she still needs time and attention herself. Even if she doesn't demand it, set aside some time each day to spend with her alone.

Health Watch

Some physical conditions are especially common during the first couple of weeks after birth. If you notice any of the following in your baby, contact your pediatrician.

Abdominal Distention. Most babies' abdomens normally stick out, especially after a large feeding. Between feedings, however, the belly should feel quite soft. If your child's abdomen feels swollen and hard, and if he has not had a bowel movement for more than one or two days or is vomiting, call your pediatrician. Most likely the problem is due to gas or constipation, but it could also signal a more serious intestinal problem.

Birth Injuries. The baby can be injured during birth if labor is particularly long or difficult, or if she is very large. Quite often the injury is a broken collarbone, which will heal quickly if the arm on that side is kept relatively motionless; your pediatrician will advise you how to do this. Incidentally, after a few weeks a small lump may form at the site of the fracture, but don't be alarmed; this is a positive sign that new bone is forming to mend the injury.

Muscle weakness is another common birth injury, caused during labor by pressure or stretching of the nerves attached to the muscles. These muscles, usually weakened on one side of the face or one shoulder or arm, generally return to normal after several weeks. In the meantime, ask your pediatrician to show you how to nurse and hold the baby to promote healing.

Blue Baby. Blue hands and feet are nothing to worry about in a newborn. His face, tongue, and lips may turn a little blue occasionally when crying hard, but once he becomes calm, his color in these areas should quickly return to normal. Likewise, if his hands and feet turn a bit blue from cold, they should return to pink as soon as they are warm. Persistently blue skin coloring is a sign that the heart or lungs are not operating properly, and the baby is not getting enough oxygen in the blood. Immediate medical attention is essential.

Coughing. If your baby eats very fast or is trying to drink water for the first time, she may choke, cough, and sputter a bit; but the coughing should stop as soon as she adjusts to a familiar feeding routine. If she coughs persistently or routinely chokes during feedings, consult your pediatrician. These symptoms could indicate an underlying problem in the lungs or digestive tract.

Excessive Crying. All newborns cry, often for no apparent reason. If you've made sure that your baby is fed, burped, warm, and dressed in a clean diaper, the best tactic is probably to hold him and talk or sing to him until he stops. You cannot "spoil" a baby this age by giving him too much attention. If this doesn't work, wrap him snugly in a blanket or try some of the tactics listed on pages 52–3.

You'll become accustomed to your baby's normal pattern of crying. If it ever sounds peculiar—for example, like shrieks of pain—or if it persists for an unusual length of time, it could mean a medical problem. Call the pediatrician and ask for advice.

Forceps Marks. When forceps are used to help during a delivery, the baby may have red marks or even superficial scrapes on her face and head where the metal pressed against her skin. These should disappear within a few days. Sometimes a firm, flat lump develops in one of these areas because of minor damage to the tissue under the skin, but this, too, usually will go away within two months.

Jaundice. Many normal, healthy infants develop a yellowish tinge to their skin in the first few days of life. This condition, called "physiologic jaundice," is a sign that the blood contains an excess of bilirubin, a chemical formed during the normal breakdown of old red blood cells. Everyone's blood contains small amounts of bilirubin, but newborns tend to have higher levels because they have extra red blood cells at birth and their immature livers may have trouble processing the additional bilirubin that exists.

As bilirubin levels rise above normal, the jaundice will appear first on the face, then on the chest and abdomen, and finally on the legs. Typically, after worsening for a few days the jaundice will subside without treatment. If the bilirubin level is extremely high and does not decline, there's a risk of damage to the nervous system. Your doctor will order blood tests to determine the cause and may recommend treatment with phototherapy. In this procedure the baby is placed under fluorescent-type lights for a day or two until the liver matures enough to handle the bilirubin load. Normal daylight has a similar effect, but is not intense enough to

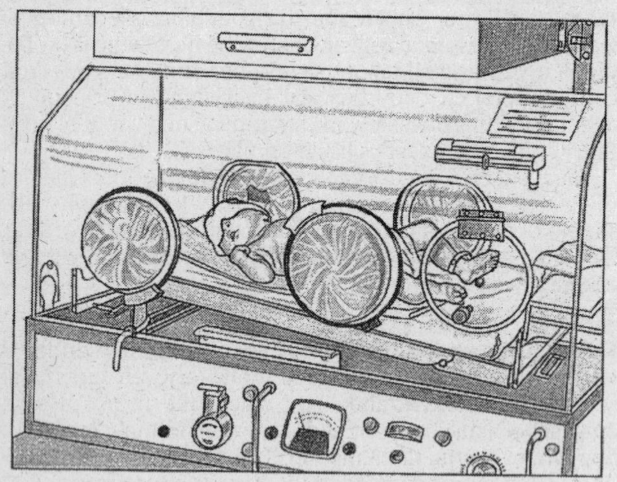

In phototherapy treatment for jaundice, the baby is placed under fluorescent-type lights for a day or two.

help. Direct sunlight is *not* more effective, and should be avoided because of the danger of sunburn.

Breastmilk, incidentally, sometimes interferes with the liver's ability to process bilirubin, so breastfeeding may prolong jaundice in some newborns. When that happens, your pediatrician may recommend that you consider halting breastfeeding briefly (no more than forty-eight hours) to help decrease the bilirubin levels. This approach will be taken only when absolutely necessary, since the baby's frequent sucking at the breast during these first few days is crucial to stimulate the mother's milk supply.

Lethargy and Sleepiness. Every newborn spends most of his time sleeping. As long as he wakes up every few hours, eats well, seems content, and is alert part of the day, it's perfectly normal for him to sleep the rest of the time. But if he's rarely alert, does not wake up on his own for feedings, or seems too tired or uninterested to eat, you should consult your pediatrician. This lethargy—especially if it's a sudden change in his usual pattern—may be a symptom of a serious illness.

Respiratory Distress. It may take your baby a few hours after birth to form a normal pattern of breathing, but then she should have no further difficulties. If she does show any of the following warning signs, however, notify your pediatrician immediately.

- Fast breathing (more than sixty breaths in one minute)
- Retractions (sucking in the muscles between the ribs with each breath, so that her ribs stick out)
- Flaring of her nose
- Grunting while breathing
- Persistent blue skin coloring

Umbilical Cord. You'll need to keep the stump of the umbilical cord clean and dry as it shrivels and, within a few weeks, eventually falls off. At each diaper change, use a cotton swab (soaked in rubbing alcohol and then squeezed) to clean away the wet, sticky material that sometimes collects where the base of the stump meets the skin. This will help dry the cord, as will exposing it to air. Also keep the diaper folded below the cord to keep urine from soaking it. You may notice a few drops of blood on the diaper around the time the stump falls off; this is normal. If the stump becomes infected, however, it will require medical treatment, so alert your pediatrician if you notice any of these signs of infection:

- Pus at the base of the cord
- Red skin around the base of cord
- Crying when you touch the cord or the skin next to it. (If your baby cries when the alcohol is applied, that is normal, because it's cold, but crying at the touch of your finger is not.)

Umbilical Granuloma. Occasionally, after the umbilical cord has fallen off, the remaining area will continue to be moist and may swell slightly. This is called an umbilical granuloma. If it is small, your pediatrician will treat it by applying a drying medication called silver nitrate. If this is not successful, or if the area continues to enlarge or ooze, it may have to be tied off and surgically removed. This is a minor procedure that does not require anesthetic or a hospital stay.

Umbilical Hernia. If your baby's umbilical cord seems to push outward when he cries, he may have an umbilical hernia. This is a small hole in the muscular part of the abdominal wall that allows tissue to bulge out when there's pressure inside the abdomen (for example, when the baby cries). This is not a serious condition, and it usually heals by itself in the first twelve to eighteen months. (It takes longer to heal in African-American babies.) In the unlikely event that it doesn't, the hole may need to be surgically closed.

Your Newborn's First Physical Exams

Your baby should have one thorough physical examination within her first twenty-four hours and a follow-up at some point before you and she leave the hospital. If you take your baby home early (less than twenty-four hours after delivery), your pediatrician should see the baby again at two to three days of age for follow-up. This visit will allow him to check for problems such as those listed earlier.

These early visits to the pediatrician are also opportunities to ask questions about baby care and relieve any worries you may have. Don't hesitate to ask questions that sound unimportant; the answers may provide valuable information and be reassuring to you.

Blood Tests

In all states, newborns are required to be checked for certain serious diseases. One of these is called phenylketonuria (PKU). It causes mental retardation, which can be prevented if the condition is detected early and treated with a special diet. Tests also are done for hypothyroidism (a problem that can lead to mental retardation) and, in some states, for sickle-cell anemia (a blood disease found chiefly among African-Americans) and other disorders. These tests involve pricking the baby's heel to obtain a small blood sample on which the laboratory work can be performed. The PKU test is best done as close as possible to the time of discharge from the nursery. If the test is done before twenty-four hours of age, you will have to visit your pediatrician to have this blood test done a second time. The repeat test should be completed no later than the third week of life.

6

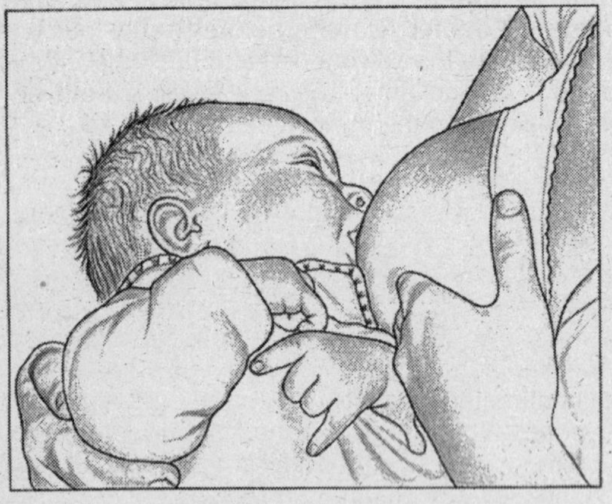

The First Month

Growth and Development

In the very beginning, it may seem that your baby does nothing but eat, sleep, cry, and fill his diapers. By the end of the first month, he'll be much more alert and responsive. Gradually he'll begin moving his body more smoothly and with much greater coordination—especially in getting his hand to his mouth. You'll realize that he listens when you speak, watches you as you hold him, and occasionally moves his own body to respond to you or attract your attention. But before we explore his expanding capabilities, let's look at the changes that will occur in his physical appearance during the first month.

Physical Appearance and Growth

When your baby was born, her birthweight included excess body fluid that was lost during her first few days. Most babies lose about one tenth of their birthweight during the first five days, then regain it over the next five, so that by about day ten they usually are back to their original birthweight. You can plot your own infant's growth on the charts on pages 150–53.

Most babies grow very rapidly after regaining their birthweight, especially during growth spurts which occur around seven to ten days, and again between three and six weeks. The average newborn gains weight at a rate of ⅔ ounce (20 to 30 grams) per day, and by one month weighs about 9 pounds (4 kilograms). She grows between 1 and 1½ inches (2.5 to 4 centimeters) during this month. Boys tend to weigh slightly more than girls (by less than 1 pound, or 400 grams). They also tend to be slightly longer than girls at this age (by about ½ inch, or 1.25 centimeters).

Your pediatrician will pay particular attention to your child's head growth, because it reflects the growth of her brain. The skull should grow faster during the first four months than at any other time in her life. The measurement around the average newborn's head is about 13¾ inches (35 centimeters), and grows to about 14¾ inches (37.75 centimeters) by one month. Because boys tend to be slightly larger than girls, their heads are larger, though the average difference is less than ⅓ inch (1 centimeter).

During these first weeks your baby's body gradually will straighten from the tightly curled position she held inside the uterus during the final months of pregnancy. She'll begin to stretch her arms and legs, and may arch her back from time to time. Her legs and feet may continue to rotate inward, giving her a bowlegged look. This condition usually will correct itself gradually over the next five to six months. If the bowlegged appearance is particularly severe or associated with pronounced curving in of the front part of the foot, your pediatrician may suggest a splint or a cast to correct it, but these circumstances are extremely unusual. (See *Bowlegs*, page 553; *Pigeon Toes [Intoeing]*, page 556.)

If your baby was born vaginally and her skull appeared misshapen at birth, it soon will resume its normal shape. Any bruising of the scalp or swelling of the eyelids that occurred during birth will be gone by the end of the first week or two. Any red spots in the eyes will disappear in about three weeks.

To your dismay, you may discover that the fine hair that covered your infant's head when she was born will soon begin falling out. If she rubs the back of her head on her bedding, she may develop a temporary bald spot there, even if the rest of her hair remains. This loss is insignificant. The bare spots will be covered with new hair in a few months.

Another normal development is "baby acne." These are pimples that break out on the face, usually during the fourth or fifth week of life. They are thought to be due to stimulation of oil glands in the skin by hormones passed across the placenta during pregnancy. This condition may be made worse if the baby lies in sheets laundered in harsh detergents or soiled by milk that she's spit up. If your baby does have baby acne, place a soft, clean receiving blanket under her head and wash her face gently once a day with a mild baby soap to remove milk or detergent residue.

Your newborn's skin may also look blotchy, ranging in color from pink to blue. Her hands and feet in particular may be colder and bluer than the rest of her body. The blood vessels leading to these areas are more sensitive to temperature changes and tend to shrink in response to cold. As a result, less blood gets to the exposed skin, causing it to look pale or bluish. If you move her arms and legs, however, you'll notice that they quickly turn pink again.

Your baby's internal "thermostat," which causes her to perspire when she's too hot or shiver when she's too cold, won't be working properly for some time. Also, in these early weeks, she'll lack the insulating layer of fat that will protect her from sudden temperature shifts later on. For these reasons, it's important for you to dress her properly—warmly in cool weather and lightly when it's hot. Don't automatically bundle her up just because she's a baby.

By the third week, the stump from the umbilical cord should have dried and fallen off, leaving behind a clean, well-healed area. Occasionally a raw spot is left after the stump is gone. It may even ooze a little blood-tinged fluid. Just keep it clean and dry and it will heal by itself. If it is not completely closed and dry in two weeks, consult your doctor.

Reflexes

Much of your baby's activity in his first weeks of life is reflexive. For instance, when you put your finger in his mouth, he doesn't *think* about what to do, but sucks by reflex. When confronted by a bright light, he will tightly shut his eyes, because that's what his reflexes make him do. He's born with many of these automatic responses, some of which remain with him for months, while others vanish in weeks.

In some cases, reflexes change into voluntary behavior. For example, your baby is born with a "rooting" reflex that prompts him to turn his head toward your hand if you stroke his cheek or mouth. This helps him find the nipple at feeding time. At first he'll root from side to side, turning his head toward the nipple and then away in decreasing arcs. But by about three weeks he'll simply turn his head and move his mouth into position to suck.

Sucking is another survival reflex present even before birth. If you had an ultrasound test done during pregnancy, you may have seen your baby sucking his thumb. After birth, when a nipple (either breast or bottle) is placed in your baby's mouth and touches the roof of his mouth, he automatically begins to suck. This motion actually takes place in two stages: First, he places his lips around the areola and squeezes the nipple between his tongue and palate. (Called *expression*, this action forces out the milk.) Then comes the second phase, or the milking action, in which the tongue moves from the areola to the nipple. This whole process is helped by the negative pressure, or suction, that secures the breast in the baby's mouth.

Coordinating these rhythmic sucking movements with breathing and swallowing is a relatively complicated task for a new infant. So, even though this is a reflexive action, not all babies suck efficiently at first. With practice, however, the reflex becomes a skill that they all manage well.

As rooting, sucking, and bringing his hand to his mouth become less reflexive and more directed, your infant will start to use these movements to console himself. Have you already seen him nestling into his blanket or gnawing on his hand when he's tired? You may want to encourage these consoling techniques by giving him a pacifier or helping him find his thumb.

Newborn Reflexes

The following are some of the reflexes you will see your baby perform during her first weeks. Not all infants acquire and lose these reflexes at exactly the same time, but this table will give you a general idea of what to expect.

Reflex	*Age When Reflex Appears*	*Age When Reflex Disappears*
Moro reflex	Birth	2 months
Walking/Stepping	Birth	2 months
Rooting	Birth	4 months
Tonic neck reflex	Birth	4–5 months
Palmar grasp	Birth	5–6 months
Plantar grasp	Birth	9–12 months

Another, more dramatic reflex present during these first few weeks is called the Moro reflex. If your baby's head shifts positions abruptly or falls backward, or he is startled by something loud or abrupt, he will react by throwing out his arms and legs and extending his neck, then rapidly bringing his arms together as he cries loudly. The Moro reflex peaks during the first month and then disappears after two months.

One of the more interesting automatic responses is the tonic neck reflex, otherwise known as the fencing posture. You may notice that when your baby's head turns to one side, his arm on that side will straighten, with the opposite arm bent, as if he's fencing. Do not be surprised if you don't see this response, however. It is subtle, and if your baby is disturbed or crying, he may not perform it. It disappears at five to seven months of age.

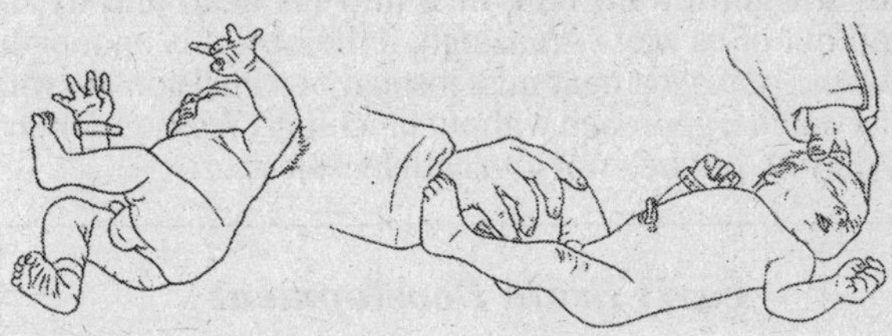

Moro reflex **Tonic neck reflex**

You'll see still another reflex when you stroke the palm of your baby's hand and watch him immediately grip your finger. Or stroke the sole of his foot, and watch it flex as the toes curl tightly. In the first few days after birth, your baby's grasp will be so strong that it may seem he can hold his own weight—but don't try it. He has no control over this response and may let go suddenly.

Aside from his "herculean" strength, your baby's other special talent is stepping! He can't support his own weight, of course, but if you hold him under the arms (being careful to support his head as well) and let his soles touch a flat surface, he'll place one foot in front of the other and "walk." This reflex will disappear after two months, then recur as the learned voluntary behavior of walking toward the end of the first year.

Although you may think of your baby as utterly defenseless, he actually has several protective reflexes. For instance, if a blanket or a pillow falls over his eyes, nose, or mouth, he'll shake his head from side to side and flail his arms to push it away so he can breathe and see. Or if an object

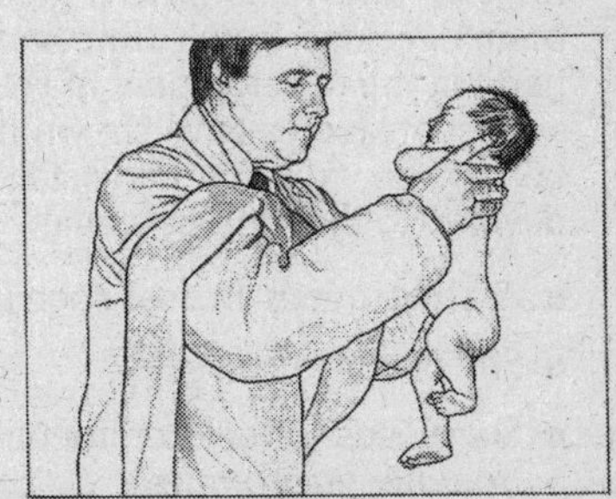

Walking/stepping reflex

comes straight toward him, he'll turn his head and try to squirm out of its way. (Amazingly, if the object is on a path that would make it a near miss instead of a collision, he will calmly watch it approach without flinching.) Yes, he's dependent on you, but he's not totally defenseless.

Early Brain Development

As a parent, you have always known that your actions affect your child. You laugh, she laughs. You praise him, he gloats. You frown at her misbehavior, she saddens. You are at the center of your child's universe.

Research shows that during the first three years of a baby's life, the brain grows and develops significantly and patterns of thinking and responding are established. What does this mean for you as a parent? It means that you have a very special opportunity to help your baby develop appropriately and thrive socially, physically, and cognitively throughout her life. The first years last forever.

For years, people have mistakenly believed that the baby's brain is an exact replica of the genetic codes of her parents. For example, if the mother is a good artist, then the baby has more potential to possess the same artistic skills when she grows up. While genetics plays a role in determining your child's skills and abilities, new research highlights the equally significant role that environment plays. Just recently, neuroscientists realized that the experiences that fill a baby's first days, months, and years have a great impact on how the brain develops. Both nature and nurture work hand in hand in the development of young children.

Recent studies have shown that children need certain elements in the early stages of life to grow and develop to their full potential:

- A child needs to feel special, loved, and valued.
- She needs to feel safe.
- She needs to feel confident about what to expect from her environment.

- She needs guidance.
- She needs a balanced experience of freedom and limits.
- She needs to be exposed to a diverse environment filled with language, play, exploration, books, music, and appropriate toys.

While it may seem that what goes on in a baby's brain would be relatively simple compared to an adult's, in fact, a baby's brain is twice as active as an adult's brain. Neuroscientists are especially focusing on the first three years of a baby's life because they have identified these as times of critical importance. During these years the human brain has the greatest potential for learning. Not only is learning occurring rapidly, but basic ways of thinking, responding, and solving problems are established. For example, notice how easy it is for a child to pick up words from a foreign language. How difficult is that same task for an adult?

What does this mean for you as a parent? It means that *you* and the environment that you create for your baby will influence the way she deals with her emotions, the way she interacts with people, the way she thinks, and the way she grows physically. By creating an appropriate environment for your child, you are allowing normal brain development to take place. You may wonder what is considered an "appropriate" environment. It's one that is "child-centered" and provides opportunities for learning that are geared to your child's development, interests, and personality. Fortunately, the components of a good environment include basic things that many parents want to provide for their children: proper nutrition; a warm, responsive, and loving family as well as other caregivers; fun playtime; consistent positive reinforcement; engaging conversation; good books to read and to listen to; music to stimulate brain activities; and the freedom to explore and learn from their surroundings.

Review the following elements of children's health, and how each one contributes to a child's brain development:

- *Language.* Direct face-to-face communication between parents and other caregivers and their young children supports language development, as does reading to them.
- *Early Identification of Developmental Problems.* Many developmental and medical problems can be usefully treated if detected early. Children with disabilities and other special health care needs can also greatly benefit from close monitoring of early brain development.
- *Stimulating Environment.* Exploring and problem solving in a variety of safe places promotes learning.
- *Positive Parenting.* Raising a child in a loving, supportive, and respectful environment enhances self-esteem and self-confidence, and has a great impact on the child's development.

More and more researchers are discovering how much the environment plays a role in shaping a baby's life. This new science helps us understand exactly how significant our role is in the development of the child's brain. How nurturing and responsive to your infant you are as a parent will play a critical role in shaping your baby's future.

To build a positive environment for your baby in your home and in your community, follow these suggestions:

- ***Get good prenatal care.*** Since brain development begins in the womb, good prenatal care can help ensure the healthy development of your child's brain. Start prenatal care early, see your doctor regularly, and be sure to follow her instructions. Eating a balanced, healthy diet and avoiding drugs, alcohol, and tobacco are just a few steps you can take to contribute to your child's future health.

- ***Try to create a "village" around you.*** Since it's hard to raise a child on your own, seek support from your family, friends, and community. Talk to your pediatrician about parent-support groups and activities.
- ***Interact with your child as much as possible.*** Talk with your child, read, listen to music, draw pictures, and play together. These kinds of activities allow you to spend time focused on your child's thoughts and interests. This, in turn, can make your child feel special and important. You can also teach the language of communication that your child will use to form healthy relationships over a lifetime.
- ***Give your child plenty of love and attention.*** A warm and loving environment helps children feel safe, competent, and cared for, as well as feel concern for others.
- ***Provide consistent guidelines and rules.*** Be sure you and other caregivers are working with the same rules. Also, be sure your own rules and guidelines are consistent while taking into account your child's growing competency. Consistency helps children feel confident about what to expect from their environment.

States of Consciousness

As you get to know your baby, you'll soon realize that there are times when he's very alert and active, times when he's watchful but rather passive, and times when he's tired and irritable. You may even try to schedule your daily activities to capitalize on his "up" times and avoid overextending him during the "down" periods. Don't count on this schedule, however. These so-called "states of consciousness" will change dramatically in this first month.

There are actually six stages of consciousness through which your baby cycles several times a day. Two are sleep states; the others are waking states.

State 1 is deep sleep, when the baby lies quietly without moving and is relatively unresponsive. If you shake a rattle loudly in his ear, he may stir a little, but not much. During lighter, more active sleep (State 2), the same noise will startle him and may awaken him. During this light sleep you can also see the rapid movements of his eyes beneath his closed eyelids. He will alternate between these two sleep states, cycling through both of them within a given hour. Sometimes he'll "retreat" into these sleep states when he's overstimulated, as well as when he's physically tired.

As your baby wakes up or starts to fall asleep, he'll go through State 3. His eyes will roll back under drooping eyelids and he may stretch, yawn, or jerk his arms and legs. Once awake, he'll move into one of the three remaining states. He may be wide awake, happy, and alert but relatively motionless (State 4). Or he may be alert, happy, and very active (State 5). Or he may cry and flail himself about (State 6).

If you shake a rattle by your baby's ear when he's happy and alert (States 4 and 5), he'll probably become quiet and turn his face to look for the source of this strange sound. This is the time when he'll appear most responsive to you and the activity around him, and be most attentive and involved in play.

Your Baby's States of Consciousness

State	*Description*	*What Your Baby Does*
State 1	Deep sleep	Lies quietly without moving
State 2	Light sleep	Moves while sleeping; startles at noises
State 3	Drowsiness	Eyes start to close; may doze
State 4	Quiet alert	Eyes open wide, face is bright; body is quiet
State 5	Active alert	Face and body move actively
State 6	Crying	Cries, perhaps screams; body moves in very disorganized ways

In general, it's a mistake to expect much attention from a baby who is crying. At these times he's not receptive to new information or sensations; what he wants instead is comforting. The same rattle that enchanted him when he was happy five minutes earlier will only irritate him and make him more upset when he's crying. As he gets older you may sometimes be able to distract him with an attractive object or sound so that he stops crying, but at this early age the best way to comfort him usually is to pick him up and hold him. (See *Responding to Your Baby's Cries, page 51).*

As your baby's nervous system becomes more developed, he'll begin to settle into a pattern of crying, sleeping, eating, and playing that matches your own daily schedule. He may still need to eat every three to four hours, but by the end of the month he'll be awake for longer periods during the day and be more alert and responsive at those times.

Colic

Does your infant have a regular fussy period each day when it seems you can do nothing to comfort her? This is quite common, particularly between 6:00 P.M. and midnight—just when you, too, are feeling tired from the day's trials and tribulations. These periods of crankiness may feel like torture, especially if you have other demanding children or work to do, but fortunately they don't last long. The length of this fussing usually peaks at about three hours a day by six weeks, and then declines to one or two hours a day by three months. As long as the baby calms within a few hours and is relatively peaceful the rest of the day, there's no reason for alarm.

If the crying does not stop, but intensifies and persists throughout the day or night, it may be caused by colic. About one fifth of all babies develop colic, usually between the second and fourth weeks. They cry inconsolably, often screaming, extending or pulling up their legs, and passing gas. Their stomachs may be enlarged or distended with gas. The crying spells can occur around the clock, though they often become worse in the early evening.

Unfortunately, there is no definite explanation for why this happens. Most often, colic means simply that the infant is unusually sensitive to stimulation. As she matures, it will decrease, and generally it stops by three months. Sometimes, in breastfeeding babies, colic is a sign of sensitivity to a food in the mother's diet. The discomfort is only rarely caused by sensitivity to milk protein in formula. Colicky behavior may also signal a medical problem, such as a hernia or some type of illness.

Perhaps you'll find it reassuring that there's a time limit to this problem, but that doesn't stop the crying now. It may be that you simply will have to wait it out, but there are also several things that might be worth trying. First, of course, consult your pediatrician to rule out any medical reason for the crying. Then ask him which of the following would be most helpful:

- If nursing, eliminate milk products, caffeine, onions, cabbage, and any other potentially irritating foods from your diet. If bottle-feeding, try a formula that has no cow's milk. If food sensitivity is causing the discomfort, the colic should decrease within a day or two of these changes.
- Walk your baby in a body carrier to soothe her. The motion and body contact will reassure her, even if her discomfort persists.
- Rock her, run the vacuum in the next room, or place her where she can hear the clothes dryer. Steady rhythmic motion and sound may help her fall asleep.
- Introduce a pacifier. While some breastfed babies will actively refuse it, it will provide instant relief for others. (See page 191.)
- Lay your baby tummy-down across your knees and gently rub her back. The pressure against her abdomen may help relieve her pain.
- Swaddle her in a blanket so that she feels secure and warm.
- When you're feeling tense and anxious, have someone else look after the baby—and get out of the house. Even an hour or two away will help you maintain a positive attitude. No matter how impatient or angry you feel, do not shake the baby. Shaking an infant hard can cause blindness, brain damage, or even death.

Where We Stand

Shaking a baby is a serious form of child abuse that appears mostly in babies younger than 6 months of age. The act of severely shaking a baby—usually a caregiver's response to a baby's constant crying or irritability—can cause serious physical and mental damage, or even death.

The First Smile

One of the most important developments during this month is the appearance of your baby's first smiles and giggles. These start during sleep, for reasons that are not understood. They may be a signal that the baby feels aroused in some way or is responding to some internal impulse. While it's great fun to watch a newborn smile his way through a nap, the real joy comes near the end of this month when he begins to grin back at you during his alert periods.

Those first loving smiles will help you tune in even more closely to each other, and you'll soon discover that you can predict when your baby will smile, look at you, make sounds, and equally important, pause for time-out from play. Gradually you'll recognize each other's patterns of responsiveness so that your play together becomes a kind of dance in which you take turns leading and following. By identifying and responding to your baby's subtle signals, even at this young age, you are telling him that his thoughts and feelings are important and that he can affect the world around him. These messages are vital to his developing self-esteem.

Movement

For the first week or two, your baby's movements will be very jerky. Her chin may quiver and her hands may tremble. She'll startle easily when moved suddenly or when she hears a loud sound, and the startling may lead to crying. If these movements are very pronounced or disturbing, you can contain them by holding the baby tightly against your body or swaddling her in a blanket. But by the end of the first month, as her nervous system

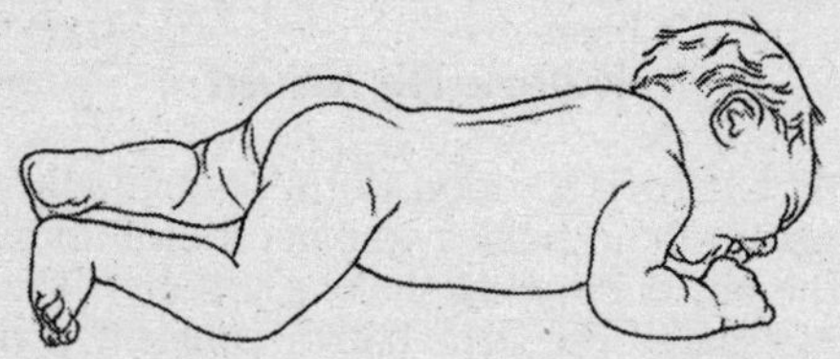

matures and her muscle control improves, these shakes and quivers will give way to much smoother arm and leg movements that look almost as if she's riding a bicycle. Lay her on her stomach now and she will make crawling motions with her legs and may even push up on her arms.

Movement Milestones By the End of This Period

- Makes jerky, quivering arm thrusts
- Brings hands within range of eyes and mouth
- Moves head from side to side while lying on stomach
- Head flops backward if unsupported
- Keeps hands in tight fists
- Strong reflex movements

The baby's neck muscles also will develop rapidly, giving her much more control over her head movements by the end of this month. Lying on her stomach, she may lift her head and turn it from one side to the other. However, she won't be able to hold her head securely until about three months, so make sure you support it whenever you're holding her.

Your baby's hands, a source of endless fascination throughout much of this first year, will catch her eyes during these weeks. Her finger movements are limited, since her hands are clenched in tight fists most of the time. But she can flex her arms and bring her hands to her mouth and into her line of vision. While she can't control her hands precisely, she'll watch them closely as long as they're in view.

Vision

Your baby's vision will go through many changes this first month. He was born with peripheral vision (the ability to see to the sides), and he'll gradually acquire the ability to focus closely on a single point in the center of his visual field. He likes to look at objects held about 8 to 15 inches in front of him, but by one month he'll focus briefly on things as far away as 3 feet.

At the same time, he'll learn to follow, or track, moving objects. To help him practice this skill, you can play tracking games with him. For example, move your head slowly from side to side as you hold him facing you; or pass a patterned object up and down or side to side in front of him (making sure it's within his range of focus). At first he may only be able to follow large objects moving slowly through an ex-

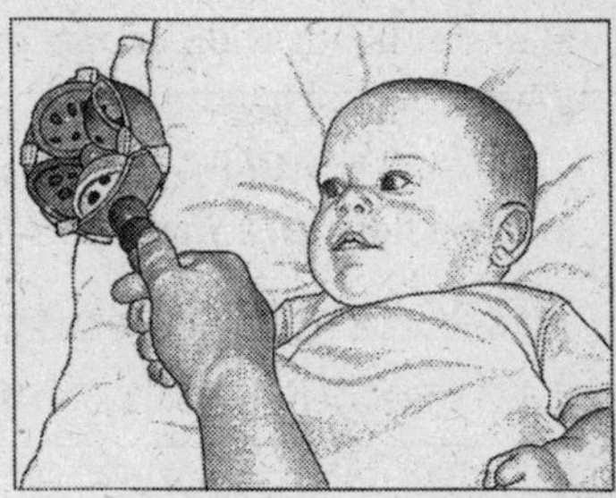

Your baby likes to look at objects held about 8 to 15 inches in front of him.

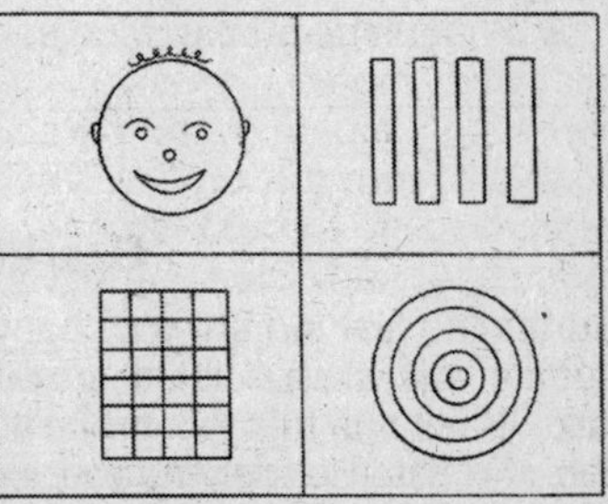

He is most attentive to black-and-white pictures or high-contrast patterns, such as sharply contrasting stripes, bull's-eyes, checks, and very simple faces.

tremely limited range, but soon he'll be tracking even small, speedy movements.

At birth your baby was extremely sensitive to bright light, and his pupils were constricted (small) to limit the amount of light that entered his eyes. At two weeks of age, his pupils will begin to enlarge, allowing him to experience a broader range of shades of light and dark. As his retina (the light-sensitive tissue inside the eyeball) develops, his ability to see and recognize patterns also will improve.

The more contrast there is in a pattern, the more it will attract his attention, which is why he is most attentive to black-and-white pictures or high-contrast patterns, such as sharply contrasting stripes, bull's-eyes, checks, and very simple faces.

If you show your infant three identical toys—one blue, one yellow, one red—he probably will look longest at the red one, although no one yet understands why. Is it the color red itself? Or is it the brightness of this color that attracts newborn babies? We do know that color vision doesn't fully mature before about four months, so if you show your baby two related colors, like green and turquoise, he probably can't tell the difference at this age.

Visual Milestones By the End of This Period

- Focuses 8 to 12 inches away
- Eyes wander and occasionally cross
- Prefers black-and-white or high-contrast patterns
- Prefers the human face to all other patterns

Hearing

During the first month, your baby will pay close attention to human voices, especially high-pitched ones speaking "baby talk." When you talk to her, she'll turn her head to search for you and listen closely as you sound out different syllables and words. Watch carefully and you may even see her make subtle movements of her arms and legs in time with your speech.

Your infant also will be sensitive to noise levels. If you make a loud clicking sound in her ear or bring her into a noisy, crowded room, she may "shut down," becoming as unresponsive as if she had heard nothing. Or she may be so sensitive that she startles, erupts into crying, and turns her entire body away from the noise. (Extremely sensitive babies also will cry when exposed to a very bright light.) Substitute the sound of a soft rattle or quiet music and she'll become alert and turn her head and eyes to locate the source of this interesting sound.

Not only does your baby hear well, but even at this age, she'll remember some of the sounds she hears. Some mothers who repeatedly read a story aloud during late pregnancy have found that their babies seemed to recognize the story when it was read to them again after birth—the babies became quiet and looked more attentive. Try reading your favorite children's story aloud for several days in a row at times when your baby is alert and attentive. Then wait a day or two and read it again. Does she seem to recognize it?

Hearing Milestones By the End of This Period

- Hearing is fully mature
- Recognizes some sounds
- May turn toward familiar sounds and voices

Smell and Touch

Just as he prefers certain patterns and sounds, your baby is very particular about tastes and smells. He will breathe deeply to catch a whiff of milk, vanilla, banana, or sugar, but will turn up his nose at the smell of alcohol or vinegar. By the end of his first week, if he's nursing, he'll turn toward his own mother's breast pad but will ignore the pads of other nursing mothers. This radarlike system helps direct him at feeding times, and warns him away from substances that could harm him.

Your baby is equally sensitive to touch and the way you handle him. He'll nestle into a soft piece of flannel or satin, but pull away from scratchy burlap or coarse sandpaper. Stroke him gently with your palm and he'll relax and become quiet. If you pick him up roughly, he'll probably take offense and start to cry. If you pick him up gently and rock him slowly, he'll become quiet and attentive. Holding, stroking, rocking, and cuddling will calm him down when he's upset and make him more alert when he's drowsy. It also sends a clear message of your love and affection for him. Long before he understands a word you say, he'll understand your moods and feelings from the way you touch him.

Smell and Touch Milestones By the End of This Period

- Prefers sweet smells
- Avoids bitter or acidic smells
- Recognizes the scent of his own mother's breast milk
- Prefers soft to coarse sensations
- Dislikes rough or abrupt handling

Temperament

Consider these two babies, both from the same family, both girls:

The first infant is calm and quiet, happy to play by herself. She watches everything that happens around her, but rarely demands attention herself. Left on her own, she sleeps for long periods and eats infrequently.

The second baby is fussy and startles easily. She thrashes her arms and legs, moving almost constantly whether awake or asleep. While most newborns sleep fourteen hours a day, she sleeps only ten, and wakens whenever there's the slightest activity nearby. She seems in a hurry to do everything at once, and even eats in a rush, gulping her feedings and swallowing so much air that she needs frequent burping.

Both these babies are absolutely normal and healthy. One is no "better" than the other, but because their personalities are so far apart, the two will be treated very differently, right from birth.

Like these babies, your infant will demonstrate many unique personality traits from the earliest weeks of life. Discovering these traits is one of the most exciting parts of having a new baby. Is she very active and intense, or relatively slow-going? Is she timid when faced with a new situation, like the first bath, or does she enjoy it? You'll find clues to her personality in everything she does, from falling asleep to crying. The more you pay attention to these signals, and learn to respond appropriately to her unique personality, the calmer and more predictable your life will be in the months to come.

While most of these early character traits are built into the newborn's hereditary makeup, their appearance may be delayed if your baby is born quite prematurely. Premature

Developmental Health Watch

If, during the second, third, or fourth weeks of your baby's life, she shows any of the following signs of developmental delay, notify your pediatrician.

- Sucks poorly and feeds slowly
- Doesn't blink when shown a bright light
- Doesn't focus and follow a nearby object moving side to side
- Rarely moves arms and legs; seems stiff
- Seems excessively loose in the limbs, or floppy
- Lower jaw trembles constantly, even when not crying or excited
- Doesn't respond to loud sounds

babies don't express their needs—such as hunger, fatigue, or discomfort—as clearly as other newborns. They may be extrasensitive to light, sound, and touch for several months. Even playful conversation may be too intense for them, and cause them to become fussy and look away. When this happens, it's up to the parent to stop and wait until the baby is alert and ready for more attention. Eventually most of these early reactions will fade away, and the baby's own natural character traits will become more evident.

Babies who are underweight at birth (less than 5.5 pounds), even if they're full-term, may also be less responsive than other newborns. At first they may be very sleepy and not seem very alert. After a few weeks they seem to wake up, eating eagerly but still remaining irritable and hypersensitive to stimulation between feedings. This irritability may last until they grow and mature further. The more they are protected from overstimulation and comforted through this fussy period, the more quickly it will pass.

From the very beginning your baby's temperamental traits will influence the way you treat her and feel about her. If you had specific ideas about child-rearing before she was born, reevaluate them now to see if they're really in tune with her character. The same goes for expert advice—from books, articles, and especially from well-meaning relatives and friends—about the "right way" to raise a child. The truth is, there is no right way that works for every child. You have to create your own guidelines based on your baby's unique personality, your own beliefs, and the circumstances of your family life. The important thing is to remain responsive to your baby's individuality. Don't try to box her into some previously set mold or pattern. Your baby's uniqueness is her strength, and respecting that strength from the start will help lay the best possible foundation for her high self-esteem and for loving relationships with others.

Toys Appropriate for Your Baby's First Month

- Mobile with highly contrasting colors and patterns
- Unbreakable mirror attached securely to inside of crib
- Music boxes and record or tape players with soft music
- Soft, brightly colored and patterned toys that make gentle sounds

Basic Care

Feeding and Nutrition

(See Chapter 4 for additional information.)

Breastmilk or formula should be your baby's basic source of nutrition for the first twelve months. But while you don't have to worry much about his diet, you need to establish a regular pattern of feedings and make sure that he's getting enough calories for growth.

Establishing a pattern of feedings does not mean setting a rigid timetable and insisting that he eat a full 4 ounces at each feeding. It's much more important to listen to your baby's signals and work around his needs. If he is bottle-fed, he probably will cry at the end of his feeding if he is not getting enough. On the other hand, if he is getting an adequate amount in the first ten minutes, he may stop and fall asleep. Breastfed babies behave a little differently in that they do not always cry when they are hungry, and the only way to be sure yours is getting enough milk is to watch his weight gain. Also, he should be fed at least every three to four hours and not be allowed to sleep through a feeding until at least four weeks of age.

At the beginning of the second week and again between three and six weeks, your baby will go through growth spurts that may make him hungrier than usual. Even if you don't notice any outward growth, his body is changing in important ways and needs extra calories during these times. Be prepared to feed him more often if he's breastfed, and if he's bottle-fed, try giving him slightly more at each feeding.

If your baby has a nutritional problem, he's likely to start losing weight. There are some signals that may help you detect such a problem.

If he's breastfeeding, one warning signal is a lack of fullness in your breasts after one week. If they don't drip milk at the start of each feeding, the baby may not be providing enough stimulation when he sucks. Some other trouble signs are listed below. These also may be signs of medical problems that are unrelated to your baby's nutrition. You should call your pediatrician if they persist.

Too Much Feeding:

- If bottle-fed, the baby is consuming more than 4 to 6 ounces (120 to 180 cc) at each feeding.
- He vomits most or all the food after a complete feeding.
- Stools are loose and very watery, eight or more times a day.

Too Little Feeding:

- If breastfed, the baby stops feeding after ten minutes or less.
- He wets fewer than four diapers.
- His skin remains wrinkled beyond the first week.
- He does not develop a rounded face by about three weeks.
- He appears hungry, searching for something to suck shortly after feedings.
- He becomes more yellow, instead of less, after the first week.

Feeding Allergy or Digestive Disturbance:

- Your baby vomits most or all food after a complete feeding.

- He produces loose, very watery stools eight or more times a day.
- If breastfeeding, he becomes more yellow, instead of less, after the first week.

Most babies this age begin to spit up occasionally after feedings. That's because the muscular valve between the esophagus (the passage between throat and stomach) and the stomach is immature. Instead of closing tightly, it remains open enough to allow the contents of the stomach to come back up and gently spill out of the mouth. This is normal and won't harm your baby.

Carrying Your Baby

A newborn or very young infant who has not developed head control needs to be carried in a way that keeps her head from flopping from side to side or snapping from front to back. This is done by cradling the head when carrying the baby in a lying position, and supporting the head and neck with your hand when carrying the baby upright.

Pacifiers

Many parents have strong feelings about pacifiers. Some oppose their use because of the way they look, or they resent the notion of "pacifying" a baby with an object.

A very young infant who has not developed head control needs to be carried in a way that keeps her head from flopping from side to side or snapping from front to back.

Others believe—incorrectly—that using a pacifier can harm a baby. Pacifiers do not cause any medical or psychological problems. If your baby wants to suck beyond what nursing or bottle-feeding provides, a pacifier will satisfy that need.

A pacifier is meant to satisfy your baby's noneating sucking needs, not to replace or delay meals. So offer a pacifier to your baby only after or between feedings, when you are sure he is not hungry. If he is hungry, and you offer a pacifier as a substitute, he may become so angry that it interferes with feeding. Remember, the pacifier is for your baby's benefit, not your convenience, so let him decide whether and when to use it.

Some babies use a pacifier to fall asleep. The trouble is, they often wake up when it falls out of their mouths. Once your baby is older and has the hand coordination to find and replace it, there is no problem. However, when he's younger he may cry for you to do this for him. Babies who suck their fingers or hands have a real advantage here, because their hands are always readily available.

When shopping for a pacifier, look for a one-piece model that has a soft nipple (some models can break into two pieces). It should be dishwasher-safe so you can either boil it or run it through the dishwasher before your baby uses it. Until he's six months old the pacifier should be cleaned this way frequently, so he's not exposed to any increased risk of infection, as his immune system is still maturing. After that, the likelihood of his picking up an infection in that way is minimal, so you can just wash it with soap and rinse it in clear water.

Pacifiers are available in two sizes, one for the first six months and another for children after that age. You'll also

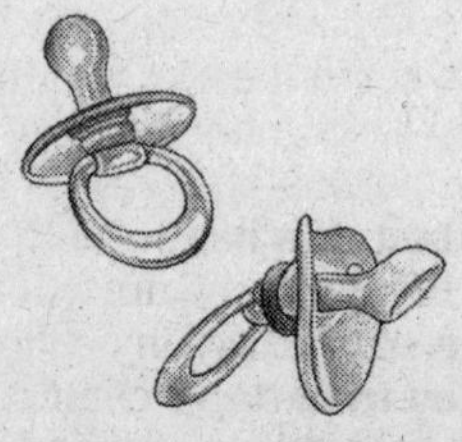

find a variety of nipple shapes, from squarish "orthodontic" versions to the standard bottle type. Once you decide which your baby prefers, buy some extras. Pacifiers have a way of disappearing or falling on the floor or street when you need them most. You might attach the pacifier to your baby's clothes using a *very short* cord or ribbon with a clip at the end. However, *never* try to solve this problem by fastening the pacifier with a cord around your baby's neck. That could interfere with his breathing or choke him. Also, for safety reasons, do not make your own pacifiers out of a bottle nipple. Babies have pulled the nipple out of such homemade pacifiers and choked on them.

Going Outside

Fresh air and a change of surroundings are good for both you and your baby, even in her first month, so take her out for walks when the weather is nice. Be careful to dress her properly for these outings, however. Her internal temperature control isn't fully mature until the end of her first year. This makes it difficult for her to regulate her body temperature when she's exposed to excessive heat or cold. Her clothing must do some of this work for her by keeping heat in when she is in a cold location and letting heat escape when she's in a very warm place. In general, she should wear one more layer than you do.

Your infant's skin also is extremely susceptible to sunburn during the first six months, so it's important to keep her out of direct and reflected sunlight (off of water, sand, or concrete, for example) as much as possible. If you must take her out in the sun, use sunblock with a sun protective factor (SPF) of 15 or more to protect her skin. Also dress her in lightweight and light-colored clothing, with a bonnet or hat to shade her face. If she is lying or sitting in one place, make sure it is shady, and adjust her position to keep her in the shade as the sun moves.

Another warning for the hot-weather months: Do not let baby equipment (car seats, strollers) sit in the sun for a long period of time. When that happens, the plastic and metal parts can get hot enough to burn your infant. Check the temperature of the surface of any such equipment before you allow your baby to come in contact with it.

In uncomfortably cold or rainy weather, keep your baby inside as much as possible. If you have to go out, bundle her up in warm sweaters or bunting bags over her other clothes, and use a warm hat to cover her head and ears. You can shield her face from the cold with a blanket when you're outside.

To check whether she's clothed well enough, feel her hands and feet and the skin on her chest. Her hands and feet should be slightly cooler than her body, but not cold. Her chest should feel warm. If hands, feet, and chest feel cold, take her to a warm room, unwrap her, and feed her something warm or hold her close so the heat from your body warms her. Until her temperature is back to normal, extra layers of clothing will just trap the cold, so use these other methods to warm her body before wrapping her in additional blankets or clothing.

Finding Temporary Child-Care Help

Most mothers need some help when they bring a new baby home. If Dad can take a few days off from work during the first week or two, the problem is usually solved. If he cannot, and the family finances won't allow you to hire help, the next best choice is a close relative or friend. It is wise to make these arrangements in advance rather than waiting until after the delivery to seek help.

Some areas have a visiting nurse or homemaking service. This will not solve your middle-of-the-night problems, but it will give you an hour or two during the day to catch up on work or simply rest a little. These arrangements, too, should be made in advance.

Be selective about the help you seek. Look for assistance from those who will really support you. Don't forget, your goal is to reduce the stress level in your home, not add to it.

Before you start interviewing or asking friends or family for assistance, decide exactly what kind of help will work best for you. Ask yourself the following questions:

- Do you want someone who can help you tend the baby, or do the housework, or cook meals—or a little bit of everything?
- During what hours do you want help?
- Do you need someone who can drive (to pick up other children at school, shop for groceries, run errands, and the like)?

Once you know what you need, make sure the person you choose to help out understands and agrees to your requests.

Your Baby's First Sitter

Sometime in the first month or two, you'll probably need to leave your baby for the first time. The more confidence you have in your baby-sitter, the easier this experience will be for you, so you may want to have your first sitter be someone very close and trusted—a grandparent, close friend, or relative who's familiar with both you and the infant.

After you've survived the first separation, you may want to look for a regular baby-sitter. Start by asking your friends for recommendations. If they have no suggestions, ask your pediatrician if she knows of any local child-care agencies or referral services. If that still doesn't yield any names, contact the placement services at local colleges for a listing of students who baby-sit. You can also find the names of baby-sitters in community newspapers, telephone directories, and church and grocery store bulletin boards, but remember that no one screens the people in these listings.

Interview every candidate in person and with your baby present. You should be looking for someone who is affectionate, capable, and supports your views about child care. If you feel comfortable with the individual after you've talked awhile, let her hold the baby so you can see how she handles him. Although experience, references, and good health are important, the best way to judge a baby-sitter is by giving her a trial run while you're home. It will give your baby and the baby-sitter a chance to get to know each other before they're alone together, and it will give you an opportunity to make sure you feel comfortable with the sitter.

Whenever you leave your baby with a sitter, give her a list of all emergency phone numbers, including those where you or other close family members can be contacted if problems arise. Establish clear guidelines about what to do in an emergency. Make sure the sitter knows how to treat a child who is choking or not breathing (see *Choking,* page 397; *Cardiopulmonary Resuscitation and Mouth-to-Mouth Resuscitation,* page 392). Ask the sitter to jot down any notes or questions she has about your child during the day. Let friends and neighbors know about your arrangement so they can help if there's an emergency and ask them to tell you if they suspect any problems in your absence.

Traveling with Your Baby

Traveling with your baby during her infancy is probably the easiest traveling the two of you will ever do. For the first few months, all she cares about is her own comfort, which amounts to a full stomach, a clean diaper, and a comfortable place to sit or lie. If you can satisfy these basic needs, your baby probably will travel with minimum protest. The key is to maintain her normal patterns as much as possible.

Long trips involving a change of time zones can disturb your baby's sleep schedule, so try to plan your activities according to the schedule your child is on, and allow several days for her to adjust to a time change. If she is waking very early in the morning, plan to start your own activities earlier. Be ready to stop earlier, too, because your little one will be getting tired and cranky long before the clock says it's time to go to bed. Always remember to perform a safety inspection of any cribs when checking into a hotel (see *Cribs*, page 30).

If you're going to remain in a new time zone for more than two or three days, your baby's internal time clock will gradually shift to coincide with the time zone you're in. You'll have to adjust mealtimes to match the times when her body is telling her she's hungry. Mom and Dad—and even older children—may be able to postpone meals to fit the new time zone, but a baby isn't able to make those adjustments.

Your baby will adapt to her new environment more quickly if you bring some familiar things from home. If she has a favorite blanket that she always sleeps with, make sure it goes with you on your trip. A few familiar rattles and toys will provide some comfort and reassurance, too. Use her regular soap, a familiar towel, and bring along one of her tub toys to make her more at ease during baths. At meals give her her normal foods. This is not the time to try out a new formula or introduce her to strange tastes.

When packing for a trip with your baby, it's usually best to use a separate bag for her things. This makes it easier to find items quickly when you want them, and reduces the chance that you'll forget an important one. You'll also need a large diaper bag for such things as bottles, small toys, snacks, lotion, diapers, and baby wipes. Keep this bag with you at all times.

When traveling by automobile, make sure your infant is safely strapped into her car seat. For more information on car seats see page 330. The back seat is the safest place for children to ride. Rear-facing seats should never be placed in

Tips for Safe Air Travel with Babies

- Ensure that your car seat has received FAA approval. Check that the label on the restraint reads: "This restraint is certified for use in motor vehicles and aircraft."
- Check the width of your car seat. While airline seats vary in width, a car seat no wider than 16 inches should fit in most coach seats. Even if the armrests are moved out of the way, a car seat wider than 16 inches is unlikely to fit properly into the frame of the aircraft seat.
- Be sure to ask your airline for its policy regarding a child traveling in a car seat. In many cases, airlines will let you seat your child under two years of age in your car seat in an empty airplane seat without having to pay a fare for your child's travel. Many airlines have discounted rates for a child under the age of two. Purchasing an airline ticket (discounted or full fare) is the only way to guarantee that you will be able to use a car seat.
- If you purchase a ticket for your child, reserve adjoining seats. A car seat must be placed in a window seat so it will not block the escape path in an emergency. A car seat may not be placed in an exit row.
- If you need to change planes to make a connecting flight, it can be very challenging to transport a car seat, a child, and luggage through a busy airport. Most airlines will help parents make the connection if they can arrange for assistance in advance.

the front seat of a car with a passenger-side air bag. At this age a baby should always ride in the rear-facing position. If you're renting an automobile, reserve a car seat ahead of time or bring your own with you. If a rented car seat seems too large, you can use rolled-up diapers to center your baby. If you're not sure how to secure her safely on a plane or train, ask a flight attendant or a conductor to help you. Unless you buy a ticket for the baby, you'll be expected to carry the baby on your lap. When there is extra room on board, you may be able to get a separate seat for the baby without paying for it (see box on 197).

If your baby is bottle-fed, bring not only enough formula for the expected travel time, but some extra in case any unexpected delays occur. The attendant or conductor will help you refrigerate the formula until it is needed. If you're nursing and you are concerned about privacy, ask the attendant for some blankets you can use as a screen.

THE FAMILY

A Special Message to Mothers

One reason why this first month can be especially difficult is that you are still recovering physically from the stress of pregnancy and delivery. It may take weeks before your body is back to normal, your incisions (if you had an episiotomy or C-section) have healed, and you're able to resume everyday activities. You may also experience strong mood swings due to changes in the amount of hormones in your body. These changes can prompt sudden crying episodes for no apparent reason, or feelings of mild depression for the first few weeks. These emotions may be intensified by the exhaustion that comes with waking up every two or three hours at night to feed and change the baby.

If you experience these so-called "postpartum blues," they may make you feel a little "crazy," embarrassed, or even that you're a "bad mother." Difficult as it may be, try to keep these emotions in perspective by reminding yourself that they're *normal* after pregnancy and delivery. Even fathers sometimes feel sad and unusually emotional after a new baby arrives (possibly a response to the psychological intensity of the experience). To keep the blues from dominating your life—and your enjoyment of your new baby—avoid isolating yourself in these early weeks. Try to nap when your baby does, so you don't get overtired. If these feelings persist past a few weeks or become severe, consult your pediatrician or your own physician about getting extra help.

Visitors can often help you combat the blues by celebrating the baby's arrival with you. They may bring welcome gifts for the baby or—even better during these early weeks—offer food or household help. But they can also be exhausting for you and overwhelming for the baby, and may expose him to infection. So strictly limit the number of visitors during the first couple of weeks, and keep anyone with a cough, cold, or contagious disease away from your newborn. Ask all visitors to call in advance, and keep the visits brief until you're back to a regular schedule. If the baby seems unsettled by all the attention, don't let anyone outside the family hold or come close to him.

If you become overwhelmed with phone calls, and you have a telephone answering machine, use it to give yourself a little peace. Record a message that gives the baby's sex, name, birth date, time, weight, and length. Then turn on the machine and turn off the ringing mechanism on your phone. That allows you to return the calls on your own schedule without feeling stressed or guilty every time the bell rings. If you don't have an answering machine, leave your phone off the hook or muffle the sound of the bell with a pillow.

With a new baby, constant visitors, an aching body, unpredictable mood swings, and, in some cases, other siblings demanding attention, it's no wonder the housework gets neglected. Resign yourself ahead of time to knowing that the wash may not get done as often as it should, the house will get dustier than usual, and a lot of meals will be frozen or take-out. You can always catch up next month. For now, concentrate on recuperating and enjoying your new baby.

A Special Message to Fathers

This can be a very stressful time for parenting couples. It's almost impossible to find time—much less energy—for each other, between the seemingly constant demands of the baby, the needs of other children, household chores, and

Become as involved as possible in caring for and playing with the new baby. You'll get just as emotionally attached to her as her mother will.

the father's work schedule (in our society, few fathers have the option of taking paternity leaves, which can help reduce these tensions). Nights spent feeding, diapering, and walking the floor with a crying baby quickly take their toll in fatigue. If both parents don't make up for this by relieving each other and taking naps, exhaustion can drive a large and unnecessary wedge between them.

At this time, some fathers also feel shut off from the infant and from the mother's attention and affections, especially if the baby is breastfed. The problem is not helped by the fact that sexual intercourse is usually prohibited by the obstetrician for these first few weeks. Even if it were allowed, many women simply aren't interested in sexual activity for a while after delivery because of the physical exhaustion and emotional stress they may be experiencing at this time.

This conflict and the jealous feelings that may arise at this time are temporary. Life soon settles into a fairly regular routine that will once again give you some time to yourselves, and restore your sex life and social activities to normal. Meanwhile, make an effort for just the two of you to spend some time together each day, and remember, you're entitled to hold, hug, cuddle, and kiss each other as well as the baby!

A positive way for men to deal with these issues is to become as involved as possible in caring for and playing with the new baby. When you spend this extra time with your baby, you'll get just as emotionally attached to her as her mother will.

This is not to say that moms and dads play with babies the same way. In general, fathers play to arouse and excite their

Once the infant arrives, you can expect your older child to be very proud and protective.

babies, while mothers generally concentrate on more low-keyed stimulation such as gentle rocking, quiet interactive games, singing, and soothing activities. Fathers tend to roughhouse more, making lots of noise, and move the baby about more vigorously. The babies respond in kind, laughing and moving more with Dad than they do with Mom. From the baby's viewpoint, both play styles are equally valuable and complement each other beautifully, which is another reason why it's so important to have *both* of you involved in the care of the baby.

Siblings

With all the excitement over the new baby's arrival, siblings often feel neglected. They may still be a little upset over their mother's hospitalization, especially if this was their first prolonged separation from her. Even after Mom returns home, they may have trouble understanding that she's tired and cannot play with them as much as they're used to. Compound this with the attention she's now devoting to the baby—attention which just a couple of weeks ago belonged to them!—and it's no wonder that they may feel jealous and left out. It's up to both parents to find ways to reassure the siblings that they're still very much loved and valued, and help them come to terms with their new "competition."

Here are some suggestions to help soothe your older children and make them feel more involved during the first month home with your new baby.

1. If possible, have the siblings visit Mother and baby in the hospital.
2. When Mom comes home from the hospital, bring each sibling a special gift to celebrate.
3. Set aside a special time to spend alone with each sibling every day. Make sure that both Mom and Dad have time with each child, individually and together.
4. While you're taking pictures of the new baby, take some of the older children—alone and with the baby.
5. Ask the grandparents or other close relatives to take the older children on a special outing—to the zoo, a movie, or just to dinner. This special attention may help them through moments when they feel abandoned.
6. Especially during the first month, when the baby's feedings are so frequent, older children can get very jealous of the intimacy you have with the baby during feedings. Show them that you can share this intimacy by turning feeding times into story times. Reading stories that specifically deal with issues of jealousy encourages a toddler or preschooler to voice his feelings so that you can help him become more accepting.

Health Watch

The following medical problems are of particular concern to parents during the first month. (For problems that occur generally throughout childhood, check the listings in Part II.)

Breathing Difficulties. Normally, your baby should take from twenty to forty breaths per minute. This pattern is most regular when he is asleep and healthy. When awake, he may occasionally breathe rapidly for a short period, then take a brief pause (less than ten seconds) before returning to normal breathing. If he has a fever, his breathing may increase by about two breaths per minute for each degree of temperature elevation. A runny nose may interfere with breathing because his nasal passages are narrow and fill easily. This condition is eased by using a cool-mist humidifier and gently suctioning the nose with a rubber aspirating bulb (ordinarily given to you by the hospital). Occasionally, mild salt-solution nose drops are used to help thin the mucus and clear the nasal passages.

Diarrhea. A baby has diarrhea if she produces loose, very watery stools more than six to eight times a day. This is usually caused by a viral infection. The danger, especially at this young age, is of losing too much water and becoming dehydrated. The first signs of dehydration are a dry mouth and a significant decrease in the number of wet diapers. But don't wait for dehydration to occur. Call your pediatrician if the stools are very loose or occur more often than after each feeding (six to eight per day).

Excessive Sleepiness. Since each infant requires a different amount of sleep, it's difficult to tell when a baby is excessively drowsy. If your infant starts sleeping much more than usual, it might indicate the presence of an infection, so notify your pediatrician. Also, if you are nursing and your baby sleeps more than five hours without a feeding in the first month, you must consider the possibility that he is not getting enough milk or perhaps is being affected, through the breastmilk, by a medication that you are taking.

Eye Infections. (See also *Tear Production Problems,* page 499.) Some babies are born with one or both tear ducts partially or totally blocked. They typically open by about two weeks, when tear production begins. If they don't, the blockage may cause a watery or mucus tearing. In this case, the tears will back up and flow over the eyelids instead of draining through the nose. This is not harmful, and the ducts generally will open without treatment. You may also help open them by gently massaging the inner corner of the eye and down the side of the nose. However, do this only at the direction of your pediatrician.

If the ducts remain blocked, thus keeping the tears from draining properly, infection can easily occur. These infections produce a white discharge in the corner of the eye. The eyelashes become sticky and may dry together at night so the eyelid can't open. Such infections usually are treated with special drops or ointment that your doctor will prescribe after examining the eye. Sometimes all that's needed is a gentle cleansing with sterile water. When the lashes are sticky, dip a cotton ball in sterile water, and use it to gently wipe from the part of the lid nearest the nose to the outside. Use each cotton ball just once, and then discard it. Use as many cotton balls as you need to clean the eye thoroughly.

Although this type of mild infection may recur several times during your baby's first months, it will not damage the eye and she probably will outgrow it, even without more serious treatment. Only rarely does this tear-duct blockage require surgical care.

If the eye itself is bloodshot or pinkish, there probably is a more serious infection, called conjunctivitis, and you should notify your pediatrician at once.

Fever. Whenever your baby is unusually cranky or feels warm, take his temperature. (See *Taking a Rectal Temperature,* page 78.) If his rectal temperature reads higher than 100 degrees F. (37.8 degrees C.) on two separate readings, and he's not overly bundled up, call your pediatrician at once. Fever in these first few weeks can signal an infection, and babies this age can quickly become seriously ill.

Floppiness. Newborn infants all seem somewhat floppy because their muscles are still developing, but if your baby feels exceptionally loose or *loses* muscle tone, it could be a sign of a more serious problem, such as an infection. Consult your pediatrician immediately.

Hearing. Pay attention to the way your baby responds to sounds. Does she startle at loud or sudden noises? Does she become quiet or turn toward you when you talk to her? If she does not respond normally to sounds around her, ask your pediatrician about formal hearing testing. This testing might be particularly appropriate if your infant was extremely premature, if she was deprived of oxygen or had a severe infection at birth, or if your family has a history of hearing loss in early childhood. If there is any suspicion of hearing loss, your infant should be tested as early as possible, as a delay in diagnosis and treatment is likely to interfere with normal language development.

Jaundice. Jaundice, the yellow color that often appears in the skin shortly after birth, sometimes persists into the second week of life in a baby who is breastfed (see page 163). It occurs because some individuals' breastmilk interferes with the liver's ability to break down bilirubin, the blood product that causes the yellow color. Sometimes breastfeeding must be stopped for twenty-four to forty-eight hours in order to clear the jaundice. Once it disappears, you may resume breastfeeding, because this type of jaundice rarely recurs. If it does, a second interruption of breastfeeding might be recommended, or the baby might be changed to formula-feeding. Your pediatrician will help you make this decision.

Jitters. Many newborns have quivery chins and shaky hands, but if your baby's whole body seems to be shaking, it could be a sign of low blood sugar or calcium levels, or some type of seizure disorder. Notify your pediatrician so he can determine the cause.

Rashes and Infections. Common newborn rashes include the following:

1. **Cradle Cap (seborrheic dermatitis)** appears as scaly patches on the scalp. Washing the hair and brushing out the scales daily helps control this condition. It usually disappears on its own within the first few months, but may have to be treated with a special shampoo. (See *Cradle Cap and Seborrheic Dermatitis*, page 563.)
2. **Fingernail or Toenail Infections** will appear as a redness around the edge of the toenail or fingernail, which may seem to hurt when touched. These infections may respond to warm compresses, but usually need to be examined by a doctor.
3. **Umbilical Infections** often appear as redness around the umbilical stump. They should be examined by your pediatrician.
4. **Diaper Rash.** See instructions for handling this problem on page 66.

Thrush. White patches in the mouth may indicate that your baby has thrush, a common yeast infection. This condi-

Sudden Infant Death Syndrome (SIDS)

Approximately one or two newborns out of every one thousand die in their sleep, for no apparent reason, between the fourth and sixteenth weeks of life. These babies generally are well cared for and show no obvious symptoms of illness. Their autopsies turn up no identifiable cause of death, so the terms *Sudden Infant Death Syndrome (SIDS)* or *crib death* are used.

SIDS occurs most often in winter among males who had a low birthweight. Premature infants and babies with a family history of SIDS, and babies of mothers who smoke and those who sleep in the prone (stomach) position (see page 54) also appear to be at increased risk. There are many theories about the cause of SIDS, but none has been proven. Infection, milk allergy, pneumonia, and child abuse all have been disproven as causes. The most believable theory at this time is that there is a delay in maturation of arousal centers in the brains of certain babies, which predisposes them to stop breathing (known as apnea) under certain conditions.

If your baby occasionally stops breathing or turns blue, your pediatrician probably will want to hospitalize him to make sure there are no treatable causes for the episodes and to assess the severity of the condition. If the apnea is severe, you may be advised to learn cardiopulmonary resuscitation (CPR) and use a home monitor while the baby sleeps. This device measures his respiration rate and sounds an alarm if it goes too low. If your baby was born prematurely, the pediatrician may choose to control the apnea with medications such as caffeine or theophylline, which stimulate respiration.

Along with the normal feelings of grief and depression, many parents who lose a child to SIDS feel guilty, and become extremely protective of older siblings or any babies born afterward. Help for parents is available through local groups or through the National SIDS Alliance in Maryland. Ask your pediatrician about resources in your area.

tion is treated with an oral antifungal medication prescribed by your pediatrician.

Vision. Watch how your baby looks at you when she is alert. When you're about 8 to 15 inches from her face, do her eyes follow you? Will she follow a light or small toy passing before her at the same distance? At this age, the eyes may appear crossed, or one eye may occasionally drift inward or outward. This is because the muscles controlling eye movement are still developing. Both eyes should be able to move equally and together in all directions, however, and she should be able to track slowly moving objects at close range. If she can't, or if she was born severely premature or needed oxygen as a newborn, your pediatrician may refer you to an eye specialist for further examination.

Vomiting. If your baby starts forcefully vomiting (shooting out several inches rather than dribbling from the mouth), contact your pediatrician at once to make sure the baby does not have an obstruction of the valve between the stomach and the small intestine (pyloric stenosis; see page 440). Any vomiting that persists for more than twelve hours or is accompanied by diarrhea or fever also should be evaluated by your pediatrician.

Weight Gain. Your baby should be gaining weight rapidly (½ to 1 ounce per day) by the middle of this month. If he isn't, your pediatrician will want to make sure that he's getting adequate calories in his feedings and that he is absorbing them properly. Be prepared to answer the following questions:

- How often does the baby eat?
- How much does he eat at a feeding, if bottle-feeding? How long does he nurse, if breastfeeding?
- How many bowel movements does the baby have each day?
- What is the amount and thinness or thickness of the stools?
- How often does the baby urinate?

If your baby is eating well and the contents of his diapers are normal in amount and consistency, there is probably no cause for alarm. Your baby may just be getting off to a slow start, or his weight could even have been measured wrong. Your pediatrician may want to schedule another office visit in two or three days to reevaluate the situation.

Safety Check

Car Seats

- Your baby should ride in a properly installed, federally approved car seat *every time* she is in the car. At this age, she should ride in the rear-facing position, in the back seat. Never place a rear-facing car seat in the front seat of a car with a passenger-side airbag.

Bathing

- When bathing the baby in the sink, seat him on a washcloth to prevent slipping, and hold him under the arms.
- Adjust the temperature of your water heater to less than 120 degrees so the hot water can't scald him.

Changing Table

- Never leave your baby unattended on any surface above the floor. Even at this young age, she can suddenly extend her body and flip over the edge.

Suffocation Prevention

- If you use baby powder, shake it out away from your infant's face so he doesn't inhale it.
- Keep the crib free of all small objects (safety pins, small parts of toys, etc.) that he could swallow.
- Never leave plastic bags or wrappings where your baby can reach them.

Fire Prevention

- Dress your baby in clothing treated with flame-retardant chemicals.

- Install smoke detectors in the proper places throughout your home.

Supervision

- Never leave your baby alone in the house, yard, or car.

Necklaces and Cords

- Don't attach pacifiers, medallions, or other objects to the crib or body with a cord.
- Don't place a string or necklace around the baby's neck.

Jiggling

- Be careful not to jiggle or shake the baby's head too vigorously.
- Always support the baby's head and neck when moving her body.

7

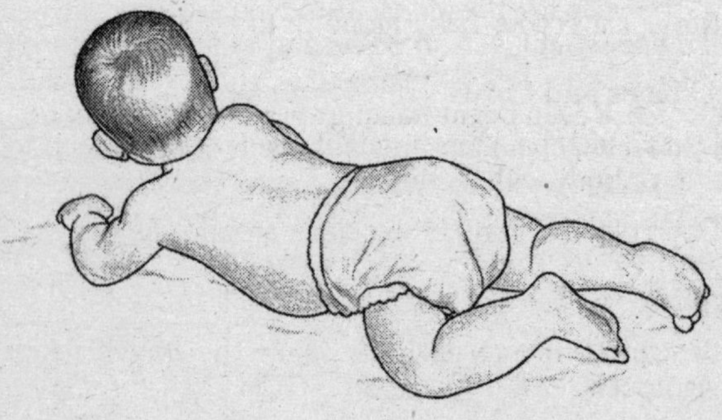

Age One Month Through Three Months

By the beginning of your baby's second month, much of the awe, exhaustion, and uncertainty that you felt immediately after her birth have given way to self-confidence. You probably have settled into a fairly routine (if still grueling) schedule around her feedings and naps. You've adjusted to having a new member of the family and are beginning to understand her general temperament. And you probably have already received the crowning reward that makes all the sacrifice worthwhile: her first true smile. This smile is just a glimmer of the delights in store over the next three months.

Between one and four months, your baby will undergo a dramatic transformation from a totally dependent newborn to an active and responsive infant.

She'll lose many of her newborn reflexes while acquiring more voluntary control of her body. You'll find her spending hours inspecting her hands and watching their movements. She'll also become increasingly interested in her surroundings, especially the people close to her. She'll quickly learn to recognize your face and voice, and will often smile when she sees or hears you. Sometime during her second or third month, she'll even begin "talking" back to you in gentle but intentional coos and gurgles. With each of her new discoveries or achievements, you'll see a new part of your child's personality emerging.

Occasionally there will be moments in which your baby's development seems to be going backward. For example, she may have been sleeping through the night for several weeks—and then suddenly starts waking up every three hours again. What should you make of this? It's probably a sign that she's about to take a major developmental leap forward. In a week or two she'll probably be sleeping through the night again and taking fewer naps, and she'll be considerably more alert and responsive to people and events around her. Developmental progress like this is often preceded by what appears to be a slight setback. As frustrating as it may be at first, you'll soon learn to read the signals, anticipate, and appreciate these periods of change.

Growth and Development

Physical Appearance and Growth

From months one through four, your baby will continue growing at the same rate he established during his first few weeks of life. Each month he'll probably gain between 1½ and 2 pounds (0.7 to 0.9 kg) and grow 1 to 1½ inches (2.5 to 4 cm). His head size will probably increase in circumference by about ½ inch (1.25 cm) each month. These figures are only averages, however, so you shouldn't be concerned as long as your baby's development matches one of the normal curves on the growth charts on pages 150–53.

At two months the soft spots on your baby's head should still be open and flat, but by four months the soft spot at the back should be closed. Also, his head may seem out of proportion, because it is growing faster than the rest of his body. This is quite normal; his body will soon catch up.

At two months your baby will look round and chubby, but as he starts using his arms and legs more actively, muscles will develop and fat will begin to disappear. His bones also will grow rapidly, and as his arms and legs "loosen up," his body and limbs will seem to stretch out, making him appear taller and leaner.

Movement

Many of your baby's movements will still be reflexive at the beginning of this period. For example, she may assume a "fencing" position every time her head turns (tonic neck reflex; see page 172) and throw out her arms if she hears a loud noise or feels that she's falling (Moro reflex, page 172). But as we've mentioned, most of these newborn reflexes will peak and begin to fade by the second or third month. She may temporarily seem less active after the reflexes have diminished, but now her movements, however subtle, are intentional ones and will build steadily toward mature activity.

By her fourth-month birthday, your baby will be able to hold up her head and chest as she supports herself on her elbows.

One of the most important developments of these early months will be your baby's increasing neck strength. Try placing her on her stomach, and see what happens. Before two months she'll struggle to raise her head to look around. Even if she succeeds for only a second or two, that will at least allow her to turn for a slightly different view of the world, and move her nose and mouth away from any pillows or blankets that might be in the way. These momentary "exercises" also will strengthen the muscles in the back of her neck so that, by her four-month birthday, she'll be able to hold up her head and chest as she supports herself on her elbows. This is a major accomplishment, giving her the freedom and control to look all around at will, instead of just staring at her crib mattress or the mobile directly overhead.

For you, it's also a welcome development because you no longer have to support her head quite so much when carrying her. If you use a front or back carrier, she'll now be able to hold her own head up and look around as you walk.

A baby's control over the front neck muscles and abdominal muscles develop more gradually, so it will take a little longer for your baby to be able to raise her head when lying on her back. At one month, if you gently pull your baby by the arms to a sitting position, her head will flop backward; by four months, however, she'll be able to hold it steady in all directions.

Your infant's legs also will become stronger and more active. During the second month they'll start to straighten from their inward-curving newborn position. Though her kicks will remain mostly reflexive for some time, they'll quickly gather force, and by the end of the third month she might even kick herself over from front to back. (She probably won't roll from back to front until she's about six months old.) Since you cannot predict when she'll begin rolling over, you'll need to be especially vigilant whenever she's on the changing table or any other surface above floor level.

The newborn stepping reflex will disappear at about six weeks, and you may not see your baby step again until she's ready to walk. By three or four months, however, she'll be able to flex and straighten her legs at will. Lift her upright with her feet on the floor and she'll push down and straighten her legs so that she's virtually standing by herself (except for the balance you're providing). Then she'll try bending her knees and discover that she can bounce herself.

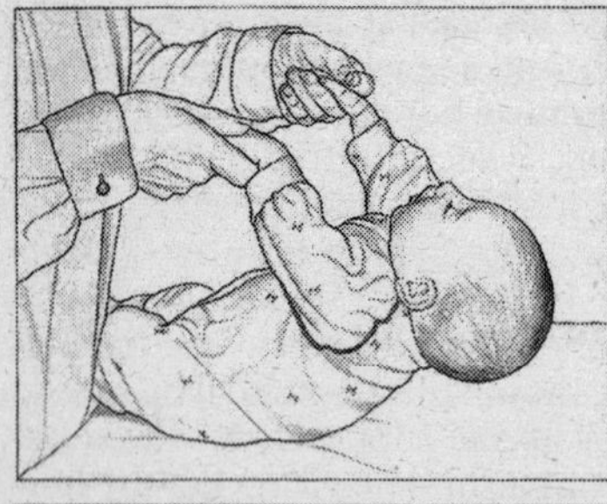

At one month, if you gently pull your baby by the arms into a sitting position, her head will flop backward (so always support your baby's head when picking her up).

By four months, however, she'll be able to hold her head steady in all directions.

Your baby's hand and arm movements also will develop rapidly during these three months. In the beginning her hands will be tightly clenched with her thumb curled inside her fingers; if you uncoil the fingers and place a rattle in her palm, she'll grasp it automatically, yet she won't be able to

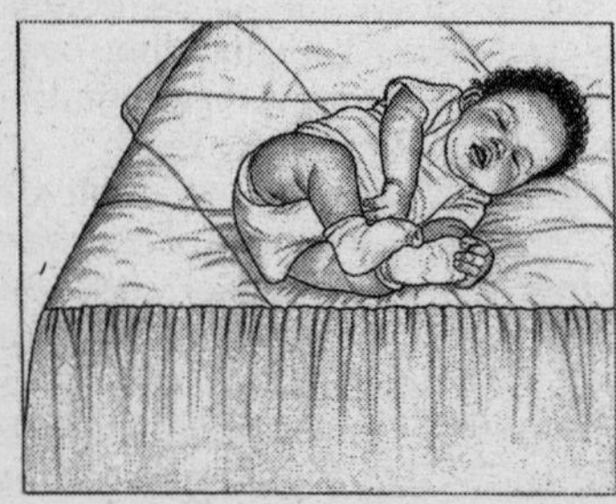

Since you can't predict when she'll be rolling over, you'll need to be especially vigilant.

shake it or bring it to her mouth. She'll gaze at her hands with interest when they come into view by chance or because of reflexive movements, but she probably won't be able to bring them to her face on her own.

Movement Milestones By the End of This Period

- Raises head and chest when lying on stomach
- Supports upper body with arms when lying on stomach

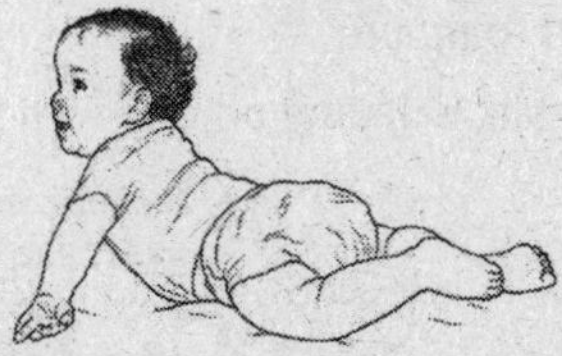

- Stretches legs out and kicks when lying on stomach or back

- Opens and shuts hands

- Pushes down on legs when feet are placed on a firm surface

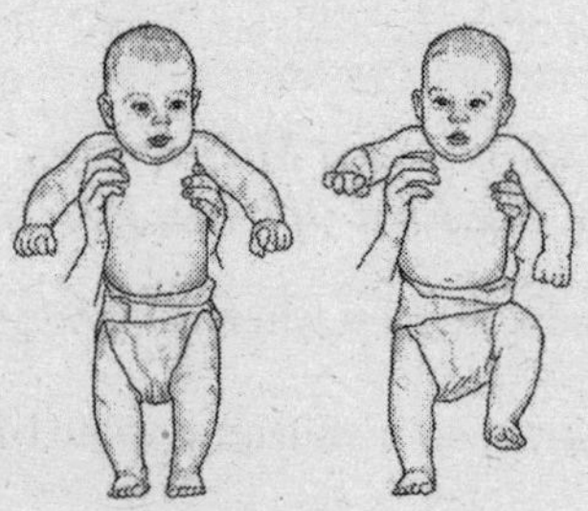

- Brings hand to mouth
- Takes swipes at dangling objects with hands

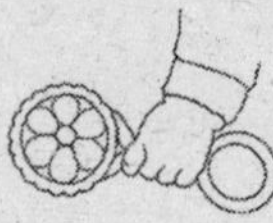

- Grasps and shakes hand toys

However, many changes will occur within just a month or two. Suddenly your baby's hands will seem to relax and her arms will open outward. During the third month her hands will be half open most of the time, and you'll notice her carefully opening and shutting them. Try placing a rattle in her palm and she'll grip it, perhaps bring it to her mouth, and then drop it only after she's explored it fully. (The more lightweight the toy, the better she'll be able to control it.) She'll never seem to grow bored with her hands themselves; just staring at her fingers will amuse her for long stretches of time.

Your baby's attempts to bring her hands to her mouth will be persistent, but mostly in vain at first. Even if her fingers occasionally reach their destination, they'll quickly fall away. By four months, however, she'll probably have finally mastered this game and be able to get her thumb to her mouth and keep it there whenever she wishes. Put a rattle in her palm now and she'll clench it tightly, shake it, mouth it, and maybe even transfer it from hand to hand.

Your baby also will be able to reach accurately and quickly—not only with both hands but with her entire body. Hang a toy overhead and she'll reach up eagerly with arms and legs to bat at it and grab for it. Her face will tense in concentration and she may even lift her head toward her target. It's as if every part of her body shares in her excitement as she masters these new skills.

By two months, your baby's eyes are more coordinated and can work together to move and focus at the same time.

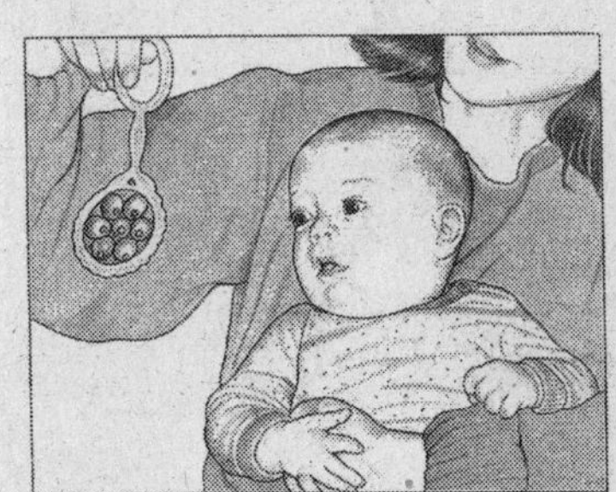

Vision

At one month your baby still can't see very clearly beyond 12 inches or so, but he'll closely study anything within this range: the corner of his crib, the play of lights, the shadows on the wall, the shapes of his mobile. The human face is his favorite image, however. As you hold him in your arms his attention is drawn automatically to your face, particularly your eyes. Often the mere sight of your eyes will make him smile. Gradually his visual span will broaden so that he can take in your whole face instead of just a single feature like your eyes. As this happens he'll be much more responsive to facial expressions involving your mouth, jaw, and cheeks. He'll also love flirting with himself in the mirror. Buy an unbreakable mirror that's specially made to attach inside cribs and playpens, so he can entertain himself when you're not nearby.

In his early weeks your baby will have a hard time tracking movement. If you wave a ball or toy quickly in front of him, he'll seem to stare through it, or if you shake your head, he'll

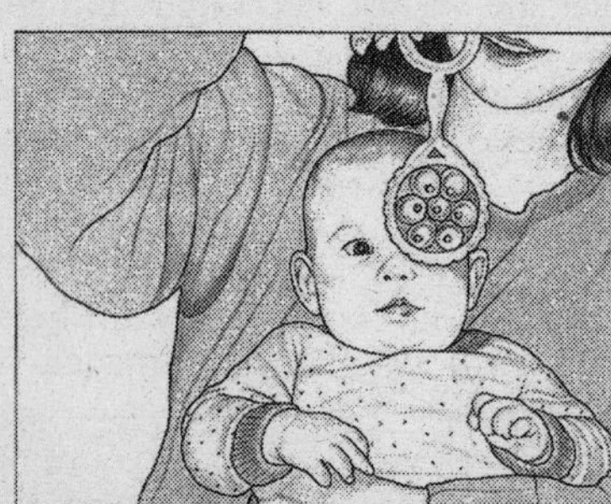

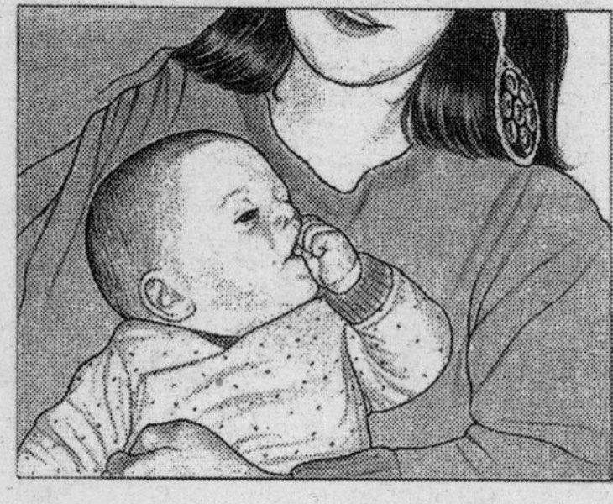

Soon he'll be able to track an object moving through an entire half-circle in front of him.

lose his focus on your eyes. But this will change dramatically by two months, when his eyes are more coordinated and can work together to move and focus at the same time. Soon he'll be able to track an object moving through an entire half-circle in front of him. This increased visual coordination also will give him the depth perception he needs to track objects as they move toward and away from him. By three months he'll also have the arm and hand control needed to bat at objects as they move above or in front of him; his aim won't be very good for a long time to come, but the practice will help him develop his hand-eye coordination.

Your baby's distance vision is also developing at this time. You may notice at three months that he's smiling at you halfway across the room, or studying a toy several feet away. By four months you'll catch him staring at the distant television screen or looking out the window. These are clues that his distance vision is fully developed.

Visual Milestones By the End of This Period

- Watches faces intently
- Follows moving objects
- Recognizes familiar objects and people at a distance
- Starts using hands and eyes in coordination

Your infant's color vision will mature at about the same rate. At one month he'll be quite sensitive to the brightness or intensity of color; consequently, he'll prefer to look at bold patterns in sharply contrasting colors or in black-and-white. The soothing pastels we usually associate with a newborn's nursery, in fact, are not appreciated by young infants because of their limited color vision. By about four months your baby will finally be responsive to the full range of colors and their many shades.

As his eyesight develops, your infant naturally will seek out more stimulating things to see. Around one month his favorite patterns will be simple linear images such as big stripes or a checkerboard. By three months he'll be much more interested in circular patterns (bull's-eyes, spirals). This is one reason why faces, which are full of circles and curves, are so appealing to him.

Hearing and Making Sounds

Just as your baby naturally prefers the human face over any other visual pattern, she also prefers the human voice to other sounds. Her mother's voice is her absolute favorite, because she associates it with warmth, food, and comfort. Babies like the high-pitched voices of women in general—a fact that most adults seem to understand intuitively and respond to accordingly, without even realizing it.

Just listen to yourself the next time you talk to your baby. You'll probably notice that you raise the pitch of your voice, slow your rate of speech, exaggerate certain syllables, and widen your eyes and mouth more than normal. This dramatic approach is guaranteed to capture almost any baby's attention—and usually make her smile.

By listening to you and others talk to her, your baby will discover the importance of speech long before she understands or repeats any specific words herself. By one month she'll be able to identify you by voice, even if you're in another room, and as you talk to her she'll be reassured, comforted, and entertained. When she smiles and gurgles back at you, she'll see the delight on your face and realize that talk is a two-way process. These first conversations will teach her many of the subtle rules of communication, such as turn-taking, vocal tone, imitation and pacing, and speed of verbal interaction.

At about two months you may begin hearing your infant repeat some vowel sounds (ah-ah-ah, ooh-ooh-ooh), especially if you've been talking to her often with clear, simple words and phrases. Along the way, it's easy to fall into a habit of baby talk, but you should try to mix your conversations with adult language and phase out the baby talk after she's six months old.

By four months your infant will babble routinely, often amusing herself for long periods by producing strange new sounds (muh-muh, bah-bah). He'll also be more sensitive to your tone of voice and the emphasis you put on certain words or phrases. As you move through each day together she'll learn from your voice when you're going to feed her, change her diapers, go out for a walk, or put her down to sleep. The way you talk will tell her a great deal about your mood and personality, and the way she responds will tell you a lot about her. If you speak in an upbeat or comforting way, she may smile or coo. Yell or talk angrily, and she'll probably startle or cry.

Hearing and Speech Milestones By the End of This Period

- Smiles at the sound of your voice
- Begins to babble
- Begins to imitate some sounds
- Turns head toward direction of sound

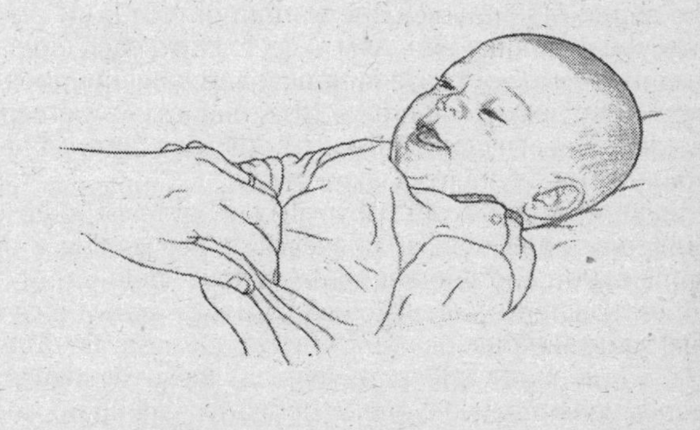

Emotional and Social Development

By the second month your baby will spend much of each day watching and listening to the people around him. He learns that they will entertain and soothe him, feed him, and make him comfortable. He feels good when they smile at him, and he seems to know instinctively that he can smile, too. Even during his first month he'll experiment with primitive grins and grimaces. Then, during the second month, these movements will turn to genuine signals of pleasure and friendliness.

Have you experienced his first true smile yet? It's a major turning point for both you and your infant. In case there was any doubt in your mind, all the sleepless nights and erratic days of these first weeks suddenly seem worthwhile at the sight of that first grin, and you'll do everything in your power to keep those smiles coming. For his part, your baby will suddenly discover that just by moving his lips he can have two-way "conversations" with you, as his grins bring him even more attention than usual and make him feel good. Smiling will also give him another way besides crying to express his needs and exert some control over what happens to him.

At first your baby may actually seem to smile past you without meeting your gaze, but don't let this disturb you. Looking away from you gives him some control and protects him from being overwhelmed by you. It's his way of taking in the total picture without being "caught" by your eyes. This way, he can pay equal attention to your facial expressions, the sound of your voice, the warmth of your body, and the way you're holding him. As you get to know each other he'll gradually hold your gaze for longer and longer periods, and you'll find ways to increase his "tolerance"—perhaps by holding him at a certain distance, adjusting the level of your voice, or modifying your expressions.

By three months your baby will be a master of "smile talk." Sometimes he'll start a "conversation" by aiming a broad smile at you and gurgling to catch your attention. At other times he'll lie in wait, watching your face until you give the first smile and then beaming back his enthusiastic response. His whole body will participate in these dialogues. His hands will open wide, one or both arms will lift up, and his arms and legs will move in time with the rhythms of your speech. His facial movements may also mirror yours. As you talk he may open his mouth and widen his eyes, and if you stick out your tongue, he may do the same!

Of course your baby probably won't act this friendly with everyone. Like adults, your infant will prefer certain people to others. And his favorites, naturally, will be his parents. Then, at about three or four months, he'll become intrigued by other children. If he has brothers or sisters, you'll see him beaming as soon as they start talking to him. If he hears

As you get to know each other he'll gradually hold your gaze for longer and longer periods.

children's voices down the street or on television, he may turn to find them. This fascination with children will increase as he gets older.

Grandparents or familiar sitters may receive a hesitant smile at first, followed by coos and body talk once they've played with him awhile. By contrast, strangers may receive no more than a curious stare or a fleeting smile. This selective behavior tells you that even at this young age, he's starting to sort out who's who in his life. Although the signals are subtle, there's no doubt that he's becoming very attached to the people closest to him.

This unspoken give-and-take may seem like no more than a game, but these early exchanges play an important part in his social and emotional development. By responding quickly and enthusiastically to his smiles and engaging him often in these "conversations," you'll let him know that he's important to you, that he can trust you, and that he has a certain amount of control in his life. By recognizing his cues and not interrupting or looking away when he's "talking," you'll also show him that you are interested in him and value him. This contributes to his developing self-esteem.

As your baby grows, the way the two of you communicate will vary with his needs and desires. On a day-to-day basis you'll find that he has three general levels of need, each of which shows a different side of his personality:

1. When his needs are urgent—when he's very hungry or in pain, for instance—he'll let you know in his own special way, perhaps by screaming, whimpering, or using desperate body language. In time you'll learn to recognize these signals so quickly that you can usually satisfy him almost before he himself knows what he wants.
2. While your baby is peacefully asleep, or when he's alert and entertaining himself, you'll feel reassured that you've met all his needs for the moment. This will give you a welcome opportunity to rest or take care of other business. The times when he's playing by himself provide you with wonderful opportunities to observe—from a distance—how he is developing new skills such as reaching, tracking objects, or manipulating his hands.
3. Each day there will be periods when your baby's obvious needs are met but he's still fussy or fitful. He may let you know this with a whine, agitated movements, or spurts of aimless activity between moments of calm. He probably won't even know what he wants, and any of several responses might help calm him. Playing, talking, singing, rocking, and walking may work sometimes; on other occasions, simply repositioning him or letting him "fuss it out" may be the most successful strategies. You also may find that while a particular response calms him down momentarily, he'll soon become even fussier and demand more attention. This cycle may not break until you either let him cry a few minutes or distract him by doing something different—for example, taking him outside or feeding him. As trying as these spells can be, you'll both learn a lot about each other because of them. You'll discover how your baby likes to be rocked, what funny faces or voices he most enjoys, and what he most likes to look at. He'll find out what he has to do to get you to respond, how hard you'll try to please him, and where your limits of tolerance lie.

Social/Emotional Milestones By the End of This Period

- Begins to develop a social smile
- Enjoys playing with other people, and may cry when playing stops
- Becomes more communicative and expressive with face and body
- Imitates some movements and facial expressions

Over time your baby's periods of acute need will decrease, and he'll be able to entertain himself for longer stretches. In part, this is because you're learning to anticipate and care for many of his problems before he's uncomfortable. But also, his nervous system will be maturing, and as a result, he'll be better able to cope with everyday stresses by himself. With greater control over his body, he'll be able to do more things to amuse himself and he'll experience fewer frustrations. The periods when he seems most difficult to satisfy probably won't disappear entirely for a few years, but as he becomes more active it will be easier to distract him. Ultimately, he should learn to overcome these spells on his own.

During these early months, don't worry about spoiling him with too much attention. Observe your baby closely and

Developmental Health Watch

Although each baby develops in her own individual way and at her own rate, failure to reach certain milestones may signal medical or developmental problems requiring special attention. If you notice any of the following warning signs in your infant at this age, discuss them with your pediatrician.

- Still has Moro reflex after four months
- Doesn't seem to respond to loud sounds
- Doesn't notice her hands by two months
- Doesn't smile at the sound of your voice by two months
- Doesn't follow moving objects with her eyes by two to three months
- Doesn't grasp and hold objects by three months
- Doesn't smile at people by three months
- Cannot support her head well at three months
- Doesn't reach for and grasp toys by three to four months
- Doesn't babble by three to four months
- Doesn't bring objects to her mouth by four months
- Begins babbling, but doesn't try to imitate any of your sounds by four months
- Doesn't push down with her legs when her feet are placed on a firm surface by four months
- Has trouble moving one or both eyes in all directions
- Crosses her eyes most of the time (occasional crossing of the eyes is normal in these first months).
- Doesn't pay attention to new faces, or seems very frightened by new faces or surroundings
- Still has the tonic neck reflex at four to five months

respond promptly when he needs you. You may not be able to calm him down every time, but it never hurts to show him that you care. In fact, the more promptly and consistently you comfort your baby's fussing in the first six months, the less demanding he's likely to be when he's older. At this age he needs frequent reassurance in order to feel secure about himself and about you. By helping him establish this sense of security now, you're laying a foundation for the confidence and trust that will allow him gradually to separate from you and become a strong, independent person.

Toys and Activities Appropriate for a One- to Three-Month-Old

- Images or books with high-contrast patterns
- Bright, varied mobile
- Unbreakable mirror attached to inside of crib
- Rattles
- Sing to your baby
- Play varied music from music boxes, records, or tapes

BASIC CARE

Feeding

Ideally, your baby will continue on his diet of breastmilk or formula without any additions from ages one month to four months. The amount he consumes at each feeding should gradually increase from about 4 or 5 ounces during the second month, to 5 or 6 ounces by four months. His daily intake should reach about 30 ounces by four months. Ordinarily, this will supply all his nutritional needs at this age.

If your baby seems persistently hungry after what you think are adequate feedings, consult your pediatrician for advice. When a breastfeeding infant is not gaining weight, your milk supply may have decreased and a supplemental bottle or two may be the answer. If it's clear that he's getting enough milk but is still hungry, the doctor may advise you to start solid foods. Solids should be introduced only near the end of this period, however, because younger babies have a tendency to push the food out with their tongues, which makes spoon-feeding difficult. Also, young infants may not be able to tolerate certain solid foods. If you do need to introduce solids, start with the least allergenic food, which is rice cereal, and thin it as much as possible with breastmilk or formula. (For more information about introducing solids, see Chapter 8.)

Even if you don't make any additions to your baby's diet, you'll probably notice a change in his bowel movements during these months. His intestines can now hold more and absorb a greater amount of nutrients from the milk, so the stools will tend to be more solid. The gastrocolic reflex is also diminishing, so he should no longer have a bowel movement after each feeding. (See *Bowel Movements*, page 64.) In fact, between two and three months, the frequency of stools in both breastfed and bottle-fed babies may decrease dramatically; some breastfed babies have only one bowel movement every three or four days, and a few perfectly healthy breastfed infants have just one a week. As long as your baby is eating well, gaining weight, and his stools are not too hard or dry, there's no reason to be alarmed by this drop in frequency.

Sleeping

By two months your baby will be more alert and social, and will spend more time awake during the day. This will make her a little more tired during the dark, quiet hours when no one is on hand to entertain her. Meanwhile, her stomach capacity will be growing, so that she needs less frequent feedings; as a result she may start skipping one middle-of-the-night feeding and sleep from around 10:00 P.M. through to daylight. By three months, most (but not all) infants consistently sleep through the night (seven or eight hours without waking).

If your infant does not start sleeping through the night by

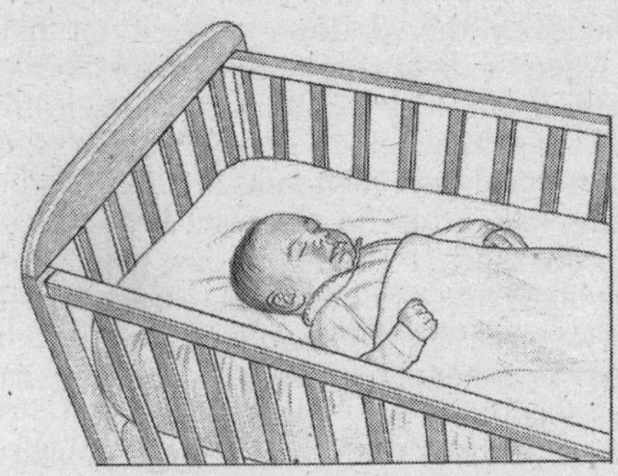

three months, you may need to give her some encouragement by keeping her awake longer in the afternoon and early evening. Play with her actively at these times, or let her join the rest of the family in the kitchen or living room so she's not tempted to drift to sleep before bedtime. Increase the amount of her feeding right before bed as well (if she's breastfeeding, increase the amount of time she nurses), so she doesn't wake up too early because she's hungry.

Even after your baby has established a fairly regular and reasonable sleep pattern, problems can develop. For example, it's common for babies at this age to get their days and nights mixed up so that they're doing most of their sleeping during the day. Although this situation may seem to occur without warning, it usually develops over several days. The baby begins by sleeping more during the day, which causes her to sleep less at night. If she's fed and comforted when she wakes up at night, she'll adopt this new sleep cycle quite naturally. To prevent or break this habit, induce your baby to go back to sleep as quickly as possible during the night. Don't turn up the lights, talk, or play with her. If you need to feed and change her, try to disturb her as little as possible when doing so. Then keep her awake as much as possible during the day, and don't put her down for the night before 10:00 or 11:00 P.M. Remember, at this age, babies should be put to sleep on their back. If you're patient and consistent, her sleep pattern will soon start to respond. (See *Helping Your Baby Sleep,* page 54.)

Many infants also wake up too early in the morning to suit

their parents. Sometimes this problem can be solved by putting shades on the windows to block out the morning sun; then when the baby awakens, perhaps after a few minutes of fussing, she may fall back to sleep. If this doesn't work, however, it may help to keep her up an extra hour at night. Unfortunately, not all infants are able to sleep late in the morning; some wake up automatically, and are ready to start the day at dawn. If that's your own baby's pattern, you really have little choice but to adapt to her schedule. As she gets older (age six to eight months) having favorite toys in her crib may keep her occupied so you can have a few more minutes to sleep.

Sometimes you may think your baby is waking up when she's actually going through a phase of very light slumber. She could be squirming, startling, fussing, or even crying—and still be asleep. Or she may be awake but on the verge of drifting off again if left alone. Don't make the mistake of trying to comfort her during these moments; you'll only awaken her further and delay her going back to sleep. Instead, if you let her fuss and even cry for a few minutes, she'll learn to get herself to sleep without relying on you. Some babies actually need to let off energy by crying in order to settle into sleep or rouse themselves out of it. As much as fifteen to twenty minutes of fussing won't do your infant any harm. Just be sure she's not crying out of hunger or pain, or because her diaper is wet. Though it may be difficult just to let her cry for even a minute or two, you and she will be much better off in the long run.

Siblings

By the second month, although you may be used to having a new baby in the house, your older children may still be having a hard time adjusting. Especially if the baby is your second child, your first probably resents giving up the central place in the household. No longer the primary focus of the family, he may do everything in his power to recapture that position—and that usually involves misbehaving.

Sometimes your older child might display his frustration by talking back, doing something he knows is forbidden, or literally shouting for attention. He might also regress, suddenly wetting his bed or having daytime accidents even though he's been toilet-trained for months. Having each par-

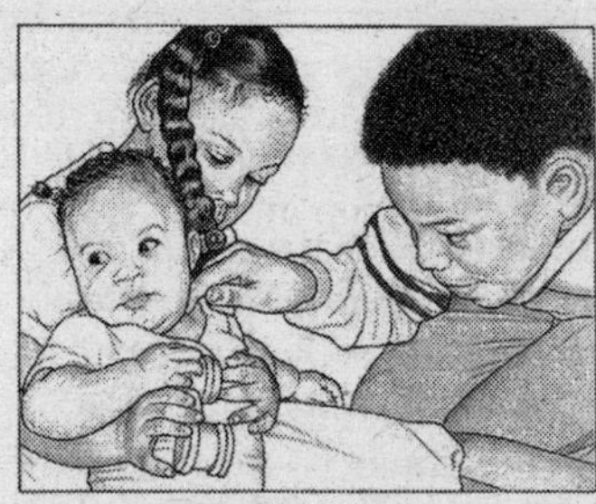

Invite older siblings to play with the baby.

ent take time with him alone each day should help resolve these problems.

However, if the older child takes out his anger on the baby—pulling away his bottle or even hitting him—you'll need to take more direct action. Sit down and talk with him, and be prepared to hear things such as "I wish that baby had never come here." Try to keep these and his other feelings in mind as you confront him. Reassure him that you still love him very much, but explain firmly that he must not hurt the baby. Make an extra effort to include him in all family activities, and invite him to play with the newborn. Make him feel like an important "big kid" by giving him specific baby-related jobs, such as carrying the diaper bag, putting away toys, or helping dress the baby. At the same time, set clear and consistent rules, such as never picking up the baby without permission.

Set clear and consistent rules, such as never picking up the baby without permission.

Stimulating Infant Brain Growth: Age One Month Through Three Months

- Provide healthful nutrition as your baby grows; have periodic checkups and timely immunizations from a regular source of medical care.
- Give consistent warm, physical contact—hugging, skin-to-skin, body-to-body contact—to establish your infant's sense of security and well-being.
- Talk or sing to your baby during dressing, bathing, feeding, playing, walking, and driving. Use simple, lively phrases and address your baby by name.
- Be attentive to your baby's rhythms and moods. Learn to read her cues and respond to her when she is upset as well as when she is happy. Babies cannot be spoiled.
- Provide colorful objects of different shapes, sizes, and textures; your face is by far the most interesting visual object at this age.
- If you speak a foreign language, use it at home.
- Avoid subjecting your baby to stressful or traumatic experiences, physical or psychological.
- Make sure other people who provide care and supervision for your baby understand the importance of forming a loving and comforting relationship with your child and also provide consistent care.

HEALTH WATCH

The following medical problems are common between the ages of two months and four months. Check Part II of this book for other illnesses and conditions that occur throughout childhood.

Diarrhea. (See also *Diarrhea,* page 421.) If your baby has a vomiting spell followed a day or two later by diarrhea, she probably has a viral infection in her intestinal tract. If you're breastfeeding, your pediatrician will probably suggest that you continue nursing her as usual. If you're bottle-feeding, she may advise you to limit the baby's intake for a day or two to a special solution containing electrolytes (such as salt and potassium) and sugar. When milk-feeding is restarted, you may be advised to use a soy formula for a few days. This is because diarrhea washes out the enzymes needed to digest the sugar in cow's milk.

Ear Infections. (See also *Ear Infection,* page 485.) Although ear infections are more common in older babies, they occasionally occur in infants under three months. Babies are prone to ear infections because the tube that connects the nasal passages to the middle ear is very short, making it easy for a cold in the nose to spread to the ear. If the infection becomes severe or is not treated, the eardrum may break and the infected fluid will pass through it and out the ear canal. With proper treatment, however, the eardrum will heal with no permanent damage.

The first sign of an ear infection is usually irritability, especially at night. Your baby also may use his hand to pull or swipe at his ear. As the infection advances, it may produce a fever. If you suspect that your baby has an ear infection, call the doctor as soon as possible. If an ear examination confirms that an infection is present, the doctor will prescribe a course of antibiotics.

Rashes and Skin Conditions. Many of the rashes seen in the first month may persist through the second or third. In addition, eczema may occur any time after one month. Eczema, or atopic dermatitis (see also *Eczema,* page 565), produces dry, scaly, and often red patches, usually on the face, in the bends of the elbows, and behind the knees. In young infants, elbows and knees are the most common locations. The patches are extremely itchy, which may make your baby irritable. Ask your pediatrician to prescribe treatment. Don't use any over-the-counter lotions or creams unless he specifically recommends them. To prevent a recurrence of the rash, make sure you use only the mildest of soaps to wash your baby and her clothes, and dress her only in soft clothing (no wool or rough weaves). Bathe her no more than three times a week, since frequent baths may further dry her skin.

Upper Respiratory Infections (URI). (See also *Colds/ Upper Respiratory Infection*, page 482.) Many babies have their first cold during these months. Breastfeeding provides some immunity, but it is not complete protection by any means, especially if another member of the family has a respiratory illness. The infection can spread easily through droplets in the air or by hand contact. (Exposure to cold temperatures or drafts does *not* cause colds.) Washing hands, covering mouths while sneezing or coughing, and refraining from kissing when you have a cold will help prevent the infection from spreading to others.

Most respiratory infections in young babies are mild, producing a cough, runny nose, and slightly elevated temperature, but rarely a high fever. A runny nose, however, can be troublesome for an infant. He cannot blow his nose, so the mucus blocks the nasal passages. Before three or four months of age, an infant doesn't breathe well through his mouth, so this blockage of his nose causes more discomfort for him than for older children. A congested nose also often disturbs his sleep because he wakes up when he's not able to breathe. It can interfere with feeding, too, since he must interrupt sucking in order to breathe through his mouth.

To help reduce this problem, use a cool-mist humidifier in his room. If congestion does occur, use a bulb syringe to suction the mucus from his nose, especially before feedings and when it's obviously blocked. If you put a few drops of normal saline (prescribed by your pediatrician) into his nose first, this will thin the mucus, making it easier to suction. Squeeze the bulb first; *then* insert the tip gently into the nostril and slowly release the bulb. Although acetaminophen will lower an elevated temperature and calm him if he's irritable, you should give it to a baby this age *only* on your pediatrician's advice. *Do not use aspirin.* (See *Medication*, page 595.)

Ordinarily, you won't need to take your baby to the doctor when he has an upper respiratory infection. You should call, however, if any of the following occurs:

- He develops a persistant cough.
- He loses his appetite and refuses several feedings.

- He runs a fever: *Anytime your baby has a rectal temperature higher than 101 degrees, you should contact your pediatrician.*
- He seems excessively irritable.
- He seems unusually sleepy or hard to awaken.

Immunization Alert

At birth, and again at one to two months, your baby should receive:

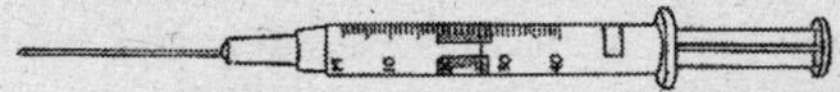

- Hepatitis B vaccine

At two months, and again at four months, your baby should receive:

- DTaP or DTP vaccine (DTaP is preferred)
- Polio vaccine. Talk to your pediatrician about what schedule to receive.
- Hib vaccine. (This may cause a slight fever and some soreness where it's injected. The vaccine helps prevent meningitis, pneumonia, and joint infection caused by *Haemophilus influenzae* type b bacteria.)

(For detailed information, see page 84 and Chapter 24, "Immunizations.")

Safety Check

Falls

- Never place the baby in an infant seat on a table, chair, or any other surface above floor level.
- Never leave your baby unattended on a bed, couch, table, chair or changing table.

Burns

- Never hold your baby while smoking, drinking a hot liquid, or cooking by a hot stove or oven.

- Never allow anyone to smoke around your baby.
- Before placing your baby in the bath, always test the water temperature with the inside of your wrist or forearm.
- Never heat your baby's milk (or, later on, food) in a microwave oven.

Choking

- Routinely check all toys for sharp edges or small parts that could be pulled or broken off.
- If you use a crib gym or other suspended toys for the crib, make sure they are fastened securely and tightly so the baby cannot pull them down or entangle herself in them.

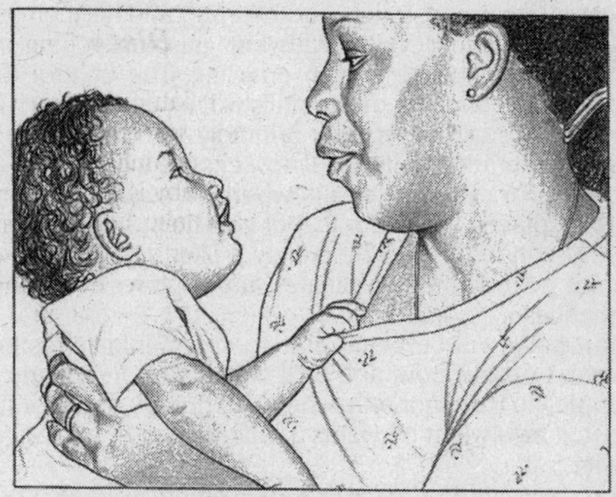

AGE FOUR MONTHS THROUGH SEVEN MONTHS

By your infant's four-month birthday you'll probably have a daily routine for his feeding, napping, bathing, and going to sleep at night. This routine will provide a predictability that will help your baby feel secure while allowing you to budget your time and activities. The schedule should be flexible, however, to allow for spur-of-the-moment fun. Short strolls when the sun finally appears on a dreary day, an unexpected lunch visit from grandparents, or a family excursion to the zoo or park are all wonderful excuses to break the routine. Being open to impulse will make your life together more enjoyable and help your baby learn to adapt to all the changes facing him in his life ahead.

For the time being, the most important changes are

taking place within him. This is the period when he'll learn to coordinate his emerging perceptive abilities (the use of senses like vision, touch, and hearing) and his increasing motor abilities to develop skills like grasping, rolling over, sitting up, and possibly even crawling. The control that's evident in his budding motor skills will extend to every part of his life. Instead of reacting primarily by reflex, as he did during his earlier months, he'll now choose what he will and won't do. For example, as a newborn he sucked on almost anything placed in his mouth, but now he has definite favorites. Though in the past he merely looked at a strange new toy, now he mouths, manipulates, and explores every one of its qualities.

Your baby will be better able to communicate his emotions and desires now, and he'll voice them frequently. For example, he'll cry not only when he's hungry or uncomfortable, but also when he wants a different toy or a change in activity.

You may find that your five- or six-month-old also occasionally cries when you leave the room or when he's suddenly confronted by a stranger. This is because he's developing a strong attachment for you and the other people who regularly care for him. He now associates you with his own well-being and can distinguish you from other people. Even if he doesn't cry out for you, he will signal this new awareness by curiously and carefully studying a stranger's face. By eight or nine months, he may openly object to strangers who come too close. This signals the start of a normal developmental stage known as "stranger anxiety."

During these months before stranger anxiety hits full force, however, your child will probably go through a period of delightful "show-offmanship," smiling and playing with everyone he meets. His personality will be coming out in full bloom, and even people meeting him for the first time will notice many of his unique character traits. Take advantage of his sociability to acquaint him with people who will help care for him in the future, such as baby-sitters, relatives, or child-care workers. This won't guarantee clear sailing through the stranger-anxiety period, but it may help smooth the waters.

You'll also learn during these months, if you haven't before, that there is no formula for raising an ideal child. You and your baby are each unique, and the relationship between the two of you is unique as well. So what works for one baby may not for another. You have to discover what succeeds for *you* through trial and error. While your neighbor's infant may fall asleep easily and sleep through the night, your baby may need some extra holding and cuddling to settle him down at bedtime and again in the middle of the night. While your first baby might have needed a great deal of hugging and comforting, your second might prefer more time alone. These individual differences don't necessarily indicate that your parenting is "right" or "wrong"; they just mean that each baby is unique. Over these first months and years you will get to know your child's individual traits, and you'll develop patterns of activity and interaction that are designed especially for him. If you remain flexible and open to his special traits, he'll help steer your actions as a parent in the right direction.

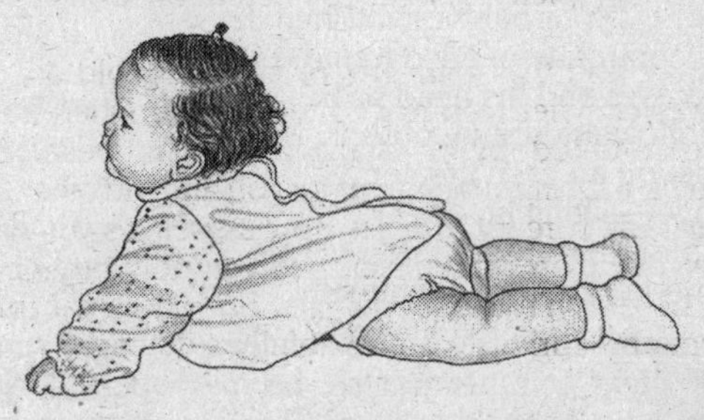

Growth and Development

Physical Appearance and Growth

Between four and seven months your baby will continue to gain approximately 1 to 1 ¼ pounds (.45 to .56 kilograms) a month. By the time she reaches her eight-month birthday, she probably will weigh about two and a half times what she did at birth. Her bones also will continue to grow at a rapid rate, and as a result during these months her length will increase by about 2 inches (5 centimeters) and her head circumference by about 1 inch (2.5 centimeters).

Your baby's specific weight and height are not as important as her *rate* of growth. By now you should have established her position on the growth curve on page 151. Continue to plot her measurements at regular intervals to make sure she keeps growing at the same rate. If you find that she's beginning to follow a different curve, or gaining weight or height unusually slowly, discuss it with your pediatrician.

Movement

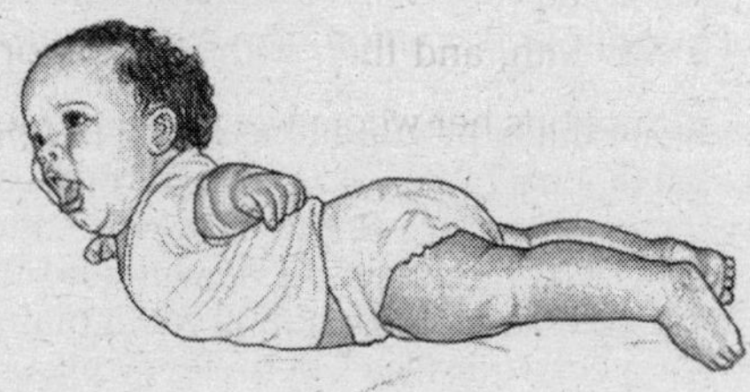

In his first four months your baby established the muscle control he needed to move both his eyes and his head so he could follow interesting objects. Now he'll take on an even greater challenge—sitting up. He'll accomplish this in small steps as his back and neck muscles gradually

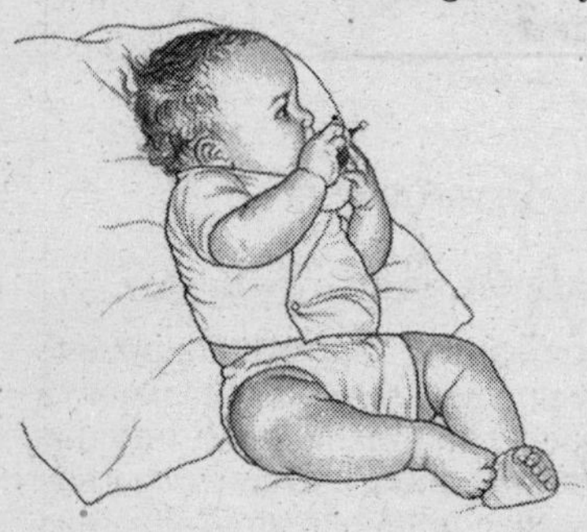

strengthen and he develops better balance in his trunk, head, and neck. First he'll learn to raise his head and hold it up while lying on his stomach. You can encourage this by placing him on his stomach and extending his arms forward; then hold a rattle or other attractive toy in front of him to get his attention and coax him to hold his head up and look at you. This also is a good way to check his hearing and vision.

Movement Milestones By the End of This Period

- Rolls both ways (front to back, back to front)
- Sits with, and then without, support of her hands
- Supports her whole weight on her legs
- Reaches with one hand
- Transfers object from hand to hand
- Uses raking grasp (not pincer)

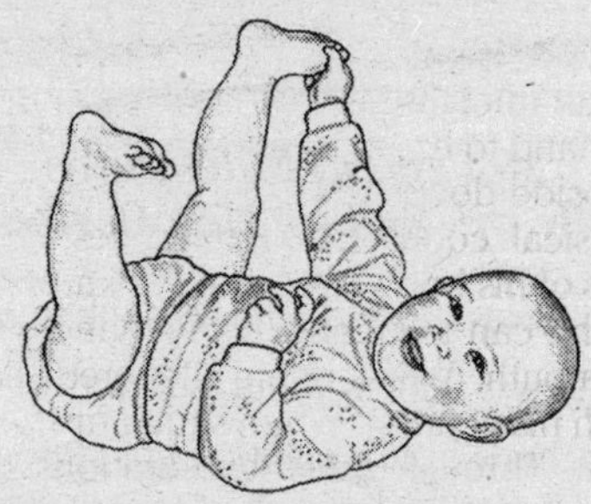

Once he's able to lift up his head, your baby will start pushing up on his arms and arching his back to lift his chest. This strengthens his upper body so he can remain steady and upright when sitting. At the same time he may rock on his stomach, kick his legs, and "swim" with his arms. These abilities, which usually appear at about five months, are necessary for rolling over and crawling. By the end of this period he'll probably be able to roll over in both directions. Most babies are able to roll first from the stomach to the back and later in the opposite direction, though doing it in the opposite sequence is perfectly normal, too.

Once your baby is strong enough to raise his chest, you can help him "practice" sitting up. Hold him up or support his back with pillows or a couch corner as he learns to balance himself. Soon he'll learn to "tripod," leaning forward as he extends his arms to balance his upper body. Bright, interesting toys placed in front of him will give him something to focus on as he gains his balance. It will be some time before he can maneuver himself into a sitting posture without your assistance, but by six to eight months, if you position him upright, he'll be able to remain sitting without leaning forward on his arms. Then he can discover all the wonderful things that can be done with his hands as he views the world from this new vantage point.

By the fourth month your baby can easily bring interesting objects to his mouth. During his next four months he'll begin to use his fingers and thumbs together in a mitten or clawlike grip or raking motion, and he'll manage to pick up many things. He won't develop the pincer grasp using his index finger and thumb until he's about nine months old, but by the sixth to eighth month he'll learn how to transfer objects from hand to hand, turn them from side to side, and twist them upside down.

As his physical coordination improves, your baby will discover parts of his body that he never knew existed. Lying on his back, he can now grab his feet and toes and bring them to his mouth. While being diapered, he may reach down to touch his genitals. When sitting up, he may slap his knee or thigh. Through these explorations he'll discover many new and interesting sensations. He'll also start to understand the function of each body part. For example, when you place his newly found feet on the floor, he may first curl his toes and stroke the carpet or wood surface, but soon he'll discover he can use his feet and legs to practice "walking" or just to bounce up and down. Watch out! These are all preparations for the next major milestones: crawling and standing.

Toys Appropriate for a Four- to Seven-Month-Old

- Unbreakable mirror attached to inside of crib or playpen
- Soft balls, including some that make soft, pleasant sounds
- Textured toys that make sounds
- Toys that have fingerholds
- Musical toys, such as bells, maracas, tambourines (make sure none of the parts can become loose)
- See-through rattles that show the pieces making the noise

- Old magazines with bright pictures for you to show her
- Baby books with board, cloth, or vinyl pages

Vision

As your baby works on her important motor skills, have you noticed how closely she watches everything she's doing? The concentration with which she reaches for a toy may remind you of a scientist engrossed in research. It's obvious that her good vision is playing a key role in her early motor and cognitive development. Conveniently, her eyes become fully functional just when she needs them most.

Although your baby was able to see at birth, her total visual ability has taken months to develop fully. Only now can she distinguish subtle shades of reds, blues, and yellows. Don't be surprised if you notice that she prefers red or blue to other colors; these seem to be favorites among many infants this age. Most babies also like increasingly complex patterns and shapes as they get older—something to keep in mind when you're shopping for picture books or posters for your child's nursery.

By four months your baby's range of vision has increased to several feet or more, and it will continue to expand until, at about seven months, her eyesight will be more mature. At the same time, she'll learn to follow faster and faster movements with her eyes. In the early months, when you rolled a ball across the room, she couldn't coordinate her eyes well enough to track it, but now she'll easily follow the path of moving objects. As her hand-to-eye coordination improves, she'll be able to grab these objects as well.

A mobile hung over the crib or in front of the infant seat is an ideal way to stimulate a *young* baby's vision. However, by about five months your baby will quickly get bored and search for other things to watch. Also by this age, she may be sitting up and might pull down or tangle herself in a mobile. *For this reason, mobiles should be removed from cribs or playpens as soon as your baby is able to pull or hold herself upright.*

Still another way to hold your baby's visual interest is to keep her moving—around your home, down the block, to the store, or out on special excursions. Help her find things to look at that she's never seen before, and name each one out loud for her.

A mirror is another source of endless fascination for babies this age. The reflected image is constantly changing, and even more important, it responds directly to your child's own movements. This is her clue that the person in the mirror is actually herself. It may take your baby a while to come to this realization, but it probably will register during this period.

In general, then, your infant's visual awareness should clearly *increase* during these four months. Watch how she responds as you introduce her to new shapes, colors, and objects. If she doesn't seem to be interested in looking at new things, or if one or both eyes turn in or out, inform your pediatrician. (See also Chapter 18, "Eyes.")

Vision Milestones By the End of This Period

- Develops full color vision
- Distance vision matures
- Ability to track moving objects matures

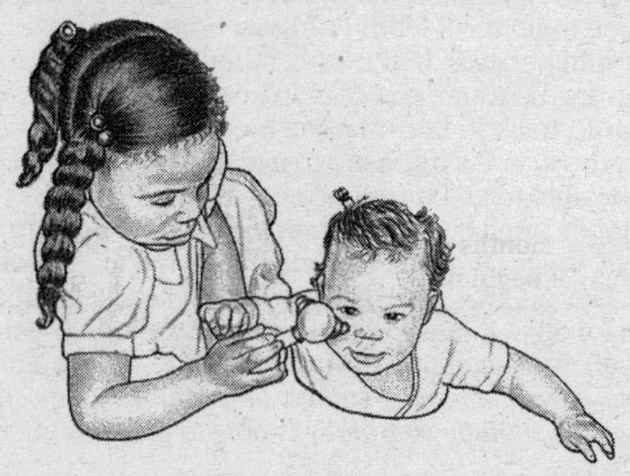

Language Development

Your baby learns language in stages. From birth he *receives* information about language by hearing people make sounds and watching how they communicate with one another. At first he is most interested in the pitch and level of your voice. When you talk to him in a soothing way, he'll stop crying because he hears that you want to comfort him. By contrast, if you shout out in anger he probably will cry, because your voice is telling him something is wrong. By four months he'll begin noticing not only the way you talk but the individual sounds you make. He'll listen to the vowels and consonants, and begin to notice the way these combine into syllables, words, and sentences.

As well as receiving sounds, your baby also has been producing them from the very beginning, first in the form of cries and then as coos. At about four months he'll start to babble, using many of the rhythms and characteristics of his native language. Though it may sound like gibberish, if you listen closely you'll hear him raise and drop his voice as if he were making a statement or asking a question. Encourage him by talking to him throughout the day. When he says a recognizable syllable, repeat it back to him and then say some simple words that contain that sound. For example, if his sound of the day is "bah," introduce him to "bottle," "box," "bonnet," and "Baa, Baa, Black Sheep."

By four months your baby will begin noticing not only the way you talk but the individual sounds you make.

Your participation in your baby's language development will become even more important after six or seven months, when he begins actively imitating the sounds of speech. Up to that point he might repeat one sound for a whole day or even days at a stretch before trying another. But now he'll become much more responsive to the sounds he hears you make, and he'll try to follow your lead. So introduce him to simple syllables and words like "baby," "cat," "dog," "go," "hot," "cold," and "walk," as well as "Mama" and "Dada." Although it may be as much as a year before you can interpret any of his babbling, your baby can understand many of your words well before his first birthday.

If he doesn't babble or imitate any sounds by his seventh month, it could mean a problem with his hearing or speech development. A baby with a partial hearing loss still can be startled by loud noises or will turn his head in their direction, and he may even respond to your voice. But he will have difficulty imitating speech. If your infant does not babble or produce a variety of sounds, alert your pediatrician. If he has had frequent ear infections he might have some fluid remaining in his inner ear, and this could interfere with his hearing.

Language Milestones By the End of This Period

- Responds to own name
- Begins to respond to "no"
- Distinguishes emotions by tone of voice
- Responds to sound by making sounds
- Uses voice to express joy and displeasure
- Babbles chains of consonants

A very young baby's hearing can be checked by using special equipment, but your observations are the early warning system that tells whether such testing is needed. If you suspect a problem, you might ask your pediatrician for a referral to a children's hearing specialist.

Cognitive Development

During your baby's first four months, did you have doubts that she really understood much that was happening around her? This parental reaction is not surprising. After all, although you knew when she was comfortable and uncomfortable, she probably showed few signs of actually *thinking.* Now, as her memory and attention span increase, you'll start to see evidence that she's not only absorbing information but also applying it to her day-to-day activities.

During this period, one of the most important concepts she'll refine is the principle of cause and effect. She'll probably stumble upon this notion by accident somewhere between four and five months. Perhaps while kicking her mattress, she'll notice the crib shaking. Or maybe, she'll realize that her rattle makes a noise when she hits or waves it. Once she understands that she can *cause* these interesting reactions, she'll continue to experiment with other ways to make things happen.

Your baby will quickly discover that some things, like bells and keys, make interesting sounds when moved or shaken.

When she bangs certain things on the table or drops them on the floor, she'll start a chain of responses from her audience.

When she bangs certain things on the table or drops them on the floor, she'll start a chain of responses from her audience, including funny faces, groans, and other reactions that may lead to the reappearance—or disappearance—of the object. Before long, she'll begin intentionally dropping things to see you pick them up. As annoying as this may be at times, it's one important way for her to learn about cause and effect and her personal ability to influence her environment.

It's important that you give your baby the objects she needs for these experiments and encourage her to test her "theories." But make sure that everything you give her to play with is unbreakable, lightweight, and large enough that she can't possibly swallow it. If you run out of the usual toys or she loses interest in them, plastic or wooden spoons, unbreakable cups, jar or bowl lids, and boxes are endlessly entertaining and inexpensive.

Another major discovery that your baby will make during this period is that objects continue to exist when they're out of her sight—a principle called *object permanence.* During

Cognitive Milestones By the End of This Period

- Finds partially hidden object
- Explores with hands and mouth
- Struggles to get objects that are out of reach

her first few months she assumed that the world consisted only of things that she could see. When you left her room, she assumed you vanished; when you returned you were a whole new person to her. In much the same way, when you hid a toy under a cloth or a box, she thought it was gone for good and wouldn't bother looking for it. But sometime after four months she'll begin to realize that the world is more permanent than she thought. You're the same person who greets her every morning. Her teddy bear on the floor is the same one that was in bed with her the night before. The block that you hid under the can did not actually vanish after all. By playing hiding games and observing the comings and goings of people and things around her, your baby will continue to learn about object permanence for many months to come.

Developmental Health Watch

Because each baby develops in his own particular manner, it's impossible to tell exactly when or how your baby will perfect a given skill. The developmental milestones listed in this book will give you a general idea of the changes you can expect, but don't be alarmed if your own baby's development takes a slightly different course. Alert your pediatrician, however, if your baby displays any of the following signs of possible developmental delay for this age range.

- Seems very stiff, with tight muscles
- Seems very floppy, like a rag doll
- Head still flops back when body is pulled up to a sitting position
- Reaches with one hand only
- Refuses to cuddle
- Shows no affection for the person who cares for him
- Doesn't seem to enjoy being around people
- One or both eyes consistently turn in or out
- Persistent tearing, eye drainage, or sensitivity to light

- Does not respond to sounds around him
- Has difficulty getting objects to his mouth
- Does not turn his head to locate sounds by four months
- Doesn't roll over in either direction (front to back or back to front) by five months
- Seems inconsolable at night after five months
- Doesn't smile spontaneously by five months
- Cannot sit with help by six months
- Does not laugh or make squealing sounds by six months
- Does not actively reach for objects by six to seven months
- Doesn't follow objects with both eyes at near (1 foot) and far (6 feet) ranges by seven months
- Does not bear some weight on legs by seven months
- Does not try to attract attention through actions by seven months
- Does not babble by eight months
- Shows no interest in games of peekaboo by eight months

Emotional Development

Between four and seven months your baby may undergo a dramatic change in personality. At the beginning of this period, she may seem relatively passive and preoccupied with getting enough food, sleep, and affection. But as she learns to sit up, use her hands, and move about, she's likely to become increasingly assertive and more attentive to the world outside. She'll be eager to reach out and touch everything she sees, and if she can't manage on her own, she'll demand your help by yelling, banging, or dropping the nearest object at hand. Once you've come to her rescue, she'll probably forget what she was doing and concentrate on you—smiling, laughing, babbling, and imitating you for many minutes at a stretch. While she'll quickly get bored with even the most engaging toy, she'll never tire of your attention.

The more subtle aspects of your baby's personality are determined largely by her constitutional makeup or temperament. Is she rambunctious or gentle? Easygoing or easily upset? Headstrong or compliant? To a large extent these are inborn character traits, and they'll become increasingly apparent during these months. You won't necessarily find all of these characteristics enjoyable all the time—especially not when your determined six-month-old is screaming in frustration as she lunges for the family cat. But in the long run, adapting to her natural personality is best for both of you.

Strong-willed and high-strung babies require an extra dose of patience and gentle guidance. They often don't adapt to changing surroundings as easily as calmer babies, and will become increasingly upset if pushed to move or perform before they're ready. For an irritable infant, language and cuddling will sometimes do wonders to calm her nerves. Distracting her can also often help refocus her energy. For instance, if she screams because you won't retrieve the toy she dropped for the tenth time, move her to the floor so she can reach the toy herself.

The shy or "sensitive" baby also requires special attention, particularly if you have more boisterous children in the household who overshadow her. When a baby is quiet and undemanding, it's easy to assume she's content, or if she doesn't laugh or smile a lot, you may lose interest in playing with her. But a baby like this often needs personal contact even more than other children. She may be easily overwhelmed and needs you to show her how to be assertive and become involved in the activities around her. How should you do this? Give her plenty of time to warm up to any situation, and make sure that other people approach her slowly. Let her sit on the sidelines before attempting to involve her directly with other children. Once she feels secure, she'll gradually become more responsive to the people around her.

Also let your pediatrician know if you have any concerns about your baby's emotional development. Your pediatrician can help if she knows there are problems, but they can be difficult to detect in a routine office visit. That's why it's important for you to call the doctor's attention to your concerns, and describe your day-to-day observations. Write them down so you don't forget them.

Social/Emotional Milestones By the End of This Period

- Enjoys social play
- Interested in mirror images
- Responds to other people's expressions of emotion

BASIC CARE

Introducing Solid Foods

At four months your baby's diet should consist of breastmilk and/or formula (with added vitamins or iron if your pediatrician recommends it), but by four to six months you can begin adding solid foods. Some babies are ready for solids as early as three months, but most have not lost their tongue-thrust reflex at that age. Because of this reflex, the young infant will push his tongue against a spoon or anything else inserted into his mouth, including food. Most babies lose this reflex at about four months. Coincidentally, the baby's energy needs increase around this age, making it an ideal time to start adding different calories through solids.

You may start solid food at whichever feedings during the

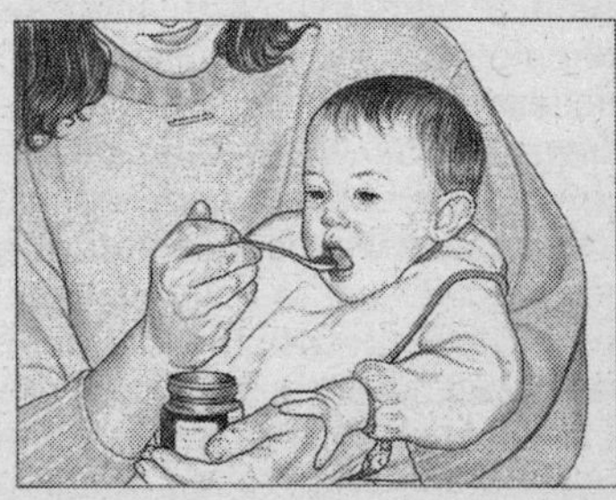

Start with half a spoonful or less (about a quarter of a teaspoonful) and talk your baby through the process.

day are most acceptable to you and your baby. However, remember that as he gets older he will want to eat with the other family members. To minimize the chances of choking, make sure your baby is sitting up, either in your lap or in an infant seat, when you introduce solids. If he cries or turns away when you try to feed him, don't force the issue. It's more important that you both enjoy his mealtimes than for him to start these foods by a specific date. Go back to nursing or bottle-feeding exclusively for a week or two, then try again.

Always use a spoon to feed your baby solids unless, at your pediatrician's recommendation, you are thickening the formula for an infant with gastroesophageal reflux (spitting up stomach contents). Some parents try putting solid foods in a bottle or infant feeder with a nipple, but feeding a baby this way can drastically increase the amount of food he takes in at each feeding and lead to excessive weight gain. Besides, it's important for your baby to get used to the process of eating—sitting up, taking bites from a spoon, resting between bites, and stopping when he's full. This early experience will help lay the foundation for good eating habits throughout his life.

Even standard baby spoons may be too wide for a child this young, but a small coffee spoon will work well. Start with half a spoonful or less (about a quarter of a teaspoonful) and talk your baby through the process ("Mmm, see how good this is"). He probably won't know what to do the first time or two. He may look confused or insulted, wrinkle his nose, and roll the food around his mouth or reject it entirely. This is an understandable reaction, considering how different his feedings have been up to this point.

One way to ease the transition to solids is to give your infant a little milk first, then switch to very small half-spoonfuls of food, and finally finish off with more milk. This will prevent him from being overly frustrated when he's very hungry, and it will link the satisfaction of nursing with this new experience of spoon-feeding.

No matter what you do, most of the first few solid-food feedings are sure to wind up outside his mouth on his face and bib, so increase the size of his feedings very gradually, starting with just a teaspoonful or two, until he gets the idea of swallowing solids.

For most babies the first solid food is rice cereal, followed by oatmeal and barley. Generally, it's a good idea to introduce wheat and mixed cereals last, since they may cause allergic reactions in very young babies.

You may use premixed baby cereals in a jar or dry varieties to which you add formula, breastmilk, or water. The prepared products are convenient, but the dry ones are richer in iron and can be varied in consistency to suit your baby. Whichever you choose, make sure that it's made for babies. This assures you that it contains the extra nutrients your infant needs at this age.

Once your baby has accepted cereal, slowly start introducing him to other foods. One possible order is strained vegetables (except corn, which is difficult for most infants to digest before six months), fruit, and meat. Give your baby just one new food at a time, and wait at least two to three days before starting another. After each new food, watch for allergic responses such as diarrhea, rash, or vomiting. If any of these occur, eliminate the suspect food from his diet until you've consulted your pediatrician. Within two or three months your baby's daily diet should include breastmilk or formula, cereal, vegetables, meats, and fruits, distributed among three meals. Because it frequently is associated with allergy, egg is started last.

Once your baby sits up, you can give him finger foods to help him learn to feed himself. Make sure anything you give him is soft, easy to swallow, and breaks down into small pieces that can't possibly choke him. Well-cooked cut-up green beans, peas, potatoes, and small pieces of wafer-type cookies or crackers are good examples. Don't give him any food that requires chewing at this age.

At each of his three daily meals, he should be eating about 4 ounces, or the amount in one small jar of strained baby food. (Because canned adult-type foods generally contain added salt and preservatives, they should not be fed to babies.)

You may start juice at this time also. However, because many young babies are sensitive to orange juice, it is a good idea to delay introducing it and other citrus fruits until about the sixth month. Fruit juices—or large amounts of fruit in general—can make the stool acidic and irritating to the skin. This can cause a rash that is bright red and painful when the baby is wiped during his diaper change. Contact with air and the application of a heavy, protective diaper ointment usually will heal the rash, but you may also want to decrease the fruit and/or juice intake for a while.

If your infant seems to be thirsty between feedings, put him to the breast or offer him extra formula. During the hot months when he's losing fluid through perspiration, 2 to 4 ounces of water or extra feedings of breastmilk or formula will help prevent dehydration.

What if you want your baby to have fresh food instead of canned or dehydrated? In that case, use a blender or food processor, or just mash softer foods with a fork. Everything should be soft, unsalted, well cooked, and unseasoned. Cooked fresh vegetables and stewed fruits (see the box on the next page for exceptions) are the easiest to prepare. Though you can feed your baby mashed raw bananas, all other fruits should be cooked until soft. Refrigerate any food you don't use immediately, and then inspect it carefully for signs of spoilage before giving it to your baby. Unlike commercial foods, your own are not bacteria-free, so they will spoil more quickly.

By the time your baby is six or seven months old, he'll probably sit up well enough to use a high chair during mealtime. To ensure his comfort, the seat of the chair should be covered with a pad that's removable and washable, so you can clean out the food that will probably accumulate there. Also, when shopping for a high chair, look for one with a detachable tray with raised rims. (See page 322 for safety recommendations.) The rims will help keep dishes and food from sliding off during your baby's more rambunctious feeding sessions. The detachable tray can be carried straight to the sink for cleaning, a feature you're bound to appreciate in the months to come (although there still may be days when the only solution is to put the entire chair in the shower for a complete wipe-down!).

As your baby's diet expands and he begins feeding himself more regularly, discuss his personal nutritional needs with your pediatrician. The latest evidence indicates that obesity in adulthood is largely the result of hereditary influences, but if your child establishes poor eating habits in infancy, they could lead to health problems later on.

Do Not Home-Prepare These Foods

Beets, Turnips, Carrots, Collard Greens, Spinach. In some parts of the country, these vegetables contain large amounts of nitrates, a chemical that can cause an unusual type of anemia (low blood count) in young infants. Baby-food companies are aware of this problem and screen the produce they buy for nitrates; they also avoid buying these vegetables in parts of the country where nitrates have been detected. Since you cannot test for this chemical yourself, it's safer to use commercially prepared forms of these foods, especially while your child is an infant. If you choose to prepare them at home anyway, serve them fresh and don't store them. Storage of these foods may actually increase the amount of nitrates in them.

Your pediatrician will help you determine whether your baby is overfed, not eating enough, or eating too many of the wrong kinds of foods. By familiarizing yourself with the caloric and nutritional contents of what he eats, you can make sure he's eating a proper diet. Be aware of the food habits of others in your family. As your baby eats more and more "table foods" (this usually starts at eight to ten months in quantities similar to those used for baby foods), he'll imitate the way you eat—including using the salt shaker and nibbling on salty snacks and processed foods. For his sake as well as your own, cut your salt use to a minimum.

What if you're concerned that your baby is *already* overweight? Get your pediatrician's advice before making any dietary adjustments. During these months of rapid growth, your infant needs the proper balance of fat, carbohydrates, and protein. So it's not wise to switch a baby this age to skim milk, for example, or to other low-fat substitutes for breastmilk or formula. A better solution might be to slightly reduce the portions of the things he eats. This way, he'll continue to receive the variety of nutrients he needs.

As soon as you start giving your baby solid foods, his stools will become more solid and variable in color. Due to the added sugars and fats, they'll have a much stronger odor, too.

Peas and other green vegetables may turn the stool deep green; beets may make it red. (Beets sometimes make urine red as well.) If his meals aren't strained, his stools may contain undigested particles of food, especially hulls of peas or corn, and the skin of tomatoes or other vegetables. All of this is perfectly normal. His digestive system is still immature and needs time before it can fully process these new foods. If the stools are extremely loose, watery, or full of mucus, however, it may mean the digestive tract is irritated. In this case, consult your pediatrician to determine if your infant has a digestive problem.

Dietary Supplements

In formula-fed infants, the formula supplies all the vitamins that are necessary, and thus no vitamin supplements are required. African-American breastfed babies should continue receiving supplemental vitamin D, because they are more resistant to the vitamin-D-generating process caused by sunlight.

For the first four months your breastfed baby needed no additional iron. The iron she had in her body at birth was enough to see her through her initial growth. But now the reserves will be running low and her need for iron will increase as her growth speeds up. Fortunately, once you start her on solid foods, she'll receive iron from iron-fortified baby cereals, green vegetables, and meat. Four level tablespoons of fortified cereal, diluted with milk or formula, provides 7 mg of iron. (See also *Supplementation for Breastfed and Bottle-Fed Infants,* page 134.)

Weaning from Breast to Bottle

Many nursing mothers begin to wean their babies between four and seven months so they can return to work or resume other activities away from the child. But even if you don't plan to stop breastfeeding until much later, you still may want to start giving your baby an occasional bottle of either breastmilk or formula so you can spend more than a few hours away from him at a stretch, and so that his father, grandparents, or siblings have a chance to feed him every now and then. Bottle-feeding also gives you more flexibility when you take him out or travel.

In any event, you should continue to breastfeed or provide infant formula until your baby is one year old. After that, whole cow's milk can be given.

Don't expect smooth sailing if your baby has never been given a bottle before. He probably will object to it the first few times, especially if his mother tries to give it to him. By this age he associates his mother with nursing, so it's understandable if he's confused and annoyed when there's a sudden change in the routine. Things may go more smoothly if his father or another family member feeds him—and Mom stays out of the room. After he's gotten used to the idea, then she can take over, but he should get lots of cuddling, stroking, and encouragement to make up for the lost skin-to-skin contact.

Once your baby has learned to take an occasional bottle, it should be relatively easy to wean him from the breast. The time needed to wean him, however, will vary, depending on the emotional and physical needs of both child and mother. If your baby adapts well to change and you're ready for the transition, you can make a total switch in one or two weeks. For the first two days, substitute one bottle of formula for one breastfeeding per day. (Don't express milk during this time.) On the third day, use a bottle for two feedings. By the fifth day, you can jump to three or four bottle-feedings.

Once you've stopped breastfeeding entirely, breastmilk production will cease very quickly. In the meantime, if your breasts should become engorged, you may need to express milk for the first two or three days to relieve the discomfort. Mild fluid restriction or wearing a breast binder can also help. Within a week the discomfort should subside.

Many women prefer to wean more slowly, even when their babies cooperate fully. Breastfeeding provides a closeness between mother and baby that's hard to duplicate any other way, and, understandably, you may be reluctant to give up such intimacy. In this case you can continue to offer a combination of the breast and the bottle for up to one year, or slightly beyond. Don't force him to keep breastfeeding if he resists, however. Many babies lose interest between nine and twelve months, or when they learn to drink from a cup. It's important for you to remember that this is not a personal rejection, but a sign of your child's growing independence.

However, breastfeeding can continue as part of the routine feeding beyond the first year of life.

Sleeping

Most babies this age still need at least two naps a day, of from one to three hours each, one in the morning and the other in the afternoon. In general it's best to let your baby sleep as long as she wants, unless she has trouble falling asleep at her normal nightly bedtime. If this becomes a problem, wake her up earlier from her afternoon nap.

By four months your baby should be sleeping through at least one nighttime feeding and perhaps through the entire night. "Through the night" could mean from 7:00 P.M. to 7:00 A.M., or from 10:00 P.M. to 6:00 A.M., depending on your baby's own internal clock; but at this age she should be able to go at least eight hours without being fed.

Because your baby is more alert and active now, she may have trouble winding down at the end of the day. A consistent bedtime routine will help. Experiment to see what works best, taking into consideration both the activities in the rest of the household and your baby's temperament. A warm bath, a massage, rocking, a story or lullaby, soft music, and a breast- or bottle-feeding will all help relax her and put her in a bedtime mood. Eventually, she'll associate these activities with going to sleep, and that will help relax and soothe her.

Instead of letting your baby fall asleep during this ritual, settle her in her crib while she's still awake so she learns to fall asleep on her own. Gently put her head down, whisper your good-night, and leave the room. If she cries, don't rush back in. She may calm down after a few minutes and fall asleep on her own.

But what if she's still crying lustily at the end of five minutes? Go in and comfort her for about a minute, without picking her up, and then leave. Let her know that you love her and are available if she needs you, but don't stay in the room. If she continues to cry, wait a little longer than five minutes before going back in again to repeat the sequence. Be consistent and firm. As hard as this is on you, it's harder on your baby if she senses you are wavering. The real reward will come when she awakens in the middle of the night and goes back to sleep without your help.

Many babies cry some every night, leading parents to

wonder if the prolonged crying can hurt her psychologically. If you actually time your baby's crying, you may find that it doesn't last that long—it just *seems* forever. If parents are steadfast, most babies will cry less each night until they finally go to sleep with only a token protest. But even if your infant cries for a long time (twenty to thirty minutes), there is no evidence that she'll be hurt by it.

Crying that goes on for more than twenty minutes may need to be checked to see if there is not some problem (such as an open diaper pin), but such interruptions should be short. Do not stop to play. The important thing is for you to keep your perfectly natural feelings of frustration and, perhaps, anger in check, so you can be firm in a calm and loving way when your baby resists sleep.

When your child awakens in the middle of the night, give her a few minutes to fall back to sleep before you go to her. If she continues to cry, talk to her and comfort her, but don't bring her to your bed. Also, unless you have reason to believe she's really hungry (for example, if she fell asleep earlier than usual and missed a feeding), don't feed her. As tempting as it may be to calm her down with food or cuddling in your bed, she'll soon come to expect these responses when she wakes up at night, and she won't go back to sleep without them.

When a baby wakes up more than once a night, there may be something disturbing her sleep. If the child is still sleeping in your room by six months, it's time to move her out; she may be waking up because she hears you or senses your presence when you're nearby. If she's still in a bassinet, she's probably feeling cramped; by this age she needs room to stretch and move in her sleep, and she should be in a full-size crib with bumpers to cushion her when she rolls to the sides. Still another problem may be a room that's too dark. She needs enough light to reassure herself that she's in familiar surroundings, and a simple night-light can solve this problem.

Teething

Teething usually starts during these months. The two bottom front teeth (central incisors) usually appear first, followed about four to eight weeks later by the four upper teeth (central and lateral incisors), and then about one month later by the two lower incisors. The first molars come in next, followed by the canine or eye teeth.

If your child doesn't show any teeth until much later, don't worry. This may be determined by heredity, and it doesn't mean that anything is wrong.

Teething *occasionally* may cause mild irritability, crying, low-grade temperature (but not over 100 degrees), excessive drooling, and a desire to chew on something hard. More often, the gums around the new teeth will swell and be tender. To ease your baby's discomfort, try gently rubbing or massaging the gums with one of your fingers. Teething rings are helpful, too, but they should be made of firm rubber (the teethers that you freeze tend to get too hard, and thus can cause more harm than good). Pain relievers and medications that you rub on the gums are not necessary or useful, either, since they wash out of the baby's mouth within minutes. If your child seems particularly miserable or has a fever higher than 100 degrees, it's probably not because he's teething, and you should consult your pediatrician.

How should you clean the new teeth? Simply brush them with a soft child's toothbrush, or wipe them with gauze at the end of the day. To prevent cavities, never let your baby fall asleep with a bottle, either at nap time or at night. By avoiding this situation, you'll keep milk from pooling around the teeth and creating a breeding ground for decay.

Swings and Playpens

Many parents find that mechanical swings, especially those with cradle attachments, can calm a crying baby when nothing else seems to work. If you use one of these devices, don't put your baby in the seat of the swing until she can sit on her own (usually between seven and nine months). Use only swings that stand firmly on the floor, not the ones that hang suspended from door frames. Also, don't use a swing more than half an hour, twice a day; while it may quiet your baby, it is no substitute for your attention.

Once your baby starts to move about, you may need to start using a playpen (also called a play yard). But even before she crawls or walks, a playpen offers a protected place where she can lie or sit outdoors as well as in rooms where you have no crib or bassinet. (See *Playpens,* page 324, for specific recommendations.) Remember to never leave the side of the playpen down. If the baby gets used to it now, she may be more willing to stay in it as she gets older. Don't count on this, though; while some babies don't mind being enclosed, others resist it vigorously.

Stimulating Infant Brain Growth: Age Four Months Through Seven Months

- Provide a stimulating, safe environment where your baby can begin to explore and roam freely.
- Give consistent warm, physical contact—hugging, skin-to-skin, body-to-body contact—to establish your infant's sense of security and well-being.
- Be attentive to your baby's rhythms and moods. Respond to her when she is upset as well as when she is happy.
- Talk or sing to your baby during dressing, bathing, feeding, playing, walking, and driving. Check with your pediatrician if your baby doesn't seem to hear sounds or doesn't imitate your words.
- Engage your child in face-to-face talk. Mimic her sounds to show interest.
- Read books to your baby every day.
- If you speak a foreign language, use it at home.
- Engage in rhythmic movement with your child, such as dancing together with music.
- Avoid subjecting your baby to stressful or traumatic experiences, physical or psychological.
- Introduce your child to other children and parents; this is a very special period for infants.
- Encourage your child to reach for toys.
- Make sure other people who provide care and supervision for your baby understand the importance of forming a loving and comforting relationship with your child.

- Encourage your child to begin to sleep for extended periods at night; if you need advice about this important step in your infant's development, ask your pediatrician.
- Spend time on the floor playing with your child every day.
- Choose quality child care that is affectionate, responsive, educational, and safe. Visit your child-care provider frequently and share your ideas about positive caregiving.

BEHAVIOR

Discipline

As your baby becomes more mobile and inquisitive, he'll naturally become more assertive as well. This is wonderful for his self-esteem, and should be encouraged as much as possible. When he wants to do something that's dangerous or disrupts the rest of the family, however, you'll need to take charge.

For the first six months or so, the best way to deal with such conflicts is to distract him with an alternative toy or activity. Standard discipline won't work until his memory span increases around the end of his seventh month. Only then can you use a variety of techniques to discourage undesired behavior.

When you finally begin to discipline your child, it should never be harsh. Often, the most successful approach is simply to reward desired behavior and withhold rewards when he does not behave as desired. For example, if he cries for no apparent reason, make sure there's nothing wrong physically; then when he stops, reward him with extra attention, kind words, and hugs. If he starts up again, wait a little longer before turning your attention to him, and use a firm tone of voice as you talk to him. This time, don't reward him with extra attention or hugs.

The main goal of discipline is to teach a child limits, so try to help him understand exactly what he's doing wrong when he breaks a rule. If you discover him doing something that's not allowed, like pulling your hair, let him know that it's wrong by calmly saying "no," stopping him, and redirecting his attention to an acceptable activity.

If your child is touching or trying to put something in his mouth that he shouldn't, gently pull his hand away as you tell him this particular object is off limits. But since you do want to encourage him to touch *other* things, avoid saying "Don't touch." More pointed phrases, like "Don't eat the flowers" or "No eating leaves," will convey the message without confusing him.

Because it's still relatively easy to modify his behavior at this age, this is a good time to establish your authority. Be careful not to overreact, however. He's still not old enough to misbehave intentionally, and won't understand if you punish him or raise your voice. So instead, remain calm, firm, consistent, and loving in your approach. If he learns now that you have the final word, it may make life much more comfortable for both of you later on, when he naturally becomes more headstrong.

Siblings

If your baby has a big brother or sister, you may start to see increasing signs of rivalry at about this time. Earlier, the baby was more dependent, slept a lot, and didn't require your constant attention. But now that she's becoming more demanding, you'll need to ration your time and energy so you have enough for each child individually as well as all of them together. This is even more important—and more difficult—if you go back to work.

One way to give some extra attention to your older child is to set aside special "big brother" or "big sister" chores that don't involve the baby. This allows you to spend some time together and get the housework done. Be sure to show the child how much you appreciate this help.

You might also help sibling relations by including the older child in activities with the baby. If the two of you sing a song or read a story, the baby will enjoy listening. The older child can also help take care of the baby to some extent, assisting you at bathtime or changing time. But unless the child is at least ten, don't leave him alone with the baby, even if he's trying to be helpful. A youngster this age can easily drop or injure an infant without realizing what he's doing.

HEALTH WATCH

Don't be surprised if your baby catches his first cold or ear infection soon after his four-month birthday. Now that he can actively reach for objects, he'll come into physical contact with many more things and people, so he'll be much more likely to contract contagious diseases.

The first line of defense is to keep your baby away from anyone you know is sick. Be especially careful of infectious diseases like chickenpox or measles (see *Chickenpox*, page 562; *Measles*, pages 567, 574). If someone in your play group has caught one of these diseases, keep your infant out of the group until you're sure no one else is infected.

No matter how you try to protect your baby, of course, there will be times when he gets sick. This is an inevitable part of growing up, and will happen more frequently as he has more direct contact with other children. It's not always easy to tell when a baby is ill; but there are some signs that will tip you off. Does he look pale or have dark circles under his eyes? Is he acting less energetic or more irritable than usual? If he has an infectious disease, he'll probably have a fever (see Chapter 20, "Fever") and he may be losing weight due to loss of appetite, diarrhea, or vomiting. Some difficult-to-detect infections of the kidneys or lungs also can prevent weight gain in babies. At this age, weight loss could also mean that the baby has some digestive problem such as an allergy to wheat or milk protein (see *Milk Allergy*, page 436) or lacks the digestive enzymes needed to digest certain solid foods. If you suspect that your baby may be ill but can't identify the exact problem, or you have any concerns about what is happening, call your pediatrician and describe the symptoms that worry you.

The most common illnesses that occur at this age include the following (all are described in Part II of this book).

Bronchiolitis	Diarrhea	Viral Infections
Colds (URI's)	Earache/Ear Infection	Vomiting
Conjunctivitis	Fever	
Croup	Pneumonia	

Your Baby and Antibiotics

Antibiotics are among the most powerful and important medicines known. When used properly they can save lives, but when used improperly, antibiotics can actually harm your infant.

Two main types of germs—viruses and bacteria—cause most infections. Viruses cause all colds and most coughs and sore throats. Common viral infections are never cured by antibiotics. Your baby recovers from these common viral infections when the illness has run its course. *Antibiotics should not be used to treat viral infections.*

Antibiotics can be used to treat bacterial infections, but some strains of bacteria have become resistant to certain antibiotics. If your child is infected with resistant bacteria, she might need to be treated in the hospital, with more powerful medicines given by vein (IV). A few new strains of bacteria are already untreatable. To protect your child from antibiotic-resistant bacteria, use antibiotics only when your pediatrician has determined that they might be effective, since repeated or improper use of antibiotics contribute to the increase in resistant bacteria.

When are antibiotics needed? When are they not needed?

These complicated questions are best answered by your pediatrician, as the answer depends on the specific diagnosis. If you think your child might need treatment, contact your pediatrician.

- *Ear infections:* Most types need antibiotics, but some do not.
- *Sinus infections:* Antibiotics are needed for some long-lasting or severe cases, but just because your infant's mucus is yellow or green does not mean that your baby has a bacterial infection. It is normal for the mucus to get thick and change color during a viral cold.

- *Bronchitis:* Infants rarely need antibiotics for bronchitis.
- *Sore throat:* Most cases are caused by viruses. Only strep throat, which must be diagnosed by a laboratory test, requires antibiotics.
- *Colds:* Colds are caused by viruses and may sometimes last for two weeks or more. Antibiotics have no effect on colds. Your pediatrician may have suggestions for comfort measures while the cold runs its course.

Viral infections may sometimes lead to bacterial infections. But treating viral infections with antibiotics to prevent bacterial infections does not work, and may lead to infection with resistant bacteria. Keep your pediatrician informed if the illness gets worse or lasts a long time, so that proper treatment can be given as needed.

If an antibiotic is prescribed, make sure your baby takes the entire course. Never save antibiotics for later use.

Immunization Alert

At four months your baby should receive:

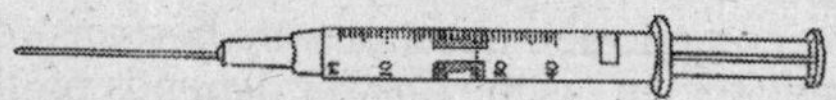

- Second DTaP or DTP vaccine
- Second polio vaccine
- Second Hib vaccine

And at six months:

- Third DTaP or DTP vaccine
- Third polio vaccine (generally given at twelve to eighteen months, but can be given at six to eighteen months if using the oral polio vaccine only)
- Third Hib vaccine may be needed depending upon vaccine type given for doses one and two.

- Third Hepatitis B vaccine can be given between six and eighteen months.

Safety Check

Car Seats

- Buckle the baby into an approved, properly installed car seat before you start the car. Keep the seat rear-facing until your infant is 20 pounds and one year of age. The back seat is the safest place for all children to ride. Never place a rear-facing car seat in the front seat of a car with a passenger-side air bag.

Drowning

- Never leave a baby alone in a bath or near a pool of water, no matter how shallow it is. Infants can drown in just a few inches of water.

Falls

- Never leave the baby unattended in high places, such as on a tabletop or in a crib with the sides down. If she does fall and seems to be acting abnormally in any way, call the pediatrician immediately.

Burns

- Never smoke, eat, drink, or carry anything hot while holding a baby.
- Prevent scalding by reducing the water heater setting to 120 degrees or lower.

Choking

- Never give a baby any food or small object that could cause choking. All foods should be mashed, ground, or soft enough to swallow without chewing.

Age Eight Months Through Twelve Months

During these months, your baby is becoming increasingly mobile, a development that will thrill and challenge both of you. Being able to move from place to place gives your baby a delicious sense of power and control—her first real taste of physical independence. And while this is quite exhilarating for her, it's also frightening, since it comes at the time when she's most likely to be upset by separation from you. So, as eager as she is to move out on her own and explore the farthest reaches of her domain, she may wail if she wanders out of your sight or you move too far from her.

From your point of view, your baby's mobility is a source of considerable concern as well as great pride.

Crawling and walking are signals that she's developing right on target, but these achievements also mean that you'll have your hands full keeping her safe. If you haven't already fully child-proofed your home, do it now. (Read Chapter 10, on safety.) At this age your baby has no concept of danger and only a limited memory for your warnings. So the only way to protect her from the hundreds of hazards in your home is to secure cupboards and drawers, place dangerous and precious objects out of her reach, and make perilous rooms like the bathroom inaccessible unless she's supervised.

By child-proofing your home, you'll also give your baby a greater sense of freedom. After all, fewer areas will be off limits, and thus you can let her make her own discoveries without your intervention or assistance. These personal accomplishments will promote her emerging self-esteem; you might even think of ways of facilitating them, for example:

1. Fill a low kitchen cupboard with safe objects and let your baby discover it herself.
2. Place some kiddie gardening tools in a corner of the garden for her to find when she's in the yard with you.
3. Equip your home with cushions of assorted shapes and sizes and let her experiment with the different ways she can move over and around them.

Knowing when to guide a baby and when to let her do things for herself is part of the art of parenting. At this age your baby is extremely expressive and will give you the cues you need to decide when to intervene. When she's acting frustrated rather than challenged, for instance, don't let her struggle alone. If she's crying because her ball is wedged under the sofa out of her reach, or she's climbed up the stairs and can't get down, she needs your help. At other times, however, it's important to let her solve her own problems. Don't let your own impatience cause you to intervene any more than absolutely necessary. You may be tempted to feed your nine-month-old, for instance, because it's faster and less messy than letting her feed herself. However, that also deprives her of a chance to learn a valuable new skill. The more opportunities you can give her to discover, test, and strengthen her new capabilities, the more confident and adventuresome she'll be.

Growth and Development

Physical Appearance and Growth

Your baby will continue to grow rapidly during these months. The typical eight-month-old boy weighs between 14½ and 17½ pounds (6½ to 8½ kg). Girls tend to weigh half a pound less. By his first birthday, the average child has tripled his birthweight and is 28 to 32 inches (71 to 81 cm) tall. Head growth between eight and twelve months slows down a bit from the first six months. Typical head size at eight months is 17½ inches in circumference (45 cm); by one year it's 18 inches (47 cm). Each baby grows at his own rate, however, so you should check your baby's height and weight curves on the growth chart on page 150–53 to make sure he's following the pattern established in his first eight months.

When your baby first stands, you may be surprised by his posture. His belly will protrude, his rear end will stick out, and his back will have a forward sway to it. It may look unusual, but this stance is perfectly normal from the time he starts to stand until he develops a confident sense of balance sometime in the second year.

Your baby's feet also may look a little odd to you. When he lies on his back, his toes may turn inward so that he appears pigeon-toed. This common condition usually disappears by eighteen months. If it persists, your pediatrician may show you some foot or leg exercises to do with your baby. If the

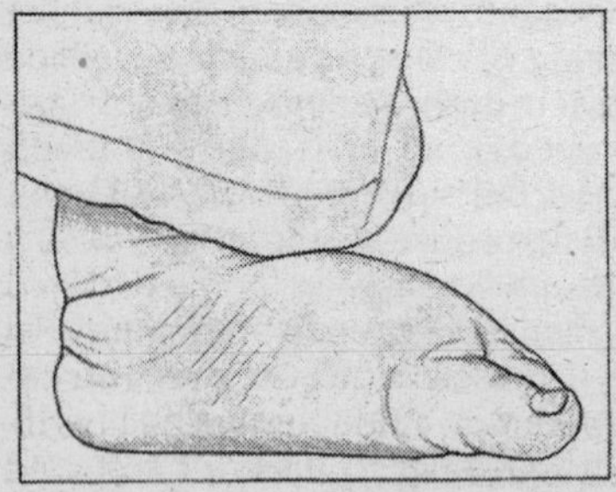

At this age your child's feet will seem flat because the arch is hidden by a pad of fat. But in two to three years this fat will disappear and his arch will be evident.

problem is severe, your pediatrician may recommend casts and refer you to a pediatric orthopedist. (See *Pigeon Toes,* page 556.)

When your baby takes his first teetering steps, you may notice quite a different appearance—his feet may turn *out*ward. This occurs because the ligaments of his hips are still so loose that his legs naturally rotate outward. During the first six months of his second year, the ligaments will tighten and his feet should then point nearly straight.

At this age your baby's feet will seem flat because the arch is hidden by a pad of fat. But in two to three years this fat will disappear and his arch will be evident.

Movement

At eight months your baby probably will be sitting without support. Though she may topple over from time to time, she'll usually catch herself with her arms. As the muscles in her trunk grow stronger she'll also start leaning over to pick up toys. Eventually she'll figure out how to roll down onto her stomach and get back up to a sitting position.

When she's lying on a flat surface, your baby is now in constant motion. When on her stomach, she'll arch her neck so she can look around, and when on her back she'll grab her feet (or anything else nearby) and pull them to her mouth. But she won't be content to stay on her back for long. She can turn over at will now, and flip without a moment's notice. This can be especially dangerous during diaper changes, so you may want to retire her changing table, using instead the floor or a bed from which she's less likely to fall. Never leave her alone for an instant at any time.

All this activity strengthens muscles for crawling, a skill that usually is mastered between seven and ten months. For a while she may simply rock on her hands and knees. Since her arm muscles are better developed than her legs, she may even push herself backward instead of forward. But with time and practice she'll discover that, by digging with her knees and pushing off, she can propel herself forward across the room toward the target of her choice.

A few babies never do crawl. Instead, they use alternative methods such as scooting on their bottoms or slithering on their stomachs. As long as your baby is learning to coordinate each side of her body and is using each arm and leg equally, there's no cause for concern. The important thing is that she's able to explore her surroundings on her own and is strengthening her body in preparation for walking. If you feel your baby is not moving normally, discuss your concern with the pediatrician.

How can you encourage your baby to crawl? Try presenting her with intriguing objects placed just beyond her reach. As she becomes more agile, create miniature obstacle courses using pillows, boxes, and sofa cushions for her to crawl over and between. Join in the game by hiding behind one of the obstacles and surprising her with a "peekaboo!" Don't ever leave your baby unsupervised among these props, though. If she falls between pillows or under a box, she might not be able to pull herself out. This is bound to frighten her, and she could even smother.

Stairs are another ready-made—but potentially dangerous—obstacle course. While your baby needs to learn how to go up and down stairs, you should not allow her to play on them alone during this time. If you have a staircase in your home she'll probably head straight for it every chance she gets, so place sturdy gates at both the top and the bottom to close off her access. The gates should have small openings and a solid piece across the top; old-fashioned accordion gates can strangle children who get their heads caught in the openings. (See illustration in Chapter 10, pages 320–21.)

As a substitute for real stairs, let your baby practice climbing up and down steps constructed of heavy-duty foam

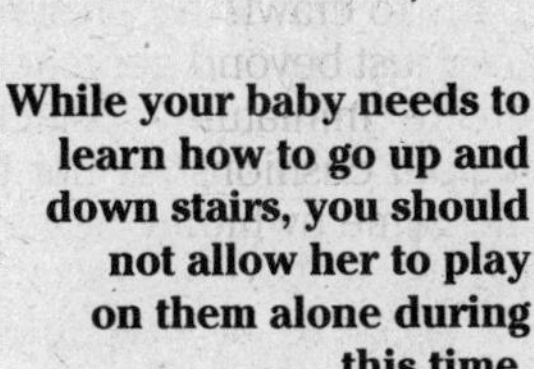

While your baby needs to learn how to go up and down stairs, you should not allow her to play on them alone during this time.

blocks or sturdy cardboard cartons covered in fabric. At about a year of age, when your baby has become a competent crawler, teach her to go down real stairs backward. She may take a few tumbles before she understands the logic of going feet first instead of head first, so practice on carpeted steps and let her climb only the first few. If your home doesn't have carpeted stairs, let her perfect this skill when you visit a home that does.

Although crawling makes a huge difference in how your baby sees the world and what she can do in it, don't expect her to be content with that for long. She'll see everyone else around her walking, and that's what she'll want to do, too. In preparation for this big step, she'll pull herself to a standing position every chance she gets—although when she first starts, she may not know how to get down. If she cries for your help, physically show her how to bend her knees so she can lower herself to the floor without falling. Teaching her this skill will save you many extra trips to her room at night when she's standing in her crib and crying because she doesn't know how to sit down.

Once your baby feels secure standing, she'll try some tentative steps while holding on to a support. For instance, when your hands aren't available she'll "cruise" alongside furniture. Just make sure that whatever she uses for support has no sharp edges and is properly weighted or securely attached to the floor so it won't fall on her.

Soon he'll manage to keep himself up and moving until you catch him several steps later.

Movement Milestones By the End of This Period

- Gets to sitting position without assistance
- Crawls forward on belly
- Assumes hands-and-knees position
- Creeps on hands and knees
- Gets from sitting to crawling or prone (lying on stomach) position
- Pulls self up to stand

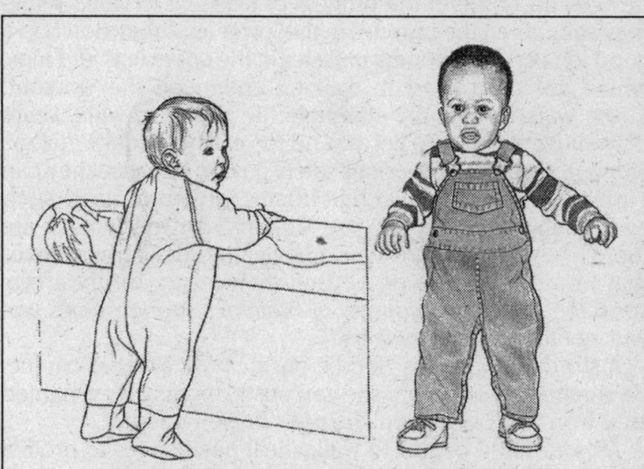

- Walks holding on to furniture
- Stands momentarily without support
- May walk two or three steps without support

As her balance improves she may occasionally let go, only to grab for support when she feels herself totter. The first time she continues forth on her own, her steps will be shaky. At first she may take only one step before dropping, either in surprise or relief. Soon, however, she'll manage to keep herself up and moving until you catch her several steps later. As miraculous as it may seem, most children advance from these first steps to quite confident walking in a matter of days.

Although both of you will feel excited over this dramatic development, you'll also find yourself unnerved at times, especially when she stumbles and falls. But even if you take pains to provide a safe and soft environment, it's almost impossible to avoid bumps and bruises. Just be matter-of-fact about these accidents. Offer a quick hug or a reassuring word and send your little one on her way again. She won't be unduly upset by these falls if you're not.

At this stage, or even earlier, many parents start using a baby walker. Contrary to what the name suggests, these devices do not help the process of learning to walk. While they strengthen the muscles in the lower legs, they don't do a good job of strengthening muscles in the *upper* legs and hips, which are used most in walking and need the workout. These walkers actually eliminate the desire to walk, since they allow the baby to get around too easily. To make matters worse, they present a serious safety hazard because they can easily tip over when the child bumps into an obstacle such as a small toy or a throw rug. Children in walkers also are more likely to fall down stairs and get into dangerous places that would otherwise be beyond their reach. *For these reasons, the American Academy of Pediatrics strongly urges parents not to use baby walkers.*

A sturdy wagon or a "kiddie push car" is a better choice. Be sure the toy has a bar she can push, and that it's weighted so it won't tip over when she pulls herself up on it.

As your child begins to walk she'll need shoes to protect her feet. Wedges, inserts, high backs, reinforced heels, special arches, and other features designed to shape and support the feet make shoes more expensive but have no proven benefit for the average child. So look instead for comfortable shoes with nonskid soles that will help your baby avoid slipping on smooth floors; sneakers are fine. Her feet will grow rapidly during these months, and her shoes will have to keep pace. Her first pair of shoes probably will last two to three months, but you should check the fit of her shoes as often as monthly during this formative period.

Many babies' first steps are taken around their first birthday, though it's perfectly normal for children to start walking a little earlier or later. At first your baby will walk with feet wide apart to improve her shaky sense of balance. During those initial days and weeks, she may accidentally get going too fast and fall when she tries to stop. As she becomes more confident she'll learn how to stop and change directions. Before long she'll be able to squat to pick something up and then stand again. When she reaches this level of accomplishment she'll get enormous pleasure from push-pull toys—the noisier the better.

Hand and Finger Skills

Your baby's mastery of crawling, standing, and walking are bound to be his most dramatic accomplishments during these months, but don't overlook all the wonderful things he's learning to do with his hands. At the beginning of this period he'll still clumsily "rake" things toward himself, but by the end he'll grasp accurately with his thumb and first or second finger. You'll find him practicing this pincer movement on any small object, from dust balls to cereal, and he may even try to snap his fingers if you show him how.

Milestones in Hand and Finger Skills By the End of This Period

- Uses pincer grasp
- Bangs two cubes together
- Puts objects into container
- Takes objects out of container
- Lets objects go voluntarily
- Pokes with index finger
- Tries to imitate scribbling

As your baby learns to open his fingers at will, he'll delight in dropping and throwing things. If you leave small toys on the tray of his high chair or in his playpen, he'll fling them down and then call loudly for someone to retrieve them so he can do it again. If he throws hard objects such as blocks, he might do some damage and probably will increase the noise level in your household considerably. Your life will be a little calmer if you redirect him toward softer objects such as balls of various sizes, colors, and textures. (Include some with beads or chimes inside so they make a sound as they roll.) One activity that not only is fun but allows you to observe your baby's developing skills is to sit on the floor and roll a large ball toward him. At first he'll slap randomly at it, but eventually he'll learn to swat it so it rolls back in your direction.

With his improved coordination, your baby can now investigate the objects he encounters more thoroughly. He'll pick them up, shake them, bang them, and pass them from hand to hand. He'll be particularly intrigued by toys with moving parts—wheels that spin, levers that can be moved, hinges that open and close. Holes also are fascinating because he can poke his fingers in them and, when he becomes a little more skilled, drop things through them.

Blocks are another favorite toy at this age. In fact, nothing motivates a baby to crawl quite as much as a tower waiting to be toppled. Toward the end of this period your child may even start to build towers of his own by stacking one block on top of another.

Language Development

Toward the end of the first year, your baby will begin to communicate what she wants by pointing, crawling, or gesturing toward her target. She'll also imitate many of the gestures she sees adults make as they talk. This nonverbal communication is only a temporary measure, however, while she learns how to phrase her messages in words.

Do you notice the coos, gurgles, and screeches of earlier months now giving way to recognizable syllables, like "ba," "da," "ga," and "ma"? Your child may even stumble on words such as "mama" and "bye-bye" quite accidentally, and when you get excited she'll realize she's said something meaningful. Before long she'll start using "mama" to summon you or attract your attention. At this age, she may also say "mama" throughout the day just to practice saying the word. Ultimately, however, she'll use words only when she wants to communicate their meanings.

Even though you've been talking to your baby from birth, she now understands more language, and thus your conversations will take on new significance. Before she can say many, if any, words, she'll probably be comprehending more than you suspect. For example, watch how she responds when you mention a favorite toy across the room. If she looks toward it, she's telling you she understands. To help her increase her understanding, just keep talking to her as much as possible. Tell her what's happening around her, particularly as you bathe, change, and feed her. Make your language simple and specific: "I'm drying you with the big blue towel. How soft it feels!" Verbally label familiar toys and objects for her, and try to be as consistent as possible—that is, if you call the family pet a cat today, don't call it a kitty tomorrow.

Language Milestones By the End of This Period

- Pays increasing attention to speech
- Responds to simple verbal requests
- Responds to "no"
- Uses simple gestures, such as shaking head for "no"
- Babbles with inflection
- Says "dada" and "mama"
- Uses exclamations, such as "Oh-oh!"
- Tries to imitate words

Picture books can enhance this entire process, too, by reinforcing her budding understanding that everything has a name. Choose books with large board, cloth, or vinyl pages that she can turn herself. Also look for simple but colorful illustrations of things your baby will recognize.

Whether you're reading or talking to her, give her plenty of opportunities to join in. Ask questions and wait for a response. Or let her take the lead. If she says "Gaagaagaa," repeat it back and see what she does. Yes, these exchanges may seem meaningless, but they tell your baby that communication is two-way and that she's a welcome participant. Paying attention to what she says also will help you identify the words she understands and make it more likely that you'll recognize her first spoken words.

These first words, incidentally, often aren't proper English. For your baby a "word" is any sound that consistently refers to the same person, object, or event. So if she says "mog" every time she wants milk, then "mog" should be treated with all the respect of a legitimate word. When you speak back to her, however, use "milk," and eventually she'll make the correction herself.

There's a tremendous variance in the age at which babies begin to say recognizable words. Some have a vocabulary of two to three words by their first birthday. More likely, your baby's speech at twelve months will consist of a sort of gibberish that has the tones and variations of intelligible speech. As long as she's experimenting with sounds that vary in intensity, pitch, and quality, she's getting ready to talk. The more you respond to her as though she were speaking, the more you'll stimulate her urge to communicate.

Cognitive Development

An eight-month-old is curious about everything, but he also has a very short attention span and will move rapidly from one activity to the next. Two to three minutes is the most he'll spend with a single toy, and then he'll turn to something new. By twelve months he may be willing to sit for as long as fifteen minutes with a particularly interesting plaything, but most of the time he'll still be a body in motion, and you shouldn't expect him to be any different.

Ironically, although toy stores are brimming with one expensive plaything after another, the toys that fascinate babies most at this age are ordinary household objects like wooden spoons, egg cartons, and plastic containers of all shapes and sizes. Your baby will be especially interested in things that

Variations of Peekaboo

The possible variations of peekaboo are almost endless. As your baby becomes more mobile and alert, create games that let her take the lead. Here are some suggestions.

1. Drape a soft cloth over her head and ask, "Where's the baby?" Once she understands the game she'll pull the cloth away and pop up grinning.

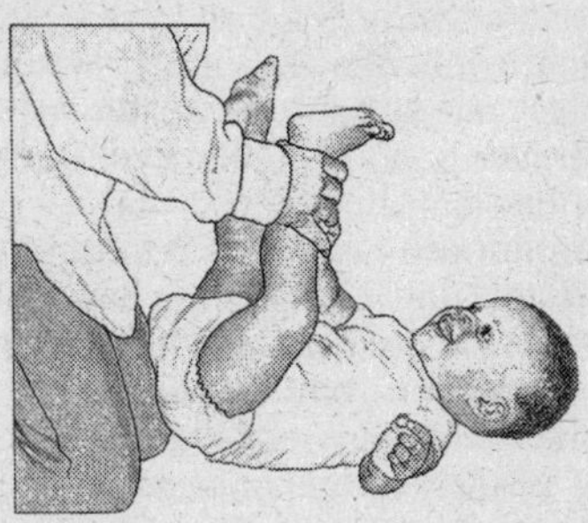

2. With baby on her back facing toward you, lift both her legs together—"Up, up, up"—until they conceal your face from her. Then open them wide—"Peekaboo!" As she gets the idea, she'll move her legs herself. (This is a great game at diaper-changing time.)

3. Hide yourself behind a door or a piece of furniture, leaving a foot or arm in her view as a clue. She'll be delighted to come find you!

4. Take turns with your baby "hiding" your head under a large towel and letting her pull the towel off and then putting it over her head and pulling it off.

differ just a bit from what he already knows, so if he's bored with the oatmeal box he's been playing with, you can renew his interest by putting a ball inside or turning it into a pull toy by tying a string to it. These small changes will help him learn to detect small differences between the familiar and the unfamiliar. Also, when you choose playthings, remember that objects too much like what he's seen before will be given a quick once-over and dismissed, while things that are too foreign may be confusing or frightening. Look instead for objects and toys that gradually help him expand his horizons.

Often your baby won't need your help to discover objects that fall into this middle ground of newness. In fact, as soon as he can crawl he'll be off in search of new things to conquer. He'll rummage through your drawers, empty out wastebaskets, ransack kitchen cabinets, and conduct elaborate experiments on everything he finds. (Make sure there's nothing that can hurt him in those containers, and keep an eye on him whenever he's into these things.) He'll never tire of dropping, rolling, throwing, submerging, or waving objects to find out how they behave. This may look like random play to you, but it's your baby's way of finding out how the world works. Like any good scientist, he's observing the properties of objects, and from his observations he'll develop ideas about shapes (some things roll and others don't), textures (things can be scratchy, soft, or smooth), and sizes (some things fit inside each other). He'll even begin to understand that some things are edible and others aren't, though he'll still put everything into his mouth just to be sure. (Again, make sure there's nothing dangerous lying around that he can put in his mouth.)

His continuing observations during these months also will help him understand that objects continue to exist even when they're out of his sight. This concept is called "object permanence." At eight months, when you hide a toy under a scarf, he'll pick up the scarf and search for the toy underneath—a response that wouldn't have occurred three months earlier. Try hiding the toy under the scarf and then removing it when he's not looking, however, and your eight-month-old will be puzzled. By ten months he'll be so certain that the toy still exists that he'll continue looking for

Cognitive Milestones By the End of This Period

- Explores objects in many different ways (shaking, banging, throwing, dropping)
- Finds hidden objects easily

- Looks at correct picture when the image is named
- Imitates gestures
- Begins to use objects correctly (drinking from cup, brushing hair, dialing phone, listening to receiver)

it. To help your baby learn object permanence, play peekaboo with him. By switching from one variation of this game to another, you'll maintain his interest almost indefinitely.

As he approaches his first birthday your baby will become increasingly conscious that things not only have names but that they also have particular functions. You'll see this new awareness weave itself into his play as a very early form of fantasy. For example, instead of treating a toy telephone as an interesting object to be chewed, poked, and banged, he'll put the receiver to his ear just as he's seen you do. You can encourage important developmental activities like this by offering him suggestive props—a hairbrush, toothbrush, cup, or spoon—and by being an enthusiastic audience for his performances.

Emotional Development

During these four months your child may sometimes seem like two separate babies. First there's the one who's open, affectionate, and outgoing with you. But then there's another who's anxious, clinging, and easily frightened around unfamiliar people or objects. Some people may tell you that your baby is fearful or shy because you're "spoiling" her, but don't believe it. Her widely diverse behavior patterns aren't caused by you or your parenting style; they occur because she's now, for the first time, able to tell the difference between familiar and unfamiliar situations. If anything, the predictable anxieties of this period are evidence of her healthy relationship with you.

Anxiety around strangers is usually one of the first emo-

The predictable anxieties of this period are evidence of your child's healthy relationship with you.

tional milestones your baby will reach. You may think something is wrong when this baby of yours who, at the age of three months, interacted calmly with people she didn't know is now beginning to tense up when strangers come too close. This is normal for this age, and you need not worry. Even relatives and frequent babysitters with whom your baby was once comfortable may prompt her to hide or cry now, especially if they approach her hastily.

At about the same time, she'll become much more "clutchy" about leaving you. This is the start of separation anxiety. Just as she's starting to realize that each object is unique and permanent, she'll also discover that there's only one of you. When you're out of her sight she'll know you're *somewhere,* but not with her, and this will cause her great distress. She'll have so little sense of time that she won't know when—or even whether—you'll be coming back. Once she gets a little older, her memory of past experiences with you will comfort her when you're gone, and she'll be able to anticipate a reunion. But for now she's only aware of the present, so every time you leave her sight—even to go to the next room—she'll fuss and cry. When you leave her with someone else she may scream as though her heart will break. At bedtime she'll refuse to leave you to go to sleep, and then she may wake up searching for you in the middle of the night.

How long should you expect this separation anxiety to last? It usually peaks between ten and eighteen months, and then fades during the last half of the second year. In some ways this phase of your baby's emotional development will be especially tender for both of you, while in others it will be painful. After all, her desire to be with you is a sign of her attachment to her first and greatest love—namely you. The intensity of her feeling as she hurtles into your arms is irresistible, especially when you realize that no one—including your baby herself—will ever again think you are quite as perfect as she does at this age. On the other hand, you may feel suffocated by her constant clinging, while experiencing guilt whenever you leave her crying for you. Fortunately, this emotional roller coaster eventually will subside along with her separation anxiety. But in the meantime, try to downplay your leave-taking as much as possible. Here are some suggestions that may help.

Social/Emotional Milestones By the End of This Period

- Shy or anxious with strangers
- Cries when mother or father leaves
- Enjoys imitating people in his play
- Shows specific preferences for certain people and toys
- Tests parental responses to his actions during feedings. (What do you do when he refuses a food?)
- Tests parental responses to his behavior. (What do you do if he cries after you leave the room?)
- May be fearful in some situations
- Prefers mother and/or regular caregiver over all others
- Repeats sounds or gestures for attention
- Finger-feeds himself
- Extends arm or leg to help when being dressed

1. Your baby is more susceptible to separation anxiety when she's tired, hungry, or sick. If you know you're going to go out, schedule your departure so that it occurs after she's napped and eaten. And try to stay with her as much as possible when she's sick.
2. Don't make a fuss over your leaving. Instead, have the person staying with her create a distraction (a new toy, a visit to the mirror, a bath). Then say good-bye and slip away quickly.
3. Remember that her tears will subside within minutes of your departure. Her outbursts are for your benefit, to persuade you to stay. With you out of sight, she'll soon turn her attention to the person staying with her.

4. Help her learn to cope with separation through short practice sessions at home. Separation will be easier on her when *she* initiates it, so when she crawls to another room (one that's baby-proofed), don't follow her right away; wait for one or two minutes. When *you* have to go to another room for a few seconds, tell her where you're going and that you'll return. If she fusses, call to her instead of running back. Gradually she'll learn that nothing terrible happens when you're gone and, just as important, that you always come back when you say you will.
5. If you take your baby to a sitter's home or a child-care center, don't just drop her off and leave. Spend a few extra minutes playing with her in this new environment. When you do leave, reassure her that you'll be back later.

Acquainting Your Baby With a Sitter

Is your baby about to have a new baby-sitter for a few hours? Whenever possible, let your infant get to know this new person while you're there. Ideally, have the sitter spend time with him on several successive days before you leave them alone. If this isn't possible, allow yourself an extra hour or two for this get-acquainted period before you have to go out.

During this first meeting, the sitter and your baby should get to know each other very gradually, using the following steps.

1. Hold the baby on your lap while you and the sitter talk. Watch for clues that your child is at ease before you have the sitter make eye contact with him. Wait until the baby is looking at her or playing contentedly by himself.

2. Have the sitter talk to the baby while he stays on your lap. She should not reach toward the child or try to touch him yet.

3. Once the baby seems comfortable with the conversation, put him on the floor with a favorite toy, across from the sitter. Invite the sitter to slowly come closer and play with the toy. As the baby warms up to her, you can gradually move back.

4. See what happens when you leave the room. If your baby doesn't notice you're missing, the introduction has gone well.

This leisurely introduction can be used with anyone who hasn't seen the child within the past few days, including relatives and friends. Adults often overwhelm babies of this age by coming close and making funny noises or, worse yet, trying to take them from their mothers. You have to intervene when this occurs. Explain to these well-meaning people that your baby needs time to warm up to strangers and that he's more likely to respond well if they go slowly.

If your baby has a strong, healthy attachment to you, her separation anxiety probably will occur earlier than in other babies, and she'll pass through it more quickly. Instead of resenting her possessiveness during these months, maintain as much warmth and good humor as you can. Through your actions, you're showing her how to express and return love. This is the emotional base she'll rely on in years to come. (Also see *Separation and Stranger Anxiety,* page 369).

From the beginning, you've considered your baby to be a unique person with specific character traits and preferences. She, however, has had only a dim notion of herself as a person separate from you. But now her sense of identity is coming into bloom. As she develops a growing sense of herself as an individual, she'll also become increasingly conscious of you as a separate person.

One of the clearest signs of her own self-awareness is the way your baby watches herself in the mirror at this age. Up to about eight months, she treated the mirror as just another fascinating object. Perhaps, she thought, the reflection was another baby, or maybe it was a magical surface of lights and shadows. But now her responses will change, indicating she understands that one of the images belongs to her. While watching the mirror, for example, she may touch a smudge on her own nose or pull on a stray lock of her hair. You can reinforce her sense of identity by playing mirror games. When you're looking in the mirror together, touch different body parts: "This is Jenny's nose. . . . This is Mommy's nose." Or move in and out of the mirror, playing peekaboo with the reflections. Or make faces and verbally label the emotions you are conveying.

Transitional Objects

Almost everyone knows about the cartoon character Linus and his blanket. He drags it around wherever he goes, nibbling on its corner or curling up with it when the going gets tough. Security objects such as blankets are part of the emotional support system every child needs in his early years.

Your baby may not choose a blanket, of course. He may prefer a soft toy or even the satin trim on Mom's bathrobe. Chances are, he'll make his choice between months eight and twelve, and he'll keep it with him for years to come. When he's tired, it will help him get to sleep. When he's separated from you, it will reassure him. When he's frightened or upset, it will comfort him. When he's in a strange place, it will help him feel at home.

These special comforts are called "transitional objects," because they help children make the emotional transition from dependence to independence. They work, in part, because they feel good: They're soft, cuddly, and nice to touch. They're also effective because of their familiarity. This so-called "lovey" has your baby's scent on it and it reminds him of the comfort and security of his own room. It makes him feel that everything is going to be okay.

Despite myths to the contrary, transitional objects are not a sign of weakness or insecurity, and there's no reason to keep your infant from using one. In fact, a transitional object can be so helpful that you may want to help him choose one and build it into his nighttime ritual. From early infancy you might try keeping a small, soft blanket or toy in his crib. He may ignore it at first, but if it's always there he'll probably take to it eventually.

You can also make things easier for yourself by having two *identical* security objects. This will allow you to wash one while the other is being used, thus sparing your baby (and yourself) a potential emotional crisis and a very bedraggled "lovey." If your baby chooses a large blanket for his security object, you can easily turn it into two by cutting it in half. He has little sense of size and won't notice the change. If he's chosen a toy instead, try to find a duplicate as soon as possible. If you don't start rotating them early, your child may refuse the second one because it feels too new and foreign.

Parents often worry that transitional objects promote thumb sucking, and in fact they sometimes (but not always) do. But it's important to remember that thumb or finger sucking is a normal, natural way for a baby to comfort himself. He'll gradually give up both the transitional object and the sucking as he matures and finds other ways to cope with stress.

Toys Appropriate for an Eight- to Twelve-Month-Old

- Stacking toys in different sizes, shapes, colors
- Cups, pails, and other unbreakable containers
- Unbreakable mirrors of various sizes
- Bath toys that float, squirt, or hold water
- Large building blocks
- "Busy boxes" that push, open, squeak, and move

- Squeeze toys
- Large dolls and puppets
- Cars, trucks, and other vehicle toys made of flexible plastic, with no sharp edges or removable parts
- Balls of all sizes (but not small enough to fit in the mouth)
- Cardboard books with large pictures
- Records, tapes, music boxes, and musical toys
- Push-pull toys
- Toy telephones
- Paper tubes, empty boxes, old magazines, egg cartons, empty plastic soda/juice/milk bottles (well rinsed)

As the months pass and your baby's self-concept becomes more secure, she'll have less trouble meeting strangers and separating from you. She'll also become more assertive. Before, you could count on her to be relatively compliant as long as she was comfortable. But now, more often than not, she'll want things her own particular way. For instance, don't be surprised if she turns up her nose at certain foods or objects when you place them in front of her. Also, as she becomes more mobile, you'll find yourself frequently saying no, to warn her away from things she shouldn't touch. But even after she understands the word, she may touch anyway. Just wait—this is only a forerunner of power struggles to come.

Your baby also may become afraid of objects and situations that she used to take in stride. At this age, fears of the dark, thunder, and loud appliances like vacuum cleaners are common. Later you'll be able to subdue these fears by talking about them, but for now, the only solution is to eliminate the source of the fears as much as possible: Put a night-light in her room, or vacuum when she's not around. And when you can't shield her from something that frightens her, try to anticipate her reaction and be close by so she can turn to you. Comfort her, but stay calm so she understands that you are not afraid. If you reassure her every time she hears a clap of thunder or the roar of a jet overhead, her fear gradually will subside until all she has to do is look at you to feel safe.

Developmental Health Watch

Each baby develops in his own manner, so it's impossible to tell exactly when your child will perfect a given skill. Although the developmental milestones listed in this book will give you a general idea of the changes you can expect, don't be alarmed if his development takes a slightly different course. Alert your pediatrician if your baby displays any of the following signs of *possible* developmental delay in the eight-to-twelve-month age range.

- Does not crawl
- Drags one side of body while crawling (for over one month)
- Cannot stand when supported
- Does not search for objects that are hidden while he watches
- Says no single words ("mama" or "dada")
- Does not learn to use gestures, such as waving or shaking head
- Does not point to objects or pictures

Basic Care

Feeding

At this age your baby needs between 750 and 900 calories each day, about 400 to 500 of which should come from breastmilk or formula (approximately 24 ounces a day). But don't be surprised if her appetite is less robust now than it was during the first eight months. This is because her rate of growth is slowing, and she also has so many new and interesting activities to distract her.

At about eight months you may want to introduce "junior" foods. These are slightly coarser than strained foods and are packaged in a larger jar—usually 6 to 8 ounces. They require more chewing than baby foods. You can also expand your baby's diet to include soft foods such as puddings, mashed potatoes, yogurt, and gelatin. Eggs are an excellent source of protein, but feed her only the yolks at first, since their nutritional value is higher and they're less likely to cause allergies than the whites. In one or two months you can give her the whole egg. As always, introduce one food at a time, then wait two or three days before trying something else to be sure your child doesn't develop an allergic reaction.

At about eight to nine months, as your baby's ability to use her hands improves, give her her own spoon and let her play with it at mealtimes. Once she's figured out how to hold it, dip it in her food and let her try to feed herself. But don't expect much in the beginning, when more food is bound to go on the floor and high chair than into her mouth. A plastic cloth under her chair will help minimize some of the cleanup.

Be patient, and resist the temptation to grab the spoon away from her. She needs not only the practice but also the knowledge that you have confidence in her ability to feed herself. For a while you may want to alternate bites from her spoon with bites from a spoon that you hold. Once she consistently gets her own spoon to her mouth (which might not be until after her first birthday), you may keep filling her spoon for him to decrease the mess and waste, but leave the actual feeding to her.

In the early weeks of self-feeding, things may go more smoothly when she's really hungry and is more interested in eating than playing. Although your baby now eats three meals, just like the rest of the family, you may not want to impose her somewhat disorderly eating behavior upon everyone else's dinnertime. Many families compromise by feeding the baby most of her meal in advance, and then letting her occupy herself with finger foods while the others eat their meal.

Finger foods for babies include crunchy toast, well-cooked pasta, small pieces of chicken, scrambled egg, cereals, and chunks of banana. Try to offer a selection of flavors, shapes, colors, and textures, but always watch her for

In the early weeks of self-feeding, things may go more smoothly when she's really hungry and is more interested in eating than playing.

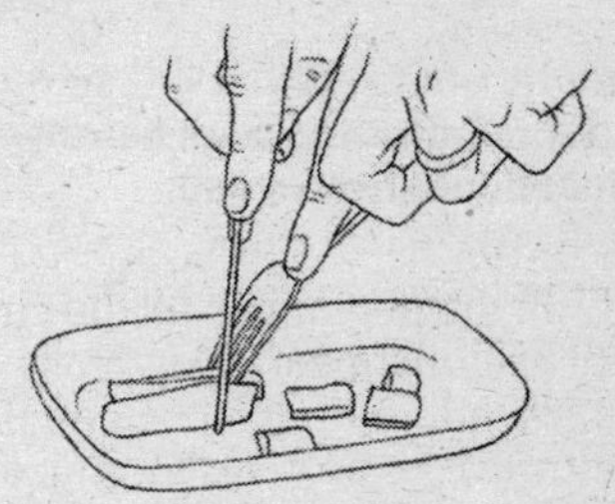

choking in case she bites off a piece too big to swallow (see *Choking*, page 397). Also, because she's likely to swallow without chewing, never offer a young child spoonfuls of peanut butter, large pieces of raw carrot, nuts, grapes, popcorn, uncooked peas, celery, hard candies, or other hard round foods. Choking can also happen with hot dogs or meat sticks (baby-food "hot dogs"), so these should always be cut lengthwise and then into smaller pieces before being fed to an infant of this age.

Weaning to a Cup

Once your baby is feeding himself more often, it's a natural time to introduce him to drinking from a cup. To get started, give him a trainer cup that has two handles and a snap-on lid with a spout, or use small plastic juice glasses. Either option will minimize spillage as he experiments with different ways to hold (and most likely to throw) the cup.

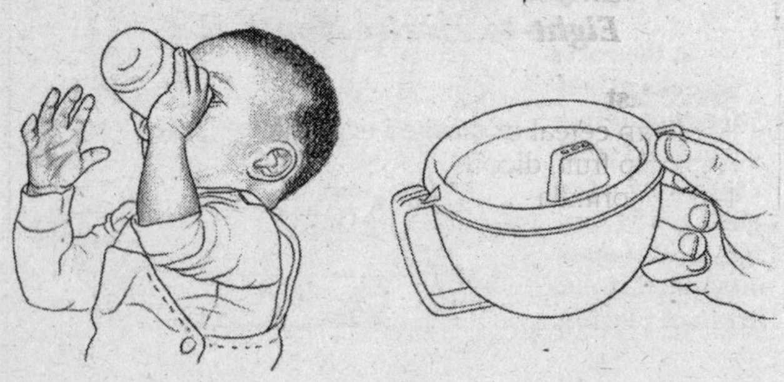

Six months may pass before your baby is willing to take all his liquid from a cup.

In the beginning, fill the cup with water and offer it to him at just one meal a day. Show him how to maneuver it to his mouth and tip it so he can drink. Don't become dismayed, however, if he treats the cup as a plaything for several weeks; most babies do. Just be patient until he's finally able to get most of the liquid down his throat—not dribbling down his chin or flying around the room—before you fill the cup with juice or milk or give it to him at other meals.

There are advantages to drinking from a cup: It will improve your baby's hand-to-mouth coordination, and it will begin to prepare him for the weaning process, which frequently occurs around this age. Your baby's readiness for this will be signaled by his:

1. Looking around while nursing or taking the bottle
2. Mouthing the nipple without sucking
3. Trying to slide off your lap before the feeding is finished

Even under the best of circumstances, weaning may not take place overnight. Six months may pass before your baby is willing to take all his liquid from a cup. Even so, you can start the process and proceed gradually, letting his interest

Sample One-Day Menu for an Eight- to Twelve-Month-Old

Breakfast
¼–½ cup cereal or mashed egg yolk
¼–½ cup fruit, diced
4–6 oz. formula

Snack
½ cup apple juice
¼ cup diced cheese or cooked vegetables

Lunch
¼–½ cup yogurt or cottage cheese
¼–½ cup yellow vegetables
4–6 oz. formula

Snack
½ cup apple juice
1 teething biscuit or cracker
¼ cup diced cheese or meat

Dinner
¼ cup diced poultry, meat, or tofu
¼–½ cup green vegetables
¼ cup noodles, pasta, rice, or potato
¼ cup fruit
4–6 oz. formula

Before Bedtime
6–8 oz. formula or water. (If formula, follow with water or brush teeth afterward.)

Discontinuing the Bottle

Most pediatricians recommend that the bottle be given up entirely at around age one and almost certainly by eighteen months. As long as your baby is drinking from a cup, he doesn't need to take liquids from a bottle anymore. Unfortunately, weaning your baby from the bottle is not as easy as it sounds. To help things along, eliminate the midday bottle first, then the evening and morning ones; save the bedtime bottle for last, since it's often the most difficult for your youngster to give up.

For a child who has trouble falling asleep or who wakes up at night, it's easy to get into the habit of using food or a bottle to comfort him. But at this age he no longer needs anything to eat or drink during the night. If you are still feeding him at that time, you should stop. Even if he demands a bottle and drinks thirstily, midnight feedings are still a comfort rather than a nutritional necessity. The bottle soon turns into a crutch and prevents his learning to fall back to sleep on his own. If he cries for only a short time, try letting him "cry himself back to sleep." After a few nights he'll probably forget all about the bottle. If this doesn't happen, consult your pediatrician and read the other sections on sleep in this book (see, for example, page 54 and page 303).

Incidentally, giving your toddler a drink or other snack *before* bedtime is perfectly fine. In fact, it may help him fall asleep. A short breastfeeding, a drink of cow's milk or other liquid, or even some fruit or another nutritious food will do. If the snack is a bottle, you can gradually phase it out by substituting a cup.

Whatever the snack, have your child finish it before brushing his teeth. Otherwise the food or liquid will remain in his mouth all night, promoting tooth decay. If he needs some comfort to get to sleep, let him use a cuddly toy, blanket, or his thumb—but not a bottle.

and willingness guide you. You'll probably find it easiest at first to substitute a cup for the bottle or breast at the midday feeding. Once he's adjusted to this change, try doing the same in the morning. The bedtime feeding probably will be the last one abandoned, and for good reason: Your baby has become accustomed to this source of nighttime comfort and calming, and it will take him some time to give it up. If he's sleeping through the night and not waking up hungry, he doesn't physically need the extra nourishment from bedtime breast- or bottle-feeding. In this case, you might break the habit in stages, first by substituting a bedtime bottle with water instead of milk, and then by switching to a drink of water from a cup.

During this process you may be tempted to put milk or juice in his bottle to help him go to sleep, but don't do it. If he falls asleep while feeding, the milk or juice will pool around his teeth, and this can cause his incoming teeth to decay—a condition known as nursing-bottle syndrome. To make matters worse, drinking while lying flat on his back can also contribute to middle-ear infections, since the liquid may actually flow through the eustachian tube into the middle ear.

There's still one more disadvantage to prolonged bottle feeding: The bottle can become a security object, particularly if your baby keeps it beyond about age one. To avoid this, don't let him carry or drink from a bottle while playing. Restrict the use of a bottle to feedings when he's sitting down or being held. At all other times, give him a cup. If you never allow him to take the bottle with him, he won't realize that bringing it along is even an option. Don't relent once this decision has been made, or it could prompt him to demand a bottle again long after he has "officially" been weaned.

Sample One-Day Menu for a One-Year-Old

This menu is planned for a one-year old child who weighs approximately 21 pounds.

1 tablespoon = ½ ounce (15 cc)
1 teaspoon = ⅓ tablespoon (5 cc)
1 cup = 8 ounces (240 cc)

Breakfast
½ cup iron-fortified breakfast cereal or 1 cooked egg (not more than 3 eggs per week)
¼ cup whole milk (with cereal)
½ cup orange juice
Add to cereal one of the following:
½ banana, sliced
2–3 large sliced strawberries

Snack
1 slice toast or whole wheat muffin
1–2 tablespoons cream cheese or peanut butter (spread)
1 cup whole milk

Lunch
½ sandwich—tuna, egg salad, peanut butter, or cold cuts
½ cup cooked green vegetables
½ cup apple juice

Snack
1–2 ounces cubed cheese, or 2–3 tablespoons pitted and diced dates
1 cup whole milk

Dinner
2–3 ounces cooked meat, ground or diced
½ cup cooked yellow or orange vegetables
½ cup pasta, rice, or potato
½ cup whole milk

Sleeping

At eight months your baby probably still takes two regular naps, one in the morning and one in the afternoon. She's also likely to sleep as much as twelve hours at night without needing a middle-of-the-night feeding. But be aware of some possible problems ahead: As her separation anxieties intensify in the next few months, she may start to resist going to bed, and she may wake up more often looking for you.

During this difficult period you may need to experiment with several strategies to find those that help your baby sleep. For example, some infants go to sleep more easily with the door open (so they can hear you); others develop consoling habits such as sucking their thumbs or rocking. As previously mentioned, your baby might also adopt a special blanket or stuffed animal as a transitional object, which comforts her when you're not nearby. Anything that's soft and huggable and can be stroked or sucked will serve this purpose. You can encourage your infant to use a transitional object by providing her with an assortment of small blankets or soft toys. But avoid resorting to a pacifier; if she depends on it to fall asleep, she'll cry for you to retrieve it each time it falls out of her mouth during the night.

Once your baby dozes off, her sleep patterns will be quite predictable. After one or two hours of deep sleep, she'll move into a stage of lighter snoozing, and she may partially awaken before returning to deeper sleep. For the rest of the night, there will be alternating periods of deeper and then lighter sleep. During the lighter periods, which may occur four to six times a night, she may even open her eyes, look around, and cry for you. This can be an exasperating experience, particularly if you've just become used to getting a full night's sleep. However, take comfort in the fact that most babies go through this stage, largely because of separation anxiety. She just needs to be reassured that you're still there when she wakes up. She also must learn to put himself back to sleep, and it's up to you to teach her. To do so, use the same techniques you relied on to get her to sleep in the first place (see *Sleeping*, page 54). Handled properly, this period of nighttime awakenings should last no more than a few weeks.

Here are some additional suggestions to help this stage pass more quickly. First of all, don't do anything that will reward your baby for calling you in the middle of the night. Go to her side to make sure she's all right, and tell her that you're nearby if she really needs you; but don't turn on the light, rock her, or walk with her. You might offer her a drink of water, but don't feed her, and certainly don't bring her to your bed. If she's suffering from separation anxiety, taking her in your bed will only make it harder for her to return to her own crib.

When you do check on her, try to make her as comfortable as possible. If she's gotten tangled in her blanket or stuck in a corner of her crib, rearrange her. Also make sure she isn't sick. Some problems, such as ear infections or the croup, can come on suddenly in the night. Once you're sure there's no sign of illness, then check her diaper, changing her only if she's had a bowel movement or if her diaper is uncomfortably wet. Do the change as quickly as possible in dim light and then settle her back in her crib under her blanket. Before leaving the room, whisper a few comforting words about how it's time to sleep. If she continues to cry, wait five minutes, then come back in and comfort her for a short time. Continue to return briefly every five to ten minutes until she's asleep.

To repeat, this period can be extremely difficult for parents. After all, it's emotionally and physically exhausting to listen to your baby cry, and you'll probably respond with a combination of pity, anger, worry, and resentment. But remember, her behavior is not deliberate. Instead, she's reacting to anxieties and stresses that are natural at her age. If you stay calm and follow a consistent pattern from one night to the next, she'll soon be putting herself to sleep. Keep this objective in sight as you struggle through the "training" nights. It will ultimately make life much easier for both of you.

Stimulating Infant Brain Growth: Age Eight Months Through Twelve Months

- Talk to your baby during dressing, bathing, feeding, playing, walking, and driving, using adult talk; check with your pediatrician if your baby does not seem to respond to sound or if syllables and words are not developing.

- Be attentive to your baby's rhythms and moods. Respond to her when she is upset as well as when she is happy.
- Encourage your baby to play with blocks and soft toys, which helps her develop eye-hand coordination, fine-motor skills, and a sense of competence.
- Provide a stimulating, safe environment where your baby can begin to explore and roam.
- Give consistent warm, physical contact—hugging, skin-to-skin, body-to-body contact—to establish your child's sense of security and well-being.
- Read to your baby every day.
- If you speak a foreign language, use it at home.
- Avoid subjecting your child to stressful or traumatic experiences, physical or psychological.
- Play games like peekaboo and pattycake to stimulate your baby's memory skills.
- Introduce your child to other children and parents.
- Provide age- and developmentally appropriate toys that are safe and inexpensive.
- Teach your baby to wave "bye-bye" and to shake her head "yes" and "no."
- Make sure other people who provide care and supervision for your baby understand the importance of forming a loving and comforting relationship with your child.
- Respect your baby's periodic discomfort around people who may not be her primary caregivers.
- Spend time on the floor playing with your child every day.
- Choose quality child care that is affectionate, responsive, educational, and safe. Visit your child-care provider frequently and share your ideas about positive caregiving.

Behavior

Discipline

Your baby's desire to explore is almost impossible to satisfy. As a result, he'll want to touch, taste, and manipulate everything he can get into his hands. In the process, he's bound to find his way into places and situations that are off limits. So although his curiosity is vital to his overall development and shouldn't be discouraged unnecessarily, he can't be allowed to jeopardize his own safety or to damage valuable objects. Whether he's investigating the burners on your stove or pulling up plants in your flower bed, you need to help him stop these activities.

Keep in mind that the way you handle these early incidents will lay the foundation for future discipline. Learning *not* to do something that he very much wants to do is a major first step toward self-control. The better he learns this lesson now, the less you'll have to intervene in years to come.

So what's your best strategy? As we suggested earlier, distraction usually can deal effectively with undesirable behavior. Your baby's memory is still short, and thus you can shift his focus with minimal resistance. If he's headed for something he shouldn't get into, you don't necessarily have to say no. Overusing that word will blunt its effect in the long run. Instead, pick him up and direct him toward something he *can* play with. Look for a compromise that will keep him interested and active without squelching his natural curiosity.

You should reserve your serious discipline for those situations where your child's activities can expose him to real danger—for example, playing with electric cords. This is the time to say no firmly, and remove him from the situation. But don't expect him to learn from just one or two incidents. Because of his short memory, you'll have to repeat the scene over and over before he finally recognizes and responds to your directions.

To improve the effectiveness of your discipline, consistency is absolutely critical. So make sure that everyone responsible for caring for your baby understands what your child is and isn't allowed to do. Keep the rules to a minimum, preferably limited to situations that are potentially dangerous to your baby. Then make sure he hears "no" *every time* he strays into forbidden territory.

Immediacy is another important component of good discipline. React as soon as you see your baby heading into trouble, not five minutes later. If you delay your reprimand, he won't understand the reason you're angry and the lesson will be lost. Likewise, don't be too quick to comfort him after he's been scolded. Yes, he may cry, sometimes as much in surprise as distress; but wait a minute or two before you reassure him. Otherwise, he won't know whether he really did something wrong.

As you refine your own disciplinary skills, don't overlook the importance of responding in a positive way to your baby's *good* behavior. This kind of reaction is equally important in helping him learn self-control. If he hesitates before reaching for the stove, notice his restraint and tell him how pleased you are. And give him a hug when he does something nice for another person. As he grows older his good behavior will depend, in large part, on his desire to please you. If you make him aware now of how much you appreciate the good things he does, he'll be less likely to misbehave just to get your attention.

Some parents worry about spoiling a baby this age by giving him too much attention, but you needn't be concerned about that. At eight to twelve months your baby still has a limited ability to be manipulative. You should assume that when he cries, it's not for effect but because he has real needs that aren't being met.

These needs will gradually become more complex, and as they do you'll notice more variation in your baby's cries—and in the way you react to them. For example, you'll come running when you hear the shattering wail that means something is seriously wrong. By contrast, you may finish what you're doing before you answer the shrill "come-here-I-want-you" cry. You'll also probably soon recognize a whiny, muffled cry that means something like "I could fall asleep now if everyone would leave me alone." By responding appropriately to the hidden message behind your baby's cries, you'll let him know that his needs are important, but you'll only respond to deserving calls for attention.

Incidentally, there probably will be times when you won't be able to figure out exactly why your baby is crying. In these cases, he himself may not even know what's bothering him. The best response is some comfort from you, combined with consoling techniques that he chooses for himself. For instance, try holding him while he cuddles his favorite stuffed animal or special blanket, or take time to play a game or read a story with him. Both of you will feel better when he's cheered up. Remember that his need for attention and affection is just as real as his need for food and clean diapers.

Siblings

As your baby becomes more mobile, she'll be better able to play with her siblings, and those brothers and sisters usually will be glad to cooperate. Older children, particularly six- to ten-year-olds, often love to build towers for an eight-month-old to destroy. Or they'll lend a finger to an eleven-month-old just learning to walk. A baby this age can be a wonderful playmate to her siblings.

However, while the baby's mobility can turn her into a more active participant in games with her brothers and sisters, it will also make her more likely to invade their private territory. This may violate their budding sense of ownership and privacy, and it can present a serious safety hazard for the baby, since the toys of older children often contain small, easily swallowed pieces. You can ensure that everyone is protected by giving older siblings an enclosed place where they can keep and play with their belongings without fear of a "baby invasion."

Also, now that the baby can reach and grab just about everything in sight, sharing is another issue that must be dealt with. Children under three just aren't capable of shar-

A baby this age can be a wonderful playmate to his siblings.

ing without lots of adult prodding and, in most cases, direct intervention. As much as possible, try to sidestep the issue by encouraging both children to play with their own toys, even if they're doing so side by side. When they do play together, suggest looking at books or listening to music, rolling a ball back and forth, or playing hide-and-seek games—in other words, activities requiring limited cooperation.

SAFETY CHECK

Car Seats

- Buckle the baby into an approved, properly installed car seat before you start the car. Be sure to keep him rear-facing until he weighs at least 20 lbs and is at least one year of age.

Falls

- Use gates at the top and bottom of stairways, and to doors of rooms with furniture or other objects that the baby might climb on or that have sharp or hard edges against which he might fall.
- Do not allow an infant to climb on a narrow-based ladder-back chair, since the child will try to "climb the ladder" and the chair will tip over, causing a head injury and possible leg or arm fractures.

Burns

- Never carry hot liquids or foods near your baby or while you're holding him.
- Never leave containers of hot liquids or foods near the edges of tables or counters.
- Do not allow your baby to crawl around hot stoves, floor heaters, or furnace vents.

Drowning

- Never leave your baby alone in a bath or around containers of water, such as buckets, wading pools, sinks, or open toilets.

Poisoning and Choking

- Never leave small objects in your baby's crawling area.
- Do not give your baby hard pieces of food.
- Store all medicines and household cleaning products up and out of his reach.
- Use safety latches on drawers and cupboards that contain objects that might be dangerous to him.

10

KEEPING YOUR CHILD SAFE

Everyday life is full of well-disguised dangers for children: sharp objects, shaky furniture, reachable hot water faucets, pots on burning stoves, hot tubs, swimming pools, and busy streets. By adulthood we've learned to navigate this minefield so well that we no longer think of things like scissors and stoves as hazards. And that's the problem. To protect your baby from the dangers she'll encounter in and out of your home, you have to see the world as she does, and you must recognize that she cannot yet distinguish hot from cold or sharp from dull.

Keeping your child physically safe is your most basic responsibility—and a never-ending one. Each year, 1 million children seek medical care because of unintentional injury. Forty to fifty thousand suffer permanent damage—and almost seven thousand under the age of fifteen die.

As might be expected, automobile crashes account for a large number of the injuries and deaths. But many children are injured and killed by equipment designed specifically for their use. In one recent twelve-month period, falls from highchairs sent nine thousand children to the hospital. Each year, toys cause more than 165,000 injuries serious enough to require treatment in hospital emergency rooms. Even cribs account for about fifty deaths annually.

These are grim statistics, but they are not inevitable. In the past, injuries were called "accidents" because they seemed unpredictable and unavoidable. Today, we know that injuries are not random; instead, they follow distinct patterns. By understanding these patterns, parents can take the precautions that will prevent most, if not all of those injuries.

Why Children Get Injured

Every childhood injury involves three elements: factors related to the baby, the object that causes the injury, and the environment in which it occurs. To keep your child safe, you must be aware of all three.

Let's start with your baby. His age makes a tremendous difference in the kind of protection he needs. The three-month-old who sits cooing in an infant seat requires quite different supervision from that needed by the ten-month-old who's started walking or the toddler who has learned to climb. So at each stage of your child's life, you must think again about the hazards that are present and what you can do to eliminate them. Repeatedly, as your baby grows, you must ask: How far can he move and how fast? How high can he reach? What objects attract his attention? What can he do today that he couldn't do yesterday? What will he do tomorrow that he can't do today?

During the first six months of life, you can secure your infant's safety by never leaving him alone in a dangerous situation. But once he begins to move, he'll create dangers of his own—first by rolling off the bed, then by creeping into places he shouldn't be, and finally by actively seeking out things to touch and taste.

As your baby begins to move about, you will certainly tell him "No" whenever he approaches something potentially hazardous, but he may not really understand the significance of your message. Many parents find the ages between six months and twelve months extremely frustrating, because the child doesn't seem to learn from these reprimands. Even if you tell him twenty times a day to stay away

His curiosity may take him to the top shelf of the refrigerator, into the medicine cabinet, and under the sink.

from the toilet, he's still in the bathroom every time you turn your back. At this age your baby is not being willfully disobedient; his memory just isn't developed enough for him to recall your warning the next time he's attracted by the forbidden object or activity. What looks like naughtiness is actually the testing and retesting of reality—the normal way of learning for a baby of this age.

Young children are extraordinary mimics, so they may try to take medicine just as they've seen Mom doing, or they may play with a razor just like Dad. Unfortunately, their notions of cause and effect aren't as advanced as their motor skills. Yes, your child may realize that tugging on the cord pulled the iron down on his head *after* it falls, but his ability to *anticipate* many similar consequences is still months away.

Most of your efforts to prevent injury should focus on objects and surroundings. By designing an environment in which the obvious hazards have been removed, you can allow your baby the freedom he needs to explore.

Some parents feel they don't need to "child-proof" their homes because they intend to supervise their infants closely. And in fact, with constant vigilance, most injuries *can* be avoided. But even the most conscientious parents can't watch a baby every moment. Most injuries occur not when parents are alert and at their best, but when they are under stress. The following situations are often associated with injuries:

- Hunger and fatigue (i.e., the hour or so before dinner)
- Mother's pregnancy
- Illness or death in the family
- Changes in the baby's regular caregiver
- Tension between parents
- Sudden changes in the environment, such as moving to a new home or going on vacation

All families experience at least some of these stresses some of the time. Child-proofing eliminates or reduces the opportunities for injury so that even when you are momentarily distracted—for example, by the ring of the telephone or doorbell—your baby is less likely to encounter situations and objects that can cause him harm.

The pages that follow include advice about how to minimize dangers in and out of the home. The intention is not to frighten you, but to alert you to hazards—particularly those that, on the surface, might seem harmless—so you can take the sensible precautions that will keep your infant safe *and* allow him the freedom he needs to grow up happy and healthy.

SAFETY INSIDE YOUR HOME

Room to Room

Your life-style and the layout of your home will determine which rooms should be child-proofed. Examine every room in which your baby spends any time (for most families, that means the entire house). It's tempting to exclude a formal dining or living room that remains behind closed doors when not in use; but remember, the rooms that are forbidden to your infant are the ones she'll want most to explore as soon as she's old enough. Any areas not child-proofed will require extra vigilance on your part, even if their entrances are normally locked or blocked.

At the very least, your baby's room should be a place where everything is as safe as it can be.

Nursery

Cribs. Your baby's crib needs to be safe, meeting present safety standards that can minimize the risk of falls and other accidents. These guidelines are described fully in *Safety Alert: Cribs* (see chapter 1 pages 30–33).

Changing Tables. Although a changing table makes it easier to dress and diaper your baby, falls from such a high surface can be serious. Don't trust your vigilance alone to prevent falls, but also consider the following recommendations:

1. Choose a sturdy, stable changing table with a 2-inch guardrail around all four sides.
2. The top of the changing table should be concave, so that the middle is slightly lower than the sides.

3. Don't depend on a safety strap alone to keep your baby secure. *Never leave an infant unattended on a dressing table, even for a moment, whether strapped or not.*

4. Keep powder and other diapering supplies within your reach, so you don't have to leave your baby's side to get them. Never let him play with the powder container while you change him. If he accidentally opens and shakes it, he's likely to inhale particles of powder, which can injure his lungs.

5. If you use disposable diapers, store them out of your infant's reach and cover them with clothing when he wears them. Babies can suffocate if they tear off pieces of the plastic liner and swallow them.

Kitchen

The kitchen is such a dangerous room for young children that some experts recommend they be excluded from it. That's a difficult rule to enforce, because parents spend so much time there and most young children want to be where the action is. It's probably more realistic to eliminate the most serious dangers by taking the following precautions:

1. Store strong cleaners, lye, furniture polish, dishwasher soap, and other dangerous products in a high cabinet and out of sight. If you must store some items under the sink, buy a "kiddie lock" that refastens automatically every time you close the cupboard (most hardware and department stores have them). Never transfer dangerous sub-

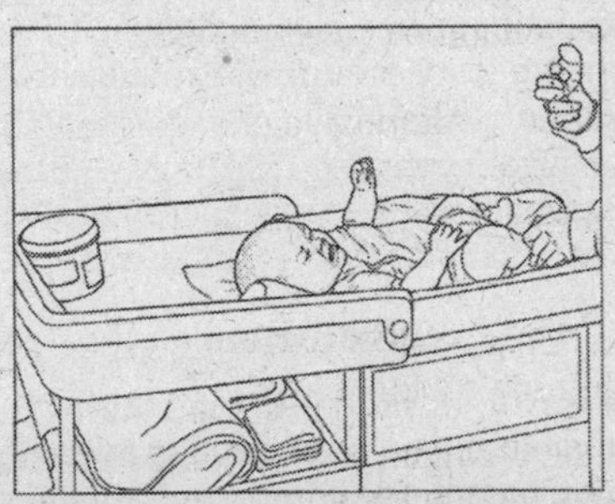

stances into containers that look as if they might hold food.

2. Keep knives, forks, scissors, and other sharp instruments separate from "safe" kitchen utensils, and in a latched drawer. Store sharp cutting appliances such as food processors out of reach or in a locked cupboard.
3. Unplug appliances when they are not in use so your baby cannot accidentally turn them on. Don't allow electrical cords to dangle where your baby can reach and tug on them, possibly pulling a heavy appliance down on herself.
4. Always turn pot handles toward the back of the stove so your child can't reach up and grab them. Whenever you have to walk with hot liquid—a cup of coffee, a pot of soup—be sure you know where your baby is so you don't trip over her.
5. If you have a gas stove, turn the dials firmly to the off position, and if they're easy to remove, do so when you aren't cooking so that your child can't accidentally turn the stove on. If they cannot be removed easily, block the access to the stove as much as possible.
6. Keep matches out of reach and out of sight.
7. Don't warm baby bottles in a microwave oven. The liquid heats unevenly, so there may be pockets of milk hot enough to scald your baby's mouth when she drinks. Also, there have been incidents in which overheated baby bottles have exploded when they were removed from the microwave.
8. Keep a fire extinguisher in your kitchen. (If your home has more than one story, mount an extinguisher in a conspicuous place on each floor.)
9. Make sure all drawers have stops, so your baby can't pull the drawer out on top of himself.

Bathroom

The simplest way to avoid bathroom injuries is to make this room inaccessible unless your child is accompanied by an adult. This may mean installing a latch on the door at adult height so a young child can't visit when you aren't around. Also, be sure any lock on the door can be unlocked from the *outside*, just in case your child accidentally locks himself in.

The following suggestions will prevent injuries when your child is using the bathroom:

1. Babies can drown in only a few inches of water, so *never leave them alone in the bath, even for a moment.* If you can't ignore the doorbell or the phone, wrap your baby in a towel and take him along when you go to answer them. Bath seats and rings are meant to be bathing aids, and will not prevent drowning if the baby is left unattended.
2. Install no-slip strips on the bottom of the bathtub. Put a cushioned cover over the water faucet so your baby won't be hurt if he bumps his head against it.
3. Get in the habit of closing the lid of the toilet. A curious child who tries to play in the water can lose his balance and fall in.
4. To prevent scalding, don't set your hot water heater higher than 120 degrees Fahrenheit (48 degrees Celsius).
5. Keep all medicines in containers with safety caps. Remember, however, that these caps are child-*resistant*, not childproof, so store all medicines and cosmetics in a *locked* cabinet. Don't keep toothpaste, soaps, shampoos, and other frequently used items in the same cabinet. Instead, store them in a hard-to-reach cabinet equipped with a safety latch or locks.
6. If you use electrical appliances in the bathroom, particularly hair dryers and razors, be sure to unplug them when they aren't in use. Better yet, use them in another room where they cannot possibly come in contact with water. Your electrician can install special bathroom wall sockets (ground fault circuit interrupters) that can lessen the likelihood of electrical injury when an appliance falls into the sink or bathwater.

Garage and Basement

Garages and basements tend to be places where potentially lethal tools and chemicals are stored. In almost all homes, these areas should be locked and strictly off-limits to children. To minimize the risk on those occasions when children do gain access to the garage and basement:

1. Keep paints, varnishes, thinners, pesticides, and fertilizers in a locked cabinet or locker. Be sure these substances are always kept in their original, labeled containers.
2. Store tools in a safe area out of reach. Be sure power tools are unplugged when you finish using them.
3. Do not allow your baby to play near the garage or driveway where cars may be coming and going.
4. If you have an automatic garage door opener, be sure your infant is nowhere near the door before you open or close it. Keep the opener out of reach and out of sight. Make sure the automatic reversing mechanism is properly adjusted.
5. If, for some reason, you must store an unused refrigerator or freezer, remove the door so that a child cannot become trapped if he crawls inside.

All Rooms

Certain safety rules and preventive actions apply to *every* room. The following safeguards against commonplace household dangers will protect not only your baby, but your entire family:

1. Install smoke detectors throughout your home, check them monthly to be sure they are working, and change the batteries annually. Develop a fire escape plan and practice it so you'll be prepared if an emergency does occur. (See *Burns*, page 390.)
2. Put safety plugs in all unused electrical outlets so your baby can't stick her finger or a toy into the holes. If she won't stay away from outlets, buy the plastic covers that block unused sockets and make it impossible for her to pull plugs out of sockets that are in use.
3. To prevent slipping, carpet your stairs where possible. Be sure the carpet is firmly tacked down at the edges. When your baby is just learning to crawl and walk, install safety

gates at both top and bottom of stairs. Avoid accordion-style gates, which can trap an arm or a neck.

4. Certain houseplants may be harmful. Your regional Poison Center will have a list or description of plants to avoid. (See *Poisoning*, page 411.)
5. Check your floors constantly for small objects that a baby might swallow, such as coins, buttons, beads, pins, and screws. This is particularly important if someone in the household has a hobby that involves small items.
6. If you have hardwood floors, don't let your young child move around in stocking feet. Socks make slippery floors even more dangerous.
7. Attach cords for Venetian blinds and drapes to floor mounts that hold them taut, or wrap these cords around wall brackets to keep them out of reach. Cords with loops should be cut and equipped with safety tassels. Babies can strangle on them if they are left loose.
8. Pay attention to the doors between rooms. Glass doors are particularly dangerous, because a baby may bang into them, so fasten them open if you can. Swinging doors can knock a baby down, and folding doors can pinch little fingers, so if you have either, consider removing them until your baby is old enough to understand how they work.
9. Check your home for furniture pieces with hard edges and sharp corners that could injure your baby if she fell

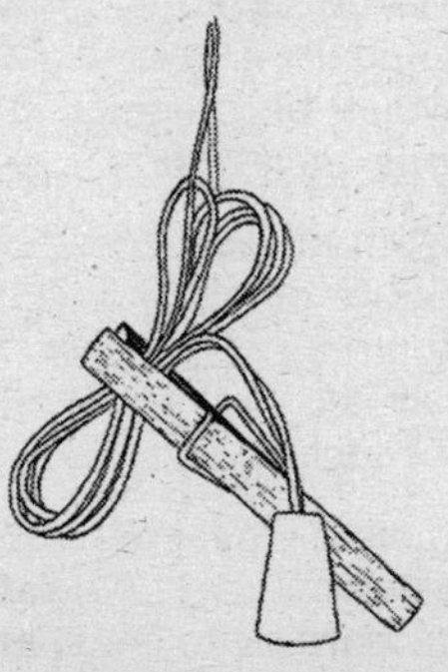

against them (coffee tables are a particular hazard). If possible, move this furniture out of traffic areas, particularly when your baby is learning to walk. You also can buy cushioned corner- and edge-protectors that stick onto the furniture.

10. Test the stability of tall pieces of furniture such as floor lamps and bookshelves. If they seem unsteady, anchor the bookcases to the wall and put floor lamps behind other furniture so your child can't pull them over.
11. Open windows from the top if possible. If you must open them from the bottom, install window bars or screens that only an adult or older child can push out from the inside. Never put chairs, sofas, low tables, or anything else a baby might climb on in front of a window. This gives her access to the window and creates an opportunity for a serious fall.
12. Never leave plastic bags lying around the house, and don't store children's clothes or toys in them. Bags from the dry cleaner are particularly dangerous. Knot them before you throw them away so that it's impossible for your baby to crawl into them or pull them over her head.
13. Think about the potential hazard to your baby of anything you put into the trash. Any trash container into which dangerous items will go—for example, spoiled food, discarded razor blades, or batteries—should have a child-resistant cover.
14. To prevent burns, check your heat sources. Fireplaces, wood stoves, and kerosene heaters should be screened

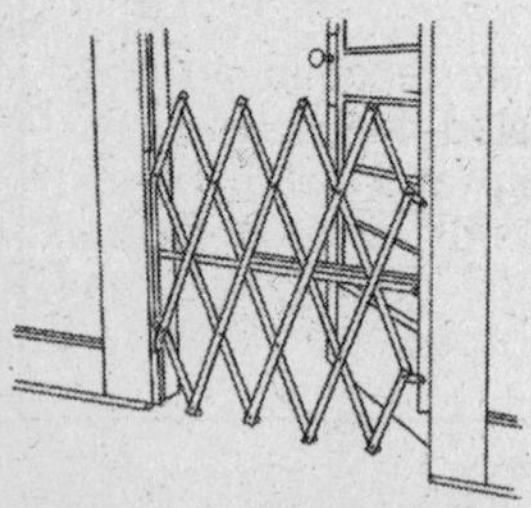

Unsafe, accordion-style gate

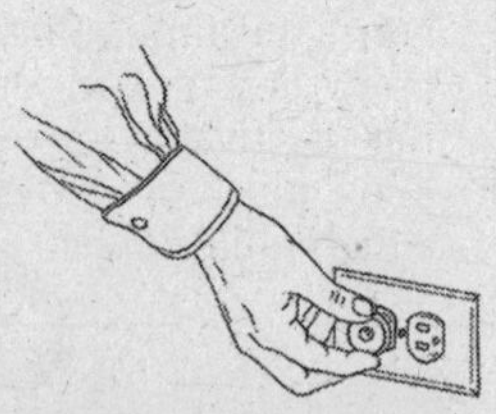

Safety plug in unused outlets

Safe, horizontal-style gate with slats 2⅜ inches apart

so that your baby can't get near them. Check electric baseboard heaters, radiators, and even vents from hot-air furnaces to see how hot they get when the heat is on. They, too, may need to be screened.

15. If you elect to have a firearm in the house (this should be avoided whenever possible), keep it unloaded and locked up. Lock ammunition in a separate cupboard.
16. Alcohol can be very toxic to a baby. Keep all alcoholic beverages in a locked cabinet and *remember to empty* any unfinished drinks immediately.

Where We Stand

The American Academy of Pediatrics strongly supports gun control legislation. We believe that handguns, deadly air guns, and assault weapons should be banned.

Until handguns are banned, we recommend that handgun ammunition be regulated, that restrictions be placed on handgun ownership, and that the number of privately owned handguns be reduced. Handguns must be removed from the environments in which children live and play.

Baby Equipment

During the past twenty years, the Consumer Product Safety Commission has taken an active role in setting standards to assure the safety of equipment manufactured for children and infants. Because many of these rules went into effect in the early 1970's, you must pay special attention to the safety of used furniture made before then. The following guidelines will help you select the safest possible baby equipment, whether used or new, and utilize it properly.

High Chairs

Falls are the most serious danger associated with high chairs. To minimize the risk of your baby falling:

1. Select a chair with a wide base, so it can't be tipped over if someone accidentally bumps against it.
2. If the chair folds, be sure the locking device is secure each time you set it up.
3. Strap your baby in with the safety strap whenever he sits in the chair. Never allow him to stand in the high chair.
4. Don't place the high chair near a counter or table. Your baby may be able to push hard enough against these surfaces to tip the chair over.

5. Don't leave your baby unattended in a high chair and don't allow older children to climb or play on it, as this could tip it over.
6. A cantilevered high chair that hooks on to a table is not a substitute for a more solid one. But if you plan to use such a model when you eat out or when you travel, look for one that locks on to the table. Be sure the table is heavy enough to support your baby's weight without tipping. Also, check to see whether his feet can touch a table support. If he can push against it, he may be able to dislodge the seat from the table.

Infant Seats

Infant seats are not car seats, so not all the same regulations apply. Use care in selecting an infant seat. Check the weight guidelines provided by the manufacturer, and don't use the seat after your baby has outgrown it. Here are some other safety guidelines to follow:

1. Never use an infant seat as a substitute for a car seat. Infant seats are designed only for propping a baby up, so that she can see or be fed more easily.
2. Always use the strap and harness when your baby is in the seat.
3. Choose a seat with an outside frame that allows the infant to sit deeply inside. Be sure the base is wide, so it is difficult to tip over.
4. Look at the bottom of the infant seat to see whether it's covered with a nonskid material. If it isn't, cut thin pieces of rubber, and glue them to the base so that the seat is less likely to slip when it's on a smooth surface.
5. Always carry your baby securely strapped into the seat, and use both your arms *under* the frame to hold it. Although some infant seats have carrying handles, using them alone will allow the seat to tip if the baby's weight is distributed unevenly. Even with the strap on, the weight of her head could pull her down and out.
6. The most serious injuries associated with infant seats occur when a baby falls from a high surface. Therefore,

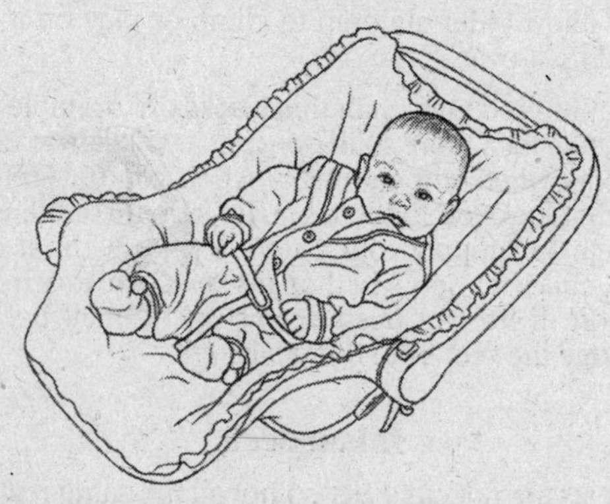

it's not wise to put the seat above floor level. Even there, an active, squirming baby can tip the seat over, so place the seat on a carpeted area near you and away from sharp-edged furniture. Also, infant seats may tip over when placed on soft surfaces, such as beds or upholstered furniture; these are not safe places for infant seats.

Playpens

Most parents depend on playpens (sometimes called play yards) as a safe place to put a baby when Mom or Dad isn't available to watch him every moment. Yet playpens, too, can be dangerous under certain circumstances. To prevent mishaps:

1. Never leave the side of a mesh playpen lowered. A baby who rolls into the pocket created by the slack mesh can become trapped and suffocate.
2. Once your baby is able to sit, remove any toys that have been tied across the top of the playpen, so he cannot become entangled in them.
3. When your baby can pull himself to a standing position, remove all boxes and large toys that he could use to help him climb out.

Mesh playpen in safe position, sides up

4. Babies who are teething often bite off chunks of the vinyl or plastic that cover the top rails, so you should check them periodically for tears and holes. If the tears are small, repair them with heavy-duty cloth tape; if they are more extensive, you may need to replace the rails.
5. If you use a playpen built before 1974, be sure the mesh is free of tears and that the openings are less than ¾ of an inch across, so that your infant cannot get caught in it. Slats on wooden playpens should be no more than 2 ⅜ inches apart, so your baby's head cannot become trapped between them.
6. Circular enclosures made from accordion-style fences are extremely dangerous, because babies can get their heads caught in the diamond-shaped openings and the V-shaped border at the top of the gate. Never use such an enclosure, either indoors or out. Octagonal playpens made of plastic mesh are safe, following the guidelines for playpen use.

Walkers

The American Academy of Pediatrics does not recommend using baby walkers. Baby walkers are advertised for use when a child is old enough to sit securely, yet not steady enough to walk; they are involved in more than 28,000 injuries in the United States every year. The AAP recommends that you select a stationary product such as a bouncer. Avoid jump seats or swings that fasten in doorways. Also, some "walkers" may have no wheels, retractable wheels, or allow only rotating motion.

If you decide to use a walker anyway, take note of the following precautions, and remember injuries will occur even in the best of circumstances:

1. If you select a walker with an X-frame, be aware that the frame can trap small fingers. Look for spacers between the collapsing components, and for locking devices that prevent this action. Also be sure that coil springs, if present, have protective covers.
2. To prevent tipping, all walkers should have at least six wheels. For maximum stability, the wheel base should be wider and longer than the seat height.
3. Use the walker only on a smooth, flat floor where there are no carpets, door thresholds, or other obstructions that could cause it to tip over.
4. Be sure stair guards and gates are securely closed before putting a baby in a walker.
5. Never leave a baby unattended in a walker.

Pacifiers

Pacifiers that are improperly constructed can choke an infant if they come apart. For maximum safety:

1. Do not use the top and nipple from a baby bottle as a pacifier, even if you tape them together. If the baby sucks hard, the nipple may pop out of the ring and choke her.
2. Purchase pacifiers that cannot possibly come apart. Those molded of one solid piece of rubber are particularly safe. If you are in doubt, ask your pediatrician for a recommendation.
3. The shield between the nipple and the ring should be at least 1½ inches across, so the infant cannot take the entire pacifier into her mouth. Also, the shield should be made of firm plastic with ventilation holes.
4. After retrieving your baby's pacifier for the thousandth time, you may think about tying it to her hand or around her neck. Don't. The danger of strangulation is too great.
5. Pacifiers deteriorate over time. Inspect them periodically to see whether the rubber is discolored or torn. If so, replace them.

Toy Boxes and Toy Chests

A toy box can be dangerous for two reasons: Its hinged lid can fall on your baby's head or body while he's searching for a toy, and he could be trapped inside. If possible, store toys on open shelves so that your young child can get them easily. If you must use a toy box:

1. Look for one with no top, or choose one that has a lightweight removable lid or sliding doors or panels.

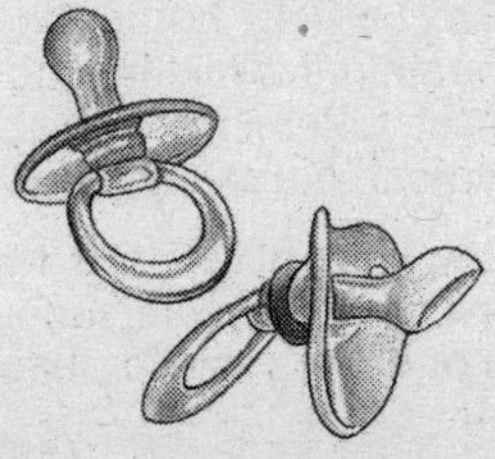

2. If you use a toy box with a hinged lid, be sure it has a support or friction hinge that holds the lid open at any angle to which the lid is opened. If your toy box didn't come with such a support, install one yourself—or remove the lid.
3. Look for a toy box with rounded or padded edges and corners, or add the padding yourself, so your baby won't be injured if he falls against it.
4. Children occasionally get trapped inside toy boxes, so be sure your box has ventilation holes or a gap between the lid and the box. Don't block the holes by pushing the box tight against a wall. Be sure the lid doesn't latch.

Toys

Most toy manufacturers are conscientious in trying to produce safe toys, but they cannot always anticipate the way a baby might use—or abuse—their products. If your baby is injured by an unsafe product or you would like to report a product-related injury, call the toll-free number of the Consumer Product Safety Commission: 1-800-638-CPSC (the number for the speech- or hearing-impaired is 1-800-638-8270). The Commission keeps a record of complaints and initiates recalls of dangerous toys, so your phone call may protect not only your child but others. You can also contact the Commission through the Internet: Info@cpsc.gov or http://www.cpsc.gov. In addition, the hotline and Web site are invaluable resources for obtaining information about product recalls or consumer alerts. When selecting or using toys, always observe the following safety guidelines:

1. Match all toys to your baby's age and abilities. Manufacturers' guidelines can help, but in the end you must decide whether your infant is mature and skilled enough to use a plaything safely. Remember, the age on toy packaging is for educational, not safety purposes.
2. Rattles—probably your baby's first toys—should be at least 1 ⅝ inches across. An infant's mouth and throat are very flexible, so one that's smaller than that could cause choking.

3. All toys should be constructed of sturdy materials that won't break or shatter even when a baby throws or bangs them.

4. Check squeeze toys to be sure the squeaker can't become detached from the toy.

5. Before giving your baby a stuffed animal or a doll, be certain the eyes and nose are firmly attached. Remove all ribbons. Don't allow your infant to suck on a pacifier or any other accessory that comes packaged with a doll and is small enough to be swallowed.

6. Swallowing and/or inhaling small parts of toys are serious dangers to babies. Inspect toys carefully for small parts that could fit in your infant's mouth and throat. Look for toys labeled for children three and under, because they must meet federal guidelines requiring that they have no small parts likely to be swallowed or inhaled.

7. Toys with small parts that are purchased for older children should be stored out of the reach of babies. Impress upon your older youngster the importance of picking up all the pieces from such toys when she's finished playing with them.

8. Don't let a baby play with balloons: She may inhale a balloon if she tries to blow it up. If a balloon pops, be sure to pick up and discard all the broken pieces.

9. To prevent both burns and electrical shocks, don't give young children (under age ten) a toy that must be plugged into an electrical outlet. Instead, buy toys that are battery-operated.

10. Toys with mechanical parts should be inspected carefully for springs, gears, or hinges that could trap a baby's fingers, hair, or clothing.

11. To prevent cuts, check toys before you purchase them to be sure they don't have sharp edges or pointed pieces. Avoid toys with parts made of glass or rigid plastic that could shatter.

12. Don't allow your young child to play with very noisy toys, including squeeze toys with unexpectedly loud

squeakers. Noise levels at or about 100 decibels—the sound of the typical cap gun at close range—can damage hearing.

13. Projectile toys are not suitable for babies or older children, because they can so easily cause eye injuries. Never give a child a toy gun that actually fires anything except water.

Safety Outside the Home

Even if you create the perfect environment for your baby inside your home, he'll also be spending a lot of time outside, where surroundings are somewhat less controllable. Obviously, your personal supervision will remain the most valuable protection. However, even a well-supervised child will be exposed to many hazards. The information that follows will show you how to eliminate many of these hazards and reduce the risk that your baby will ever be injured.

Car Seats

Each year, car crashes claim the lives of many children. Many of these deaths could be prevented if the youngsters were properly restrained. Contrary to what many people believe, a parent's lap is actually the most perilous place for a baby to ride. In case of a car crash, you probably wouldn't be able to hold on to your baby. But even if you could, your body would crush hers as you were thrown against the dashboard and windshield. The single most important thing you can do to keep your baby safe in the car is to buy, install, and use a federally approved car seat.

Car seats are required by law in all fifty states and U.S. territories. Unfortunately, recent studies show that many parents are not properly using them. The most common mistakes are placing rear-facing seats in front of an air bag, facing car seats in the wrong direction, and failing to harness the infant into the seat. Also, some parents don't use the seat on short trips. They are not aware that most fatal crashes occur within five miles of home and at speeds of less than twenty-five miles per hour. For all these reasons, children continue to be at risk. It's not enough to have a car seat—you must use it correctly, every time.

Infant Car Seat

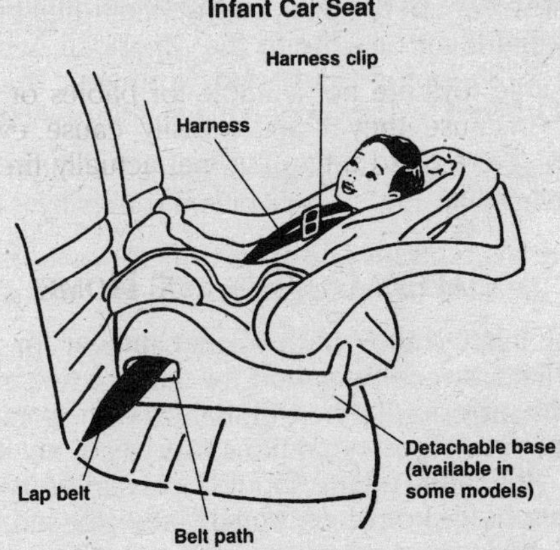

Convertible Car Seat

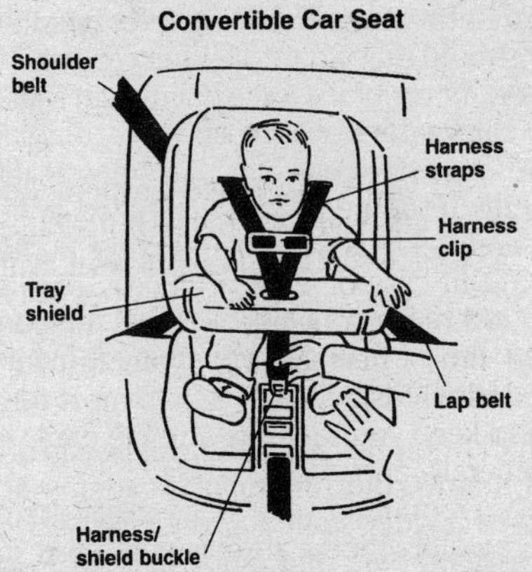

Choosing a Car Seat

Here are some guidelines you can use to help you select a car seat:

1. All new car seats sold today must meet federal safety guidelines. Don't use a seat made before 1981, the year these regulations went into effect. The abbreviated table

on pages 333–339 lists some of the seats that are available. For a more complete up-to-date list, including prices, ask your pediatrician or write to the American Academy of Pediatrics, Shopping Guide, 141 Northwest Point Boulevard, P.O. Box 927, Elk Grove Village, Illinois 60009.

2. Always use a car seat, starting with your baby's first ride home from the hospital. Buy the seat before your baby is born.

3. Read the instructions and your vehicle's owner's manual and try the seat in your car to ensure proper installation.

4. For small infants or low-birthweight babies, a car seat without a shield is recommended for the first few months at least, as it provides the best fit. Babies with special health problems or medical conditions may need other restraint systems. Premature infants should be observed in a car seat before discharge from the hospital to see if the semireclined position adds to or causes possible breathing problems. Your pediatrician may recommend using a crash-tested car bed so your baby can lie flat. Whenever possible, a premature infant should ride where an adult can watch his breathing. However, never place a rear-facing car seat in the front seat with a passenger-side air bag.

5. Be sure the seat can be installed properly and easily in your car. Some cars have seat belt configurations, seating positions, or vehicle seats that do not work with car seats.

6. Look for a car seat with harnesses that are easy to adjust when the seat is in your car; you're more likely to use the seat if it's convenient.

7. For information on the special travel needs of premature and small infants, the American Academy of Pediatrics has endorsed a video called *Special Delivery: Safe Transportation of Premature and Small Infants.* To order, send $50 to Automotive Safety for Children Program, Riley Hospital for Children, 575 West Drive, Room 004, Indianapolis, Indiana 46202–5225.

1997 Shopping Guide to Car Seats

All products listed meet current Federal Motor Vehicle Safety Standard 213.

Infant car seats can be used from birth to at least 20 pounds and at least one year of age. The advantage of using infant car seats is that they are small and portable and fit newborns best. The disadvantage is that they must be replaced by a convertible seat when a baby outgrows the seat, usually within the first year. When using an infant seat, make sure that it is made for use in a vehicle. Never use an infant carrier in place of a car seat. **Remember, infant seats are always used rear-facing.**

Manufacturer/ Name	*Harness Type*	*Features*	*Price Range*
INFANT SEATS		**(Birth to 20 lbs unless noted)**	
Britax Rock-a-tot	3-Point	For use up to 22 lbs	$79-89
Century Assura 565 Series	3-Point	Correct recline indicator	$29–39
Century Assura Premiere	3-Point	Detachable base that is smaller to fit contoured vehicle seats. Raised belt slots adapt to more of today's seat belt systems. Correct recline indicator. Also available with stroller.	$49–59
Century Smart Fit	3-Point	Detachable base that is smaller to fit contoured vehicle seats. Raised belt slots adapt to more of today's seat belt systems. Correct recline indicator. Also available with stroller.	$60–70

1997 Shopping Guide to Car Seats (*Continued*)

Manufacturer/ Name	*Harness Type*	*Features*	*Price Range*
Cosco Arriva	3-Point	For use up to 22 lbs. Some models have detachable base. Some models have correct recline indicator. Also available with stroller.	$35–55
Cosco Dream Ride Plus	3-Point	Can use as car bed with passenger-side airbag. Use side-facing as car bed; rear-facing as car seat. Converts to swing.	$59
Cosco TLC	3-Point		$20–25
Cosco Turnabout	3-Point	For use up to 22 lbs. Some models have detachable base. Some models have correct recline indicator. Harness system adjusts automatically. Also available with stroller.	$55–75
Evenflo Joy Ride	3-Point	Harness adjuster located in compartment behind seat. Also available with stroller.	$25–45
Evenflo On My Way	3-Point	Detachable base. Can use without base. Also available with stroller.	$55–65
Evenflo Travel Tandem	3-Point	Detachable base. Can use without base. Harness adjuster located in compartment behind seat.	$45–55

Manufacturer/ Name	*Harness Type*	*Features*	*Price Range*
Gerry Guard with Glide	3-Point	For use up to 22 lbs. Can use as glider. Must be converted for use as car seat.	$50–55
Gerry Secure Ride	3-Point	For use up to 22 lbs.	$40
Kolcraft Infant Rider	3-Point		$50–60
Kolcraft Rock 'n Ride	3-Point	For use up to 18 lbs. Harness height is not adjustable.	$30–35
Kolcraft Travel About	3-Point	Detachable base. Can use without base.	$60–70

Convertible Car Seats can be used from birth to about 40 pounds. These are seats that are used rear-facing for infants and forward-facing for toddlers. Infants should ride rear-facing until at least 20 lbs and one year of age. The advantage of convertible seats is that they can be used longer. The disadvantages are that they are bulkier than infant seats, are less portable, and may not fit newborn infants well.

Convertible seats have three types of harnesses: **5-Point Harness**—five straps: two at the shoulders, two at the hips, one at the crotch; **T-Shield**—a padded T-shaped or triangular shield attached to shoulder straps that buckles into the seat at the crotch; **Overhead or Tray-Shield**—a padded, tray-like shield that swings down around the child.

For small newborns, shields are often too high and too far from the body to fit correctly. A 5-point harness fits small newborns best because it can be adjusted to fit snugly.

Each model has its own correct belt routes for use when facing forward and facing rearward. On different models, the belt paths are different. Do not guess—to protect your child, follow instructions for your seat exactly.

1997 Shopping Guide to Car Seats (*Continued*)

Manufacturer/ Name	*Harness Type*	*Features*	*Price Range*
CONVERTIBLE SEATS		**(Birth to approximately 40 lbs)**	
Babyhood Baby Sitter	5-Point		$89–99
Britax Freeway	5-Point	Toddler seat only (20–40 lbs.). Cannot be used rear-facing for infants. Includes built-in "lock off" clamp in place of a locking clip. Adjustable recline.	$159–169
Century 1000 STE, 1500 Prestige	5-Point	Rear-facing up to 20 lbs. Adjustable crotch buckle.	$49–75
Century 2000 STE, 2500 Prestige	T-Shield	Rear-facing up to 20 lbs. Adjustable crotch position.	$59–85
Century 3000 STE, 3500 Prestige	Tray Shield	Rear-facing up to 20 lbs. Adjustable crotch buckle. Prestige model has adjustable shield.	$59–89
Century Smart Move	5-Point or Tray Shield	Rear-facing up to 30 lbs. Full recline for newborns and low birth-weight infants. Moves to upright position for more protection in a frontal collision.	$109–139

Manufacturer/ Name	*Harness Type*	*Features*	*Price Range*
Cosco Olympian	T-Shield, Tray Shield	Rear-facing up to 22 lbs. Adjustable tray shield. Harness system adjusts automatically.	$80–100
Cosco Regal Ride	5-Point, T-Shield, or Tray Shield	Rear-facing up to 22 lbs.	$65–85
Cosco Touriva	5-Point, T-Shield, or Tray Shield	Rear-facing up to 22 lbs.	$40–60
Early Development Guardian Comfort	5-Point, T-Shield, or Tray Shield	Rear-facing up to 20 lbs. Harness designed like vehicle seat belts—locks upon impact. Adjustable recline.	$80–100
Early Development Guardian Folder	5-Point, T-Shield, or Tray Shield	Rear-facing up to 20 lbs. Seat folds for travel or storage. Available with either automatic or manual belt adjustment. Adjustment recline. Tray shield model has adjustable shield.	$90–120
Early Development Guardian Express	5-Point	Rear-facing up to 20 lbs. Manual belt adjustment.	$50–60
Evenflo Champion	Tray Shield	Rear-facing up to 20 lbs. Optional tether available.	$50–70

1997 Shopping Guide to Car Seats (*Continued*)

Manufacturer/ Name	*Harness Type*	*Features*	*Price Range*
Evenflo Medallion	5-Point or Tray Shield	Rear-facing up to 22 lbs. Front access to vehicle belt for easier installation. Adjustable recline. Tray shield model has adjustable shield.	$110–160
Evenflo Scout	5-Point or T-Shield	Rear-facing up to 20 lbs. Optional tether available.	$39–60
Evenflo Trooper	5-Point or Tray Shield	Rear-facing up to 20 lbs. Adjustable shield. Optional tether available.	$60–70
Evenflo Ultara I	Tray Shield	Rear-facing up to 20 lbs. Adjustable shield. Adjustable recline. Optional tether available.	$80–100
Evenflo Ultara V	5-Point	Rear-facing up to 20 lbs. Adjustable recline. Optional tether available.	$80–100
Gerry One-Click	Tray Shield	Rear-facing up to 22 lbs. Harness system adjusts automatically. Optional tether available.	$80–90
Gerry Pro-Tech	5-Point	Rear-facing up to 22 lbs. Optional tether available.	$60–65
Kolcraft Auto-Mate	5-Point	Rear-facing up to 20 lbs. Harness adjuster located on both sides of seat.	$50–60

Manufacturer/ Name	*Harness Type*	*Features*	*Price Range*
Kolcraft Performa	Tray Shield	Rear-facing up to 20 lbs. Harness adjuster located on both sides of seat.	$50–70
Kolcraft Secure Fit	Tray Shield	Rear-facing up to 20 lbs. Three-position adjustable shield. Harness adjuster located on both sides of seat.	$60–80
Renolux Formula	5-Point	Rear-facing up to 20 lbs. Adjustable recline. Removable headrest.	$ Not available
Safeline Sit 'n Stroll	5-Point	Rear-facing up to 25 lbs. Converts to stroller.	$159–169

For current information about child safety seat recalls, safety notices, and replacement parts, call the Auto Safety Hotline at (800) 424-9393.

Installing a Car Seat

1. The back seat is the safest place for all children to ride. Infants in rear-facing car seats should never be in the front seat when there is a passenger-side air bag.
2. Be sure to follow the manufacturer's installation instructions precisely and check the vehicle's owner's manual for installation procedures.
3. Thread the seat belt in your car through the correct spaces or paths in the car seat. Be sure the belt stays tight. Many lap/shoulder belts allow the passenger to move freely even when they are buckled. If your car has this type of seat belt, you will need to use a locking clip to secure the car seat. Locking clips are provided with all new car seats. See instructions that come with the car seat for information on how to use the locking clip.

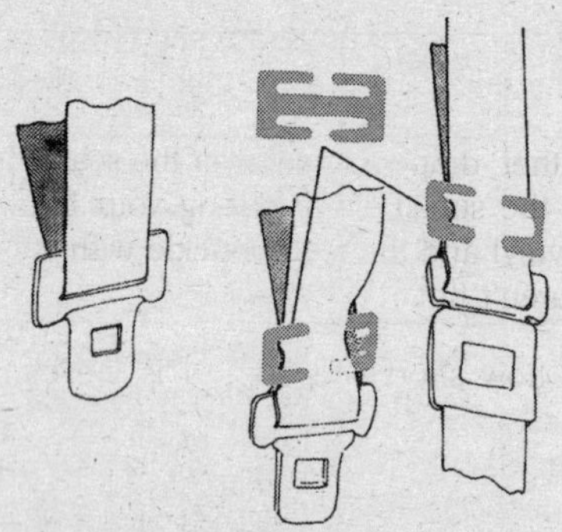

Locking clip placed to keep straps snug

4. A seat for an infant should be installed facing the rear. When your child weighs over 20 pounds and is one year of age, he can move into a properly secured, forward-facing toddler seat or a "convertible seat" used in the forward-facing position.
5. Adjust the straps in the car seat to your baby's size. The shoulder straps should come through slots level with or just below his shoulders. The straps should be flat, not twisted, and should be adjusted to fit snugly. The crotch strap should be kept short.

Use of the Car Seat

1. A car seat can protect your baby only if she sits in it every time she rides in the car—no exceptions. If you have two cars, buy two seats or transfer the seat to the car in which your baby will be traveling. If you are renting a car, find out if the rental car has a passenger-side air bag. If so, never place a rear-facing car seat in the front seat. ***The safest place for all children to ride is in the back.***
2. Many babies go through a stage when they protest every time you put them in the seat. But remember that you cannot drive until everyone is buckled up. That's a hard-and-fast rule.
3. Be sure the harness straps are snug against your child's body. Dress your baby in clothes that allow the straps to go

between her legs. Keep the straps snug by adjusting them to allow for the thickness of your child's clothes.

4. In hot weather, drape a towel over the seat when you leave the car in the sun. Before putting your baby in the seat, touch the vinyl and the metal buckle with your hand to be sure they aren't hot.

5. No matter how short your errand is, never leave a baby alone in a car. She might get overheated or too cold, if the outside temperature is extreme, or she may become frightened and panicky when she realizes she's alone. Any child alone in a car is a target for abduction.

6. Always use your own seat belt. In addition to setting a good example, you'll reduce your own risk of injury or death in a crash by 60 percent.

7. Keep your baby in a convertible car seat until she outgrows it, then move her to a booster seat when her ears extend above the car seat back. The boosters that provide the best protection are those that hold the child with a harness or the combination lap/shoulder belts. Raised seats with only a padded barrier in front of the child but no harness are convenient but provide less protection, but they are better than poorly fitting lap belts used alone.

Air Bag Safety

- The safest place for *all* infants and children under 12 years of age to ride is in the back seat.
- *Never* put an infant under 1 year of age in the front seat of a car with an air bag.
- Infants must always ride in rear-facing car seats in the back seat until they are at least 20 pounds AND 1 year of age.

- All children should be properly secured in car safety seats, booster seats, or shoulder/lap belts correct for their size.
- Seat belts must be worn correctly at all times by all passengers to provide the best protection.
- If no other arrangement is possible and a child *must* ride in the front seat, move the vehicle seat back as far as it can go, away from the air bag. Be sure the child is properly buckled. Keep in mind that your child may still be at risk for injuries from the air bag.

Keeping Your Baby Happy and Safe on the Road

As hard as you may try to enforce car seat and seat belt use, your baby may resist these constraints as he gets older. Here are some tips to keep him occupied and content—and also safe—while the car is in motion:

- Ensure your newborn's comfort by padding the sides of his car seat with rolled towels to prevent slouching.
- Place a small rolled towel between the crotch strap and your baby to prevent his lower body from sliding too far forward.
- If your infant's head flops forward, tilt the seat backward until it is level by wedging firm padding, such as a rolled towel, under the front of the base of the seat.
- Older babies love to climb, and may want desperately to get out of the car seat. If this describes your baby, remind yourself that this is only a phase, and in a calm but stern voice insist that he stay in his seat whenever the car is on the road.
- Entertain your baby by talking or singing with him as you drive. However, never do this to the point that it distracts you from paying attention to your driving.

Where We Stand

All fifty states require that children ride in car safety seats. Also, the American Academy of Pediatrics urges that all newborns discharged from hospitals be brought home in infant car safety seats. The AAP has established car seat guidelines for low-birthweight infants, which include riding in a rear-facing seat and supporting the infant with ample padding. A convertible safety seat is recommended as a child gets older.

Babies should always ride in car safety seats—preferably in the back seat—because it is safest. Never use a rear-facing car safety seat in the front seat of a car equipped with a passenger-side air bag. A baby should never ride in an adult's arms.

Baby Carriers—Backpacks and Front Packs

Back and front carriers for infants are very popular, although most babies outgrow front carriers by the age of three months. For your baby's—and your own—comfort and safety, follow these guidelines when purchasing and using baby carriers:

1. Take your baby with you when you shop for the carrier so that you can match it to his size. Make sure the carrier supports his back, and that the leg holes are small enough so he can't possibly slip through. Look for sturdy material.
2. If you buy a backpack, be sure the aluminum frame is padded, so that your baby won't be hurt if he bumps against it.
3. Check the pack periodically for rips and tears in the seams and fasteners.
4. When using a back carrier, be sure to bend at the knees, not the waist, if you need to pick something up. Otherwise, the baby may tip out of the carrier and you may hurt your back.

5. Babies over five months may become restless in the back carrier, so be sure the restraining straps are always used. Some babies will brace their feet against the frame, changing their weight distribution. Make sure your baby is seated properly before you walk.

Strollers and Baby Carriages

Because infants outgrow baby carriages so quickly, many manufacturers now make low carriages that can be converted into strollers when the baby is bigger. Look for safety features and take the following precautions:

1. If you use bumpers in your baby carriage, or if you string toys across it, fasten them securely so they can't fall on top of the baby. Remove such toys as soon as the baby can sit or get on all fours.
2. If the carriage is collapsible, be sure your baby cannot reach the release mechanism. This mechanism should always be locked upright before you put your baby in the carriage.
3. Once your baby is able to sit alone, stop using the carriage, because falls from them are very common after this

point. If you must continue to use the carriage for some reason, or if you have an extremely active baby, harness her and attach the harness to the side of the carriage so she cannot lean out while you're walking.

4. Both carriages and strollers should have brakes that are easy to operate. Use the brake whenever you are stopped, and be sure your infant can't reach the release lever. A brake that locks two wheels provides an extra measure of safety.
5. Select a stroller with a wide base, so it won't tip over.
6. Babies' fingers can become caught in the hinges that fold the stroller, so keep your baby at a safe distance when you open and close it.
7. Don't hang bags or other items from the handles of your stroller—they can make it tip backward. If the stroller has a basket for carrying things, be sure it is placed low and near the rear wheels.
8. The stroller should have a seat belt and shoulder harness, and it should be used whenever your child goes for a ride. For infants, roll up baby blankets to be used as bumpers on either side of the seat.
9. Never leave your child unattended in a baby carriage or stroller.
10. If you purchase a twin stroller, be sure the footrest extends all the way across both sitting areas. If there are separate footrests, a baby's foot can become trapped between them.

Shopping Cart Safety

It is estimated that more than twenty-five thousand shopping-cart-related injuries occur each year. The vast majority involve young children, and the most frequent kinds of injuries are fractures, internal injuries, and concussions.

The design of shopping carts makes it possible for them to tip over when a baby is in the cart or in the seat designed to fit on the cart. Until shopping carts are redesigned, you need to know that seats attached to the top of shopping carts or built into them won't prevent a baby from falling out if he isn't properly restrained; these seats also won't prevent the cart from tipping over even if the baby is restrained.

You should put your baby in a shopping cart seat only when he is able to sit up; make sure he is carefully strapped in. Never leave a baby alone in a shopping cart.

Bicycles

If you like to ride a bicycle, you'll probably consider getting a child carrier that attaches to the back of the bike. You should be aware that even with the best carrier and safety helmet, your child is at risk for serious injury—and children under one year of age should not be put into a child carrier. It is wiser to wait to enjoy bicycling together until your child is old enough to ride with you on his own two-wheeler.

Playgrounds

Whether it's a swing set in the backyard or the more elaborate apparatus in the park, there are many positive things to say about playground equipment. The use of this equipment encourages children to test and expand their physical abilities. However, there are some inevitable dangers. Your baby should participate only in playground activities that are appropriate for his age and development. The risks can also be minimized when equipment is well designed and children are taught basic playground manners. Here are some guidelines you can use in selecting playground equipment and sites for your child:

1. Make sure there is sand, wood chips, or rubberized matting under swings, seesaws, and jungle gyms, and that these surfaces are well maintained. On concrete or asphalt, a fall directly on the head can be fatal—even from a height of just a few inches.
2. Wooden structures should be made from all-weather wood, which is less likely to splinter. Examine the surfaces periodically to be sure they are smooth.
3. Conduct a periodic inspection of equipment, looking especially for loose joints, open chains that could come loose, and rusted cotter pins. On metal equipment, check

for rusted or exposed bolts as well as sharp edges and points. At home, cover them with protective rubber. In a public playground, report the hazard to the appropriate authorities.

4. Be sure swings are made of soft and flexible material. Insist that your child sit in the middle of the seat, holding on with both hands. Don't allow two children to share the same swing. Teach your child never to walk in front of or behind a swing while another youngster is on it.

Your Backyard

Your backyard can be a sanctuary for your baby if you eliminate potential hazards. Here are some suggestions for keeping your yard safe:

1. If you don't have a fenced yard, teach your child the boundaries within which she should play. Always have a responsible person supervise outdoor play.
2. Check your yard for dangerous plants, which are a leading cause of poisoning. If you are unsure about any of the plants in your yard, call your local poison center and request a list of poisonous plants common in your area. If you find any, either replace them or securely fence and lock that area of the yard away from your baby.
3. Teach your child never to pick and eat anything from a plant, no matter how good it looks, without your permission. This is particularly important if you let her help out in a vegetable garden where there's produce that could be eaten.
4. If you use pesticides or herbicides on your lawn or garden, read the instructions carefully. Don't allow babies to play on a treated lawn for at least forty-eight hours.
5. Don't use a power mower to cut the lawn when young children are around. The mower may throw sticks or stones with enough force to injure them. Never have your baby on a riding mower even when you are driving.
6. When you cook food outdoors, screen the grill so your baby cannot touch it. Explain that it is hot like the stove in the kitchen. Store propane grills so your baby cannot reach the knobs. Be sure charcoal is cold before you dump it.
7. Young children should never play unattended near traffic.

Water Safety

Water is one of the most ominous hazards your baby will encounter. Infants can drown in only a few inches of water. Though swimming classes for young children are widely available, the American Academy of Pediatrics does not recommend them for children under four. There are two reasons:

1. You may be lulled into being less cautious because you think your child can swim.
2. Young children who are repeatedly immersed in water may swallow so much of it that they develop water intoxication. This can result in convulsions, shock, and even death.

If you do enroll a child under one in a swimming program, particularly a "Daddy-" or "Mommy-and-Me" class, think of it primarily as an opportunity to enjoy playing in the water together. Be sure the class you choose adheres to guidelines established by the national YMCA. Among other things, these guidelines forbid submersion of young children and encourage parents to participate in all activities. But remember that even a child who knows how to swim needs to be watched constantly. Whenever your baby is near water, follow these safety rules:

1. Be aware of small bodies of water your infant might encounter, such as fish ponds, ditches, fountains, rain barrels, watering cans—even the bucket you use when you wash the car. Babies may be drawn to places and things like these and need constant supervision to be sure they don't fall in.
2. Children who are swimming—even in a shallow toddler's pool—should be watched by an adult, preferably one who knows CPR. (See *Cardiopulmonary Resuscitation and Mouth-to-Mouth Resuscitation*, page 392). Inflatable pools should be emptied and put away after each play session.
3. Don't allow your baby to use inflatable toys or mattresses to keep him afloat. These toys may deflate suddenly or your baby may slip off them into water that is too deep for him.
4. If you have a swimming pool at home, it should be completely surrounded with a 5-foot fence that has a self-

locking gate. Keep the gate closed and locked *at all times*. Be sure your child cannot manipulate the lock.

5. If your pool has a cover, remove it completely before swimming. Also, never allow your baby to crawl or walk on the pool cover; water may have accumulated on it, making it as dangerous as the pool itself. Your baby could also fall through it and become trapped underneath.
6. Keep a safety ring with a rope beside the pool at all times. If possible, have a phone in the pool area with emergency numbers clearly marked.
7. Spas and hot tubs are dangerous for babies, who can easily drown or become overheated in them. Don't allow babies to use these facilities.
8. Your baby should always wear a life preserver when he is in the water or rides in a boat. A life preserver fits properly if you can't lift it off over your baby's head after he's been fastened into it. For the child under age one, the life preserver also should have a flotation collar to keep the head upright and the face out of the water.
9. Adults should not drink alcohol when they are swimming. It presents a danger for them as well as for any children they might be supervising.

Where We Stand

The American Academy of Pediatrics feels strongly that parents should never—even for a moment—leave children alone near open bodies of water, such as lakes or swimming pools, nor near water in homes (bathtubs, spas). For backyard pools, rigid, motorized pool covers are not a substitute for four-sided fencing, since pool covers are not likely to be used appropriately and consistently. Parents should learn CPR and keep a telephone and emergency equipment (such as life preservers) at poolside.

Safety Around Animals

Children are more likely than adults to be bitten by domesticated animals, including your own family pet. This is particularly true when a new baby is brought into the home. At such times the pet's response should be observed carefully, and he should not be left alone with the infant. After the two- or three-week "get acquainted" period, the animal usually ignores or actually enjoys the baby. However, it is always wise to be cautious when the animal is around, regardless of how much your pet seems to enjoy the relationship.

If you want to get a pet as a companion for your baby, wait until she is mature enough to handle and care for the animal—usually around age five or six. Babies and young children have difficulty distinguishing an animal from a toy, so they may inadvertently provoke a bite through teasing or mistreatment. Remember that you have ultimate responsibility for your baby's safety around any animal, so take the following precautions:

1. Look for a pet with a gentle disposition. An older animal is often a good choice for a child, because a puppy or kitten may bite out of sheer friskiness. Avoid older pets raised in a home without children, however.
2. Treat your pet humanely so he will enjoy human company. Don't, for example, tie a dog on a short rope or chain, since extreme confinement may make him anxious and aggressive.
3. Never leave a baby alone with an animal. Many bites occur during periods of playful roughhousing, because the baby doesn't realize when the animal gets overexcited.
4. Teach your baby not to put her face close to an animal.
5. Don't allow your baby to tease your pet by pulling its tail or taking away a toy or a bone. Make sure she doesn't disturb the animal when it's sleeping or eating.
6. Have all pets—both dogs and cats—immunized against rabies.
7. Obey local ordinances about licensing and leashing your pet. Be sure your pet is under your control at all times.

8. Find out which neighbors have dogs, so your baby can meet the pets with which she's likely to have contact. Teach your child how to greet a dog: She should stand still while the dog sniffs her; then she can slowly extend her hand to pet the animal. Teach your child not to approach or pet animals without owner's OK.
9. To avoid bites by wild creatures, notify the health department whenever you see an animal that seems sick or injured, or one that is acting strangely. Don't try to catch the animal or pick it up. Teach your baby to avoid all undomesticated animals.
10. Dog owners should be aware that their dog may react aggressively when strangers approach their baby.

When planning ways to keep your child safe, remember that she is constantly changing. Strategies that successfully protect her from danger when she's one year old may no longer be adequate in later months and years. Review your family's home and habits often to make sure your safeguards remain appropriate for your child's age.

11

PART-TIME CARE FOR YOUR BABY

Who will care for your baby during the hours when you are away? Sooner or later you're bound to face this question. Whether you need someone to care for him a few hours a week or nine hours a day, you'll want to feel confident about the person who does it. But finding the right individual to care for your baby can be a big challenge. This chapter provides suggestions to make your search easier. It also contains guidelines for preventing, recognizing, and resolving problems once you've made your choice.

The most difficult and crucial part of finding good part-time care is judging the character and abilities of the caregiver. If she (many, though not all, caregivers are women) is not a member of your family, chances are you'll meet this person only a few times before entrusting your child to her. Even so, you'll want to feel as confident about her as if she were a member of your family. While it's impossible to be 100 percent sure about anyone under these circumstances, you can tell a great deal about caregivers by observing them at work for a day or two and carefully checking references. Never entrust your child to anyone until you've taken time to watch her with your child and other children, and you feel confident in her abilities and dedication.

WHAT TO LOOK FOR IN A CAREGIVER: GUIDELINES FOR BABIES (ALSO, SEE CHAPTER 6, PAGE 194.)

Most babies thrive when they're cared for by supportive adults who are warmly affectionate and help them

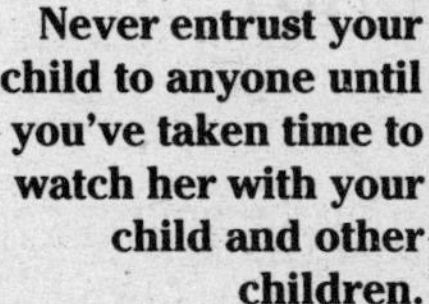
Never entrust your child to anyone until you've taken time to watch her with your child and other children.

work out solutions while protecting them from making choices that could lead to serious injury. The following list describes many things you should look for when you're observing someone who might take care of your infant. These guidelines apply not only to child-care workers but also to baby-sitters. They're also good to keep in mind as you play with your baby yourself or supervise small groups of children.

A good caregiver should:

- listen carefully to children and observe their behavior.
- set reasonable limits for children and maintain those limits consistently.
- tell children why certain things are not allowed, and offer acceptable alternatives.
- deal with difficult situations as they arise and before they get out of control.
- follow through on what you tell children.
- join children at play without disrupting their activity.
- reward childrens' efforts and relieve their "hurts" with an affectionate physical gesture, such as a hug or a pat.
- talk naturally and conversationally with the children about what they are doing.
- limit adult conversations in the childrens' presence.
- show respect for the childrens' ideas and decisions.
- avoid offering children choices when there is no choice.

- allow children to make mistakes and learn from them (as long as there is no danger involved in doing so).

Choices in Part-time Care

In addition to the *general* suggestions mentioned above, you need to identify your *specific* needs and desires. Your list of questions should include:

- Where do I want my baby to be during the day: at home? in someone else's home? in a child-care center? If away from home, in what part of town?
- What days and hours do I need part-time care each week?
- How will I handle my infant's transportation to and from the program (if it's away from home)?
- What backup arrangements can I make? How will I handle days when my baby is sick or when my baby's caregiver is unavailable because of illness or personal business? What are the arrangements for holidays, summertime, vacations?
- What can I realistically afford?
- How large a program would I like for my baby?
- What qualifications would I like the caregiver(s) to have?
- How do I want my baby disciplined?
- What other basic conditions would make me feel comfortable about leaving my infant with someone else?

About half of all parents keep the part-time care of their babies within their own families, either by sharing the responsibility between the parents or by letting the infant stay with relatives during work hours. Usually this is one of the better arrangements, because the baby is familiar with the people caring for her. If you have family members or friends whom you would like to care for your infant and who live nearby, you should ask yourself if you would be comfortable with their care and whether they'd be willing to provide part-time care either on a regular basis or as a backup if other arrangements fail. Consider also, when possible, that offering payment for these services makes the arrangement fairer and creates an additional incentive for a member of your family to help you.

Other options are to bring someone into your own home or to take your baby to another person's home or a child-care center. Your financial resources, the age and needs of your child, and your own preferences about child rearing will help you decide which choice is best.

In-Home Care

If you are returning to work while your child is still an infant, your first choice for child care may be to bring someone into your own home who can look after him and perhaps help with the housework. This person may come to your home on a regular basis, or live with you. You can find such a person by asking your friends for recommendations, scanning or placing ads in the paper (especially local publications for parents), and checking with agencies that specialize in child care.

In-home caregivers are not required to be licensed, so you'll have to check references very carefully. When you have a candidate, ask for her work record during the past four or five years and talk to each of her former employers. Don't be afraid to ask detailed and personal questions about whether she's reliable and capable. Also, ask about her approach to discipline, scheduling, feeding, and comforting, to try to determine if she is right for your baby and your style of child rearing.

The person you ultimately choose will quickly become part of your family, so make sure you hire someone who respects your values, beliefs, and life-style. To the extent possible, involve the whole family in the decision, and arrange for a trial period under your supervision before you make a final commitment.

Arranging for child care at home has the following advantages and disadvantages:

Advantages:

1. Your baby stays in familiar surroundings and receives individualized care and attention.

2. She isn't exposed to the illnesses and negative behavior of other children.
3. When your infant is sick, you don't have to stay home from work or make different arrangements to take care of her.
4. Your caregiver may do some light housework as well. (If this is one of your expectations, make that clear from the start.)
5. You needn't worry about transportation for your baby (unless you plan that the caregiver will take her on outings).

Disadvantages:

1. You may have difficulty finding someone who is willing to accept the wages, benefits, and confinement of working in the home, or you may find the costs of qualified in-home care prohibitive.
2. Since you will be considered an employer, you must meet minimum-wage, Social Security, and tax-reporting requirements. (If you use a part-time care agency, your costs may be higher, but you won't have to manage the government reporting and tax payments yourself.)
3. The presence of a caregiver may infringe on your family's privacy, especially if she lives in your home. Furthermore, she may bring her own needs and problems with her, which could involve more of your own time and energy than you bargained for.
4. Because the caregiver is alone with your baby most of the time, you have no way of knowing exactly how she is performing her job.
5. You are dependent on your caregiver's reliability. If she gets sick, has a family crisis, finds a better job, or wants to take a vacation without warning you, you'll be left frantically searching for a replacement.

Family Child Care

Many people provide informal care in their homes for small groups of children, including babies, often looking after their own children or grandchildren at the same time. Some offer evening care or care for children with special needs. Family day care generally is less expensive and more flexible than that offered by formal child-care centers.

Family child-care homes can be more intimate and less stressful environments than a large child care center. But good supervision isn't necessarily guaranteed in these settings. If there is only one caregiver, and a particular child needs her attention at a given moment, the other youngsters will be ignored.

Some family child-care providers are formally licensed and registered. Licensing regulations vary from state to state and can be obtained from the appropriate local authorities. Also, the American Academy of Pediatrics can provide general information on the basic requirements for family child-care homes and the new national standards for a safe and healthy child-care center. (Send request for information to the American Academy of Pediatrics, Dept. C—Child Care, 141 Northwest Point Boulevard, P.O. Box 927, Elk Grove Village, Illinois 60009.)

However, the majority of family child-care homes are not licensed. For that reason you must be careful to observe the caregiver's work and check her references and certification before making a decision about such care for your child.

Family child care has the following advantages and disadvantages:

Advantages:

1. In good family child-care settings, there is a favorable adult/child ratio. The total number of children should be no more than about three if some of the children are infants.

2. Your baby has all the comforts of being in a home, and can be involved in many of the same household activities he'd find at your own house.

3. There may be playmates. This provides more opportunities for social stimulation than if your baby were cared for alone at home.

4. Family child care is very flexible, so special arrangements usually can be made to meet your child's individual interests and needs.

Disadvantages:

1. You cannot observe what happens to your baby in your absence. While some providers carefully organize activities that are appropriate and stimulating for children, others use TV as a baby-sitter while they do housework. (Be aware that the same thing could be true of people who care for your child in your own home.)
2. It may be difficult for you to get satisfactory references for a particular caregiver.
3. Most family child-care providers work without supervision or advice from other adults.

For the names of family child-care homes in your area, contact the local agency that licenses or registers them, or use a local referral agency that lists them. Check with these agencies about homes advertised in the paper or on neighborhood bulletin boards, since these may not be licensed. Call Child Care Aware at 1-800-424-2246 for the child-care resource and referral agency nearest you. References from parents of children the same age as yours can also be very helpful.

Before committing to a particular family child-care home:

- Check references, licensing, accreditation, and inspection status (if any).
- Call the parents of children who are in, or recently were in, child care there, and ask about their impression and experiences.
- Find out how many children (including the caregiver's children) are actually cared for in the home at various times of the day and on different days.
- Ask what other adults live in or visit the house and might come and go while your child is there.
- Ask about substitute arrangements in case the caregiver (or someone in his family) becomes ill.
- Ask how the caregiver would handle an emergency situation involving one or more of the children or himself.
- Make sure the caregiver and facility (if licensed) complies with standard health and safety requirements such as those

endorsed by the American Academy of Pediatrics as national standards. If your pediatrician does not have these available in her office, she can help you get them. (Also see discussion in *Making a Final Selection*, page 361.)

Child-Care Centers

Child-care centers are also called day-care or child-development centers. Many child-care centers are open from 6:00 or 7:00 A.M. to 6:00 P.M., thus meeting the needs of most working parents. These facilities usually care for groups of ten or more children, often in a church, community center, or school. Although most are licensed for children from two and a half to six years, many offer care for infants. A growing number of centers participate in accreditation programs. For more information about accreditation of centers, contact The National Association for the Education of Young Children, 1509 16th Street NW, Washington, D.C. 20036–1426.

Child-care centers are the fastest-growing form of part-time care in the United States. They can be found in several different versions, each with its own characteristics, strengths, and weaknesses.

Chain Centers have become a thriving national industry. Many of the larger ones have a wide variety of activities and programs that appeal to both parents and children (child-development programs, structured curricula, and centrally managed personnel and facility routines). Because of centralized management, they may not exhibit unique features found in individually run facilities.

Independent For-Profit Centers usually are small operations run by a small staff. They generally have no agency, church, or other support, so they must depend on enrollment fees to pay the overhead and earn a narrow profit for the owners. Because many of these programs are built around one or two dedicated people, they can be quite excellent—as long as those individuals remain actively involved with day-to-day operations. Unfortunately, such programs do not always maintain their high standards, because of staff turnover or ownership changes.

Nonprofit Centers often are linked with churches, synagogues, community centers, universities, or organizations like the YMCA or YWCA. They may have access to public funding, permitting discounted fees for lower-income families. Any profits earned from enrollment are put back into the program, thus directly benefiting the children. However, these centers are also subject to undesirable changes due to the need to meet the demands of the sponsoring organization. Many also rely on parent involvement for fund-raising events and other aspects of operating the centers.

There are several advantages and disadvantages to child-care centers:

Advantages

1. Because local child-care centers are easier to regulate and observe, more information is generally available about them than about other child-care choices.
2. Many centers have structured programs designed to meet children's developmental needs.
3. Most centers have several caregivers, so you are not dependent on the availability of just one person.
4. Workers in these centers tend to be better supervised than caregivers in other settings.
5. You can often arrange shorter hours or fewer days of care if you work only part-time.

Disadvantages:

1. Regulations for child-care centers vary widely: Strict standards applied to publicly funded centers may not apply to privately financed ones, and many states exempt church-run facilities from even minimum requirements. To save on personnel costs, the center may provide less qualified and consistent adults to care for infants and toddlers than is desirable.
2. Good programs may have waiting lists for admission because they are in such demand.
3. Because these arrangements serve more children and have larger staffs, your baby may receive less personalized attention than in smaller programs.

Child-care centers generally are listed in the phone book or can be identified by calling your local health or welfare agency. Many communities have resources and referral agencies that help parents find appropriate care. For a resource and referral agency near you, call Child Care Aware at 1-800-424-2246. Ask your pediatrician or other parents with children in child care to recommend a center from these lists.

Making a Final Selection

When considering a particular child-care setting, you need to know all of the rules and practices that would affect your baby. If the program is formal enough to have a printed handbook, this may answer many of your questions. Otherwise, ask the program director about the following (some of which apply to in-home or family child-care as well):

1. What are the hiring requirements for staff members? In most good programs, caregivers must have at least two years of college, pass minimum health requirements, and receive basic immunizations. Ideally, they will have some background in early child development and perhaps have children themselves. Directors generally must have a college degree or many years of experience qualifying them as experts in both child development and administration.

2. How many staff members are available per child? The general rule to follow is: the younger the child, the more adults there should be in each group. Each baby should be assigned to one caregiver as the primary person responsible for that baby's care.

   How many children are in each group? Generally, smaller groups offer babies a better chance to interact with and learn from one another. For babies from birth to 12 months of age, the ideal child/staff ratio is 3:1; and the ideal group size is 6.

3. Is there any problem with frequent staff changes? This may suggest that there may be problems with the facility's operations. Ideally, most caregivers should have been with the program for several years. Unfortunately, because wages of caregivers are low, a high turnover rate is common.

4. What are the goals of the program? Some are very organized and try to teach children new skills, or attempt to change or mold their behavior. Others are very relaxed, with an emphasis on helping babies develop at their own

pace. Still others fall somewhere in between. Decide what you want for your child, and make sure the program you choose meets your desires. Avoid those that offer no personalized attention or support for your baby. Generally, these care for large groups of children with too few staff members.

5. What are the admission procedures? Quality child-care programs require some background information on each baby. Be prepared for very specific questions about your child's individual needs, developmental level, and health status. You may also be asked about your own child-rearing desires and any other children in your family. Be concerned if the center has no interest in any of this information.
6. Does the child-care provider have a valid license and recent health certificate, and does the provider enforce health and immunization requirements for children in the program? Standard immunizations and regular checkups should be required for all children and staff members.
7. How are illnesses handled? Parents should be notified if a staff member or child contracts a significant communicable disease (not just a cold, but problems like chickenpox, measles, or hepatitis). The program also should have a clear policy regarding sick children. You should know when to keep your baby home and how the center will respond if he becomes ill during the day.
8. What are the costs? How much will you have to pay to start, and how often will you make installment payments? What do the payments specifically cover? Will you need to pay when your child is absent for illness or vacations with the family?
9. What happens on a typical day? Ideally, there should be a mix of physical activity and quiet times. Some activities should be group oriented and others individualized. There should be set times for meals and snacks. While a certain amount of structure is desirable, there should also be room for free play and special events.
10. How much parental involvement is expected? Some programs rely heavily on parent participation, while others request very little. At the least, quality programs should

welcome your opinions and allow you to visit your child during the day. Do *not* consider any program that is closed to parents for part or all of the day.

11. What are the general procedures? A well-organized program should have clearly defined rules and regulations regarding:

- Hours of operation
- Transportation of children
- Field trips
- Meals and snacks
- Administration of medication and first aid
- Emergency evacuations
- Notification of child's absence
- Weather cancellations
- Withdrawal of children from the program
- Supplies or equipment that parents must provide
- Special celebrations
- How parents may contact the staff during the day and at night
- Exclusion of children for certain illnesses

Once you've received the basic information, you should inspect the building and grounds during operating hours to see how the caregivers interact with the children. Your first impressions are especially important, since they'll influence all your future dealings with the program. If you sense warmth and a loving approach to the children, you'll probably feel comfortable placing your own baby there. If you see a worker spank one of the youngsters, you should reconsider sending your own baby, even if that's the only sign of abusiveness you notice.

Try to observe the daily routine, paying attention to how the day is organized and what activities are planned for the children. Watch how food is prepared and find out how often the children are fed. Check how frequently the babies are diapered. While touring the child-care home or center, also check to see if the following basic health and safety standards are being met:

- The premises are clean and reasonably neat (without discouraging play by the children).
- There is plenty of play equipment, and it is in good repair.
- The equipment is appropriate for the developmental skills of the children in the program.
- Babies are closely supervised when climbing on playthings, roughhousing, or playing with blocks (which are sometimes thrown) and other potentially dangerous toys.
- There are safe indoor and outdoor areas where the children have active (large-muscle) play each day, with cushioning material under climbing equipment that meets the guidelines of the Consumer Product Safety Commission.
- Areas where food is handled are clearly separate from toilets and diaper-changing areas.
- Diaper-changing areas are cleaned and sanitized after each infant's use.
- Handwashing sinks are available and used by the children and staff next to the toilets, changing areas, and where food is prepared and served.
- Potty (or training) chairs should be avoided because they increase the risk of spreading germs that cause diarrhea.
- Babies are supervised at all times, even when napping.
- Caregivers who handle diaper changing or toileting wash their hands carefully after diapering and toileting. Where possible, these caregivers do not prepare food or serve food to the group.

Once you're satisfied that a particular program will provide your child with a safe, loving, healthy environment, let him test it out while you're present. Watch how the caregivers and your child interact, and make sure that all of you are comfortable with the situation.

A Child-Care Checklist

The following checklist can be used to help you evaluate caregivers and child-care programs. Ideally, the answer to every question will be yes, but realistically there are bound to be a few no's. Look carefully at the questions that receive "no" responses, and decide how important these issues are to you.

Does the caregiver:

1. feel like someone with whom you can develop an open relationship?
2. impress you as someone your baby will enjoy, and who enjoys working with children?
3. agree with your beliefs about child rearing and discipline, and respect your family's cultural and religious values?
4. provide the right activities, materials, and equipment to help children learn and grow?
5. encourage good health habits, such as washing hands before eating?
6. know basic first aid?
7. have enough time for each child in his care?
8. help each child to feel good about herself?
9. take time to discuss your child with you regularly?
10. enjoy cuddling your baby?
11. properly care for your infant's physical needs, such as feeding and diapering?
12. spend plenty of time holding, talking, and playing with your child?
13. help your baby find interesting things to look at, touch, and hear?
14. provide a safe environment for children who are beginning to crawl and walk?
15. have a regular medical examination and TB test?

Does the child-care home or center have:

1. an up-to-date license?
2. a convenient location near your home or work?
3. an open-door policy allowing parents to visit at any time?
4. enough indoor and outdoor space so children can move freely and safely?
5. an adequate number of caregivers to meet the needs of all the children?
6. equipment that is safe, clean, and suitable for the ages of the children in the program?
7. enough heat, light, and ventilation?
8. a clear policy for the care of sick children, and a separate area to care for sick children? (An isolated area is not necessary, but a quiet place to rest should be available.)
9. a clean, safe place to change diapers?
10. cribs with firm mattresses covered in heavy plastic?
11. separate cribs and linens for each baby?
12. acceptable safety standards? These should include:
    - Cushioning material in the fall zone of any climbing equipment, indoors or out
    - A first-aid kit
    - Smoke detectors and enough exits in case of fire
    - Covered radiators and protected heaters
    - Strong screens or bars on windows above the first floor, and gates at the top and bottom of stairs
    - Safety caps on all electrical outlets

- Medicines and poisonous substances stored out of children's reach and locked if possible

Are there opportunities:

1. to play both quietly and actively, indoors and out?
2. to play both alone and in groups?
3. to use materials and equipment that help develop new skills and abilities?
4. to learn to get along and share with others?
5. to learn about different cultures through art, music, and games?
6. to crawl and explore safely?
7. to play with objects and toys that help develop the senses of touch, sight, and hearing (such as mobiles, rattles, crib gyms, nesting toys, balls, and blocks)?

After completing this checklist, if you are still uncertain about your child's care arrangement, discuss your concerns with your pediatrician.

Building a Relationship with Your Baby's Caregivers

For your child's sake, you need to develop a good relationship with the person or people who care for her in your absence. The better you get along with her caregiver, the more comfortable your baby will feel as she interacts with both of you. The better you communicate with each other about her, the more continuity there will be in her care throughout the day.

One way to build this relationship is by talking with the caregiver—even briefly—each time you leave or return for your baby. If something exciting or upsetting happened during the early morning, it might affect your baby's behavior during the rest of the day, so the caregiver should know about it. When you take her home, you should be told about any important events that occurred in your absence, from a change in bowel movements or eating patterns to a new way of playing or her first steps. Also, if she's showing symptoms of a developing illness, you and the caregiver should discuss the situation and agree on what to do if these symptoms get worse.

A rivalry may develop between you and the caregiver for your baby's affection and control of her behavior. For example, you may hear "Funny, she never does that for me" when she misbehaves. Don't take this seriously—all children usually save their worst behavior for the people they trust most.

If you treat caregivers as partners, they will feel that you respect them and probably will be more enthusiastic about looking after your baby. Here are some ways to build this sense of partnership on a daily basis:

- Talk to the caregiver about things your baby has done that are particularly funny or interesting. Explain that sharing this kind of information is important to you, and encourage two-way communication.
- Extend basic courtesy to your baby's caregivers.
- Provide materials and suggestions for special projects the caregivers can do with your baby and/or the group.
- Help out before you leave your baby by spending a few minutes getting her settled. If she's in a child-care center, help her put away her things and join an activity. If she is being cared for at home, get her involved in an activity before you depart. Make sure your baby always knows you are leaving. Say good-bye before you disappear, but leave without prolonging your departure. Don't just "slip away."
- Help plan and carry out special activities with the caregiver.

Periodically, the two of you also should have longer discussions to review any problems and plan for future changes in your child's care. Try to schedule these extended conversations at a time when you won't be rushing to get somewhere and at a place where there won't be distractions. If possible, arrange for someone else to care for your baby while you are talking. Allow enough time to discuss all the facts and opin-

Tips to Make It Easier When You Leave Your Baby

Just getting the day started is challenging: You have to get the whole family dressed and fed, leaving enough time to get to the child-care facility and then to work on schedule. The biggest struggle in all of this comes the moment you leave your child. Separating is hard, whatever your child's age, but especially difficult during the first year of life. Here are some suggestions to make this morning ritual a little easier for both of you.

Your Child's Developmental Stage	Your Response
0 to 7 months In early infancy your baby primarily needs love, comforting, and good basic care to satisfy his physical needs.	Though this period may be a difficult time of separation for you, young infants generally will accommodate well to a consistent child-care worker in almost any setting. During the initial settling-in period, your presence should last for up to one hour. This can be shortened by the end of one to two weeks.
7 to 12 months This is when stranger anxiety normally occurs. Your baby may suddenly be reluctant to stay with anyone outside his family. The unfamiliar setting of a child-care center may also upset him.	If possible, do not start child care during this period. If your baby is already in such a program, take a little extra time each day before you say good-bye. Create a short good-bye ritual, perhaps involving a favorite toy. Above all, be consistent from day to day.

Your Child's Developmental Stage	Your Response
One Year and older This is when separation anxiety peaks and your child has the most difficulty with your leaving. He may not believe you will really return, and may weep and cling to you as you try to get out the door.	Be understanding but firm and persistent. Once you have left, do not reappear unless you are prepared to stay or to take your child with you.

ions that both of you have on your minds, and agree on specific objectives and plans.

Most parents find that this discussion goes more smoothly if they've made a list of important topics beforehand. You should also start the conversation on a positive note by talking about some of the things the caregiver is doing that please you. Then move on to your concerns. After presenting your own thoughts, ask for her opinions and listen carefully. Remember, there is little that's strictly right or wrong when it come to child rearing, and most situations have several "right" approaches. So try to be open-minded and flexible in your discussions. Close the conversation with a specific plan of action and a date to meet again. Both of you will be more comfortable if something concrete comes out of the meeting, even if it's only a decision to stay on the same course for another month or two.

Resolving Conflicts that Arise Over Your Baby's Care

Let's presume that you've chosen a child-care setting carefully. Does that mean your problems are over? Probably not.

Whenever two or more people share responsibility for a child, some conflicts eventually are bound to arise. In many cases you can resolve a disagreement about child care simply by talking through the problem. You may find that the conflict is nothing more than a misunderstanding or a misreading of the situation. Other times, especially when several people are involved in the care of your child, you may need a more organized approach to resolving problems. The following step-by-step strategy can help:

1. Define the problem clearly. Make sure you understand who is involved, but avoid blaming anyone. For example, what if your baby has been hitting or biting other children in her child-care program? Find out whom she has hit or bitten, and which caregivers were on hand at the time. Ask what they observed before you decide whether the problem is solely your baby's. Perhaps she was provoked. Maybe you can suggest an alternate way in which the caregivers can respond if the incident recurs.
2. Listen to everyone's ideas, in order to find other possible solutions.
3. Agree on a specific plan of action with clearly defined time limits and assignments to each of the caregivers—including you.
4. Consider everything that could go wrong with the plan you've devised, and decide how these problems might be avoided or handled if they occur.
5. Put the plan into action.
6. Meet again at a specified time to decide whether the plan is working. If it's not, go through the process again to decide what changes need to be made.

What to Do When Your Child Is Sick

If your baby is like most others, he'll get his share of illnesses, whether or not he's in a child-care program. In most cases these illnesses will be colds or other respiratory infections, which tend to occur more often between early fall and late spring. At times he may get one infection right after another, and be sick for weeks. If both parents have full-time jobs, this can be a big problem.

Even babies who are only mildly ill may be sent home from child-care programs, and for good reason. A sick baby may be contagious and risks giving his illness to another child. Also, a sick baby may need extra care and attention, which most programs are poorly equipped to provide.

Some states have regulations that actually require child-care programs to send sick children home. This makes sense, particularly when a baby has a fever and is acting sick, is sneezing or coughing, is vomiting, or has diarrhea, since it is under those circumstances that contagious diseases are spread to others.

Respiratory diseases, however, are contagious well before any symptoms appear. By the time anyone realizes the baby is sick, he's probably already spread the infection, and excluding him won't do much to contain it at that point. Nevertheless, few child-care workers want to accept the responsibility of caring for a sick infant with anything more than a very minor illness.

Ideally, you'll be able to stay home when your baby is sick. However, if you work full-time, this may be difficult. Talk to your employer ahead of time to see if arrangements can be made for you to be home when your baby is sick. You might suggest bringing your work home with you, or try to identify in advance coworkers who can substitute for you when this situation arises.

If your job and your spouse's require full-time attendance, you'll have to make other arrangements for a sick baby. These are days when you might arrange alternate care for him, preferably where both the caregiver and the setting are familiar. If you rely on a relative or hire a sitter to stay with him, make sure she understands the nature of the illness and how it should be treated.

If your baby requires medication, write out detailed instructions. Tell the caregiver why it's being given, how it should be stored and administered (in what doses and at what intervals), what side effects to look for, and what to do if they occur. Explain that medicine should not be disguised as food or described as candy; instead, the baby should be told what the medicine is and why he needs to take it. Ask the caregiver to record the time each dose is given. If your baby is in a child-care center, you might be asked to sign a consent for the caregiver to administer the medication.

In a few communities there are services that specialize in care for mildly ill babies or older children. These include:

Home-Based Programs

1. Family child-care homes that are equipped to care for both sick and well children. If a baby becomes ill in such a program, she can continue attending in a segregated area if possible.
2. Family child-care homes that care only for sick children. Some of these are associated with well-child care centers.
3. Agencies or child-care centers that provide caregivers who can work in your home.

Center-Based Programs

1. Regular child-care centers that have trained staff members to care for sick babies and older children in the usual child-care setting, but apart from the main group of well children.
2. Centers that offer a separate "get-well room" for sick babies and older children, staffed by a caregiver.
3. Sick-child care centers that are set up specifically to care for ill babies and older children.

In sick-child programs, caregivers adjust the activity level of the youngsters to the child's ability to participate, and the babies receive a lot of cuddling and personal attention. These programs should pay extra attention to hygiene for both caregivers and babies. The premises and equipment, especially toys, should be cleaned thoroughly and often. Disposable toys may be necessary in some situations, depending on the nature of the illnesses involved. A pediatrician and public health consultant should be on call for every sick-child care facility.

Controlling Infectious Diseases in Child-Care Programs

Whenever children gather in groups, their risk of getting sick increases. Babies are particularly affected, since they tend to place their hands and play objects in their mouths, making it even easier to spread infectious diseases.

It's impossible for adults to keep toys and other objects in the child-care center in perfect sanitary condition. However, there are many precautions and practices that can help control the spread of infection. Immunizations, for example, can greatly reduce outbreaks of serious infectious diseases. Centers should require children to be immunized (at appropriate ages) against diphtheria, tetanus, pertussis, polio, measles, mumps, rubella, *Haemophilus influenzae* type b, hepatitis B, chickenpox, and possibly viral influenza. The immunity of caregivers should be checked, and if there is any doubt, they should receive appropriate immunizations as well.

In addition to requiring immunizations, child-care programs should be extremely careful about maintaining good hygiene. If a center cares for infants, toddlers, and toilet-trained youngsters, each group should have a separate area, each with its own accessible sink for hand washing. Staff should wash their hands after changing diapers, blowing noses, and before touching food. The facility and all equipment should be cleaned at least daily. Changing tables, toilets, and anything that goes in the babies' mouths should be washed, then sprayed with or dipped in a sanitizing solution and allowed to air-dry.

As a parent, you also can help control the spread of disease in your child's center by keeping her home when she has an illness that's contagious or requires extra attention. (Your center should issue guidelines to help you determine when to do this.) Also notify her caregiver as soon as *anyone* in your family is diagnosed as having a serious communicable disease, and request that all parents be alerted when any child in the program has a serious or highly contagious infectious illness.

As she grows, teach your child proper hygiene and hand-washing habits so that she's less likely to spread illnesses herself. And finally, educate yourself about the illnesses that are most common in child-care settings, so you know what to expect and how to respond if they occur in your infant's program. These include the following:

Colds and Other Respiratory Infections

The most common infections are caused by viruses that produce the symptoms of a cold, fever or crankiness, or result in ear infections. Because infants in child care are exposed to many people while they're so young, they often get these infections at an earlier age than do infants cared for at home. However, after infancy the risk begins to decrease for children in stable child-care arrangements. Infections caused by the bacteria *Haemophilus influenzae* type b are an important exception to this. They are two or three times more common among children in child care. Fortunately, the chances of contracting this illness can be significantly decreased by immunizing infants with the Hib vaccine starting at two months of age.

Diarrheal Diseases

Gastrointestinal diseases are less common than respiratory infections. The average baby has one or two episodes of diarrhea a year. These illnesses can spread easily in day-care homes and centers that have poor hand-washing practices, careless handling of diapers, or unsanitary food practices. Even when the staff is vigilant, however, a single infected child can pass the disease to others.

If your infant has diarrhea, check with your pediatrician or the staff at the center before leaving him that day. If he has a mild form of the illness, then several days away from the center should minimize the chances that he'll transmit it to other children. But if a more serious cause is suspected, then further tests to identify the responsible agent (bacteria, virus, or parasite) will need to be done before the baby returns. (See *Diarrhea,* page 421.)

Hepatitis A

If a youngster in a child-care program gets hepatitis A, a viral infection of the liver, it can spread easily to other children and caregivers. In infants (as well as preschool children), most infections are asymptomatic or cause mild, nonspecific symptoms. Older infected children may have mild fever, nausea, vomiting, diarrhea, and/or jaundice (a yellowish skin color). However, the adults who contract this illness usually experience these problems to a much greater degree. The spread of hepatitis can be controlled by giving injections of gamma globulin, but several staff members and parents may be infected before anyone realizes there's a problem. For this reason, whenever hepatitis A is diagnosed in anyone even remotely connected with the program, parents and staff should be alerted and a doctor consulted to decide how best to stop the disease from spreading. (See *Hepatitis,* page 428.) There are now hepatitis A vaccines available, but they are approved only for children ages two years and older. These vaccines are suggested for certain international travelers and adults employed in certain high-risk occupations such as a child-care facility.

Cytomegalovirus (CMV) Infection

Cytomegalovirus usually causes only mild illness, and many babies show no symptoms at all. However, this virus is dangerous to any pregnant woman who is not immune to it, because infection may cause serious defects in her unborn child. The virus is transmitted easily through direct contact with body fluids (tears, urine, saliva). Fortunately, most adult women are already immune to this disease, but if you are pregnant, have a baby in child care, or work in a child-care home or center yourself, you have an increased risk of exposure to CMV and should discuss the problem with your physician.

HIV (AIDS Virus) and Hepatitis B

HIV (AIDS virus) and Hepatitis B virus produce serious chronic infections. HIV infection, when it develops into full-blown AIDS, is a fatal illness. Children who get HIV or Hepatitis B infections usually acquire these viruses from their infected mother during pregnancy or at the time of birth. Both diseases are transmitted from one child to another only by passage of blood from an infected child into the body of someone not infected. Because this type of contact does not occur in the course of usual child-care activities, children with these infections are not a danger to others. In order to be sure that no transmission of these serious illnesses can occur, all bloody injuries should be handled wearing protective gloves, and all blood-contaminated surfaces or clothing should be washed and disinfected. Hepatitis B vaccines are universally recommended in the first few months of life (see the Recommended Childhood Immunization Schedule, page 82); in some states, they are required for entry into child care.

Safety Walk Checklist

Next time you walk through your baby's child-care home or center, use the following checklist to make sure the facility is safe, clean, and in good repair. If there is a problem with any item on the list, bring it to the attention of the director or caregiver and follow up later to be sure it was corrected.

Indoors

- Floors are smooth, clean, and have a nonskid surface.
- Climbers are mounted over impact-absorbent surfaces.
- Medicines, cleaning agents, and tools are out of babies' reach.
- First-aid kit is fully supplied and out of babies' reach.
- Walls and ceilings are clean and in good repair, with no peeling paint or damaged plaster.
- Children are never left unattended.
- Toys do not contain lead or have any signs of chipping paint, rust, or small pieces that could break off. (The weight or softness of the material may provide clues that the toys are made of lead.)
- High chairs have wide bases and safety straps.
- Babies are not allowed to take bottles to bed.
- Electrical outlets are covered with childproof caps.
- Electric lights are in good repair, with no frayed or dangling cords.
- Heating pipes and radiators are out of reach or covered so babies cannot touch them.
- Hot water is set at or below 120 degrees Fahrenheit (92 degrees Celsius) to prevent scalding.

- There are no poisonous plants or disease-bearing animals (such as water turtles).
- Trash containers are covered.
- Exits are clearly marked and easy to reach.
- No smoking is allowed in the child-care facility.
- Windows are securely screened.

Outdoors

- Grounds are free of litter, sharp objects, and animal droppings.
- Play equipment is smooth, well anchored, and free of rust, splinters, and sharp corners. All screws and bolts are capped or concealed.
- No play equipment is higher than 6 feet.
- Swing seats are lightweight and flexible, and there are no open or S-shaped hooks.
- Slides have wide, flat, stable steps with good treads, rounded rims along the sides to prevent falls, and a flat area at the end of the slide to help children slow down.
- Metal slides are shaded from the sun.
- Sandboxes are covered when not in use.
- Childproof barriers keep babies and older children out of hazardous areas.
- Playground surfaces are made of 12 inches of wood chips, shredded tires, or other impact-absorbing material in areas where falls are more likely to occur (under monkey bars, slides).

Preventing and Dealing with Injuries in Child-Care Programs

Many injuries that occur at home or in child-care settings are predictable and preventable. While the staff is largely responsible for your baby's safety, you can contribute to the prevention of injuries by helping them to identify potential hazards in the facility and by observing the safety practices of caregivers when you leave or return for your infant. For instance, you can take "safety walks" through the center, to make sure all equipment is in proper working condition, and to find other ways to reduce risks.

Safety for children (and adults) in and around cars is a special concern. The center should have large, sheltered, and well-marked pickup and drop-off points. Parents should be protected from stormy weather as they get their children into and out of car seats and seat belts, and into the building. CHILDREN AT PLAY or similar signs should be placed along the street near the center. If your child shares a ride to and from child care, be sure the other drivers are using appropriate seat restraints for the children. The driver must check the vehicle to be sure that everyone is safely buckled in before pulling away and that everyone has left the vehicle before locking up at the parking spot. Also, care should be taken that the children are released to recognized adults at the child-care facility or at day's end at the child's home.

If your child-care program includes swimming, make sure appropriate safety precautions are followed. If a pool is at or near the child-care center itself, it should be surrounded by a childproof fence with a locked gate. For hygienic reasons, portable wading pools should be avoided.

Car Pool Safety

If you drive children in a car pool, you must be as responsible for every child in the car as you are for your own. This means making sure that everyone buckles up, not overloading the car, disciplining children who disobey safety rules, and checking that your insurance covers everyone on board. In addition, make sure that you and other drivers observe the following precautions:

- If possible, have each child's own parents or another responsible adult buckle her into the car and take her out when she returns home.

- Turn all babies and children over to the direct supervision of a child-care staff member.
- Place all hard objects, such as lunch boxes or toys, on the floor.
- Close and lock all car doors, but only after checking that everyone's fingers and feet are inside.
- Open the passenger window only a few inches, and lock all power window and door controls from the driver's seat if possible.
- Remind children about safety rules and proper behavior before starting out.
- Plan your routes to minimize travel time and avoid hazardous conditions.
- Pull over if any child in the group gets out of control or misbehaves. If any child presents a problem consistently, exclude her from the car pool until her conduct improves.
- Have available emergency contact information for each child who rides in the car.
- Ideally, equip each vehicle with a fire extinguisher and first-aid kit.

Part-Time Care for Children with Special Needs

If your child has a developmental disability or a chronic illness, don't let that keep him out of pre-school or child care. In fact, quality part-time care may be extremely good for him. He may actually benefit more than other children from the social contact, physical exercise, and variety of experiences of a group program.

The time he spends in a child-care program will be good for you, too. Tending a baby with a disability can be extremely demanding of time, energy, and emotions. It can also be expensive, requiring both parents to work. The challenge is to find an excellent program that encourages normal childhood activities and at the same time meets his special needs.

Federal law (the Individuals with Disabilities Education Act, formerly known as the Amendments to the Education for All Handicapped Children Act) requires all states to develop special education programs for preschool (three-to-five-year-old) children with developmental disabilities. This act also gives states the option to develop special education programs for infants and toddlers with developmental disabilities or delays. Parents should check with their pediatrician or their state Education or Health Department regarding the availability of these early intervention programs:

Start your search with your pediatrician by asking if your baby is capable of participating in a group program, and requesting referrals to suitable centers. Sometimes there will be only one choice available, but often, especially in larger communities, you will have several from which to choose. The one you select should meet the same basic requirements outlined earlier for other child-care programs, plus the following.

1. The program should include babies and older children with and without chronic illnesses and disabilities, to the extent possible. Having normal relationships with typically developing playmates helps a child with a disability feel more relaxed and confident socially, and helps build his self-esteem. The arrangement also benefits the typically developing child by teaching him to look past the surface differences, and helping him develop sensitivity and respect for *all* people.
2. The staff should be specially trained to provide the specific care your child requires.
3. The program should have at least one physician consultant who is active in the development of policies and procedures affecting the type of special needs present among the children in the group.
4. All children should be encouraged to be as independent as their abilities allow, within the bounds of safety. They should be restricted only in activities that might be dangerous for them or that have been prohibited by doctor's orders.

5. The program should be flexible enough to adapt to slight variations in your child's abilities. For example, this may include altering some equipment or facilities for physically challenged or visually or hearing-impaired babies.
6. The program should offer special equipment and activities to meet the special needs of babies. The equipment should be in good repair, and the staff should be trained to operate it correctly.
7. The staff should be familiar with each child's medical and developmental status. If a child has a chronic disease, the staff should be able to recognize its symptoms and determine when the child needs medical attention.
8. The staff should know how to reach each child's physician in an emergency, and should be qualified to administer any necessary medications.

These are very general recommendations. Because special needs vary so widely, it's impossible to tell you more precisely how to determine the best program for your own baby. If you're having trouble deciding among the programs your pediatrician has suggested, go back and discuss your concerns with her. Your pediatrician will work with you to make the right choice.

Whatever your child's special needs, how he will be cared for in your absence is one of the most difficult decisions you will have to make as a parent. The information you have just read should help you. However, remember that you know your baby better than anyone, so rely most heavily on your needs and impressions when choosing or changing a child-care arrangement.

PART II

12

EMERGENCIES

The information and policies in this section, such as first-aid procedures for the choking baby and CPR, are constantly changing. Ask your pediatrician or other qualified health professional for the latest information on these procedures.

It is rare for children to become seriously ill with no warning. Based on your baby's symptoms, you should usually contact your pediatrician for advice. Timely treatment of symptoms can prevent an illness from getting worse or turning into an emergency.

A true emergency is when you believe a severe injury or illness is threatening your baby's life or may cause permanent harm. In these cases, a baby needs emergency medical treatment immediately. Discuss with your baby's pediatrician in advance what you should do in case of a true emergency.

Many true emergencies involve sudden injuries. These injuries are often caused by the following:

- Car crashes, falls, or other violent impacts
- Poisoning
- Burns or smoke inhalation
- Choking
- Near drowning
- Firearms or other weapons
- Electric shocks

Other true emergencies can result from either medical illnesses or injuries. You can often tell that these emergencies are happening if you observe that your child is doing or has any of the following symptoms:

- Acting strangely or becoming more withdrawn and less alert
- Increasing trouble with breathing
- Bleeding that does not stop
- Skin or lips that look blue or purple (or gray for darker-skinned children)
- Rhythmical jerking and loss of consciousness (a seizure)
- Unconsciousness
- Major mouth or facial injuries
- Increasing or severe persistent pain
- A cut or burn that is large or deep
- Any loss of consciousness, confusion, a bad headache, or vomiting several times *after a head injury*
- Decreasing responsiveness when you talk to your baby

Call your baby's pediatrician or poison center at once if your baby has swallowed a suspected poison or another person's medication, even if your baby has no signs or symptoms.

Always call for help if you are concerned that your baby's life may be in danger or your baby is seriously hurt.

In Case of a True Emergency:

- Stay calm.
- If it is needed and you know how, start rescue breathing or CPR (cardiopulmonary resuscitation).
- If you need immediate help, call 911. If you do not have 911 service in your area, call your local emergency ambulance service or county emergency medical service. Otherwise, call your baby's pediatrician's office and state clearly that you have an emergency.
- If there is bleeding, apply continuous pressure to the site with a clean cloth.
- If your baby is having a seizure, place her on a carpeted floor with her head turned to the side, and stay with your baby until help arrives.

After you arrive at the emergency department, make sure you tell the emergency staff the name of your child's pediatrician, who can work closely with the emergency department and can provide them with additional information about your baby. Bring any medication your baby is taking and her immunization record with you to the hospital. Also bring any suspected poisons or other medications your baby might have taken.

Important Emergency Phone Numbers Keep the following phone numbers handy by taping them on or near your phone:

- Your home phone and address
- Your baby's pediatrician
- Emergency medical services (ambulance) (911 in most areas)
- Police (911 in most areas)
- Fire department (911 in most areas)
- Poison center
- Hospital
- Dentist

It is important that caregivers know where to find emergency phone numbers. If you have 911 service in your area, make sure your older children and your caregiver know to dial 911 in case of an emergency. Be sure they know your home address and phone number, since an emergency operator would ask for this information. Always leave your caregiver the phone number and address where you can be located.

Remember, for medical emergency, always call 911, EMS, or your baby's pediatrician. If your baby is seriously ill or injured, it may be safer for your baby to be transported by emergency medical services.

BITES

Animal Bites

Many parents assume that children are most likely to be bitten by strange or wild animals, but in fact most bites are inflicted by animals the child knows, including the family pet. Although the injury often can be minor, biting does at times cause serious wounds, facial damage, and emotional problems.

As many as 1 percent of all visits to pediatric emergency centers during the summer months are for the treatment of human or animal bite wounds. An estimated 4.7 million dog bites, 400,000 cat bites, 45,000 snake bites, and 250,000 human bites occur annually in the United States. The incidence of infection following cat bites can be more than 50 percent, and that following dog or human bite wounds can be 15 to 20 percent.

Treatment

If your baby is bleeding from an animal bite, apply firm continuous pressure to the area for five minutes or until the blood flow stops. Then wash the wound gently with plenty of soap and water, and consult your pediatrician.

If the wound is very large, or you cannot stop the bleeding, continue to apply pressure and call your pediatrician to find out where your baby should be taken for treatment. If the wound is so large that the edges won't come together, it will probably need to be sutured (stitched). This will help reduce scarring but, in an animal bite, increases the chance of infection, so your doctor may prescribe preventive antibiotics.

Contact your pediatrician whenever your baby receives an animal bite that breaks the skin, no matter how minor the injury appears. The doctor will need to check whether your infant has been adequately immunized against tetanus (see immunizations schedule on page 82) or might require protection against rabies. Both of these diseases can be spread by animal bites.

Rabies is a viral infection that can be transmitted by an infected animal. It causes high fever, difficulty in swallowing, convulsions, and ultimately death. Fortunately, rabies is so rare today that no more than five cases have been reported in the United States each year since 1960. Nevertheless, because the disease is so serious and the incidence has been increasing in animals, your pediatrician will carefully evaluate the bite for the risk of contracting this disease. The risk probably depends a great deal on the animal and the circumstances surrounding the bite. Bites from wild animals such as bats, skunks, raccoons, and foxes are much more dangerous than those from tame, immunized (against rabies) ones such as dogs and cats. The health of the animal also is important, so if possible, the animal should be captured and confined for later examination by a veterinarian. *Do not destroy the animal.* If it *has* been killed, however, the brain can still be examined for rabies, so call your pediatrician immediately for advice on how to handle the situation.

If the risk of rabies is high, your pediatrician immediately will give injections of medications to prevent it. If the biting animal is a healthy dog or cat, he will have you observe the bite for ten days, initiating your baby's treatment only if the animal shows signs of rabies. If the animal is a wild one, commonly identified as a rabies risk, it usually is euthanized immediately so that its brain can be examined for signs of rabies infection.

Like any other wound, a bite can become infected. Notify your pediatrician immediately if you see any of the following signs of infection.

- Pus or drainage coming from the bite, or swelling or tenderness immediately around the bite (redness normally continues for two to three days, and is not a cause for alarm)
- Red streaks that appear to spread out from the bite
- Swollen glands above the bite

(See also *Safety Around Animals*, page 350.)

Antibiotic therapy may be recommended by your pediatrician for a baby who has:

- Moderate or severe bite wounds
- Puncture wounds, especially if the bone, tendon, or joint has been penetrated

- Facial bites
- Hand and foot bites
- Genital area bites
- Wounds in a baby who is immunocompromised or asplenic

Your pediatrician should provide a follow-up visit to inspect any wound for signs of infection within forty-eight hours.

Human Bites

Children often experience a human bite by a sibling or a playmate. If your baby is bitten by another person, you should call your pediatrician immediately in order to describe the severity of the injury. This can be especially important if the biter's teeth pierced your baby's skin or the injury is large enough to require stitches.

Be sure to carefully wash a serious bite with cool water and soap before going to the pediatrician. Your pediatrician will check your baby's tetanus and hepatitis B vaccine status and assess the risk for other infections. For a bite that barely breaks the skin, such as a cut or scrape, a good washing with soap and water, followed by bandaging and close follow-up, is all that is needed.

Burns

Burns are divided into three categories, according to their severity. First-degree burns are the mildest and cause redness and perhaps slight swelling of the skin (like most sunburns). Second-degree burns cause blistering and considerable swelling. Third-degree burns may appear white or charred, and cause serious injury not just to the surface but also to the deeper skin layers.

There are many different causes of serious burns in babies, including sunburn, hot water scalds, and those due to fire, electrical contact, or chemicals. All of these can cause permanent injury and scarring to the skin.

Treatment

Your *immediate* treatment of a burn should include the following:

1. As quickly as possible, soak the burn in cool water. Don't hesitate to run cool water over the burn long enough to cool the area and relieve the pain immediately after the injury. *Do not use ice.*
2. Cool any smoldering clothing immediately by soaking with water, then remove any clothing from the burned area unless it is stuck firmly to the skin. In that case, cut away as much as possible.
3. If the injured area is not oozing, cover the burn with a sterile gauze pad.
4. If the burn is oozing, cover it lightly with sterile gauze if available and immediately seek medical attention. If sterile gauze is not available, cover burns with a clean sheet or towel.
5. Do not put butter, grease, or powder on a burn. All of these so-called home "remedies" can actually make the injury worse.

For anything more serious than a superficial burn, or if redness and pain continue for more than a few hours, consult a physician. *All* electrical burns and burns of the hands, mouth, or genitals should receive immediate medical attention. Chemicals that cause burns may also be absorbed through the skin and cause other symptoms. Call your pediatrician or poison center, after washing off all the chemical (for treatment of a chemical contact to a baby's eyes, see *Poison in the Eye,* page 414).

If your physician thinks the burn is not too serious, he may show you how to clean and care for it at home using medicated ointments and dressings. Although a pediatrician may be more inclined to hospitalize a baby for initial care, he will almost certainly choose hospitalization under the following circumstances:

- If the burns are third-degree
- If 10 percent or more of the body is burned

- If the burn involves the face, hands, feet, or genitals, or crosses a moving joint

When treating a burn at home, watch for any increase in redness or swelling, or the development of a bad odor or discharge. These can be signs of infection, which will require medical attention.

Prevention

Chapter 10, "Keeping Your Baby Safe," provides ways to safeguard your child against fire and scalding at home. For added protection, here are a few more suggestions:

- Install smoke detectors in all sleeping rooms, hallways outside sleeping rooms, kitchen, and living rooms, with *at least* one on every floor of the house. Test them regularly. Change batteries regularly or on a specific date.
- Practice home fire drills. Make sure every family member knows how to leave any area of the home safely in case of fire.
- Have several working fire extinguishers readily available.
- Lock up flammable liquid in the home.
- Lower the temperature of your hot water heater to below 120 degrees Fahrenheit, 48.8 degrees Celsius.
- Don't use inadequate extension cords or old, possibly unsafe electrical equipment.
- Keep matches and lighters away from babies and older children.
- Avoid fireworks.

Cardiopulmonary Resuscitation (CPR) and Mouth-to-Mouth Resuscitation

Reading about CPR is not enough to teach you how to perform it. *The Academy strongly recommends that all parents and anyone who is responsible for the care of children should complete a course in basic CPR and treatment for choking*. This training is vital if you own a swimming pool or live near water. Contact your local chapter of the American Heart Association or Red Cross to find out where and when certified courses are given in your community.

CPR can save your baby's life if his heart stops beating or he has stopped breathing for any reason—drowning, poisoning, suffocation, smoke inhalation, choking, infections of the respiratory tract, or suspected sudden infant death syndrome (SIDS). This procedure is most likely to be successful if it is begun immediately after the heart or breathing stops. The following danger signs can alert you that CPR may be needed soon:

- Unresponsiveness, with no evidence of effective breathing
- Extreme wheezing or difficulty in breathing (such as with obstruction from an aspirated foreign body)
- Blue lips or skin associated with extreme difficulty in breathing
- Rapid or labored breathing (grunting or pulling in of muscles between the ribs with respirations)
- Drooling, or difficulty in swallowing with trouble breathing
- Extreme paleness

If your baby displays any of these signs and you are with someone else, have that person call for emergency help while you begin the steps below. If you are alone, go ahead and follow these steps immediately after shouting or calling for help.

Step 1. Rapidly evaluate your baby's condition. Is he unconscious? Firmly shake, tap, or shout as though trying to awaken him. Assume he is unconscious if he doesn't respond after three attempts.

Is he breathing? Place your ear directly over his mouth and listen for breathing. If he is breathing with difficulty, arrange to get him immediately to an emergency medical facility while continuing to monitor to assure he has not stopped breathing. If you don't hear breathing, look to see whether his chest is moving up and down.

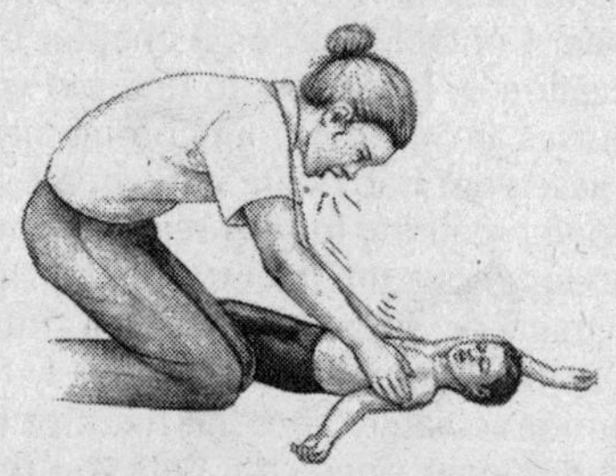

Step 1

Step 2. If your baby is not breathing, position him on his back on a firm flat surface.

If you suspect that he has injured his neck or spine (a possibility in a fall or automobile crash), move him carefully so that his neck does not bend. If you find your baby face-down, support his head to keep his neck from twisting while you roll him over.

Step 3. Open your baby's airway by tilting his head back to lift his chin.

Be careful not to push his head back too far, because that could block the airway in an infant. To clear the tongue from the back of the throat, lift the chin up gently with one hand while pushing down on the forehead with the other hand. A good way to open the airway is to lift the chin by pushing up on the bones at the back of the jaw. In some cases, simply opening the airway will allow your baby to breathe on his own. If it doesn't, look into the throat to see whether it is blocked by a foreign object or a piece of food. If so, follow the instructions under *Choking* (see page 397).

Step 4. If your baby still is not breathing, and he does not appear to be choking, give mouth-to-mouth resuscitation.

1. Take a deep breath.
2. Place your mouth over your baby's nose and mouth, making as tight a seal as possible.
3. Give two rescue breaths, blowing enough air into your baby so you can see his chest rise slightly. Then pause,

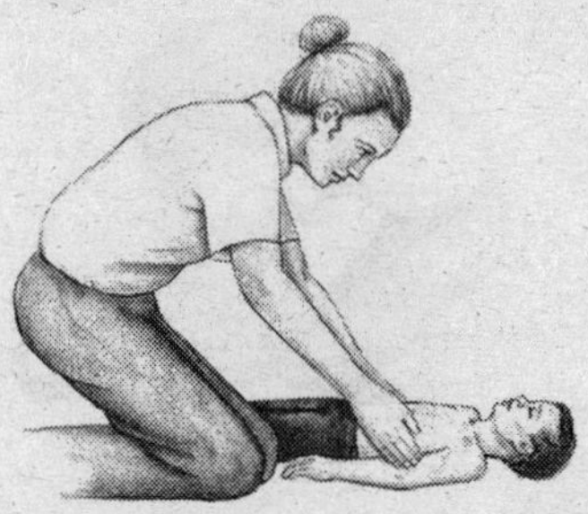

Step 2

removing your mouth from his so the air can escape, and take another deep breath. *With an infant, be careful not to blow with too much force, because this can be dangerous.* If *no* air seems to be getting into the chest, the airway is still blocked, and you will need to repeat Step 3.

4. If your baby's chest does rise as you breathe into his mouth, continue to breathe for him at a rate of approximately one breath every three seconds (twenty per minute), until he is breathing on his own.

5. A baby who stops breathing is very likely to vomit, complicating rescue breathing. If there is no suspected neck injury, turn the baby's head to the side to allow fluid to drain out. Wiping deep inside with an absorbant towel may help (do not use much force, to avoid pushing vomit down the windpipe), as may any available equipment to suction the mouth (bulb, syringe, turkey baster, etc.).

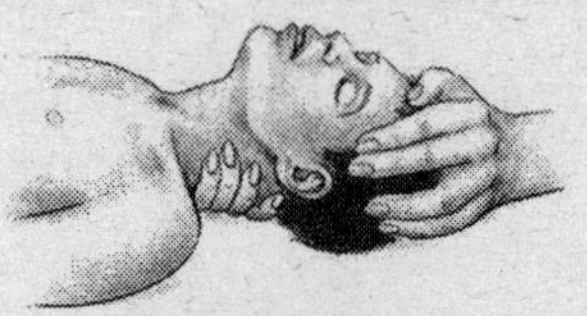

Step 3

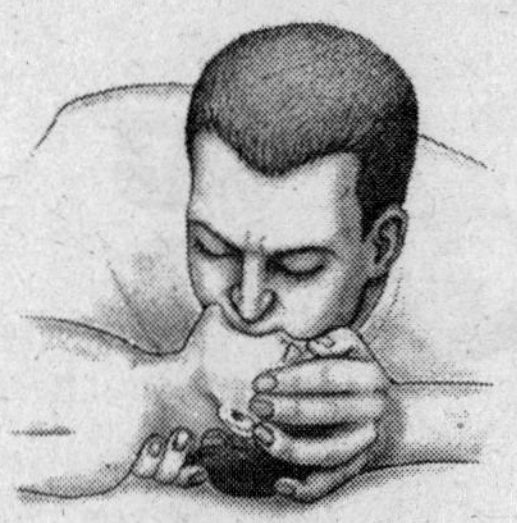

Step 4

Step 5. Check your baby's pulse after the two rescue breaths. With an infant under one year, find the artery in the front of and above the elbow. If the heart is beating, you should feel a pulse with your fingers gently touching this point. Do not press hard.

Step 6. If you can't feel a pulse, assume the heart has stopped, and begin chest compressions (CPR) to keep the blood circulating to the vital organs.

Proceed as follows (with the baby on a flat, firm surface):

1. Place two or three fingers on the breastbone one finger width below the nipple line. Press down ½ to 1 inch, at a rate of about one hundred times per minute. *Be careful not to apply too much pressure.*

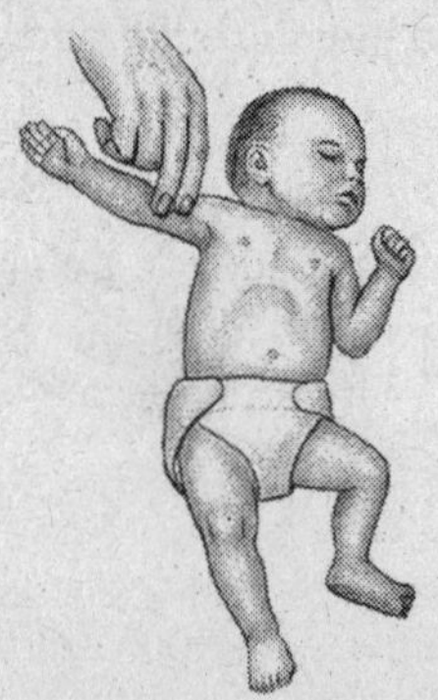

Step 5

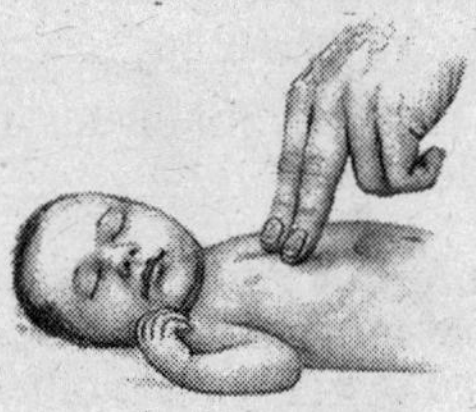

Step 6

2. After five compressions, give the baby one breath, as described in Step 4. Continue five-compressions/one-breath, five-compressions/one-breath until you feel a pulse in the artery, indicating that the heart is pumping once again.

Step 7. Get emergency medical help.

If you are alone with your baby, call immediately for emergency help or after one minute of CPR. Be sure to give your location and the number of the phone from which you are calling. The paramedics who arrive on the scene will determine his condition and treat him appropriately.

CHOKING

Choking occurs whenever a person inhales something other than air into her windpipe. Among children, choking often is caused by liquid that "goes down the wrong way." The baby will cough, wheeze, gasp, and gag until the windpipe is cleared, but this type of choking is not usually harmful.

Choking becomes life-threatening when an infant swallows or inhales an object, often food, that blocks the flow of air to the lungs. If this happens, your infant will not be able to make normal sounds, and her face will turn from bright red to blue. This is an emergency that calls for immediate first aid. There is no time to call the doctor; you must deal with it immediately. If someone else is available, have him call for medical assistance while you continue your first-aid efforts.

How to Respond

The way to handle a choking incident depends upon the condition and age of the child. For infants up to one year of age, follow these guidelines:

For a Baby Coughing but Able to Breathe and Talk: Coughing is the natural mechanism for expelling an object from the throat. Instead of trying some other maneuver that might make the obstruction worse, let your infant cough. In particular, don't try to remove the object with your fingers; that could push it farther into the throat and totally block the windpipe.

For a Baby Who Cannot Breathe and Is Turning Blue: This requires immediate first aid. Because the infant's internal organs are fragile, *be gentle,* and use the following steps: (Do not use the Heimlich maneuver recommended for older children and adults.)

1. Place the infant facedown on your forearm in a head-down position with the head and neck stabilized. Rest your forearm firmly against your body for additional support.

   For a large infant, you may instead lay the baby facedown over your lap, with her head lower than her trunk and firmly supported.

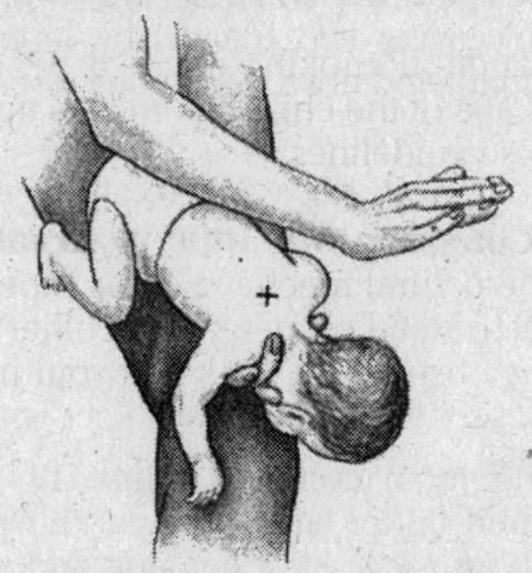

2. Give five back blows rapidly with the heel of the hand between the shoulder blades.

3. If she still cannot breathe, turn the infant over onto her back, resting on a firm surface, and deliver five rapid chest compressions over the breastbone, *using only two fingers.*

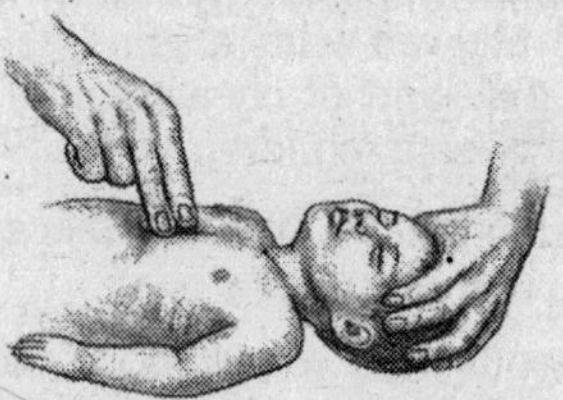

4. If she is still not breathing, open the airway using the tongue-jaw lift technique, and attempt to see the foreign body. Do not try to pull out the object unless you can see it. But if you see it, sweep it out with your finger.

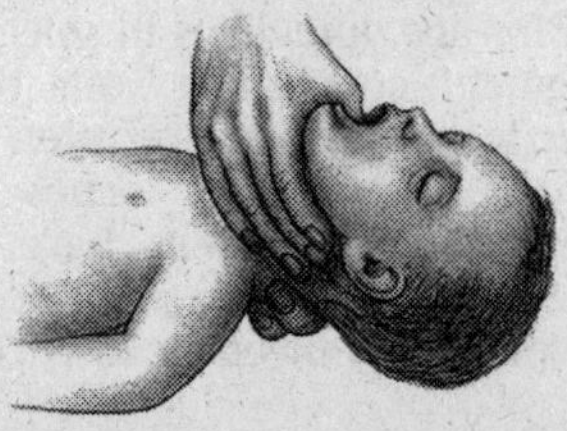

5. If she doesn't start breathing on her own; try to start her breathing by giving two breaths by mouth-to-mouth, or mouth-to-mouth-and-nose, technique (see Step 4, page 394).
6. Continue to repeat steps 1 through 5 as you call for emergency medical help (from your local emergency service).

Prevention

Choking is the most common cause of non-intentional death in children under age one. Ask your pediatrician for information about preventing choking and what to do if it should occur. Also see Chapter 10, "Keeping Your Baby Safe."

Objects such as safety pins and coins cause choking, but food is responsible for most incidents. You must be particularly watchful when your baby is sampling new foods, around the age of one. Here are some additional suggestions for preventing choking:

- Don't give babies hard, smooth foods (such as peanuts) that must be chewed with a grinding motion. Children don't master that kind of chewing until age four. Peanuts should not be given to children until age seven or older.
- Cut or break food into bite-size pieces and encourage your baby to chew thoroughly.
- Avoid giving your baby round foods such as meat sticks, hot dogs, carrot sticks, celery sticks, grapes, and hard candies.

  All of these can lodge easily in her throat.

Because babies put everything into their mouths, small nonfood objects are also responsible for many choking incidents. Look for age guidelines in selecting toys, but use your own judgment concerning your baby. Government regulations specify that toys for children under age three cannot have parts less than 1¼ inches in diameter and 2¼ inches long. If older siblings have toys with small parts, keep them out of the reach of your baby. Also, be aware that the following objects have been associated with choking:

- Uninflated balloons and pieces of broken balloon.
- Baby powder. Don't allow your baby to play with the powder container when you change her diaper.
- Items from the trash. Be especially alert for eggshells and pop tops from beverage cans.
- Safety pins. Be sure they are closed and out of reach when not in use.
- Coins. Don't give babies coins or other small objects as a reward or treat.

Despite these precautions, choking can occur at any time. You must familiarize yourself with the procedures for dealing with it, so that you can act quickly in an emergency. If you feel unsure, seek out an approved first-aid course such as those sponsored by the American Heart Association or the American Red Cross, or view a videotape such as those available from the American Academy of Pediatrics. To receive a Parent Resource Guide, send a self-addressed, business-size envelope to:

American Academy of Pediatrics
Attn: Dept C,PRG
P.O. Box 927
Elk Grove Village, Illinois 60009–0927

Cuts and Scrapes

Your baby's natural curiosity and eagerness are likely to produce some scrapes and cuts along the way. The shrieks and cries that accompany these injuries may bring terror to your heart, but his reaction usually will be far more severe than the actual damage. In most cases, good treatment will require little more than cleansing the injury and providing plenty of reassurance (and perhaps a kiss on the minor bump or bruise).

Scrapes

Most minor injuries in young children are scrapes, or abrasions, which means that the outer layers of skin have literally been scraped off. If the abrasion covers a large area, it may appear to be very bloody, although the actual amount of blood lost usually is very small. The only treatment required is cleansing, since dirt can lead to infection. The area should be rinsed first with water to flush away debris, and then washed vigorously with warm water and soap. Iodine and other antiseptic solutions generally should be avoided. They have little protective value, but can add to the pain and discomfort.

Most abrasions "scab" over quickly without treatment, and this is the best natural remedy. Scrapes that are large or oozing should be covered with a sterile (germ-free) dressing. These can be obtained at your local pharmacy either in the form of an adhesive bandage or a separate gauze pad that is held in place by roller gauze or adhesive tape. The sterility of the dressing is guaranteed as long as the covering envelope is not opened or has not become wet. Care should be taken to be sure dressings around such areas as the fingers or toes are not so tight as to interfere with circulation.

Some dressings are made of materials such as Telfa, which are less likely to adhere to the raw surface of a wound, but the best way to prevent sticking is to apply an antibiotic cream (such as triple antibiotic ointment) to the wound before covering it with the dressing. The wound should be examined daily and the dressing changed at that time or whenever it becomes dirty or wet. If a bandage sticks when you try to remove it, soak it off with warm water.

Once a firm scab has formed, a covering usually is not necessary or recommended. Most wounds will require a dressing for only two or three days.

Call your pediatrician if you can't get a wound clean, or if you notice drainage of pus, increasing tenderness or redness around the site, or fever. These are signs that the wound may be infected. If necessary, the doctor can use a local anesthetic to prevent severe pain while cleaning out dirt and debris that you are not able to remove. If the wound is infected, she may prescribe antibiotics orally or in the form of an ointment or cream.

Cuts, Lacerations, and Bleeding

A cut or laceration is a wound that breaks through the skin and into the tissues beneath. Because the injury is deeper than a scrape, there are more likely to be problems such as bleeding, and there is the possibility of damage to nerves and tendons. The following simple guidelines will help you prevent serious bleeding and other problems such as scarring when your baby gets a cut.

1. **Apply pressure.** Almost all active bleeding can be stopped by applying direct pressure with clean gauze or cloth over the site for five minutes. The most common mistake is interrupting the pressure too early in order to peek at the wound. This may result in more bleeding or in the buildup of a clot that can make it harder to control the problem with further pressure. If bleeding starts again after five minutes of continuous pressure, reapply pressure and call your doctor for help. Do not use a tourniquet on an arm or leg unless you are trained in its use, since this can cause severe damage if left on too long.
2. **Stay calm.** The sight of blood frightens most people, but this is an important time to stay in control. You'll make better decisions if you are calm, and your baby will be less likely to get upset by the situation. Remember, with direct pressure you will be able to control bleeding from even the most severe lacerations until help can arrive. Relatively minor cuts to the head and face will bleed more than cuts to other parts of the body because of the greater number of small superficial blood vessels in the skin of the head. In these situations, it's especially important to keep calm and apply steady pressure to control bleeding.
3. **Seek medical advice for serious cuts.** No matter how much (or how little) bleeding occurs, call your doctor if the laceration is deep (through the skin) or more than ½ inch (1.2 cm) long. Deep cuts can severely damage underlying nerves and tendons, even if the wound on the surface does not appear serious. Long lacerations and those located on the face, chest, and back are more likely to leave disfiguring scars. In these situations, if the wound is properly sutured (stitched), the scar probably will be much less apparent. If in doubt about whether sutures are needed, call your doctor for advice. To reduce unsightly scarring, sutures should be placed within eight hours after injury occurs.

   You should be able to treat short, minor cuts yourself, as long as the edges come together by themselves or with the aid of a "butterfly" bandage, and if there is no numbness beyond the wound. However, have your doctor examine your baby if there is any possibility that foreign matter such as dirt or glass is trapped in it. Your baby may not like to let you examine a laceration thoroughly because of the pain involved. The pediatrician, however, can use a local anesthetic, if necessary, to ensure a thorough exam.

4. **Cleanse and dress the wound.** If you feel comfortable handling the problem, wash the wound with plain water and examine it carefully to be sure it is clean, apply an antibiotic ointment, then cover it with a sterile dressing. It's easy to underestimate the extent or severity of a laceration, so even if you choose to treat it yourself, don't hesitate to call your pediatrician for advice. If any redness, swelling, or pus appears around the wound, or if bleeding recurs, consult your physician as soon as possible.

   Antiseptics such as iodine, Mercurochrome, and alcohol are not necessary and increase the discomfort for your baby, so do not use them on cuts. Tetanus shots are not necessary after most abrasions and lacerations, if your baby's immunizations are current.

Prevention

It is almost impossible for a curious and active baby to get by without some scrapes and minor cuts, but there are things you can do to decrease the number your baby will have and to minimize their severity. Keep potentially dangerous objects like sharp knives, easily breakable glass objects, and firearms out of his reach. At regular intervals, make a safety check of your house, garage, and yard. If you find objects that are potentially dangerous because your baby can "get into them," store them securely out of his reach.

See also Chapter 10, "Keeping Your Baby Safe."

DROWNING

With babies, drowning can happen even in only a few inches of water. They may panic, struggle, inhale water, and suffocate. Drowning refers to death that occurs in this way. When a baby is rescued before death occurs, we refer to the episode as a near drowning.

What You Should Do

As soon as your baby is out of the water, check to see if she is breathing on her own. If she is not, begin CPR immediately (see page 392). If someone else is present, send him or her to call for emergency medical help, but don't spend precious moments looking for someone, and don't waste time trying to drain water from your baby's lungs. Concentrate instead on giving her artificial respiration and CPR until she is breathing on her own and has a pulse of between eighty and one hundred beats per minute. Vomiting of swallowed water is very likely during CPR. Only when the baby's breathing has resumed and her pulse has returned to normal should you stop and seek emergency help. Once the paramedics arrive, they will administer oxygen and continue CPR if necessary. You can then call your pediatrician for further instructions.

Any baby who has come close to drowning should be given a complete medical examination, even if she seems all right. If she stopped breathing, inhaled water, or lost consciousness, she should remain under medical observation for at least twenty-four hours to be sure there is no damage to her respiratory or nervous system.

A baby's recovery from a near drowning depends upon how long she was deprived of oxygen. If she was underwater only briefly, she is likely to recover completely. Longer periods without oxygen can cause damage to the lungs, heart, or brain. An infant who doesn't respond quickly to CPR may have more serious problems, but it's important to keep trying, because sustained CPR has revived babies who have appeared lifeless or who have been immersed in very cold water for lengthy periods.

Prevention

Babies should never be left alone in a bath, and all children are in danger if they play unsupervised in or near water. Therefore, watch constantly when a baby is in a bath or near a body of water such as a swimming pool, lake, or river. Babies who are crawling need to be kept away from bodies of water of any size, not just pools.

Innocent exploration of the toilet or a bucket of water by a walking child can lead to tragedy. Never leave water standing where your baby can get to it. Empty or cover plastic wading pools when not in use. Drain wash water promptly from basins. Keep the lid down on the toilet, and, if your baby is very active and curious, close and latch the bathroom door. Don't leave buckets with even a few inches of water or cleaning solutions where babies can explore. Never leave a baby standing beside a tub while the water is running, or alone in a tub filled with water. (For more information on water safety, see page 348).

Electric Shock

When the human body comes in direct contact with a source of electricity, the current passes through it, producing what's called an electric shock. Depending upon the voltage of the current and the length of contact, this shock can cause anything from minor discomfort to serious injury to death.

Babies most often experience electric shock when they bite into electrical cords or poke metal objects like forks or knives into unprotected outlets or appliances. These injuries also can take place when electric toys are used incorrectly, or when electric current makes contact with water in which an infant is sitting or standing. Lightning accounts for about one fifth of the cases that occur. Christmas trees and their lights are a seasonal hazard.

What You Should Do

If your baby comes in contact with electricity, *always* try to turn the power off first. In many cases you'll be able to pull the plug or turn off the switch. If this isn't possible, consider an attempt to remove the live wire, *but not with your bare hands*, which would bring you in contact with the current yourself. Instead, try to cut the wire with a wood-handled ax or well-insulated wire cutters, or move the wire off the infant using a dry stick, a rolled-up magazine or newspaper, a rope, a coat, or another thick, dry object that won't conduct electricity, such as a piece of wood.

If you can't remove the source of the current, try to pull the baby away. Again, *do not touch the baby with your bare hands* when he's attached to the source of the current, since his body will transmit the electricity to you. Instead, use a nonconducting material such as rubber (or those described above) to shield you while freeing him. (*Caution:* None of these methods can be guaranteed safe unless the power can be shut off.)

As soon as the current is turned off (or the baby is removed from it), check the baby's breathing, pulse, skin color, and ability to respond to you. If his breathing or heartbeat has stopped, or seems very rapid or irregular, immediately use CPR (see page 392) to restore it, and have someone call for emergency medical help. At the same time, avoid needlessly moving the baby, since a spinal fracture may have occurred with such a severe electrical shock.

If the baby is conscious and it seems the shock was minor, check him for burned skin, especially if his mouth was the point of contact with the current. Then call your pediatrician. Electrical shock can cause internal organ damage that may be difficult to detect without a medical examination. For that reason *all* infants who receive a significant electric shock should see a doctor.

In the pediatrician's office, any minor burns resulting from the electricity will be cleansed and dressed. The doctor may order laboratory tests to check for signs of damage to internal organs. If the baby has severe burns or any sign of brain or heart damage, he will need to be hospitalized.

Prevention

The best way to prevent electrical injuries is to cover all outlets, make sure all wires are properly insulated, and provide adult supervision whenever infants are in an area with potential electrical hazards. Small appliances are a special hazard around bathtubs or pools. (See also Chapter 10, "Keeping Your Baby Safe.")

FINGERTIP INJURIES

Children's fingertips get smashed sometimes, usually getting caught in closing doors. Too often, those doors are shut by parents unaware that little fingers are in danger. The baby is unable to recognize the potential danger.

Because fingertips are exquisitely sensitive, your baby will let you know immediately that she's been injured. Usually the damaged area will be blue and swollen, and there may be a cut or bleeding around the cuticle. The skin, tissues below the skin, and the nail bed, as well as the underlying bone and growth plate, may all be affected. If bleeding occurs underneath the nail, it will turn black or dark blue, and the pressure from the bleeding may be painful.

Home Treatment

When the fingertip is bleeding, wash it with soap and water, and cover it with a soft, sterile dressing. An ice pack or a soaking in cold water may relieve the pain and minimize swelling.

If the swelling is mild and your baby is comfortable, you can allow the finger to heal on its own. But be alert for any increase in pain, swelling, redness, or drainage from the injured area, or a fever beginning twenty-four to seventy-two hours after the injury. These may be signs of infection, and you should notify your pediatrician.

When there's excessive swelling, a deep cut, blood under the fingernail, or the finger looks as if it may be broken, call your doctor immediately. And by all means, do not attempt to straighten a fractured finger on your own.

Professional Treatment

If your doctor suspects a fracture, he may order an X ray. If the X ray confirms a fracture, or if there's damage to the nail bed where nail growth occurs, an orthopedic consultation may be necessary. A fractured finger can be straightened and set under local anesthesia. An injured nail bed also must be repaired surgically to minimize the possibility of a nail deformity developing as the finger grows. If there's considerable blood under the nail, the pediatrician may drain it by making a small hole in the nail, which should relieve the pain.

Although deep cuts may require stitches, often all that's necessary is sterile adhesive strips (thin adhesive strips similar to butterfly bandages). If there's a fracture underneath a cut, this is considered an "open" fracture and is susceptible to infection in the bone. In this case, antibiotics will be prescribed. Depending on your child's age and immunization status, the doctor also may order a tetanus booster.

Head Injury/Concussion

It's almost inevitable that your child will hit her head every now and then. Especially when she's a baby, these collisions may upset you, but your anxiety is usually worse than the bump. Most head injuries are minor, causing no serious problems. Even so, it's important to know the difference between a head injury that warrants medical attention and one that needs only a comforting hug.

If your child suffers a brief, temporary loss of consciousness after a hard blow to the head, she is said to have had a concussion. If a child has a concussion, it doesn't necessarily mean that her brain has been damaged, but it does indicate that the brain centers for consciousness have been momentarily disturbed.

Treatment

If a child's head injury has been mild, she'll remain alert and awake after the incident, and her color will be normal. She may cry out due to momentary pain and fright, but the crying should last no more than ten minutes and then she'll go back to playing as usual.

Occasionally, a minor head injury also will cause slight dizziness, nausea, and headache, and the child might vomit once or twice. Even so, if the injury seems minor and there's not a significant cut (one that's deep and/or actively bleeding) which might require medical attention or possibly stitches (see *Scrapes and Cuts*, page 401), you can treat your child at home. Just wash the cut with soap and water. If there's a bruise, apply a cold compress. This will help minimize the swelling if you do it in the first few hours after the injury.

Even after a minor head injury, you should observe your child for twenty-four to forty-eight hours to see if she develops any signs of more severe damage. Although it's *very rare*, children can develop serious brain injury after a seemingly minor bump on the head that causes no immediate obvious problems. When brain injury does occur, it's usually due to internal bleeding and almost always shows up within one to two days of the original incident. If your child develops any of the following symptoms, consult your pediatrician immediately:

- She seems excessively sleepy or lethargic during her usual wakeful hours, or you cannot awaken her while she's asleep at night. (You should try to awaken her once or twice during the first night if she's had a hard blow to the head.)

- She has a headache that won't go away (even with acetaminophen), or vomits more than once or twice. Headache and vomiting occur commonly after head trauma, but they are usually mild and last only a few hours.
- She's persistently and/or extremely irritable. With an infant who cannot tell you what she's feeling, this may indicate a severe headache.
- Any significant change in your child's mental abilities, coordination, sensation, or strength warrants immediate medical attention. Such changes would include weakness of arms or legs, slurred speech, crossed eyes, or difficulty with vision.
- She becomes unconscious again after being awake for a while, or she has a seizure (convulsion) or starts to breathe irregularly. These are signs of disturbed brain activity and, possibly, a serious head injury.

If your child loses consciousness *at any time* after hitting her head, the pediatrician should be notified. If she doesn't awaken within a few minutes, she needs *immediate medical attention.* Call for help while you follow these steps:

1. Move your child as little as possible. *If you suspect that she might have injured her neck, do not attempt to move her. Changing the position of her neck might make her injuries worse.* One exception: Move her only if she's in danger of being injured further where she is (for example, on a ledge or in a fire).
2. Check to see if she's breathing. If she isn't, perform CPR (see page 392).
3. If she's bleeding severely from a scalp wound, apply direct pressure with a clean cloth over the wound.
4. If trained ambulance personnel are readily available, it's safer to await their arrival than to try taking your child to the hospital yourself.

Loss of consciousness following a head injury may last only a few seconds or as long as several hours. If you find the child after the injury happened, and you are not sure if she lost consciousness, notify the pediatrician.

Most children who lose consciousness for more than a few minutes will be hospitalized overnight. Hospitalization is essential for children with severe brain injury and irregular breathing or convulsions. Fortunately, with modern pediatric intensive care, many children who have suffered serious head injury—and even those who have been unconscious for several weeks—may eventually recover completely.

Poisoning

Most babies who swallow poison are *not* permanently harmed, particularly if they receive immediate treatment. If you think your baby has been poisoned, stay calm and act quickly.

You should suspect poisoning if you ever find your baby with an open or empty container of a toxic substance, especially if she is acting strangely in any way. Be alert for these other signs of possible poisoning.

- Unexplained stains on her clothing
- Burns on her lips or mouth
- Unusual drooling, or odd odors on her breath
- Unexplained nausea or vomiting
- Abdominal cramps without fever
- Difficulty in breathing
- Sudden behavior changes, such as unusual sleepiness, irritability, or jumpiness
- Convulsions or unconsciousness (only in very serious cases)

Treatment

Any time your baby has ingested a poison of any kind, your pediatrician should be notified. However, your regional poison center will provide the *immediate* information and guidance you need when you first discover that your infant has been poisoned. These centers are staffed twenty-four hours a day with experts who can tell you what to do without delay. The number of your regional poison center should be listed on the inside cover of your telephone book. You also should write that number on a piece of paper that is attached to or located near every phone in your home, along with other emergency numbers. *If an emergency exists and you cannot find the number, dial 911 or Information and ask for the poison center.*

The immediate action you need to take will vary with the type of poisoning. The poison center can give you specific instructions if you know the particular substance your baby has swallowed. However, carry out the following instructions before calling them.

Swallowed Poison. First, get the poisonous substance away from your baby. If she still has some in her mouth, try to make her spit it out, or remove it with your fingers. Keep this material along with any other evidence that might help determine what she swallowed.

Next, check for these signs:

- Severe throat pain
- Excessive drooling
- Breathing difficulty
- Convulsions
- Excessive drowsiness

If any of these are present, get emergency medical help immediately by calling for an ambulance or having someone drive you to the nearest emergency center. Take the poison container and remnants of material with you to help the doctor determine what was swallowed. *Do not make your baby vomit,* as this may cause further damage, and *do not follow instructions about poisoning on the label* of the container, as these are often out of date or incorrect.

If your baby is not showing these serious symptoms, call your regional poison center. They will need the following information in order to help you:

- Your name and phone number.
- Your baby's name, age, and weight. Also be sure to mention any serious medical conditions she may have or medications she is taking.
- The name of the substance your baby swallowed. Read it off the container, and spell it if necessary. If ingredients are listed on the label, read them, too. If your baby has swallowed a prescription medicine, and the drug is not named on the label, give the center the name of the pharmacy and its phone number, the date of the prescription and its number. Try to describe the tablet or capsule, and mention any imprinted numbers on it. If your baby swallowed another substance, such as a part of a plant, provide as full a description as possible to help identify it.
- The time your baby swallowed this poison (or when you found her), and the amount you think she swallowed.

If the poison is extremely dangerous, or because of the age of your child, you may be told to make her vomit and/or take her directly to the nearest emergency room for medical evaluation. Otherwise, you will be given instructions to follow at home.

If you are advised to make your baby vomit, consult with your doctor for the recommended dose of syrup of ipecac (keep this on hand). Also, have your baby drink a glass of water. If she doesn't vomit within twenty minutes, repeat the dose *once.* Get a large basin or bowl, and when your baby starts to vomit, place her over your lap, with her face down and her head lower than her hips. Catch the vomit in the basin so it can be inspected. Save it until your pediatrician or the poison center tells you to discard it. If your baby continues to vomit for more than two hours after being given syrup of ipecac, or shows any of the symptoms described earlier, again contact your pediatrician.

In some cases vomiting may be dangerous, so never make a baby vomit unless the poison center instructs you to do so. Strong acids (such as toilet bowl cleaner) or strong alkalis (such as lye, drain or oven cleaner, or dishwasher detergent) can burn the throat, and vomiting will only increase the damage. In such cases you probably will be advised to have the baby drink milk or water. Also, sometimes induction of vomiting may interfere with administration of activated charcoal or oral antidote.

Poison on the Skin. If your baby spills a dangerous chemical substance on her body, remove her clothes and rinse the skin with lukewarm—not hot—water. If the area shows signs of being burned, continue rinsing for at least fifteen minutes, no matter how much your baby may protest. Then call the poison center for further advice. Do not apply ointments or grease.

Poison in the Eye. Flush your baby's eye by holding her eyelid open and pouring a steady stream of lukewarm water into the inner corner. A baby is sure to object to this treatment, so get another adult to hold her while you rinse the eye. If that's not possible, wrap her tightly in a towel and clamp her under one arm so you have one hand free to hold the eyelid open and the other to pour in the water. Continue flushing the eye for fifteen minutes. Then call the poison center for further instructions. Do not use an eyecup, eye drops, or ointment. If there is any question of continued pain or severe injury, seek emergency assistance immediately.

Poison Fumes. In the home, poisonous fumes are most likely to be produced by an idling automobile in a closed garage; leaky gas vents; and wood, coal, or kerosene stoves that are improperly vented or maintained. If your baby is exposed to fumes or gases from these or other sources, get her into fresh air immediately. If she is breathing, call the poison center for further instructions. If she has stopped breathing, start CPR (see page 392) and don't stop until she breathes on her own or someone else can take over. If you can, have someone call for emergency medical help immediately; otherwise, try one minute of CPR and then call for emergency assistance.

Prevention

Young children, especially those between ages one and three, are poisoned most commonly by things in the home, such as drugs and medications, cleaning products, plants, cosmetics, pesticides, paints, and solvents. This happens because tasting and mouthing things is a natural way for children to explore their surroundings, and because they imitate adults without understanding what they are doing. Although more poisonings occur in children over the age of one year old, poison-proof your home now in anticipation of an increasing risk of these problems down the road.

Most poisonings occur when parents are distracted. If you are ill or under a great deal of stress, you may not watch your child as closely as usual. The hectic routine of getting dinner on the table at the end of the day causes so many lapses in parental attention that late afternoon is known as "the arsenic hour" by poison center personnel.

The best way to prevent poisonings is to store all toxic substances, locked, where your baby cannot possibly get to them, even when you are not directly watching her. Also, supervise her even more closely whenever you're visiting a store or home that has not been child-proofed. Be especially attentive when your child is visiting another home, or a grandparent's home, where child-proofing has not been as vigilant. (See also Chapter 10, "Keeping Your Baby Safe.")

Poison-Proofing Your Home

- Store drugs and medications in a medicine cabinet that is locked or out of reach. Do not keep toothpaste in the same cabinet.
- Buy and *keep* medication in containers with child-proof caps. Discard prescription medicines when the illness for which they were prescribed has passed.
- Do not take medicine in front of small children; they may try to imitate you later. Never tell them that a medicine is candy in order to get them to take it.
- Check the label every time you give medication, to be sure you are giving the right medicine in the correct dosage. Mistakes are most likely to occur in the middle of the night, so always turn on the light when handling any medication.
- Read labels on all household products before you buy them. Try to find the least toxic ones for the job, and buy only what you need to use immediately.

- Store hazardous products in locked cabinets that are out of your baby's reach. Do not keep detergents and other cleaning products under the kitchen or bathroom sink unless they are in a cabinet with a safety lock.
- Never put poisonous or toxic products in containers that were once used for food, especially empty drink bottles, cans, or cups.
- Never run your car in a closed garage. Be sure that coal, wood, or kerosene stoves are properly maintained. If you smell gas, turn off the stove or gas burner, leave the house, and then call the gas company.
- Keep a small bottle of syrup of ipecac on hand. (Store it with your other medicines, out of the baby's reach.) This is available without prescription at most pharmacies. Use it only when and as directed by the poison center or your pediatrician. Ask your pediatrician for the recommended dose.
- Post the poison center number near every telephone in your home, along with other emergency numbers. Be sure that your caregiver knows how to use these numbers.

13

Abdominal/Gastrointestinal Tract

Abdominal Pain

Although children of all ages experience abdominal pain occasionally, the causes of such pain in infants tend to be quite different from those of older children. So, too, is the way babies react to the pain. While an older youngster may rub her abdomen and tell you she's having a "bellyache" or "tummyache," a very young infant will show her distress by crying and pulling up her legs or by passing gas (which is usually swallowed air). Vomiting or excessive burping may also accompany the crying in babies.

Fortunately, most stomachaches disappear on their own, and are not serious. However, if your baby's distress continues or worsens over a period of three to five hours, or if she has a fever or extreme change in appetite or energy level, you should notify your pediatrician immediately. These symptoms may indicate that a more serious disorder is causing the pain.

Common Causes of Abdominal Pain in Infancy

1. **Colic** usually occurs in infants between the ages of ten days and three months of age. While no one knows exactly what causes it, colic seems to produce rapid and severe contractions of the intestine which probably are responsible for the baby's pain. The discomfort often is more severe in the late afternoon and early evening, and may be accompanied by inconsolable crying, pulling up of the legs, frequent passage of gas, and general irritability. (See Chapter 6, "The First Month.")

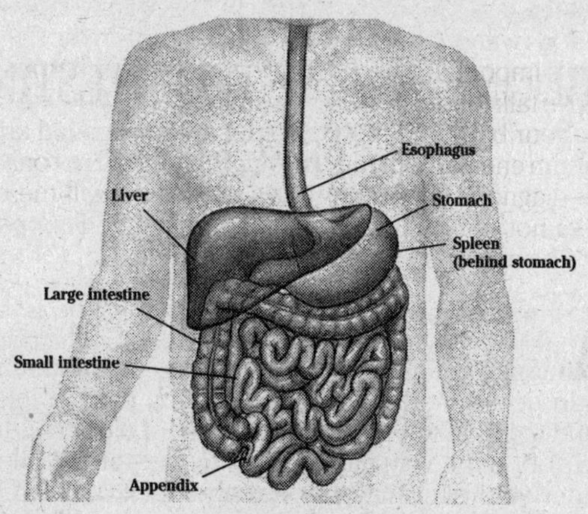

Abdomen/Gastro-intestinal Tract

How should you respond? You may need to try a variety of approaches (detailed on page 179).

2. **Constipation** often is blamed for abdominal pain, but it's rarely a problem in younger infants. Older babies who have started solid foods, however, do sometimes become constipated, and may experience abdominal discomfort while having a bowel movement. If this appears to be your infant's problem, try the following:

   - Add a small amount of water to the diet.
   - Decrease constipating foods, such as rice, banana, or cereal.

   If these simple measures don't seem to help, consult the section on *Constipation* (page 420), and talk to your pediatrician. Never give a baby laxatives or other types of stool loosening or softening medications without first consulting your pediatrician.

3. **Intussusception** is another rare cause of abdominal pain in young infants, usually occurring in the first year of life. This particular problem is due to one part of the intestine telescoping on itself. This creates a blockage that causes severe pain. The child will intermittently and abruptly cry and

pull her legs toward her stomach. This will be followed by periods without pain, often without any distress.

It is important to recognize this cause of abdominal pain and to talk to your pediatrician immediately. She will want to see your baby and perhaps order an X ray called an air or barium enema. Sometimes doing this test will not only make the diagnosis but also unblock the intestine. If the enema does not unblock the intestine, an emergency operation may be necessary to correct the problem.

4. **Viral or bacterial infection** of the intestine is usually associated with diarrhea and/or vomiting. Infectious gastroentitis often presents with abdominal pain.

5. **Urinary tract infection (UTI)** can occur during infancy, but it only occasionally produces abdominal pain at that age. More commonly, symptoms in babies include fever and irritability. If your pediatrician suspects a UTI, he will examine the baby and her urine. If an infection is present, an antibiotic will be prescribed. This will eliminate both the infection and the abdominal pain. (See *Urinary Tract Infections*, page 531).

6. **Intestinal infection (gastroenteritis):** Viruses are the most frequent cause of intestinal infection and the abdominal pain that results from such infection. However, intestinal infection can be caused by bacteria or parasites—organisms, larger than bacteria or viruses, that are frequently found in unsanitary water or food supplies. When infection occurs, there are usually abdominal cramps, diarrhea, and/or vomiting. (See *Diarrhea*, page 421, and *Vomiting*, page 439.) The pain generally lasts one or two days and then disappears. One exception is an infection caused by the *Giardia lamblia* parasite. This infestation may produce periodic recurrent pain not localized to any one part of the abdomen. The pain may persist for a week or more, and can lead to a marked loss of appetite and weight. Treatment with appropriate medication can cure this infestation and the abdominal pain that accompanies it.

7. **Milk allergy** is a reaction to the protein in milk which results in cramping abdominal pain. (See *Milk Allergy*, page 436.)

CONSTIPATION

Bowel patterns vary in children just as they do in adults. Because of this, it is sometimes difficult to tell if your baby is truly constipated. One infant may go two or three days without a bowel movement and still not be constipated, while another might have relatively frequent bowel movements but have difficulty passing the stool. In general, it is best to watch for the following signals before suspecting constipation:

- In a newborn, firm stools less than once a day
- At any age, stools that are hard and dry and associated with painful bowel movements
- Episodes of abdominal pain relieved after having a large bowel movement
- Blood in or on the outside of the stools
- Soiling between bowel movements

Constipation generally occurs when the muscles at the end of the large intestine tighten, preventing the stool from passing normally. The longer the stool remains there, the firmer and drier it becomes, making it even more difficult to pass without discomfort. Then, because the bowel movement is painful, your baby may consciously try to hold it back, making the problem still worse.

The tendency to constipation seems to run in families. It may start in infancy and remain as a lifetime pattern, becoming worse if the child does not establish regular bowel habits, or withholds stool.

Treatment

Mild or occasional episodes of constipation may be helped by the following suggestions:

If your constipated child is between six months and twelve months of age and recently has started cow's milk, return to his previous formula. This may be helpful, since infant formula tends to be less constipating than unmodified cow's milk. Constipation due to breastmilk is unusual, but if your breastfed infant is constipated it is probably due to a reason other than diet. Do *not* substitute formula for breastmilk unless your doctor tells you to do so.

If your child is eating solid foods and has problems with constipation, you may need to add high-fiber foods to his daily diet. These include prunes, apricots, plums, high-fiber vegetables (such as peas, beans, broccoli), and whole-grain cereals and bread products. Increasing the daily consumption of water may also help.

In more severe cases the pediatrician may prescribe a mild laxative or enema. Follow such prescriptions exactly. Never give your child a laxative without your doctor's advice.

Prevention

Parents should become familiar with their baby's normal bowel patterns and the typical size and consistency of their stools. This is helpful in determining when constipation occurs and how severe the problem is. If the infant does not have regular bowel movements each day or two, or appears uncomfortable when they are passed, talk with your pediatrician about dietary changes that may help his bowel habits become more regular.

Diarrhea

Your baby's bowel movements normally will vary in number and consistency, depending on her age and diet. Breastfed newborns may have up to twelve small bowel movements a day, but by the second or third month may have some days without any. Most babies under one year of age produce less than 5 ounces of stool per day.

An occasional loose stool is not cause for alarm. If, however, the bowel pattern *suddenly changes* to loose, watery stools that occur more frequently than usual, your child has diarrhea.

Diarrhea occurs when the inner lining of the intestine is injured. The stools become loose because the nutrients that your baby eats and drinks are not properly digested or absorbed by the intestine. Also, the injured lining tends to leak fluid. Minerals and salt are lost along with the fluid. This loss can be made even worse if your infant is fed food or beverages that contain large amounts of sugar, since unabsorbed sugar draws even more water into the intestine, increasing the diarrhea.

When the body loses too much water and salt, dehydration results. This can be prevented by replenishing the diarrhea losses with adequate amounts of fluid and salt, as described under *Treatment.*

The medical term for intestinal inflammation is *enteritis.* When the problem is accompanied by or preceded by vomiting, as it often is, there is usually some stomach and small intestinal inflammation as well, and the condition is called *gastroenteritis.*

Babies with viral diarrheal illnesses (see the box below) often have vomiting, fever, and irritability as well. (See *Vomiting,* page 439; Chapter 20, "Fever.") Their stools tend to be greenish-yellow in color, and have a significant amount of water with them. (If they occur as often as once an hour, they usually won't have any solid material at all.) If the stools appear red or blackish, they might contain blood. Bleeding may arise from the injured lining of the intestine or, more

Causes of Diarrhea

In babies, the intestinal damage that produces diarrhea is most often caused by viruses called *enteroviruses.*

Other causes are:

- Bacteria (salmonella, shigella, *E. coli,* campylobacter)
- Parasitic infections *(Giardia)*
- Food or milk allergy
- Side effects from oral medications (most commonly antibiotics)
- Food poisoning (from things such as mushrooms, shellfish, or contaminated food)
- Infections outside the gastrointestinal tract, including the urinary tract, the respiratory tract, and even the middle ear. (If your baby is taking an antibiotic for such an infection, the diarrhea may become more severe.)
- Rotavirus infections

likely, may simply be due to irritation of the rectum by frequent, loose bowel movements. In any event, if you notice this or any other unusual stool color, you should mention it to your pediatrician.

Treatment

There are no effective medications for treating viral intestinal infections, the cause of most cases of diarrhea in infants. Antibiotics should be used only to treat certain types of bacterial or parasitic intestinal infections, which are much less common. When these other conditions are suspected, your pediatrician will ask for stool specimens to test in the laboratory. Other tests also may be done.

Over-the-counter antidiarrheal medications are not recommended for babies. They often worsen the intestinal injury, and they do not stop the body's loss of water and salt if an infection is present. Instead, they cause the fluid and salt to remain *within* the intestine. When this occurs, the baby can become dehydrated without your being aware of it, and without necessarily showing weight loss, because the diarrhea *appears* to stop. For this reason, always consult your pediatrician before giving your child any medication for diarrhea.

Mild Diarrhea. If your baby has a small amount of diarrhea, but is not dehydrated (see the box on page 425 for signs of dehydration), does not have a high fever, and is active and hungry, the diet need not be changed and breastmilk or formula can be continued. You should *not* give a "clear liquid diet" consisting solely of sweetened beverages (juices, Jell-O, or soda pop), because their high sugar content may make the diarrhea worse.

If your baby has mild diarrhea and is vomiting, substitute a commercially available electrolyte solution for her normal diet. These solutions will be recommended by your pediatrician, to maintain normal body water and salt levels until the vomiting has stopped. In most cases, they're needed for only one to two days. Once the vomiting has subsided, gradually restart the normal diet.

Never give boiled milk (skimmed or otherwise) to any baby with diarrhea. Boiling the milk allows the water to evaporate, leaving the remaining part dangerously high in salt and mineral content. (In fact, you should not even give a well infant boiled milk.)

Significant Diarrhea. If your baby has a watery bowel movement every one to two hours, or more frequently, and/or has signs of dehydration (see the box on page 425), consult his pediatrician. She may advise you to withhold all solid foods for at least twenty-four hours and to avoid liquids that are high in sugar (Jell-O, soft drinks, full-strength fruit juices, or artificially sweetened beverages), high in salt (packaged broth), or very low in salt (water and tea). She probably will have you give him only commercially prepared electrolyte solutions, which contain the ideal balance of salt and minerals. (See the table on page 427.) Breastfed babies usually are treated in a similar fashion except in very mild cases, where breastfeeding may be continued.

If your baby has diarrhea and you are concerned that he may be becoming dehydrated, call your pediatrician and withhold all foods and milk beverages until she gives you further instructions. *Take your baby to the pediatrician or nearest emergency room immediately if you think he is moderately to severely dehydrated.* A commercially prepared electrolyte solution should be given in the meantime. For severe dehydration, hospitalization is sometimes necessary so that your baby can be rehydrated intravenously. In milder cases all that may be necessary is to give your child an electrolyte replacement solution according to your pediatrician's directions. The table on page 427 indicates the approximate amount of this solution to be used.

Once your baby has been on an electrolyte solution for twelve to twenty-four hours and the diarrhea is decreasing, you gradually may expand the diet to include foods such as applesauce, pears, bananas, and flavored gelatin. Milk can be withheld for one to two days except in the case of young, bottle-fed babies, who can be given half-strength formula to start (add an equal volume of water to your baby's usual full-strength formula). If the baby is breastfed, you can continue breastfeeding while giving the electrolyte solution.

It is usually unnecessary to withhold food for longer than twenty-four hours, as your baby will need some normal nutrition to start to regain lost strength. After you have started giving your baby food again, the stools may remain loose, but that does not necessarily mean that things are not going well. Look for increased activity, better appetite, more frequent urination, and the disappearance of any of the signs of dehydration. When you see these, you will know your child is getting better.

Diarrhea that lasts longer than two weeks (chronic diarrhea) may signify a more serious type of intestinal problem.

Signs and Symptoms of Dehydration (Loss of Significant Amounts of Body Water)

The most important part of treating diarrhea is to prevent your child from becoming dehydrated. Be alert for the following warning signs of dehydration, and notify the pediatrician immediately if any of them develop.

Mild to Moderate Dehydration:

- Plays less than usual
- Urinates less frequently (wets fewer than six diapers per day)
- Parched, dry mouth
- Fewer tears when crying
- Sunken soft spot of the head

Severe Dehydration (in addition to the symptoms and signs listed above):

- Very fussy
- Excessively sleepy
- Sunken eyes
- Cool, discolored hands and feet
- Wrinkled skin
- Goes several hours without urinating

When diarrhea persists this long, the pediatrician will want to do further tests to determine the cause, and to make sure your baby is not becoming malnourished. If malnutrition is becoming a problem, the pediatrician may recommend a special diet or special type of formula.

If your baby drinks too much fluid, especially too much juice or sweetened beverages, a condition commonly referred to as "toddler's diarrhea" could develop. This causes ongoing loose stools but shouldn't affect appetite or growth, or cause dehydration. Although toddler's diarrhea is not a dangerous condition, the pediatrician may suggest that you limit the amounts of juice and sweetened fluids your infant drinks. Plain water can be given to babies whose thirst does not seem to be satisfied by their normal dietary and milk intake.

When diarrhea occurs in combination with other symptoms, it could mean that there is a more serious medical problem. Notify your pediatrician immediately if the diarrhea is accompanied by any of the following:

- Fever that lasts longer than twenty-four to forty-eight hours
- Bloody stools
- Vomiting that lasts more than twelve to twenty-four hours
- Vomited material that is green-colored, blood-tinged, or like coffee grounds in appearance
- A distended (swollen-appearing) abdomen
- Refusal to eat or drink
- Severe abdominal pain
- Rash or jaundice (yellow color of skin and eyes)

If your baby has another medical condition, or is taking medication routinely, it is best to tell your pediatrician about any diarrheal illness that lasts more than twenty-four hours without improvement, or anything else that really worries you.

Prevention

The following guidelines will help lessen the chances that your baby will get diarrhea:

1. Most forms of infectious diarrhea are transmitted from direct hand-to-mouth contact following exposure to contaminated fecal (stool) material. Promote sanitary measures in your household and in your child's day-care center.
2. Avoid drinking raw (unpasteurized) milk and eating foods that may be contaminated. (See *Food Poisoning*, page 422.)
3. Avoid the unnecessary use of medications, especially antibiotics.
4. If possible, breastfeed your baby through early infancy.
5. Do not give your baby unlimited amounts of sweetened beverages or juice.

(See also *Milk Allergy*, page 436; *Vomiting*, page 439; *Abdominal Pain*, page 417.)

Estimated Oral Fluid and Electrolyte Requirements by Body Weight

Body Weight, in Pounds	*Minimum Daily Fluid Requirements, in Ounces**	*Electrolyte Solution** Requirements for Mild Diarrhea, in Ounces for 24 Hours*
6–7	10	16
11	15	23
22	25	40
26	28	44

*Note: This is the *smallest* amount of fluid that a normal baby requires. Most children drink more than this.
**Commercially available electrolyte solutions include Pedialyte®, Rehydralyte®, and Infalyte®.

Hepatitis

Hepatitis is an inflammation of the liver that, in children, is almost always caused by one of several viruses. In some infants it may cause no symptoms, while in others it can provoke fever, jaundice (yellow skin), loss of appetite, nausea, and vomiting. There are at least five forms of hepatitis, each categorized according to the type of virus that causes it:

1. Hepatitis A, also called infectious hepatitis or epidemic jaundice
2. Hepatitis B, also known as serum hepatitis or transfusion jaundice
3. Non-A, non-B hepatitis, also known as Hepatitis C
4. Hepatitis D, or delta virus hepatitis, which causes disease in persons acutely or chronically ill with Hepatitis B
5. Hepatitis E, caused by a recently recognized virus

Approximately 400,000 cases of hepatitis occur in the United States each year. About half of these are caused by hepatitis B, forty out of every hundred by hepatitis A, and nearly all of the remainder are of the non-A, non-B variety.

Children, especially those in low socioeconomic groups, have the highest incidence of hepatitis A infection. However, because they often have no symptoms, their illness may go unrecognized.

Hepatitis A can be transmitted from person to person, or through contaminated food or water. Commonly, human feces are infected with the virus, so in a day-care or household setting, the infection can be spread when hands are not washed after having a bowel movement or changing the diaper of an infected infant. Anyone who drinks water contaminated with infected human feces or who eats raw shellfish taken from polluted areas may also become infected. A baby infected with hepatitis A virus will become ill from two to six weeks after the virus is transmitted. The illness usually disappears within one month after it begins.

While hepatitis A is rarely transmitted via contaminated blood, semen, or saliva, hepatitis B is sometimes spread through these body fluids. The incidence of hepatitis B infection is now greatest among adolescents, young adults, and in the newborns of women who are infected with the virus. When a pregnant woman has acute or chronic hepatitis B, she may transmit the infection to her newborn at the time of delivery.

The use of sterile disposable needles and the screening of all blood and blood products has essentially eliminated the risk of transmission of hepatitis B in hospitals and doctors' office.

Most cases of transfusion-related hepatitis are now due to non-A, non-B infection.

There are at least two non-A, non-B hepatitis viruses. Infection with these viruses commonly produces mild symptoms, with a gradual onset of fatigue and jaundice. In many cases this form of hepatitis may last for several months, even years, and can occasionally result in severe liver disease and even death. More common in adults than children, this form of hepatitis has become the most frequent type of hepatitis acquired after a transfusion.

The delta virus appears to be a defective or incomplete virus that is transmitted by routes similar to those of hepatitis B. Delta virus infection only occurs in the presence of acute or chronic hepatitis B infection.

Signs and Symptoms

Your baby could have hepatitis without your even being aware of it, since many affected children have few, if any, symptoms. In some babies the only signs of disease may be malaise and fatigue for several days. In others there will be a fever followed by the appearance of jaundice (the sclera, or whites of the eyes, develop noticeable yellowish color). This jaundice is due to an abnormal increase in bilirubin (a yellow pigment) in the blood, caused by the liver inflammation.

With hepatitis B, fever is less likely to occur, although the baby may suffer loss of appetite, nausea, vomiting, abdominal pain, and malaise, in addition to jaundice.

If you suspect that your baby has jaundice, notify your pediatrician. She will order blood tests to determine if hepatitis is causing the problem, or if it is due to another condition. You should contact your doctor any time vomiting and/or abdominal pain persist beyond a few hours, or if appetite loss, nausea, or malaise continues for more than a few days. These all may be indicators of hepatitis.

Treatment

There is no specific treatment for hepatitis. As with most viral infections, the body's own defense mechanisms usually will overcome the infecting agent. Although you do not need to rigidly restrict the diet or activity of your baby, you may need to make adjustments depending on his appetite and energy levels. Avoid aspirin and acetaminophen, because of the risk of toxicity due to inadequate liver function. Also, infants on certain medications for long-term illnesses should have their dosages carefully reviewed by the pediatrician, again to avoid the toxicity that might result because the liver is unable to handle the usual medication load.

Most babies with hepatitis do not need to be hospitalized. However, if loss of appetite or vomiting is interfering with your baby's fluid intake and posing a risk of dehydration, your pediatrician may recommend that he be hospitalized. You should contact your doctor immediately if your baby appears very lethargic, unresponsive, or delirious, as these may indicate that his illness is worsening and hospitalization is indicated.

The great majority of babies with hepatitis recover uneventfully. Cirrhosis (scarring of the liver) occasionally follows recovery, but only in severe cases. Death occurs very rarely. There is no chronic infection following hepatitis A, but about 10 of every 100 people infected with hepatitis B become chronic carriers of the virus. A much higher percentage of infants who are born to mothers with acute or chronic hepatitis B become chronic carriers if not properly immunized with the vaccine developed for protection against the hepatitis B virus. As chronic hepatitis B carriers, they would be at risk for the development of liver cancer many years later. A majority of persons injected with hepatitis C may eventually develop a chronic liver problem. Transmission from an infected mother to an infant can occur. There are now hepatitis A vaccines available. These vaccines, first licensed in 1995, are suggested for certain international travelers and adults employed in certain high-risk occupations such as those working in a child-care facility or hospital.

Prevention

Thorough handwashing before eating and after using the toilet is the most important preventive measure against hepatitis. If your baby is in child care, you should check to be sure that members of the staff wash their hands after handling diapers and before feeding the children.

Hepatitis is not transmitted by simply being in the same child-care facility or room with an infected person, or by playing with him. It can occur only if there has been a direct or indirect exposure to the blood, bodily fluids, or excretions of a person with hepatitis. This could happen during kissing, mouthing of toys, or sharing food or utensils.

If you find out that your baby has been exposed to a person with hepatitis, you should immediately contact your pediatrician, who will determine if the exposure has placed your infant at risk. If there's a chance of infection, the doctor may administer an injection of gamma globulin or a hepatitis vaccine, depending on which hepatitis virus was involved.

Prior to foreign travel with your baby, consult your physician to determine the risk of exposure to hepatitis in the countries you plan to visit. In certain situations, gamma globulin and/or a hepatitis A vaccine may be indicated.

It is now recommended that all newborn infants, children, and adolescents be immunized against Hepatitis B (see immunization schedule on page 82).

HYDROCELE (COMMUNICATING HYDROCELE, INFANT HERNIA)

The testicles of the developing male grow inside his abdominal cavity, moving down through a tube (the inguinal canal) into the scrotum as he nears birth. When this movement takes place, the lining of the abdominal wall (peritoneum) is pulled along with the testes to form a sac connecting the testicle with the abdominal cavity. The opening into the abdominal space usually closes. If it does not, and the passage remains open, the fluid which normally surrounds the abdominal organs will flow through it and collect in the scrotal area. This is called a communicating hydrocele (pronounced hy-dro-seal).

As many as half of all newborn boys have this problem; however, it usually disappears within one year without any

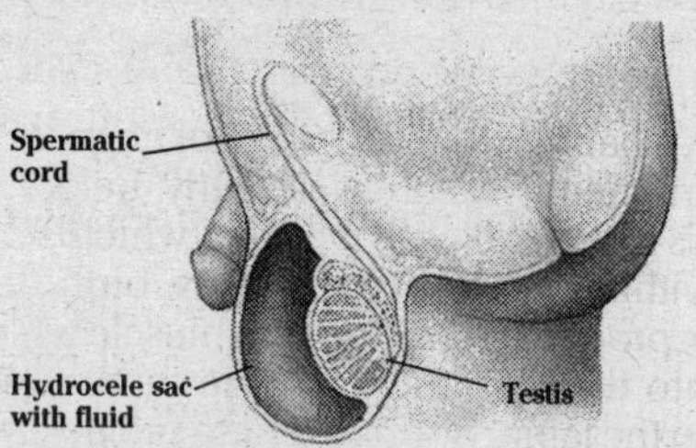

treatment. Although most common in the newborn, hydroceles also can develop later in childhood, most often in association with a hernia (see below).

If your son has a hydrocele, he probably will not complain, but you or he will notice that one side of his scrotum is swollen. In an infant this swelling decreases at night or when he is resting or lying down. When he gets more active or is crying, it increases, then subsides when he quiets again. Your pediatrician will make the final diagnosis by shining a bright light through the scrotum, to show the fluid surrounding the testicle.

If your baby is born with a hydrocele, your pediatrician will examine it at each regular checkup until around one year of age. During this time your child should not feel any discomfort in the scrotum or the surrounding area. If he seems to be tender in this area or has unexplained discomfort, nausea, or vomiting, call the doctor at once. These are signs that a piece of intestine may have entered the scrotal area along with abdominal fluid. (See *Inguinal Hernia*, below.) If this occurs and the intestine gets trapped in the scrotum, your son probably will require immediate surgery to release the trapped intestine and close the opening between the abdominal wall and scrotum.

If the hydrocele persists beyond one year without causing pain, a similar surgical procedure may be recommended. In this relatively minor operation, the excess fluid is removed and the opening into the abdominal cavity closed.

Inguinal Hernia

If you notice a small lump or bulge in your baby's groin area or an enlargement of the scrotum, you may have discovered an inguinal hernia. This condition, which is present in five of every hundred children (most commonly in boys), occurs when an opening in the lower abdominal wall allows the child's intestine to squeeze through.

A hernia in a baby is due to a failure of normal protrusions from the peritoneum to close properly before birth. The peritoneum is a large, balloonlike sac which surrounds all the organs within the abdomen. Before birth, this sac has two fingerlike projections through the muscle walls which, in boys, lead into the scrotum alongside the testicles and, in girls, lead into the labia. Normally, these projections separate from the rest of the peritoneum before birth, producing in boys protective sacs for the testicles inside the scrotum. When these extensions do not close properly, a small portion of the bowel may push through into the groin or scrotum, producing a hernia. If the opening is very small and only abdominal fluid comes down into the sac, it is called a hydrocele (see page 431).

Most hernias do not cause any discomfort, and you or the pediatrician will discover them only by seeing the bulge. While this kind of hernia must be treated, it is not an emergency condition. You should, however, notify your doctor, who may instruct you to have the baby lie down and elevate his legs. Sometimes this will cause the bulge to disappear. However, your doctor will still want to examine the area as soon as possible.

Rarely, a piece of the intestine gets trapped in the hernia, causing swelling and pain. (If you touch the area, it will be

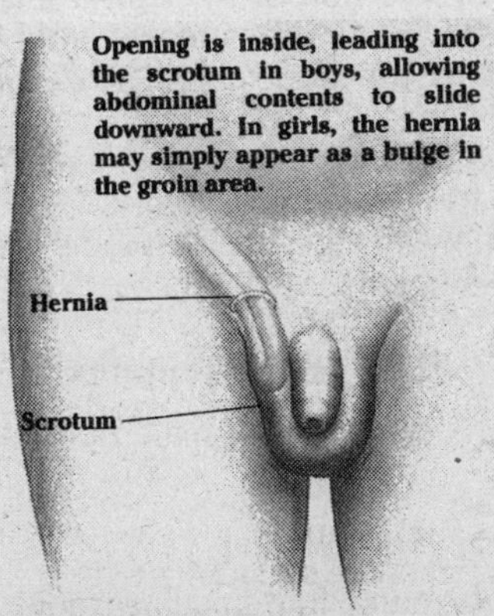

tender.) This condition is called an incarcerated (trapped) hernia, and does require immediate medical attention.

Treatment

Even if the hernia is not incarcerated, it still needs to be surgically repaired as soon as possible. The surgeon also may check the other side to see if it, too, needs to be corrected, since it is very common for the same defect to be present there.

If the hernia is causing pain, it may indicate that a piece of intestine has become trapped, or incarcerated. In that case, your pediatrician will want to be consulted immediately. He may try to move the trapped piece of intestine out of the sac. Even if this can be done, the hernia still needs to be surgically repaired soon thereafter. If the intestine remains trapped despite the physician's efforts, emergency surgery must be performed to prevent permanent damage to the intestine.

Malabsorption

Sometimes babies who eat a balanced diet suffer from malnutrition. The reason for this may be malabsorption, the body's inability to absorb nutrients from the digestive system into the bloodstream.

Normally, the digestive process converts nutrients from the diet into small units that pass through the wall of the intestine and into the bloodstream, where they are carried to other cells in the body. If the intestinal wall is damaged by a virus or bacterial infection or by parasites, its surface may change so that digested substances cannot pass through. When this happens, the nutrients will be eliminated through the stool.

Malabsorption commonly occurs in a normal baby for a day or two. It rarely lasts much longer. However, if two or more of the following signs or symptoms seem to persist, notify your pediatrician.

Signs and Symptoms

Possible signs and symptoms of malabsorption include the following:

- Abdominal pain and vomiting
- Frequent, loose, bulky, foul-smelling stools

- Increased susceptibility to infection
- Loss of fat and muscle
- Increase in bruises and bone fractures
- Dry, scaly skin rashes
- Personality changes
- Slowing of growth and weight gain (may not be noticeable for several months)

Not all babies who have absorption problems display these symptoms. Some simply consume more food to make up for the nutrients they're losing. In others, the digestive surface of the intestine heals so quickly there is no significant discomfort or damage. In these cases, malabsorption is no cause for concern.

Treatment

When an infant suffers from malnutrition, malabsorption is just one of the possible causes. She might be undernourished because she's not getting enough of the right types of food, or has digestive problems that prevent her body from digesting them. She also might have a combination of these problems. Before prescribing a treatment, the pediatrician must determine the cause. This can be done in one or more of the following ways:

- You may be asked to list the amount and type of food your baby eats.
- The pediatrician may test the infant's ability to digest and absorb specific nutrients. For example, the doctor might have her drink a solution of milk sugar (lactose) and then measure the level of hydrogen in the breath afterward. This is known as a lactose hydrogen breath test.
- The pediatrician may collect and analyze stool samples. In healthy babies, only a small amount of the fat consumed each day is lost through the stool. If too much is found in the stool, it is an indication of malabsorption.
- Collection of sweat from the skin, called a "sweat test," may be performed to see if cystic fibrosis (see page 587) is

present. This is a disease in which there are insufficient amounts of certain enzymes necessary for proper digestion and an abnormality in the sweat.

- In some cases the pediatrician might request a specialist to take a small piece of the wall of the small intestine (a biopsy) and have it examined under the microscope for signs of infection, inflammation, or other injury.

Ordinarily, these tests are performed before any treatment is begun; although a seriously sick baby might be hospitalized in order to receive special feedings while her problem is being evaluated.

Once the physician is sure the problem is malabsorption, she will try to identify a specific reason for its presence. When the reason is infection, the treatment usually will include antibiotics. If malabsorption occurs because the intestine is too active, certain medications may be used to counteract this, so that there's time for the nutrients to be absorbed.

Sometimes there's no clear cause for the problem. In this case, the diet may be changed to include foods or special nutritional formulas that are more easily tolerated and absorbed.

MILK ALLERGY

Everyone has heard of children who are allergic to ordinary cow's milk. It's actually a rare occurrence. Only 1 child in 100 develops a true intolerance to milk. It usually appears in the first few months of life, when an infant's digestive system is still quite immature.

If other family members have allergies, your baby may be more likely to develop a milk allergy. This likelihood will increase further if he's fed cow's milk formula from birth. Breastfeeding will delay if not prevent the onset of a milk allergy. Once in a while a very sensitive breastfed baby may develop this condition because milk products consumed by the mother may be passed to the baby through the breastmilk.

The symptoms of milk allergy may appear anywhere from a few minutes to a few hours after the baby consumes the product, but the most severe symptoms usually occur within half an hour. The most common symptoms are:

- Colic: inconsolable crankiness or fussiness, often interfering with normal sleep. (See *Colic,* page 417.)
- Vomiting and/or diarrhea. (See pages 439 and 421.)

Less common symptoms are

- Constipation (see page 420.)
- Bleeding in the digestive tract

If the respiratory system is affected by the milk allergy, the baby also may have chronic nasal stuffiness, a runny nose, cough, wheezing, or difficulty in breathing. The allergy can also cause eczema, hives, swelling, itching, or a rash around the mouth and on the chin due to contact with milk. (See *Eczema,* page 565; *Hives,* page 569; *Cough,* page 456.)

If you suspect your baby has an allergy to milk, tell your pediatrician, and be sure to mention whether there's a family history of allergy. Take your infant to the doctor's office or emergency room *immediately* if he:

- Has difficulty breathing
- Turns blue
- Is extremely pale or weak
- Has generalized hives
- Develops swelling in the head and neck region
- Has bloody diarrhea

Treatment

If your pediatrician suspects that a milk allergy is present, he will first try eliminating milk and milk products completely for a period of time to see if there is any improvement. If there is, your baby may then be given a milk trial—that is, a controlled introduction of milk to the diet. This will reveal whether the symptoms decrease or disappear when milk is avoided, and if they reappear when it's introduced again.

This trial of milk should be carried out cautiously and under the supervision of a physician. Infants who are allergic to milk can become quickly sick, even if exposed to only a small amount.

Your pediatrician can use several appropriate medications to treat the symptoms of milk allergy. These include antihistamines, decongestants, and antiasthma medication (if wheezing is among your infant's allergy symptoms). The most important treatment, however, is to eliminate milk and milk products from your baby's diet (or from yours if you're breastfeeding). When milk is avoided completely for a long enough period of time, most infants will eventually outgrow the allergy. Your baby has about a 50 percent chance of outgrowing it by age one.

In the meantime, babies with milk allergy must avoid cheese, yogurt, ice cream, and cow's milk formula as well as any food that contains milk. You must also check all processed food labels for *casein, caseinate,* and *whey;* they are all milk products and must be avoided, too. A bottle-fed infant will need a milk substitute such as a soybean formula. If he's also sensitive to soy protein (some infants are allergic to both soy and milk), your doctor will suggest still another milk substitute. Some milk-sensitive babies can tolerate diluted evaporated milk, because the heating process used in making this product alters some of the milk protein. Goat's milk should not be used as a substitute because of its similarity to cow's milk.

If your breastfed infant develops a milk allergy, you'll have to have a milk-free diet yourself. (You'll also need to start taking calcium and vitamin supplements.) When you wean your baby, delay feeding him cow's milk as long as possible, and give it very cautiously at first, at the direction of your doctor.

You may be tempted to "cheat" on the milk-free diet once your baby's symptoms lessen or disappear. Don't! If you give him even small quantities of milk or its products, he may continue to have mild symptoms or an ongoing hidden reaction and he may even develop other food allergies. In the process, you also may prolong the milk allergy and reduce his chance of outgrowing it.

We can't overemphasize the importance of a milk-free diet for an infant with milk allergy. If it's ignored, his allergy may lead to potentially serious complications, including dehydration due to severe vomiting or diarrhea; loss of weight from chronic diarrhea; anemia caused by gastrointestinal bleeding; infected eczema; severe difficulty breathing; and occasionally an inflammation of the lungs resembling recurrent pneumonia. The very worst complication, acute shock, is rare but can be fatal.

Prevention

In general, breastfeeding a baby is the best way to prevent the onset of milk allergy. Particularly if anyone in the immediate family is allergy-prone, you should plan to breastfeed your baby for as long as possible, preferably for six months or more. While doing so, you'll need to minimize or perhaps eliminate your own intake of milk products. And when you eventually introduce other foods to your baby, you'll want to do it gradually (a new one at one- or two-week intervals), watching for the signs of allergy mentioned previously.

If you cannot breastfeed, ask your pediatrician to guide you in selecting an appropriate formula.

Vomiting

Since many common childhood illnesses can cause vomiting, you should expect your baby to have this problem from time to time. Usually, it ends quickly without treatment, but this doesn't make it any easier for you to watch. That feeling of helplessness—combined with the fear that something serious might be wrong and the desire to do something to make it better—may make you tense and anxious. To help put your mind at ease, learn as much as you can about the causes of vomiting and what you can do to treat your baby when it occurs.

First of all, there's a difference between real vomiting and just spitting up. Vomiting is the forceful throwing up of stomach contents through the mouth. Spitting up (most commonly seen in infants under one year of age) is the easy flow of stomach contents out of the mouth, frequently with a burp.

Vomiting occurs when the abdominal muscles and diaphragm contract vigorously while the stomach is relaxed. This reflex action is triggered by the "vomiting center" in the brain after it has been stimulated by:

- Nerves from the stomach and intestine when the gastrointestinal tract is either irritated or swollen by an infection or blockage
- Chemicals in the blood (drugs, for example)
- Psychological stimuli from disturbing sights or smells
- Stimuli from the middle ear (as in vomiting caused by motion sickness)

The common causes of spitting up or vomiting vary according to age. During the first few months, for instance, most infants will spit up small amounts of formula, usually within the first hour after being fed. This "cheesing," as it is often called, is simply the occasional movement of food from the stomach, through the tube (esophagus) leading to it, and out of the mouth. It will occur less often if a child is burped frequently and if active play is limited right after meals. This spitting up tends to decrease as the baby becomes older, but may persist in a mild form until ten to twelve months of age. Spitting up is not serious and doesn't interfere with normal weight gain. (See *Spitting Up*, page 140.)

Occasional vomiting may occur during the first month. If it appears repeatedly, or is unusually forceful, call your pediatrician. It may be just a mild feeding difficulty, but could also be a sign of something more serious.

Between two weeks and four months of age, persistent forceful vomiting may be caused by a thickening of the muscle at the stomach exit. This prevents food from passing into the intestines, and is known as *hypertrophic pyloric stenosis.* It requires immediate medical attention. Surgery usually is required to open the narrowed area. The important sign of this condition is forceful vomiting occurring approximately fifteen to thirty minutes or less after every feeding. Any time you notice this, call your pediatrician as soon as possible.

Occasionally, the spitting up in the first few weeks to months of life gets worse instead of better, that is, even though it's not forceful, it occurs all the time. This happens when the muscles at the lower end of the esophagus become overly relaxed and allow the stomach contents to back up. This condition usually can be controlled by the following:

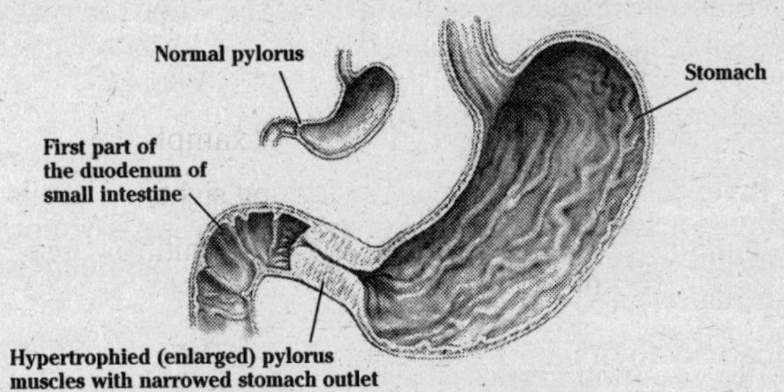

1. Thicken the milk with small amounts of baby cereal.
2. Avoid overfeeding.
3. Burp the baby frequently.
4. Leave the infant in a quiet, upright position for at least thirty minutes following feeding. If this is not effective, you may want to put the baby in a prone or prone-elevated position (prone with head elevated).

After the first few months of life, the most common cause of vomiting is a stomach or intestinal infection. Viruses are by far the most frequent infecting agents, but occasionally bacteria and even parasites may be the cause. The infection also may produce fever, diarrhea, and sometimes nausea and abdominal pain. The infection is usually contagious, so if your infant has it, chances are some of her playmates also will be affected.

Occasionally, infections outside the gastrointestinal tract will cause vomiting. These include infections of the respiratory system, infections of the urinary tract (see page 531), otitis media (see page 485), and pneumonia (see page 460), as well as meningitis (see page 534). Some of these conditions require immediate medical treatment, so be alert for the following trouble signs, whatever your baby's age, and call your pediatrician if they occur:

- Blood or bile (a green-colored material) in the vomitus
- Severe abdominal pain

- Strenuous, repeated vomiting
- Swollen abdomen
- Lethargy or severe irritability
- Convulsions
- Signs or symptoms of dehydration, including dry mouth, absent tears, depression of the "soft spot," and decreased urination
- Inability to drink adequate amounts of fluid
- Vomiting continuing beyond twenty-four hours

Treatment

In most cases, vomiting will stop without specific medical treatment. You should never use over-the-counter or prescription remedies unless they've been specifically prescribed by your pediatrician for your child and this particular illness.

When your infant is vomiting, keep her lying on her stomach or side as much as possible. This will minimize the chances of vomit being inhaled into the upper airway and lungs.

When there is continued vomiting, you need to make certain that dehydration doesn't occur. (*Dehydration* is a term used when the body loses so much water that it can no longer function efficiently.) If allowed to reach a severe degree, it can be serious and life-threatening. To prevent this from happening, make sure your baby consumes enough extra fluids to restore what has been lost through throwing up. If she vomits these, notify your pediatrician.

For the first twenty-four hours or so of any illness that causes vomiting, keep your infant off solid foods, and encourage her to suck or drink clear fluids, such as water, sugar water (½ teaspoon [2.5 cc] sugar in 4 ounces [120 cc] of water), popsicles, gelatin water (1 teaspoon [5 cc] of flavored gelatin in 4 ounces of water), or preferably an electrolyte solution (ask your pediatrician which one), instead of eating. Liquids not only help to prevent dehydration, but also are less likely than solid foods to stimulate further vomiting.

Here are some guidelines to follow for giving your baby fluids *after* she has vomited:

1. Wait for two to three hours after the last vomiting episode, and then give 1 to 2 ounces of cool water every half hour to one hour for four feedings.
2. If she retains this, give 2 ounces of electrolyte solution alternated with 2 ounces of clear liquids every half hour.
3. If this is retained for two feedings, add half-strength formula or milk (depending upon age), and continue increasing the quantity slowly to 3 to 4 ounces every three or four hours.
4. After twelve to twenty-four hours with no additional vomiting, gradually return your child to her normal diet, but continue to give her plenty of clear fluids.

If your baby also has diarrhea (see page 421), ask your pediatrician for instructions on giving liquids and restoring solids to her diet.

If your infant can't retain any clear liquids or the symptoms become more severe, notify your pediatrician. She will examine your baby and may order blood and urine tests or Xrays to make a diagnosis. Occasionally, hospital care may be necessary.

14

BEHAVIOR

THE "HYPERREACTIVE" BABY

Every baby has her own way of reacting to the world around her. Some infants are particularly excitable and active, and are difficult to calm and settle down for feeding and sleeping. Others are much quieter and less responsive to the stimuli around them. Both of these types of infants are developing normally, even though their behavior can be dramatically different.

Parents of an excitable baby may believe that their child is "hyperactive." But true hyperactivity occurs in older children, and is typically diagnosed in preschool or school-age youngsters. It is a condition that affects about 1 in 20 children under age twelve. These youngsters have trouble sitting still, are easily distracted, often act on impulse, and have difficulty paying attention when listening to or watching events around them. When their condition combines hyperactivity and distractibility, physicians call their condition "attention deficit hyperactivity disorder," or ADHD.

But the situation is different for babies. When they are overly active or "hyperresponsive," it is a reflection of their inborn temperament, not ADHD. They do not have an emotional disorder or a condition that needs treatment. Instead, they have their own personality traits and unique style of reacting to the stimuli in their lives. They may move a lot. They may be fussy, and cry more than the average infant. But their behavior is well within the range of normal.

A baby who is hyperreactive or hyperresponsive will not necessarily develop hyperactivity or ADHD later in childhood, although this is sometimes the case. Many babies "outgrow" this tendency toward excitability and outbursts of motor activity.

How to Respond

If your baby is hyperresponsive, there are steps you can take to help control her excitable temperament. For example, create an environment that is as calming as possible. Speak to her quietly. Touch her gently. Lift her slowly. Avoid loud television noise or blaring music around her.

Many hyperreactive babies become calmer when they are swaddled. Wrap them securely in a blanket. Carry them in a "front pack," which gives them loose person-to-person contact.

As a hyperresponsive infant begins to crawl and walk, she may be more prone to accidents (falls down steps, for example), or she might be more likely to explore bathrooms or kitchen cupboards. So you need to become more vigilant, and ensure that her environment is carefully monitored for safety.

If you're concerned about your infant's temperament, particularly if there is a change in her activity level, talk to your pediatrician. He will probably offer reassurance that everything is quite normal.

SEPARATION AND STRANGER ANXIETY

At some point in the first year of life, your baby will show signs of distress around strangers. He may cling to you in the presence of unfamiliar people. He might cry when others approach him. He may refuse to be held by anyone except you and your spouse.

Most babies begin to show obvious awareness of so-called strangers, or people outside of their normal environment, in the latter half of their first year. In many babies, it may start at about nine months of age; in others, it can begin earlier, at about six months old. The way they react to these strangers may be interpreted by adults as anxiety.

At about this same time, babies may develop separation anxiety. When they're left with a baby-sitter, or dropped off at a child-care center, they may burst into tears and cling to their parent's leg. The intensity of these responses can vary from one baby to another, and is often a reflection of a baby's temperament; those who already tend to be hyperresponsive to stimuli in their environment may react with more crying and clinging than a baby who is generally calmer and more tranquil.

In many children, these reactions to strangers and separation begin to wane at about their first birthday. In other youngsters, however, these responses may peak in the second year of life, and continue well into the toddler years. As upsetting as it can be to see your baby so distressed, keep in mind that this phenomenon is quite normal, and does not require a doctor's attention.

Ironically, this reaction to strangers is a positive sign, in that it indicates that the baby is well attached to his parent. Because he has bonded so strongly with his primary caregiver, he becomes distressed when other people enter his life, or when he is separated from the parent to whom he has established this strong, healthy relationship.

How to Respond

Keep in mind that separation and stranger anxieties are a normal part of your child's development. This is a transitory stage that will subside over time. However, there are steps you can take to make these predictable moments of stress as tolerable as possible. For example, when a baby-sitter comes to your home, have her arrive 15 to 30 minutes before you leave, so that your baby can become familiar with the sitter while you are still present. When you drop off your baby at a child-care facility, spend a few minutes playing with him before departing. You may be able to leave without your baby shedding tears by having the caregiver or child-care provider distract him for a few moments, perhaps with a toy.

For a more complete discussion of these anxiety-producing phenomena, see *Emotional Development,* pages 221–27.

TELEVISION

Your child will probably view his first television program during infancy. If you own a TV set or VCR, it will gradually become an important part of his life and will teach him many lessons, some good and some bad.

During the early years of life, your child can benefit a great deal from watching educational programming such as *Sesame Street, Mister Rogers' Neighborhood,* nature programs, and broadcasts of concerts or dance. Educational television is not a substitute for reading or playing, but it can enrich your child's life.

Unfortunately, most television programming is not good for children. Even if your child watches only cartoons, he'll see characters hitting, shooting, or otherwise harming each other at a rate of about twenty times per hour. Television also exposes children to sexuality, drugs, and alcohol use at a time when they are too young to understand these issues.

What You Can Do

Media-wise families are well equipped to enjoy the positive benefits of television and to minimize the negative effects. Media education includes smart, limited use of TV in your home, plus an understanding of how TV programming and advertising work. If you do not make a conscious effort to control your child's television viewing, it could become one of the most important negative influences in his life.

For many children, TV serves as a substitute for friends, caregivers, teachers, and even parents. It is the easiest way to be entertained, and quickly becomes habit-forming unless limits are set.

As a general policy your baby should not watch television and your young child should watch no more than one to two hours of television a day. It is easy to enforce this rule when he is a toddler, but it becomes more difficult as he grows older and more independent, so you should start early. If your child never gets used to watching a lot of TV, he won't develop a habit that may be difficult to break later in life. Limit his viewing to programs like *Sesame Street* and other educational programs.

You can help improve television programming for children by contacting the networks, commercial sponsors, or local broadcasters. Voice your complaints and your preferences. If there is a program you especially like, be sure to let the local station manager know, because quality programs often have low ratings, and your support can help keep them on the air.

Become involved in local advocacy groups for better children's TV; join local, community-based coalitions for "Turn Off the Violence" events; and urge local schools to teach media literacy.

Where We Stand

Although the American Academy of Pediatrics does not hold television solely responsible for violence in our society, we believe that televised violence has a clear effect upon the behavior of children and contributes to the frequency with which violence is used to resolve conflict. The absence of consequences of the TV violence that children see, and the rapidity with which difficulties are resolved by the use of violence, increase the likelihood that violence will be among the first strategies that a child selects, rather than the last.

Both parents and broadcasters must be held responsible for the television that children see. We urge parents to limit the amount of TV that their children view, to monitor what their children are watching, and to watch TV with them to help them learn from what they see.

The American Academy of Pediatrics strongly supports legislative efforts to improve the quality of children's programming.

The primary goal of commercial children's television is to sell products, from toys to junk food, to youngsters. Young children in particular cannot distinguish between programs and their commercials, nor do they fully understand that commercials are designed to sell them (and their parents) something.

Television is also guilty of distorting reality on matters such as drugs, alcohol, tobacco, sexuality, family relations, and sex roles.

THUMB AND FINGER SUCKING

Do not be upset if your baby begins sucking his thumb or fingers. This habit is very common and has a soothing and calming effect. Some experts feel that nine out of every ten children engage in this activity at some time in their early life. It is largely the result of the normal rooting and sucking reflexes present in all infants. There actually is evidence that some infants suck their thumbs and fingers even before delivery, and some, particularly finger suckers, will show that behavior immediately after being born.

Because sucking is a normal reflex, thumb and finger sucking can be considered a normal habit. The only time it might cause you concern is if it continues too long or affects the shape of your child's mouth or the alignment of his teeth. Over half of thumb or finger suckers stop by age six or seven months. Sometimes young children, especially when they are feeling most vulnerable, even until age eight or so, will still occasionally suck their thumb. Thumb sucking beyond the fifth birthday may cause changes in the roof of the mouth (palate) or in the way the teeth are lining up. It is then that you and your dentist might become concerned.

15

CHEST AND LUNGS

ASTHMA

Children who cough and/or make a high-pitched wheezing or whistling sound as they breathe may have asthma, a lung disorder affecting the bronchial tubes. However, in infants under six months of age, asthma is rarely diagnosed. Between ages six and twelve months, some babies do develop what is called early-onset asthma, and are often described as having "hyperresponsive" or "reactive" airways.

The bronchial tubes are small airways that connect the main air passages (bronchi) to the place in the lung where the oxygen and carbon dioxide exchange takes place during normal breathing. These tubes are surrounded by smooth muscles that are very sensitive. When stimulated they go into spasm, making the small breathing passages even narrower. In addition, the lining (mucous membrane) of the breathing tubes becomes swollen and inflamed, and produces more of its protective fluid, called mucus.

The airway inflammation is the most important aspect of the disease. The inflammation leads to airway reactivity, which causes the smooth airway muscles to go into spasm. This results in narrowing of these airways, which in turn causes the whistling or wheezing sound heard particularly when the child exhales.

A reactive airway in babies means that the lungs may be responsive to environmental triggers such as inhaling cold air or air pollutants, including cigarette smoke. However, the most common triggers of an attack of asthma in these babies are viral infections, which inflame the lining of the bronchial tubes and stimulate the muscles surrounding them.

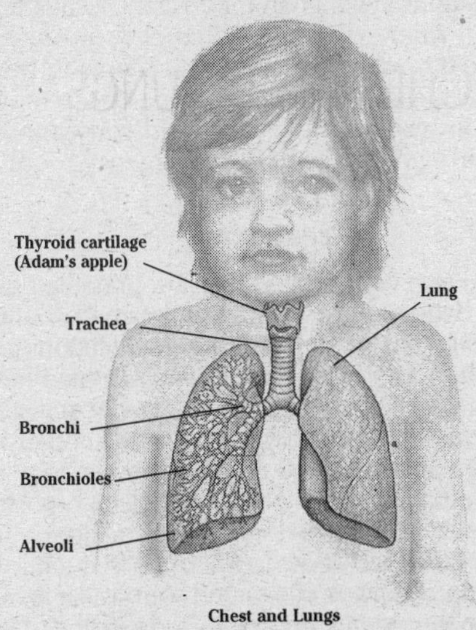

Chest and Lungs

Signs and Symptoms

Recurring episodes of wheezing and coughing in babies (ages 6 to 12 months) are often the earliest signs of asthma or hyper-responsive airways. However, some babies who experience these symptoms may not have classic asthma, and as they grow older, they may no longer experience these episodes. Nevertheless, if a child wheezes and coughs in the latter months of the first year of life, early-onset asthma is a potential diagnosis that needs to be considered. An upper respiratory infection can cause a cough and wheezing that become worse at night or upon contact with an irritant like cigarette smoke.

When to Call the Pediatrician

If your baby under the age of one year has recurring episodes of coughing and wheezing, contact your pediatrician. Positive allergy tests (to allergens such as pollen or pets) are uncommon in babies, and are not routinely performed; viral infections are most likely to cause airway reactivity in these babies.

When asthma is diagnosed, talk with the pediatrician

about the situations in which immediate medical attention is required. As a rule, call your pediatrician at once if your baby has *severe* trouble breathing and seems to be getting worse. Some of these episodes may be life-threatening, and if your baby is in respiratory distress, and you cannot reach your doctor, take your baby to the emergency room.

Treatment

Asthma should always be treated under your pediatrician's supervision. For babies whose symptoms are chronic and recurrent, the pediatrician may prescribe medications such as cromolyn sodium, which is inhaled by mist from a nebulizer, and can reduce the airway inflammation and reactivity. This is frequently combined with a bronchodilator, another inhaled medication that can open up the airways. Babies tend to tolerate these inhaled drugs better than oral medications. However, during a severe episode, an oral steroid may be prescribed for a short period of time (3 to 5 days), which can frequently stop an attack and may prevent an emergency room visit or hospitalization. Short-term steroids are not associated with the side effects of long-term steroid administration.

Prevention

The most important and successful ways to keep your baby from having asthmatic episodes are:

- Give medications according to your pediatrician's directions. Do not stop medications too soon, give them less often than recommended, or switch to other drugs or treatments without first discussing the change with the doctor. If you do not understand why something is being done to your infant, or why a particular medication is being given, ask for an explanation.
- Keep your baby away from the things that trigger her attacks, such as cigarette smoke. Keeping a diary of when the attacks occur and what preceded them may help you identify the triggering substances. Whenever possible, learn to anticipate the attacks. If your infant has asthma with viral infections, talk to your pediatrician about whether to begin giving medication at the start of the viral infection, and precisely what drugs to administer.

Bronchiolitis

Bronchiolitis is an infection of the small breathing tubes (bronchioles) of the lungs. It occurs most often in infants. (Note: The term *bronchiolitis* is sometimes confused with bronchitis, which is an infection of the larger, more central airways.)

Bronchiolitis is almost always caused by a virus, most commonly the respiratory syncytial virus (RSV). Other viruses that can cause this condition are parainfluenza, influenza, measles, and adenovirus. The infection causes inflammation and swelling of the bronchioles, which in turn causes blockage of air flow through the lungs.

Most adults and many children who are infected by RSV get only a cold. In infants, however, the infection is more likely to lead to bronchiolitis. This is because their airways are smaller and are more easily blocked when infection and inflammation occur.

Almost half the infants who develop bronchiolitis go on to develop asthma later in life. We do not know why these babies are more susceptible, but it is likely that the RSV infection is the first trigger for the airway reaction.

RSV infection is the most likely cause of bronchiolitis from October through March. During the other months, bronchiolitis is usually caused by other viruses.

The RSV is spread by contact with secretions from an infected person. It often spreads through families, day-care centers, and hospital wards. Careful hand washing can help prevent this.

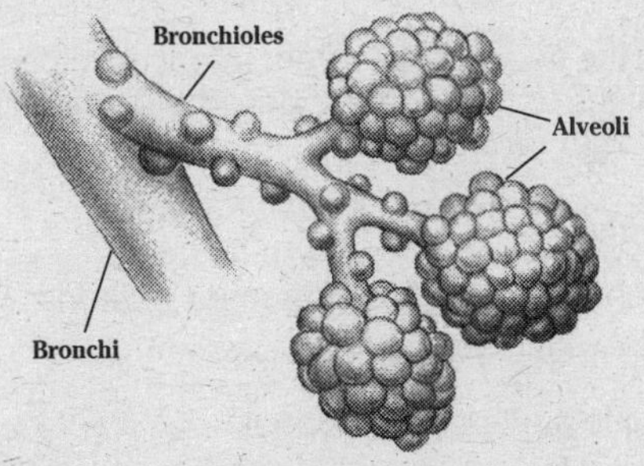

Signs and Symptoms

If your infant has bronchiolitis, it will start with signs of an upper respiratory infection (a cold): runny nose, mild cough, and sometimes fever. After a day or two the cough becomes more pronounced, the baby begins to breathe more rapidly, and with more difficulty:

- He may dilate his nostrils and squeeze the muscles under his rib cage in efforts to get more air in and out of his lungs.
- He will use the muscles between the ribs and above the collarbone to help him breathe.
- When he breathes he may grunt and tighten his abdominal muscles.
- He will make a high-pitched whistling sound, called a wheeze, each time he exhales.
- He may not take fluids well because he is working so hard to breathe that he has difficulty sucking and swallowing.
- As his breathing difficulty increases you may notice a bluish tint around the lips and fingertips. This indicates that his airways are so blocked that an inadequate amount of oxygen is getting into the blood.

If your baby shows any of these signs of breathing difficulty, or if his fever lasts more than three days (or is present at all in an infant under three months), call your pediatrician immediately.

Also call the pediatrician if your infant develops any of the following signs or symptoms of dehydration, which also can be present with bronchiolitis:

- Dry mouth
- Taking less than his normal amount of fluids
- Shedding no tears when he cries
- Urinating less often than normal

If your baby has any of the following conditions, notify your pediatrician as soon as you suspect that he has bronchiolitis:

- Cystic fibrosis
- Congenital heart disease
- Bronchopulmonary dysplasia (seen in some infants who have been on a respirator as newborns)
- Low immunity
- Organ transplant
- A cancer for which he is receiving chemotherapy

Home Treatment

There are no medications you can use to treat RSV infections at home. All you can do during the early phase of the illness is ease your baby's cold symptoms. You can relieve some of the nasal stuffiness with a humidifier, nasal aspirator, and perhaps some mild salt-solution nasal drops prescribed by your pediatrician. (See the treatment for *Colds/Upper Respiratory Infection*, page 482.) Also make sure your baby drinks lots of fluid during this time so he does not become dehydrated. (See *Diarrhea*, page 421.) He may prefer clear liquids rather than milk or formula. Because of the breathing difficulty, he also may feed more slowly and may not tolerate solid foods very well.

Professional Treatment

If your baby is having mild to moderate breathing difficulty, your pediatrician may try using a bronchodilating drug (one that opens up the breathing tubes) before considering hospitalization. These drugs seem to help a small number of patients.

Unfortunately, some infants with bronchiolitis need to be hospitalized, either for breathing distress or dehydration. The breathing difficulty is treated with oxygen and bronchodilating drugs, which are inhaled periodically. Occasionally, another medicine, called theophylline, is used. The dehydration will be treated with a special liquid diet or by fluids given intravenously.

Recently effective treatment has involved the use of RSV-specific antibodies. Though still controversial, this is used in the very ill, hospitalized infant with bronchiolitis, as it may be effective.

Very rarely an infant will not respond to any of these treatments and might have to be assisted by a breathing machine (respirator). This usually is only a temporary measure to help him until his body is able to overcome the infection.

Prevention

The best way to protect your baby from bronchiolitis is to keep him away from the viruses that cause it. When possible, avoid close contact with children or adults who are in the early (contagious) stages of respiratory infections. If your baby is in a day-care center where other children might have the virus, make sure that those who care for him wash their hands thoroughly and frequently.

COUGH

Coughing is almost always an indication of an irritation in your baby's air passages. When the nerve endings in the throat, windpipe, or lungs sense the irritation, a reflex causes air to be ejected forcefully through the passageways.

Coughs usually are associated with respiratory illnesses such as colds/upper respiratory infection (see page 482), bronchiolitis (see page 453), croup (see page 458), or pneumonia (see page 460). If your baby's cough is accompanied by fever, irritability, or difficulty in breathing, he probably has such an infection.

To a large extent, the location of the infection determines the sound of the cough: An irritation in the larynx (voice box), such as croup, causes a cough that sounds like the bark of a dog or seal; irritation of the larger airways such as the trachea (windpipe) or bronchi is characterized by a deeper, raspy cough that gets worse in the morning.

A chronic or long-lasting cough without fever may indicate that your baby has accidentally inhaled a small object such as a peanut into his windpipe or lungs (see *Choking*, page 397). Allergies can cause chronic cough, too, because mucus drips down the back of the throat, producing a dry, hard-to-stop cough, particularly at night. An infant who coughs only at night also may have a mild form of asthma (see page 450).

Occasionally a cough is caused by a temporary irritation, such as breathing strong fumes from drying paint, tobacco smoke, or insecticide sprays. In this case, the cough will go away when the baby gets into fresh air. In rare situations, the infant may continue to have a dry, periodic cough long after the physical cause has been cleared. Though this can be bothersome (more to you than to your baby), the cough usually will eventually disappear. If it becomes a habit, however, your physician will be able to recommend ways of discouraging it.

When to Call the Pediatrician

An infant under two months of age who develops a cough should be seen by the doctor. For older infants, consult your physician if:

- The coughing makes it difficult for your child to breathe.
- The coughing is painful, persistent, and accompanied by whooping, vomiting, or turning blue.
- The cough lasts longer than one week.
- The cough appears suddenly and is associated with fever.
- The coughing begins after your child chokes on food or any other object. (See *Choking*, page 397.)

Your pediatrician will try to determine the cause of your infant's cough. Most often, it will be a symptom of a cold or flu, and he will recommend lots of rest. He also may suggest an over-the-counter or prescription cough medicine if the symptoms are severe enough to warrant it.

When the cough is caused by another medical problem, such as a bacterial infection, it will be necessary to treat that condition before the cough will clear. Occasionally, when the cause of a chronic cough is not clear, further tests such as chest X rays or tuberculosis skin tests may be necessary.

Treatment

The treatment for a cough depends upon its cause. But, whatever the cause, it is always a good idea to give your baby extra fluids. Adding moisture to the air with a humidifier or vaporizer also may make your infant more comfortable, especially at night.

A cold-water humidifier is just as effective as a hot-water vaporizer and is considerably safer if accidentally knocked over. However, be sure to clean the device thoroughly with detergent and water each morning, so it doesn't become a breeding ground for harmful bacteria or fungi.

Consult your pediatrician before giving your child any cough medicine.

Croup

Croup is an infection that causes a swelling of the voice box (larynx) and windpipe (trachea) which narrows the airway just below the vocal cords and makes breathing noisy and difficult.

There are different types of croup:

Viral croup is the most common and is the result of a viral infection in the voice box and windpipe. This condition usually starts with a cold, which gradually develops into croup's barking cough. As your child's airway swells and secretions increase, her breathing will become noisy and labored. She may make a coarse musical sound each time she breathes in, called "stridor." Some children have a fever as high as 104 degrees Fahrenheit (40 degrees Celsius), but most have a lower grade of fever.

Spasmodic croup is often most frightening because it comes on suddenly in the middle of the night. Your child will go to bed with a mild cold and awaken in a few hours gasping for breath. She also will be hoarse and have a distinctive cough (see page 456) that sounds like the bark of a seal. This type of croup is usually caused by a mild upper respiratory infection (see page 482).

As your child tires from the effort of breathing, she may stop eating and drinking. She also may become too fatigued to cough, though the stridor will become more audible with each breath. The danger with croup accompanied by stridor is that the airway will continue to swell, further narrowing your child's windpipe and making it difficult and perhaps impossible to breathe.

Croup can occur at any time of the year, but it is more common between October and March. Some youngsters

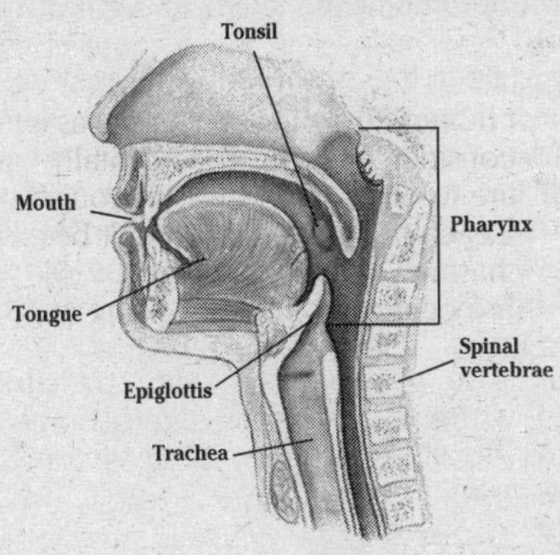

are particularly prone and seem to get croup whenever they have a respiratory illness. Children generally are most susceptible to it between six months and three years. After three, the condition is uncommon because the windpipe is larger, so swelling is less likely to interfere with breathing.

Treatment

If your child awakens in the middle of the night with croup, take her into the bathroom and steam it up by turning on the shower with the hottest available water. Close the door and sit in the steamy bathroom with your child. Inhaling the warm, humidified air should ease her breathing within fifteen to twenty minutes, but she will still have the barking cough.

For the rest of that night and the two or three nights that follow, use a cold-water vaporizer or humidifier in your child's room. Sometimes another episode of croup will occur the same night or the next. If it does, repeat the steam treatment in the bathroom. Steam is almost always effective, but if it doesn't seem to be working, take your child outdoors for a few minutes. Inhaling the cold, moist night air may open up her air passages so she can breathe more freely. If that does not help, call your pediatrician. If your child's breathing becomes a serious struggle or if your child looks blue, call for emergency medical services. (In most areas, dial 911.)

Do *not* try to open the airway with your finger. Breathing is being obstructed by swollen tissue beyond your reach, so you can't clear it away. Besides, putting your finger in your child's throat will make her even more agitated, which will make her breathing even more difficult. For similar reasons, don't make your child vomit. If she does happen to throw up, hold her head down and then quickly sit her back up in the steamy room.

With either type of croup, call your pediatrician right away—even if it's the middle of the night. Also, pay attention to your child's breathing. Call for emergency medical services *immediately* if:

- She makes a whistling sound that gets louder with each breath.
- She can't speak or make verbal sounds for lack of breath.
- She seems to be struggling to get a breath or is turning blue.
- She has a bluish mouth or fingernails.
- She has stridor when resting.
- She drools or has extreme difficulty swallowing saliva.

If your child has viral croup and is not breathing better after the steam treatment, your pediatrician may prescribe steroid medication to reduce swelling. Steroids can be inhaled, taken by mouth, or given by injection. Treatment with a few doses of steroids should do no harm. For spasmodic croup, your pediatrician may recommend a bronchodilator to help your child's breathing.

Antibiotics, which treat bacteria, are not helpful because croup is almost always caused by a virus or allergy. Cough syrups are of little use because they do not affect the larynx or trachea, where the infection is located. They also may interfere with your child's ability to cough up the secretions produced by the infection.

In most serious cases, which are quite rare, your child will not get enough oxygen into her blood. Your doctor may then hospitalize her.

tions, most children today can easily recover from them if they receive proper medical attention.

Most pneumonias follow a viral upper-respiratory-tract infection. Typically, the viruses that cause these infections (respiratory syncytial virus [RSV], influenza, parainfluenza, adenovirus) spread to the chest and produce pneumonia there. Other viruses, such as those related to measles, chickenpox, herpes, infectious mononucleosis, and rubella, may travel from various parts of the body to the lungs, where they also can cause pneumonia.

Pneumonia can also be caused by bacterial infections. Some of these are spread from person to person by coughing or by direct contact with the infected person's saliva or mucus. Also, if a viral infection has weakened a child's immune system, bacteria that ordinarily are harmless may begin to grow in the lung, adding a second infection to the original one.

Babies whose immune defenses or lungs are weakened by other illnesses such as cystic fibrosis or cancer (as well as by the chemotherapy used to treat cancer) are more likely to develop pneumonia, as are infants whose airways or lungs are abnormal in any other way.

Because most forms of pneumonia are linked to viral or bacterial infections that spread from person to person, they're most common during the fall, winter, and early spring, when children spend more time indoors in close contact with others. The likelihood that a baby will develop pneumonia is *not* affected by how she is dressed, by the temperature of the air she is in, or by whether she is exposed to fresh air when ill.

Signs and Symptoms

Like many infections, pneumonia usually produces fever, which in turn may cause sweating, chills, flushed skin, and general discomfort. The baby also may lose her appetite and seem less energetic than normal. She may seem pale and limp, and cry more than usual.

Because pneumonia can cause breathing difficulties, you may notice these other, more specific symptoms, too:

- Cough (see page 456)
- Fast, labored breathing

- Increased activity of the breathing muscles below and between the ribs and above the collarbone
- Flaring (widening) of the nostrils
- Wheezing
- Bluish tint to the lips or nails, caused by decreased oxygen in the bloodstream

Although the diagnosis of pneumonia can usually be made on the basis of the signs and symptoms, a chest X ray is sometimes necessary to make certain and to determine the extent of lung involvement.

Treatment

When pneumonia is caused by a virus, there is no specific treatment other than rest and the usual measures for fever (see Chapter 20). Cough suppressants containing codeine or dextromethorphan should not be used, because coughing is necessary to clear the excessive secretions caused by the infection. Viral pneumonia usually disappears after a few days, though the cough may linger up to several weeks. Ordinarily, no medication is necessary.

Because it is often difficult to tell whether the pneumonia is caused by a virus or by bacteria, your pediatrician may prescribe an antibiotic. All antibiotics should be taken for the full prescribed course and at the specific dosage recommended. You may be tempted to discontinue them early, since your baby will feel better after just a few days, but if you do this, some bacteria may remain and the infection might return.

Your baby should be checked by the pediatrician as soon as you suspect pneumonia. You should check back with the doctor if your baby shows any of the following warning signs that the infection is worsening or spreading:

- Fever lasting more than two or three days despite the use of antibiotics
- Breathing difficulties
- Evidence of infection elsewhere in the body: red, swollen joints, bone pain, neck stiffness, vomiting

Many pediatricians recommend hospitalizing infants under four months old who have pneumonia.

(See also: Chapter 20, "Fever"; *Colds/Upper Respiratory Infection,* page 482.)

WHOOPING COUGH (PERTUSSIS)

Pertussis, or whooping cough, is uncommon now, as the pertussis vaccine has made most children immune. (This is the "P" or "aP" part of the DTP or DTaP vaccine given to all infants beginning at two months of age; the other parts are for the prevention of diphtheria and tetanus.) Before the vaccine was developed, there were several hundred thousand cases of whooping cough each year in the United States. Now there are approximately four thousand.

This illness is called pertussis because it is caused by the pertussis bacterium, which attacks the lining of the breathing passages (bronchi and bronchioles), producing severe inflammation and narrowing of the airways. Severe coughing is a prominent symptom. If not recognized properly, the bacteria may spread to those in close contact with the infected person, through her respiratory secretions.

Infants under one year of age are at greatest risk of developing severe breathing problems and life-threatening illness from whooping cough. Because the baby is short of breath, she inhales deeply and quickly between coughs. These breaths (particularly in older infants) frequently make a "whooping" sound, which is how this illness got its common name. The intense coughing scatters the pertussis bacteria into the air, spreading the disease to other susceptible persons.

Pertussis often acts like a common cold for a week or two. Then the cough gets worse, and the older infant may start to have the characteristic "whoops." During this phase (which can last two weeks or more) the baby often is short of breath and can look bluish around the mouth. She also may tear, drool, and vomit. Infants with pertussis become exhausted, and develop complications such as susceptibility to other infections, pneumonia, and seizures. Pertussis can be fatal in some infants, but the usual course is for recovery to b[illegible] after two to four more weeks. The cough may not di[illegible] for months, and may return with subsequent [illegible] infections.

When to Call the Pediatrician

Pertussis infection starts out acting like a cold. You should consider the possibility of whooping cough if the following conditions are present:

- The very young infant has not been fully immunized and/or has had exposure to someone with a chronic cough or the disease.
- The baby's cough becomes more severe and frequent, or her lips and fingertips become dark or blue.
- She becomes exhausted after coughing episodes, eats poorly, vomits after coughing, and/or looks "sick."

Treatment

If your pediatrician determines that your infant has whooping cough, he may admit her to the hospital. Depending upon the age of the baby and the severity of the illness, treatment will include:

- Antibiotics (If given during the active coughing stage, this will not shorten the length of the illness, but will make the child less contagious.)
- Close observation, sometimes in an intensive-care setting
- Oxygen and intravenous fluids

Prevention

The best way to protect your baby against pertussis is with DTaP (preferred) or DTP immunizations at two months, four months, and six months of age, and booster shots at twelve to eighteen months and before entering school. The recently approved new vaccine, DTaP, known as the "accellular" type, has fewer side effects than DTP, including less fever, irritability, and probably less risk of brain injury. The risk to your baby from pertussis disease is greater than risking serious reactions from either DTaP or DTP.

Therefore, the *American Academy of Pediatrics urges par- to continue immunizing their infants against pertussis but to be aware of the following reactions that can occur, and the conditions under which the vaccine should not be used.*

Severe reactions to the DTP or DTaP vaccine that should alert you and your pediatrician not to give another pertussis immunization:

- Allergic reaction (hives or rash within minutes of the injection, or shock)
- Acute severe central nervous system disorder within seven days of receiving injection, which is otherwise unexplained

In addition, there are certain adverse reactions which occur in relation to DTP or DTaP vaccines which are considered precautions to further administration of these vaccines. Because these events have not been proven to cause permanent injury, the benefits of future vaccinations versus risks need to be carefully weighed by you and your pediatrician. Adverse reactions in this category are:

- Fever of 105 degrees Fahrenheit (40.6 degrees Celsius) or greater
- Prolonged, continuous crying
- An episode of limpness or paleness
- Unusual high-pitched cry
- Convulsions

In addition to the above, there are certain babies who probably should never get the "P" part of the injection in the first place: Any infant with a progressive neurological disorder or a neurologic (nervous system) condition that increases the likelihood of developing a seizure.

Fortunately, the number of babies to whom these rules apply is very small. Do not make the mistake of refusing to immunize your infant if she is normal and healthy. The benefits of the vaccine far outweigh the risks. As DTaP, a less reactive but equally effective vaccine, gradually replaces DTP, the risks of vaccination should decrease even further.

16

DEVELOPMENTAL DISABILITIES

It's natural to compare your baby with others his age. When the neighbor's baby walks at ten months, for example, you may worry if yours does not crawl until twelve months. Usually, however, such differences are not significant. Each baby has his own unique rate of development, so some learn certain skills faster than others.

Only when a baby lags far behind, or fails altogether to reach the developmental milestones outlined in Chapters 5 through 9 of this book, or loses a previously acquired skill, is there reason to suspect a mental or physical problem serious enough to be considered a developmental disability. Disabilities that can be identified during childhood include mental retardation, language and learning disorders, cerebral palsy, autism, and sensory impairments such as vision and hearing loss. (Some pediatricians include seizure disorders in this category, but a large percentage of children who have seizures develop normally.)

Each of these disabilities can vary greatly in severity. For example, one baby with mild cerebral palsy may have no obvious disability other than a slight lack of coordination, while another with a severe form may never be able to walk or feed himself. Also, some babies have more than one disability, each requiring different care.

If your child does not seem to be developing normally, he should have a complete medical and developmental evaluation, perhaps including a consultation with a developmental pediatrician who is a specialist in this field. This will give your pediatrician the information needed to determine whether a true disability exists and, if so, how it should be managed. Depending on the results of the evaluation, the doctor

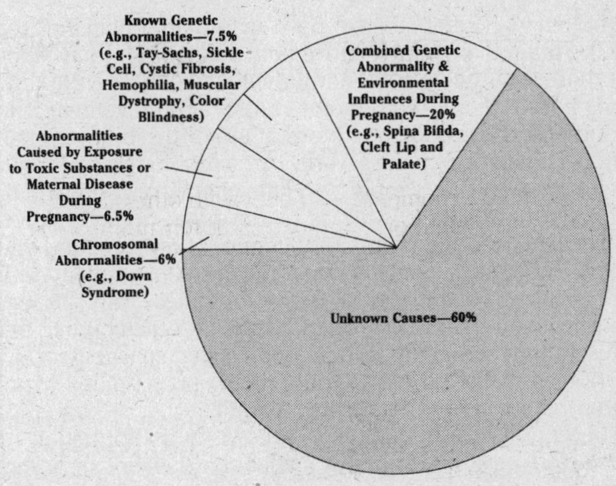

may recommend physical, speech and language, or occupational therapy at various stages of your baby's life. Educational intervention or psychological counseling also might be necessary. A child development center affiliated with a medical school should be able to help you arrange these consultations. In some states and cities these evaluations are offered free of charge, or are partially paid for by local government. Your local board of education can tell you if this is the case in your area.

Today, every child over the age of three years who has a developmental disability is entitled by federal law to special education in a preschool or school program, and most states also offer special programs for infants and toddlers who have developmental delays or disabilities, or who are at risk for these difficulties.

The families of children with disabilities also need special support and education. It's not so easy to accept the fact that a child has a developmental problem. To understand what the child is facing and how he can be helped to realize his full potential, each member of the family should be educated about the specific problem and counseled about how to deal with it.

Cerebral Palsy

Children with cerebral palsy have an impairment in the area of the brain that controls movement and muscle tone. Many of these youngsters have normal intelligence, even though they have difficulty with motor control and movement. The condition causes different types of motor disability in each child. Depending on the severity of the problem, a child with cerebral palsy may simply be a little clumsy or awkward, or he may be unable to walk as he develops. Some children have weakness and poor motor control of one arm and one leg on the same side of the body (this is called hemiparesis). Many have problems in all four extremities, with the legs mostly involved: this is called diplegia. In some children the muscle tone generally is increased (called spasticity or hypertonia), while others are abnormally limp (called hypotonia). Speech may be affected as well.

Cerebral palsy frequently is caused by malformation or damage to the brain during pregnancy, delivery, or immediately after birth. Premature birth is associated with an increased risk of cerebral palsy. A baby can also get cerebral palsy from *very severe* jaundice after birth, or later on in infancy from a brain injury or an illness affecting the brain. In most cases the cause is unknown.

Signs and Symptoms

The signs and symptoms of cerebral palsy vary tremendously because there are many different types and degrees of disability. The main clue that your baby might have cerebral palsy is a delay in achieving the motor milestones listed in Chapters 5 through 9 of this book. Here are some specific warning signs:

In a Baby Over Two Months:

- Head lags when you pick him up while he's lying on his back.
- He feels stiff.
- He feels floppy.
- When held cradled in your arms, he seems to overextend

his back and neck, constantly acts as if he is pushing away from you.

- When you pick him up, his legs get stiff and they cross or "scissor."

In a Baby Over Six Months:

- He continues to have the asymmetrical tonic neck reflex (see page 172).
- He reaches out with only one hand while keeping the other fisted.

In a Baby Over Ten Months:

- He crawls in a lopsided manner, pushing off with one hand and leg while dragging the opposite hand and leg.
- He scoots around on buttocks or hops on knees, but does not crawl on all fours.

If you have any concerns about your baby's development, talk to your pediatrician at your routine visit. Because children's rates of development do vary so widely, it is sometimes difficult to make a definite diagnosis of mild cerebral palsy in the first year or two of life. Often a consultation with a developmental pediatrician or pediatric neurologist will assist in the diagnosis. A CAT/CT or MRI of the head may be recommended to determine whether a brain abnormality exists. Even when a firm diagnosis is made during these early years, it often is difficult to predict how severe the disability will be in the future.

Treatment

If your pediatrician suspects that your baby has cerebral palsy, you will be referred to an early intervention program. These programs are staffed by early childhood educators; physical, occupational, and speech and language therapists; nurses; social workers; and medical consultants. In such a program you'll learn how to become your child's own teacher and therapist. You will be taught what exercises to do with your baby, what positions are most comfortable and beneficial to him, and how to help with specific problems such as feeding difficulties. Through these programs you can also meet other parents of children with similar disabilities, and share experiences, concerns, and solutions.

The most important thing you can do for your child is to help him develop competence and grow up feeling good about himself. When he is old enough to ask or understand, explain to him that he has a disability, and reassure him that he'll be able to make adjustments in order to succeed in life. Encourage him to perform the tasks he is ready for, but do not push him to do things at which you know he will fail. The professionals at early intervention centers can help you evaluate your child's abilities and teach you how to reach appropriate goals.

Do not make the mistake of searching for magical cures or undertaking controversial treatments. They will waste your time, energy, and money. Instead, ask your pediatrician, or contact the United Cerebral Palsy Association, for information about resources and programs available in your area.

Associated Problems

Mental Retardation. It has been estimated that more than one half of children with cerebral palsy have problems with intellectual functioning (thinking, problem solving). Many are classified as mentally retarded, while others have average abilities with some learning disorders. Some have perfectly normal intelligence.

Seizures. One out of every three people with cerebral palsy has or will develop seizures. (Some start having them years after the brain is damaged.) Fortunately, these seizures can usually be controlled with anticonvulsant medications. (See also page 537.)

Vision Difficulties. Because the coordination of the eye muscles is often affected by the brain damage, more than three out of four children with cerebral palsy have strabismus, a problem with one eye turning in or out, with or without nearsightedness. If this problem is not corrected early, the vision in the affected eye will get worse and eventually will be lost permanently. This makes it extremely important to have your baby's eyes checked regularly by your pediatrician. (See also *Strabismus*, page 494.)

Limb Shortening and Scoliosis. Of those babies with cerebral palsy affecting only one side of the body, over half will develop a shortening of the involved leg and arm. The difference between the legs is rarely more than two inches, but an orthopedic surgeon should be consulted if shortening is noticed. Later in childhood, depending on the degree of difference between the legs, a heel or sole lift may be prescribed to fit into the shoe on the shorter side. This is done to prevent a tilt of the pelvis, which can lead to curvature of the spine (scoliosis) when standing or walking.

Hearing Loss. Some children with cerebral palsy have a complete or partial hearing loss. This most often happens when the cerebral palsy is a result of *severe* jaundice at birth. If you find that your baby does not blink to loud noises by one month or is not turning his head toward a sound by three to four months, or is not saying words by twelve months, discuss it with your pediatrician. (See also page 478.)

Joint Problems. In children with spastic forms of cerebral palsy, it is often difficult to prevent "contracture," an extreme stiffening of the joints caused by the unequal pull of one muscle over the other. A physical therapist, developmental pediatrician, or physiatrist (doctor of physical medicine) can teach you how to stretch the muscles to try to prevent the onset of contracture. Sometimes braces, casting, or medication may be used to improve joint mobility and stability.

Congenital Abnormalities

Thanks to improved medical care during pregnancy, and the progress in early detection of chromosomal and other genetic abnormalities through amniocentesis, chorionic villus sampling, or other newer diagnostic tests, there are fewer and fewer newborns with congenital problems. About three of every hundred babies born in the United States have congenital abnormalities that will affect the way they look, develop, or function, in some cases for the rest of their lives.

Congenital abnormalities are caused by problems in the development of the infant before birth. There are five categories, grouped according to the cause of the abnormality:

Chromosome Abnormalities. Chromosomes are the structures that carry the genetic material inherited from one generation to the next. Normally, twenty-three chromosomes come from the father and twenty-three from the mother, and all are found in the center of every cell in the body except the red blood cells. The genes carried on the chromosomes determine how the baby will grow, what she will look like, and to a certain extent how she will function.

When a child does not have the normal forty-six chromosomes, or when pieces of the chromosomes are missing or duplicated, she may look and behave differently from others her age, and she may develop serious health problems as well. *Down syndrome* is an example of a condition that can occur when a baby is born with an extra chromosome.

Single Gene Abnormalities. Sometimes the chromosomes are normal in number but one or more of the genes on them is abnormal. Some of these genetic abnormalities can be passed on to the baby if one of the parents is affected with the same abnormality. This is known as autosomal dominant inheritance.

Other genetic problems can be passed to the infant only if both parents carry the same defective gene. (Cystic fibrosis, Tay-Sachs disease, and sickle-cell anemia are all examples of this type of abnormality.) In these cases both parents are normal but one in four of their children would be expected to be affected. This is known as autosomal recessive inheritance.

A third type of genetic abnormality is called sex-linked, and generally is passed on to boys only. Girls may carry the abnormal gene that causes these disorders, but not show the actual disease herself. (Examples of this problem include hemophilia, color blindness, and the common forms of muscular dystrophy.)

Damaging Conditions During Pregnancy. Certain illnesses during pregnancy, particularly during the first nine weeks, can cause serious congenital abnormalities—German measles and diabetes, for example. Excess alcohol consumption and the use of certain drugs during pregnancy significantly increase the risk that a baby will be born with abnormalities. Certain medications, if taken during pregnancy, also can cause permanent damage to the fetus, as can certain chemicals that can pollute air, water, and food. Before using any medication during pregnancy, women should check with their doctors.

Combination of Genetic and Environmental Problems. Spina bifida and cleft lip and palate are types of congenital abnormalities that may occur when there is a genetic tendency for the condition combined with exposure to certain environmental influences within the womb during critical stages of the pregnancy.

Unknown Causes. The vast majority of congenital abnormalities have no known cause. This is particularly troubling for parents who plan to have more children, because there is no way to predict if the problem will occur again. If you and your family have experienced such a situation, ask your pediatrician for a referral to a genetic counseling service. These individuals or groups have expertise with a variety of genetic abnormalities and may be able to advise you as to the proper course of action.

Learning to Live with the Problem

If your newborn has a congenital abnormality, the first hours and days of her life will be very difficult for you. At the same time that you are learning about your infant as she is, you probably will be mourning the perfect baby you'd imagined she would be. Meanwhile, all your relatives and friends are calling to hear the "good news." One way to relieve the social pressure you're bound to feel is to appoint one family member and one friend to inform other friends and relatives about your newborn's condition.

If you have other children, you'll need to explain the situation to them as soon as possible. It is difficult to predict how siblings will react to such news; but, whether they show it or not, many feel guilty. They may have felt jealous and resentful about the baby during the pregnancy, perhaps even wished secretly that the baby would never come. If so, when they learn that their new brother or sister has a problem, they may feel that their wishes were responsible. Encourage them to ask questions, answer them in terms that they can understand, and be sure to explain that the problem is no one's fault.

Try not to blame yourself for what's happened, either. Except in cases where the congenital abnormality is caused by the mother's use of drugs or alcohol during pregnancy, there is nothing that could have been done to prevent an abnormality of this kind. Don't allow yourself to feel guilty or responsible. Guilt will only get in the way of the love and affection that are especially vital in these special circumstances.

As overwhelmed as you may be by the problems facing your family and your newborn, this child needs to receive all the nurturing and affection you would give any baby. It's easy to forget this during the first days of her life, when you are confronting many difficult decisions and feeling anxious, fearful, and disappointed. Yet this is precisely the time when touching, holding, and comforting are especially critical to the baby and to you.

Coping with the Medical Necessities

Congenital abnormalities are so diverse, and require such different types of treatment, that it would be impossible to discuss them all in this section. Instead, we will look only at the medical management of the two most common problems, Down syndrome and spina bifida.

Down syndrome. Approximately one out of every eight hundred babies is born with Down syndrome. Fortunately, with the use of amniocentesis, Down syndrome can be detected prenatally. This problem, which is caused by the presence of an extra chromosome, results in a number of physical abnormalities, including up-slanted eyes with extra folds of skin at the inner corners, flattening of the bridge of the nose, a relatively large tongue, and a decrease in the muscle and ligament tone of the body.

A major serious effect of Down syndrome is mental retardation. All but a very small number of these children develop more slowly than average, though the extent of the delay can vary widely from one youngster to the next. Some seem to border on normal development, while others are severely retarded. However, even though babies with Down syndrome may be retarded in development as children and young adults, most eventually are able to feed and dress themselves and to be toilet trained. Many, with special education, can learn basic job skills.

Early detection of Down syndrome is very important, since many babies with the disorder have related abnormalities of the heart, intestinal tract, and/or blood which require prompt treatment. Early detection also allows parents to adjust to the situation and gather support and information. Once suspected, the condition is confirmed by a blood test (it takes a few days to produce results). Since newborns with Down syndrome usually have no medical problems that require immediate treatment, most can leave the hospital after the normal newborn stay.

If you have a newborn with Down syndrome, your pediatrician may recommend a special early intervention program for you and your baby. If so, you should begin it as soon as possible. These programs apply specially designed services to help your child make the most of her developmental and physical capabilities.

You will probably hear about other types of "therapy" that are *not* proven or recommended, such as multivitamin ("orthomolecular") treatments and a system known as "patterning," which focuses on the child's behavior. These approaches receive a lot of media attention because they claim to have great success, but no long-term benefits have ever been proven for them, and large doses of some vitamins may be harmful. These programs also may delay effective methods of treatment and be very expensive. If you hear of any treatments that you think may help your baby, always discuss them first with your pediatrician to see if they are valid before spending your money or trying them.

In addition to developmental delay, Down syndrome can result in physical problems as your baby gets older. Her growth should be closely watched, since extremely slow growth in height and/or excessive weight gain may indicate a lack of thyroid hormone, a problem that affects many youngsters with Down syndrome. Even without thyroid problems, chances are that she'll be shorter and weigh less than average for her age. Some children with Down syndrome also have heart problems that may require medication or surgery.

Another problem, which affects fifteen of every hundred children with Down syndrome, is an abnormality in the ligaments of the neck that can cause serious spinal injury if the neck is extended (bent backward) during exercise. When your child is older, consult your pediatrician for advice regarding the need for your child's neck to be x-rayed before she's allowed to participate in vigorous athletic activities (especially tumbling and gymnastics). If X rays show this abnormality, her physical activities should be limited to movements that cannot cause injury.

For all its difficulties, raising a baby with Down syndrome can be deeply rewarding. Children with this condition are usually loving and openly affectionate, and will thrive if nurtured and loved in return. As with all children, each achievement they make can be a triumph shared by everyone in the family.

Spina bifida. Spina bifida occurs when the spinal bones fail to close properly during early formation. Spina bifida occurs less often than Down syndrome, or in about one in one thousand births. It is, however, the most common of the *physically* disabling congenital abnormalities. A parent who has one child with spina bifida has a greater chance (one out of a hundred) of having another. This increased frequency appears to be due to some combined effect of heredity and environment. There are now tests available to screen for spina bifida early in pregnancy.

A newborn with spina bifida appears at first glance to be normal, except for a small sac protruding from the spine. However, the sac contains spinal fluid and damaged nerves that lead to the lower body. Within the first few days, surgery must be performed to remove the sac and close the opening in the spine. Unfortunately, little can be done to repair the damaged nerves.

Most babies with spina bifida develop further problems later on, including:

Hydrocephalus. Approximately seventy of every hundred children with spina bifida eventually develop hydrocephalus, caused by an excessive increase in the fluid that normally cushions the brain from injury. The increase occurs because the spina bifida abnormality blocks the path through which the fluid ordinarily flows. This condition is serious and, if not treated, may lead to death.

The pediatrician should suspect hydrocephalus if the baby's head is growing more rapidly than expected. The condition is confirmed by a computerized X ray of the head, called a CT scan or magnetic resonance imagery (MRI). If hydrocephalus is present, surgery will be necessary to relieve the fluid buildup.

Muscle weakness or paralysis. Because the nerves leading to the lower part of the body are damaged, the muscles in the legs may be very weak or even paralyzed in infants with spina bifida. Their joints also tend to be very stiff, and many babies with this disorder are born with abnormalities of the hips, knees, and feet. Surgery can be performed to correct some of these problems, and the muscle weakness can be treated with physical therapy and special equipment such as braces and walkers. Many children with spina bifida eventually can stand and some do walk, though the learning process is often long and extremely frustrating.

Bowel and bladder problems. Often the nerves that control bowel and bladder function are damaged in infants with spina bifida. As a result, these babies are more likely to develop urinary tract infections and damage to the kidneys due to abnormal urine flow. Special techniques are available to develop urinary control and minimize infections.

Bowel control also is a problem but usually can be accomplished by children with this disorder. It may, however, take a great deal of time, patience, careful dietary management (to keep stool soft), and the occasional use of suppositories or other bowel stimulants.

Infection. Parents of babies who have spina bifida and hydrocephalus or urinary tract problems must be ever alert for signs of infection. Fortunately, the types of infections that occur in these cases usually can be treated effectively with antibiotics.

Educational and social problems. Seven out of ten children with spina bifida have developmental and learning disabilities that will require some sort of special education. Many will also need psychological counseling and tremendous emotional support in order to deal with their medical, educational, and social problems.

Parents of a baby with spina bifida will need more than one physician to manage their child's medical care. In addition to the basic care your pediatrician delivers, this disorder will require a team approach that involves neurosurgeons, orthopedic surgeons, urologists, rehabilitation experts, physical therapists, psychologists, and social workers. Many medical centers run special spina bifida clinics, which offer the services of all these health professionals in one location. Having all members of the team together makes it easier for everyone to communicate, and usually provides better access to information and assistance when parents need it.

Resources

Information and support for parents are available from various organizations:

The National Down Syndrome Congress
1605 Chantilly Drive
Suite 250
Atlanta, GA 30324
(1-800-232-NDSC)

The Spina Bifida Association of America
4590 MacArthur Boulevard, NW
Suite 250
Washington, D.C. 20007–4226

For information about congenital abnormalities, write:

The March of Dimes Resource Center
1275 Mamaroneck Avenue
White Plains, NY 10605

Hearing Loss

Most babies experience mild hearing loss when fluid accumulates in the middle ear in response to allergies or colds. This hearing loss is temporary. In many babies, perhaps one in ten, fluid stays in the middle ear because of *ear infection* (see page 485). They don't hear as well as they should during the infections, and sometimes have delays in talking. Much less common is the permanent kind of hearing loss that always endangers normal speech and language development. This difficulty varies from mild or partial to complete or total.

Although they can occur at any age, the most serious effects come from hearing losses that are present from birth or develop during infancy and the toddler years. Hearing loss during this time demands immediate attention, because it directly affects the child's ability to understand and produce spoken language. Even a temporary severe hearing loss during infancy can make it very difficult for the child to learn proper oral language.

There are two main kinds of hearing loss:

Conductive hearing loss. When a baby has a conductive hearing loss, there may be an abnormality in the structure of the outer ear canal or middle ear, or there may be fluid in the middle ear that interferes with the conduction of sound.

Sensorineural hearing loss (also called nerve deafness). This type of hearing impairment is caused by an abnormality of the inner ear or the nerves that carry sound messages from the inner ear to the brain. The loss can be present at birth or occur shortly thereafter. If there is a family history of deafness, the cause is likely to be inherited (genetic). If the mother had rubella (German measles), cytomegalovirus (CMV), or another infectious illness that affects hearing during pregnancy, the fetus could have been infected and may lose hearing as a result. The problem also may be due to a malformation of the inner ear. The cause of severe sensorineural hearing loss is most often unknown. In such cases the probability that the hearing loss is genetic is high even when no other family members are affected. Future brothers and sisters of the child have a greatly increased risk of also being hearing impaired.

Hearing loss must be diagnosed as soon as possible, so that the child isn't delayed in learning language, a process that begins the day she is born. If you and/or your pediatrician suspect that your baby has a hearing loss, insist that a formal hearing evaluation be performed promptly. Although some family doctors, pediatricians, and well-baby clinics can test for fluid in the middle ear, a common cause of hearing loss, they cannot measure hearing precisely. Your baby should be taken to an audiologist, who can perform this service. She may also be seen by an ear, nose, and throat doctor (an otolaryngologist).

Babies may be given a test called brain-stem evoked-response audiometry. This allows the doctor to test your infant's hearing without having to rely on her cooperation. This test may not be available in your immediate area, but the consequences of undiagnosed hearing loss are so serious that your doctor may advise you to travel to where it can be done.

Treatment

The treatment of a hearing loss will depend on its cause. If it is a mild conductive hearing loss due to fluid in the middle ear, the doctor may simply recommend that your baby be retested in a few weeks to see whether the fluid has cleared by itself. Use of antihistamines or decongestants is an ineffective treatment for fluid in the middle ear. Antibiotics are of limited value, but a trial for one to two weeks is usually worth it. (See *Ear Infection*, page 485.)

If there is no improvement in hearing over a three-month period, and there is still fluid behind the eardrum, the doctor may recommend referral to an ear, nose, and throat (ENT) specialist, and drainage of the fluid through ventilating tubes, which are surgically inserted through the eardrum. This is a minor operation and takes only a few minutes, but the baby must receive a general anesthetic for it to be done properly, so she usually will spend part of the day in a "one-day surgery center" of a hospital. Even with the tubes in place, future infections can occur, but the tubes help reduce the amount of fluid and decrease your baby's risk of repeated infection. They also improve the hearing. Often, the pediatrician will place the baby on a low-dose antibiotic regimen to decrease the possibility of infection.

If a conductive hearing loss is due to a malformation of the outer or middle ear, a hearing aid may restore hearing to normal or near-normal levels. However, a hearing aid will work only when it's being worn. You must make sure it is on and functioning at all times, particularly in the very young child. Reconstructive surgery may be considered when the child is much older.

Parents of babies with sensorineural hearing loss usually are most concerned about whether their child will learn to talk. The answer is that all children with a hearing impairment can be taught to speak, but not all will learn to speak clearly. Some children learn to lip-read well, while others never fully master the skill. But speech is only one form of language. Most learn a combination of spoken and sign language. Written language also is very important because it is the key to educational and vocational success. Learning excellent oral language is highly desirable, but not all people who are born deaf can master this. Sign language is the primary way deaf people communicate with one another, and the way many express themselves best.

When to Call the Pediatrician

Here are the signs and symptoms that should make you suspect that your baby has a hearing loss, and alert you to call your pediatrician:

- Your baby doesn't startle at loud noises by one month or turn to the source of a sound by three to four months of age.
- He doesn't notice you until he sees you.
- He concentrates on gargles and other vibrating noises that he can feel, rather than experimenting with a wide variety of vowel sounds and consonants. (See *Language Development* in Chapters 8 and 9.)
- Speech is delayed or hard to understand, or he doesn't say single words such as *dada* or *mama* by one year of age.
- He seems to hear some sounds but not others. (Some hearing loss affects only high-pitched sounds; some babies have hearing loss in only one ear.)
- He seems not only to hear poorly but also has trouble holding his head steady, or is slow to sit or walk unsupported. (In some babies with sensorineural hearing loss, the part of the inner ear that provides information about balance and movement of the head is also damaged.)

17

Ears, Nose, and Throat

Colds/Upper Respiratory Infection

Your baby probably will have more colds, or upper respiratory infections, than any other illness. If your child is in day care, or if there are older school-age children in your house, she may be particularly susceptible, since colds spread easily among children who are in close contact with one another. That's the bad news, but there is some good news, too: Most colds go away by themselves and do not lead to anything worse.

Colds are caused by viruses, which are extremely small infectious organisms (much smaller than bacteria). A sneeze or a cough may directly transfer a virus from one person to another. The virus may also be spread indirectly, in the following manner:

1. A child or adult infected with the virus will, in coughing, sneezing, or touching her nose, transfer some of the virus particles onto her hand.
2. She then touches the hand of a healthy person.
3. This healthy person touches her newly contaminated hand to her own nose, thus introducing the infectious agent to a place where it can multiply and grow, the nose or throat. This soon gives rise to the symptoms of a cold.
4. The cycle then repeats itself, with the virus being transferred from this newly infected child or adult to the next susceptible one, and so on.

Once the virus is present and multiplying, your baby will develop these familiar symptoms and signs:

- Runny nose (first, a clear discharge; later, a thicker, slightly colored one)
- Sneezing
- Slight fever (101–102 degrees Fahrenheit [38.3–38.9 degrees Celsius]), particularly in the evening
- Decreased appetite
- Sore throat and, perhaps, difficulty swallowing
- Cough
- On-and-off irritability
- Slightly swollen glands

If your baby has a typical cold without complications, the symptoms should gradually disappear after three to four days.

Treatment

A baby older than three months with a cold usually doesn't need to see a doctor unless the condition becomes more serious. If she is three months or younger, however, call the pediatrician at the first sign of illness. With a young baby, symptoms can be misleading, and colds can quickly develop into more serious ailments, such as bronchiolitis (see page 453), croup (see page 458), or pneumonia (see page 460).

For a baby older than three months, call the pediatrician if:

- The noisy breathing of a cold is accompanied by the nostrils' widening with each breath, or difficulty with moving breath in and out.
- The lips or nails turn blue.
- Clear mucus becomes thick, runny, and green.
- She has a cough that just won't go away (for more than one week).
- She has pain in her ear (see *Ear Infection*, page 485).

- Her temperature is over 102 degrees Fahrenheit (39.0 degrees Celsius).
- She is excessively sleepy or cranky.

Your pediatrician may want to see your infant, or he may ask you to watch her closely and report back if she doesn't improve each day and is not completely recovered within one week from the start of her illness.

Unfortunately, there's no cure for the common cold. Antibiotics may be used to combat *bacterial* infections, but they have no effect on viruses, so the best you can do is to make your baby comfortable. Make sure she gets extra rest and drinks extra or increased amounts of fluids. If she has a fever, give her acetaminophen or ibuprofen. Ibuprofen is approved for use in children six months of age and older; however, it should never be given to babies who are dehydrated or who are vomiting continuously. (Be sure to follow the recommended dosage for your infant's age.) Never give her any other kind of cold remedy without first checking with your pediatrician. Over-the-counter treatments often dry the respiratory passages or make the nasal secretions even thicker. In addition, they tend to cause side effects such as drowsiness.

If your infant is having trouble nursing because of nasal congestion, clear her nose with a rubber suction bulb before each feeding. When doing so, remember to *squeeze the bulb part of the syringe first, gently stick the rubber tip into one nostril, then slowly release the bulb.* This slight amount of suction will draw the clogged mucus out of the nose, and should allow her once again to breathe and suck at the same time. You'll find that this technique works best when your baby is under six months of age. As she gets older, she'll fight the bulb, making it difficult to suction the mucus.

If the secretions in your baby's nose are particularly thick, your pediatrician may recommend that you liquefy them with saline nose drops, which are available without a prescription. Using a dropper that has been cleaned with soap and water and well rinsed with plain water, place two drops in each nostril fifteen to twenty minutes before feeding, and then immediately suction with the bulb. *Never use nose drops that contain any medication, since it can be absorbed in excessive amounts. Use only normal saline nose drops.*

Placing a cool-mist humidifier (vaporizer) in your baby's

room will also help keep nasal secretions more liquid and make her more comfortable. Set it close to her so that she gets the full benefit of the additional moisture. Be sure to clean and dry the humidifier thoroughly each day to prevent bacterial or mold contamination. *Hot-water vaporizers are not recommended since they can cause serious scalds or burns.*

One final note about medications: *Cough medicines or cough/cold preparations should never be given to a baby (or any child under three years of age) unless prescribed by your pediatrician.* Coughing is a protective mechanism that clears mucus from the lower part of the respiratory tract, and ordinarily there's no reason to suppress it.

Prevention

If your baby is under three months old, the best prevention against colds is to keep her away from people who have them. This is especially true during the winter, when many of the viruses that cause colds are circulating in larger numbers. A virus that causes a mild illness in an older child or an adult can cause a more serious one in an infant.

Ear Infection

Early in your baby's life, there's a significant chance that he'll get an ear infection when he has a cold. This happens because fluid often accumulates in the middle ear during colds and upper respiratory infections. If this fluid becomes infected by bacteria, it causes pain in the ear and inflammation of the eardrum. Doctors refer to this middle-ear infection as "acute otitis media."

Ear infections are a particularly common problem among babies, because they are susceptible to viral upper respiratory infections, and because their tiny eustachian tubes, which normally drain fluid from the middle ear, don't function properly during an infection.

Children under one year of age who spend time in group day-care settings get more ear infections than those cared for at home, primarily because they are exposed to more viruses. Also, infants who self-feed when lying on their backs are susceptible to ear infections, since this may allow small amounts of formula to enter the eustachian tube, causing

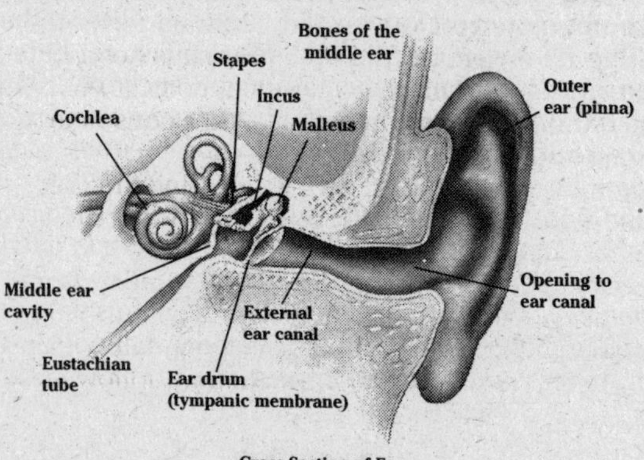

Cross Section of Ear

blockage. Babies in certain ethnic groups, notably Native Americans and Eskimos, seem to have more ear infections, too. This may be due to the shape of the eustachian tube in these groups.

Signs and Symptoms

Ear infections are usually, but not always, painful. While a baby can't tell you that his ear hurts, he may pull at his ear and cry. Babies with ear infections may cry even more during feedings, because sucking and swallowing cause painful pressure changes in the middle ear. Lying down leads to changes in ear pressure, so a baby with an ear infection may have trouble sleeping. Fever is another warning signal; ear infections often are accompanied by elevated temperatures ranging from 100 to 104 degrees Fahrenheit (38 to 40 degrees Celsius).

You might see blood-tinged yellow fluid or pus draining from the infected ear. This kind of discharge means that the eardrum has developed a small hole (called a perforation). This hole usually heals by itself without complications, but you will want to describe the discharge to your pediatrician.

You may also notice that your baby's hearing ability has decreased. This occurs because the fluid behind the eardrum interferes with sound transmission. But the hearing loss is almost always temporary; normal hearing will be restored once the middle ear is free of fluid. Occasionally, when ear infections recur, fluid may remain behind the eardrum for several weeks and continue to interfere with hearing. If you feel your infant's hearing is not as good as it was before his ear became infected, consult your pediatrician. If you remain concerned, request a consultation with a hearing specialist.

Ear infections are most common during the cold and flu "season" of winter and early spring.

Treatment

Whenever you suspect an ear infection, call your pediatrician as soon as possible. In the meantime, follow these steps to make your child more comfortable:

- If he has a fever, cool him using the procedures described in Chapter 20, on fever.
- Give liquid acetaminophen in the dose appropriate for his age.
- Do not use eardrops unless your pediatrician authorizes them after seeing your baby.

The pediatrician will look into your baby's ears with a lighted instrument called an otoscope. To determine whether there is fluid in the middle-ear space behind the eardrum, the doctor may attach a piece of rubber tubing to the otoscope and blow gently into the ear to check for sensitivity and eardrum movement. There is a test that can objectively measure whether there is fluid in the middle ear. This test uses an instrument that produces a printed report called a tympanogram. If a fever is present, the doctor will perform an overall examination to determine whether your baby has any other problem in addition to an ear infection.

To treat infections of the middle ear, the doctor will prescribe an antibiotic. These are available as flavored liquids. Eardrops are sometimes used to relieve pain but should be used only on your pediatrician's advice. Unless your baby's ear infections are associated with allergies, antihistamines and decongestants probably won't help.

An antibiotic is the primary treatment for an ear infection. Your doctor will specify the schedule for giving it to your infant; it may be two, three, or four times a day. Follow the schedule precisely. There should be clear signs of improvement and disappearance of ear pain and fever within three days.

When your baby starts feeling better, you may be tempted to discontinue the medication, but don't! Some of the bacteria that caused the infection may still be present. Stopping the treatment too soon may allow them to multiply again and permit the infection to return with full force. The only way to protect your infant against a second infection is to give him the antibiotic for the full period recommended by your pediatrician (usually ten days).

Your pediatrician will want to see your baby after the medication is gone, to check if any fluid is still present behind the eardrum. This can occur even if the infection has been controlled. This condition, known as "otitis media with effusion," is extremely common: Five out of every ten children still have some fluid three weeks after an ear infection is treated. In nine out of ten cases the fluid will disappear within three months without additional treatment.

On occasion an ear infection won't respond to the first antibiotic prescribed, so if your infant's fever persists or he shows signs of ear pain for more than three days, call the pediatrician. To determine if the antibiotic is working, your doctor, or a consulting ear, nose, and throat (ENT) specialist, may take a sample of the fluid from the ear. This is done by inserting a needle through the eardrum. If the analysis of this sample reveals that the infection is caused by bacteria resistant to the antibiotic your infant has been taking, your pediatrician will prescribe a different one. In very rare instances, an ear infection may linger even though other drugs are used. In these cases, a baby may be hospitalized so that antibiotics can be given intravenously, and the ear can be drained surgically.

Should a baby with an ear infection be kept home? It won't be necessary if he's feeling well, as long as someone at day care can administer his medication properly. Talk with your baby's caregiver, and review the dosage and the times when it should be given. You also should check to be sure that storage facilities are available if the medication must be refrigerated. Medicine that doesn't require refrigeration should be kept in a locked cabinet separate from other items, and its container should be clearly identified with your baby's name and the proper dosage.

If your baby's eardrum is perforated, he'll be able to engage in most activities, although he may not be permitted in a swimming pool. Ordinarily, there's no reason to prevent him from flying in an airplane.

Prevention

Occasional ear infections cannot be prevented. In some babies, ear infections may be related to seasonal allergies, which also can cause congestion and block the natural drainage of fluid from the ear to the throat. If your baby seems to get ear infections more frequently when his allergies flare up, mention this to your pediatrician, who may suggest additional testing. And what about babies who recover from one ear infection only to get another shortly thereafter? If your baby has had several ear infections during the season, your pediatrician may suggest preventive antibiotics to reduce the chances of still another infection. These drugs usually are prescribed at a low dosage which is taken once or twice a day. Although ear infections may recur while this medicine is being taken, they usually happen much less often.

Repeated ear infections can be very trying for you and your baby. However, rest assured that it is only a temporary problem that *will* improve as he gets older.

Sore Throat

The terms *sore throat,* and *tonsillitis* are often used interchangeably, but they don't necessarily mean the same thing. Tonsillitis refers to tonsils that are inflamed. When your baby has a sore throat, the tonsils may be inflamed, or the inflammation may affect the surrounding part of the throat but *not* the tonsils.

In infants, the most frequent cause of sore throats is a viral infection. No specific treatment is required when a virus is responsible, and the baby should get better over a three- to five-day period. Often, infants who have sore throats due to viruses also have a cold at the same time. They may develop a mild fever, too, but they generally aren't very sick.

One particular virus (called Coxsackie), seen most often during the summer and fall, may cause the baby to have a somewhat higher fever, more difficulty swallowing, and a sicker overall feeling. If your infant has a Coxsackie infection, she also may have one or more blisters in her throat, which your pediatrician will look for during the examination.

Treatment

Any time your baby has a sore throat that persists, whether or not it is accompanied by fever, stomachache, or extreme fatigue, you should call your pediatrician. That call should be made even more urgently if your baby seems extremely ill, or if she has difficulty breathing or extreme trouble swallowing (causing her to drool). This may indicate a more serious infection.

Prevention

Most types of throat infections are contagious, being passed primarily through the air on droplets of moisture, so it makes sense to keep your baby away from people who have symptoms of this condition. However, most people are "contagious" before their first symptoms appear, so often there's really no practical way to prevent your baby from contracting the disease.

In the past when a baby had frequent sore throats, her tonsils might have been removed in an attempt to prevent further infections. But this operation, called a tonsillectomy, is much less often recommended today. Even in difficult cases, treatment with antibiotics is usually the best solution.

18

EYES

Your baby relies on the visual information he gathers to help him develop throughout infancy. If he has difficulty seeing properly, he may have problems in learning and relating to the world around him. For this reason it is important to detect eye deficiencies as early as possible. Many vision problems can be corrected if treated early but become much more difficult to care for later on.

Your infant should have his first eye examination by a pediatrician at birth to check for problems that may be present then. Routine vision checks should then be part of every visit to the pediatrician's office. If your family has a history of serious eye diseases or abnormalities, your pediatrician may refer your baby to an ophthalmologist (an eye specialist with a medical degree) for an early examination and follow-up visits if necessary.

If an infant is born prematurely, he will be checked for a vision-threatening condition called "retinopathy of prematurity." This is especially true if the baby required oxygen over a prolonged period of time during the early days of life. The risk is greater in the more premature, lower-birthweight infant. While this condition cannot be prevented, in most cases—if detected early—it can be treated successfully. All neonatologists are aware of the threat of retinopathy and will advise parents of the necessity for ophthalmological evaluations. Parents should also be advised that all premature babies are at greater risk for developing astigmatism, myopia, and strabismus and that they therefore should be screened periodically throughout childhood.

How much does a newborn baby see? Until fairly recently it was thought that the newborn infant could

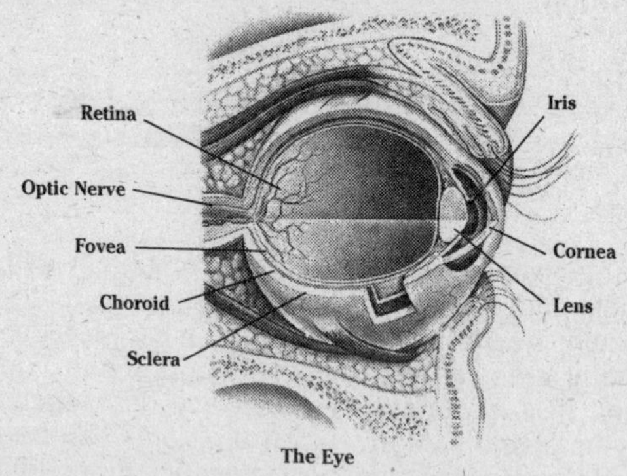

The Eye

see very little; however, the information now available indicates that even during the early weeks of life, an infant can see light and shapes and can detect movement. Far vision remains quite blurry, with the optimal focal length being 8 to 15 inches, roughly the distance from his eyes to yours as you are nursing or feeding your baby.

Until your baby learns to use both eyes together, his eyes may "wander," or move randomly. This random movement should be decreasing by two to three months of age. Around three months of age, your baby will probably focus on faces and close objects and follow a moving object with his eyes. By four months of age, your baby should be using his vision to detect various objects close to him, which he will probably reach for and grasp. By six months of age the baby should be able to visually identify and distinguish between objects.

Between one and two years of age, your child's ability to see develops rapidly, so that the average two-year-old can see at approximately the 20/60 level. Between the ages of two and five years, the child's vision gradually reaches an acuity level of 20/25, and by ages seven to nine, the child with normal vision will reach the adult visual acuity level of 20/20.

If regular eye checks during pediatric visits indicate that your baby's eyes are developing normally, he should not need more formal testing until three to four years of age. By that age, most children can follow directions and describe what they see, so testing is much more reliable.

Vision Screening Recommendations

Vision screening is a very important factor in identifying vision-threatening conditions. The American Academy of Pediatrics recommends that babies be screened in stages:

1. **In the newborn nursery:** Pediatricians should examine all infants prior to their discharge from the nursery to check for infections and structural defects, cataracts, or glaucoma. All children with multiple medical problems or with a history of prematurity and/or oxygen exposure should be examined by an ophthalmologist.
2. **By the age of six months:** Pediatricians should screen infants at the time of their well-baby visits to check for alignment (eyes working together).

Further screenings should occur at ages three to four and at five years and older.

When to Call the Pediatrician

Routine eye checks can detect hidden eye problems, but occasionally you may notice obvious signs that your baby is having trouble seeing or that his eyes are not normal. Notify the pediatrician if your child shows any of the following warning signs:

- Persistent (lasting more than twenty-four hours) redness, swelling, crusting, or discharge in his eyes or eyelids
- Excessive tearing
- Sensitivity to light
- Eyes that look crooked or crossed, or that don't move together
- Head held in an abnormal or tilted position
- Frequent squinting
- Drooping eyelids
- Pupils of unequal size
- Continuous eye-rubbing

- Eyes that "bounce" or "dance"
- Inability to see objects unless he holds them close
- Eye injury
- Cloudy cornea

Depending on the symptoms your baby displays, the pediatrician will probably check for vision difficulties and/or some of the other problems discussed in the remainder of this chapter.

Vision Difficulties Requiring Corrective Lenses

Nearsightedness. The inability to see distant objects clearly is the most common visual problem in young children. This inherited trait occasionally is found in newborns, especially premature infants, but it's more often detected after two years of age.

Nearsightedness is usually the result of an eyeball that's longer than average. Less frequently, it's due to a change in the shape of the cornea or lens.

The treatment for nearsightedness is corrective lenses. Keep in mind that when your child grows rapidly, so does his eye, so he may need new lenses as often as every six months.

Farsightedness. This is a condition in which the eyeball is shorter than average, making it difficult for the lens to focus on nearby objects. Most babies are actually born farsighted, but as they grow, their eyeballs get longer and the farsightedness diminishes. Glasses are rarely needed unless the condition is excessive.

Astigmatism. Astigmatism is an uneven curvature of the surface of the cornea and/or lens. If your baby has an astigmatism, vision—both near and far—may be blurred. Astigmatism can be corrected with glasses.

Strabismus

Strabismus is a misalignment of the eyes caused by an imbalance in the muscles controlling the eye.

A newborn baby's eyes commonly and normally wander.

However, within a few weeks he learns to move his eyes together, and the wandering should disappear within a few months. If this intermittent wandering continues, or if your baby's eyes don't turn in the same direction (if one turns in, out, up, or down), the muscles controlling the eye movement on one side may be weaker than on the other. This condition, called *strabismus,* makes it impossible for the eyes to focus on the same point at the same time.

If your baby is born with strabismus, it's important for his eyes to be realigned early in life so he can focus them together on a single object. Eye exercises alone cannot accomplish this, so the treatment usually involves eyeglasses, eye drops, or surgery.

If your baby needs an operation, it is frequently done between six and eighteen months of age. The surgery is usually safe and effective, although it's common for a child to need more than one procedure. Even after surgery, your youngster still may need glasses.

Some babies look as though they have strabismus because of the way their faces are structured, but in fact their eyes are perfectly aligned. These babies may have a flat nasal bridge and broad skin folds alongside the nose, termed *epicanthus,* which can distort the appearance of the eyes. This is called *pseudostrabismus* (meaning "false eye-turn"). The baby's vision is not affected, and in most cases, as the child grows and the nasal bridge becomes more prominent, he loses the pseudostrabismic appearance.

Because of the importance of early diagnosis and treatment of the true eye-turn (or true strabismus), if you have

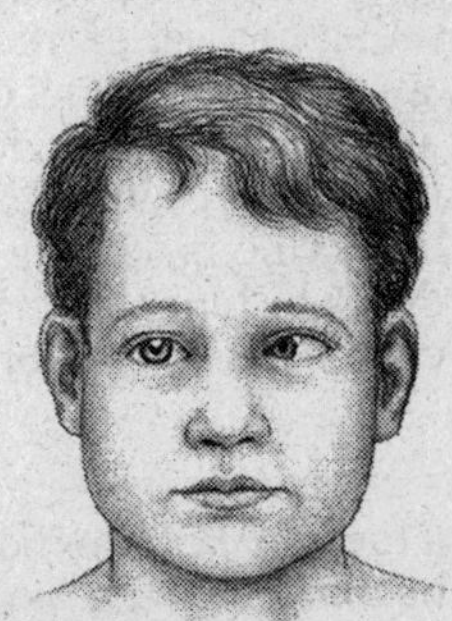

Left eye turning inward

any suspicion that your baby's eyes may not be perfectly aligned and working together, it should be brought to the attention of your pediatrician, who can best determine whether your baby has an actual problem.

Strabismus may be present at birth (congenital strabismus) or it may develop later in childhood (acquired strabismus). Strabismus may develop if your baby has another visual impairment, sustains an eye injury, or develops cataracts. The sudden onset of strabismus should always be reported to your pediatrician immediately. Although very rare, it may indicate the development of a tumor or other serious nervous system problem. In all cases, it is important to diagnose and treat strabismus as early in your infant's life as possible. If an eye-turn is not treated early, the baby may never develop the ability to use both eyes together (binocular vision); and if both eyes are not used together, it is common for one to become "lazy," or amblyopic.

AMBLYOPIA

Amblyopia is a fairly common eye problem that develops when a child has one eye that doesn't see well or is injured, and begins to use the other eye almost exclusively. The idle eye then relaxes and becomes even weaker. In general, the problem must be detected by the age of three years in order to treat and successfully restore normal vision in the affected eye by age six. If this situation persists for too long (past the age of five or six years), vision may be lost permanently in the unused eye.

Once an ophthalmologist corrects the problems in the unused eye, your baby may need to wear a patch over the "good" eye for periods of time. This forces her to use—and strengthen—the eye that has become "lazy." Patching therapy will be continued for as long as necessary to bring the weaker eye up to its potential. This could take weeks, months, or even up to age nine years or older. As an alternative to the patch, the ophthalmologist might prescribe eyedrops to blur vision in the good eye, thereby forcing your child to use the amblyopic eye.

EYE INFECTIONS

If the white of your baby's eye and the inside of his lower lid become red, he probably has a condition called conjunctivitis. Also known as "pinkeye" or "red eye," this inflammation usually signals an infection, but may be due to other causes such as an irritation, an allergic reaction, or (rarely) a more serious illness. It's often accompanied by tearing and discharge, which is the body's way of trying to heal or remedy the situation.

If your baby has a red eye, he needs to see the pediatrician as soon as possible. The doctor will make the diagnosis and prescribe the necessary medication, and also will show you how to cleanse the eyelids. *Never put previously opened medication or someone else's eye medication into your baby's eye. It could cause serious damage.*

In the newborn baby serious eye infections may result from exposure to bacteria during passage through the birth canal—which is why all infants are treated with antibiotic eye ointment or drops in the delivery room. Such infections must be treated early to prevent serious complications. Eye infections that occur after the newborn period may be unsightly, because of the redness of the eye and the yellow discharge that usually accompanies them, and they may make your baby uncomfortable, but they are rarely serious. Several different viruses, or occasionally bacteria, may cause them, and topical antibiotics (eye drops prescribed by your pediatrician) are the usual treatment.

Eye infections typically last up to one week and may be contagious. Except to administer drops or ointment, you should avoid direct contact with your baby's eyes or drainage from them until the medication has been used for several days and there is evidence of clearing of the redness. Carefully wash your hands before and after touching the area around the infected eye. If your baby is in a child-care program, you should keep him home until the eyes are no longer red.

EYELID PROBLEMS

Droopy eyelid (ptosis) may appear as an enlarged or heavy upper lid; or, if it is very slight, it may be noticed only because the affected eye appears somewhat smaller than the other eye. Ptosis usually involves only one eyelid, but both may be affected. Your baby may be born with a ptosis, or it may develop later. The ptosis may be partial, causing your baby's eyes to appear slightly asymmetrical; or it may be total, causing the affected lid to completely cover the eye. If the ptotic eyelid covers the entire pupillary opening of your infant's eye, or if the weight of the lid causes the cornea to assume an irregular shape (astigmatism), it will threaten normal vision development and must be corrected as early as possible. If vision is not threatened, surgical intervention, if necessary, is usually delayed until the child is four or five years of age, when the eyelid and surrounding tissue are more fully developed and a better cosmetic result can be obtained.

Most **birthmarks** and growths involving the eyelids of the newborn are benign; however, because they may increase in size during the first year of life, they sometimes cause parents to become concerned. Most of these birthmarks and growths are not serious and will not affect your baby's vision. Many decrease in size after the first year of life and eventually disappear entirely without treatment. However, any irregularity should be brought to the attention of your pediatrician so that it can be evaluated and monitored.

Some babies are born with or develop **tumors** that can impair eyesight. In particular, a flat, purple-colored skin tumor (hemangioma), if it involves the infant's upper eyelid, may put the baby at risk for glaucoma (a condition where pressure increases inside the eyeball). Any infant having such a mark should be examined periodically by an ophthalmologist.

Small dark moles, called **nevi,** on the eyelids or on the white part of the eye itself rarely cause any problems or need to be removed. Once evaluated by your pediatrician, these marks should only cause concern if they change in size, shape, or color.

Small, firm, flesh-colored bulges on your baby's eyelids or underneath the eyebrows are usually **dermoid cysts.** These are noncancerous tumors which are usually present from birth. Dermoids will not become cancerous if not removed; however, because they tend to increase in size during puberty, their removal during preschool years is preferred in most cases.

Two other eyelid problems—**chalazions** and **styes**—are common, but not serious. A chalazion is a cyst resulting from an infection of an oil gland, usually in the middle of the underside of the lid. This can lead to infection and swelling of the lid. A stye is a bacterial infection of the cells surrounding the sweat glands or hair follicles on the *edge* of the lid. Call your pediatrician regarding treatment of these conditions. He will probably tell you to apply warm compresses directly to the eyelid for twenty or thirty minutes three or four times a day until the signs of infection are gone. The doctor may want to examine your baby before prescribing additional treatment, such as an antibiotic ointment or drops.

Once your baby has had a stye or chalazion, she's more likely to get them again. When chalazions occur repeatedly, it's sometimes necessary to perform lid scrubs to reduce the bacterial colonization of the eyelids and open the oil gland pores.

Impetigo is a very contagious bacterial infection that may occur on the eyelid. Your pediatrician may advise you on how to remove the crust from the lid, and then prescribe an eye ointment and oral antibiotics.

TEAR PRODUCTION (OR LACRIMAL) PROBLEMS

Tears play an important role in maintaining good eyesight by keeping the eyes wet and free of particles, dust, and other substances that might cause injury or interfere with normal vision. The so-called lacrimal system maintains the continuous production and circulation of tears, and depends on regular blinking to propel tears across the surface of the eye, finally draining into the nose.

This lacrimal system develops gradually over the first three or four years of life. Thus, while a newborn will produce enough tears to coat the surface of the eyes, it probably will be about seven to eight months after birth before he "cries real tears."

Blocked tear ducts, which are very common among newborns and young babies, can cause the appearance of excessive tearing in one or both eyes, because the tears run down the cheek instead of draining through the duct and into the nose and throat. In newborns, blocked tear ducts usually occur when the membrane covering them at birth fails to disappear. Your pediatrician will demonstrate how to massage the tear duct. She also may recommend the use of barely warm compresses and, if there is infection, antibiotic drops or ointment. She'll also show you how to clean the eye with moist compresses to remove all secretions. Until the tear duct finally opens, the eye infection may not go away

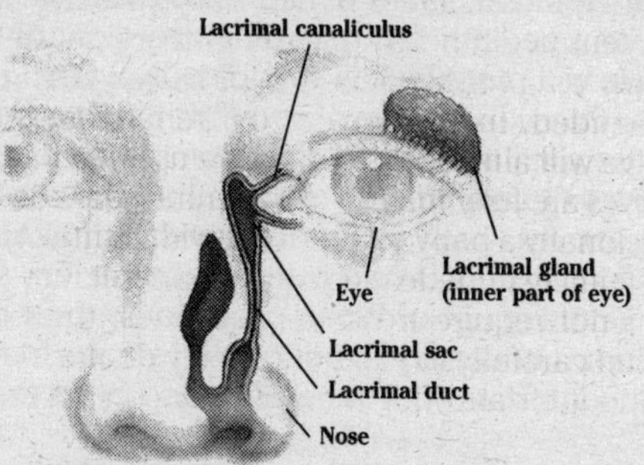

and, in fact, may move even deeper into the tear production mechanism. This condition must be watched carefully to prevent this more serious infection.

Sometimes a membrane or small cyst can cause blocked or inflamed tear ducts. When this occurs and the methods described above are unsuccessful, the ophthalmologist may decide to open the blocked sac and duct surgically. Unfortunately, sometimes this procedure must be repeated more than once.

In rare cases a baby's eyes will not tear at all. When this happens, the surface of the eyes will become inflamed, and a sticky discharge will be present. If this doesn't clear by itself, the baby will need eye drops to keep the eyes wet and prevent any damage.

Cataracts

Although we usually think of cataracts as affecting elderly people, they also may be found in infants and young children. A cataract is a clouding of the lens (the transparent tissue inside the eye that helps bring light rays to focus on the retina). While rare, congenital cataracts are nonetheless a leading cause of visual loss and blindness in children.

A cataract usually shows up as a white reflection in the center of the child's pupil. If a baby is born with a cataract that blocks most of the light entering the eye, the affected lens has to be removed surgically to permit the baby's vision to develop. Most pediatric ophthalmologists recommend that this procedure be performed during the first month of life. After the clouded lens is removed, the baby must be fitted with a contact lens or with an eyeglass correction. At the age of about two years, the placement of lenses within the eye is recommended. In addition, visual rehabilitation of the affected eye will almost always involve use of a patch until the child's eyes are fully mature (at age nine years or older).

Occasionally a baby will be born with a small cataract that will not initially impede visual development. These cataracts often do not require treatment; however, they need to be monitored carefully to ensure that they do not become large enough to interfere with normal vision. In addition, even if they are too small to pose a direct threat to visual development, cataracts may cause secondary amblyopia (loss of vision), which will need to be treated by your ophthalmologist.

In most cases the cause of cataracts in infants cannot be determined. Cataracts may be attributed to a tendency inherited from parents; they may result from trauma to the eye; or they may occur as a result of viral infections such as German measles and chicken pox or infection from other microorganisms such as toxoplasmosis. To protect the unborn child from cataracts as well as from other serious disorders, pregnant women should take care to avoid unnecessary exposure to infectious diseases. In addition, as a precaution against toxoplasmosis, pregnant women should avoid handling cat litter or eating raw meat, both of which may contain the organism that causes this disease.

EYE INJURIES

When dust or other small particles get in your baby's eyes, the cleansing action of tears will usually wash them out. If that fails to occur, or if a serious accident affecting the eye takes place, call your pediatrician or take your baby to the nearest emergency room after heeding the following emergency guidelines:

Chemicals in the Eye. Flush the eye with water for fifteen minutes, making sure you get the water into the eye itself. Then take the baby to the emergency room.

Large Particle in the Eye. If the particle won't come out with tears or by flushing with water, call your pediatrician.

The doctor will remove the object or, if necessary, refer you to an ophthalmologist. Sometimes such particles cause scratches on the cornea (corneal abrasions). These are quite painful but heal rapidly with eye ointment and patching. Corneal injuries also can be caused by blows or other injuries to the eye.

Cut Eyelid. Minor cuts usually heal quickly and easily, but a deep cut requires emergency medical attention, and probably will need stitches. (See *Cuts and Scrapes*, p. 401.) Even if the cut is minor, check to make sure it isn't on the border of the eyelid or near the tear duct. If it is, call your pediatrician right away for advice on how to handle the situation.

Black Eye. To reduce swelling, apply a cool pack or towel to the area for ten to twenty minutes. Then consult the doctor to make sure there is no internal damage.

19

FAMILY ISSUES

ADOPTION

If you are about to adopt or have just adopted a baby, you are likely to be experiencing conflicting emotions: Along with the excitement and delight, you understandably will feel some anxiety and apprehension. It's no different with couples who bear a child themselves, except that nature gives them nine months of preparation.

Having an understanding and supportive pediatrician will be very helpful as you begin your new job as a parent. Even before the baby actually comes to your home, the doctor can help you understand your feelings. If you are adopting a baby from overseas, the pediatrician will be able to alert you to special medical issues that may arise.

Once your baby is home with you, a visit to the pediatrician should be scheduled as soon as possible to make sure there are no existing medical problems. Future examinations should be scheduled as required by the child's age and medical needs.

Adoptive parents must face several issues and questions that natural parents do not encounter. Although most of these matters do not need to be dealt with until the baby is older, you and your spouse should begin to discuss them now, preparing yourself for the issues that are likely to arise in the future. They include the following:

- ***How and when should I tell my baby she is adopted?***

Your child should learn the truth as early as she is able to understand, which probably will be between ages two and four. It's important to adjust the information to her maturity level, so that she can make sense of it. For example, "Your parents loved you very much, but they knew they could not take care of you. So they looked for someone who also loved little children, but could not have them on their own." As she gets older and asks more specific questions, give her honest answers, but do not press information on her if she seems uncomfortable or fearful about it.

■ ***Are there special problems to watch for?***

Adopted children have no more problems than, or different problems from, any other child of the same age and background.

■ ***Should I tell others that my baby is adopted?***

If you are asked, answer the question honestly and straightforwardly. When your child is older, however, do not belabor the point or go into extensive detail if she is nearby, as that may make her uncomfortable.

Child Abuse and Neglect

The news is so full of reports about child mistreatment that you can't help but wonder how safe your baby really is. While it's a mistake to become overprotective, it is important to recognize the actual risks and familiarize yourself with the signs of abuse. More than 2.5 million cases of child abuse and neglect are reported each year, involving physical abuse, sexual abuse, and neglect.

Sexual abuse includes inappropriate touching of a baby's breasts or genitalia. Physical abuse involves injuring an infant's body by burning, beating, or breaking bones. A bruise indicates that body tissue has been damaged and blood vessels have broken.

Child neglect can include physical neglect (withholding food, clothing, shelter, or other physical necessities), emotional neglect (withholding love, comfort, or affection), or medical neglect (withholding needed medical care).

Most child abuse occurs within the family, often by parents or relatives who themselves were abused as children. Neglect and mistreatment of babies are also more common in families living in poverty, and among parents who are teenagers or are drug or alcohol abusers. While there has been a recent increase in child abuse outside the home, it is still true that children are most often abused by a caregiver or someone they know, not a stranger.

Shaken Baby Syndrome

In recent years, pediatricians have used the term "shaken baby syndrome" to describe the serious injuries that can occur when a baby is severely or violently shaken. Babies have very weak neck muscles and do not yet have full support of their heavy heads. When they are shaken, their fragile brains move back and forth within their skulls. This can be fatal or cause serious injuries such as:

- blindness or eye damage
- delay in normal development
- seizures
- damage to the spinal cord (paralysis)
- brain damage

Shaken baby syndrome usually occurs when a parent or other caregiver shakes a baby because of anger or frustration, often because the baby would not stop crying. Although shaken baby syndrome is a serious form of child abuse, many parents are unaware of the injuries that shaking can cause. Remember, it is never okay to shake a baby.

If you or someone else shakes your baby, the most important step is to get medical care right away. Immediately take your baby to the pediatrician or emergency room. Don't let embarrassment, guilt, or fear get in the way of your baby's health or life.

If your baby's brain is damaged or bleeding inside from severe shaking, it will only get worse without treatment. Getting medical care right away may save your infant's life, and prevent serious health problems from developing.

Be sure to tell your pediatrician or other doctor if you know or suspect that your baby was shaken or abused in another way. A doctor who is not aware that an infant has been shaken may assume that the baby is vomiting or having trouble breathing because of an illness. Mild symptoms of shaken baby syndrome are very much like those of infant colic, feeding problems, and fussiness. Your pediatrician should have complete information so that she can treat your infant properly.

Signs and Symptoms

It's not always easy to recognize when a child has been abused. Parents also tend to overlook symptoms because they don't want to face the truth. This is a serious mistake. A child who has been abused needs treatment as early as possible. The longer he continues to be abused, the less likely he is to make a full recovery.

The best way to check for signs of abuse is to be alert to any unexplainable changes in your child's body. Be alert for any injury (bruise, burn, fracture, abdominal or head injury) that cannot be explained.

Getting Help

If you suspect your child has been abused, get help immediately through your pediatrician or a local child protective agency.

Physicians are legally obligated to report all suspected cases of abuse or neglect to state authorities. Your pediatrician also will detect and treat any medical injuries or ailments, recommend a therapist, and provide necessary information to investigators. The doctor may also testify in court if necessary to obtain legal protection for the baby or criminal prosecution of a sexual abuse suspect.

If your baby has been abused, you may be the only person who can help him. There is *no* good reason to delay reporting your suspicions of abuse. Denying the problem will only make the situation worse, allowing the abuse to continue unchecked and decreasing your child's chance for a full recovery.

Preventing Abuse

The major reasons for mistreatment of babies within the family are often parental feelings of isolation, stress, and frustration. Taking care of a baby can be challenging, especially when an end to his crying seems nowhere in sight. If you have tried to calm your crying baby but nothing seems to work, it's important to stay in control of your temper. Remember, it's never okay to shake, throw, or hit your baby. If you feel as though you could lose control:

- Take a deep breath and count to ten.
- Take time out and let your baby cry alone.
- Call someone close to you for emotional support.
- Call your pediatrician. There may be a medical reason why your baby is crying.

Parents need support and as much information as possible in order to raise their infants responsibly. They need to be taught how to cope with their own feelings of frustration and anger without venting them on babies. They also need the companionship of other adults who will listen and help during times of crisis. Support groups through local community organizations are often helpful first steps to diminish some of the isolation or frustration they may be feeling.

Part-time Care and Child Abuse

The media sometimes publicize frightening stories about child abuse in child-care settings. As a result, many parents are reluctant to leave their baby in the hands of anyone outside their families. The truth is that child abuse in child-care settings is extremely rare. More often, child-care homes and centers are places where children who are abused *elsewhere* can get help.

Still, for your own peace of mind, you can minimize any chance of abuse by inspecting your child's program fully before enrolling him, and making unannounced visits after he starts going there.

How will you know if your baby is being physically abused, in child care or elsewhere? You might be alerted by changes in his behavior or appearance. Pay special attention to the following:

- Any injury that does not have a reasonable explanation
- Repeated injuries, even if apparently accidental
- Changing accounts from the caregiver about injuries to a baby
- Hand-shaped bruises; burns in patterns that don't look accidental; marks in the shape of a cord, belt, or other object
- Bruises, infections, and bleeding around the genital or anal area

As a general guideline, if your baby has seemed comfortable in his child-care program for a while but then suddenly starts to protest, look for explanations—but don't automatically assume the worst. This shift of attitude may simply reflect a developmental change. Between seven and nine months, for example, most babies suddenly become afraid of "strangers," which could include anyone other than Mom and Dad. But if you can't reasonably explain your child's change in behavior, consult your pediatrician for advice before launching an investigation of the child-care program.

One- and Two-Child Families

Most newly married couples today plan to have only one or two children, compared with three or more back in the early 1960's. The reasons for this shift include a trend toward later marriage, more emphasis on careers for women, more effective methods of contraception, and the rising cost of rearing and educating children.

There are some very clear benefits to having a small family:

- Each child receives more parental attention and educational advantages, which generally raises her self-esteem.
- Children in small families, especially first and only children, tend to have higher school and personal achievement levels than do children of larger families.
- The financial costs of maintaining a household are lower.
- It is easier for both parents to combine careers with family life.
- The general stress level is lower because there often are fewer conflicts and less rivalry.

There are also some trade-offs, especially in one-child families. When all the expectations, hopes, and fears are focused on just one child, parents easily can become overprotective and indulgent without even realizing it. The child may have fewer opportunities to meet other children or to develop a sense of independence. She may be pushed to overachieve, and she may receive so much doting attention that she becomes self-centered and undisciplined.

Here are tips to help you keep these feelings in the proper perspective as your baby matures:

- Make sure your expectations of your infant are realistic for her age. Get to know other families with children the same age, and watch how these parents raise their offspring: when they're protective, and when they let go; how they discipline the children; how much responsibility they expect of them.
- Maintain your own adult social life as a couple (or as an individual, if you are a single parent). Taking a few hours off from each other will help both you and your baby develop your individual identities. The earlier you start this pattern of personal time (at least once a week, even during infancy), the easier it will be for you both to accept the increasing definition of personality that needs to occur as she grows older.
- Let your baby get to know other trusted grown-ups by having them baby-sit, and by including the baby in group activities with other families.

- Give her plenty of opportunities to play with other children her age through play groups.
- If you are worried about your baby's health or development, get advice from your pediatrician as soon as possible.

Single-Parent Families

Single-parent families are becoming more common. Most children of divorce spend at least some years in single-parent households. Another increasingly large group live with single parents who were never married. A smaller number have widowed parents.

From a parent's viewpoint, there are some benefits to being single. You can raise the baby according to your own beliefs, principles, and rules, with no need for conflict or resolving differences. Single parents often develop closer bonds with their children. When the father is the single parent, he may become more nurturing and more active in his child's daily life than most fathers in two-parent households. Children in single-parent households may become more independent and mature because they have more responsibility within the family.

Single parenthood is not easy, though, for parents or children. It generally means less income and a lower standard of living. If you can't arrange or afford child care, getting and holding a job may be difficult. (See Chapter 11, "Part-time Care for Your Baby.") Without another person to share the day-in, day-out job of raising the infant and maintaining the household, you may find yourself socially isolated.

Here are some suggestions that may help you meet your own emotional needs while raising your infant:

- Take advantage of all available resources in finding help in caring for your baby. Use the guide to part-time care in Chapter 11.
- Maintain your sense of humor as much as possible. Try to see the positive or humorous side of everyday surprises and challenges.
- For your family's sake as well as your own, take care of yourself. See your doctor regularly, eat properly, and get enough rest, exercise, and sleep.

- Set a regular time when you can take a break without your baby. Relax with friends. Go to a movie. Pursue hobbies. Join groups. Do things that interest *you.* Pursue a social life of your own.
- Don't feel guilty because your child has only one parent. There are plenty of families in the same situation. You didn't "do it to her," and you don't need to penalize yourself or spoil her to make amends. Feeling and acting guilty won't help anyone.
- Don't look for problems where none exist. Many children grow up very well in single-parent homes, while others have a great many problems in two-parent homes. Being a single parent doesn't necessarily mean you'll have more problems or have more trouble resolving them.
- Create as large a support network for yourself as possible. Keep active lists of relatives, friends, and community services that can help with child care. Establish friendships with other families who will let you know of community opportunities (cultural events, etc.) and are willing to exchange baby-sitting.
- Talk to trusted relatives, friends, and professionals such as your pediatrician about your baby's development, and relationships within the family.

Smaller Extended Families

Until the last few generations, most American families were two-parent ones; living nearby, perhaps even in the same house, were grandparents, aunts, uncles, and cousins. The women were primarily responsible for caring for the children and running the household while the men worked outside the home. In many ways, this formula worked well: There were plenty of adults to look after the children. There was a built-in support system and roles were clearly defined. The children benefited the most because they had so many close social contacts and received love from so many different directions.

The extended family is not as common in American society today. Due to career obligations, opportunities, and the desire to go to new places, fewer and fewer newly married couples choose to or can live near their parents or close relatives.

Without regular contact with these relatives, parents and children need to create alternative support systems. As your child grows, keep in mind that a close friendship with another family, participation in a surrogate or foster grandparent program, or in Big Brothers or Sisters, can help replace the missing ties. For many families, religious congregational activities are a source of support and close friendships. Many other community programs such as youth and neighborhood activity centers also can fulfill these needs.

Even if your relatives are scattered, try to strengthen your child's sense of family by keeping in touch by phone and letters. When your child becomes a little older, encourage him to draw pictures for relatives, and to send his own letters when he learns to write. Exchange photographs, and make them into a photo album that grows with your child. If you have a tape recorder or video camera, make tapes of your family as "audio/video letters" to bring you closer together.

The overall intent is to balance the intimate connections of a small nuclear family with continued meaningful contacts with loved ones outside the immediate family. The values fostered and nurtured through these family relationships will be important ones for your baby to model and incorporate into his way of living when he grows up.

STEPFAMILIES

When a baby is born into a blended family—where one or both parents had been married before and may have had children from those relationships—there may be special issues that need to be dealt with by mothers and fathers, many of them involving the older siblings (or half-siblings) of the new baby. The addition of a newborn always requires adjustments, and his presence can be both joyful and stressful for the rest of the family.

The older children may feel jealous of the new baby and compete for the love of the parents. The siblings who have only one biological parent in the household may feel the baby is getting more attention than they are. These youngsters may act out in order to gain parental attention.

With time, most blended families do manage to sort through any conflicts that arise, but it requires a great amount of patience and commitment on the part of the adults, as well as the willingness to get professional help if serious problems should develop. Perhaps the most important factor in healthy stepfamilies is for parents to be equally supportive, affectionate, and loving of all children in the family.

TWINS

Having twins means much more than simply having two babies at once, and this challenge goes beyond having twice the work or pleasure. Twins quite frequently are born early and therefore tend to be smaller than the average newborn, so you may need to consult your pediatrician even more frequently than you would with a single baby. Feeding twins, whether by breast or bottle, also requires some special strategies, and the doctor can provide advice and support. (See Chapters 1 and 4.)

Raising Twins

From the very beginning it's important that you recognize your twin babies as two separate individuals. If they are identical it's easy to treat them as a "package," providing them with the same clothing, toys, and quality of attention. But as similar as they may appear physically, emotionally they are different, and in order to grow up happy and secure as individuals, they need you to support their differences. As one twin explained, "We're not twins. We're just brothers who have the same birthday!"

Both identical and fraternal twins may become either competitive or interdependent as they grow. Sometimes one twin acts as the leader and the other as the follower. Whatever the specific quality of their interaction, however, most twins develop very intense relationships early in life simply because they spend so much time with each other.

If you also have other children, your twin newborns may prompt more than the usual sibling rivalry. They will require a large amount of your time and energy, and will attract a great deal of extra attention from friends, relatives, and strangers on the street. You can help your other children accept, and maybe even take advantage of, this unusual situation by offering them "double rewards" for helping with the new babies and encouraging even more involvement in the daily baby-care chores. It also becomes even more es-

Twins: Fraternal vs. Identical

Identical twins come from the same egg, are always the same sex, and look very much alike. However, they have their individual personalities, styles, and temperament. We expect them to act alike and develop in similar ways as they grow up. Because of their many similarities, they may develop extremely close emotional bonds, possibly excluding even other family members to some extent. **Fraternal twins** come from two separate eggs, which are fertilized at the same time. They may or may not be the same sex, and they will not be identical in appearance, temperament, or behavior. Because of these differences, they often do not form the extremely close relationship found between identical twins.

Characteristic	*Identical*	*Fraternal*
Sex	Same	Same or different
Appearance	Identical	Many similarities, but not identical
Placenta	One	Two
Chorion bag*	One or two	Two
Amniotic sac**	One or two	Two
Blood types	Identical	May be identical

* the cellular, outermost extraembryonic membrane
** membrane around the fetus

sential that you spend some special time each day alone with the other children doing their favorite activities.

Twins are not always happy about being apart, especially if they've established strong play habits and preferences for each other's company. For this reason, it's important to begin separating them occasionally as early as possible. If they resist strongly, try a gradual approach using very familiar children or adults to play with them individually but in the same room or play area.

As much as you appreciate the individual differences between your twins, you no doubt will have certain feelings for them as a unit. There is nothing wrong with this, since they do share many similarities and are themselves bound to develop a dual identity—as individuals and as twins. Helping them understand and accept the balance between these two identities will be one of the most challenging tasks facing you as the parent of twins. Your pediatrician can advise you on how to cope with the special parenting problems involved with twins. He also can suggest helpful reading material or refer you to organizations involved with helping parents who have multiple births.

WORKING MOTHERS

In the United States today, more than half of mothers with young children work, compared to 30 percent in the 1970's. Working mothers are the rule rather than the exception. Women have been moving into the work force not only for career satisfaction but also because they and their families need the income. More than one fourth of all children live in single-parent homes, with their mothers providing most of their support. About 80 percent of married working women have husbands who earn less than $30,000 a year. For the children in many of these families, the alternative to a working mother is poverty.

In some families, mothers continue to work because they have careers that they have spent years developing. Most employers in this country are not sympathetic to working mothers who wish to take time off to be with their babies and young children. If these women stop working, even for a year or two, they may give up some of the advantages they have earned or risk losing certain career opportunities.

As more women enter the work force, more and more children are cared for by adults other than their parents. Relatives sometimes take on child-care duties, or children are enrolled in child-care programs. Working mothers are almost five times as likely to have their infants in a child-care center than nonemployed mothers.

Some people still think that a "good mother" is one who gives up work to stay home with her children. However, there is no scientific evidence that says children are harmed when their mothers work. A child's development is more influenced by the amount of stress in the family, how the family feels about the mother's working, and the quality of child care. A child who is emotionally well-adjusted, well loved, and well cared for will thrive regardless of whether the mother works outside the home.

Problems can arise if a woman does not want to work or if her husband does not want her to work. If a woman works because she needs the money, she may have to take a job that she does not like. In that case, she needs to be careful not to bring her frustration and unhappiness home, where it will spill over into family relationships.

Family relationships may suffer if both parents want to work but only one has a job. Problems also can occur if there is competition or resentment because one parent is earning more money than the other. Such conflicts can strain the marriage. With both parents working, the need for mutual support and communication is even more important.

Even when there are no problems, however, a two-career family has to deal with issues that do not come up in other families. Parents may feel so divided between family and career that they have little time for a social life or each other. Both parents should share household and child-care responsibilities so that one will not end up doing most of the work and feeling resentful. Parents will lose nine to twelve work days per year due to the need to tend to a sick child, to care for their baby when child-care arrangements have broken down, or to take their baby to necessary appointments.

A woman's decision to return to work must take into account her own needs as well as those of her family. If you are considering returning to work, try to delay your return until three or four months after your baby is born, so you have time to firmly establish the initial parent-child relationship. Take the time to prepare yourself and your family, so that the adjustment is as easy as possible for everyone. Try to time your return to work so that stress is minimal. If at all possible, your return should not coincide with other major family changes, such as moving or changing schools, or personal crises such as illness or death in the family; arrange trustworthy child care as far in advance as possible.

As a working parent, you are bound to be concerned about the loss of time with your baby. You may worry that you will miss some of his important milestones, like his first step or word. You may even feel jealous of the time your baby spends with the caregiver. These are all normal feelings, but try to separate your own needs from concerns about your child's welfare.

Parents all wish for the best start for their baby. Unfortunately, quality child care can be expensive and often hard to find. Many parents end up spending a large share of their paychecks for child care and still are not happy with the quality of the care their baby receives. Lower-income families are less likely to have their infant in a quality center, and are more likely to have multiple changes in their child-care arrangements, than middle- to higher-income families.

Finding quality child care is important. Standards for child-care settings may vary depending on the type of child care. Parents can, however, improve their baby's child-care programs by becoming actively involved. You can visit the program regularly and talk with the caregiver often and extensively. You can also get involved in fund-raising, donate supplies, volunteer to help, or work with the staff to develop more stimulating activities for the children.

Taking an active role in your baby's care not only helps ensure his well-being, but also may reduce any guilt or misgivings parents may feel about working. Having quality child care and a good relationship with the caregiver can also ease some of the worry.

Good child care helps your baby grow in every way and promotes his physical, social, and mental development. It offers support to working parents. Your pediatrician wants your baby to grow and develop with enjoyment in a setting that supports you as a parent. For more information on choosing a child-care arrangement for your family, ask your pediatrician about the brochure "Child Care: What's Best for Your Family" by the American Academy of Pediatrics (also see Chapter 11).

20

FEVER

Your baby's normal temperature will vary with his age, his activity, and the time of day. Babies tend to have higher temperatures than older children, and everyone's temperature is highest between late afternoon and early evening, and lowest between midnight and early morning. Ordinarily, a rectal reading of 100 degrees Fahrenheit (37.8 degrees Celsius) or less, or an oral reading of 99 degrees Fahrenheit (37.2 degrees Celsius) or less, is considered normal, while higher readings indicate fever.

By itself, fever is *not* an illness. In fact, usually it is a positive sign that the body is fighting infection. Fever stimulates certain defenses, such as the white blood cells, which attack and destroy invading bacteria. However, fever can make your baby uncomfortable. It increases his need for fluids and makes his heart rate and breathing faster.

Fever most commonly accompanies respiratory illnesses such as croup or pneumonia, ear infections, flu, severe colds, and sore throats. It may also occur with infections of the bowel or urinary tract, and with a wide variety of viral illnesses.

In children between six months and five years, fever can trigger seizures, called *febrile convulsions*. These usually happen during the first few hours of a febrile illness. The child may look "peculiar" for a few moments, then stiffen out, twitch, and roll his eyes. He will be unresponsive for a short time, and his skin may appear a little darker than usual during the episode. The entire convulsion usually will last no more than three or four minutes, and may be over in a few seconds, but it can seem like a lifetime to a frightened parent. It is reassuring to know that febrile convulsions almost always are harmless, though they should be reported promptly to your pediatrician.

A rare but serious problem which is easily confused with fever is *heat-related illness*, or *heat stroke*. This is caused not by infection or internal conditions, but by surrounding heat. It can occur when a baby is in a very hot place, for example a hot beach in midsummer or an overheated closed car on a summer day. Leaving babies unattended in closed cars is the cause of several deaths a year; never leave a baby unattended in a closed car, even for a few minutes. Heat stroke also can occur if a baby is overdressed in hot, humid weather. Under these circumstances the body temperature can rise to dangerous levels (above 105 degrees Fahrenheit [40.5 degrees Celsius]), which must be reduced quickly by cool-water sponging, fanning, and removal to a cool place. After the baby has been cooled, he should be taken immediately to a pediatrician or emergency room. Heat stroke is an emergency condition.

Upper Limits of Normal Temperatures

Method	*Time*	*Birth to Three Years*
Rectal temperature (Mercury thermometer)	2 minutes	100.4 F (38 C)
Rectal temperature (Digital thermometer)	1 minute	100.4 F (38 C)

Whenever you think your baby has a fever, take his temperature with a thermometer. (See *Which Thermometer Is Best?*) Feeling the skin (or using temperature-sensitive tape) is not accurate, especially when the baby is experiencing a chill. Until your child reaches the age of three years old, take his temperature rectally with a mercury rectal thermometer (see *Taking a Rectal Temperature,* page 78).

When to Call the Pediatrician

If your infant is *2 months or younger* and has a rectal temperature of 100.4 degrees Fahrenheit (38.1 degrees Celsius) or higher, call your pediatrician immediately. *This is an absolute necessity.* The doctor will need to examine the baby to rule out any serious infection or disease.

You also may need to notify the doctor if your infant is

between three and six months and has a fever of 101 degrees Fahrenheit (38.3 degrees Celsius) or greater, or is older than six months and has a temperature of 103 degrees Fahrenheit (39.4 degrees Celsius) or higher. Such a high temperature may indicate a significant infection or dehydration, which may require treatment. However, in most cases your decision to call the pediatrician also will depend upon associated symptoms such as sore throat, earache, or cough. If a high fever persists for more than twenty-four hours, however, it is best to call even if there are no other complaints or findings.

If your infant has a febrile convulsion, he should be examined by your pediatrician as soon as possible, particularly if this is the first time it has occurred, or if it is more severe or prolonged than others he has had. You need to be sure that the seizure is due to fever and not to a more serious condition such as meningitis (see page 534).

Home Treatment

Fevers under 101 degrees Fahrenheit (38.3 degrees Celsius) generally do not need to be treated unless your baby is uncomfortable or has a history of febrile convulsions. Even higher temperatures are not in themselves dangerous or significant unless your infant has a history of convulsions or a chronic disease. It is more important to watch how your baby is behaving. If he is eating and sleeping well, and has periods of playfulness, he probably doesn't need any treatment. If he seems to be bothered by the fever, however, you can treat it in the following ways:

Acetaminophen Dosage Table

Dosages may be repeated every four hours, but should not be given more than five times in twenty-four hours. (*Note:* Milliliter is abbreviated as ml; 5 ml equals 1 teaspoon [tsp].)

Age	*Weight*	*Drops 80 mg/0.8 ml*	*Elixir 160 mg/5 ml*
0–3 mos.	6–11 lbs. (2.7–5 kg)	0.4 ml	
4–11 mos.	12–17 lbs. (5.5–7.7 kg)	0.8 ml	½ tsp
12–23 mos.	18–23 lbs. (8.2–10.5 kg)	1.2 ml	¾ tsp

We do not recommend using aspirin to treat a simple fever.

Which Thermometer Is Best?

Mercury

How to Use: Shake the thermometer until the mercury line falls below 96 degrees Fahrenheit. Then clean the thermometer in lukewarm soapy water, or swab it with rubbing alcohol. Rinse with cool water.

Rectal (for infants and young children up to the age of three years): Coat the bulb with petroleum jelly. Hold your baby in a diapering position, facedown, or on her side with her knees drawn up, and gently insert the thermometer about one inch into her rectum. Keep the thermometer in place for two to three minutes.

Pros:

- Less expensive
- Very accurate

Cons:

- Fragile
- Numbers are small and hard to read
- Fussy babies may not sit still for this type of reading

Axillary (for infants over three months old): Place the bulb of a rectal thermometer in your baby's armpit, and hold her arm tightly against her chest. Wait four to five minutes before removing.

Pros:

- Easier to use

Cons:

- Less accurate

Digital

How to Use: Wipe with soapy water or rubbing alcohol, then rinse with cool water. Turn on the switch, and place the sensor with a nonpetroleum lubricant into the baby's rectum. Hold in place for about one minute (until you hear an electronic beep). You can also use a digital thermometer in your infant's armpit.

Pros:

- Easy to read
- Beeps when ready

Cons:

- Needs batteries
- Fussy babies may not sit still for this type of reading

Tympanic

How to Use: Position the end gently in the ear canal. Press the start button.

You will get a digital reading of your infant's temperature within seconds.

Pros:

- Very quick reading
- Easy to use on fussy or uncomfortable children

Cons:

- Needs to be placed correctly in the ear canal for an accurate reading
- Needs batteries
- Cost: about $60 to $70

Ibuprofen Dosage Table

Dosages may be repeated every six to eight hours, but should not be given more than four times in twenty-four hours. (Note: Milliliter is abbreviated as ml; 5 ml equals 1 teaspoon [tsp].)

*Age**	*Weight***	*Drops 40 mg/1.5 cc*
6–11 mos.	12–17 lbs.	1.5 cc
12–23 mos.	18–23 lbs.	3 cc

*Note: Age is provided as a convenience only. Dosing for fever should be based on baseline temperature and weight.

**Weight given corresponds to the exact dosage and is representative of the age range.

We do not recommend using aspirin to treat a simple fever.

Medication

There are several medications that can reduce body temperature by blocking the mechanisms that cause a fever. These so-called antipyretic agents include acetaminophen, ibuprofen, and aspirin. All three of these drugs appear to be equally effective at reducing fever. *However, since aspirin may cause or be associated with side effects such as stomach upset, intestinal bleeding, and (most seriously) Reye syndrome, we do not recommend using it to treat a simple fever.* Ibuprofen use is approved for children six months of age and older; however, ibuprofen should never be given to babies who are dehydrated or vomiting continuously.

Ideally, the dose of acetaminophen should be based on a baby's weight, not his age. The dose of ibuprofen should be based on baseline temperature and weight, not his age. (See the dosage tables, page 522.) However, the dosages listed on the labels of acetaminophen bottles (which are usually calculated by age) are generally safe and effective unless your baby is unusually light or heavy for his age.

Be sure to read and follow the instructions on the manufacturer's label when using any medication. Following the instructions is important to ensure that your baby receives the proper dosages. Acetaminophen may be contained in other over-the-counter medications, such as cold preparations. Read all medication labels to ensure your baby is not receiving multiple doses of the same medicine. As a general rule, do not give a baby under two years acetaminophen or any other medication without the advice of your pediatrician.

Sponging

In most cases, using oral acetaminophen is the most convenient way to treat a fever. However, in some cases you might want to combine this with tepid sponging, or just use sponging alone.

Sponging is preferred over acetaminophen if:

- Your baby is known to be allergic to, or is unable to tolerate, antipyretic (antifever) drugs (a rare case).

It is advisable to *combine* sponging with acetaminophen if:

- Fever is making your baby uncomfortable.
- He has a temperature over 104 degrees Fahrenheit (40 degrees Celsius).
- He has a history of febrile convulsions or someone else in your immediate family has had them.
- He is vomiting and may not be able to retain the medication.

To sponge your baby, place him in his regular bath (tub, bathinette, or baby bath), but put only 1 to 2 inches of tepid water (85 to 90 degrees Fahrenheit, or 29.4 to 32.2 degrees Celsius) in the basin. If you do not have a bath thermometer, test the water with the back of your hand or wrist. It should feel just slightly warm. Do not use cold water, since that will be uncomfortable and may cause shivering, which can raise his temperature. Seat your baby in the water—it is more comfortable than lying down. Then, using a clean washcloth or sponge, spread a film of water over his trunk, arms, and legs. The water will evaporate and cool the body. Keep the room at about 75 degrees Fahrenheit (23.9 degrees Celsius), and continue sponging him until his temperature has reached an acceptable level (see the table of Normal Temperatures). *Never put alcohol in the water; it can be absorbed into the skin, which can cause serious problems such as coma.*

Usually, sponging will bring down the fever in thirty to forty-five minutes. However, if your baby is resisting actively, stop and let him just sit and play in the water. If being in the tub makes him more upset and uncomfortable, it is best to take him out even if his fever is unchanged. Remember, fever in the moderate range (less than 102 degrees Fahrenheit [38.9 degrees Celsius]) is in itself not harmful.

Other Suggestions for Mild Fever

- Keep your baby's room comfortably cool, and dress him lightly.
- If the room is warm or stuffy, place a fan nearby to keep the cool air moving.

- Encourage him to drink extra fluid (water, diluted fruit juices, gelatin-flavored water). There is no reason to discontinue giving your baby the milk he normally drinks.
- Your baby does not have to stay in his room or in bed when he has a fever, but he should not overexert himself.
- If the fever is a symptom of a highly contagious disease, keep your baby away from other youngsters and elderly people.

Treating a Febrile Convulsion

If your infant has a febrile convulsion, act immediately to prevent injury:

- Place him on the floor or bed away from any hard or sharp objects.
- Turn his head to the side so that any saliva or vomit can drain from his mouth.
- Do not put anything into his mouth; he will not swallow his tongue.
- Call for emergency medical help if the convulsion lasts more than two or three minutes or is particularly severe (difficulty breathing, choking, blueness of the skin, several convulsions in a row).

21

Genitourinary Tract

Hypospadias

Ordinarily in boys, the opening through which urine passes (the meatus) is located at the tip of the penis. In rare cases, and for reasons that are unknown, this opening may appear on the underside of the penis—a condition known as *hypospadias.*

Because hypospadias involves a malformation of the skin in this area, it may cause abnormal erections (called chordees) and sexual problems in adulthood. The meatus may direct the urinary stream downward, and in very rare cases there may be some blockage during urination. One of the most important reasons to correct severe hypospadias, however, is to prevent the psychological complications that can arise quite early in childhood when playmates notice the abnormal appearance of the penis.

Treatment

After detecting hypospadias in your newborn, the pediatrician probably will advise against circumcision until after consultation with a urologist. This is because circumcision makes future surgical repair more difficult.

Mild hypospadias may require no treatment, but moderate or severe forms require surgical repair. This operation may be done as early as six months or as late as eighteen months of age, but usually is recommended around the first birthday. Very often this surgery can be performed on an outpatient basis. In some severe cases more than one operation may be needed to repair the defect completely. After surgery your baby will have normal urinary and sexual function, and a nearly normal-appearing penis.

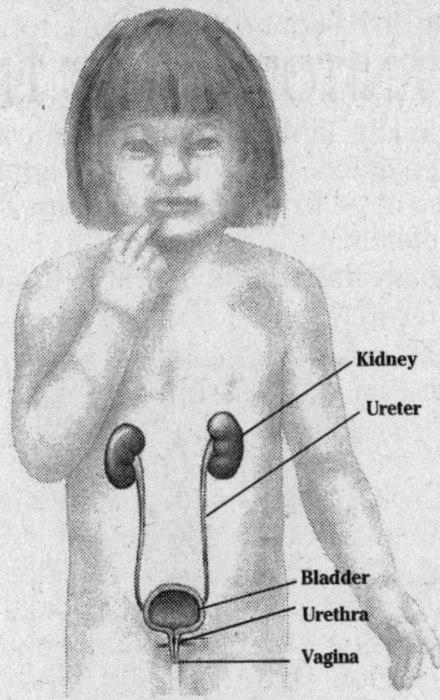

Genitourinary System

Labial Adhesions

Ordinarily, the lips of skin (labia) surrounding the entrance to the vagina are separated. In rare cases they grow together to block the opening, partially or completely. This condition, called *labial adhesions,* may occur in the early months of life or, less frequently, later on if there is constant irritation and inflammation in this area. In these latter cases, the problem is usually traceable to diaper irritation, contact with harsh detergents, or panties made with synthetic fabric. Usually, labial adhesions do not cause symptoms, but they can lead to difficulty with urination and increase a girl's susceptibility to urinary tract infection. If the vaginal opening is completely blocked, there is a buildup of urine or vaginal secretions behind the obstruction.

Treatment

If the opening of your daughter's vagina appears to have closed, or looks partially blocked, notify your pediatrician. She will examine her and advise you if any treatment is necessary.

At first, the doctor will gently attempt to spread the labia. If the connecting tissue is weak, this mild pressure may expose the opening. If the connecting tissue is too strong, the doctor may prescribe a cream that contains the female hormone estrogen for you to apply to the area as you very gently and gradually pull the labia apart over a period of time. Once the labia are separated, you will need to apply the cream for a short while (three to five days) until the skin on both sides heals completely.

Occasionally the adhesions will return once the cream is

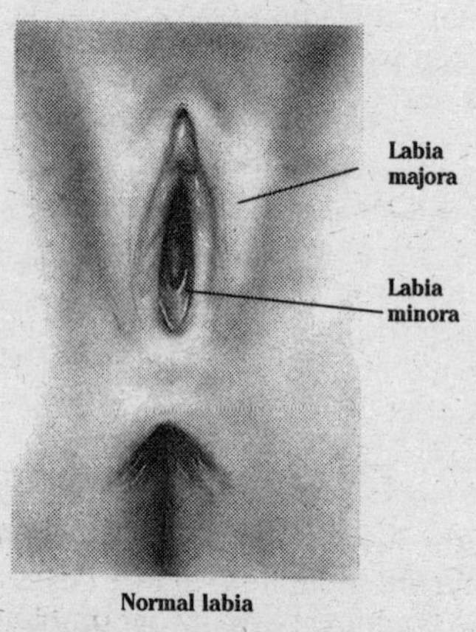

Normal labia

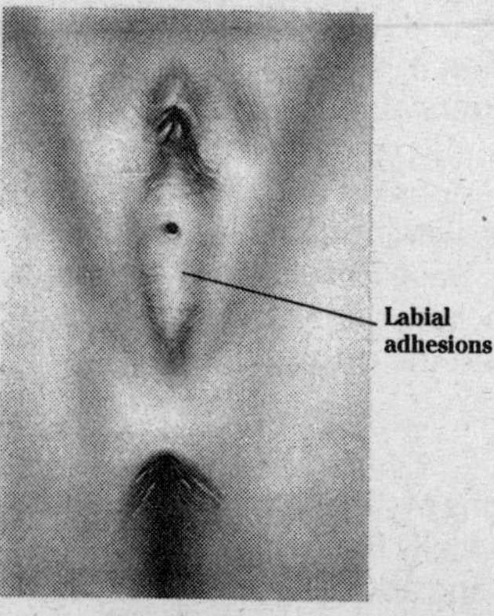

With adhesions

discontinued. Know that they disappear permanently at puberty. In very rare cases, the adhesions (scarlike tissue that grows between the labia and holds them together) are so thick that they block the flow of urine. In this rare case, they will need to be separated. This must be done by the physician.

UNDESCENDED TESTICLES (CRYPTORCHIDISM)

During gestation, the testes develop in the abdomen of the male fetus. As he nears birth, they descend through a tube (the inguinal canal) into the scrotum. In a small number of boys, especially those who are premature, one or both testicles fail to descend by the time of birth. In many of these boys, descent will occur during the first nine months of life. In some, however, this does not happen.

All boys will have normal elevation of testes under certain situations, such as sitting in warm water. However, under normal conditions, testes should be low in the scrotum.

The cause of undescended testicles cannot be explained in most cases. However, in some boys the following factors may play a role:

- There may not have been enough of certain hormones from the mother or the developing testicles to stimulate their normal maturation.
- The testes themselves may be abnormal in their response to these hormones.
- There may be a physical blockage that prevents descent.

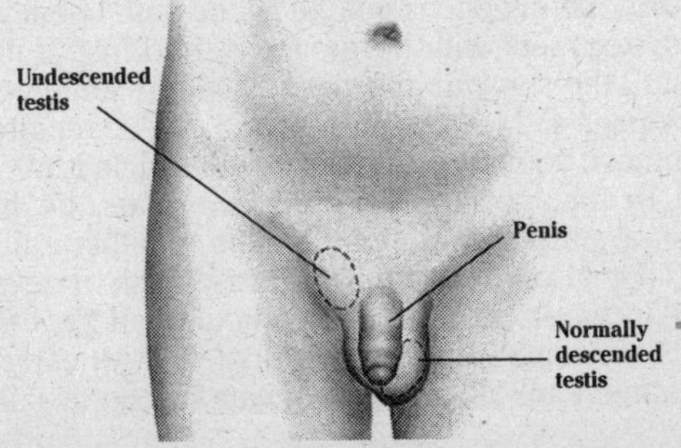

- In some cases there may be a link with hormonal preparations taken by the mother during pregnancy (which is one reason why pregnant women are advised to avoid such medications).

If your baby boy has undescended testicles, his scrotum will be small and appear underdeveloped. If only one testicle is undescended, the scrotum may look asymmetrical (full on one side, empty on the other). If the testicles are sometimes present in the scrotum and at other times (such as when he is cold or excited) are absent, and located above the scrotum, they are said to be "retractile." This condition usually is self-correcting as the baby becomes more mature.

The undescended testicle may be twisted, and in the process, its blood supply may be blocked, causing pain in the inguinal (groin) or scrotal area. If this situation is not corrected, the testicle can be severely and permanently damaged. So if your son has an undescended testicle and seems to be having pain in the groin or scrotal area, call your pediatrician immediately.

Undescended testicles should be reevaluated at each regular checkup. If they do not descend into the scrotum by age one to two, treatment should be started.

Treatment

Undescended testicles may be treated with hormone injections and/or surgery. The lower the testes, the more likely that the hormone injections will be successful. Usually, but not always, treatment with hormones is tried first; if that is unsuccessful, the surgical approach is taken. Sometimes a hernia (see page 432) is also present and can be repaired at the same time. If your son's undescended testicle is allowed to remain in that position for over two years, he has a higher than average risk of being unable to father children (infertility). He also has a slightly increased risk of developing testicular tumors in adult life, particularly if the testicle is left in its abnormal position. Fortunately, with early and proper treatment, all of these complications can usually be avoided.

Urethral Valves

Urine leaves the bladder through a tube called the urethra, which in boys passes through the penis. During early fetal development, there are tiny "valves" at the beginning of the urethra which block the passage of urine. These normally disappear well before birth so that urine can flow freely out the end of the penis. In some boys, however, the valves remain after birth, and may cause serious problems by interfering with the flow of urine. They are called *posterior urethral valves.*

Often these valves are detected by ultrasound during pregnancy, but many times they are not discovered until the newborn period, when the pediatrician finds that the baby's bladder is distended and enlarged. Other warning signals include a continual dribbling of urine and a weak stream during urination. If you notice these symptoms, notify your pediatrician at once.

Posterior urethral valves require immediate medical attention to prevent serious urinary tract infections or damage to the kidneys. If the blockage is severe, the urine can back up through the ureters (the tubes between the bladder and the kidneys), creating pressure that can damage the kidneys.

Treatment

If a baby is having urinary blockage due to posterior urethral valves, the pediatrician may pass a small tube up the penis into the bladder to relieve the obstruction temporarily. Then X rays of the bladder and kidneys will be ordered to confirm the diagnosis and to see if any damage has occurred to the upper urinary tract. A pediatric urologist will then perform surgery to remove the obstructing valves.

Urinary Tract Infections

Urinary tract infections are common among young children, particularly girls. They generally are caused by bacteria that enter through the urethra, though they also can be caused by bacteria carried through the bloodstream to the kidneys from another part of the body. As the bacteria move through the urinary tract, they may cause infection in different locations. *Urinary tract infection* is a general term used for all the following specific infections:

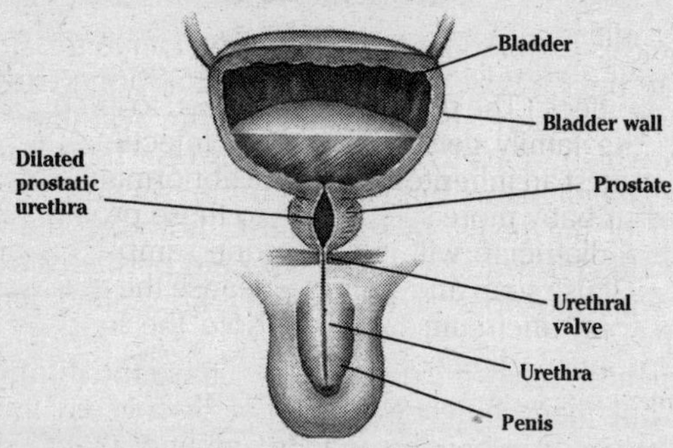

- Urethritis—infection of the urethra
- Cystitis—infection of the bladder
- Pyelonephritis—infection of the renal pelvis and kidney

The area most commonly infected is the bladder (cystitis). Usually, cystitis is caused by bacteria that get into the urinary tract by contamination of the urethra with stool. The urethra is very short in girls, allowing bacteria to get into the bladder easily. Thus, they tend to have urinary tract infections more frequently than boys.

Cystitis can cause lower abdominal pain, tenderness, pain during urination, frequent urination, blood in the urine, and fever. Infection of the upper urinary tract (the kidneys) will cause a more general abdominal pain and higher fever, but is less likely to cause frequent and painful urination.

Urinary tract infections must be treated with antibiotics as quickly as possible, so you should notify your pediatrician promptly if you suspect your baby has developed one. A urinalysis also should be performed if your baby suffers vague symptoms that cannot be explained, since these can be caused by a chronic urinary tract infection.

Treatment

The pediatrician will measure your baby's blood pressure and examine her for lower abdominal tenderness that might indicate a urinary tract infection. The doctor will want to know what your baby has been eating and drinking, because certain foods can irritate the urinary tract, causing symptoms similar to those of an infection. (Drinks containing citrus juice, carbonation, and caffeine are especially likely to have this effect.) The doctor also will need to know if anyone else in the family gets urinary tract infections, since this might suggest an inherited structural abnormality that would make your baby more susceptible to these problems.

Your pediatrician will need a urine sample for analysis. First, you'll use soap and water to cleanse the urethral opening (with an uncircumcised boy, hold the foreskin back). Then, a special urine collector will be taped over the penis or vaginal opening until voiding occurs.

The urine will be examined under the microscope for any sign of blood cells or bacteria, and special tests (cultures) will be done to identify the bacteria that are present. An antibiotic will be started immediately if an infection is suspected, although it may need to be changed after the final results of the culture are obtained (up to forty-eight hours later).

Antibiotics usually are prescribed for a ten-day-to-two-week period. After several days your pediatrician may request another urine sample, to check the effectiveness of the treatment. If it does not seem to be working, the prescription will be changed. Otherwise, the same medication will be continued for another week.

Make sure your baby takes the full course of medication prescribed. Otherwise, the bacteria may grow again, causing further infection and more serious damage to the urinary tract. After your baby's treatment is complete, another urine sample will be taken to make sure that the infection is completely gone and no bacteria remain.

Most specialists now feel that after your baby's first serious urinary tract infection, further tests should be done (ultrasound, X rays, or renal scanning examinations). Your pediatrician also may conduct other tests to check kidney function. If any of these examinations indicates a structural abnormality that should be corrected, your doctor will recommend that your child see a genitourinary surgeon.

22

Head, Neck, and Nervous System

Meningitis

Meningitis is an inflammation of the tissues that cover the brain and spinal cord. The inflammation sometimes affects the brain itself. Meningitis is a very serious disease that occurs rarely. When it does, however, we see it most commonly in babies and young children under five years old. With early diagnosis and proper treatment, a child with meningitis has an excellent chance of getting well without any complications.

The most serious kind of meningitis is caused by bacteria (several different types are involved). Babies and toddlers under the age of two are at greatest risk for this form of the disease. Meningitis also can be caused by viruses and other organisms such as fungi or parasites. The viral form usually is not very serious, except in young infants less than three months of age.

The bacteria that cause meningitis often can be found in the mouths and throats of healthy babies. But this does not necessarily mean that these infants will get the disease. That doesn't happen unless the bacteria get into the bloodstream.

We still don't understand exactly why some babies get meningitis and others don't, but we do know that certain groups of children are more likely to get the illness. These are the following:

- Babies, especially those under two months of age. (Because their immune systems are not well developed, the bacteria can get into the bloodstream more easily.)

- Children with recurrent sinus infections
- Children with recent serious head injuries and skull fractures
- Children who have just had brain surgery
- Children with severe burns that may be chronically infected
- Children with certain chronic conditions such as cystic fibrosis, cancer, sickle-cell anemia, or illnesses requiring continuous respirator care or intravenous infusions

Before antibiotics (drugs that combat bacteria) were developed, 90 percent of the children with meningitis died. Of the 10 percent who survived, most were left retarded or deaf, or had convulsions. Now, the outlook is much brighter. With prompt diagnosis and treatment, 70 percent of the children who get meningitis recover without any complications. Even most of those with complications usually have only minor ones that last just a short time. Hearing loss, however, remains an important, frequently found, long-lasting problem. Meningitis must be detected early and treated aggressively in order to be cured. This is why it's so important for you to notify your pediatrician immediately if your baby displays any of the following warning signs.

If your infant is less than two months old: The presence of fever, decreased appetite, listlessness, or increased crying or irritability warrants a call to your doctor. At this age, the signs of meningitis can be very subtle and difficult to detect, and thus it's better to call early and be wrong than to call too late.

If your baby is two months to two years old: This is the most common age for meningitis. Look for symptoms such as fever, nausea, vomiting, decreased appetite, excessive crankiness, or excessive sleepiness. (His cranky periods might be extreme and his sleepy periods might make it impossible to arouse him.)

Treatment

If, after an examination, your pediatrician is concerned that your baby may have meningitis, she will do a blood test to check for a bacterial infection, and will also obtain some spinal fluid by performing a spinal tap, or lumbar puncture (LP). This procedure involves inserting a special needle into your child's lower back to draw out the fluid. Any signs of

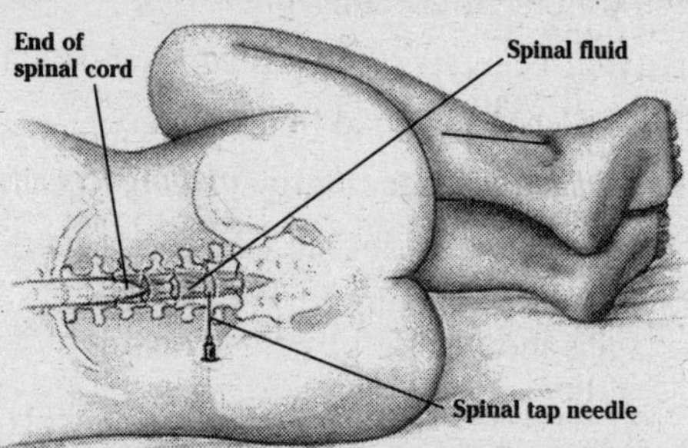

A spinal tap is taken from the space below the spinal cord so that the needle will not touch the spinal cord.

infection in this fluid will confirm that your baby has meningitis. In that case he'll need to be admitted to the hospital for intravenous antibiotics and fluids, and for careful observation for complications. During the first days of treatment your baby may not be able to eat or drink, so intravenous fluid will be used to provide the medicine and nutrition he needs. For certain types of meningitis, this may be necessary for seven to twenty-one days, depending on the age of the child and the bacteria identified.

Prevention

Some types of bacterial meningitis can now be prevented with vaccines or antibiotics. Ask your pediatrician about the following:

Hib Vaccine. This vaccine will decrease the chance of children becoming infected with *Haemophilus influenzae* type b (Hib) bacteria. The vaccination is given by injection to children beginning at two months of age. (See Immunization Alert in Chapter 8, page 268.)

Pneumovax. This vaccine is effective in preventing some infections caused by the *pneumococcus* bacteria. It is recommended for administration only to those babies who are most susceptible to such infections: children with abnormal immune systems, sickle-cell disease, certain kidney problems, and other chronic conditions.

Rifampin. If your baby has been exposed—either at home or during day care—to a child with meningitis caused by *Haemophilus influenzae* or the *meningococcus* bacteria, he should be placed on this antibiotic to prevent him from becoming infected. In some cases adults who are exposed (by means of close intimate contact) to someone with bacterial meningitis should also be placed on this medication for a period of time. Your pediatrician will tell you how often and how long to use it. If your baby shows any of the signs of meningitis, even though he is on the medication, call your pediatrician immediately.

Seizures and Convulsions

Seizures are sudden temporary changes in physical movement or behavior caused by abnormal electrical impulses in the brain. Depending upon how many muscles are affected by the electrical impulses, a seizure may cause sudden stiffening of the body or complete relaxation of the muscles, which temporarily can make a person appear to be paralyzed. Sometimes these seizures are referred to as "fits" or "spells." The terms *convulsion* and *seizure* can be used interchangeably.

Febrile convulsions (seizures caused by high fever) occur in three or four out of every hundred children between infancy and age five. A febrile convulsion can cause reactions as mild as a rolling of the eyes or stiffening of the limbs, or as startling as a generalized convulsion with twitching and jerking movements that involve the whole body. Febrile convulsions usually last less than five minutes, and ordinarily the baby's behavior quickly returns to normal.

Treatment

Most seizures will stop on their own and do not require immediate medical treatment. If your baby is having a convulsion, you should protect her from injuring herself by moving her to a semisitting position or laying her on her side with her hips higher than her head, so she will not choke if she vomits.

If the convulsion does not stop within two or three minutes, is unusually severe (difficulty breathing, choking, blueness of the skin, having several in a row), call for emergency medical help. Do *not* leave the infant unattended, however. After the seizure stops, call the pediatrician immediately and arrange to meet in the doctor's office or the nearest emergency room.

If your baby has a fever, the pediatrician will check to see if there is an infection.

With a febrile convulsion, the doctor may simply advise you to control the fever using acetaminophen and sponging. However, if a bacterial infection is present, an antibiotic will probably be prescribed. If a serious infection such as meningitis (infection of the lining of the brain) is responsible for the seizure, your baby will have to be hospitalized for further treatment.

SINUSITIS

Sinusitis is an inflammation of one or more of the sinuses (bony cavities) around the nose. It usually occurs as a complication of a viral upper respiratory infection or allergic inflammation. These conditions cause swelling of the lining of the nose and sinuses. This swelling blocks the openings that normally allow the sinuses to drain into the back of the nose, so the sinuses fill with fluid. Since the sinuses can't drain properly, the bacteria will multiply there, causing an infection.

There are several signs of sinusitis that should alert you to call your pediatrician:

- The persistence of symptoms of a cold or upper respiratory infection, including cough and nasal discharge last-

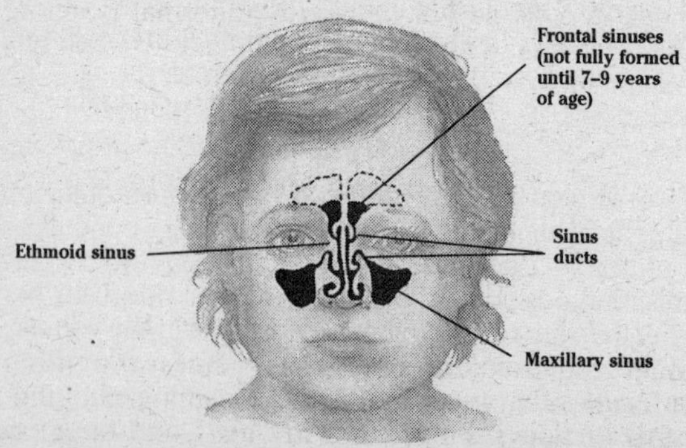

ing for more than ten days, without any improvement. The nasal discharge may be thick and yellow, clear, or whitish, and the cough usually will continue during the day as well as at night. In some cases a baby with sinusitis will have swelling around the eyes when he wakes up in the morning.

- Your baby's cold is severe and is accompanied by high fever and thick yellow nasal discharge.

Treatment

If your pediatrician thinks your baby has sinusitis, she will prescribe an antibiotic, usually for a fourteen-to-twenty-one-day period. Once your baby is on the medication, his symptoms should start to go away very quickly. In most cases the nasal discharge will clear and the cough will improve over a week or two. *But even though he may seem better, he must continue to take the antibiotics for the prescribed length of time.*

On the other hand, if there's no improvement after two to four days, your pediatrician might want to conduct some further tests, after which a different medication may be prescribed or an additional one added for a longer period of time.

Wryneck (Torticollis)

Wryneck is a condition that causes a baby to hold her head or neck in a twisted or otherwise abnormal position. She may lean her head toward one shoulder and, when lying on her stomach, always turn the same side of her face toward the mattress. This can cause her head to flatten on one side and her face to appear uneven or out of line. If not treated, wryneck may lead to permanent facial deformity or unevenness and to restricted head movement.

There are several different causes of wryneck. These include:

Congenital Muscular Torticollis. By far the most common cause of wryneck among babies is injury to the muscle that connects the breastbone, head, and neck (sterno-

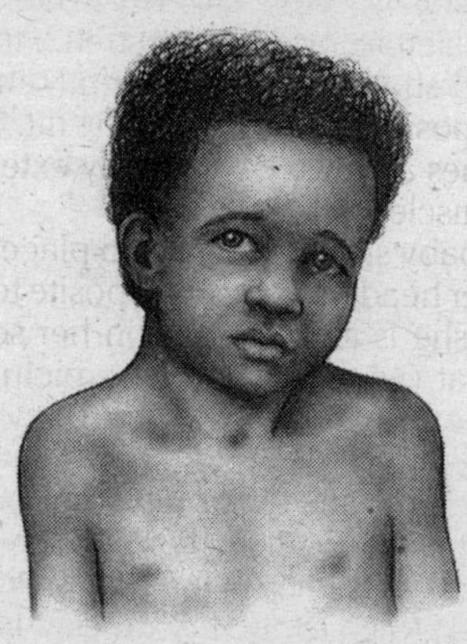

cleidomastoid muscle). The injury may occur during birth (particularly breech and difficult first-time deliveries), but it also can occur while the baby is still in the womb. Whatever the cause, this condition usually is detected in the first six to eight weeks of life when the pediatrician notices a small lump on the side of the baby's neck in the area of the damaged muscle. Later, the muscle contracts and causes the head to tilt to one side.

Klippel-Feil Syndrome. In this condition, which is present at birth, the tilt of the neck is caused by an abnormality of the bones at the top of the spine. Babies with Klippel-Feil syndrome may have a short, broad neck, low hairline, and very restricted neck movement.

Treatment

Each type of wryneck requires a slightly different treatment. It is very important to seek such treatment early, so that the problem is corrected before it causes permanent deformity.

Your pediatrician will examine your baby's neck and may order X rays of the area in order to identify the cause of the problem. X rays of the hip may also be ordered, as some infants with congenital muscular torticollis also have been found to have dislocation of the hip. If the doctor decides that the problem is muscular torticollis due to a birth-related injury to the sternocleidomastoid muscle, you will be instructed in an exercise program to stretch the neck muscles. The doctor will show you how to gently move your baby's head in the opposite direction from the tilt. You'll need to do this several times a day, very gradually extending the movement as the muscle stretches.

When your baby sleeps, it is best to place her on her back or side, with her head positioned opposite to the direction of the tilt. When she is awake, position her so that things she wants to look at (windows, mobiles, pictures, activity) are on the side away from the injury. In that way, she'll stretch the shortened muscle while trying to see these objects. These simple strategies cure this type of wryneck in the vast majority of cases, preventing the need for later surgery.

If the problem is not corrected by exercise or position change, your pediatrician will refer you to an orthopedic surgeon. In some cases it may be necessary to surgically remove the damaged section of muscle.

If your baby's wryneck is caused by something other than congenital muscular torticollis, and the Xrays show no spinal abnormality, other treatment involving rest, a special collar, traction, application of heat to the area, medication, or rarely even surgery may be necessary.

23

HEART

CONGENITAL HEART DISEASE

About 8 to 10 of every 1000 children are born with a congenital heart defect (a heart problem at birth). The defect can range from a structural abnormality of the heart's chambers, to a malfunctioning heart valve, to arteries or veins that are improperly connected or abnormally formed.

Most defects develop early in pregnancy, typically in the eighth to twelfth week of fetal development. About one-third of these babies have a heart disorder that is life-threatening, and surgery must be done within the first few days or weeks after birth if the patient is to survive.

The cause of nearly all congenital heart defects is never identified, although researchers are investigating possible roles of genetic and environmental factors. Parents should not blame themselves for their baby's heart condition; it is not caused by anything that the mother or father did or didn't do.

The two most common congenital heart defects are the following:

A *ventricular septal defect* is characterized by a hole in the septum (the wall or partition) between the two ventricles, or pumping chambers, of the heart. This allows blood to pass abnormally from the left side of the heart to the right side. The increased workload on the heart may lead to abnormal growth of the baby and breathing difficulties. In some instances, as the heart has to work harder, congestive heart failure can develop.

An *atrial septal defect* occurs when there is a hole in the septum between the atria (upper or receiving chambers) of the heart. Because the pressure in the atrial chambers is lower than in the ventricular chambers, this problem tends to cause less of a workload

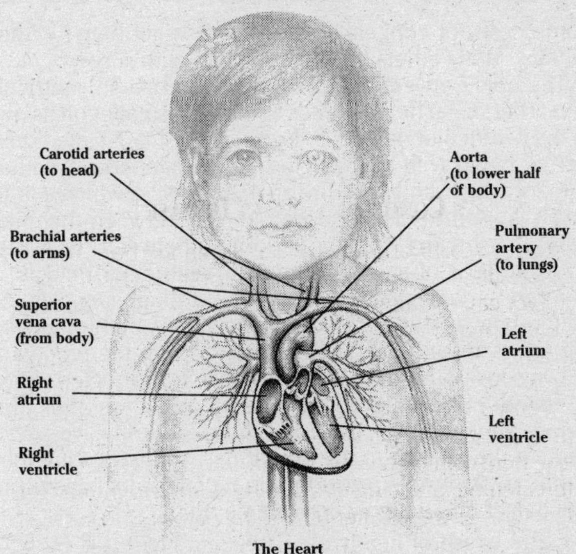

The Heart

upon the heart than ventricular septal defects. Many children with this condition have no symptoms and function well, particularly in the early years of life. A pediatrician may detect the problem, however, during a routine physical exam. Eventually, sometimes not until adulthood, those with atrial septal defects may experience symptoms such as irregular heart rhythms, and in some cases, heart failure.

There are other, less common types of congenital heart defects. One of them, called *transposition of the great arteries,* occurs when the two arteries coming out of the heart are reversed—that is, the aorta comes from the right ventricle instead of the left one; and the pulmonary artery comes from the left ventricle. Thus, oxygenated blood does not circulate properly through the body.

Transposition of the great arteries is the most common cause of cyanotic heart disease at birth, which gives the baby's skin a bluish hue (hence the term "blue baby"). It can usually be diagnosed immediately after birth because of the baby's blueness, and the diagnosis is confirmed by echocardiography (sound-wave imaging of the heart).

Treatment

Some cases of congenital heart disease get better without therapy. Many others can be corrected with surgery.

The hole between the pumping chambers in ventricular and atrial septal defects tends to become smaller on its own; in the ventricular defects, if the hole was small to medium in size to begin with, it may close up spontaneously without surgery. Larger holes require an operation, in which a fabric patch is used to close up the opening between the chambers. This surgery may be performed between six months and one year of age in those with ventricular defects. By contrast, atrial septal defects are most often surgically corrected between two and four years of age. Both operations are very safe, and most babies do well after the procedure.

Transposition of the great vessels can be corrected with an operation performed about three to four days after birth, before the child ever leaves the hospital. It involves reconnecting the arteries to the appropriate pumping chambers. Refinements in this procedure in recent years have turned this defect into a highly correctable one.

Prevention

Although there is no known way to prevent most congenital heart defects, a pregnant woman can help ensure the health of her baby by avoiding alcohol, cocaine, and other drugs, and by taking steps to avoid contracting rubella (German measles). If you have a family history of congenital heart disease—that is, if you or your spouse, or a previously born child has this condition—your doctor may monitor the fetus for possible heart problems.

Heart Murmur

Technically, a heart murmur is simply a noise heard between the beats of the heart. When a doctor listens to the heart, she hears a sound something like *lub-dub, lub-dub, lub-dub.* Most often, the period between the *lub* and the *dub,* and the *dub* and the *lub* is silent. If there is any sound during this period, it is called a "murmur." Although the word is unsettling, murmurs are *extremely* common, and usually normal, occurrences. Many times they are called "innocent murmurs," caused simply by the way blood is flowing through the heart.

However, heart murmurs that can be heard during the first six months of life usually are *not* innocent, and they require the attention of a pediatric cardiologist. Your infant will be observed for changes in skin color (turning blue) as well as breathing or feeding difficulties. He also may undergo additional tests, such as a chest X ray, ECG, and an echocardiogram. The echocardiogram creates a picture of the inside of the heart by using sound waves.

Kawasaki Disease

Kawasaki disease is a serious and perplexing disease, the cause of which is unknown. Some researchers believe, however, that it is caused by a virus or bacteria. Signs of this disease include:

- Fever, usually quite high, that lasts for at least five days and doesn't respond to treatment. This sign should be present to consider the disease in the acutely ill child.

In addition, four of the six following signs are present in the typical case:

- Rash over some or all of the body, often more severe in the diaper area, especially in infants under six months of age
- Redness and swelling of the palms and soles
- Red, swollen, and cracked lips and/or a strawberry tongue
- Red, inflamed eyes, especially the sclerae (white part)
- A swollen gland, particularly on one side of the neck
- Irritability or listlessness. Babies with Kawasaki disease are usually more cranky or more lethargic than usual. They may also complain of abdominal pain, headache, and/or joint pain.

Kawasaki disease causes inflammation of the blood vessels. In some cases this includes the arteries of the heart (the coronary arteries). This inflammation weakens the walls of the blood vessels. In most cases the blood vessels return to normal after several months, but in some cases they remain weakened and may even balloon out, causing aneurysms (blood-filled swellings of the blood vessels).

Kawasaki disease occurs most frequently in Japan and Korea and in individuals of Japanese and Korean ancestry, but it can be found among all racial groups and on every continent. In the United States alone, there are more than three thousand reported cases a year, typically among older infants and preschoolers.

Kawasaki disease does not appear to be contagious. It is extremely uncommon for two children in the same household to get the disease. Likewise, it does not spread in child-care centers, where there is daily close contact. Although Kawasaki disease can occur in community outbreaks, particularly in the winter and early spring, no one knows the cause. The peak age of occurrence in the United States is from six months to five years. There is evidence to suggest that Kawasaki disease may be linked to a yet-to-be-identified infectious agent, such as a virus or bacteria. However, despite intense research, no bacteria, virus, or toxin has been identified as a cause of the disease. No specific test makes the diagnosis. The diagnosis is established by fulfilling the signs of illness mentioned above and by excluding other possible diseases.

Treatment

Because the cause of Kawasaki disease is unknown, it can be treated but not prevented. If it is diagnosed early enough, large doses of intravenous gamma globulin (a mixture of human antibodies) can minimize the risk of a baby developing aneurysms. In addition to gamma globulin, the infant should receive aspirin, initially in high doses, then, after the fever is gone, in lower doses. Aspirin can decrease the tendency of blood to clot in damaged blood vessels. Although it's appropriate to use aspirin to treat Kawasaki disease, use of aspirin to treat minor illnesses (such as a cold or influenza) in children has been linked with a serious disease called Reye syndrome. Always consult your pediatrician before giving aspirin to your baby.

24

IMMUNIZATIONS

Routine immunizations are available to protect your child against ten major childhood diseases: polio, measles (page 574), mumps, German measles (rubella; page 567), chickenpox (page 562), whooping cough (pertussis; page 463), diphtheria, tetanus, haemophilus infections (meningitis; page 534, and epiglottitis, and hepatitis B (page 428). Any of these diseases can disable or kill, so your children should be immunized against them. Immunizations also are available against influenza, rabies, pneumococcus, and hepatitis A for special circumstances.

When your child is given a vaccine, he actually receives that part of the "weakened" or killed infectious organism that is able to stimulate his body to produce antibodies against it. These antibodies then protect him against the disease, should he ever come in contact with it. Except for the oral polio vaccine, all of the immunizations are injections.

Certain children may need protection against influenza virus (flu vaccine) or rabies virus (rabies vaccine). Pneumoccocal vaccine may be useful in children over age two years who have problems with their immune system. Your pediatrician will tell you if this is necessary.

> The American Academy of Pediatrics recommends the schedule of immunizations appearing on page 82. Please see that page for complete details.

Side Effects

Each of the vaccines has some potential side effects. These are listed below:

Diphtheria, Tetanus, and Pertussis (given together in a single vaccine). The side effects for the diphtheria and tetanus portions of the vaccine are similar: pain and swelling at the site of the injection and, on rare occasions, skin rash within twenty-four hours. The pertussis portion of the vaccine may cause heat, redness, and tenderness at the injection site in about half the children who receive it. It may also cause fever and irritability. Inflammation of the brain also has been known to occur following vaccination, although it is so rare (1 in 110,000 immunizations) that it is not definitely known whether it is caused by the vaccine or by some other substance or infection.

These side effects and complications must be weighed against the fact that the disease itself causes far more complications than the vaccine. There is a new type of pertussis vaccine that does not use the whole killed bacteria itself, but only part of it. This is called "acellular type" and is listed as DTaP. It is now approved for infants starting with the first dose (at two months) and is associated with far fewer reactions.

Polio. OPV, or oral polio vaccine, does not require injections. Even though OPV contains a weakened polio vaccine virus, it can on very rare occasions cause vaccine-associated paralytic polio (VAPP) in a baby with a compromised immune system. It may also cause VAPP in a person who is in close contact with a child who has received the oral vaccine, if that person has not been properly immunized (the virus will be present in the child's stool shortly after vaccination). The chances of this occurring are very rare, however. The all-OPV schedule may be recommended if your baby is allergic to the antibiotics neomycin or streptomycin, which are used in the production of IPV.

IPV, or inactivated polio vaccine, has not been shown to cause any major problems except mild soreness at the site of the injection. IPV does not cause VAPP. Your baby may need to get the all-IPV schedule if he, or anyone with whom he is in close contact, has a weakened immune system as the result of a disease such as cancer or AIDS. The IPV schedule may also be recommended for children who are receiving radiation or chemotherapy treatments or for those undergoing long-term steroid treatment for chronic illnesses.

By getting two doses of IPV followed by two doses of OPV (the combination schedule), your baby can get the benefits of both vaccines—excellent protection against polio with fewer injections; protection from epidemic polio; and less risk of contracting VAPP.

Chickenpox Vaccine. Adverse reactions from the chickenpox vaccine generally are mild and include redness, stiffness, soreness, and swelling where the shot was given; tiredness; fussiness; fever; and nausea. Also, a rash of a few small bumps or pimples may develop at the spot where the shot was given or, infrequently, on other parts of the body. This can occur up to one month after immunization and can last for several days.

Measles, Mumps, and Rubella. These vaccines usually are given together in one injection. The measles part of the vaccine sometimes causes a mild rash and fever five to twelve days after it is given. Very rarely, children will have slight swelling over the jaw, as if they had mild mumps from the mumps vaccine. The rubella part of the vaccine sometimes causes joint pains and swelling or, very rarely, an inflammation of the nerves of the arms or legs.

Haemophilus Influenza Type B (Hib) Vaccine. Your baby might be sore, red, or swollen around the site of the injection. This occurs in a very small number of cases (one out of every sixty-seven). Mild fever may develop.

Influenza. The newer vaccines have few side effects except for one or two days of soreness at the injection site; febrile reactions are infrequent.

Rabies. The new vaccines have few or no side effects in children.

Treatment for Side Effects

Before immunizing your baby, your pediatrician should review with you what reactions you can expect and how to treat them. Generally, fever is managed with acetaminophen. For local reactions your pediatrician may recommend that you apply cool compresses for symptomatic relief.

If your baby has any reaction that makes him uncomfortable for more than four hours, notify your pediatrician, who will want to note it in your baby's records and prescribe appropriate treatment.

Children Who Should Not Receive Certain Vaccines

These vaccines do not cause serious reactions in most children. However, there are cases where they should not be given.

Diphtheria and Tetanus. If your baby has had a serious reaction (petechial rash, hives, or anaphylaxis) to a previous dose of these vaccines, he should not receive another one. Fever of 105 degrees Fahrenheit (40.5 degrees Celsius) or greater, and fainting or collapse due to a previous dose, require careful consideration before administering additional doses of vaccine containing these components.

Pertussis. If your baby has had a seizure *before* getting the pertussis vaccine, your pediatrician may delay giving the aP or P part of the DTP until the cause of the seizure is known, and at least six months have gone by without the occurrence of another seizure. If your baby had a serious reaction to a previous dose of pertussis vaccine, careful consideration to future doses of the P or aP part may be given and Pediatric D-T will be substituted. Serious reactions include high fever (105 degrees Fahrenheit [40.5 degrees Celsius] or greater), seizures, prolonged high-pitched and peculiar crying or screaming, or collapse. Severe reactions (contraindications) that should alert you and your pediatrician not to give any more doses of DTaP or DTP and substitute Pediatric D-T are allergic reactions and/or otherwise unexplained inflammation of the brain within seven days of the injection.

Chickenpox Vaccine. Although the chickenpox vaccine is approved for use in otherwise healthy children, there are certain groups of people, such as children with a weakened immune system or pregnant women, who should not receive it. Talk to your pediatrician about whether your baby falls into any of the high-risk categories and should not be vaccinated against chickenpox.

Measles, Mumps. Because these vaccines contain a small amount of egg protein, there are differing opinions about whether or not your healthy child should receive these vaccines, if he is highly allergic to eggs. However, your pediatrician may want to consult with an allergist or immunologist, who will advise you and your child's doctor before a decision is made concerning the use of the vaccine. Two doses prior to adolescence (age eleven to twelve years) are recommended.

Rubella. All healthy children not severely allergic to neomycin should be given this vaccine twice before adolescence. It should not be given to a pregnant woman but may be given to her other children without endangering her pregnancy.

Rabies. There are no reasons not to give the rabies vaccine when it is needed.

Influenza. Flu vaccines are prepared from egg protein, so babies who are allergic to eggs should not receive them.

Hib Vaccine. There are no reasons for withholding this vaccine unless your baby has a sensitivity to one or more of its ingredients. Your pediatrician will help you determine this.

Live Virus Vaccines (polio, measles, mumps, rubella, and varicella). No live virus vaccine should be given to an immunodeficient or immunosuppressed baby. Because measles disease is more dangerous to an HIV-infected infant than is measles vaccine, such children may receive MMR (but not oral polio or varicella vaccines). Babies who cannot receive oral polio vaccine can be safely vaccinated with inactivated polio vaccine (IPV).

Personal Immunization Chart

Keep a record of your baby's immunization by filling in this chart. Fill in the date each time your infant is immunized. If you need more of these records, contact the American Academy of Pediatrics, 141 Northwest Point Boulevard, P.O. Box 927, Elk Grove Village, Illinois 60009–0927.

	DTaP or DTP	*Polio*	*MMR*	*Hepatitis B*	*Hib*	*Tetanus-Diphtheria*	*Chickenpox*
Birth							
1–2 months							
2 months							
4 months							
6 months							
6–18 months							
12–15 months							
15 months							
15–18 months							
4–6 years							
11–12 years							
14–16 years							

25

Musculoskeletal Problems

Bowlegs

If your baby's legs seem to curve outward at the knees, there's probably no reason for concern. Look around, and you'll see that few young children have truly straight legs. In fact, many children between the ages of one and two appear quite bowlegged. Their legs may not look straight until the age of nine or ten.

Bowlegs usually are just variations of normal, and they require no treatment. Ordinarily the legs straighten out and look perfectly normal by adolescence. Bracing, corrective shoes, and exercise are not helpful and, in fact, can hinder a child's physical development and cause emotional difficulty.

Rarely, bowlegs are the result of a disease. Arthritis, injury to the growth plate around the knee, infection, tumor, and rickets all can cause changes in the curvature of the legs. Here are some signs that suggest a child's bowlegs may be caused by a serious problem:

- The curvature is extreme.
- Only one side is affected.
- Your baby is also unusually short for his age.

If your baby's condition fits any of these descriptions, you should talk to your pediatrician, who can determine the exact cause and prescribe the necessary treatment. In some cases, the pediatrician will refer you to a pediatric orthopedist for consultation and possible corrective surgery.

Elbow Injuries

Pulled elbow (also known as "nursemaid's elbow") is a common, painful injury among children under four

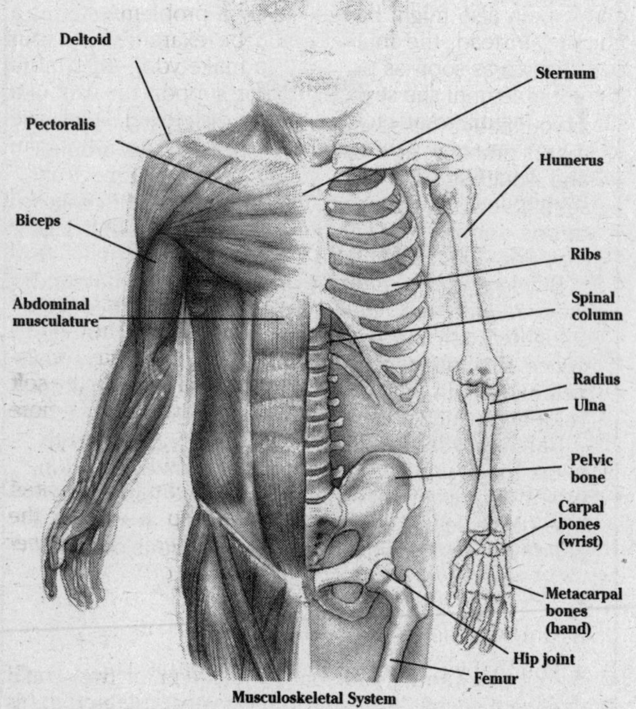

Musculoskeletal System

years old. It occurs when nearby soft tissue slips into the elbow joint and is trapped there. This can happen because your child's elbow joint is loose enough to separate slightly when her arm is pulled to full length (when she's being lifted, yanked, or swung by the hand or wrist, or if she falls on her outstretched arm). The nearby tissue slides into the space created by the stretching and is trapped there when the joint returns to its normal position.

Nursemaid's elbow usually doesn't cause swelling, but your child will complain that it hurts. She probably will hold her arm close to her side, with her elbow slightly bent and her palm turned toward her body. If you try to straighten the elbow or turn her palm upward, she will resist because of the pain.

Treatment. Don't try to treat this injury yourself, because elbow pain also might be caused by a problem such as a fracture. Instead, the injury should be examined by your pediatrician as soon as possible. To make your child more comfortable until she sees the doctor, support the arm in a sling made from a soft cloth, such as a dish towel. Don't give her food, water, or pain medication unless your physician advises you to do so.

The doctor will check the injured area for swelling and tenderness, and any limitation of motion. If an injury other than nursemaid's elbow is suspected, X rays will be taken. If no fracture is noted, the doctor will gently manipulate the joint to release the trapped tissue. While this procedure causes some pain as it's being done, your child should feel relief almost immediately afterward. The doctor may recommend the use of a sling for two or three days while the soft tissue heals, particularly if several hours have passed before the injury is successfully treated.

Prevention. Nursemaid's elbow usually can be prevented by lifting your young child properly. Grasp her under the arms or around her body. *Do not pull or lift her by holding her hands or wrists, and never swing her by the arms.*

Flatfeet

At some point during your baby's first year or two, you'll probably notice that he seems to have very little arch to his feet. This flat-footedness, which may persist well into later childhood, occurs because children's bones and joints are very flexible, causing their feet to flatten when they stand. Also, young babies have a fat pad on the inner border of their feet that hides the arches. You can still see the arch if you lift your baby up on his toes, but it disappears when he comes down on his heels. Often the foot also turns out, increasing the weight on the inner side and making it appear even more flat.

This natural flat-footedness usually disappears by age six as the feet become less flexible and the arches develop. Only

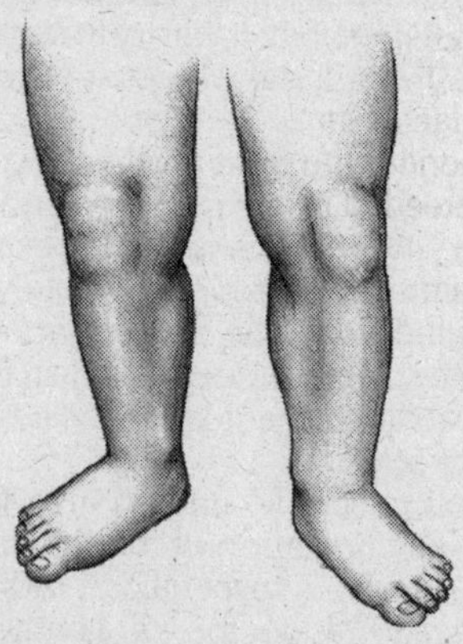

about one or two out of every ten children will continue to have this kind of flat-footedness into adulthood. Even for these youngsters, however, as long as the feet remain flexible, there's no cause for concern and no need for treatment. In fact, all the special shoes, inserts, and exercises that are promoted and sold only cause more problems than the flatfeet themselves, and will *not* develop an arch in your child's foot.

There are other forms of flat-footedness that may need to be treated differently. For instance, a baby may have tightness of the heel cord (Achilles tendon) that limits the motion of his foot. This tightness can result in a flatfoot, but it usually can be treated with special stretching exercises to lengthen the heel cord.

PIGEON TOES (INTOEING)

If your baby's feet turn inward, he is said to be pigeon-toed, or have in-toeing. It's a very common problem that may involve one or both feet, and occurs for a variety of reasons.

In-toeing usually is due to a turning in of the front part of the foot (the forefoot), and is called *metatarsis adductus* (see Figure 1). It may be due to the baby's position in the uterus or other causes.

You can be suspicious if:

- When you look at the foot from the bottom while the infant is resting, you see that the front portion turns inward.
- The outer side of your baby's foot (opposite his big toe) is curved like a half-moon.

Usually this condition is mild and will resolve before the baby's first birthday. Sometimes it is more severe, or is accompanied by other foot deformities that result in a problem called "clubfoot." This condition requires a consultation with a pediatric orthopedist and early casting or splinting.

Treatment

Some experts feel no treatment is necessary for in-toeing in an infant under six months of age. For severe *metatarsis adductus* in infancy, brief, early casting is appropriate. In cases where there are different opinions, it is best to follow the advice of your own pediatrician. It does appear that the majority of infants who have in-toeing in early infancy will outgrow it with no treatment.

If your baby's in-toeing persists after six months, or if it is rigid and difficult to straighten out, your doctor may recommend a series of casts applied over a period of three to six weeks. The pediatrician will also refer you to a pediatric orthopedist. The main goal is to correct the condition before your infant starts walking.

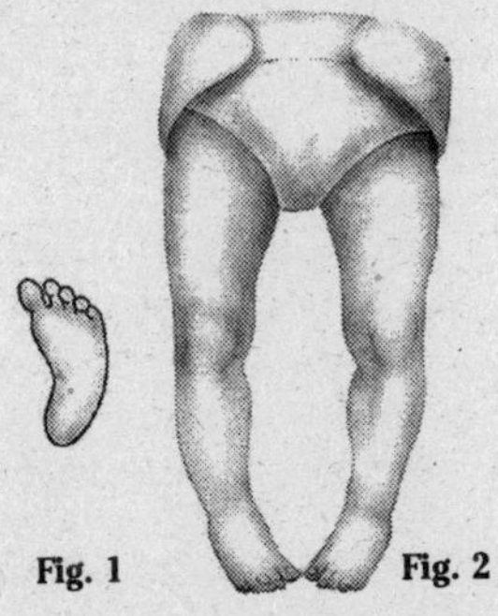

Fig. 1 Fig. 2

Because in-toeing so often corrects itself over time, it is very important *not* to use nonprescribed "treatments" such as corrective shoes, twister cables, daytime bracing, exercises, shoe inserts, and back manipulations. These do not correct the problem and are, in fact, harmful because they interfere with normal play or walking, and may even cause additional deformity.

26

SKIN

BIRTHMARKS AND HEMANGIOMAS

Dark-Pigmented Birthmarks (Nevi or Moles)

Nevi, or moles, are either congenital (present at birth) or acquired. They are composed of so-called nevus cells, similar to those that give dark pigment to the skin, so these spots are dark brown or black.

Congenital Nevi. Small nevi present at birth are relatively common, occurring in one of every hundred Caucasian children. They tend to grow with the baby and usually don't cause any problems. Rarely, however, these moles may develop into a type of serious skin cancer (melanoma) at some later time, usually during or after adolescence. Therefore, while you don't have to *worry* about them right away, it's a good idea to watch them carefully and have them checked by your pediatrician at regular intervals or if there is any change in appearance (color, size, or shape). She may refer you to a pediatric dermatologist who will advise you on removal and any follow-up care.

But there's also a much more serious type of nevus—a large congenital one that varies in size from as small as a half-dollar to as large as this book. It might be flat or raised, may have hair growing from it (though hair can also be seen in small, insignificant nevi), and can be so large that it covers an arm or a leg. Fortunately, these are very rare (occurring in one of every twenty thousand births). However, they are much more likely than the smaller ones to develop into a melanoma, so early consultation with a pediatric dermatologist is advisable.

Acquired Nevi, or Moles. Most Caucasian people develop ten to thirty pigmented nevi, or moles, throughout the course of their lives. They usually occur after the age of five, but sometimes develop earlier. These *acquired* moles are seldom a cause for worry. However, if your baby develops one that's larger than a pencil eraser, is an irregular shape, or has multiple colors within its structure, your pediatrician should examine it.

Blood Vessel Birthmarks on the Skin (Hemangiomas)

Your young infant has a red raised bump growing rapidly on his forehead, and a flat, dark red patch on one arm. They're quite unsightly, but are they harmful?

Hemangiomas are birthmarks that occur when a certain area of the skin develops an abnormal blood supply during early childhood. This, in turn, causes the tissue to enlarge over the course of several weeks or months and become reddish-blue. When the condition involves only the capillaries (the smallest blood vessels), the birthmark is called a "strawberry hemangioma." When the blood vessels are larger, the hemangioma may be of a different type and have a different appearance.

Flat Angiomata (Stork Bites). These most common blemishes on the skin usually appear on the eyelids or back of the neck. They usually disappear over the first months of life and are not serious.

Hemangiomas. Strawberry hemangiomas (sometimes called "strawberry patches"), another common form of this condition, are found in at least two of every hundred babies born. Although they frequently are not noticeable at birth, they appear within the first month of life as a red raised dot. They can occur on any area of the body, but are most commonly seen on the head, neck, and trunk. Usually, a baby has just a single strawberry hemangioma, but occasionally these marks will be scattered over several parts of the body.

If your infant develops a strawberry hemangioma, have your pediatrician examine it so he can follow its course from the start. During the first six months of life strawberry hemangiomas usually grow very rapidly, which can be quite alarming. But they soon stop enlarging, and almost always disappear by the time the child is nine years old.

Quite often, the large reddish-purplish appearance of these birthmarks so upsets parents that they want to have them removed immediately. However, since the vast majority will gradually reduce in size over the second to third year of life, it's generally best to leave them alone. Studies have shown that when this type of hemangioma is left untreated, there are few complications or cosmetic problems. By contrast, those that are treated either with medication or surgery have a far greater chance of complications or unwanted changes in appearance.

At times, strawberry hemangiomas may need to be treated or removed—namely, when they occur close to vital structures, such as the eye, throat, or mouth; when they seem to be growing much faster than usual; or when they are likely to bleed profusely or become infected. Such uncommon conditions will require careful evaluation and management by your pediatrician and pediatric dermatologist.

Very rarely, hemangiomas are found in large numbers on the face and upper trunk. On such occasions, hemangiomas also may be present on organs inside the body. If this is suspected, your pediatrician may need to conduct further tests.

Port Wine Stains. Port wine stains are flat malformations of small blood vessels, usually present at birth, which enlarge as the baby grows. They are dark red and often found on the face or limbs (usually only on one side of the body). Unlike the hemangiomas, these port wine stains don't go away, although they sometimes fade. Even so, they rarely cause any problems. On occasion, however, if they are found on the upper eyelid and/or forehead, there is a chance of a related problem in the underlying brain structures (Sturge-Weber syndrome). Or, if the birthmark is present immediately around the eye, there is a possibility that glaucoma (see page 498) may develop in that eye.

Port wine stains should be examined from time to time to evaluate their size, location, and appearance. If an older child becomes very unhappy with this birthmark, a special covering makeup can be used. Laser treatment has been successful in many cases, but other types of surgery are rarely recommended. (See also *How Your Newborn Looks*, page 143.)

CHICKENPOX

Chickenpox is one of the most common childhood illnesses. This highly contagious infection causes an itchy, blisterlike rash that can cover most of the body. Children often get a mild fever along with the rash.

After your baby is exposed to the virus that causes chickenpox, it can take ten to twenty-one days for the rash to appear. Small blisters, which may have a red area around them, will begin to appear on the body and scalp, then spread to the face and to the arms and legs. Normally, the blisters will crust over and then heal, but tiny sores and possibly small scars may develop if your baby scratches them and they become infected. There also may be minor darkening of the skin around some of the blisters, but this will gradually disappear after the rash is gone.

Treatment

From your own childhood, you may remember just how itchy chickenpox can be. You should try to discourage your baby from scratching, because that can cause additional infection. Acetaminophen (in the appropriate dose for your infant's age and weight) may decrease the discomfort and also reduce any fever she has. Trimming her fingernails and bathing her daily with soap and water can also help prevent secondary bacterial infection. Oatmeal baths, available without prescription from your pharmacy, will ease the itch. A prescription medicine (acyclovir) also decreases the severity of the symptoms if started within twenty-four hours of the onset of the disease. The medicine, while not needed by everyone, is especially valuable for babies with eczema (a skin disorder).

Do not give your baby aspirin or any medication that contains aspirin or salicylates when she has chickenpox. These products increase the risk of Reye syndrome, a serious illness that involves the liver and brain. If you are not sure about what medications you can safely use at this time, ask your pediatrician for advice.

Incidentally, the doctor probably won't need to see your baby unless her temperature rises above 102 degrees Fahrenheit (38.9 degrees Celsius) or lasts longer than four days. But let the pediatrician know if areas of the rash become very red, warm, or tender; this may indicate a bacterial infection requiring antibiotics and a special oral anti-itch medication. And be sure to call your pediatrician *immediately* if your baby develops any of these signs: vomiting, nervousness, confusion, convulsions, lack of responsiveness, increasing sleepiness, or poor balance.

Babies may be contagious one to two days before the rash starts, and for twenty-four hours after the last new blister appears (usually five to seven days). Only individuals who have never had chickenpox are susceptible, however, so if your baby has playmates who already have had the infection, and she is feeling well, she can play with them even while the rash is active. But keep her away from youngsters who have never had the disease or who aren't sure that they've had it. After she's recovered from the chickenpox, your child will be immune to it for the rest of her life.

Prevention

A vaccine to protect against chickenpox is recommended for all healthy children between twelve and eighteen months of age who have never had the disease. Until your baby has received the vaccine at one year of age, the only sure way to protect her is to avoid exposure. Protection from exposure is important for newborn infants, especially premature babies, in whom the disease can be more severe. Most infants whose mothers have had chickenpox may be immune to the disease for the first few months of life.

Cradle Cap and Seborrheic Dermatitis

Your beautiful one-month-old baby has developed scaliness and redness on his scalp. You're concerned and think maybe you shouldn't shampoo as usual. You also notice some redness in the creases of his neck and armpits, and behind his ears. What is it and what should you do?

When this rash occurs on the scalp alone, it's known as cradle cap. But although it may start as scaling and redness of the scalp, it also can be found later in the other areas mentioned above. It can extend to the face and diaper area, too, and when it does, pediatricians call it seborrheic dermatitis (because it occurs where there are the greatest number of oil-producing sebaceous glands). Seborrheic dermatitis is a noninfectious skin condition and is a form of eczema that's very common in infants, usually beginning in the first weeks of life and slowly disappearing over a period of weeks or months. Unlike atopic or contact eczema (see page 565), it's rarely uncomfortable or itchy.

What's the exact cause of this rash? No one knows for sure. However, it certainly is influenced by the hormonal changes of pregnancy, which stimulate the oil glands. This overproduction of oil may have some relationship to the scales and redness of the skin.

Treatment

If your baby's seborrheic dermatitis is confined to his scalp (and is, therefore, just cradle cap), you can treat it yourself. Don't be afraid to shampoo the hair; in fact, you should wash it (with a mild baby shampoo) more frequently than before. This, along with soft brushing, will help remove the scales.

As for baby oil, it's not very helpful or necessary. Many parents tend to use the unperfumed baby oil or mineral oil and do nothing else. But this allows scales to build up on the scalp, particularly over the rear soft spot, or fontanelle. If you decide to use oil, use only a little, rub it into the scales, and then shampoo and brush it out. Stronger medicated shampoos (antiseborrhea shampoos containing sulfur and 2 percent salicylic acid) may loosen the scales more quickly, but since they also can be irritating, use them only after consulting your pediatrician. The doctor also may prescribe some additional medication to treat the scales and redness.

If frequent shampooing doesn't improve the cradle cap, or if the rash spreads to your baby's face, neck, and crease areas, call your pediatrician, who will probably suggest a stronger, scale-dissolving shampoo and might also prescribe a cortisone cream or lotion. One-percent hydrocortisone cream is a commonly used preparation.

Once the condition has improved, how can you prevent it from recurring? In most cases, just by frequent hair washing with a mild baby shampoo. Occasionally, a stronger medicated shampoo may be needed, but let your pediatrician make the decision. Also, after the child's first birthday, the condition will not come back until puberty.

Sometimes, yeast infections will become superimposed on the affected skin, most likely in the crease areas rather than on the scalp. If this occurs, the area will become extremely reddened and quite itchy. In this case, your pediatrician might prescribe some specific antiyeast cream containing the medicine nystatin. If this is necessary, apply a small amount to the area three or four times a day, and rub it in well.

Rest assured that seborrheic dermatitis is not a serious infection. Nor is it an allergy to something you're using, or due to poor hygiene. It will go away without any scars and your baby will be beautiful again!

ECZEMA

Eczema is a general term used to describe a number of different skin conditions. It usually appears as reddened skin that becomes moist and oozing, occasionally resulting in small, fluid-filled bumps. When eczema becomes chronic (persists for a long time), the skin tends to thicken, dry out, and become scaly with coarse lines.

There are two main types of eczema: atopic dermatitis and contact dermatitis.

Atopic Dermatitis

Atopic dermatitis often occurs in infants who have allergies or a family history of allergy or eczema, although the problem is not necessarily caused by an allergy. Atopic dermatitis usually first occurs between two and six months of age, with itching, redness, and the appearance of small bumps on the cheeks, forehead, or scalp. This rash may then spread to the arms or trunk. Although atopic dermatitis is often confused with other types of dermatitis, especially seborrheic dermatitis, severe itching and the absence of previous allergy are clues that this is the problem. In many cases the rash disappears or improves by two or three years of age.

Contact Dermatitis

Contact dermatitis occurs when the skin comes in contact with an irritating substance. One form of this problem results from repeated contact with irritating substances such as citrus juices, bubble baths, strong soaps, certain foods and medicines, and woolen or rough-weave fabrics. In addition, one of the most common irritants is the infant's own saliva. Contact dermatitis doesn't itch as much as atopic dermatitis and usually will clear when the irritant is no longer present.

Another form of contact dermatitis develops after skin contact with substances to which the baby is allergic. The most common of these are:

- Glues and dyes used in the manufacture of shoes (They produce a reaction on the tops of the toes and feet.)
- Dyes used in clothing (These cause rashes in areas where the clothing rubs or where there is increased perspiration.)
- Nickel jewelry or snaps on jeans or pants
- Plants (especially poison ivy, poison oak, and poison sumac see page 570)
- Medications such as neomycin ointment

This rash usually appears within several hours after contact (one to three days with poison ivy). It is somewhat itchy, and may even have small blisters.

Treatment

If your baby appears to have a rash that looks like eczema, your pediatrician will need to examine it to make the correct diagnosis and prescribe the proper treatment. In some cases, she may arrange for a pediatric dermatologist to examine it.

Although there is no cure for atopic dermatitis, it generally can be controlled and often will go away after several months or years. The most effective treatment is to prevent the skin's becoming dry and itchy. To do this:

- Avoid frequent long, hot baths, which tend to dry the skin.
- Use skin moisturizers (e.g., creams or ointments) regularly and frequently to decrease the dryness and itchiness.

- Avoid harsh or irritating clothing (wool or coarse-weave material).
- If there is oozing or exceptional itching, use tepid (lukewarm) compresses on the area, followed by the application of prescribed medications.

Your pediatrician usually will suggest a medicated cream or ointment to control inflammation and itching. These preparations often contain a form of cortisone, and should be used only under the direction of your doctor. In addition, other lotions or bath oils might be prescribed. It's important to continue to apply the medications for as long as your pediatrician directs. Stopping too soon will cause the condition to recur.

In addition to the skin preparations, your child also may need to take an antihistamine to control the itching, and antibiotics if the skin becomes infected.

The treatment of allergic contact dermatitis is similar, although your pediatric dermatologist or allergist also will want to find the cause of the rash by taking a careful history or by conducting a series of patch tests. These tests are done by placing a small patch of a common irritant (allergen) against your baby's skin. If the skin reacts with redness and itching, that substance should be avoided.

Alert your pediatrician if any of the following occurs:

- Your baby's rash is severe and is not responding to home treatment.
- There is any evidence of fever or infection (such as blisters, redness, yellow crusts, pain, or oozing of fluid).
- The rash spreads or another rash develops.

German Measles (Rubella)

Rubella, or German measles, is a relatively uncommon disease today, thanks to the availability of an effective vaccine against the virus that causes it. However, babies can be born with a form of rubella, which occurs when rubella infects an unvaccinated, susceptible woman in the first three months of her pregnancy. In these cases, rubella can cause severe, irreversible damage (congenital rubella) to the unborn fetus. Babies born with congenital rubella may have eye disorders (cataracts, glaucoma, small eyes), heart problems, deafness, severe mental retardation, and other evidence of central nervous system damage.

Before the rubella vaccine was developed, German measles tended to occur in epidemics every six to nine years among children and adults, with symptoms such as a fever (100–102 degrees Fahrenheit [37.8–38.9 degrees Celsius]), swollen glands (typically on the back of the neck and the base of the skull), and a rash. Since the vaccine was introduced in 1968, however, there have been no significant epidemics. Today, with the routine use of two doses of the MMR (measles, mumps, rubella) vaccine, the number of cases of rubella has decreased to record low levels.

What You Can Do

If your child is diagnosed as having the congenital form of rubella, your pediatrician can advise you on the best way to manage his complex and difficult problems. Infants born with congenital rubella are often infectious for a year after birth, and therefore should be kept out of any group child-care setting, where they could expose other susceptible children or adults to the infection.

Prevention

Prevention of congenital rubella through maternal immunization is the best approach. Vaccination should be considered in all girls and women who have not previously received two doses of the MMR (measles, mumps, rubella) vaccine, and are known not to be pregnant or anticipating becoming pregnant within three months. A susceptible pregnant woman should never be immunized; she also should be extremely careful to avoid contact with any child or adult who may be infected with the virus.

Hair Loss

Almost all newborns lose some or all of their hair. This is *not* abnormal; in fact, it is to be expected. The baby hair falls out before the mature hair comes in. Thus, hair loss occurring during the first six months is *not* a cause for concern.

Very commonly, a baby will lose her hair by rubbing her scalp against the mattress. As she starts to move more and sit up, this type of hair loss will correct itself.

In very rare cases, babies may be born with alopecia (baldness), which can occur by itself or in association with certain abnormalities of the nails and the teeth. Because alopecia can be a sign of other medical or nutritional problems, hair loss should be brought to your pediatrician's attention whenever it occurs after six months of age. The pediatrician will look at your child's scalp, determine the cause, and prescribe treatment. Sometimes referral to a pediatric dermatologist is necessary.

HIVES

If your baby has an itchy rash that consists of raised red bumpy areas with pale centers, and no scales or dry skin over the lesions, he probably has hives (welts). This allergic reaction may be all over the body or just in one region, such as the face. The location may change, with the hives disappearing in one area of the body and appearing in another, often in a matter of hours.

Among the most common causes of hives are allergies to:

- Foods (berries, cheese, nuts, eggs, milk, sesame oils, shellfish)
- Drugs, either over-the-counter or prescribed (Penicillin and aspirin are two frequent culprits.)
- Pollen from trees, grass, ferns
- Plants
- Response to infection (so-called infectious hives)
- Cold water
- Bites or stings from bees or other insects

Most often, it is difficult to pinpoint the cause.

Treatment

An antihistamine will relieve the itching of hives. Many of them can be obtained without a prescription, but you should ask your doctor to recommend one. You may need to use this type of medication for one to three days, and give it as often as every four to six hours. Applying cool compresses to the area of itching and swelling also may help.

Still other treatments may be necessary if internal parts of the body are involved in the allergic reaction as well. If your baby is wheezing or having trouble swallowing, emergency treatment should be sought. The doctor usually will prescribe a more effective antihistamine, and may even give an injection of Adrenalin to stop the allergic response. If the allergy causing the hives also results in severe breathing difficulties, your pediatrician will help you obtain a special emergency-care kit for possible use with such reactions in the future.

Prevention

In order to prevent subsequent outbreaks of hives, your doctor will try to determine what is causing the allergic reaction. If the rash is confined to a small area of skin, it probably was caused by something your baby touched (plants and soaps are frequent culprits). But if it spreads all over her body, something she ate or inhaled is most likely to blame.

Frequently, there's a pattern to the appearance of the hives that provides a clue to the allergy. For example, does it usually happen after meals? Does it seem to occur more during certain seasons, or when traveling to particular places? If you discover a specific pattern, alter the routine to see if your baby improves. You will need to consider every food your baby eats, even those that she has eaten without difficulty in the past. Sometimes, hives will occur if your baby eats an unusually large amount of a food to which she is only mildly allergic.

Once you've discovered the cause of the problem, try keeping your baby away from it as much as possible. If you know in advance that she will or may be exposed, send or bring along an antihistamine. If her allergy is to insects, keep a bee-sting kit available. (See *Insect Bites and Stings*, below.)

Insect Bites and Stings

Your baby's reaction to a bite or sting will depend on her sensitivity to the particular insect's venom. While most babies have only mild reactions, those who are allergic to certain insect venoms can have severe symptoms that require emergency treatment.

Treatment

Although insect bites can be irritating, they usually begin to disappear by the next day and do not require treatment by a doctor. To relieve the itchiness that accompanies bites by mosquitos, flies, fleas, and bedbugs, apply ice to the area or calamine lotion freely onto any part of your baby's body except the areas around her eyes and genitals. If your baby is stung by a wasp or bee, soak a cloth in cold water and press it over the area of the sting to reduce pain and swelling. Call your pediatrician before using any other treatment, including creams or lotions containing antihistamines or home remedies such as baking soda, meat tenderizer, tobacco juice, ammonia, or vinegar. If the itching is severe, the doctor may prescribe cortisone ointment or oral antihistamines.

If your baby disturbs a bee nest, get her away from the nest as quickly as possible. An alarm pheromone is emitted at the base of a honey bee's sting, which other bees detect, making them more likely to sting your baby.

It is very important to remove a bee stinger quickly and completely from the skin. The quick removal of a bee stinger will prevent a large amount of venom from being pumped into the skin. If the stinger is visible, remove it by gently scraping it off horizontally with a credit card or your fingernail. You can also remove a bee stinger by pinching it out with a pair of tweezers or your fingers. Bee stings and mosquito bites may be more swollen on the second or third day after the incident.

Keep your baby's fingernails short and clean to minimize the risk of infection from scratching. If infection does occur anyway, the bite will become redder, larger, and more swollen. In some cases you may notice red streaks or yellowish fluid near the bite. Have your pediatrician examine any infected bite, because it may need to be treated with antibiotics.

Call for medical help immediately if your baby has any of these other symptoms after being bitten or stung:

Insect/Environment	*Characteristics of Bite or Sting*	*Special Notes*
Mosquitoes Water (pools, lakes, birdbaths)	Stinging sensation followed by small, red, itchy mound with a tiny puncture mark at center.	Mosquitoes are attracted by bright colors, sweat, and sweet odors such as perfumes, scented soaps, and shampoos.
Flies Food, garbage, animal waste	Painful, itchy bumps. May turn into small blisters.	Bites often disappear in a day but may last longer.
Fleas Cracks in floor, rugs, pet fur	Small bump that looks like a hive. Often in groups where clothes fit tightly (waist, buttocks).	Fleas are most likely to be a problem in homes with pets.
Bedbugs Cracks of walls, floors, crevices of furniture, bedding	Itchy red bumps surrounded by a blister. Usually two or three in a row.	Bedbugs are most likely to bite at night and are less active in cold weather.
Fire ants Mounds in pastures, meadows, lawns, and parks	Immediate pain and burning. Swelling up to one-half inch. Cloudy fluid in area of bite.	Fire ants usually attack intruders. Some children have reactions such as difficulty in breathing, fever, and stomach upset.
Bees and wasps Flowers, shrubs, picnic areas, beaches	Immediate pain and rapid swelling.	A few babies have severe reactions such as difficulty in breathing and swelling all over the body.

Insect/Environment	*Characteristics of Bite or Sting*	*Special Notes*
Ticks Wooded areas	May not be noticeable. Hidden in hair or on skin.	Don't remove ticks with matches, lighted cigarettes, or nail polish remover. Grasp the tick firmly with tweezers near the head. Gently remove the tick; don't leave any parts of it embedded in the skin.

- Sudden difficulty in breathing
- Weakness, collapse, or unconsciousness
- Hives or itching all over the body
- Extreme swelling near the eye, lips, or penis that makes it difficult for the baby to see, eat, or urinate.

Prevention

Some babies with no other known allergies may have severe reactions to insect bites and stings as well. If you suspect that your baby is allergy-prone, discuss the situation with your doctor. He may recommend a series of hyposensitization injections. In addition, he will prescribe a special kit for you to keep on hand for use if your child is stung.

It is impossible to prevent *all* insect bites, but you can minimize the number your baby receives by following these guidelines:

- Avoid areas where insects nest or congregate, such as garbage cans, stagnant pools of water, uncovered foods and sweets, and orchards and gardens where flowers are in bloom.
- When you know your baby will be exposed to insects, dress her in long pants and a lightweight long-sleeved shirt.

- Avoid dressing your baby in clothing with bright colors or flowery prints, because they seem to attract insects.
- Don't use scented soaps, perfumes, or hair sprays on your baby, because they also are inviting to insects.

Insect repellents are generally available without a prescription, but they should be used sparingly on infants. The most effective insecticides include DEET (diethyltoluamide). Repellents appropriate for use on infants should contain *no more than 10 percent DEET* because the chemical, which is absorbed through the skin, can cause harm. The concentration of DEET varies significantly from product to product, so read the label of any product you purchase. Repellents are effective in preventing bites by mosquitoes, ticks, fleas, chiggers, and biting flies, but have virtually no effect on stinging insects such as bees, hornets, and wasps. Contrary to popular belief, giving antihistamines continuously throughout the insect season does not appear to prevent reactions to bites.

The table on pages 572–573 summarizes information about common stinging or biting insects.

MEASLES

Thanks to measles vaccine, this disease is relatively uncommon in America today. In 1996, only about three hundred cases occurred in the United States. However, people still get measles. The measles virus is passed through the air droplets transmitted by an infected person. Anyone who breathes the droplets and is not immune to the disease can become infected.

Signs and Symptoms

For the first eight to twelve days after being exposed to the measles virus, your baby probably will have no symptoms; this is called the incubation period. Then he may develop an illness that seems like a common cold, with a cough, runny nose, and pinkeye (conjunctivitis; see page 496). The cough may be severe at times, and will last for about a week, and your baby probably will feel miserable.

During the first one to three days of the illness, the coldlike symptoms will become worse, and he'll develop a fever that may run as high as 103 to 105 degrees Fahrenheit (39.4 to 40.5 degrees Celsius). The fever will last until two to three days after the rash first appears.

After two to four days of illness, the rash will develop. It usually begins on the face and neck, and spreads down the trunk and out to the arms and legs. It starts as very fine red bumps, which may join together to form larger splotches. If you notice tiny white spots, like grains of sand, inside his mouth next to the molars, you'll know the rash is soon to follow. The rash will last five to eight days. As it fades, the skin may peel a little.

Treatment

Although there is no licensed antiviral treatment for the disease in the United States, it is important that the pediatrician examine your baby to determine that measles is, in fact, the cause of the illness. Many other conditions can start in the same way, and measles has its own complications (such as pneumonia) that the doctor will want to watch for. When you call, describe the fever and rash so that the doctor knows it may be measles. When you visit the office, the pediatrician will want to separate your baby from other patients, so that the virus is not transmitted to them.

Your baby is contagious from several days before the rash breaks out until the fever and rash are gone. During this period he should be kept at home (except for the visit to the doctor) and away from anyone who is not immune to the illness.

At home, make sure your baby drinks plenty of fluids, and give acetaminophen in the proper dose to control fever. The conjunctivitis that accompanies measles can make it painful for the baby to be in bright sunshine, so you may want to darken his room to a comfortable level for the first few days.

Sometimes bacterial infections develop on top of the measles. These most often include pneumonia (see page 460), and ear infection (see page 485). These must be seen by the pediatrician and usually require antibiotic treatment.

Prevention

Almost all children who receive two doses of the MMR (measles, mumps, rubella) vaccine after their first birthday are protected against measles for life. (See Chapter 24, "Immunizations.") Up to five percent of children may not respond to the initial vaccination. For this reason, a second dose is recommended either at age five or upon entry to middle school (ages eleven to twelve), depending on your specific state requirements. Your pediatrician will tell you what is best for your child.

If your baby has been exposed to someone who has measles, or if someone in your household has the virus, notify your pediatrician at once. The following steps can help keep your baby from getting sick:

1. If he is under one year old or has a weakened immune system, he can be given immune globulin (gamma globulin) up to six days following exposure. This temporarily may protect him from becoming infected, but will not provide extended immunity.
2. An infant six to eleven months of age may receive measles vaccine alone (not MMR) if exposed to the disease or if residing in a community where exposure is highly likely or in an epidemic situation.

Roseola Infantum

Your ten-month-old doesn't look or act very ill, but she suddenly develops a fever between 102 degrees Fahrenheit (38.9 degrees Celsius) and 105 degrees Fahrenheit (40.5 degrees Celsius). The fever lasts for three to seven days, during which time your baby has less appetite, mild diarrhea, slight cough, and runny nose, and seems mildly irritable and a little sleepier than usual. Her upper eyelids appear slightly swollen or droopy. Finally, *after her temperature returns to normal,* she gets a slightly raised, spotty, pink rash on her trunk. "Oh, no!" you say. "It's measles!" But the rash spreads only to her upper arms and neck and fades after just twenty-four hours. What's the diagnosis? Most likely it's a disease called *roseola*—a contagious viral illness. Its incubation period is seven to fourteen days. The key to this diagnosis is that the rash appears *after* the fever is gone.

Treatment

Whenever your infant has a fever of 102 degrees Fahrenheit (38.9 degrees Celsius) or higher for twenty-four hours, call your pediatrician, even if there are no other symptoms. If the doctor suspects the fever is caused by roseola, he will suggest ways to control the temperature and advise you to call again if your infant becomes worse or the fever lasts for more than three or four days. For a baby who has other symptoms or appears more seriously ill, the doctor may order a blood count, urinalysis, or other tests.

Since most illnesses that cause fever are contagious, it's wise to keep your baby away from other children, at least until you've conferred with your pediatrician. Once she is diagnosed as having roseola, don't let her play with other children until the rash clears.

While your baby has a fever, dress her in lightweight clothing and give her acetaminophen in the appropriate dose for her age and weight. (See Chapter 20, "Fever.") If her temperature goes over 104 degrees Fahrenheit (40 degrees Celsius), she may be more comfortable if you give her a sponge bath with barely cool water. Also don't worry if her appetite is decreased, and encourage her to drink extra fluids. As soon as her rash is gone, she may return to all normal activities, including contact with other children.

Although this disease is rarely serious, be aware that early in the illness when fever climbs very quickly, there's a chance of convulsions (see *Seizures and Convulsions*, page 537). There may be a seizure regardless of how well you treat the fever, so it's important to know how to manage convulsions even though they're usually quite mild and occur only briefly, if at all, with roseola.

SCABIES

Scabies is caused by a microscopic mite that burrows under the top layers of skin and deposits its eggs. The rash that results from scabies is actually an allergic reaction to the mite's body, eggs, and excretions. Once the mite gets into the skin, it takes two to four weeks for the rash to appear.

In an infant, the rash appears as itchy, fluid-filled bumps. They may be scattered and isolated and are often found on the palms and soles. Because of scratch marks, crusting, or a secondary infection, this annoying rash is often difficult to identify.

According to legend, when Napoleon's troops had scabies, one could hear the sound of scratching at night from over a mile away! A bit of exaggeration perhaps, but it illustrates two key points to remember if you think your baby has scabies: It's very itchy and very contagious. Scabies is spread only person to person, but this happens extremely easily. If one person in your family has the rash, the others almost certainly will get it, too.

Treatment

If you notice that your baby (and possibly others in the family) is scratching constantly, suspect scabies and call the pediatrician, who will examine the rash and may gently scrape a skin sample from the affected area to look at under the microscope for evidence of the mite or its eggs. If scabies turns out to be the diagnosis, the doctor will prescribe one of several antiscabies medications. Most are lotions that are applied over the entire body, then washed off after several hours. Although one treatment is usually sufficient, it may need to be repeated.

Some experts feel the whole family must be treated—even those members who don't have a rash. Any live-in help, sleep-over visitors, or frequent baby-sitters also should receive care.

To prevent infection caused by scratching, cut your baby's fingernails, and if the itching is very severe, ask your pediatrician to prescribe an antihistamine or other anti-itch medication. If your baby shows signs of bacterial infection in the scratched scabies, notify the pediatrician. She may want to prescribe an antibiotic or other form of treatment.

Following treatment, the itching could continue for two to four weeks, because this is an allergic rash. If it persists past four weeks, call your doctor, because the scabies may have returned and need retreatment.

Incidentally, there is some controversy over the possible spread of scabies from clothing or linen. Evidence indicates that this occurs very rarely. However, for peace of mind, you may want to wash your linens and bedclothes in hot water. There's no need, though, to decontaminate the baby's room or the house, since the mite usually lives only in people's skin.

Sunburn

While those with darker coloring tend to be less sensitive to the sun, no one, regardless of complexion, is immune to sunburn and its associated disorders, and babies especially need to be protected from the sun's burning rays. Like other burns, sunburn will leave the skin red, warm, and painful. In severe cases it may cause blistering, fever, chills, headache, and a general feeling of illness.

Your baby doesn't actually have to be burned, however, in order to be harmed by the sun. The effects of exposure build over the years, so that even moderate exposure during childhood can contribute to wrinkling, toughening, and perhaps cancer of the skin in later life. Also, some medications can cause a skin reaction when the person taking them is exposed to sunlight, and some medical conditions may make people more sensitive to the effects of the sun.

Treatment

The signs of sunburn usually appear six to twelve hours after exposure, with the greatest discomfort during the first twenty-four hours. If your baby's burn is just red, warm, and painful, you can treat it yourself. Apply cool compresses to the burned areas or bathe in cool water. You also can give acetaminophen to help relieve the pain. (Check the package for appropriate dosage for her age and weight.)

If the sunburn causes blisters, fever, chills, headache, or a general feeling of illness, call your pediatrician. Severe sunburn must be treated like any other serious burn, and if it's very extensive, hospitalization is sometimes required. In addition, the blisters can become infected, requiring treatment with antibiotics.

Sometimes, extensive or severe sunburn also can lead to dehydration (see *Diarrhea*, page 421, for signs of dehydration) and in some cases fainting (heatstroke). Such cases need to be examined by your pediatrician or the nearest emergency facility.

Prevention

Many parents incorrectly assume that the sun is dangerous only when it's shining brightly. In fact, it's not the visible light rays but rather the invisible ultraviolet rays that are harmful. Your child actually may be exposed to more ultraviolet rays on foggy or hazy days because she'll feel cooler and therefore stay outside for a longer time. Exposure is also greater at higher altitudes. Even a big hat or umbrella is not absolute protection because ultraviolet rays reflect off sand, water, snow, and many other surfaces.

Try to keep your child out of the sun when the peak ultraviolet rays occur (between 10 A.M. and 4 P.M.). In addition, follow these guidelines:

- Dress your child in lightweight cotton clothing with long sleeves and long pants.
- Use a beach umbrella or similar object to keep her in the shade as much as possible.
- Have her wear a hat with a wide brim.
- Always use a sunscreen to block the damaging ultraviolet rays. Choose a sunscreen made for children with a sun protection factor (SPF) of at least 15 (check the label). Apply the protection half an hour before going out. Many sunscreens are waterproof, but even these may need to be reapplied every three or four hours if your child spends a lot of time in the water. Consult the instructions on the bottle.
- Babies under six months of age should be kept out of direct sunlight. If adequate clothing and shade are not available, sunscreen may be used on small areas of the body, such as the face and the backs of the hands.

(See also *Burns,* page 390.)

27

Chronic Conditions and Diseases

Coping with Chronic (Long-Term) Health Problems

We tend to think of childhood as a carefree and healthy time of life, but some children face chronic health problems during these early years. (By *chronic*, we mean conditions that last for at least three months, or require at least a month of hospitalization.) While most long-term health problems in children are relatively mild, any type of lengthy illness or disability is stressful for the family.

The specific medical treatment of many chronic conditions is discussed elsewhere, under the names of those conditions. (See index.) The information that follows is aimed at helping parents deal with the emotional and practical challenges of living with any baby who has a long-term illness or disability.

Getting Help

If your baby is born with a serious medical problem, or develops a chronic medical condition early in life, you may face some of the following stresses and decisions:

- The realization that your child is not perfectly healthy often leads to feelings of disappointment and guilt, and fear for her future. In trying to deal with these feelings, you may find yourself struggling with unexplained emotional swings ranging from hopefulness to despair and depression.
- You will need to select and work with a team of medical professionals who can help your baby.

- You may face decisions about treatment or surgery.
- You may have to accept responsibility for giving your baby certain medications, using special equipment, or performing special therapies.
- You will be called on to provide the time, energy, money, and emotional commitment necessary for your baby to receive the best possible treatment.
- In adapting your life to meet your baby's needs without neglecting other family members, you will face many difficult choices, some of which may require compromise solutions.

To avoid becoming overwhelmed, it is helpful to select one medical person as the overall coordinator of your baby's medical care. This person may be your pediatrician or another health professional who is most closely involved with your baby's treatment. It should be someone who knows your family well, makes you feel comfortable, and is willing to spend time answering your questions and working with other doctors and therapists involved in your baby's care.

Not all of your baby's special needs will be medical, of course. She eventually may require special schooling, counseling, or other therapy. Your family may need outside financial or governmental assistance. The person who coordinates your baby's medical care should also provide some guidance in obtaining this extra help, but the best way to make sure you and your baby get the services and support you need is to learn about the resources and regulations that apply to special services for children with chronic illnesses or disabilities. You should also find out what you can do if the services your family receives do not meet your baby's needs.

Balancing the Needs of Family and Child

For a while, the baby with special needs may take all your attention, leaving little for other family members and your outside relationships. While this is normal, everyone will suffer unless you find some way to restore a sense of balance and routine to your activities. Neither your sick baby nor the rest of the family will benefit if the health problem becomes the central and overwhelming issue in your family's life.

Eventually your baby's medical care must become a part of your daily routine rather than the focus of it.

While it's natural to want to protect your sick baby, he will need your encouragement far more than your protection. Rather than concentrating on what she cannot do, try to focus instead on what she *can* do. If given a chance to participate in normal activities with children her age, she probably will do things that surprise everyone.

Establishing this sense of normalcy is difficult if your baby's condition is uncertain. You may find yourself withdrawing from your friends because you're so worried about your baby, and you may hesitate to plan social activities if you're not sure she'll be well enough to attend. If you give in to these feelings all the time, resentment is bound to build up, so try not to let this happen. Even if there is a chance that your baby's condition may worsen unexpectedly, take the risk and plan special outings, invite friends to your home, and get a baby-sitter from time to time so you can go out for an evening. Both you and your baby will be better off in the long run if you take this approach.

Special Tips

The following are suggestions that may help you cope more effectively with your baby's condition:

- Whenever possible both parents should be included in discussions and decisions about your baby's treatment. Too often, mothers go alone to medical appointments and then must explain what was said to the father. This may prevent the father from getting some of his own questions answered or learning enough about the choices.
- Don't be offended if your baby's doctors ask personal questions about your family life. The more they know about your family, the better they can help you manage your baby's care. If your baby will need a wheelchair, the doctor may ask about your home in order to suggest the best places for wheelchair ramps. If you have concerns about the doctor's suggestions, discuss them with him so you can reach an acceptable plan of action together.
- Remember that although you and your doctor want to be

optimistic about your child's condition, you must be honest about it. If things are not going well, say so. Work with the doctor to adjust the treatment or find a solution that will make the situation as good as possible.

- Call on friends and family members for support. You cannot expect to handle the strain created by your baby's chronic condition all by yourself. Asking close friends to help you meet your own emotional needs will in turn help you to meet your infant's.
- Remember that your baby needs to be loved and valued as an individual. If you let the medical problems overshadow your feelings for her as a person, they may interfere with the bond of trust and affection between you. Don't let yourself become so worried that you cannot relax and enjoy your baby.

ANEMIA

Blood contains several different types of cells. The most numerous are the red blood cells, which absorb oxygen in the lungs and distribute it throughout the body. These cells contain hemoglobin, a red pigment that carries oxygen to the tissues and carries away the waste material, carbon dioxide. When there is a decreased amount of hemoglobin available in the red blood cells, making the blood less able to carry the amount of oxygen necessary for all the cells in the body to function and grow, the condition is called anemia.

Anemia may occur for any of the following reasons:

1. Production of red blood cells slows down.
2. Too many red blood cells are destroyed.
3. There is not enough hemoglobin within the red blood cells.

Babies most commonly become anemic when they fail to get enough iron in their diet. Iron is necessary for the production of hemoglobin. This iron deficiency causes a decrease in the amount of hemoglobin in the red blood cells. A young infant may get iron-deficiency anemia if he starts drinking cow's milk too early, particularly if he is not given an iron supplement or food with iron. The deficiency occurs because cow's milk contains very little iron and the small amount present is poorly absorbed through the intestines into the body. In addition, cow's milk given to an infant under six months of age can cause irritation of the bowel and small amounts of blood loss. This results in a decrease in the number of red blood cells, which can cause anemia.

Other nutritional deficiencies, such as lack of folic acid, also can cause anemia, but this is very rare. It is probably most often seen in babies fed on goat's milk, which contains very little folic acid.

Anemia at any age can be caused by excessive blood loss. In rare cases, the blood does not clot properly, and a newborn infant may bleed heavily from his circumcision or a minor injury, and become anemic. Because vitamin K promotes blood clotting and is often lacking in newborns, an injection of this vitamin generally is given right after birth.

Sometimes the red blood cells are prone to being easily destroyed. This is called hemolytic anemia, and can result from disturbances on the surface of the red blood cells or other abnormalities in or outside the cells.

A severe condition which involves an abnormal structure of hemoglobin, seen most often in children of black African heritage, is called sickle-cell anemia. This disorder can be very severe and is associated with frequent "crises" and often repeated hospitalizations.

Finally, certain enzyme deficiencies also can alter the function of the red blood cells, increasing their susceptibility to destruction.

Signs and Symptoms

Anemia causes a mild paleness of the skin, usually most apparent as a decreased pinkness of the lips, the lining of the eyelids (conjunctiva), and the nail beds (pink part of the nails). Anemic babies also may be irritable, mildly weak, or tire easily. Those with severe anemia may have shortness of breath, rapid heart rate, and swelling of the hands and feet. If the anemia continues, it may interfere with normal growth. A newborn with hemolytic anemia may become jaundiced (turn yellow), although many newborns are mildly jaundiced and don't become anemic.

If your infant shows any of these symptoms or signs, or if you suspect he is not getting enough iron in his diet, consult your pediatrician. A simple blood count can diagnose anemia in most cases.

Babies with sickle-cell anemia may have unexplained fever or swelling of the hands and feet as infants, and they are extremely susceptible to infection. If there is a history of sickle-cell anemia in your family, make sure your baby is tested for it.

Treatment

Since there are so many different types of anemia, it is very important to identify the cause before *any* treatment is begun. Do not attempt to treat your infant with vitamins, iron, or other nutrients or over-the-counter medications unless it is at your physician's direction. This is important, because such treatment may mask the real reason for the problem and thus delay the diagnosis.

If the anemia is due to lack of iron, your baby will be given an iron-containing medication. This comes in a drop form for infants. Your pediatrician will determine how long your baby should take the iron by checking his blood at regular intervals. Do not stop giving the medication until the physician tells you it is no longer needed.

Following are a few tips concerning iron medication:

- It is best not to give iron with milk because milk blocks the absorption.
- Vitamin C increases iron absorption, so you might want to follow the dose of iron with a glass of orange juice.
- Iron medications cause the stools to become a dark black color. Don't be worried by this change.

Safety precautions: Iron medications are extremely poisonous if taken in excessive amounts. (Iron is one of the most common causes of poisoning in children under five.) *Keep this and all medication out of reach of small children.*

Prevention

Iron-deficiency anemia and other nutritional anemias can be prevented easily by making sure your baby is eating a well-balanced diet and by following these precautions:

- Do not give your infant cow's milk until he is over one year old.
- If your baby is breastfed, give him iron-fortified foods such as cereal when solid foods are introduced. Before then, he will absorb enough iron from the breastmilk. If you choose to breastfeed solely beyond 4 months, an iron supplement is recommended. However, the introduction of iron-poor solid foods will decrease the amount of iron he absorbs from the milk.
- If your baby is formula-fed, give him formula with added iron.

CYSTIC FIBROSIS

Cystic fibrosis (CF) is an inherited disease that changes the secretions of certain glands in the body. The sweat glands and the glandular cells of the lungs and pancreas are most often affected, but the sinuses, liver, intestines, and reproductive organs can also be involved. Although we have made great progress in treating this disease and its symptoms, there is still no cure. Children with cystic fibrosis now live much longer than previously.

For a baby to get cystic fibrosis, both parents must be carriers of the gene that causes it. In the United States, one out of every twenty Caucasian people is a carrier of the CF gene, and approximately one out of every 1,600 white babies is born with the disease. The illness is much less common in the African-American population (one in every 17,000 live births) and even rarer among Asians.

In the last few years, a genetic abnormality has been detected in many cystic fibrosis patients, with other gene mutations being found as more research is done. We are developing the capability to screen the population at large effectively for CF, and genetic screening and counseling is available for those with a family member with CF. Since the disease is usually fatal, this should be an important consideration for high-risk families.

Signs and Symptoms

In children with CF, the disease is not usually obvious at birth or at a very young age. The signs and symptoms vary, depending on the severity of the particular case and the organs that are involved. Some of this has been related to the amount of mutation of the most common genetic abnormality. However, all children with CF excrete excessive amounts of salt in their sweat. This may cause salt crystals to appear on their skin and gives them a salty taste when you kiss them.

CF often (though not always) seriously affects the lungs, causing mucus in the airways to be thicker than normal and more difficult to cough out. A child with CF is likely to have a persistent cough, which gets worse with colds. Since the lungs' secretions remain in the airways for longer than normal, the airways are more likely to become infected, increasing the chances of pneumonia or bronchitis.

Many children with CF are deficient in the pancreatic enzymes that help to digest food. As a result, they cannot digest fats and proteins as well as they should, which results in large, bulky, foul-smelling stools. These children grow more slowly than normal and are underweight.

You should suspect cystic fibrosis and call your pediatrician if your child has frequent pneumonia (see page 460), bulky, foul-smelling stools, or fails to grow or gain normally. The doctor will order a sweat test to measure the amount of salt your child's sweat contains. Children with cystic fibrosis excrete large quantities of salt in this manner.

Two or more tests may be required to confirm the diagnosis, since the results are not always clearly positive or negative. If your child is diagnosed as having the disease, your pediatrician will help you get the additional specialized medical help that is necessary.

Treatment

The treatment of cystic fibrosis depends upon which body system is involved with the disease (skin, lungs, digestive tract) and the severity of that involvement. In general, the goals are to:

1. Reduce secretions from the lungs
2. Replace missing or insufficient digestive enzymes
3. Reduce or replace salt loss

4. Treat promptly and vigorously the infections of the lungs that occur more frequently in these children

The Emotional Burden of Cystic Fibrosis

Because CF is a hereditary disease, many parents feel very guilty about their child's illness. But this problem is not *anyone's* fault, so you should channel your emotional energies into your child's treatment instead. Work closely with the doctors and therapists, and do not be fooled by publicized "breakthroughs" or "guaranteed cures." If you hear of a new therapy, ask your pediatrician or CF center before spending money or trying it.

It also is important to raise your child as you would if she did not have this illness. There is no reason to limit her educational or career goals. Many CF patients grow up to lead productive adult lives. Your child needs both love and discipline, and she should be encouraged to develop and test her limits.

Balancing the physical and emotional demands created by this disease is hard on both the CF patient and her family, so it is very important that you get as much support as possible. Ask your pediatrician to put you in touch with the nearest CF center and CF support groups. The Cystic Fibrosis Foundation can also help. Write to: Cystic Fibrosis Foundation, 6931 Arlington Road, Bethesda, Maryland 20814.

FAILURE TO THRIVE

If you plot your baby's weight and measurements, you should see a continuous upward trend, although there will be times when she gains very slowly and perhaps some weeks when she actually loses a little weight due to illness. It is not normal for her to stop growing, or to decrease in weight except for the small amount she loses during the first few days of life. If she does lose weight, it's a clear sign either that she's not getting enough to eat or that she's ill. The medical term for this condition is *failure to thrive*. Although it can occur in older children who are seriously ill or undernourished, it is most common and most dangerous during the active growth period of the first three years of life.

If allowed to continue for a prolonged period, this condition can become serious. Steady weight gain is especially important for infants because it indicates that they are receiving adequate nutrition and care for normal physical, mental, and emotional development.

Usually when a baby stops growing, it's due to a feeding problem that prevents her from getting as many calories as she needs. As a newborn, she may be too fussy to eat as much as she needs, or, if breastfed, she may not be getting enough milk while nursing. Some babies may require more food than their parents are able to provide.

Sometimes failure to thrive signals a medical problem. The newborn may have an infection passed on from her mother during pregnancy, or she may have a hormonal difficulty, allergy, or a digestive problem that prevents nutrients from being properly absorbed into the body. Diseases such as cystic fibrosis (page 587) or heart disease also can interfere with normal growth. If one of these is present, the baby may need a special diet as well as medical treatment.

When to Get Help

Regular charting of your baby's growth and comparison of her general development with others her age is the best way to make sure she is thriving. If she does not gain weight, grow in length, or otherwise develop normally, consult your pediatrician, who will measure and examine your baby, ask about her diet and eating patterns, and review her medical history for signs of illness that may be contributing to her failure to thrive. The physician will try to establish exactly when the growth or weight gain stopped, and ask about any incidents or events that may have contributed to this. The pediatrician may also watch the baby eating or nursing to see how much she consumes and how she responds to food. Sometimes a short period of in-hospital observation may be necessary. If the doctor discovers a physical cause for the decrease in growth rate, the appropriate treatment will be recommended.

HIV Infection and AIDS

No one who has read a newspaper or watched a television newscast in recent years could have avoided learning something about HIV infection (which frequently leads to AIDS, or acquired immune deficiency syndrome). This infection is caused by the human immunodeficiency virus (HIV).

Babies acquire infection primarily from their HIV-infected mothers, either in utero (as the virus passes across the placenta) or during delivery (when the newborn is exposed to the mother's blood and body fluids) or by ingestion of infected breastmilk. HIV infection will develop in 13 to 39 percent of infants born to HIV-infected mothers who are untreated. Zidovudine (or AZT) treatment of the mother and newborn diminishes the transmission of HIV infection from mothers to babies, so that approximately one in ten babies will be infected instead of one in four to five.

Once a baby is infected with HIV, the virus will be present in his body for life. Infants with HIV infection initially may appear well, but problems gradually develop. For example, their weight and height fail to increase appropriately within the first six months to one year. They have frequent episodes of diarrhea or minor skin infections. The lymph nodes (glands) anywhere in the body may enlarge, and there is a persistent fungus infection of the mouth (thrush). The liver and spleen may enlarge.

All the above symptoms are highly suggestive of HIV infection. Eventually, if the HIV infection progresses with the body's immune system further deteriorating, the AIDS-related infections and cancers may occur. The most common of these, pneumocystis carinii pneumonia (PCP), is accompanied by fever and breathing difficulties. PCP occurs predominantly in infants between three months and one year of age. It is possible to prevent infection with antibiotics, and it is now recommended that all babies born to HIV-infected women be placed on preventative antibiotics as early as six weeks of age. The doctor must determine if the baby is HIV infected before deciding to stop therapy.

Care of the Baby with HIV Infection

It is clear from the overwhelmingly uniform evidence that babies who are HIV positive should be played with, interacted with, and loved just like all other children. Children with HIV infections cannot transmit the disease by just being held. These babies need all we can give them, whether it be in a child-care center, on a one-to-one basis, or in any group large or small. Often, in fact, their circumstances have placed them in a situation or an environment which is less conducive to optimum growth and development. We must all do everything we can to counteract those negative factors. We must contribute to their positive outlook on life.

Common infections can cause devastating illnesses in children with HIV infection. Call the doctor immediately if your baby develops a fever, breathing difficulties, diarrhea, swallowing problems, or skin irritation, or if he's been exposed to communicable disease. In fact, any change in health status should prompt you to seek medical attention, since the baby with HIV may have little reserve to combat even minor illnesses.

Whenever seeking any medical attention for your baby, be sure to inform the physician of the HIV infection so that she can appropriately assess and care for the illness and give correct immunizations.

There are currently several licensed antiretroviral drugs for use in children. These include zidovudine (ZDV), didanosine (ddi), and lamuvudine (3TC). Others are in the process of being tested and approved. These agents suppress virus replication and have been demonstrated to improve growth and neurodevelopment and delay progression of disease. It is essential that your doctor knows about the baby's HIV infection as early in life as possible and that antiretroviral therapy be administered as the doctor advises. New treatments continue to be developed, and successful complete suppression of the virus may become a reality in the near future. There are specific therapeutic guidelines for the specific treatment of HIV-infected babies.

Immunizing the Baby Born to the HIV-Infected Mother

Your pediatrician has up-to-date guidelines for which vaccines should and shouldn't be given. Below is a summary of the current recommendations:

Babies with HIV infection (yeast infections in the mouth, frequent minor infections, enlarged lymph nodes, enlarged liver or spleen, or overwhelming infection) as well as babies with asymptomatic HIV infection should receive the following vaccines at the usual recommended age:

- DTaP (diphtheria, tetanus, pertussis vaccine)
- IPV (inactivated poliovirus vaccine), not OPV
- Hepatitis B vaccine
- Hib (*haemophilus influenzae* type b vaccine)
- Children with HIV infection should receive live measles, mumps, rubella vaccine (MMR) unless they are severely immunocompromised. Your doctor will know how to determine if vaccine is to be administered.
- HIV-infected children should not receive varicella vaccine. Studies are in progress and this recommendation may change.
- Children with HIV infection should, in addition, receive pneumococcal and influenza vaccines. Noninfected children living in a household with HIV-infected children or adults should not receive OPV because they may excrete the virus and expose the HIV-infected family members.

HIV-infected infants may experience especially severe illness due to chickenpox or measles. Following exposures to these infections, the physician should be notified and HIV-infected babies should receive special immune globulin by injection.

Parents of babies with HIV infection sometimes hide the diagnosis from relatives, feeling the infant will be shunned by them. However, most families have been very supportive; indeed, they have often taken over the responsibility for care during periods when the parents need such assistance.

If You're Pregnant

All pregnant women should be counseled about HIV and offered HIV testing. It is important for appropriate care of the mother and because treatment can reduce transmission of the virus from the mother to her infant.

In Child Care

There is no risk of HIV transmission in routine child-care activities. The virus is not spread through casual contact.

It is not transmitted through the air or by touching. Almost all babies with HIV infection can attend regular child care.

Although transmission of HIV has not occurred in child-care centers, transmission of other infectious agents requires that all these settings adopt routine precautionary procedures for handling blood, stool, and bodily secretions. The standard precaution is to immediately wash exposed skin with soap and water after any contact with blood or body fluids. Soiled surfaces should be cleaned with disinfectants such as bleach (a one-to-ten dilution of bleach to water). Disposable towels or tissues should be used whenever possible. Gloves are recommended when contact with blood occurs, and therefore gloves should be available in child-care centers. It is important to wash hands thoroughly after changing diapers.

Where We Stand

The American Academy of Pediatrics supports legislation and public policy directed toward eliminating any form of discrimination based on HIV serostatus.

Commonly Used Medications

Antibiotics	*Reason for Use*	*Side Effects*
Penicillin V	Strep throat; protection against rheumatic fever and bacterial endocarditis	Allergic reaction
Penicillin G, Benzathine	Strep throat; protection against rheumatic fever and bacterial endocarditis; gonorrhea	Soreness at injection site; allergic reaction
Amoxicillin	Ear, sinus, urinary tract infections; gonorrhea	Loose stools; skin rash; allergic reaction
Augmentin	Alternative to amoxicillin	Skin rash; allergic reaction
Azithromycin	Ear infections	Stomach upset
Biaxin®	Infections	Stomach upset
Dicloxacillin	Infections (especially skin, impetigo) caused by staph germs	Allergic reaction
Cephalexin (Keflex®)	Alternative to amoxicillin for urinary tract infection	Allergic reaction; loose stools
Erythromycin/ Sulfisoxazole (Pediazole®)	Alternative to amoxicillin for ear and sinus infections	Allergy; skin rash; stomach upset
Lorabid®	Skin infections	Stomach upset; allergy
Sulfisoxazole (Gantrisin®)	Urinary tract and ear infections	Allergy; skin rash
Trimethoprim Sulfamethoxazole (Bactrim®, Septra®)	Urinary tract and ear infections	Allergy; skin rash; nausea; vomiting

Commonly Used Medications *(Continued)*

Antibiotics	*Reason for Use*	*Side Effects*
Erythromycin (Ilosone®, E-mycin®, Pediamycin®)	Alternative to penicillin V; Mycoplasma pneumonia; Legionnaires' disease; impetigo; chlamydia infections	Nausea, vomiting; loose stools; abdominal pain
Rifampin (Rifadin®, Prevent meningitis due to Rimactane®)	*Haemophilus influenzae* B and meningococcus	Red/orange staining of urine
Ear Preparations		
Acetic acid solution (Vosol®)	External ear infections	None
Cortisporin ® otic solution or suspension	External ear infections	None
Eye Preparations		
Erythromycin (Ilotycin®) ointment (0.5%)	Conjunctivitis	Puffy eyes
Gentamicin (Garamycin®) solution (0.3%)	Conjunctivitis	Puffy eyes
Sulfacetamide (Sulamyd®) solution (10%)	Conjunctivitis	Puffy eyes
Analgesics		
Aspirin	Pain; inflammation. **Do Not Use For Fever Due To Any Infection**	Many—especially stomach upset; ringing in ears; allergic reactions

Analgesics	*Reason for Use*	*Side Effects*
Acetaminophen (Tylenol®, Tempra®, Liquiprin®, Panadol®)	Pain; fever	None with suggested dose
Ibuprofen (Motrin®, Advil®)	Pain, fever, inflammation	Stomach upset
Agents for Common Cold		
Actifed®	Common cold; upper respiratory infections	Irritability; sleep disturbances, drowsiness
Dimetapp®	Common cold; upper respiratory infections	Irritability; sleep disturbances, drowsiness
Triaminic®	Common cold; upper respiratory infections	Irritability; sleep disturbances, drowsiness
Diphenhydramine elixir (Benadryl®)	Allergic reactions; itching; motion sickness; hay fever	Drowsiness
Hydroxyzine (Atarax®)	Allergic reactions; itching; motion sickness; hay fever	Drowsiness
Robitussin®	Cough	None
Agents for Common GI Problems		
Ipecac syrup	Empty stomach by vomiting after poison ingestion	Lethargy; diarrhea; persistent vomiting
Skin Preparations		
Bacitracin Ointment	Skin infections	None when used correctly
Silver sulfadiazine	Burns	Discoloration of skin

Commonly Used Medications *(Continued)*

Skin Preparations	*Reason for Use*	*Side Effects*
Pyrethrins/ Piperonyl Butoxide (RID®)	Lice	None when used correctly
Hexagammabenzene (Kwell®)	Lice	May be toxic; follow directions and speak with physician

INDEX

Page numbers of illustrations appear in italics.